MAKE MEN OF THEM

MAKE MEN of THEM:

Introductory Readings for Cultural Anthropology

Edited by
Charles C. Hughes
Michigan State University

RAND McNALLY COLLEGE PUBLISHING COMPANY
CHICAGO

Rand McNally Anthropology Series

Human Evolution: An Introduction to the New Physical Anthropology
  J. B. Birdsell
Make Men of Them: Introductory Readings For Cultural Anthropology
  Charles C. Hughes

Forthcoming:
Handbook of Social and Cultural Anthropology
  John J. Honigmann

Cover photo: Interstampa from Black Star

Third Printing, 1973

Copyright © 1972 by Rand McNally College Publishing Company
All rights reserved
Printed in U.S.A. by Rand McNally & Company
Library of Congress Catalogue Card Number 77-178229

to
L. A. H.

ACKNOWLEDGMENTS

I am grateful to those colleagues who suggested possible readings for inclusion in this book and assisted in other ways—Dr. Joanne Eicher, Dr. Ralph Faulkingham, Dr. Moreau Maxwell, and Dr. Ralph Nicholas. And I wish particularly to thank Dr. George Axinn for bringing to my attention the splendid quotation from Benjamin Franklin's essay, "Remarks Concerning the Savages of North America," first published in 1784, which I have used as the Foreword for this book.

Many others were instrumental in helping me compile this book, my publishers—especially Lawrence J. Malley and Margaret L. Kachadurian of the Rand McNally College Department—and several typists who worried and worked through various drafts of the manuscript and whose efforts I appreciate—Alane Johnson, Albertha Brown, Mary Jones, and Jane O'Neil. Also I would like to thank all the publishers who granted me permission to print excerpts from their publications in this volume. Special credit footnotes accompany each article.

FOREWORD FROM THE PAST

"Savages we call them, because their manners differ from ours, which we think the perfection of civility; they think the same of theirs.

"Perhaps, if we could examine the manners of different nations with impartiality, we should find no people so rude as to be without any rules of politeness; nor any so polite as not to have some remains of rudeness.

"The Indian men, when young, are hunters and warriors; when old, counselors; for all their government is by the counsel or advice of the sages; there is no force, there are no prisons, no officers to compel obedience, or inflict punishment. Hence they generally study oratory; the best speaker having the most influence. The Indian women till the ground, dress the food, nurse and bring up the children, and preserve and hand down to posterity the memory of public transactions. These employments of men and women are accounted natural and honorable. Having few artificial wants, they have abundance of leisure for improvement in conversation.

"Our laborious manner of life, compared with theirs, they esteem slavish and base; and the learning on which we value ourselves, they regard as frivolous and useless. An instance of this occurred at the treaty of Lancaster, in Pennsylvania, anno 1744, between the government of Virginia and the Six Nations. After the principal business was settled the commissioners from Virginia acquainted the Indians by a speech, that there was at Williamsburgh a college, with a fund, for educating Indian youth; and that if the chiefs of the Six Nations would send down half a dozen of their sons to that college, the government would take care that they should be well provided for, and instructed in all the learning of the white people.

"It is one of the Indian rules of politeness not to answer a public proposition the same day that it is made: they think that it would be treating it as a light matter, and they show it respect by taking time to consider it, as of a matter important. They therefore deferred their answer till the day following: when their speaker began by expressing their deep sense of the kindness of the Virginia government, in making them that offer.

"'For we know,' says he, 'that you highly esteem the kind of learning taught in those colleges, and that the maintenance of our young men, while with you, would be very expensive to you. We are convinced, therefore, that you mean to do us good by your proposal; and we thank you heartily. But you who are wise must know, that different nations have different conceptions of things; and you will therefore not take it amiss, if our ideas of this kind of education happen not to be the same with yours. We have had some experience of it; several of our young people were formerly brought up at the colleges of the northern provinces; they were instructed in all your sciences; but when they came back to us they were bad runners; ignorant of every means of living in the woods; unable to bear either cold or hunger; knew neither how to build a cabin, take a deer, or kill an enemy; spoke our language imperfectly; were therefore neither fit for hunters, warriors or counselors; they were totally good for nothing. We are not, however, the less obliged by your kind offer, though we decline accepting it; and to show our grateful sense of it, if the gentlemen of Virginia will send us a dozen of their sons, we will take great care of their education, instruct them in all we know, and MAKE MEN OF THEM.*' "*

BENJAMIN FRANKLIN – 1784

CONTENTS

ACKNOWLEDGMENTS   vi

FOREWORD FROM THE PAST   vii

THE BEGINNING OF INQUIRY   1

INTRODUCTION   5

PART I: SCIENCE IS "SCIENCING"   21

Science as Perspective
THE CHARACTER OF SCIENCE *by J. Bronowski*   22

Science as Activity
SCIENCE IS "SCIENCING" *by Leslie A. White*   27

Science as Method
THE NATURE OF SCIENCE *by Ralph Ross*   36

PART II: THE ANTHROPOLOGIST "SCIENCING"   43

The "Laboratory"
IN THE COMPANY OF MAN *by Joseph B. Casagrande*   44

The Field Experience
A NEW HOME *by Elenore Smith Bowen*   46

An Ethnographic Study
SUBJECT, SCOPE, AND METHOD OF ETHNOGRAPHIC WORK
by Bronislaw Malinowski   53

Urban Ethnography
A FIELD EXPERIENCE IN RETROSPECT *by Elliot Liebow*   64

PART III: THE CULTURAL SHAPING OF BEHAVIOR   71

The "Humanity" of Man's Behavior
ON BEING HUMAN *by Marston Bates*   72

Food
VARIETY IN FOOD CUSTOMS *by John Gillin*   78

Kissing
THE NATURAL HISTORY OF A KISS *by E. Royston Pike*   83

Toilet Habits
TOILET TRAINING *by Theodor Rosebury*   87

Gesture
THE CULTURAL BASIS OF EMOTIONS AND GESTURES *by Weston La Barre*   94

Dress
CLOTHING AND ORNAMENT *by E. Adamson Hoebel*   104

Pain
SOCIOCULTURAL CORRELATES OF PAIN RESPONSE *by Victor A. Christopherson* 110

Space
SPACE SPEAKS *by Edward T. Hall*   114

Time
THE VOICES OF TIME *by Edward T. Hall*   124

Language
    SCIENCE AND LINGUISTICS *by Benjamin Lee Whorf*   129
Unconscious Patterning
    THE UNCONSCIOUS PATTERNING OF BEHAVIOR IN SOCIETY
      by Edward Sapir   135

PART IV: THE CONCEPTUALIZATION OF CULTURE   139

What We Start With
    THE ELEMENTS OF BEHAVIOR *by George C. Homans*   140
Words as Tools
    HOW WE KNOW WHAT WE KNOW *by S. I. Hayakawa*   151
Anthropological Constructs
    THE ABSTRACT OR "CONSTRUCT" NATURE OF ANTHROPOLOGICAL
      CONCEPTS *by Felix M. Keesing*   158
Operational Definitions
    OPERATIONAL DISCRIMINATIONS AMONG CONCEPTS *by A. F. C. Wallace*   165
Concepts of Culture
    THE CONCEPT OF CULTURE *by Clyde Kluckhohn and William H. Kelly*   169
Anthropology and Its Use of "Culture"
    ANTHROPOLOGICAL USE OF THE TERM "CULTURE" *by Felix M. Keesing*   185
Symbol
    A CLUE TO THE NATURE OF MAN: THE SYMBOL *by Ernst Cassirer*   192
The Symbolic Process
    SYMBOLS *by S. I. Hayakawa*   194
Symbols in Human Behavior
    THE SYMBOL: THE ORIGIN AND BASIS OF HUMAN BEHAVIOR
      by Leslie A. White   199
Symbols and Values
    SYMBOLIZATION AND VALUE *by Dorothy D. Lee*   206
Culture as Values
    SIGNIFICANCE AND VALUES *by A. L. Kroeber and Clyde Kluckhohn*   213
"Culture" as Orientation: An Example
    RELIGION AS A CULTURAL SYSTEM *by Clifford Geertz*   215
Culture, Symbols, and Society
    COMMUNICATION, SYMBOLS, AND SOCIETY *by Ralph Ross*   234

PART V: CULTURE AND THE SOCIOCULTURAL LEVEL OF EVENTS   245

Levels of Phenomena
    THE CONCEPT OF INTEGRATIVE LEVELS AND BIOLOGY *by Alex B. Novikoff*   246
Levels of Analysis
    THE HIERARCHY OF SCIENCES *by S. F. Nadel*   252
"Culture" and "Society"
    THE RELATION OF CULTURE TO "SOCIETY" *by Felix M. Keesing*   257
Cultural Dimension
    THE CULTURAL AND THE SOCIAL DIMENSIONS *by Clyde Kluckhohn*   259
Culture and the Social System
    THE CONCEPTS OF CULTURE AND OF SOCIAL SYSTEM *by A. L. Kroeber and
      Talcott Parsons*   261
Putting It All Together
    THE FUNCTIONAL PREREQUISITES OF A SOCIETY *by D. F. Aberle,
      A. K. Cohen, A. K. Davis, M. J. Levy, Jr., F. X. Sutton*   263

PART VI: CULTURE IN THE ECOSYSTEM   273

Man and Habitat
    THE ECOLOGICAL APPROACH TO THE SOCIAL SCIENCES *by F. Fraser Darling*   274
"Cultural" Ecology
    THE SIZE OF ALGONKIAN HUNTING TERRITORIES: A FUNCTION OF
        ECOLOGICAL ADJUSTMENT *by A. Irving Hallowell*   281
Sociocultural System and Ecosystem
    FROM SOCIAL SYSTEM TO ECOSYSTEM *by Otis Dudley Duncan*   288
The Unity of the Environment
    CULTURE AND ENVIRONMENT *by L. L. Bernard*   294

PART VII: THE CASE STUDIES   301

Health
    A SOUTH AFRICAN HEALTH PROGRAM (CONTINUED) *by John Cassel*   302
Wells
    THE WELLS THAT FAILED (CONTINUED) *by Allan R. Holmberg*   314
Axes
    STEEL AXES FOR STONE AGE AUSTRALIANS (CONTINUED)
        by Lauriston Sharp   319
Medicine
    MEDICINE AND FAITH IN RURAL RAJASTHAN (CONTINUED)
        by G. Morris Carstairs   328
Epilogue   340

THE BEGINNING OF INQUIRY

To study culture is to begin a learning process which links together certain kinds of events in the outer world with an idea, or a conception, that itself is symbolized and expressed by a word. That word is "culture." But we have to work at such a linking, work to sort out the appropriate and useful events from the inappropriate and irrelevant observations, for the world as nature gives it to us is a "many splendored thing," full of sufficient variety to occupy students with all kinds of interests. Some illustrations, therefore, of how "culture" is imbedded in the observed world may help get us started. For example, I give four abbreviated selections:

[1] . . . Health conditions in a community of 16,000 Zulu tribesmen in southwestern Natal in the year 1940 were extremely poor. The infant mortality rate was 276 per 1,000 live births, the crude mortality rate 38 per 1,000 population. Inadequacy of the diet was evident in the fact that more than 80 per cent of the people exhibited marked stigmata of nutritional failure and that malnutrition in the form of pellagra and kwashiorkor was rife. Frequent epidemics of typhoid, typhus fever, and smallpox contributed to the high death rate; tuberculosis, venereal disease, and dysentery were major problems.

The Polela Health Centre, an enterprise based on a new approach to the pressing health problems of these Bantu-speaking peoples, was instituted in 1940. Operating on the principle that modern medical services could and should be brought directly to the people themselves, the Centre had at its disposal the most effective known techniques for the detection and treatment of disease.

Personnel of the Centre anticipated that it would be no easy task to implement their plans in a situation where health standards were so low and the culture of the people so different from their own. They could foresee in general that difficulties would arise, but they could not, at the outset of their program, know the specific kinds of conditions that did, in fact, serve to complicate their efforts. In their attempts to put into practice ameliorative health measures, they found that some of the obstacles encountered could be surmounted with a little ingenuity; others, more resistant, could be successfully circumvented; while still others appeared virtually insuperable.

For example, the people readily agreed to plant home vegetable gardens, thus adding important nutrients to their diet, once the proper incentive

[1] Reprinted with permission. From John Cassel, "A Comprehensive Health Program Among South African Zulus," in *Health, Culture, and Community*, ed. Benjamin D. Paul, ©1955 by Russell Sage Foundation, Publishers, N.Y., pp. 15-17. The rest of this chapter (and of the other three chapters from which the problems posed here and on the next several pages are excerpted) is found in Part VII.

was discovered. On the other hand, no amount of demonstration of the nutritional importance of milk could convince the people that they should increase its use but it turned out to be unexpectedly easy to introduce milk through the back door. In another instance, a father with four advanced tubercular cases in his family agreed to hospitalize the patients after an extensive explanation as to the nature of the disease, but on fuller explanation angrily withdrew permission. Other agencies working in this and similar areas experienced like difficulties. Efforts by agricultural experts to combat extensive soil erosion by getting people to reduce the size of their cattle herds resulted in an impasse, yet the available grazing for cattle was so inadequate that the milk yield was negligible and many cattle died every winter from starvation.

In each of these instances, the intensity of effort required to motivate changes was different; in some cases effort was nominal, in others considerable, and in others great. How are these differences to be explained? What information do health workers need to have about a community to enable them to predict some of the resistances they are likely to meet, and therefore plan program priorities more realistically?

2. . . . In the village of Viru—a rural community of about 2,000 people which lies in a fertile valley of the same name on the coast of Peru 300 miles north of the capital city of Lima—intensive agriculture has been practiced for the past several thousand years. Because of peculiar geographic and climatic conditions on the coast of Peru, however, it does not rain in Viru, so that the farmers there must depend exclusively on irrigation to grow their crops. Water for this purpose comes from a small river which runs down the center of the valley and which swells periodically during the rainy season in the Andes (December until May). High in the valley which depends for its life on this small stream, the water is diverted into a complex network of irrigation ditches that run the length and breadth of the area. Consequently, little if any of the stream ever reaches the sea.

The supply of water in Viru, however, is neither great nor constant. The river is generally dry from

²Reprinted with permission. From Allan R. Holmberg, "The Wells That Failed," in *Human Problems in Technological Change*, ed. Edward H. Spicer. ©1952 by Russell Sage Foundation, Publishers, N.Y., pp. 113–14.

May until December, and even during the rainy season in the Andes water does not always descend in quantities sufficient to irrigate all the fields. For this reason, yields are often diminished; sometimes crops fail completely. At best the farmer can hope to harvest but one crop a year even though the climate in which he lives is favorable, and the land on which he farms fertile enough, to raise two. The lack of an adequate and secure water supply, therefore, may be regarded as the principal drawback to economic security and to agricultural expansion in this valley.

Most of the farmers of Viru are too poor to undertake irrigation projects of their own. Through their political representatives, however, they had for years been soliciting the Peruvian government for aid. Many promises had been made, but few had ever been fulfilled. Nevertheless, in August, 1947, the government finally decided to drill six wells in strategic parts of the valley, the water of which was to be piped to the village for household needs and for a sewage system, as well as to augment the supply of water for irrigation at those times when the river would be dry. The offer was reciprocal in the sense that it entailed a certain amount of collaboration from people of the village in such matters as the building of trails, the removal of rock, and the digging of ditches—a collaboration that was promised by the *Junta Transitoria*, or Transitory Board, then in charge of municipal affairs.

In spite of the obvious advantages of this offer, which was immediately publicized by the *Junta* (by word of mouth), the people of the village displayed a marked lack of interest in, and in some cases outright opposition to, the project even before it began. Although the government made good its offer and one technically successful well was eventually drilled—under no few difficulties, to be sure—the project was later abandoned, largely for lack of favorable response from the very people who had for years voiced the loudest complaints about the scanty water supply.

Why, then, were the people of Viru reluctant to get behind a project so likely to fulfill a long-desired village need? And in view of the fact that nothing beneficial resulted—rather, that harm was done—what could have been done to enlist the support of the village so that the project might have been a success?

3. . . . Like other Australian aboriginals, the Yir Yoront group at the mouth of the Coleman River on the west coast of tropical Cape York Peninsula originally had no knowledge of metals. Technologically their culture was of the old stone age or paleolithic type; they supported themselves by hunting and fishing, obtaining vegetable foods and needed materials from the bush by simple gathering techniques. Their only domesticated animal was the dog, and they had no domesticated plants of any kind. Unlike some other aboriginal groups, however, the Yir Yoront did have polished stone axes hafted in short handles, and these implements were most important in their economy.

Toward the end of the nineteenth century metal tools and other European artifacts began to filter into the Yir Yoront territory. The flow increased with the gradual expansion of the white frontier outward from southern and eastern Queensland. Of all the items of western technology thus made available, none was more acceptable, none more highly valued by aboriginals of all conditions than the hatchet or short-handled steel axe.

In the mid-1930's an American anthropologist was able to live alone in the bush among the Yir Yoront for thirteen months without seeing another white man. They were thus still relatively isolated and they continued an essentially independent economic life, supporting themselves entirely by means of their old stone-age techniques. Yet their polished stone axes were fast disappearing and were being replaced by steel axes, which came to them in considerable numbers directly or indirectly from various European sources to the south.

What changes in the life of the Yir Yoront still living under aboriginal conditions in the Australian bush could be expected as a result of their increasing possession and use of the steel axe?

4. . . . In one of his many Indian short stories, Rudyard Kipling describes how a young district officer persuaded a frightened village community to submit to vaccination by reminding the people that its effectiveness derived from the sacred cow, and then

by getting one or two of the leading men to be the first to undergo it. No doubt this story was founded on observation. Certainly it illustrated one way to make such a measure acceptable. Another method, adopted in the early years of this century by the chief health officer of Jodhpur State, turned upon a judicious use of showmanship. This doctor, an Irishman and a famous athlete, included in his retinue one of those emaciated beggars, blind and pock-marked who are still all too common a sight in India. When he came to a village he would summon everyone with his stentorian voice. "Take a good look at him," he would bellow, "that is what Mataji [the goddess of smallpox] does for you! And now look at this: this is what vaccination does to you!" He would then strip to the waist and display not only his vaccination scars but also his muscular torso. The demonstration was convincing.

In contrast, during my recent stay in the village of Delwara I witnessed a conspicuously less successful technique. The public vaccinator came to pay his annual visit of a few days. He was a supercilious young man from Udaipur city, who had passed a course in this specialty, and he regarded villagers as an inferior and stupid lot—especially when they refused to accept his scarifications. During his four-day stay in Delwara, the task degenerated into a hunt. I would see a herd of children and young mothers come bolting out of an alleyway with hilarity and panic mingled in their shrieks, while the vaccinator pursued them, brandishing the weapons of his trade.

It is not enough to bring new medical techniques to a community. No matter how well established these may be in Europe or America, they must be presented afresh to each new social group in a way that will command conviction and acceptance. In order to do this effectively, one has to understand the climate of ideas into which these new elements are to be introduced. A practitioner from another culture may find himself faced with situations that appear to him at first sight as incomprehensible.

For example, when I first practiced medicine in India, I found that in a case where I did nothing at all, except diagnose pregnancy, I was given great credit; in another where the patient died of diphtheria despite my treatment, I was lauded; and in a third, where I made an accurate diagnosis, I was held to blame. As a westerner, I was puzzled by these reactions. It was only gradually that I came

3Reprinted with permission. From Lauriston Sharp, "Steel Axes for Stone Age Australians," in Human Problems in Technological Change, ed. Edward H. Spicer, ©1952 by Russell Sage Foundation, Publishers, N.Y., p. 69.
4Reprinted with permission. From G. Morris Carstairs, "Medicine and Faith in Rural Rajasthan," in Health, Culture, and Community, ed. Benjamin D. Paul, © 1955 by Russell Sage Foundation, Publishers, N.Y., pp. 107-9.

to realize that they all made sense in the context of the villagers' own beliefs about sickness and its cure, and of their concept of the role of a physician. It was only after many months had passed and after numerous contretemps that I began to appreciate the reason for the misunderstandings between us. This process of learning can best be illustrated by describing some of the incidents during my apprenticeship as a country doctor in India.

INTRODUCTION

Epidemics, insufficient water, faulty nutrition, "irrational" social practices, radical changes in human relations following introduction of a simple tool— these are not trivial issues, but kinds of problems important to the well-being of many peoples around the world. As you will see in readings in Part VII, the solutions and analyses eventually arrived at for the problems outlined in the above pages involve some of the basic working ideas and strategies of the field of cultural anthropology (ideas which we will examine through various readings in Parts I–VI).

The particular problems selected are, of course, just a sampling of those that could be used to illustrate some basic cultural anthropological concepts. But these will do that job satisfactorily, while at the same time making another point that needs underscoring: science is an instrumental, problem-solving activity. This is true whether we conceive of "problems" in the highly abstract theoretical sense of an unsolved proposition or some relationship in nature that awaits unravelling—the "learning for its own sake" kind of interest—or whether we view it in terms of more "practical" and "applied" outcomes, such as are represented in these selected problems. And to pick up again on the point about science as a problem-solving activity, the core of any "discipline" in science is a focus upon certain kinds of questions being asked, a particular range of problems examined and dealt with. Insofar as cultural anthropology is a science, then, it too tends to address itself to certain kinds of issues in nature and not others. What some of those issues and problems are will become clearer and more in focus as we proceed.

This reader is not intended as an introduction to the field of anthropology as a whole. Numerous other books are available for that purpose. Rather, it concentrates on what has been labeled *cultural* anthropology and tries to be selective in its format even in that respect. The collection of readings that follows, their variety, content, and sequencing, is based upon the assumption that in learning about a new field of study it is better for the reader to proceed one step at a time, to have first of all a grasp, however general, of the most central concept or concepts and later to fill in differentiating details. In this

5

case that central concept (at least for many American anthropologists) is the concept of *culture*; and the primary function of these readings is to help the student begin developing not only an intellectual grasp of the concept, but, equally important, a sense or *feeling* for what the term means. In this light, part of that development will involve recognizing experiences that are usually below the level of awareness—to get the fish to perceive the existence of the water—and accepting taken-for-granted phenomena as something both in need of and amenable to further study. From such an exposure to the "experienced" meaning of the concept, a base is laid for considering it conceptually with regard to its properties, structure, dynamics, and manifestations in concrete societies.

This strategy of approach to an unfamiliar area of knowledge is an example of what has been called the "method of successive approximations" in science. Vilfredo Pareto, one of the founders of modern social thought, commented that:

> One must first obtain a general concept of the thing one is studying, disregarding details, which for the moment are taken as perturbations; and then come to particulars afterwards, beginning with the more important and proceeding successively towards the less important.[1]

> We shall proceed by *successive approximations*. That is to say, we shall first consider things as wholes, deliberately ignoring details. Of the latter we shall then take account in successive approximations.[2]

The principal objective lying behind this collection can then be restated in these terms as the inculcation of a *first approximation* of a *cultural frame of reference*—to provide a concept of culture you can work with, at least until you develop or adopt a different one.

We must obviously deal, first of all, with the question of what in reality the *word* "culture" refers to (a question often phrased as "What *is* culture?"). Rather than tossing you straightaway into the morass of philosophical questions of *being* and the existence of concepts, of "ultimate reality" and the like—the "is" kind of question—I have taken a more mundane route. A series of initial readings illustrate how pervasive in human life are certain phenomena we eventually will label "culture" and something of what they *do* in the observable world, that world of human beings doing the simplest, life-bound things—eating, sitting, pointing, defecating, loving, talking, seeing, thinking—in short, examples of *behavior*, of people being their animal selves. What I use is therefore initially an inductive or demonstrative approach to getting us on the same track in thinking about culture. The substance of this approach and its pertinence for a word as common in the language as "culture" has been expressed by one philosopher in the following way:

> . . . we learn the proper use of most expressions, and thus come to understand them, not with the help of definitions, but by various subtle processes of

[1]Vilfredo Pareto, *The Mind and Society: A Treatise on General Sociology*, vol. 1 of four volumes bound as two (New York: Dover Publications, Inc., 1963), p. 323. Reprinted through permission of the publisher.
[2]Ibid., p. 37.

conditioning and conjecture; these may involve confrontation with suitable instances, but will frequently amount to our making a conjecture simply on the basis of the context in which the term occurs. Fortunately for the objectives of science, there is a vast array of terms which in these non-definitional ways we learn to use with high individual consistency and interpersonal uniformity; these terms may then be chosen as antecedently understood and may serve as a basis for specifying the meaning of scientific terms by actual definitions.[3]

Why behavior as the point of entry into understanding the concept of culture? Three reasons. For one thing, behavior—what people observably do and say—is the ultimate empirical root of the evidence or the "data" on which many anthropologists (and other behavioral scientists) build much of their diverse conceptualization and theory. It is the common core of observable events out of which each kind of investigator extracts his own concerns and to which he must return when questions of empirical prediction and validity arise. Indeed, in a primary sense we can say that the cultural anthropologist does not directly study "culture"; rather, he studies, i.e., observes, behavior, utilizing (at least in part) the *concept of culture* as a tool in his analysis. Thus the very fountainhead of what we observe as anthropologists is human behavior and not some mystical entity; and if a student is to get grounding in the operational meaning of the concept of culture, the relationship of that concept to its place in the world of observable behavioral events must be included from the beginning. It must be part of that "first approximation" in understanding.

A second reason for looking at behavior in relation to gaining an understanding of the concept of culture has to do with one of the attributes of culture commonly singled out in discussions of its role in human life and social evolution. This attribute is expressed in the phrase "Culture is man's way of adaptation."

Think for a moment about that phrase, and it becomes clear that what is really being made is a complex assertion, with the middle term implicit. That implicit middle term is "behavior." The way man—any organism—adapts and survives is through differential patterns of *behavior*; the term "adaptation" cannot be considered except, ultimately, with reference to behavior. When, therefore, the phrase "culture is man's way of adapting" is asserted, what is being said is something like the following:

Behavior is (equivalent to attempts at) adaptation;
Culture (as will be apparent in Part III) shapes much of that behavior;
Therefore: in large part culture is man's way of adapting.

But there is another reason for using behavior as the point of entry into understanding culture. If a student is led from the familiar into the unfamiliar, rather than catapulted directly into the middle of new abstract ideas, there is more likelihood of those new ideas being grasped and used as part of a developing framework of knowledge. Can we then start with something very familiar, something as familiar as one's own body, daily activities, sense of

[3]Carl G. Hempel, "Introduction to Problems of Taxonomy," in *Field Studies in the Mental Disorders*, ed. Joseph Zubin (New York: Grune and Stratton, 1961), p. 35. Reprinted with permission of publisher.

self, ways of seeing and feeling? Clearly, the assumption is that if we can come to see that much of what we take for granted about "human nature" is really simply *customary* ways of doing things and is in fact neither programmed biologically nor simply the result of *unique* learning experiences of the person, we can better sense how much culture cloaks and masks "human nature" and how much our particular cultural setting is *our* "human nature." Then we can take the next step in understanding "culture," that is, conceptualizing that pattern of influences leading to "customary" behavior as one major element in a dynamic behavioral process.

Among other things, that next step involves moving from the level of the individual person as the system being studied to that of the group or population as the system. That is apparently a transition having much difficulty for some people, depending as it does upon awareness of the *process* of abstracting, upon a kind of thinking very different from an "either/or" pattern (the "individual" *or* the "group"). It is, rather, one of systems *within* systems. It is a mode of thinking (in terms of "levels of analysis") appropriate to grasping the idea of *levels of phenomena* in nature, in which units at one level—analyzable in their own right—nevertheless function as units of larger systems. Thus, for some kinds of problems, the single cell is the bounded universe; but that same cell is also at the same time functionally part of other contexts, such as organ and organism (in the same way that an individual person can be viewed in isolation or as a member of environing systems, such as family, group, society).

It is to the *group level of events* that the concept of culture primarily refers, and this point will come out repeatedly in the readings. But the concept of culture is not the only major behavioral science concept having its primary location in the group level of events. Aside from the cultural dimension in collective human life there is the *social* dimension; and although the main thrust of this collection of readings is on the cultural system as a component in human life, to leave a reader without the beginnings of understanding that social dimension would be to distort the frame of reference. A few words, then, to convey the basic idea involved in the "social" (or more accurately, "sociocultural") level as an entity in its own right, for it is from such a nuclear concept that further differentiating concepts are compounded, such as social organization, institutions, kinship systems, networks of social relations, role systems, etc.

The building block of such structures is the idea of the *social fact*, as Durkheim put it—that phenomenon which is a new "thing" in nature created by interaction of two or more persons. It is something different from the properties of those two persons considered in empirical isolation from each other, although analytically (but not observationally) the unique contribution of each to the joint end product can be seen. The essence of this idea of the "social fact," on which more complex forms and conceptions of social structure and social organization are based, is illustrated in the following example:

> Two boys, between them, lift and carry a log which neither could move alone.
> You cannot speak of either boy as carrying half the log, in any concrete sense,

for the log is not in halves. Nor can you speak of either boy as half carrying the log, for there is no such concrete fact as half carrying the log. The two boys, coordinating their efforts upon the log, perform a joint action and achieve a result which is not divisible between the component members of this elementary group. To insist that the pair of boys consists simply of the two individuals is to commit an abstraction. It leaves out the log. By acting together upon the same object, the individuals composing the group coordinate their behavior, and the total behavior consequently possesses a unity analogous to that of a group of muscles in a coordinated movement.[4]

Although, as indicated above, the principal intent in this book of readings is not that of introducing you to the study of social organization or "social anthropology," clearly some understanding of at least the basic idea involved in a "social level of analysis" is a complement to that of a "cultural level of analysis," since this dimension figures into many of the articles that follow and is, like culture, rooted in collective aspects of human behavior.

But to talk about the group level of phenomena, or the collective aspect of individual experiences, is to raise that old chestnut of relations between "personality" and "culture," or the "individual" and "society," and go right into the perplexities of where, in nature, do we locate or assign "culture"? This is the old question of the "superorganic" level of cultural events (as Kroeber, White, and others have called it) as contrasted to the individual level of experiencing and manifesting those events. To try to give you some understanding of how to handle the empirical questions of "person" versus "culture" in a conceptual way, selections are included that deal with this issue and put the drawing of such distinctions where it belongs: in the mind of the investigator who is tackling a particular problem, and not in categories supplied by observed events in nature itself. It seems to me that unless a student has a firm grasp of how the concept of culture interlocks with other concepts, and unless he knows how to go up the ladder of abstraction from those conceptualizations that take the person as their observational focus to those which (while still rooted in the actions of that person) broaden the view of a *class* of persons and of *relations among* persons, he will be impeded from the outset.

To mention "patterns" or classes of observed behavioral events as the materials the cultural anthropologist works with is to refer to one of the ways the cultural anthropologist participates in the practice of science. The humanist may well be concerned with the single event or the unique happening. But the way of science is that of attempting to interrelate *classes* of events or things. In support of this point an early section of readings (Part I) has to do with the process of doing science, of considering science itself as a kind of behavior, of science (in Leslie White's apt term) as *sciencing*. While it may appear unnecessary in this day of advanced, moon-shot technology to include readings on what science is all about, I think it still needs repeating that basic to "science" is a way of thought, a particular kind of orientation toward

---

[4]R. S. Woodworth, "A Review of *Social Psychology* by F. H. Allport," *Journal of Abnormal Psychology*, 20 (1925), 105. Reprinted with permission of publisher.

nature. If something of that *way of thinking* about the world can be conveyed, then the aims and purposes, the methods of cultural anthropology as a science, can be viewed in better perspective. Finally, given the wide range of educational backgrounds of students who become interested in studying anthropology, many of whom for example may not have had much training in science (or at least in the conceptual character of science), to assume a working familiarity with the fundamental outlook of science may be overly optimistic. However that may be, a few passages are included that discuss what science is about generally and its implications for those sciences that take problems from the field of human behavior as their concern.

The broad format of the book, then, can be briefly summarized. First is the section of readings just referred to, those having to do with science generally, not with the distinctive concepts that characterize particular *sciences*, but rather with science as a kind of human activity and way of thinking about observable events. Based on the assumption that there *is* a structure of events apart from the perceiving person (an assumption perhaps worth restating in today's "do your own thing" world), it stresses that there are resemblances among observed events that can be grouped into classes, and that concepts referring to those classes of events can be developed into theoretical frameworks that aid in understanding and predicting interrelations among such classes of events.

The next section is less abstract. It brings together several examples of anthropological inquiry that convey something of how the cultural anthropologist begins his version of "sciencing"—what it is like to be in the field, where the field experience may lead in terms of inquiry into a problem, and finally, what is something of the "meaning" in human terms of anthropology for those doing it.

There is another reason for including this section on field work in anthropology. It is to convey the sense of anthropological inquiry as a *process*, not simply as a product or finished set of findings. Abraham Kaplan draws a distinction between two very different ways in which "science" is discussed and presented to the non-specialist.[5] One way, common in many works, is that of "reconstructed logic," i.e., science is presented as a neat, lockstep progression from statement of the problem through the rigorous deductive formulation and operationalization of hypotheses to the conducting of the crucial experiment and final evaluation of findings with reference to theoretical implications. The trouble is that such a tidy picture is rarely found in fact. It leaves out the trial and error, the operation of insight and hunch, the unforeseen observation that piques the curiosity, the role of serendipity (accidental discovery), and many of the other features that characterize the actual practice of science. One implication from Kaplan's comments is that a better way to learn about both the method and spirit of the scientific endeavor at understanding is through following a "logic-in-use" paradigm instead of the reconstructed logic paradigm—to see the rough edges, the tentative hypotheses, the interplay between theory and empirical datum at many points along the

---

[5]Abraham Kaplan, *The Conduct of Inquiry: Methodology for Behavioral Science* (San Francisco: Chandler Publishing Co., 1964).

way, instead of only the final, polished product of the analyst's skill. An excellent portrayal of such a "logic-in-use" process that culminated in one of the most momentous discoveries in recent science is the book by James Watson, *The Double Helix*.

In the next section we return to what was discussed above as the empirical roots of the concept of culture: behavior and how it is pervasively shaped and constituted by certain influences based in shared, group experience. Selections deal with the observable wide variations in human groups in treatment of the body and its processes, in behavior, and in belief that lead to the question of what is it that thus shapes and molds so much of what we are, and can we devise a concept that is a shorthand way of referring to those influences?

At this point the need for transition in thought from a focus on the person, to a focus on a concept of culture itself becomes apparent, and it is here that selections are included which indicate that the kind of concept one wants to use, its appropriateness and utility in a given problem context, are in the hands of the investigator; *they are not immutably and inexorably given by the empirical events themselves*. Several selections outline the conceptual and "operational" transition from a focus on the person and his behavior to that of collective phenomena, shared attributes. We are then at the point of considering culture generically, that is, as a concept that disregards individual variations among phenomena and refers, instead, to modal and collective aspects. Knowing how it has been arrived at and how it is related to its observational base in the real world, we can begin thinking more about some of its essential features.

The next sections of readings therefore deal with two of those basic properties of the concept as it is used here: first, its intimate interrelationship with symbolism, and second, its definition as a system of values, beliefs, and orientations *to* nature. Those sections are followed by excerpts which place culture, thus conceived, in a larger system, a "sociocultural" system, in which relations between "culture" and "society" as concepts are examined. Then we further increase the range of perspective employed and think of that sociocultural system *itself* in a context, turning to such ideas as adaptation, functional interrelations, and—a more recent term in the behavioral sciences —culture as part of an *ecosystem*. Finally, in the last section (Part VII), we return to take up in fuller detail the problems posed at the beginning—the case studies that illustrate some of the working concepts of the cultural anthropologist. By this time perhaps you will be in a better position to accept the several investigators' analyses of events and the suggested resolutions of those problems, thereby gaining further insights into the concept of culture and of culture as a process in larger systems of relationships.

ON THE MATTER OF DEFINITION

I hesitate to offer a definition of "culture" for fear it might be memorized and then used rigidly, in the manner of received wisdom or revealed truth. That is the chief mischief perpetrated by nominal definitions, for they often stultify thought and inquiry instead of serving, as they should do, as encouragement to an ongoing and evolving process of understanding.

However, on the assumption that for some readers the lack of a definition may prove more unsettling than the offering of one would prove crippling, I will suggest a definition of "culture" that I have found useful in trying to convey what I mean.[6] You will, of course, use it *heuristically* (that is, in a manner serving to instruct or inform) and not dogmatically. It should be helpful in ordering and systematizing thought in reference to observation; if it does not do that adequately, having understood its intention, you should devise your own:

> "A culture" is a learned configuration of images and other symbolic elements widely shared among members of a given society or social group which, for individuals, functions as an orientational framework for behavior; and, for the group, serves as the communicational matrix which tends to coordinate and sanction behavior.

Note that the chief dimension of the above definition is that of a shared way of perceiving the world, of orienting one's self and one's behavior—a "programming" kind of usage for the concept of culture. This is a kind of definition widely shared among working anthropologists. It is a kind of definition in which a *family* of terms are prominently found, such as "values," "beliefs," "meanings," "assumptions," "ideals," "understandings," "standards," "norms," "rules," "codes," "themes," and the like, and such terms can vary along a continuum from the implicit and unexpressed to the clearly formulated and overtly stated.

But that is not the only common usage. Let's back up for a moment. To oversimplify a bit, there seem to be two broad patterns of use for the concept of culture (and, we might add, it isn't always used consistently even within this framework). The key idea in the first of the uses is the "way of life" notion—a descriptive account of the observed behavioral regularities of a group of people, as in the phrase "In this culture, people do so and so." Many synonyms exist for this kind of usage of "culture," for example, "customs" or "social heritage." With such a conception, for instance, the various aspects of belief and institutional areas of group life can be referred to and contrasted from one group to another—family life, kinship relations, economic patterns, supernatural belief systems, and so on. However, for some problems, and for some *phases* in the analytic process, this kind of usage seems to be overloading the concept of "culture" with too much responsibility and asking it to do too much.

A second major kind of conception, the kind suggested first, is more restrictive in its reference to natural events and responds to the dilemma about working responsibility. In this case, "culture" refers only to a part of the set of observations of ongoing events and behavior, and is an inference

[6]If you want a choice of other definitions, you should look into the numerous definitions discussed and analyzed in the review monograph, by A. L. Kroeber and Clyde Kluckhohn, *Culture: A Critical Review of Concepts and Definitions* (Cambridge: Harvard University), Papers of the Peabody Museum of American Archaeology and Ethnology, vol. 47, no. 1 (1952). A paperback edition is published by Vintage Books.

from those observations that is concerned with shared and patterned orientations, images, concepts of the world—with what has been called an "assumptive world"—which are part of what the person as a result of social learning brings to a situation and which influence his behavior. In this view, the term does not directly describe overt behavior, but rather is conceived as one element, dimension, or "input" into that behavior. Perhaps the most elaborate (though it is not unique) statement of this kind of conception of culture is that associated with the work of Talcott Parsons, Clyde Kluckhohn, and others at Harvard University, in which the "cultural system" is discussed as values and "value-orientations" in a concrete empirical situation. The essential questions here, for the analyst of culture, are: How does the person see the world? How does this predispose him to act in particular ways as a result of such an orientation? "Culture" is therefore seen as one element—a major element—in a "theory of action," the study of human behavior systems, the other key elements being the social system, personality system, and biological system. Kluckhohn has discussed this particular view of a concept of culture in the following way:

> The simple biological analogy of "organism and environment" is inadequate because man is a culture-bearing animal. Some sort of three-way paradigm is necessary since we have: (a) individuals, (b) the situations in which they find themselves, and (c) the modes or ways in which they are oriented to these situations. In terms of the intellectual division of labor which has generally been adhered to during this century, the study of individual organisms and their motivations has been the province of psychology and biology. Insofar as sociology has had a distinct conceptual field, it has been that of investigation of the situation. Cultural anthropology has been dealing with the modes of orientation to the situation. How the individual is oriented to his situation is, in the concrete sense, "within" the actor, but not in the analytic sense, for modal orientations cannot, by definition, be derived from observing and questioning a single individual—they are culture.[7]

In the readings that follow you will find references to both the general, "way of life" conception of culture and that of culture as a system of belief and orientation. But the main emphasis is clearly on the second usage—culture as a system of symbolic elements, a system of orientations *to* experience which not only shape individual experience but also structure many areas of social reality as well, and is not simply a descriptive summary of those experiences themselves. Some writers have likened this second view to a "coding" system which thereby selects and differentially highlights some aspects of experience over others. It also expresses the idea that culture is a process productive of an entirely unique dimension, a *meaning* dimension, in human behavior as compared to that of other animal forms. Another way of stating it is perhaps too simple but contains the basic idea: culture is the assignment of value to fact.

---

[7]Clyde Kluckhohn, "Culture and Behavior," in *Handbook of Social Psychology*, ed. Gardner Lindzey, vol. II (Reading: Addison-Wesley Publishing Co., 1954), pp. 960–61. Reprinted with permission of publisher.

ANTHROPOLOGY AND THE BEHAVIORAL SCIENCES

While concerned with the matter of definitions—with giving *some* idea, at least, of what is meant by the terms used—I might add a few words about "anthropology" itself as a discipline or field of study, especially about its relation to the other prominent social or behavioral sciences, such as sociology and psychology. What follows will not please everyone, I am sure—neither all anthropologists, nor, certainly, sociologists and psychologists. But it may be worth the effort; for to the student just entering the social or behavioral sciences as a field of study, the terms, the boundary-disputes, and the territorial questions may sometimes seem (quite rightly) not only overwhelming but also fruitless, a quarreling over mere words rather than substance. A bit said about this matter may therefore be appropriate to serve as something of a summary of a number of ideas contained in the forthcoming pages as well as to place cultural anthropology in context in the usual university or college organizational setting.

There is, obviously, a good deal of overlap among the behavioral sciences in concept, terminology, and method. But there are also differences, and many of those that exist are at the level of the philosophic framework in which the world is viewed—basic assumptions, themes, or viewpoints. Such assumptions, often implicit, are operative in the characterization and study of a problem, constituting a "hidden agenda" in discourse between one kind of behavioral scientist and another. It is possible, I believe, to isolate several such basic themes or assumptions of anthropological inquiry, which, taken together as a syndrome, influence many of the methods, techniques, and concepts employed by the practitioners of "anthropology." I prefer this kind of demonstrative definition to the simpler "anthropology is the study of man" approach, for it is more descriptive of the range of problems investigated, as will be evident in the readings that follow. Let us turn, then, to a brief consideration of themes of anthropological inquiry.[8]

1. The species-centered character of anthropology as a discipline.

One of the ways of differentiating among the several behavioral sciences is to look at their implicit intellectual targets. They often do not stay directly on target, of course; indeed, they wander quite widely. But it can be asserted that psychology, sociology, and anthropology each has a different "home base" in the process of inquiry, and that such reference points serve as basic, often unexpressed, anchoring points that influence derivative concepts, theory development, and methods of research. Thus, while admitting the oversimplification, one can say that while the central reference point of choice for sociology as a discipline is *society*, its many forms and subsystems, and that for psychology the central focus is on various psychological processes as manifested in the individual organism, for anthropology such a reference

[8]The following section has been adapted in revised form from a paper prepared for another purpose, "Anthropology and Medical Education," by Donald A. Kennedy and Charles C. Hughes, presented at the Second International Conference on Social Science and Medicine, Aberdeen, Scotland, September 4–7, 1970.

framework is man as a species, *Homo sapiens.* Indeed the etymology of the term suggests this.

Of course, the natural history of inquiry in the evolution of the various behavioral sciences has taken them into many common problem areas, so that it is sometimes difficult (and often unnecessary) to discern whether the given investigator is a "sociologist," "psychologist," or "anthropologist." Thus, for example, all three disciplines have done studies of socialization, social organization, belief systems, mental health, and numerous others. But there usually remains considerable attachment to, or "imprinting" from, that "home base" of disciplinary assumptions and orientations which give coherence to the body of concepts distinguishing each discipline and serving as corporate values for the group of scholars differentiating themselves by use of the disciplinary label.

The implicit character of what has emerged as "anthropology" (at least in the American academic scene) has been strongly influenced by the natural history and biological sciences approach to understanding events in nature. In much the same way—and with much the same inclusive scope—as there evolved disciplines or fields of study centering on other species or orders of animals and plants (e.g., mammalogy, herpetology, apiology, ornithology, pomology, etc.), so too man was taken as a legitimate object of inquiry, man and everything that pertained to him: his evolutionary past and current differentiation, his bodily form and mental functioning, his settlement patterns and social organization, his artifactual manipulations, his symbolic productions, his growth and development—in other words, nothing that was part of the life and behavior of man as an animal form was excluded by academic fiat from investigation as relevant to understanding him, however difficult it might be for any one person or group of persons to live up entirely to the demands of such an intellectual goal. But it is such open-ended commitment which, more than anything else, provides the coherent framework for anthropology as a discipline and makes it understandable why the study of man's psychobiological development, varieties, and capabilities ("physical anthropology"), his artifact assemblages ("archaeology" and "material culture"), his symbolic productions ("linguistics"), his social organizations ("social anthropology"), his belief and values systems ("cultural anthropology"), and his socially-derived personality structure ("psychological anthropology") are complementary and not dispersive areas of study.

One form of this intellectual commitment to the "study of man" made by anthropology is often expressed as the "holistic" approach to understanding the phenomenon of man and his behavior—an open-ended, "wide-angle vision" rather than a "tunnel vision" approach in working through a problem.

2. The preference for natural settings in investigations of human behavior.

Anthropology is very much a field-oriented enterprise, one in which the primary desideratum is investigation of human behavior in all kinds of natural settings—whether they be nomadic hunting and gathering bands, sedentary villages, developing cities, urban ghettos. hospital wards, factory assembly lines, aircraft crew operations, or whatever. Closely allied with this orientation is another which has implications for behavioral science methods as a whole. That is an emphasis upon, but not an exclusive concern with, observational and participant observational studies, by which is meant that the investigator becomes part of the social action he is studying.

While it can be argued that because of the investigator's presence in the research situation his findings are thereby affected, even contaminated, the counter-argument can be made that the quality of data thus obtained is worth the cost in whatever degree of artificiality of conduct may occur because of the researcher's presence. In addition, being in the action affords the chance to observe not only the real life situation of the persons being studied, but also the degree of correspondence between self-reports of attitude and behavior in imagined situations, and their actual behavior in a context of real events.

Such an observational and participant-observational method supplements, of course, and does not replace, data-gathering techniques based upon verbal interviews. It simply enlarges the scope of evidence upon which conclusions and inferences relating to the social process being studied can be based, bringing in contextual factors such as physical setting or crisis events in the daily social round and, perhaps most important, a chance for the outside investigator to see life (at least up to a point) as the people he is living with see it. It provides the context for informed empathy.

3. The pervasiveness of an ecologic perspective.

Closely intertwined with the development of anthropology as a discipline has been a concern with interrelations between man and his environment or "habitat" (to use the older and perhaps even more suggestive term). Indeed, it could not be otherwise, for the very evolution of man out of proto- and pre-hominid primate forms was strongly influenced by particular climatological and topographic features, and the pattern of transactions between environmental and sociocultural forms in any human group is a primary element in understanding the structure and dynamics of social processes.

The inclusive term for such an orientation is, of course, "ecology"—much used these days and equally as much abused, "abused" in the sense of often being conceived in an overly restrictive and too narrow a manner, such as the static sense in which it is employed to refer simply to settlement patterns or aggregate social data. But in actuality the term comes from and makes reference to the very essence of the life process: attempts at adaptive and adjustive behavior on the part of an organism or group of organisms—adaptation to environing conditions of life, which includes coping with each other (e.g., seen in matters of population density, of hierarchical power structuring and "pecking orders," etc.). The term, indeed, has the power to inform a wide range of particular investigations which relate to the dynamics of behavior, whether in individual or group terms. It may be suggested that what is called "structural-functional analysis" in behavioral science is, with sociocultural content, another expression of a basic ecologic perspective on events in nature—in other words, a subset of a more encompassing conceptual system; for the intent, as with ecology, is to see the many varieties of the functional coupling of events and structures, of which cultural and social systems are only a part.

With the human species, ecologic studies become more complicated than they do with nonhuman species, for another set of considerations is introduced into the basic dialectic of man with nature. This is elaboration of psychological transactions with the environment, taking the form of perceptions, projections, rationalizations and repressions, anticipations, aspirations, affect-laden symbolizations and images, abstractions and class concepts, etc., all heavily influenced by a specific social context but subject to idiosyncratic reworking. It is this capacity of the human organism for complex psychological relations with the environment that underlies the development of shared group systems of belief, value, and assumption (in one term "culture"), and, in turn, creates another dimension in that very environment with which the person must cope.

4. An ingrained evolutionary and diachronic perspective.

Although not all problems demand it and not all anthropologists employ it as a perspective of choice, nevertheless, built into the collective frame of reference is a strong awareness of the workings of time in shaping the observed event or form. A common feature of the "culture of anthropology" (if we can think of it in this way) is an implicit emphasis upon process and interaction of empirical events over time, whether the content be morphological or societal. Such an element of the frame of reference explains, for example, the joining together (in many introductory courses) of human evolution with the growth and development of human society and culture; indeed, to do so helps illuminate many of the most striking aspects of "human" nature, such as those features of *Homo sapiens* as a primate which underlie his capacity for culture and for a distinctly *human* mode of adaptation to the environment.

It is with respect to this theme, for example, that studies by physical anthropologists, zoologists, and ethologists of primate behavior are relevant in bringing out some of the kinds of social organizational forms that are possible given particular stages of somatic and cortical development. Although the "origin of language," for instance, will never be sharply specified in a temporal framework, the hypothesis is well-argued that survival possibilities of australopithecine or other pre-hominid forms were immensely increased when they achieved better coordination of group efforts through development of that highly effective signaling and information-storing system, language, a development itself that functionally evolved through interacting factors of habitat and morphology.

Such a "long-range" perspective is indeed enormous and, if internalized fully, forces one to acknowledge how parochial and circumscribed is the usual sense of time with which we operate. If nothing else, it is startling to realize how very tiny a portion of the span of organic life on this planet is occupied by anything that we can justifiably call *human* experience. If, for example, the origin of the earth itself is placed at about 3 billion years ago (a conservative estimate these days), and if this estimate were concretized by a book consisting of 3,000 pages (each page representing one million years), the point at which the earliest (and crudest) forms of manlike apes appear is somewhere on page 2,999; the earliest forms of "modern" man (some 50,000 years ago) close to the bottom of the very last page; the birth of Christ somewhere in the last word in the last line; and the beginning of the twentieth century as only part of the final period in that last line.

This long record of the unfolding of life and its forms accomplishes something more than mere philosophic bewilderment. It enforces an essentially dynamic and interactive point of view for all natural phenomena. Changes and modification of existing forms in nature are seen as the norm, with concepts of "structure" serving as "halfway house" concepts in the service of understanding patterns of process.

5. The pervasiveness of the symbolic dimension in human behavior.

A generation ago Ernst Cassirer said, "Man has, as it were, discovered a new method of adapting himself to his environment. Between the receptor system and the effector system, which are to be found in all animal species, we find in man a third link which we may describe as the symbolic system." The most obvious manifestation of this symbolic system in the human species is language, with its abstracting and generalizing capacities; but it is by no means the only mode in which referential symbolism makes its appearance in human behavior, nor is the influence of the symbolizing function as a shaper of meaning confined only to spoken utterances. Indeed, to follow Whitehead's phrase, "Symbolism has a tendency to run wild, like vegetation in a tropical forest," and not only other kinds of sounds (e.g., music), but also physical sensations (such as pain), material objects, clothing, adornment, artifacts, social situations and events (e.g., ritual), all and anything may function in the dual capacity of serving one kind of need while at the same time being indicators of another dimension or definition of the situation. The event or object, when used symbolically, must be interpreted in terms of that world beyond itself to which it has reference if a full understanding of its importance in human affairs is to be achieved. Consider for example something very familiar from the television screen: the clinician's white coat. Worn by anyone, even an unschooled actor, it confers—it *means*—authority, skill, and wisdom. The ability of other kinds of empirical events such as dress, seating patterns, posture, titles to convey status, i.e., to indicate, without explicitly saying so, power ranking and special privilege, is a prime ingredient in the social process. In most situations in which people find themselves the forms of symbolism, the ability of any one thing or object to serve as a stand-in for something else or some other situation, are protean—especially when the matter is viewed in a cross-cultural framework.

6. An implicit cross-cultural and comparative perspective.

Although the task is immense, anthropologists take seriously the commitment to *Man* writ large in considering their generalizations and formulating their theoretical positions. Such an almost instinctive approach derives, indeed, from several of the themes sketched in above. Insofar as the ambitious subject matter of the discipline is "man," the list of diverse instances is drawn as broadly as possible as a foundation for generalizations—from the simple bands of Bushmen in the Kalahari Desert to the high civilizations of the Andes, the ghetto dweller, the study of political elites in modern Africa, Tungus reindeer herders of northeastern Siberia, or any number of other groups. Far from simply serving an anecdotal function, contrasting and diverse ethnological data bearing on the same problem area are vital in cleansing variables of parochial content and, in consequence, more soundly based theory development.

Return for the moment to the illustration of color symbolism referred to above. To those of us in the Western tradition, the color white most commonly conjures up positive values, sanctity, cleanliness, holiness, goodness, and the like. Contrastingly, in many contexts the color black signifies the opposite values; indeed, it is culturally the predominant color of grief and mourning. But for some Chinese groups white, not black, signifies grief and bereavement, and for some Mexican Indian groups red serves a similar purpose. From the point of view of a cross-cultural perspective, it is not the color *per se* that is chosen that is important, but the fact that so many groups do have affect-laden symbols (color and otherwise) by which they "express" and thereby externalize psychological processes in response to a crisis event. Beyond color, of course, all the data of human behavior are subject to diverse cultural differentiation and expression, and one of the implicit concerns of anthropological inquiry, as a collective enterprise at least, is to place all problems in a framework comparative of culture, time, and space.

Let us hold in mind, then, these six themes of anthropology as a discipline; perhaps consider them as a minimal frame of reference, a sketch of a group of ideas that give structure to many dimensions of inquiry in the field:

1. The species-centered character of anthropology as a discipline
2. The preference for natural settings in investigations of human behavior
3. The pervasiveness of an ecologic perspective
4. An ingrained evolutionary and diachronic perspective
5. The pervasiveness of the symbolic dimension in human behavior
6. An implicit cross-cultural and comparative perspective

We can turn now to the readings themselves. Clyde Kluckhohn once epitomized the study of culture as

. . . the study of circular and interactive behavior. The prime anthropological problem is to find the right point of entrance in studying a circle.

After selections concerned with the nature of science and the anthropologist in the field, our point of entrance into that circle will be where culture intersects human life, seeing there how diverse societies take the raw material they have to work with and, through the instrument of a cultural system, make "human beings" out of members of *Homo sapiens*. Recall the Foreword (p. vii), in which Benjamin Franklin was telling of the conflict of cultures and of meaning between the Virginia colonists and the Indians of the Six Nations. The Indian spokesman put our purpose in this reader very well:

> But you who are wise must know, that different nations have different conceptions of things. . . .

PART I

SCIENCE IS "SCIENCING"

As I said in the Introduction, I don't consider it beside the point to start off with some readings on the fundamental nature of science, for this will help set the tone for what follows. One can't assume that, even these days, everybody "knows" what science is; too many seem to have either a global perception of it as some variant of magic, or else an understanding of the specifics of a *particular* science but no fundamental grasp of it as a generic process of knowing. (Then, of course, there are those who see it as having two horns —the devil in today's world that leeches the good and beautiful out of man, leaving him as only a soul-less husk of biological material.)

In this section, we are concerned with what science is about as a human activity. We will see science as the search for ordered relations in an open-ended, dynamic world of events, a search rooted in observations that are interrelated with concepts and theoretical structures. This is a common theme, of course. Bronowski states the problem generally and places it in a historical framework of the development of science as a cultural phenomenon in European societies. I have included this excerpt because he starts with fundamentals of the sciencing process which traditionally have been and remain one of the chief areas of contribution by anthropology to the behavioral sciences: the ordering and systematization of observations concerning diversity in human behavior around the world.

The article by Leslie White is justly well known, at least in part for its stress upon science as generic human activity, not as a completed thing but as a *process*. It is also relevant here insofar as it attempts to place the "science of culture" in a larger framework of general scientific approaches to various domains of natural events (although, as will be evident, I do not fully subscribe to his conceptual dictates).

The remaining selection (by Ross) stresses themes already stated—science as process, as observationally-based, as a *social* activity which is culturally cumulative and self-corrective (another of the distinctive features of science as a human activity that sets it apart from some other kinds of activities, such as religion or art).

FEATURES OF SCIENCE

Science takes many forms, but lying behind its various appearances is a common thread. This thread, or theme, is that science is a way of dealing with the world and that the language (or languages) of science comprise tools for describing and anticipating events in nature. If science, however, does link man to his surroundings (and *to himself*) in this fashion, it does so through particular kinds of methods which can be communicated and shared, and not through those of the mystic or the artist, who creates from the events of nature his own "reality." The primary link in the relation of science to the world is fundamentally that of multiple observations of recurring events (with such "observation" often utilizing mechanical and technical aids to human capacities for seeing the world, ranging from microscope to questionnaire). "Observation" in science, then, means "data"—that which is given by nature independent of the observer. Such an observational base is, however, only the necessary and not the sufficient condition for a scientific understanding of the world; fact must be joined with concept in the constant search for order, structure, predictable pattern. To speak of concepts is to speak of another of the fundamental features in man's gaining knowledge of the world around him—the process of *abstracting* and grouping together into one thing or class (that is, generalizing) events in nature that, though they are similar, in the last analysis are unique. These several themes are what Bronowski, a noted physicist (who happens also to be a poet), lays before us in excerpts from his excellent little book, *The Common Sense of Science*.

THE CHARACTER OF SCIENCE

J. BRONOWSKI

The whole structure of thought in the Middle Ages is one which we find hard to grasp today. It was an orderly structure, but the principles by which it was ordered seem to us now outlandish and meaningless. Take such a simple question as that which is said to have turned Newton's mind to the problem of gravitation: Why does an apple when it leaves the tree fall down to the ground? The question had been asked often since the fourteenth century, when the active and enquiring men of the Italian Renaissance began to take an interest in the mechanical world. For answer, they went back to one of the

Reprinted with permission of publisher. From J. Bronowski, *The Common Sense of Science* (Cambridge: Harvard University Press, 1955).

great re-discoveries of the Arabs and the Renaissance, the works of the Greek philosophers. To us, this answer smacks of the most pompous tradition of philosophy, and does less to explain the world than to shuffle it in a set of tautologies. For the Middle Ages answered the question about the apple in the tradition of Aristotle: The apple falls down and not up because it is its nature to fall down.

In putting it in this way, I have of course made a caricature of the answer. I have done so not to make fun of it but, on the contrary, in order to show that even in this extravagantly naïve form, the answer is not really childish. It would be childish only if it read "This apple falls down and not up because it is the nature of this apple at this instant to fall down". But this is not what Aristotle said. He said that the particular apple falls down now because it is the nature of all apples to fall down at all times. Simple as this notion may seem to us, it is in itself a bold and remarkable extension of the mind. The mere creation of a permanent class of apples, the mere generalisation of the concept of apples, is an act of the first importance. Of course it is simple enough to make a class of identical objects such as pennies or the capital A's in this book. But nature does not provide identical objects; on the contrary, these are always human creations. What nature provides is a tree full of apples which are all recognisably alike and yet are not identical, small apples and large ones, red ones and pale ones, apples with maggots and apples without. To make a statement about all these apples together, and about crab-apples, Orange Pippins, and Beauties of Bath, is the whole basis of reasoning.

This is so important that I must underline it. The action of putting things which are not identical into a group or class is so familiar that we forget how sweeping it is. The action depends on recognising a set of things to be alike when they are not identical. We order them by what it is that we think they have in common, which means by something that we feel to be a likeness between them. Habit makes us think the likeness obvious; it seems to us obvious that all apples are somehow alike, or all trees, or all matter. Yet there are languages in the Pacific Islands in which every tree on the island has a name, but which have no word for tree. To these islanders, trees are not at all alike; on the contrary, what is important to them is that the trees are different. In the same islands men identify themselves with the totem of their clan, say with the parrot, and it seems to them plain that they are like parrots when to us the notion seems a mere artifice, and an outrageous one.

This ability to order things into likes and unlikes is, I think, the foundation of human thought. And it is a human ability; we trace and to some extent inject the likeness, which is by no means planted there by nature for all to see. Our very example of Newton's apple shows this vividly. For Newton's instant insight, as he himself told it, was precisely to see the likeness which no one else had seen, between the fall of the apple and the swing of the moon in its orbit round the earth. The theory of gravitation rests upon this; and familiar as the likeness now is to us, and obvious, it would have

seemed merely fanciful to the Aristoteleans of the Middle Ages.

In order to act in a scientific manner, in order to act in a human manner at all, two things are necessary: fact and thought. Science does not consist only of finding the facts; nor is it enough only to think, however rationally. The processes of science are characteristic of human action in that they move by the union of empirical fact and rational thought, in a way which cannot be disentangled. There is in science, as in all our lives, a continuous to and fro of factual discovery, then of thought about the implications of what we have discovered, and so back to the facts for testing and discovery—a step by step of experiment and theory, left, right, left, right, for ever.

This union of two methods is the very base of science. Whitehead, who in his philosophy laid stress on it, dated the Scientific Revolution from the moment when Galileo and his contemporaries understood that the two methods, the empirical and the logical, are each meaningless alone, and that they must be put together. In Whitehead's view, the Middle Ages were quite as logical in their speculations about nature as we are. It is not as rationalists that we have the advantage of them; our material successes stem from joining to their logic a ruthless appeal, at each bold deductive step, back to the hard empirical facts. The moment when this was begun, and the authority of the thought and the word was put to the challenge of fact, has long been dramatised in a scene at Pisa. Galileo is said to have dropped a large and a small mass from the Leaning Tower there; and they reached the ground more or less together, in flat contradiction of the pronouncements of Aristotle and Aquinas. But history is rarely so simple or so decisive. Galileo did not make this experiment at Pisa, and those who did could not make it work. And meanwhile logic was already thinking out the experiment. Independent spirits in the bolder school of Paris had for some time doubted Aristotle's dictum that larger masses fall faster. Their logical objection can be put in this way: that since three equal masses dropped together will all fall side by side, it is at least unlikely that two of them should suddenly begin to gain on the third merely because they happen to be tied or formed together into a larger mass.

We need not wonder too nicely whether we shall take this event or that thought as zero hour for the

Scientific Revolution. No change of outlook is as direct as Whitehead implies, or as abrupt as I have sometimes dramatically pictured it. The beginnings of the Industrial Revolution go back before 1760, and the beginnings of the Scientific Revolution go back long before 1660 or indeed that earlier day, real or fabled, on the Leaning Tower of Pisa about 1600. But our concern is not with beginnings; it is with the visible substantial change, from the outlook before to the outlook after. The outlook before the Scientific Revolution was content with scholastic logic applied to a nature of hierarchies. The Scientific Revolution ended that: it linked the rational and the empirical, thought and fact, theory and practical experiment. And this has remained the content of science ever since. . . .

The ambition of the eighteenth century systematisers was to impose a mathematical finality on history and biology and geology and mining and spinning. It was a mistaken ambition and very damaging. A science is a description of the world or, better, a language for describing the world. When a science has been studied as long as astronomy, it can develop a concise description in the shorthand of laws like Newton's. But before this can happen it must have the observations not only of Tycho Brahe and Kepler, but of the Moors and the Greeks and even the Babylonians. Until a science has passed through a long stage of observation and trial, it cannot develop a system of ordering its observations; and it is mere presumption to try to fit it with so ambitious an order as Newton's.

Indeed there is no reason to think that the mathematical method is even appropriate to every science. But we need not stay to argue that in this context. What is certain here is that, even where the method of axioms ruling a substratum of elementary particles or events is appropriate, it simply cannot be applied until that science has an exceptionally full record of observations. In the eighteenth century, there was no science with an orderly history of observations except astronomy. There was in fact at the time no further scope for the mathematical method of all.

Therefore the important progress in science in the eighteenth century was made not under the domination of the mathematicians, but out of sight by two kinds of empirical workers. There were the self-made inventors of whom I have already spoken, like Brindley and the Wedgwoods and the Darby family and James Watt. And there were the observers and collectors, the eccentric virtuosi, of whom it was fashionable to make fun. They were men like Sir Hans Sloane, whose collection began the British Museum, and simple observers like Gilbert White of Selborne. They were travellers coming back with antiques from Italy and inscriptions from Turkey. Thomas Jefferson, the American statesman, is the model of the scientific observer and collector of the age. He collected everything from flints to Indian languages, and observed everything from American plants to the French Revolution; and he was at the same time a great humanist.

In England, this temper and that of the industrial inventor were combined in the little societies run by go-ahead manufacturers in the Midlands and the North. Such societies were the Manchester Philosophical Society, which discovered the chemist Dalton, and the Lunar Society of Birmingham, where men like Joseph Priestley and Josiah Wedgwood and Wilkinson and Edgeworth met. Erasmus Darwin, the grandfather of Charles Darwin, was a member of the Lunar Society. His botanical primers in verse, taking such subjects as *The Loves of the Plants*, brought the new approach into the rigid teaching of the time. . . .

The best example of the new order which was being discovered in the non-mathematical sciences is botany. It remains to this day the creation of the Swedish naturalist Linnaeus, who set out in the eighteenth century the system of classification by species and families on which it still rests. What kind of order was Linnaeus looking for? Why did his order seem so plainly more reasonable than, say, a grading of flowers by their colours?

This is the most difficult question in science. The notion of order cannot be defined on any ground except its success. It cannot be put into a science in advance at all. It is not obviously silly to classify flowers by their colours; after all, the bluer flowers do tend to be associated with colder climates and greater heights. There is nothing wrong with the system, in advance. It simply does not work as conveniently and as instructively as Linnaeus's classification by family likenesses.

Order is the selection of one set of appearances rather than another because it gives a better sense of the reality behind the appearances. Science is an orderly language for describing some events and predicting others like them. The order is a selection of appearances. And any selection itself implies, and imposes, an interpretation. If we choose a successful order, as Linnaeus did, we lead that science naturally to the discovery first of evolution and ultimately of the way that inheritance works. If we choose a far-sighted arrangement of the chemical elements in order, as the periodic table does, it leads us by steps to the theories both of molecules and of atomic structure. In each case, our choice has been an unconscious interpretation; just as the literary realist interprets life by the very act of choosing the slice of it which he holds out so faithfully and so depressingly.

We have a great deal to learn from these unassuming orders of the eighteenth century naturalists. Their odd minds were remarkably free from theoretical prejudices; they had to be, to resist the prestige of the mathematical method. And they made the language of their science in the most human way, like the making of a character. We cannot change our character, we can only enlarge it. If we are wise, then we go on learning all through life, and go on fitting what is new to what we have learnt before, piece by piece. And at the end of our life we have a full and orderly personality in which the boy, the undergraduate, the fanatic and the lover all remain and are all enlarged and fulfilled. It is the collector's and the biologist's and the historian's order: the sort of order which fills Frazer's *Golden Bough* say, with the sense of real people busy with customs which they really enjoy. It is an order which other scientists and humanists might envy. . . .

This is the important step in every science: the construction of a first order which is reasonable in itself and which holds to the experimental facts that are known. We see it with the greatest clarity in the order which Linnaeus brought to botany, which had such far-reaching effects later in evolution and then in genetics. But it was equally important in the other sciences which in the eighteenth century still had no orderly body of observations, though some of them were of great age. The obvious examples are the other biological sciences. Think of the most important of them, medicine. It is as old as recorded history; there is even some evidence that operations like trepanning were known to prehistoric man. It had a high standing at least since Greek times. It attracted some of the best medieval and Renaissance minds, particularly among the Moors and Jews of North Africa and Spain. Great discoveries had been made in it in the seventeenth century, for example by William Har-

vey about the function and power of the heart as a pump. And medicine certainly did not lack a system. Words which we still use, like "phlegmatic" and "fiery", witness the long and lasting influence of its system of four humours. For the theory of the humours was not only the theory of psychological types which Ben Jonson's plays have made familiar to us. It was a theory of medical types, founded in turn on the theory of the four elements which I sketched earlier.

The theory of humours tried to analyse diseases and temperaments into one or more of four extreme types: earthy, watery, airy or fiery. The folly of the theory was that it tried to impose a system on events which had not been sufficiently observed; and in time it came to shape the observations themselves by the system. . . .

The purpose of science is to describe the world in an orderly scheme or language which will help us to look ahead. We want to forecast what we can of the future behaviour of the world; particularly we want to forecast how it would behave under several alternative actions of our own between which we are usually trying to choose. This is a very limited purpose. It has nothing whatever to do with bold generalisations about the universal workings of cause and effect. It has nothing to do with cause and effect at all, or with any other special mechanism. Nothing in this purpose, which is to order the world as an aid to decision and action, implies that the order must be of one kind rather than another. The order is what we find to work, conveniently and instructively. It is not something we stipulate; it is not something we can dogmatise about. It is what we find; it is what we find useful.

Let me give an example. One causal mechanism in the breeding of plants is obviously their sex. No one discovered that plants have sex until the time of Queen Anne, sometime about 1710. But men had been breeding plants for thousands of years before that. Over the larger part of the world, man has actually created his culture by turning a few scraggy grasses into the wheats. His methods were not causal ones; but his work was at least as successful as anything that the rationalists of Queen Anne's day did.

In order to act, it is not necessary to have a metaphysical belief that the rules by which we are acting are universal and that all other rules are just like them. On the contrary, at bottom all general beliefs of this kind are at odds with the princi-ples of science. Laplace believed that if we knew the present completely, we could completely de-termine the future. This belief had some political and religious force for Frenchmen of the Revolu-tion. But it has no scientific meaning at all. It does not resemble a scientific statement, or for that mat-ter a literary one, because it is not a statement about reality, either now or in the future. There simply is no sense in asserting what would happen if we knew the present completely. We do not, and plainly we never can.

This is precisely what the principle of uncertainty says to modern physics. It makes no assertions at all about whether we could or could not predict the future of an electron, supposing that we knew this or that about its present. It simply points out that we cannot completely know its present. For in-stance, we can know either its whereabouts or its speed with high precision; but we cannot know both. And, in consequence, we cannot predict its future.

At bottom then, the principle of uncertainty states in special terms what was always known, which is this. Science is a way of describing reality; it is therefore limited by the limits of observation; and it asserts nothing which is outside observation. Anything else is not science; it is scholastics. The nineteenth century was dominated by Laplace's belief that everything can be described by its causes. But this is no less scholastic than the medieval be-lief, that everything is contained in the First Cause.

SCIENCE AS ACTIVITY

Leslie White has long been one of the most influential of modern American anthropologists and a frequently cited article of his follows next. As was Bronowski, White is concerned with some of the fundamental features of science; he offers not a simple verbal definition of the end products of science, but a discussion of science as a human activity, as a *process of discovery* in knowing the world around. This interest in conveying a sense of science as a human activity for dealing with reality is the basis of the title: "Science is 'Sciencing,' " i.e., the best way to grasp what science "is" is to see what *scientists do*. Science is, in other words, a dynamic activity rather than a static achievement, changing and evolving in the same way that nature, which it purports to study and understand, changes and evolves. This theme—of nature as the background process against which we superimpose our mental constructions in an attempt to understand and anticipate—reiterates what was said by Bronowski. It also looks to what will come up again later (Part IV), when Homans, Hayakawa, and others analyze the process of knowing and the nature of conceptualization.

White also introduces an idea fundamental to understanding variety in the sciences and something of their interrelationships: the idea of "levels" of phenomena and the relationship of part to whole. Today's language might be "systems" and "subsystems" in referring to the same basic notion. One of White's purposes is to establish the basis for considering "culture" to be a process or system on a level of its own, one not reducible to a psychological or biological level. As we will see later, while most social scientists work with such a concept (often phrased as a "*socio*cultural" level), not all fully accept White's view of the extent of autonomy of the "cultural" level in governing human behavior.

SCIENCE IS "SCIENCING"

LESLIE A. WHITE

Science is not merely a collection of facts and formulas. It is preëminently a way of dealing with experience. The word may be appropriately used as a verb: one *sciences*, i.e., deals with experience according to certain assumptions and with certain techniques. Science is one of two basic ways of dealing with experience. The other is art. And this word, too, may appropriately be used as a verb; one may *art* as well as science. The purpose of science and art is one: to render experience intelligible, i.e., to assist man to adjust himself to his environment in order that he may live. But although working toward the same goal, science and art approach it from opposite directions. Science deals with particulars in terms of universals: Uncle Tom disappears in the mass of Negro slaves. Art deals with universals in terms of particulars: the whole gamut of Negro slavery confronts us in the person of Uncle Tom. Art and science thus grasp a common experience, or reality, by opposite but inseparable poles.

To use the word science as a noun is not, however, without justification. The words chemistry, physiology, history, sociology, etc., are both legitimate and useful. As categories they are derived from two sources. On the one hand, they reflect analytical distinctions which may be made within the field of reality: erosion, respiration, hysteria, voting, etc., are phases or segments of experience which find their reflections in the categories geology, physiology, psychology, and political science, respectively. On the other hand, division of labor in society, essential in modern times, also finds its reflection in the same, or similar, categories. This is a fact often ignored. Psychology is a category that is a reflection of the division of society into disparate occupational groups just as truly as it is an expression of analytical distinctions which may be made in experience ("subject matter") itself. "Psychology is what *psychologists* (i.e., a guild of workers bearing the label 'psychologist') do," is as valid a definition as "psychology is the study of mind, or behavior." The one is an expression of social reality, of social derivation; the other derives from the nature of the subject matter of the study.

This dual nature of the categories becomes manifest in the recurrent protest against the partition of science into "watertight" compartments, in the impossibility of telling whether a given study is historical, sociological, or psychological. Does the story of John Brown's "insurrection" belong to psychology, sociology, economics, political science, or history? Obviously to all. Nor can the distinction between inorganic, organic and superorganic (or cultural, humanly social) withstand the categorizing process which is implicit in the division of labor in society. When Harlow Shapley studies the responses of ants to varying quantities of heat reaching them from the sun,[1] is he an astronomer or an entomologist? "Astronomy is what an astronomer does as an astronomer," whether he be studying comets, ants or the growth of trees.[2] The biologist in a certain capacity must be geologist just as the geologist must, at times, turn biologist.

The custom of viewing "science" as a vast terrain divided into a number of "fields" each tilled by its own appropriately named guild has a certain justification in utility and convenience. But it tends to obscure the nature of science as a way of interpreting reality, to spread confusion in the ranks of scientists and laymen alike. The use of the word science as a noun not only leads to jurisdictional disputes—does the study of juvenile delinquency belong to sociology or to psychology? the study of fossils to geology or to biology?—but to such ques-

---

[1] "Thermokinetics of *Liometopum apiculatum* Mayr," and "Note on the Thermokinetics of Dolichoderine Ants," *Proc. National Academy of Sciences*, VI (1920), 204–211; and X (1924), 436–439, respectively. He found a close correlation between the speed of ants and temperature, within certain temperature limits.

[2] Dr. A. E. Douglass, an astronomer at Steward Observatory, University of Arizona, has, by working out a correlation between climate and growth of trees, provided archaeologists with the most precise method for dating prehistoric remains unaccompanied by written records that has ever been devised. In this instance the astronomer has become an archaeologist. See "The Secret of the Southwest Solved by Talkative Tree Rings," *National Geographic Magazine*, December, 1929.

Reprinted with permission of publisher. From *Philosophy of Science*, vol. 5, no. 4 (October 1938), 369–89.

tions as, is history a science? is sociology a science? There is a tendency to identify "science" with some of its techniques. For example, one can perform experiments in chemistry and make accurate predictions in astronomy. Chemistry and astronomy are "sciences." Experimentation is exceedingly limited in sociology and predictions in history are seldom more than guesses. Therefore, the tendency is to say, "history and sociology are not sciences." Despite the fact that much of geology is more historical than certain studies of human culture, there is a willingness to call the one "a science" but to deny this status to the other.

Then a distinction is made between the physical sciences (frequently called by the flattering term "the exact sciences") and the "social sciences." Implicit in this distinction is the assumption that a fundamental difference obtains between the nature of physical reality and human social reality. This assumption leads to, if indeed it does not include by implication, the further assumption that the data of human society being essentially different from the data of physics ("the exact sciences") are really not susceptible to scientific treatment, hence the social sciences are really not sciences at all;[3] they are not and cannot be "scientific." The same observations are made, although with less emphasis, with reference to biology: "Biology is less scientific than physics, but more scientific than sociology." These assumptions are not only confusing; they are unwarranted. The basic assumptions and techniques which comprise the scientific way of interpreting reality are applicable equally to all of its phases, to the human-social, or cultural, as well as to the biological and the physical. This means that we must cease viewing science as an entity which is divisible into a number of qualitatively different parts: some wholly scientific (the "exact sciences"), some quasi-scientific, and some only pseudo-scientific. We must cease identifying science with one or another of its techniques, such as experimentation. We must, in short, view science as a way of behaving, as a way of interpreting reality, rather than as an entity in itself, as a segment of that reality.

Experience is the interaction of the organism and its environment.[4] Experience, or reality,[5] consists then of a multiplicity of varied interactions. Conceptually we may view reality as a one, interaction constituting a continuum of experience. Reality is analyzed on a perceptual level; it is divided into odors, sounds, tastes, etc. Conceptually, experience is analyzed with symbolic instruments—words, mathematical symbols, etc. Matter, energy, time, space, motion, etc., are conceptual devices with which we analyze reality and in terms of which we make our adjustments to it. Matter, energy, time, motion, and so on are not therefore discrete entities, but aspects or phases of a common reality. Similarly we may analyze the totality of reality, insofar as we can experience it, into equivalent component parts, or "units," which we may call events. Experience is therefore conceived by us on the one hand as a one, as a totality, and on the other as an infinite number of parts, or events.

"Whole and parts" means relationships. "Relationship," too, is another conceptual device, a symbolic instrument, with the aid of which we render experience intelligible to a degree, and by means of which we effect our adjustments to our environment. Events are related to each other. But how?

"Every event that happens in the world is determined by the space-coördinates x, y, z and the time-coördinate t."[6] The fundamental relationship, or "interval," between events is one of space-time. Whereas formerly space and time were thought of as properties of the external world independent of each other, they are now seen to be merely *aspects* of the basic and primary property, space-time. To quote Minkowski's famed phrase: "The views of space and time which I wish to lay before you have

---

[3] ". . . I think that social science is like a Welsh rabbit—not really a rabbit at all." A. E. Hooton, Professor of Anthropology at Harvard University, in his *Apes, Men, and Morons,* p. 62.

[4] The intra-organic functioning of the organism might also be included here. But since no organism exists except in an extra-organic setting, and since intra-organic functioning has significance only in terms of the interaction of organism and environment, we may confine ourselves to the latter and employ the following equation: organism $\times$ environment = experience.

[5] I shall use the term reality as synonymous with experience thus defined. This is quite unwarranted from a philosophic point of view: we can be sure that the whole of reality is not experienced by us. But from an anthropological or behavioristic point of view, the term "reality" may be justified, since any portion of reality lying outside and beyond the range of experience is not significant behavioristically. From the point of view of behavior, then, that is to say, within the scope of science (sciencing) experience and reality are coextensive and equivalent, and hence may be regarded as synonymous. The term reality is to be preferred to experience because of its philosophic connotation. Reality is our ultimate interest.

[6] Article *Space-Time,* by Albert Einstein, in *Encyclopedia Britannica,* XXI, 107 (14th ed.).

sprung from the soil of experimental physics, and therein lies their strength. They are radical. Henceforth space by itself, and time by itself, are doomed to fade away into mere shadows, and only a kind of union of the two will preserve an independent reality."[7] Thus reality confronts us, in modern thought, as a four-dimensional continuum; the process of reality in which events are manifested is a temporal-spatial (or temporal-formal) one.

Thus the primary and fundamental relationship between events is temporal-formal. But by purely logical analysis, we may distinguish the temporal aspect of the process from the spatial; although inseparable in actuality, we may occupy ourselves with either to the exclusion of the other. Thus we may distinguish three kinds of processes, one primary, the spatial-formal, and two secondary and derivative, the temporal on the one hand and the spatial, or formal, on the other. In the first category we would deal with events as being related to each other by space-time intervals; as for the other two we would in the one consider the interval (or relationship) in its temporal aspect only; and in the other the interval would be dealt with in its spatial, or formal, aspect alone.

Sciencing must adapt itself to the structure of reality; its tools must be so shaped and its techniques so ordered as to grasp reality effectively and render it intelligible, if not controllable, to us. This means, therefore, that we shall have three ways of sciencing: one which grasps the space-time property of reality in its entirety, and two subsidiary and derivative ways, each of which deals with two aspects of this property, viz., space and time respectively. All of "science" or sciencing will be found to be assignable to one or another of these three categories; there is no way of sciencing apart from these three.

"History" is that way of sciencing in which events are dealt with in terms of their temporal relationships alone. Each event is unique. The one thing that history never does is to repeat itself: Lincoln is assassinated only once. To be sure, the events which constitute history are related in ways other than temporal. This must of necessity be true since all kinds of relationships are equally attributes of a common reality. But in "history-ing" we arbitrarily

select for our consideration the connective tissue of *time*, and just as arbitrarily ignore the relationship of space.[8]

This process of reducing concrete experience to artificial abstractions, or, to put it more precisely, the act of substituting concepts, "free inventions of the human intellect" (to borrow Einstein's phrase), for the concrete experiences of the senses,[9] is not only unavoidable, it is the very essence of sciencing.

"History," or the temporal aspect of experience, is coextensive with reality; it is a property common to the inorganic, organic, and superorganic (or *cultural*, to use the anthropological term, or human-social, to use a sociological term) orders of phenomena. Stars, the solar system, the earth, rivers, lead, granite, plants and animals, species and individuals, customs and institutions, each have their respective histories. Astronomy, physics, geology, biology, psychology, sociology, and anthropology are then, in part at least, historical "sciences." There is no antagonism nor even distinction between history and science: history is simply one way of sciencing whether it be in geology or sociology. If we refuse to accept this conclusion then we are forced to its alternative: "an astronomer is a scientist when he deals with a non-temporal, repetitive process, but when he concerns himself with a chronological sequence of events (the history of the solar system, e.g.) then he is no longer a scientist."

Events are related to each other spatially, and we may deal with reality in terms of spatial, or formal, relationships, ignoring the aspect *time*.

Spatial relationships between events may be regarded as either constant or variable. Events, or material objects, whose mutual spatial relationships are regarded as constant, constitute a *structure*. This property is characteristic of all phases of reality. In the inorganic, organic, and superorganic levels it manifests itself in the forms atoms, molecules, stars, constellations, planets, orbits, strata, the elements; in skeletons, bones, muscles, organs, bodies, limbs;

[7]Address delivered at the 80th Assembly of German Natural Scientists and Physicians at Cologne, Sept. 21, 1908.

[8]To be sure, those who bear the label "historian" concern themselves with relationships other than temporal: they may wish to know *where* Lincoln was assassinated as well as when. "The temporal process" would probably be a better term for our purpose here than "history."

[9]"The relation is not analogous to that of soup to beef, but rather that of wardrobe number to overcoat," p. 353, "Physics and Reality," by Albert Einstein, *Jour. Franklin Institute*, Vol. 221, No. 3 (March, 1936).

in families, clans, societies, grammars, constitutions. When the spatial relationships uniting a number of events, or material objects, are regarded as variable, then we speak of *function*. This property likewise manifests itself on all levels of reality in atomic, molecular, meteorological, astronomic behavior; in physiological and psychological processes; and, on the superorganic level, in cultural processes. Thus the physicist, chemist, astronomer, geologist, zoologist, botanist, physiologist, psychologist, sociologist, linguist, anthropologist, etc., are all directly concerned with the spatial (non-temporal) aspect of reality, in its structural or functional aspects, or both.

We come now to the third kind of relationship, or process: the temporal-spatial.[10] This is like the two preceding processes, but different from each. As we have already noted, all three kinds of relationships are always intrinsic in any series of events, in any phase of reality. The temporal process (or "history") is a selective arrangement of events according to the principle *time*. Spatial relationships, though actually existent in these events, are disregarded: in the history of thought it is immaterial whether Newton cogitates under an apple tree or in his bath. Similarly, when dealing with spatial relationships, i.e., with structure and function, the time relationships which are inseparable from these events in objective reality are here divorced by logical analysis: the structure of the crystal, the rusting of iron, respiration, cowardice, secret societies, are studied without reference to clocks or calendars.

But in the temporal-spatial process both temporal and spatial relationships are simultaneously significant. And it is not a case of time *and* space—"up from the South at break of day . . . and Sheridan twenty miles away." The conventional historian wishes to know not only that Napoleon fought battles, but where he fought them. The zoologist and the ethnologist are interested in the distribution of species and culture traits as well as their history. These are examples of a simultaneous interest in both temporal and spatial relationships. But they are not examples of temporal-spatial relationships. Hydrogen + oxygen = hydrogen + oxygen; $t + s = t + s$. But hydrogen × oxygen = water (H_2O); $t \times s = ts$. The temporal-spatial process is not, then, equivalent to a space *and* time organiza-

tion of phenomena; it is not the *sum* of these factors but their product.

It is of interest to note in passing that in many instances in which both temporal *and* spatial relationships are involved, that one is significant only in terms of the other. Thus the thickness of a geologic stratum measured in feet indicates its age measured in years. Similarly, the distribution of a plant or animal species indicates its age[11]: the more wide the distribution the greater the age. And, using the same principle, the anthropologist has been able, in many instances, to reconstruct the history of a tool, myth, custom, or institution by inference from its geographic distribution.[12] And, of course, our clocks measure time by a repetitive movement of a mechanism through space.

The temporal-spatial process is an evolutionary, or developmental process. It is to be distinguished from the temporal process on the one hand and the formal process on the other. Like the others, this process is inherent in all experience and is manifest in all realms of reality, inorganic, organic, and superorganic. Thus we have stellar and cosmic evolution, organic evolution, and cultural evolution. This process differs from the temporal and formal processes in that in the evolutionary process, time and space are both integrally involved, they are fused, inseparable. Evolution is temporal-alteration-of-forms. A comparison of these three processes will make each one more distinct.

The temporal process is non-repetitive. In the sequence or process which is temporal (and temporal only), each event is unique; it occurs only once. The Rocky Mountains are formed only once, there is only one Würm glaciation, each raindrop is unique, each movement of every living creature is distinguished from every other movement,[13] John Brown is executed only once, each meeting of the women's sewing circle is a unique event. The spatial, or functional, process, being non-temporal, is repetitive; mountain systems may be formed re-

---

[10]It should be noted that this classification can have, logically, only three categories: t, s, and ts.

[11]I.e., it tends to. The correlation between spatial distribution and age is not always close.

[12]See A. L. Kroeber's essay, "The Culture-Area and Age-Area Concepts of Clark Wissler," in *Methods in Social Science*, Stuart A. Rice, Ed., Chicago, 1931.

[13]It *may* be. Actually they usually are not, for the reason that such distinctions except in rare instances—such as the real or imagined kick of Mrs. O'Leary's cow that started the great Chicago fire, or the honking of the geese who "saved Rome"—have no significance for *us* as ordinary human beings. But for a philosophy of science the sneeze of an anonymous monkey in the depths of a jungle is as significant as illustrating the uniqueness of each event in a temporal series as is the birth of Christ or the death of Caesar.

peatedly, ice-age may follow ice-age, raindrops fall again and again, water freezes, ice thaws and water freezes again, metal may be melted and remelted, monkeys sneeze, men die, insurrectionists are executed repeatedly, prices rise and fall and rise again, societies and clubs are organized in every age. The evolutionary process, being in part temporal in character, is non-repetitive[14]; a reptile becomes a mammal only once; radium decomposes only once; stars "die" only once.[15] Growth is also a temporal-spatial process; the term, however, is usually applied to individuals rather than to classes. Growth is a non-repetitive process: one is a child only once - second childhood is always a novelty.

Even at the cost of repetition, it might be well, for the sale of clarity, to re-emphasize the nature of the distinctions just made. Actually, each event has a four-dimensional character and has its place in a four-dimensional, space-time continuum. Thus the raindrop is an event in the process of cosmic evolution, and we may view it as such. But we may also view it in other contexts: in a purely temporal context, or in a wholly non-temporal context (in which we consider only the alteration in spatial relationships between the raindrop, the earth, the clouds, etc.). The contexts are, of course, devices of our own making. They are arbitrarily selected points of view from which we regard and consider reality; they are the forms, the channels, so to speak, within which we science.

The formal process is reversible as well as repetitive. Water freezes, ice thaws; iron rusts, iron oxide decomposes; hay becomes beef; beef may become hay again; revolt and reaction are cyclical and opposite processes in society; prices rise and fall, etc. But the temporal order of events remains immutable; it cannot be reversed. Only in *Through the Looking Glass* do Queens scream before they prick their fingers, or Alices pass the cake before they cut it. The evolutionary process being temporal as well as formal, is likewise irreversible. The stars do not reabsorb energy once emanated, mammals do not return to reptilianism, the days when knighthood was in flower can never return, "make me a child again just for tonight" is an impossible request.

The historic process and the evolutionary process are alike in being temporal in character, i.e., non-repetitive and irreversible. But, whereas the historic process is merely temporal, the evolutionary process is formal as well: it is a *temporal-sequence-of-forms*. Historically Eli Whitney and the invention of the cotton gin are inseparable events in a chronological sequence. But had Whitney died in his cradle the evolutionary process expressed in technology would have produced a machine for ginning cotton. Similarly, although Lincoln is bound historically to the emancipation of slaves and Darwin to the discovery of certain biological principles, the processes of politico-economic evolution would have achieved the one without Lincoln just as evolution of thought would have produced the other without Darwin. The invention of the calculus, which took place almost simultaneously, and independently, in the activities of Newton and Leibnitz, was the logical expression of a developmental process, i.e., it was the emergence of a new mathematical form from previous forms. Just as the invention of the calculus was not dependent upon either Newton or Leibnitz alone, so it was not necessarily dependent upon them both; it would have occurred eventually if both Newton and Leibnitz had died in infancy. The development of mathematics, like the development of technology or medicine, is an evolutionary process[16]: new forms grow out of preceding forms. But in whose person and labors a new form is to appear, and when and where it is to appear is a matter that belongs to the context history alone. From the point of view of the evolutionary process every *historical* event is an *accident* and hence unpredictable. We may predict that a cure for cancer

---

[14]Actually, this may depend upon one's point of view, or more accurately, upon the temporal scope of one's vision. To us, the cosmic process seems to be evolutionary in character: the universe is expanding (it may be assumed), or matter is being transmuted into energy. The process seems to be temporal-formal in character: non-repetitive and irreversible. But this appearance may be an illusion due to our infinitesimally brief span of observation. Were it longer, sufficiently longer, the cosmic process might reveal itself as a repetitive one: a period of contraction might follow expansion, and so on, in an endless series of pulsations; matter may be transmuted into energy and re-congealed into matter, an endless vibration of a cosmic pendulum. So, to a creature which, compared with us, had an infinitesimally brief span of observation, the repetitive and rhythmic character of respiration or the heart beat or the rusting of iron would appear to be evolutionary in character, for seeing only a minute part of the process, neither the beginning nor the end, he would observe only a temporal alteration of form, and might declare it to be a non-repetitive process. And he would be correct too, for the *process* which he observes *is* non-repetitive, just as the dying star and the decomposing radium represent non-repetitive processes to us. Thus, whether a process be labelled repetitive or evolutionary depends upon the unit of measurement. Any repetitive process is made up of a sequence of events which in themselves are non-repetitive. Conversely, any repetitive process is but a segment of a larger one which is evolutionary in character.

[15]One must not confuse *duplication* with *repetition*: there may be transitions from reptile to mammal in different races; one stellar death may follow another. These are duplications, not repetitions.

[16]Einstein and Infeld have called their recent book The *Evolution* of Physics, not the *History* of Physics, it is significant to note.

will be found, but to predict who will make the discovery and when is impossible. That the nations of Europe will be embroiled again in a great war in the not distant future is as safe a prediction as one could make; the development of technological, economic, political, and military forces makes another war inevitable. But who will strike the spark that will set off the conflagration, and when and where—what archduke or official will be shot, when, where, and by whom—it is utterly impossible to say. The passing of a star, drawing out from the sun a gigantic filament from which the planets of our solar system were formed, if a fact, is an historic fact; the process is an historic process in which specific and severally unique events take place in a purely temporal context. But this is quite a different process from that of cosmic or galactic evolution as exemplified, for instance, by the equi-partition of energy, or the transmutation of matter into energy, the dying of a star. Similarly, in the biologic realm, the narrative of the specific wanderings over the face of the earth, the struggles, intermixture, vicissitudes, etc., of the various species and races of man is quite a different story from the account of their evolutionary development.

So far, we have spoken of the inorganic, organic, and superorganic realms, or levels, of reality as if these distinctions could be taken for granted. For the sake of completeness and clarity, however, a few words on this subject are desirable.

The distinctions between these levels, or strata, of reality are valid, and are fundamental for science. The phenomena of these three levels do not differ from each other in that one is composed of one kind of basic substance, another of a different kind. They differ in the manner in which their component parts are organized into patterns or forms, respectively. Basically all reality may be assumed to be made up of a common stuff; differences in various manifestations of reality are due to differences in the forms in which reality confronts us. There are classes, or kinds, of forms amid the infinite range of specific variation. Inorganic, organic, and superorganic are labels for three qualitatively different and scientifically significant categories of forms of reality.

The category inorganic includes, of course, those phenomena which we call inanimate, lifeless. "Organic" includes living organisms. The superorganic category is composed of phenomena called by the anthropologist *culture*. Culture is a term which in-cludes such things as tools, clothing, art, social organization, religion, systems of thought, etc. Culture is an organization of extra-organic mechanisms by means of which a particular animal, man, adjusts, and strives to adjust himself to his environment in order to live securely, fully, and comfortably. Culture, in the anthropological sense, is the possession of man and of no other creature. The essential quality of this organization of such diverse phenomena as hats and ethics, amulets and politics, spears and logarithms, is the *symbol*.[17] Human beings alone of all creatures are able to use symbols: that is, they alone are able freely to endow any perceptible phenomenon (be it material object, gesture, color, sound, or odor) with a meaning which cannot be perceived with the senses.[18] Because of this ability human beings alone possess a culture. And it is cultural phenomena which comprise the category of the superorganic.

Even a casual inspection of our three categories reveals the fact that organic phenomena and superorganic phenomena are but particular kinds of organization of phenomena in the inorganic, and the organic and inorganic categories, respectively. Thus, a plant or an animal is but a peculiar form of organization of carbon, oxygen, calcium, etc. Likewise a cultural phenomenon is but a manifestation of organic (human beings) and inorganic (inanimate objects) phenomena organized in a special manner. Thus the phenomena of the organic level (for levels, or strata, are what these categories are in reality) can be dealt with in terms of inorganic phenomena: a plant or animal is so much carbon, nitrogen, hydrogen; it has weight, will fall as a rock, may be frozen, transformed by fire, and so on. Similarly, a phenomenon of culture—a man taking a Christian oath of office—may be dealt with in terms of his gestures, vocal and manual, and these, in turn, together with the book upon which the oath is taken, can be treated in terms of acous-

---

[17]Tool-using is found among sub-human creatures, such as apes. But without articulate speech which provides a means both to communicate experience and to endow it with continuity, tool-using cannot become habitual, traditional and, hence, cumulative and progressive. The apes have the beginnings of culture but they never progress beyond beginnings. They make innumerable starts, but never arrive.

[18]When an ape or man uses a random object as a tool he thereby endows that object with meaning—"poke meaning," or "strike meaning." But this endowed meaning is dependent upon the physical properties of the object-tool, and the *meaning* can be perceived with the senses. But when man endows a combination of sounds, or a color, or a gesture, with *symbolic* meaning (e.g., the word *see*, the x in algebra, the color of mourning, the tipping of a hat), the meaning is *not* dependent upon the physical properties of the symbol's *form of expression*, and hence can not be perceived with the senses.

tics, mechanics, and physical and chemical properties of the Bible, and so on.

But the fact that the phenomena of one category (except the first, the inorganic) can be "reduced" to the one, or ones, below it does not destroy the categories themselves, nor even minimize their distinctness. A projectile, a pterodactyl, a bird, a squirrel, a fish, a bat, and a bee "fly through the air." A physicist could deal with each as a projectile, in terms of mass, energy, atmospheric resistance, etc. To the physicist all of these objects are alike projectiles: the qualitative differences between them do not exist for the physicist. But merely because they do not exist for him does not mean that they cannot and should not have significance for other men of science. That which distinguishes the inanimate projectile from all the rest on the one hand and that which distinguishes bird from bat and fish on the other, escapes the physicist entirely. Likewise the essential feature of the cultural phenomenon in our example above, the Christian oath, escapes the psychologist[19] and the physiologist as well as the chemist and physicist.

Thus we see that we have three qualitatively distinct levels or strata of phenomena: the cultural, or superorganic, which is characterized by the symbol; the organic, which is characterized by the cell; and the inorganic, which is characterized by the atom, proton, electron, wave, or whatever other unit, or units, the physicist decides upon. Being distinct, the phenomena of these three categories must be studied on their respective levels.[20] That is, organic phenomena must be studied *as* organic phenomena and not as inorganic phenomena if we wish to understand organisms as organisms. A chemical analysis or a description in terms of electrons will tell us nothing of respiration, sex, or mammalianism. Similarly, in the case of culture, or superorganic phenomena, we must study it *as* superorganic phenomena and not as psychological or biological phenomena if we wish to understand culture *as* culture. Such things as Grimm's law, kinship systems, clans, logarithms, laws of cultural evolution, and so on, lie outside and above the fields of psychology and biology.

There are, however, instances in which our ends are not served by maintaining the distinctions between these three levels. We may wish to inquire into the relationship between one level and another. Inquiries of this sort are, needless to say, as legitimate and potentially profitable as any other. Thus bio-chemistry inquires into the relationship between the inorganic level and the organic. Similar inquiries are directed to the relationship between the organic category and the superorganic. Take the Oedipus complex of psychoanalysis, for example. Love of a boy for his mother and hostility for his father springs in part from his organism. But it may be derived, or at least conditioned, by the form of the family into which he is born. If the family is patriarchal the expression (if not partial derivation) of the boy's attitudes will be different from those in a society organized matrilineally, or one recognizing both lines of descent equally. Thus the Oedipus or Electra complex, as well as all other examples of *human* behavior—i.e., human behavior as distinguished from non-human, or sub-human, behavior; there is nothing peculiarly *human* about a sneeze, e.g.—are made up of elements drawn from two different categories: the biological and the cultural. The formula for human behavior is: Human behavior = Human organism × Cultural stimuli.

Studies of soil erosion inquire into the relationship between such things as farming or grazing methods, lumber industry, the prices of building materials, and reforestation; the quantity and frequency of rainfall, natural and artificial drainage structures; winds, and legislation. The search for a material that will destroy plant or animal pests may involve relationships between all three levels: the price of commodities, the organic pests and the chemicals capable of killing them.

Here again, whether we deal with reality in terms of distinct categories, or levels, of phenomena, or

[19]It might seem, at first glance, that the psychologist could give a complete account of the swearing of an oath. But a second thought shows that no psychological examination of the human organism and no amount of psychological laws of human behavior would enable one to tell why one person took an oath to Jesus on a Bible and why another took an oath to the Sun on a tobacco pipe (Plains Indians), any more than a psychologist could tell by psychology alone whether a given human organism would speak English or Chinese.

[20]It has been only recently that the superorganic level of phenomena has been recognized as a distinct stratum of reality. But even today there are many (anthropologists included) who insist upon dealing, or prefer to deal, with cultural phenomena in psychological or biological terms rather than in terms of its own order of existence. There is a close and interesting correlation between the arrangement of the strata of reality and the history of the sciences. At the bottom lies the inorganic; this was the first to be cultivated with success by the scientist in the persons of astronomers, physicists and chemists. Lying above the inorganic, and being in actuality, merely a special and peculiar form of inorganic components, is the organic. This was next in order of scientific development. Finally, superimposed upon the organic stratum is the superorganic or culture layer. The scientist has only recently invaded this realm, and, so far, his achievements here have been insignificant when compared with his triumphs in lower levels. But, given time, maturity will come here also, and with it achievement.

in terms of relationships between them, depends upon our purposes and ends. Both approaches are equally legitimate and potentially profitable.

In summary, we see that we have two classifications of reality which cut across each other at right angles: the one has to do with structure (the "atom," the cell, the symbol), the other has to do with process (temporal, formal, and temporal-formal). This gives us nine categories in which all reality and all manners of sciencing may be logically and consistently divided as indicated in the accompanying diagram.

On the inorganic level we have cosmic and galactic histories (such as they are or may be), the history of our solar system, the history of the earth or of a continent, a mountain chain, a river, or even a snowflake, encompassed within the purely temporal context. In the purely formal-functional context we have the non-temporal and repetitive, structural and functional aspects of astronomy, geology, chemistry, and physics. And in the primary category, the temporal-formal one, of which the other two are but aspects, we have cosmic, galactic, stellar,[21] and solar evolution, and the decomposition of radio-active substances.

On the organic level, in the purely temporal context, we have the histories of plants and animals, of genera, species, and individuals, both human and non-human. Our greatest concern in this category is, perhaps, with human beings: we are intensely interested in the problems of the origin, diffusion, extinction, intermixture of various species and races of mankind. But a like interest in plants and sub-human animals is not insignificant. In the formal-functional category we have studies of morphology and function; anatomy, the non-temporal, repetitive aspects of physiology and psychology belong here. And, in the temporal-formal category, we have evolution of organic forms in general, of genera, species, varieties in particular. The growth of an individual also comes within this category.

Biography, the history of a human individual, should, in most instances, be regarded as dealing with both the organic and the superorganic levels since our interest in a human individual is seldom, if ever, divorced from the culture in which he has his *human* being. Similarly with significant individuals in the subhuman animal or plant world: the cow that started the Chicago fire, the goose that saved Rome, the wolf who suckled Romulus and Remus, Man o' War, the hemlock that killed Socrates, each is significant only because it enters the context of human cultural history.

On the superorganic level we have culture history; the history of nations, reigns, tribes, institutions, tools, ideas, beliefs, etc., in the temporal context. In the formal-functional context, we have the studies of "social morphology" in sociology, cul-

---

[21]See, e.g., the discussions on "The Evolution of the Universe" by J. Jeans, R. A. Millikan, Eddington, W. de Sitter, G. Lemaître, et al, in Appendix, Report of the Centenary Meeting, British Assn. for Adv. of Science, held in London in 1931. Also, H. N. Russell's article "Stellar Evolution," in *Encyclopedia Britannica*, 14th ed.

	Temporal	Spatial-Temporal	Spatial
Super-organic	"History," Culture history, or History of Civilization	Cultural Evolution	Non-temporal, repetitive, culturally determined processes in human society
Organic	Racial history of Man History of animal and plant species, genera	Organic evolution Growth of individuals	Non-temporal, repetitive processes in organic behavior: intra-organic (physiology), extra-organic (psychology)
Inorganic	History of solar system, of the earth, a continent, mountain system, river, drop of water, a grain of sand	Cosmic, solar, stellar, galactic evolution Disintegration of radio-active substances	Non-temporal, repetitive processes in physics, chemistry, astronomy

tural anthropology, and the other "social sciences." The so-called functionalist school of cultural anthropology,[22] the "Chicago school" of sociology,[23] e.g., belong here. In the basic category, that of evolution of culture, we have at present virtually nothing. After a vigorous and bitter struggle the philosophy of evolution conquered on the organic field, but, after a few brief advances it has been routed from the superorganic field. A few giants like Herbert Spencer and Lewis H. Morgan, in the "boom" days of evolutionism in the second half of the nineteenth century were able to occupy the superorganic field for a time. But the anti-evolutionists have regained the field and have held it successfully since the turn of the century. To be sure both Morgan and Spencer committed errors in the *use* of their philosophy, but a mistake made in the use of a tool does not render the tool worthless. But sociologists and anthropologists have repudiated the philosophy of evolutionism along with the errors of some evolutionists: they have poured the baby out with the bath. But the victory of the anti-evolutionists on the superorganic level is only temporary. As social science matures, the basic concept of science and philosophy, that reality is spatial-temporal in character, will win its way on the superorganic level as it has upon the organic and inorganic levels.

It will be noted, of course, that our conventional names for "the sciences" do not readily fit our category system. But this is quite understandable: the terms *physics, zoology, sociology,* etc. have come into use as science has grown, and this growth has been more or less accidental. The concepts *time* and *space* existed long before it was discovered that *time* and *space* are but aspects of a third thing for which there is no more adequate a name than *space-time.* But the fact that the names of "the sciences" do not correspond to our nine categories in no way invalidates the categories. The maturity of science in any field can be rather accurately gauged by its vocabulary: as "a science" matures it develops its own terminology. This has taken place extensively in the physical and the biological sciences. And such words as *instinct, intelligence, race, society,* are now being found so difficult to use that it is likely they will give way soon to a more effective terminology.

For the scientific worker such terms as *psychology, botany, chemistry,* etc., will no doubt continue to be useful and satisfactory except in so far as further division of labor and specialization should make new terms necessary. But for the thinker, for the philosopher of science, new technical terms are needed. I shall not presume to supply names for our nine categories. But, since they represent a realistic and logical analysis of the field, it seems likely that as these categories obtrude themselves more and more into systematic thinking, they will eventually receive names.

The scope of each of the three levels of phenomena has interesting implications for philosophy and for human welfare. The category of the inorganic embraces the cosmos in extent; the two other levels are built up, so to speak, out of inorganic phenomena. The scientific exploration and progressive conquest of terrain on the inorganic level will have the greatest significance for philosophy (at least for much of what has been traditionally labelled "philosophy"); it will bring us closest to reality, closest to the "nature of things." Contrasted with the extent of the inorganic realm, both in time and in space, the phenomena of the superorganic appear infinitesimal and insignificant: all of life, to say nothing of human culture, appears as but a slight rash upon the epidermis of a most microscopic and insignificant cosmic speck. But to us, the cultural phenomena are anything but trivial: war and revolution, financial crises, organized crime, unemployment, poverty, and destitution may be of greater moment than the movements of the wily electron or the temperature of Antares. Insignificant in cosmic perspective, the institutions under which we live, labor and suffer are of supreme human importance. The phenomena of the cultural realm have their own distinctive properties and function in accordance with their own laws just as the phenomena of other levels do. It is possible for us to discover, with the viewpoint, assumptions and techniques of science, what these properties and laws are. And once this has been done, it will be possible to control these phenomena and bend them to our desire and will, to a greater extent than is possible in either of the other two levels, for culture is but

[22]I.e., of Bronislaw Malinowski, A. R. Radcliffe-Brown and their respective students.
[23]See *Introduction to Sociology,* by Robert E. Park and Ernest W. Burgess (Chicago, 1921). Among the students of Professors Park and Burgess: E. T. Hiller, *The Strike* (1928); F. M. Thrasher, *The Gang* (1936); A. Blumenthall, *Small-Town Stuff* (1932); N. Nelson, *The Hobo* (1923), etc.

a human by-product. This is not a plea for the development of one type of science at the expense of, or even *rather than*, another. But at the present time vast progress has already been made in the physical sciences, and even in the biological. Our control over the resources and brute forces of nature is staggering when compared with that of 1776. And we have won a large measure of success and control in the biological (especially the medical) sciences. But there is so little effective knowledge of our cultural world, so much difficulty and so little control that many sober minds are seriously wondering if

our civilization will survive the present world crisis. It is the profound conviction of the present writer that the phenomena of the cultural level are as susceptible to scientific study as the data of other levels, and that when concerted and sustained scientific attack is made upon problems in this field that the achievements and triumphs will be as great, if not greater, than in the physical and biological domains. A way must be found to divert the resources of science and society in this direction, else, indeed, our triumphs in physics, astronomy, and medicine may well turn out to be hollow ones.

SCIENCE AS METHOD

Finally, in the following excerpt by Ross, we have something of a summary of ideas discussed by Bronowski and White, but the core ideas are essential if science as an ongoing activity (and not as the static end product of activity) is to be adequately grasped: science is the interaction of observation and reason; it is cumulative; it is self-corrective; it searches for regularities in the patterning of events at many levels of conceptualization and does not reduce nature to single principles; and it matches its instruments and techniques of data gathering to the problem at hand and the evidence being sought. In all these points Ross (with Bronowski and White who precede him) sets the intellectual background in terms of which we can begin to ask the questions: What is anthropology as a science? In what respects *is* it a science? What particular aspects or phases of the scientific process as this is applied to the study of human behavior does it emphasize more than others? To these—and other—questions we will turn, beginning in Part II with the cultural anthropologist in his "laboratory"—the village, the island, or the street corner.

THE NATURE OF SCIENCE

RALPH ROSS

Science is often defined inadequately as "an organized body of knowledge." This would make cookbooks, Sears, Roebuck catalogues, and telephone books science, which they are not. Sometimes science is defined simply as rationality, but that

Reprinted with permission of publisher. From Ralph Ross, *Symbols and Civilization,* © 1957, 1962 by Harcourt Brace Jovanovich, New York.

would make much of theology and metaphysics science, which they are not. *Rationality* is logical consistency, lack of contradiction. It is to be distinguished from *reasonableness*, the quality of a mind open to arguments and evidence opposed to its beliefs: a willingness to reconsider. Rationalists can be quite unreasonable or dogmatic. Rationalist metaphysicians and theologians are often certain about premises which come from intuition or revelation. Even paranoiacs may be thought of as rationalists, for they are commonly most rigorous in reasoning. But their premises, which they cling to in spite of all evidence, are absurd.

Science is empirical, rational, general, and cumulative; and it is all four at once. Science is *empirical* in that all its conclusions are subject to test by sense experience. Observation is the base on which science rests, but scientific observation is more than keeping one's eyes open. It is observation, made by qualified observers under controlled conditions, of those things which confirm or disconfirm, verify or refute a theory. Sherlock Holmes could tell by the stains on a vest what a man had eaten for breakfast. From a number of such observations he arrived at a theory about why and how a particular crime was committed. This procedure is excellent for detection but insufficient for science, because it yields only knowledge of particular events. Science would go on to ask why and how crime, not a particular crime, is committed. Science uses facts to test general theories and general theories to make predictions about particular facts.

Scientific observation may be made of things as they exist, like the color of an apple or the temperature of the air, or it may be made of what results from an experiment. An experiment is the deliberate manipulation of conditions in order to bring about what we want to observe. If we want to test the hypothesis that a new plastic can withstand two hundred pounds of pressure without crumbling, we may have to create a situation in which such pressure is applied to a piece of the plastic, because it is unlikely that the situation already exists anywhere in the world, or, if it does, that all other factors are kept constant. In some sciences, like astronomy, we do not sufficiently control the subject matter to experiment on it—although we do control the conditions of observation—and we distinguish those sciences from others, like chemistry, in which experiment is possible, by calling the latter "experimental sciences."

Although all scientific thought *ultimately* rests on observation, there are vast portions of it which are entirely *rational:* analysis of the meanings of terms, deductions from existent theories, explorations of the logical relations among concepts and among theories. Logic is applied to science constantly because logic contains the rules of valid

thinking. The application of mathematics is often thought, erroneously, to be an index of the status of any science. Of course, the more it can be applied usefully within a science, the more advanced the science. For mathematics functions both as a language in which scientific laws are stated, giving them the utmost precision, elegance, and economy, and as the basis of measurement. Many of the most significant advances in physics, astronomy, and chemistry have depended on advances in and application of mathematics. Without calculus the work of Isaac Newton would have been impossible. Yet great scientific work in other fields, performed by men like Pasteur, Darwin, and Pavlov (with whose names pasteurization, evolution, and conditioned response in psychology are associated), has used little or no mathematics. This is true also of important contributions to social science, like those of Weber, Veblen, and Mosca. Nothing is gained by the use of mathematics when a subject is not measurable or sufficiently precise.

If observation is the base of science, general laws are its crown. The body of any science is a set of general laws, logically connected, from which the occurrence of particular events is predictable. Young sciences, like nineteenth-century biology, are chiefly taxonomic; that is, they organize and classify a subject matter so that there will be enough order in it for laws to be sought. Even less-advanced sciences, like contemporary anthropology and sociology, still record a host of particular and often isolated observations so that there will be material from which to generalize. One goal of science is the creation of a unified body of knowledge which will relate all the sciences to one another; thus from laws of physics and chemistry—which deal with matters that are basic to all things, organic and inorganic—one could move logically to laws of biology, psychology, and society. Ideally, all science would be logically deducible from a single law general enough to apply to everything.

Of course, we are so far from a single set of laws for all the sciences that we can scarcely go logically from physics to chemistry. We are closer to—though still far enough from—more limited ideals of the unity of science: unity on the basis of terms or of methods. There have been relatively successful attempts to create a common body of terms for the sciences, so that propositions of one science can be meaningful in others. And, despite great differences in the procedures and apparatus of the particular sciences, it is possible to approximate a statement of the most general methods of science so that they are applicable to all science.

Science is *cumulative* in that present knowledge is based on past knowledge, even when the new supersedes the old. The dullest freshman in an introductory physics course knows more about physics than Aristotle did, not because he is brighter than Aristotle but, among other things, because of the work of Aristotle. Scientific conclusions are held tentatively; if they were regarded as certainly true, inquiry would be terminated and mistakes would be enshrined as dogma. But science is self-corrective; its mistakes are eliminated by more science. This is perhaps the basic criterion that distinguishes science from all other ways proposed for attaining truth: intuition, authority, tradition, for example. Different intuitions, authorities, and traditions may contradict each other, but each will remain firmly convinced of its own truth. These methods can be corrected only from outside themselves, especially by logical criticism and new evidence. But science is corrigible by its own practice, through continued application of its method. And the recurrent criticism that science is unreliable because it is always changing misses the point. Science is reliable *because* its conclusions change in a successive approximation of truth. It does not claim absolute truth for any of its conclusions, but only probability. And at any time we can expect the probability of a scientific law to be greater than knowledge about the same subject from any other source. Further, science does not correct itself only by recognition of mistakes. Solving one problem opens a path to others, and they in turn may lead back to a reconsideration of the earlier problem. When we learn that something previously called an instinct, for example, is actually the result of cultural conditioning, we promptly ask whether the same is true of other "instincts." And what we discover about conditioning as a result of this new inquiry may lead to greater understanding of the first "instinct."

Of course, scientific growth is not always direct; there are many blind alleys, and errors may last for years. But many errors have worked out well in the end because they led to the study of related problems or accidental discovery of some truth. Examples include the political doctrine of a state of

nature,[1] which led to the isolation of specifically social and political characteristics of human behavior; the theory of humors, which pointed the way to discovery of a relationship between glandular secretions and temperament; and alchemy, which in the search for ways of transmuting other substances into gold helped found the science of chemistry. As Augustus De Morgan, a nineteenth-century English mathematician, said, "Wrong hypotheses, rightly worked, have produced more useful results than unguided observation."

Many scientists rule out of court all vague and fuzzy notions. Yet science has often advanced because of, not despite, just such notions when they were bold and imaginative, or were metaphors which called attention to a previously neglected relationship. One of the great men of modern physics, Max Planck, wrote:[2] "We must never forget that ideas devoid of a clear meaning frequently gave the strongest impulse to the further development of science." Of course, we cannot in general prefer vague ideas to exact ones; but the chief value of clarity in a statement is sometimes only the ease with which we can tell that it is wrong. Clarity and precision are great virtues, but they are not the only ones. Like sincerity and honesty in moral choice, they are not enough without intelligence. Clarity may coexist with error, triteness, and tautology. Cryptic and enigmatic statement, on the other hand, should not be dismissed without a hearing; there may be something precious buried in the words. And although a statement whose meaning is not exact should not end an inquiry, it may start one. Planck believed that with many ideas in science—like the reality of the external world, and the concept of causality—the question was not whether they were true but whether they were valuable.

Planck's distinction between the value and the truth of scientific ideas is not utterly exclusive;

---

[1]This is the belief that men were at first nonsocial creatures who behaved on instinct and impulse. Living together in society was thought to be the result of a rational decision which was embodied in a "social contract," stating that men would give up certain of their "natural rights" or powers to each other or to a sovereign. Some political writers knew that there probably never was a state of nature, but they continued to talk about it because it provided a useful contrast to the way men live in society, and it allowed them to distinguish the specifically social elements in human behavior from those they regarded as natural, or biological.

[2]See *Philosophy of Physics*, by Max Planck, George Allen & Unwin, Ltd., London, 1936, pp. 111 ff., for a discussion of what leads to scientific theories.

truth, too, is a value, and in science it is the ultimate value. But there are other scientific values, and they are not inconsistent with truth. If we distinguish between science as a product and science as a process, we can see that as a product—as a body of propositions about the world—what we value are answers, and we want them to be true. But as a process, what we value are questions and methods, with their attendant insights and new concepts. And the truth of the presuppositions on which questions are based may be irrelevant to the questions themselves, or of the concepts that go with them. Here the chief values are those of stimulating and guiding further inquiry.

The cumulative character of science becomes clearer in contrast with art, which does not necessarily improve. We know more about art and artistic technique than artists of the past did, but our poets, playwrights, sculptors, and musicians are not superior to Dante, Shakespeare, Michelangelo, and Bach. The reasons are simple. Every artist, no matter what he has learned from his masters, really starts from scratch. He may not only refuse to build on past artistic achievements—which make up no single body of work, anyway—but he may have to reject much of the past for the sake of his own vision. The scientific novice, however, starts his thinking with the conclusions of past science. Although he may correct some of it, he accepts most of it and goes further. And he enters a laboratory complete with instruments which his predecessors did not have, instruments making new and more exact observation and measurement possible. The artist has no such aid from instruments, for a typewriter will write no better sonnets than a quill.

Too many people believe that science is only a new body of dogma; this is harmful whether it leads people to support or to oppose science. On both sides there are excessive claims. Those who are "for" science as dogma sometimes argue that science has replaced religion. They often talk and act as though science were a new religion, and the true one. They treat scientific laws as absolute and certain. They are fascinated by the paraphernalia of science—its jargon, techniques, attitudes. This is less likely to result in science than in "scientism," an inflation of science into the only intellectual discipline and the use of science as the only measure, so that any activity that seems "scientific," whether or not it results in knowledge, is acclaimed, and

any nonscientific activity, whether or not it results in beauty or wisdom, is scorned.

Those who oppose science, thinking it to be dogma, often hold it responsible for all the failures and difficulties of the modern world, although most of these are irrelevant to science or are caused by too little rather than too much scientific method. And they think that the conclusions of science are important, but that its methods are not. One of their chief mistakes is to interpret scientific law as *prescriptive*, governing the universe through a system of divine legislation, rather than as *descriptive* of the regularities of phenomena. This notion may result from confusing two basic meanings of the word "law," a scientific meaning and a legal one. When scientific laws are interpreted as if they were legal, they are thought to have the power of commands. But such laws imply a legislator, who could only be God, or Nature personified. So scientific laws are conceived as results of a cosmic jurisprudence.[3]

If scientific laws were prescriptive, nature would obey them better than men obey the laws of the state, and the possibility of chance, adventure, and novelty would disappear. The laws of nature would have to have no purpose, and attain no ends, but merely regulate events. The belief that this is so is called *mechanism*, and it was popular in the late nineteenth century. Mechanism, more fully, is a philosophy of science that interprets all phenomena as mechanical movements of matter in a world of eternal and inexorable law blindly fulfilling itself, with no place for human freedom, art, imagination, or love—which are sometimes treated as illusions. Many artists, theologians, and humanists were appalled. They tried to keep science apart from art, theology, and personal relations; they denounced the mechanization of life and blamed science for the technology which they felt overwhelmed them. George Gissing, the Victorian novelist, wrote:[4] "I hate and fear 'science' because of my conviction that for a long time to come, if not forever, it will be the remorseless enemy of mankind. I see it destroying all simplicity and gentleness of life, all beauty of the world; I see it restoring barbarism

---

[3]The opposite error consists in treating actual legislation as if it were scientific, or "natural." So laws made by government are thought of as instances of the natural order and, in consequence, never to be changed.
[4]Quoted by George Lundberg in *Can Science Save Us?* Longmans, Green, 1947, pp. 79–80.

under the mask of civilization; I see it darkening men's minds and hardening their hearts; I see it bringing a time of vast conflict which will pale into insignificance 'the thousand wars of old,' and, as likely as not, will whelm all the laborious advances of mankind in blood-drenched choas." Gissing's statement sounds like prophecy in this day of atom and hydrogen bombs, but is it science itself that brings these things or what we do with science? We might better denounce our morals or our lack of wisdom than our science.

What was perhaps most terrifying about mechanism was the implication that everything in the world could be explained in terms of mechanics, that branch of physics which deals with the actions of forces on bodies. Thus there was, and is, the belief that science "reduces" mind, consciousness, and the objects of ordinary experience to purely physical processes, or to movements of electrical charges, and that it regards all else as the illusions of the senses. Humanists in denying this have characterized science as incapable of dealing with the distinctive qualities of man and his experience, and have suggested that other methods, loosely defined in terms of sympathetic imagination, insight, or common sense, be employed in the investigation of the specifically human.

Humanists have been right in their opposition, even if not helpful in their constructive proposals. By now the belief they attack is usually regarded by scientists and philosophers as fallacy, called reductionism. Reductionism consists in treating an experienced phenomenon as *nothing but* some other phenomenon which has fewer or different properties, and in asserting, ultimately, that an experienced phenomenon contains no properties beyond its physical elements. So every table would *really* be only atoms. Progressive reductionism works as follows. An art object is only mass and light waves, an act of love only chemical process; the chemical is only the physical and the physical only electrical charges; therefore, the art object or act of love is only a flow of electricity.

Ernest Nagel called this a caricature of physics for, he said,[5] ". . . the sciences seek to determine the precise *conditions* under which events come into being and continue to exist . . . the sciences do not *thereby deny* the existence of any traits found in

nature . . . " If the laws stating the *conditions* for the occurrence of a social event were reducible to laws of physics, we could predict on the basis of physical knowledge alone that the event would take place, and our control of events might be correspondingly increased. We might be able at will to bring about or avert the social event. Yet this reduction of the laws of society to the laws of physics would be only a statement of the physical conditions under which an event takes place. Even now, natural science can state many of the physical, chemical, physiological, and psychological conditions under which acts of art and love take place, and the social sciences can treat their social and environmental conditions. Knowledge of these conditions allows us to predict the occurrence of such acts and perhaps to institute conditions that will bring them about. But the *conditions* are not the acts themselves nor definitions of them; to treat them as equivalent is to commit the fallacy of reductionism. Neither the social nor the natural sciences can deny without absurdity the *existence* of things whose *conditions* of existence they describe.

If science is reductionist, it cuts the ground from under its own feet.[6] Science rests on observation, and the world we observe contains colors, sounds, odors, and tastes. A physical hypothesis about atoms, waves, or particles refers to things that are colorless, soundless, odorless, tasteless. Yet that hypothesis is tested by observation. How paradoxical it would be to insist that the physical phenomena described by the hypothesis are the only reality, for that would imply a denial that the world we observe in testing the hypothesis—the very reason we call it true—is real!

So science may state the conditions under which art and love occur, but it is left to the humanities, and to religion, to explore the *nature* of art and love. Yet this distinction between the nature of any phenomenon and the conditions of its occurrence is misleading if it is thought to be utterly exclusive. When we know a great deal about the physical, chemical, and physiological conditions under which love occurs, and about the social and psychological conditions as well, we may be said to know some-

---

[5]See Ernest Nagel, "Malicious Philosophies of Science," *Partisan Review*, January-February 1943, p. 47.

[6]Some scientists are, in fact, reductionist. The American psychologist John B. Watson said that thinking was nothing but subvocal talking and that in turn was only movements of the larynx. Happily, there are fewer reductionists today than in the late nineteenth and early twentieth centuries, although those who linger on get publicity disproportionate to their importance.

thing about the nature of love. Phenomena cannot be understood entirely apart from the conditions of their occurrence, but neither can they be reduced entirely to those conditions. What remains to be known about love after science has said what it can is what it feels like to love and what the significance and value of love are.

If the actual knowledge acquired by science at any time were looked at a hundred years later, much of it would turn out to be only partially true, and much actually false. Only the newer body of knowledge would then be thought of as science, and it in turn will be superseded by a still newer body. Science as method, however, despite constant refinements in procedure, has been essentially the same since about 1600. If we were forced to choose between having the conclusions of science but not its method, and scientific method but not its conclusions, there would be great advantage in choosing the latter, for the former would leave us with all the errors of our day forever fixed, while the latter, although depriving us of the scientific knowledge of the moment, would allow us to reach today's knowledge and to surpass it.

Scientific method—the general methods of science —is of two kinds, analytic and empirical. The an-alytic is linguistic and logical; it deals with ideas and meanings. The empirical is observational; it deals with matters of fact. Analytical method alone suffices for logic and mathematics, but both analysis and observation are necessary for empirical study. General methods are distinguished from procedures or techniques, which result from the application of scientific method to a particular subject matter. One application, for example, of scientific method to the subject matter of public opinion results in the questionnaire and the interview as procedures. These depend, obviously, on special characteristics of the subject: men can think and answer questions. Questionnaires and interviews would be absurd in geological investigations; there we are limited to techniques of examining rock formations, fossils, fossil casts, and fossil molds. To be sure, it would be helpful if the rocks could talk, but they cannot. As for the special instruments of particular sciences—the familiar test tubes and Bunsen burners of chemistry laboratories, microscopes for biology, telescopes for astronomy, the great cyclotrons for physics, the galvanometers and tachistoscopes for psychology—they are not parts of general scientific method, but aids in technique and procedure.

PART II

THE ANTHROPOLOGIST "SCIENCING"

If, as Bronowski asserts, "observations" (that is, data) are the very stuff of science as an activity, where does anthropology fit into this scheme? How does the anthropologist go about gathering the evidence or information ("data" is the more highfalutin term) he will use in trying to answer the problem he has set for himself? We could answer this with excerpts from some of the now numerous manuals on "field techniques," but many of them are fairly dry reading, and, perhaps, a bit premature at this point in an introduction to the field. For now, let us instead take a look at the cultural anthropologist engaging in one of the first steps in the process of inquiry. And let's look at it not so much with regard to data-gathering as a scientific process, but rather as a human encounter, one between the anthropologist as a person and the people whose behavior and activities will be the basis of his inferences and conceptual structures. The other, more technical features of data-gathering come later in your exposure to anthropology.

THE "LABORATORY"

To do cultural anthropological field work is to be "in the company of man," as Casagrande says. Interviews and first-hand observations of the life of a people are not, of course, the only kind of data the cultural anthropologist uses in probing the problem he has set for himself, but they are so central to most anthropological investigations as to be almost the *sine qua non* of the anthropological enterprise. "When are you going back into the field?"—a question often heard in hotel hallways during annual meetings of the American Anthropological Association. Indeed, in a larger sense, for most anthropologists the field experience is more than simply a data-gathering expedition; it is a participation, however brief, in another human world. And by that participation the anthropologist becomes part of what he observes—(recall what Bronowski noted about the power as well as the limits of observations as the basis of scientific conceptualization). Field work is also an encounter between two different worlds of meaning; and (due to that, among other things) for most anthropologists I know it is the source of some of the most poignant memories in all of life. In the following brief excerpt, the preface from a book about anthropological informants that can be highly recommended, Casagrande introduces well some of the themes that will be further illustrated by the three selections following it.

IN THE COMPANY OF MAN

JOSEPH B. CASAGRANDE

Most scholars in the several disciplines that deal with man and his works are devoted to the specialized study of but one rather recent variant of human culture, that of Western Man. Unlike his colleagues the anthropologist takes all mankind as his proper subject; and he is concerned with the whole range of socially learned and socially shared behavior patterns that we have come to call *culture*. As the biographer seeks to portray the life of a man, so the anthropologist as ethnographer seeks to describe and understand the *way of life* of a people.

Traditionally, the anthropologist has studied the nonliterate peoples of the world, be they the primitive hunters in the remote corners of the earth or the sophisticates of the florescent civilizations. He is interested alike in the Bushmen of the Kalahari Desert and the sculptors of Benin, in the naked Tierra del Fuegans and the empire-building Inca. In recent years anthropologists have also turned in increasing numbers to the study of peasant communities of the Old World and to the complex societies of modern nations, including their own. But despite the greater compass of his interests the anthropologist's basic methods of research, and perhaps more importantly, his way of looking at human behavior as a whole, remain those that have evolved from his work with the simpler groups.

Where there are no archives and no books other than the memories of men, the anthropologist perforce must take his primary data from life, so to speak—from the actions and words of the people

among whom he lives and works. Even if he has recourse to documents, he still relies heavily on his own observations of behavior and on the oral statements of informants. For the anthropologist the field is thus the fountainhead of knowledge, serving him as both laboratory and library. His research is necessarily done in the company of man.

Field work by its very nature is at heart a collaborative enterprise. To come as an inquisitive stranger to live among an alien people is an audacious undertaking. At the very least the anthropologist's presence on the scene must be condoned and his impertinences suffered. But the anthropologist hopes for more than this; he needs the active coöperation of the people if he is to succeed in his work. That such coöperation is so often freely given is eloquent testimony to the universal good will of men. Let it be admitted, too, that the successful outcome of field research depends not only on the anthropologist's own skills, but also on the capabilities and interest of those who teach him their ways.

Like any stranger anywhere the anthropologist on arrival in his community will be an object of curiosity. He will be visited, queried, courted, perhaps resented or suspected. He may be a nuisance and something of a social irritant. He may be a source of some pride. But in either case he will, in the natural course of events, come to terms with the people. The total process of mutual adjustment will not be unlike that, say, of any rather mysterious newcomer who comes to settle in some small provincial town.

With luck and in good time the anthropologist will find an accepted place in the community. His

Reprinted with permission of Harper and Row, Inc. From *In the Company of Man*, ed. Joseph B. Casagrande. © 1960 by Joseph B. Casagrande, pp. ix–xii.

presence will be taken for granted. The people will answer his questions, see that he is fed, invite him to ceremonies, and apprise him of events that they have learned will be of interest. They will laugh at his mistakes and breaches of native etiquette, and they will be amused or perplexed by *his* queer customs. What was strange will in time become familiar. He will become conversant with village gossip, privy to all that is both commonplace and momentous in the daily lives of the people. Individuals, too, will emerge as separate personalities, each as distinct and as predictable as those he knows back home. Indeed, he will recognize beneath the cloak of culture many of the same personality types, and he will come to respond to people as individuals whom he can like or dislike rather than as ethnic prototypes.

In the course of his work, as he sorts out individuals and his reactions to them, the anthropologist will inevitably form closer ties with some persons than with others. Some will serve him as assistant, informant, interpreter, major domo, cook, or house-boy; others may become hangers-on, attaching themselves to his household in the hope of gaining favor for an errand or a scrap of information. One or a few individuals, by virtue of their special knowledge or skills, their authority or qualities of intellect and temperament, may become his particular mentors and close associates.

The relationship between the anthropologist and a key informant has many of the attributes of other kinds of primary relationships: between student and teacher, employee and employer, friends or relatives—as a matter of fact, it is often assimilated to the latter. In some respects it is most closely paralleled by the relationship between the psychiatrist and his patient. There is much of the same depth and intimacy, the same desire to gain insight,

in the one case into the personality and in the other into the culture as it is reflected in the personality. There is the same constraint to maintain objectivity, and many of the same psychodynamic currents of transference, counter-transference, and identification are at work in the two forms of relationship. But there are marked differences. The relationship between the anthropologist and an informant usually bridges two cultures, it is less episodic, there is greater reciprocity, and it is entered into for quite different reasons. In final analysis it is unique among the various forms of human association. Whatever its emotional tone, whether it be colored by affection and respect or not, such a sustained close relationship cannot but be highly significant for both parties to it.

Immersed in the life around him, the anthropologist may experience an exhilarating sense of coming to understand another people and of being accepted by them. He may also at times undergo a shattering feeling of isolation, of strangeness and disorientation, and yearn for the comfort of accustomed things. Herein lies a dilemma, for he is neither a full participant in the life he studies, nor simply a passive background observer of it. He is something of both, a role nicely summarized in the double term, "participant-observer." Not born to the alien culture or committed to it, the anthropologist must stand at a certain psychological and emotional distance from it. If he is an objective scientist, he cannot "go native." Neither can he hold himself aloof and observe human behavior as a naturalist might watch a colony of ants; with fellow humans there is both the possibility and necessity of communication. Thus one's capacity for imaginatively entering into the life of another people becomes a primary qualification for the ethnographer.

THE FIELD EXPERIENCE

The following pages are not from a formal anthropological monograph, but I have no apologies for including them. They are taken from a semifictionalized account of field work and human reactions to it written by a well-known professional anthropologist. This brief excerpt compellingly portrays some of the problems of personal loneliness in the press of a strange and alien situation, of gradually finding ways of coping with the new problems—in short, of discovering some of the "parameters" of the "ethnographic laboratory" (as it is often put) that anthropologists and ethnographers work in. The first part of a field period is usually one of fumbling around, of feeling lost and incapable, of asking oneself "How did I get here?", of slowly readjusting one's daily habits and expectations to match a new round of tasks dictated by the situation and the job at hand, and of only gradually being accepted by the people as someone they should spend time with and worry about. It is, as Bowen says, a process of finding a new "home." Once again, for getting a good feeling of what work in the field is like, the entire book from which this is taken can be read with profit (and enjoyment).

A NEW HOME

ELENORE SMITH BOWEN

In my hut at Kako's I sat idly watching a June shower spin a wet beaded curtain beyond my open door. Against the sharp tapping of the rain I could hear the occasional crow of a rooster and the calls of frantic parents, "Come in and get dry!" For everyone knows it is mad to stay out in the rain—everyone but the children, who romp on through the puddles, slide in the mud, or stand wet and naked in the rain blissfully eating a windfall of mangoes.

It was little more than ten weeks since I had waved good-by to Sackerton, but already time had taken on a more individualistic and yet more seasonable aspect than I had been used to. Already the days of the week and the month were no more than a heading printed on my diary pages. I did try to keep count; old habit made me feel I ought to know the date. Yet, in July, when I went back to the station for supplies, I found I had lost three days.

I discarded any concern with "the right time" of day much more readily. Shortly after moving into Kako's, I forgot to wind the rackety alarm I had brought instead of my wrist watch. I set the hour approximately by the sun. I soon became more sensible. From the standpoint of work, it was convenient for me to have two hours between bath and dinner. I was fed at nine by the clock; Monday had the bath water hot at dark. I went on my own time zone: dark and seven by the clock were to

coincide. Every few weeks for the rest of my stay in the bush, I readjusted the clock, blandly telling my protesting boys that it was not working well.

I learned to forget months and to live by moons: to anticipate the full moon for its dances and story-telling; to fear the dark of the moon when witches were abroad.

Cutting through the moons was, for me, a complicated combination of weeks. First, there was the cook's seven-day curry week, highlighting Saturdays. Then there was the five-day cycle of markets by which everyone made engagements. Finally there was the seven-day beer-brewing week which culminated on a named day impartially designating "Sunday" and "beer drink." All these weeks ran concurrently, Kako's market coinciding now with curry Saturdays, now with beer Sundays, until, one day, Kako's market, Saturday and Sunday all happened at once, and none of us could figure out just how. There was no year, merely a succession of seasons and agricultural activities uncorrelated with moons or markets. The rains began when it began to rain; when it began to rain, people started to plant. One could say that a man had done his planting late, but not that the rains had come late. There was the season of yams, of guinea corn, and of millet, and the hungry season when there was little millet left and only corn to eat until the yam harvest. It was the time of hunger now. The provident were down to one meal a day, the improvident or unlucky to one every other day. Old women scolded the young wives for having sold food during the time of plenty: "Wait till you

Reprinted with permission of Curtis Brown, Ltd. From Elenore Smith Bowen, *Return to Laughter*. © 1954 by Harper Brothers, New York, pp. 63–77.

hear your children crying for hunger and have only water to give them."

"When I have children, I'll be careful," women like Ticha retorted. "But now I want money for cloths."

Meanwhile people grew thin and drank more and more beer. "From the amount of millet that will fill one man"—Udama was a thrifty woman—"one can make enough beer to make ten men feel full. That way you can save the real food for your children." Everyone looked with greedy eyes at the burgeoning yam vines.

And yet the mango rains, as this season became in my personal calendar, were for me one of the pleasantest times of the year. Early in the wet season, the rains still come tempestuously with thunder, lightning and a wind that bends branches and tosses mangoes to the ground like bright thunderbolts. In a storm these wind-felled mangoes rolled almost to my doorstep. Then, when they were thoroughly rain-chilled, I would crawl out under the eaves to gather four or five of the choicest. An epicurean feast and an act-of-God holiday.

The holiday aspect of rain was always uppermost in my mind. If I was caught out walking, I splashed happily home through the ankle-deep stream of cool, swift running water that purled down the paths. People called at me from their farm shelters —they have a catlike distaste for wet—and when the path led me through a homestead, heads popped out from under the eaves at the noise of my squelching tennis shoes: "Come inside, Redwoman," they coaxed, gently, as one tries to persuade the crazy. "Come inside. Take off your clothes and dry yourself by our fire." I only grinned in reply. They thought me quite mad anyhow, and the rain that made their bones shiver with cold was to me a respite from a steamy heat surpassed, in my experience, only by a Washington, D.C. summer. So I reveled in the rain, and, according to Ticha, gamboled in it like young sheep and goats. Then once home, I would towel myself dry and sink into a happy period of complete relaxation, too dark for reading and too wet for visitors.

"Once home"—it was not long before I felt that I had always lived here, not long before I found myself writing in my diary "at home" instead of "at Kako's." It was my home. I no longer remember just how it came about, by what individual steps my new life became so familiar that even now I can smell, touch and hear it. I have only to close

my eyes. But if my recollections of this time are as vivid as my childhood memories, they are also as disconnected and unordered: small, particular incidents, a pointillist picture evoking the entire period between moving to Kako's in May and going back to the station in July.

I remember the way Ikpoom's black and tan goat jumped my fence every morning, to drink from the waterpots by my kitchen. I can still see the wet, polished skins of women swaying back from the spring with the large-bellied waterpots on their heads. I remember when I first realized that the early morning pounding couldn't possibly be what I had so far sleepily assumed it: the throb, thump and whir of machinery. My alarm clock, typewriter and meat grinder were the only machines in miles. Over my coffee, I asked Sunday. His conviction that no one could be unacquainted with so common a sound made for a long detour through thatch rustlings and bird calls. Finally I went out to look. It was the thump of hardwood pestles in waist-high mortars accompanied by the shush-shush of grain slowly crushed between handstone and granite slab.

Most nostalgically I remember the nights. At the resthouse night had been a silence in which one lowered one's voice. I had sometimes hesitated to use my typewriter; its clatter had seemed an intrusion into something that might pounce. Common sense has little power against an African night, and to those who sit alone in the bush, the night is undomesticated and strange.

But in a large homestead like Kako's, the night is tame. Even in the dark of the moon, when people stay inside their huts, one can always hear the sound of low gossiping when people wake at night. (I found myself unique in my notion of a "good night's sleep" of so many uninterrupted hours.) In the full of the moon, everyone sat outside beside the fires which encircled the moon-washed yard like a bright necklace set in darkness. The children romped about, calling riddles to each other with shrill laughter. The old men, full of years and content, sat close to the warmth, smoking their pipes, their children and grandchildren about them. Here a young woman dressed her co-wife's hair into elaborate braids and puffs, using a bone awl, a wooden comb and liberal applications of castor oil. There a youngster sat at the loom he had brought into the brighter radius of my lamplight, and wove a cloth for his mother while he listened to his brother's wives gossip as they spun. An old woman fried that delicacy, gourd seeds in palm oil, and everyone helped himself to the half-penny worth allowable to all the members of the homestead. Two sisters out in the pale moonlight pounded grain in one large mortar, singing to the thump of their alternating pestles; every now and then one would toss the mahogany pestle high up into the air—and straight—clapping her hands in time to their song until she caught it coming down, and, thump, into the mortar just on the beat. Women sliced vegetables for sun-drying, or made potash from the ashes of yam peelings. Here an idle young man sat beside his busy wife loudly singing a song in praise of the father and mother who had reared her so well. And always, somewhere in the distance, there was the sound of gongs and drums and singing.

Through the night Kako wandered from fire to fire, settling minor quarrels, informally discussing the next day's tasks, and generally just making sure that all was well. At first I wandered in his wake, for loneliness often drove me from my hut and my work, to seek the fellowship of human beings. But Kako had little time for me, and I was glad to be made welcome at Udama's fire. Soon I had my regular place there, and was content to lean back listening to Udama's strictures on the slackness of modern manners and watching Ticha tease Ihugh's younger brother—her husband's son. It was almost flirtation, but no one, not even Udama, seemed to mind. But then, Ticha was Udama's "little wife." (A man with many wives, like Kako who had seventeen, generally places the younger ones in the care of one of the first three; these "great wives" then look after the welfare and morals of their "little wives"; they farm together, cook together, and mind each other's children.) It was natural that she should be particularly familiar with Udama's three sons, and they were all much the same age. The marked reserve with which Ticha treated the sons of Kako's other wives confirmed me in my opinion. Anyhow, her giddy jesting made Udama's fire gay with laughter.

Occasionally the contented gossip of these nights was shattered by a voice raised high in complaint to the world at large; it was usually a man who had come home to find no food prepared for him and no good reason for his wife's negligence. Soon murmurs of "Hear our brother" rose from the other fires, calls of sympathy, and perhaps even offers of food. Then, one would hear the energetic thumping of pestle in mortar as the dilatory wife, shamed by this appeal to public opinion, set about her task.

Such public complaining always worked. It was my quite innocent use of it which finally established the family relationship between myself and my boys. My cook was a very good cook, but he had a temperament and a delusion: he believed that his best creation was corn starch pudding. I loathe corn starch pudding anyhow. In his, there was enough corn starch to enable him to achieve sculpture: cubist, abstract and some attempts at realistic representations of coiled snakes. When all appeal and admonition failed, I snatched the corn starch from him and threw it into the river. The cook sulked. Things began to go wrong, each trivial and possibly accidental.

One day I told Kako, who was going off to market with his notables, that I would follow later, as soon as I had eaten. No food had been prepared. It was market day; the cook might have some legitimate excuse. I told him not to let it happen again, and turned on my heel to shout after Kako to wait: my cook had cooked me no food. From their own domestic lives, the elders found the situation familiar. By asking leading questions, they drew the story from me in its true perspective. Their loud asides taught me that the corn starch was indeed at the bottom of it all. (There's no hiding anything in such a community.)

The cook, poker-faced, slouched to the kitchen door. I realized I had started something. I hoped I wouldn't lose a good cook over it, but the affair was no longer in my hands. Kako gave his decision against the cook by calling Udama and instructing her to feed me, for my "children" were either lazy or sick. Immediately, just like the lazy wives I had so often heard similarly rebuked, my cook turned back into the kitchen and there clashed pot against pan to notify the public that he was making amends.

That evening, while I was still most uncertain about possible consequences of the whole affair, my three boys appeared in delegation to present the cook's apology and a petition. The cook would never do anything bad again. None of them would. If, inadvertently, they ever again gave me cause of complaint, would I please mention it privately and softly before I let an outsider know? We were "one family"; they were all my children; we should settle our affairs among ourselves.

After that I had no more servant trouble, no need to speak of firing or fines, no need to scold, no need to do more than state my wishes—and listen courteously to any countersuggestions. I had appealed to the community once, and I might do so again; and so, I now knew, might they. We ruled ourselves accordingly. From that day on, as befitted the "one family" we were called, we showed the world only our loyalty to one another; our differences we kept to ourselves.

During this same period my relationship to the community also underwent a noticeable change. I was no longer called "the white woman." I was "Kako's European," sometimes even "our European." Kako, for reasons of his own—which I learned only when it was almost too late for remedy—was doing his best to have me identified as his "child." His intervention between me and my cook was one step toward this end: the incident showed us as his dependents, among whom he should keep the peace. He encouraged the women of his homestead to include me in all their activities.

At the time I noticed only that finally I was being invited out, that I was no longer restricted to the self-made projects in my notebook. First Udama, then her married cousin who was living at Tar's homestead not too far from us, then all the other important matrons, began to ask me to weeding parties. I was aware that it was largely a matter of lion hunting; that my hostesses asked me for prestige's sake and not my own. Nevertheless, being asked to such parties at all made me feel a part of their daily life; it even gave me one thing about which I knew more than my own boys.

Generally women weed their own farms, but sometimes, because it is much pleasanter to get a month's work done in one day and in company, several women who have adjacent farms brew beer and summon the women of the neighborhood to weed and drink. No man between five and eighty dare venture near such a party. Each woman takes one line of yam mounds. Abreast, dancing as they move, singing obscene songs, they weed their way down to the end of the farm. Meanwhile, in any homestead within earshot, the men prick their ears at the songs and shake their heads disapprovingly if they do catch any of the words, for the songs the women sing in the evening while they drink their hostesses' beer are full of virtuous sentiments and fit for the ears of husbands.

One day I went to one of these weeding parties

close to Kako's. Since I had come with Udama who called me "daughter," I was expected to join in the weeding. My hostess showed me a short row, slightly less than the amount of work expected from an eight-year-old girl. "We know Europeans, like albinos, can't stand much sun," the woman said kindly when I flagged. "Go sit under the tree and start some yams roasting for us."

"Madam!" I looked up from the coals and saw Monday. "Madam!" He was advancing upon us, waving one of my handkerchiefs like a flag of truce and shouting loudly that I had forgotten it. "Go away," I yelled. But Monday was young, curious, and overconfident in my will to protect him; he had determined to find out what actually went on at these feminine get-togethers. Udama turned on me: had I broken my promise not to bring or tell any man? I denied my responsibility for Monday's gate-crashing; again I shouted at him to go back. Monday, still etiquette-distance away and not wanting to hear, was deaf. He came on.

With a whoop of pure anticipation, the women surged toward him; they screamed obscenities as they ran. Monday gave one frightened look; he swiveled on his heel and bolted for safety. Only the Furies could have caught him. The women, panting and laughing, returned to the tree. There they proceeded to mime in dance just what they would have done to Monday had they captured him. I appreciated his speed. When I got home to scold him, Monday still looked unsettled, but he seemed only faintly sheepish and not at all repentant. At least, he asked me to teach him some of the songs. Sedately, I refused.

Not all my social involvements were due to Kako's urging. I always felt welcomed at Poorgbilin's, and I was on familiar terms in Yabo's homestead. One day Atakpa came to fetch me. In great excitement she dragged me off with her to Poorgbilin's. Once she had me on the path, she began to explain. Only a few hours ago, Poorgbilin's fifth wife had borne her first child, a girl. Poorgbilin, as husband and as homestead head, had to name her; he had named her "Redwoman" after me, and Atakpa, who had been there visiting, had been told to bring me the news at once so that I might come give the mother two tenth-pennies "to tie around the namesake's neck." Atakpa outlined my new responsibilities: later, I was to make more gifts of coins "to tie around the waist," still later to help buy the girl's first cloth (I was vaguely surprised that Atakpa should imagine me still around thirteen years hence); I must always assist in medical matters and in payments to a diviner investigating the magical complications of my namesake's illness. I was not quite a godmother. The baby and I were one; we each took on all the relatives of the other.

Under Atakpa's eye, I handed over my gifts. I stood for a long time watching the pink-purple baby, wriggling and howling as the midwives smeared her with camwood for warmth and luck, put castor oil on her hair to keep her head cool, and painted her eyelids with antimony because it looked nice. For the first time I felt that it mattered to someone whether I came or went. In calmer moments I reflected that my pennies probably had something to do with it. On the whole, I preferred to believe Poorgbilin's statement, "Now, even if you go, your name will not be forgotten here."

I should have been content. The women accepted me. The children hunted me out. Indeed, it became difficult to find any time to myself. Once, after an afternoon rain, I went out with the fixed determination of seeing the sunset. Kako's homestead lay on the sheltered side of one of the foothills to the mountains that rose to the southeast. On the path leading down to the stream and swampland below was a convenient outcrop of bare stone where I often sat; it was not too far off the path, and yet hidden in the grass. There I went to smoke and look. A green field of yam gardens and grass, dotted with trees and occasional circles of bright thatched huts, rose gradually from the swamp. Behind, clear in the rain-washed air, the slopes of the hill Telemkpe glided through two thousand feet of grass and farms to the girdle of dark rain forest that hemmed the bare, baboon-haunted summit. Now Telemkpe was vivid in the saffron light of the storm-setting sun, a beacon before the threatening rain clouds piled high behind it. Truly, it is a country just this side of Eden.

I sat on, watching each fluctuation of beauty as the light was slowly drawn upward from the foothills. "Redwoman, Redwoman," a shrill, mosquito cloud of children was suddenly upon me. "Redwoman, didn't you see us burning the swampland? Come down with us. It's not good to sit alone." Children tugged at my clothes, unaware of anything but kindness in relieving my solitude.

At the edge of the swamp was a strip of land reclaimed and drained for growing corn and rice.

Women and children were burning the stalks of the last crop, pulled and piled to dry as well as the rains permitted. The still moist debris popped and crackled in the fire or smoldered out. The children screeched with excitement as they darted with flaming grass brands to relight the pile, then the next. My nostrils pricked with the acrid smoke. I too caught the fever. I careened about with them, burning grass, laughing, slapping at the flying sparks. The sun set unwatched.

As I walked swiftly home through the brief twilight, I held careless debate on the pleasures of solitude and of sociability. I easily concluded that the delights of solitude were the more sophisticated, but which was the better, the preferable or the more valuable (and in reference to what) was a question I dismissed with the unthinking compromise that perhaps they were complementary.

In any case, the pleasures of sociability certainly depended on being able to communicate. As my grasp of the language improved, I began to be able to relax in company: savoir-faire assumes a certain conversational facility. Much of my early desire to flee into my hut and slam the door had been due to sheer exhaustion, for it had taken an intense concentration to find even a few familiar sounds in the stream of syllables so fluently and easily directed at me. Now this flow of speech resolved itself into words, known and unknown, just as the crowds began to dissolve into a number of people, friends or strangers. Within Kako's homestead I could even recognize some of the legs—all I could see from under the low thatch—that flashed past when a storm broke, and some of the voices that called outside my door. "Come out, Redwoman, come out. It's not good to sit alone."

I should have been content, and I was—as long as I thought only in terms of enjoying myself and of feeling at home. My dissatisfaction lay wholly in the part I was being assigned. I was rapidly being absorbed in the life of the women and children. All the magic, all the law, all the politics—over half the things professionally important to me—were in the hands of the men, and so far not one man had been willing to discuss such matters with me, not one man had taken me with him to the meetings of the elders which, I knew, often took place. Was there a moot? I was at a weeding party. An inquest? I had gone to visit my namesake. A ceremony? I heard women gossip of it, afterwards. I had been identified with the women: unless I could break that association, I would leave the field with copious information on domestic details and without any knowledge of anything else.

I didn't like this situation, and I tried to change it. My efforts seemed futile. I never accepted women's invitations without first asking Kako if anything "of importance" were happening that day. Kako always smiled while he uttered the many polite phrases which boiled down to, "Don't bother your head with such things, my child. Run off and amuse yourself." On my visits I always called first on the homestead head. Poorgbilin always led me straight to my namesake, Tar to Udama's cousin.

Daily I went to Yabo's. It was always assumed that I had come to visit Atakpa or Amara. Atakpa's brother Cholo sometimes spent a few moments teasing me. Amara's father Lam would answer my point-blank questions, if I could find him. (Lam never said no to anyone; he knew when to vanish.) Yabo made no bones about snarling at me if I tried to interrupt his thoughts with my questions. One day he spoke viciously to me. I wanted to tell him a great many things, all of which would prove how immensely superior I was and how necessary it was to treat me with respect. A limited vocabulary restricted me to an irritable, "You and Kako, you are just alike. There is only one difference: *you* know nothing!" I swept about on my heel, all set for a grand exit that was quite spoiled by my having to crawl out the low doorway. I muttered my way home, composing and trying to translate into their language the speech I had wanted to make.

A few days later there was a commotion in my reception hut. Sunday, who had entered it with dignity, flew out of it and into my hut; he announced that Yabo demanded to see me. I'd had enough of Yabo's rudeness. "Tell him to wait," I snapped; I tried to recall the nasty comments I had composed on the path. Sunday saw the gleam in my eye. He hastened back out, but there he hovered between two equally fearful poles, like one of Newton's planets. "Go on, tell him!" I shouted out the door. "Tell her," growled Yabo from the reception hut. Sunday seemed permanently fixed halfway between the two of us. Both of us saw his irresolution; simultaneously we roared out of our lairs to browbeat him. Sunday sidestepped and let us collide.

My next clear recollection is of Yabo leading me by a bruising grip on my wrist out of Kako's homestead, and of Sunday panting up breathlessly be-

hind to give me a notebook before I disappeared. As soon as we reached our destination, however, I swallowed all anger: Yabo had brought me to my first funeral.

I saw the body, a stiff bundle wrapped in mats, lying in the middle of the yard. Then I noticed the people. Under one tree sat the notables and Kako. Our eyes met for a moment; his shifted. He didn't greet me. Perhaps I should have challenged him then. But I didn't. I was too glad to be there. I looked around. Under another tree, the chief mourners sat silent with bowed heads and vacant faces. A group of strangers crowded under a third tree; some of these also had their cloths tied about the waist like a sash, in sign of grief.

Yabo moved over to the elders and notables. He pulled me down beside him onto one of the hard plank benches. There was a long wait, while more and more elders came. Yabo only grunted at my questions. I located Ikpoom. Since other people were moving about, I went over to him. He told me that a woman married into this homestead had died in the night; she had five children; the strangers were her relatives; she would be buried today. We were shushed. I went back to my seat.

I was prepared for ritual, for funeral orations perhaps, for anything but what actually happened. It was a debate, conducted with all the noise and irreverence of a court case. And I understood not one word of it. First the strangers orated. Kako and his elders objected to everything they said. The strangers spoke even more hotly. En masse, they advanced to the center of the yard. The notables left me behind quite alone under our tree, as they too marched grimly out into the yard. Old men stuck out their chins pugnaciously; they shouted and waved their barbed spears in menacing gesticulation. Only the mourners remained silent and dejected under their tree. Finally Kako and some of his elders, either convinced or outshouted, returned to our tree and sat down again.

Not Yabo. He, Poorgbilin and a few others were still arguing and brandishing their spears in dangerous persuasion. It looked like the beginning of a fight; I hoped it was merely their style of rhetoric.

Kako tried to quiet Yabo, who turned upon him with a snarl. Kako jumped up, backed by his followers. He and Yabo argued bitterly. Meanwhile, the strangers unobtrusively and prudently withdrew to their own tree. In the midst of all this shouting, one of the mourners led forth five children. I caught

Ikpoom's eye and he nodded: the dead woman had been their mother. Once again I expected some note of consolation and mourning. Once more I was mistaken. I watched in astonishment as the children were bandied about by the wrist, from one elder to the next. Before long Yabo reached the end of his brief patience. He seized the eldest child and flung her at Kako.

For the first time I saw Kako lose his temper and his dignity. Roughly, screaming at Yabo, he pushed the child aside. She reeled and fell against one of the elders. Kako paid no heed; he stood rigid and tight-faced as he wrestled with his anger. By the time the child had been set on her feet again, Kako had regained his self-control. He turned to the elders; in a soft, definite voice he put his views before them. At first there was appreciative laughter for some of Yabo's heckling. But slowly, with persuasive rhetoric, Kako won over all the elders. I leaned forward, as though by straining my ears I could make myself understand words I did not know. I might as well have been deaf. I had to fall back on what I could see, and that served only to confirm a rivalry I had already guessed.

Kako had secured his backing; he now resumed his debate with the strangers. Yabo found himself completely left aside. He began to dance up and down, shouting the first words I could understand: "I'm leaving." No one paid any attention. "I'm leaving!" screeched Yabo in the falsetto of rage. He was not heard. He started to walk out of the homestead. He was not seen. The elders were absorbed in the debate between Kako and the strangers. Yabo turned. Again he announced that he was leaving. No one asked him to stay. He started off again, but this time he wanted to take me along. I protested; I wanted to see the burial. Kako, lost in the heat of argument, paid no more attention to my objections than he did to Yabo's expostulations.

I had come with him, said Yabo, and I would leave with him. And willy-nilly, as I had come, so I left. Yabo dragged me by the wrist until he could fling me before him onto the grass-enclosed path from which there was no turning. Over his shoulder he shouted vituperations at the unheeding hullabaloo in the homestead behind us. Angrily he jerked me about to face him: "It wasn't the strangers. It was Kako who killed her." Then, as though he had said too much, he shut himself in a surly silence, and shooed me along the path before him, prodding me with the butt of his spear whenever I tried to linger, opening his lips only to hiss their "giddup" for slow-moving goats and women.

Back in my hut I poured myself a drink and tried to assimilate what had happened. Yabo's violence didn't worry me; he had merely treated me as he treated his own womenfolk—with the very important difference that he would not have taken one of them along on such an occasion. He had accused Kako of murder; he must have meant poison or witchcraft; Kako had been in his homestead when the woman died. I was too unsure of myself to repeat Yabo's words to any of Kako's people. My boys wouldn't talk. I never found out just what had happened that day, before my very eyes.

I had, however, learned that I could play Yabo and Kako off against each other, though not, as yet, very skillfully. Yabo would take me any place to show that I preferred his company to the chief's; Kako could not bear to let Yabo take the lead. Neither Kako nor Yabo was, by himself, willing to tell any European anything; neither Kako nor Yabo could stand the thought that the other was the more valued, by anyone or for any reason. Yabo had set the first, necessary precedent. From then on Kako, and in his wake all the other notables, told me of funerals and expected me to attend them. Again after Yabo set the example, I was notified of moots and inquests. Some of the elders always—and all of them sometimes—were amused or annoyed by my new role, but none disputed it. Not for any merit of mine, but because of the relationship between Kako and Yabo, my work flourished like the green bay tree.

AN ETHNOGRAPHIC STUDY

Bronislaw Malinowski was one of the founders of modern cultural anthropology about whom you will be hearing a great deal if you go further into the social or behavioral sciences. His name is associated with the development of a particular set of concepts or theory, a "functional" frame of reference for the analysis of human behavior. He also produced a vast number of publications and set a model for intensive, long-term, and comprehensive ethnographic field work. His discussion of "functionalism" serves as a good example of a conceptual theme very important for most anthropologists—the "holistic" emphasis, an insistence that in the process of abstraction elements of human behavior must not be wrenched out of their relevant context of meaning and purpose. Toward this end Malinowski is concerned to observe and record a wide range of data—as wide as possible—with a subsequent narrowing of focus as the boundaries of the problem become more clear. He is as interested, for example, with recording what has recently become known in anthropological literature as the "emic" emphasis (the meaning, subjective, and value aspects of a phenomenon) as he is to record the "etic" (the objective, structural features of a phenomenon). The following excerpt is taken from the opening chapter of one of his most famous books, which deals with an elaborate and far-ranging trading cycle in Melanesia, the "Kula" ring.

SUBJECT, SCOPE, AND METHOD OF ETHNOGRAPHIC WORK

BRONISLAW MALINOWSKI

Imagine yourself suddenly set down surrounded by all your gear, alone on a tropical beach close to a native village, while the launch or dinghy which has brought you sails away out of sight. Since you take up your abode in the compound of some neighbouring white man, trader or missionary, you have nothing to do, but to start at once on your ethnographic work. Imagine further that you are a beginner, without previous experience, with nothing to guide you and no one to help you. For the white man is temporarily absent, or else unable or unwilling to waste any of his time on you. This exactly describes my first initiation into field work on the south coast of New Guinea. I well remember the long visits I paid to the villages during the first weeks; the feeling of hopelessness and despair after many obstinate but futile attempts had entirely failed to bring me into real touch with the natives, or supply me with any material. I had periods of despondency, when I buried myself in the reading of novels, as a man might take to drink in a fit of tropical depression and boredom.

Imagine yourself then, making your first entry

into the village, alone or in company with your white cicerone. Some natives flock round you, especially if they smell tobacco. Others, the more dignified and elderly, remain seated where they are. Your white companion has his routine way of treating the natives, and he neither understands, nor is very much concerned with the manner in which you, as an ethnographer, will have to approach them. The first visit leaves you with a hopeful feeling that when you return alone, things will be easier. Such was my hope at least.

I came back duly, and soon gathered an audience around me. A few compliments in pidgin-English on both sides, some tobacco changing hands, induced an atmosphere of mutual amiability. I tried then to proceed to business. First, to begin with subjects which might arouse no suspicion, I started to "do" technology. A few natives were engaged in manufacturing some object or other. It was easy to look at it and obtain the names of the tools, and even some technical expressions about the proceedings, but there the matter ended. It must be borne in mind that pidgin-English is a very imperfect instrument for expressing one's ideas, and that before one gets a good training in framing questions and understanding answers one has the uncomfortable feeling

Reprinted with permission of publisher. From Bronislaw Malinowski, *Argonauts of the Western Pacific* (New York: E. P. Dutton and Co., 1953), pp. 4–25.

that free communication in it with the natives will never be attained; and I was quite unable to enter into any more detailed or explicit conversation with them at first. I knew well that the best remedy for this was to collect concrete data, and accordingly I took a village census, wrote down genealogies, drew up plans and collected the terms of kinship. But all this remained dead material, which led no further into the understanding of real native mentality or behaviour, since I could neither procure a good native interpretation of any of these items, nor get what could be called the hang of tribal life. As to obtaining their ideas about religion, and magic, their beliefs in sorcery and spirits, nothing was forthcoming except a few superficial items of folk-lore, mangled by being forced into pidgin-English.

Information which I received from some white residents in the district, valuable as it was in itself, was more discouraging than anything else with regard to my own work. Here were men who had lived for years in the place with constant opportunities of observing the natives and communicating with them, and who yet hardly knew one thing about them really well. How could I therefore in a few months or a year, hope to overtake and go beyond them? Moreover, the manner in which my white informants spoke about the natives and put their views was, naturally, that of untrained minds, unaccustomed to formulate their thoughts with any degree of consistency and precision. And they were for the most part, naturally enough, full of the biassed and pre-judged opinions inevitable in the average practical man, whether administrator, missionary, or trader, yet so strongly repulsive to a mind striving after the objective, scientific view of things. The habit of treating with a self-satisfied frivolity what is really serious to the ethnographer; the cheap rating of what to him is a scientific treasure, that is to say, the native's cultural and mental peculiarities and independence—these features, so well known in the inferior amateur's writing, I found in the tone of the majority of white residents.[1]

Indeed, in my first piece of Ethnographic research on the South coast, it was not until I was alone in the district that I began to make some headway; and, at any rate, I found out where lay the secret of effective field work. What is then this ethnographer's magic, by which he is able to evoke the real spirit of the natives, the true picture of tribal life? As usual, success can only be obtained by a patient and systematic application of a number of rules of common sense and well-known scientific principles, and not by the discovery of any marvellous short-cut leading to the desired results without effort or trouble. The principles of method can be grouped under three main headings; first of all, naturally, the student must possess real scientific aims, and know the values and criteria of modern ethnography. Secondly, he ought to put himself in good conditions of work, that is, in the main, to live without other white men, right among the natives. Finally, he has to apply a number of special methods of collecting, manipulating and fixing his evidence. A few words must be said about these three foundation stones of field work, beginning with the second as the most elementary. . . .

Proper conditions for ethnographic work. These, as said, consist mainly in cutting oneself off from the company of other white men, and remaining in as close contact with the natives as possible; which really can only be achieved by camping right in their villages. . . . It is very nice to have a base in a white man's compound for the stores, and to know there is a refuge there in times of sickness and surfeit of native. But it must be far enough away not to become a permanent milieu in which you live and from which you emerge at fixed hours only to "do the village." It should not even be near enough to fly to at any moment for recreation. For the native is not the natural companion for a white man, and after you have been working with him for several hours, seeing how he does his gardens, or letting him tell you items of folk-lore, or discussing his customs, you will naturally hanker after the company of your own kind. But if you are alone in a village beyond reach of this, you go for a solitary walk for an hour or so, return again and then quite naturally seek out the natives' society, this time as a relief from loneliness, just as you would any other companionship. And by means of this natural intercourse, you learn to know him, and you become familiar with his customs and beliefs far better than when he is a paid, and often bored, informant.

---

[1] I may note at once that there were a few delightful exceptions to that, to mention only my friends Billy Hancock in the Trobriands; M. Raffael Brudo, another pearl trader; and the missionary, Mr. M. K. Gilmour.

There is all the difference between a sporadic plunging into the company of natives, and being really in contact with them. What does this latter mean? On the Ethnographer's side, it means that his life in the village, which at first is a strange, sometimes unpleasant, sometimes intensely interesting adventure, soon adopts quite a natural course very much in harmony with his surroundings.

Soon after I had established myself in Omarakana (Trobriand Islands), I began to take part, in a way, in the village life, to look forward to the important or festive events, to take personal interest in the gossip and the developments of the small village occurrences; to wake up every morning to a day, presenting itself to me more or less as it does to the native. I would get out from under my mosquito net, to find around me the village life beginning to stir, or the people well advanced in their working day according to the hour and also to the season, for they get up and begin their labours early or late, as work presses. As I went on my morning walk through the village, I could see intimate details of family life, of toilet, cooking, taking of meals; I could see the arrangements for the day's work, people starting on their errands, or groups of men and women busy at some manufacturing tasks. . . . Quarrels, jokes, family scenes, events usually trivial, sometimes dramatic but always significant, formed the atmosphere of my daily life, as well as of theirs. It must be remembered that as the natives saw me constantly every day, they ceased to be interested or alarmed, or made self-conscious by my presence, and I ceased to be a disturbing element in the tribal life which I was to study, altering it by my very approach, as always happens with a new-comer to every savage community. In fact, as they knew that I would thrust my nose into everything, even where a well-mannered native would not dream of intruding, they finished by regarding me as part and parcel of their life, a necessary evil or nuisance, mitigated by donations of tobacco.

Later on in the day, whatever happened was within easy reach, and there was no possibility of its escaping my notice. Alarms about the sorcerer's approach in the evening, one or two big, really important quarrels and rifts within the community, cases of illness, attempted cures and deaths, magical rites which had to be performed, all these I had not to pursue, fearful of missing them, but they took place under my very eyes, at my own doorstep, so to speak. . . . And it must be emphasised whenever anything dramatic or important occurs it is essential to investigate it at the very moment of happening, because the natives cannot but talk about it, are too excited to be reticent, and too interested to be mentally lazy in supplying details. Also, over and over again, I committed breaches of etiquette, which the natives, familiar enough with me, were not slow in pointing out. I had to learn how to behave, and to a certain extent, I acquired "the feeling" for native good and bad manners. With this, and with the capacity of enjoying their company and sharing some of their games and amusements, I began to feel that I was indeed in touch with the natives, and this is certainly the preliminary condition of being able to carry on successful field work. . . .

But the Ethnographer has not only to spread his nets in the right place, and wait for what will fall into them. He must be an active huntsman, and drive his quarry into them and follow it up to its most inaccessible lairs. And that leads us to the more active methods of pursuing ethnographic evidence. It has been mentioned at the end of Division III that the Ethnographer has to be inspired by the knowledge of the most modern results of scientific study, by its principles and aims. I shall not enlarge upon this subject, except by way of one remark, to avoid the possibility of misunderstanding. Good training in theory, and acquaintance with its latest results, is not identical with being burdened with "preconceived ideas." If a man sets out on an expedition, determined to prove certain hypotheses, if he is incapable of changing his views constantly and casting them off ungrudgingly under the pressure of evidence, needless to say his work will be worthless. But the more problems he brings with him into the field, the more he is in the habit of moulding his theories according to facts, and of seeing facts in their bearing upon theory, the better he is equipped for the work. Preconceived ideas are pernicious in any scientific work, but foreshadowed problems are the main endowment of a scientific thinker, and these problems are first revealed to the observer by his theoretical studies.

In Ethnology the early efforts of Bastian, Tylor, Morgan, the German Völkerpsychologen have remoulded the older crude information of travellers, missionaries, etc., and have shown us the importance of applying deeper conceptions and discarding crude and misleading ones.[2]

The concept of animism superseded that of "fetichism" or "devil-worship," both meaningless terms. The understanding of the classificatory systems of relationship paved the way for the brilliant, modern researches on native sociology in the field work of the Cambridge school. The psychological analysis of the German thinkers has brought forth an abundant crop of most valuable information in the results obtained by the recent German expeditions to Africa, South America and the Pacific, while the theoretical works of Frazer, Durkheim and others have already, and will no doubt still for a long time inspire field workers and lead them to new results. The field worker relies entirely upon inspiration from theory. Of course he may be also a theoretical thinker and worker, and there he can draw on himself for stimulus. But the two functions are separate, and in actual research they have to be separated both in time and conditions of work.

As always happens when scientific interest turns towards and begins to labour on a field so far only prospected by the curiosity of amateurs, Ethnology has introduced law and order into what seemed chaotic and freakish. It has transformed for us the sensational, wild and unaccountable world of "savages" into a number of well ordered communities, governed by law, behaving and thinking according to consistent principles. The word "savage," whatever association it might have had originally, connotes ideas of boundless liberty, of irregularity, of something extremely and extraordinarily quaint. In popular thinking, we imagine that the natives live on the bosom of Nature, more or less as they can and like, the prey of irregular, phantasmagoric beliefs and apprehensions. Modern science, on the contrary, shows that their social institutions have a very definite organisation, that they are governed by authority, law and order in their public and personal relations, while the latter are, besides, under the control of extremely complex ties of kinship and clanship. Indeed, we see them entangled in a mesh of duties, functions and privileges which correspond to an elaborate tribal, communal and kinship organisation. . . . Their beliefs and practices do not by any means lack consistency of

a certain type, and their knowledge of the outer world is sufficient to guide them in many of their strenuous enterprises and activities. Their artistic productions again lack neither meaning nor beauty.

It is a very far cry from the famous answer given long ago by a representative authority who, asked, what are the manners and customs of the natives, answered, "Customs none, manners beastly," to the position of the modern Ethnographer! This latter, with his tables of kinship terms, genealogies, maps, plans and diagrams, proves the existence of an extensive and big organisation, shows the constitution of the tribe, of the clan, of the family; and he gives us a picture of the natives subjected to a strict code of behaviour and good manners, to which in comparison the life at the Court of Versailles or Escurial was free and easy.[3]

Thus the first and basic ideal of ethnographic field work is to give a clear and firm outline of the social constitution, and disentangle the laws and regularities of all cultural phenomena from the irrelevances. The firm skeleton of the tribal life has to be first ascertained. This ideal imposes in the first place the fundamental obligation of giving a complete survey of the phenomena, and not of picking out the sensational, the singular, still less the funny and quaint. The time when we could tolerate accounts presenting us the natives as a distorted, childish caricature of a human being are gone. This picture is false, and like many other falsehoods, it has been killed by Science. The field Ethnographer has seriously and soberly to cover the full extent of the phenomena in each aspect of tribal culture studied, making no difference between what is commonplace, or drab, or ordinary, and what strikes him as astonishing and out-of-the-way. At the same time, the whole area of tribal culture *in all its aspects* has to be gone over in research. The consistency, the law and order which obtain within each aspect make also for joining them into one coherent whole.

An Ethnographer who sets out to study only

---

[2]According to a useful habit of the terminology of science, I use the word Ethnography for the empirical and descriptive results of the science of Man, and the word Ethnology for speculative and comparative theories.

[3]The legendary "early authority" who found the natives only beastly and without customs is left behind by a modern writer, who, speaking about the Southern Massim with whom he lived and worked "in close contact" for many years, says:—" . . . We teach lawless men to become obedient, inhuman men to love, and savage men to change." And again:—"Guided in his conduct by nothing but his instincts and propensities, and governed by his unchecked passions. . . ." "Lawless, inhuman and savage!" A grosser misstatement of the real state of things could not be invented by anyone wishing to parody the Missionary point of view. Quoted from the Rev. C. W. Abel, of the London Missionary Society, "Savage Life in New Guinea," no date.

religion, or only technology, or only social organisation cuts out an artificial field for inquiry, and he will be seriously handicapped in his work. . . .

Having settled this very general rule, let us descend to more detailed consideration of method. The Ethnographer has in the field, according to what has just been said, the duty before him of drawing up all the rules and regularities of tribal life; all that is permanent and fixed; of giving an anatomy of their culture, of depicting the constitution of their society. But these things, though crystallised and set, are nowhere *formulated*. There is no written or explicitly expressed code of laws, and their whole tribal tradition, the whole structure of their society, are embodied in the most elusive of all materials; the human being. But not even in human mind or memory are these laws to be found definitely formulated. The natives obey the forces and commands of the tribal code, but they do not comprehend them; exactly as they obey their instincts and their impulses, but could not lay down a single law of psychology. The regularities in native institutions are an automatic result of the interaction of the mental forces of tradition, and of the material conditions of environment. Exactly as a humble member of any modern institution, whether it be the state, or the church, or the army, is *of* it and *in* it, but has no vision of the resulting integral action of the whole, still less could furnish any account of its organisation, so it would be futile to attempt questioning a native in abstract, sociological terms. The difference is that, in our society, every institution has its intelligent members, its historians, and its archives and documents, whereas in a native society there are none of these. After this is realised an expedient has to be found to overcome this difficulty. This expedient for an Ethnographer consists in collecting concrete data of evidence, and drawing the general inferences for himself. This seems obvious on the face of it, but was not found out or at least practised in Ethnography till field work was taken up by men of science. Moreover, in giving it practical effect, it is neither easy to devise the concrete applications of this method, nor to carry them out systematically and consistently.

Though we cannot ask a native about abstract, general rules, we can always enquire how a given case would be treated. Thus for instance, in asking how they would treat crime, or punish it, it would be vain to put to a native a sweeping question such as, "How do you treat and punish a criminal?" for even words could not be found to express it in native, or in pidgin. But an imaginary case, or still better, a real occurrence, will stimulate a native to express his opinion and to supply plentiful information. A real case indeed will start the natives on a wave of discussion, evoke expressions of indignation, show them taking sides   all of which talk will probably contain a wealth of definite views, of moral censures, as well as reveal the social mechanism set in motion by the crime committed. From there, it will be easy to lead them on to speak of other similar cases, to remember other actual occurrences or to discuss them in all their implications and aspects. From this material, which ought to cover the widest possible range of facts, the inference is obtained by simple induction. The *scientific* treatment differs from that of good common sense, first in that a student will extend the completeness and minuteness of survey much further and in a pedantically systematic and methodical manner; and secondly, in that the scientifically trained mind, will push the inquiry along really relevant lines, and towards aims possessing real importance. Indeed, the object of scientific training is to provide the empirical investigator with a *mental chart*, in accordance with which he can take his bearings and lay his course.

To return to our example, a number of definite cases discussed will reveal to the Ethnographer the social machinery for punishment. This is one part, one aspect of tribal authority. Imagine further that by a similar method of inference from definite data, he arrives at understanding leadership in war, in economic enterprise, in tribal festivities—there he has at once all the data necessary to answer the questions about tribal government and social authority. In actual field work, the comparison of such data, the attempt to piece them together, will often reveal rifts and gaps in the information which lead on to further investigations.

From my own experience, I can say that, very often, a problem seemed settled, everything fixed and clear, till I began to write down a short preliminary sketch of my results. And only then, did I see the enormous deficiences, which would show me where lay new problems, and lead me on to new work. In fact, I spent a few months between my first and second expeditions, and over a year between that and the subsequent one, in going over all my material, and making parts of it almost ready for publication each time, though each time I knew I would have to re-write it. Such cross-fertilisation of constructive work and observation, I found most valuable, and I do not think I could have made real headway without it. I give this bit of my own history merely to show that what has been said so far is not only an empty programme, but the result of personal experience. In this volume, the description is given of a big institution connected with ever so many associated activities, and presenting many aspects. To anyone who reflects on the subject, it will be clear that the information about a phenomenon of such high complexity and of so many ramifications, could not be obtained with any degree of exactitude and completeness, without a constant interplay of constructive attempts and empirical checking. In fact, I have written up an outline of the Kula institution at least half a dozen times while in the field and in the intervals between my expeditions. Each time, new problems and difficulties presented themselves.

The collecting of concrete data over a wide range of facts is thus one of the main points of field method. The obligation is not to enumerate a few examples only, but to exhaust as far as possible all the cases within reach; and, on this search for cases, the investigator will score most whose mental chart is clearest. But, whenever the material of the search allows it, this mental chart ought to be transformed into a real one; it ought to materialise into a diagram, a plan, an exhaustive, synoptic table of cases. Long since, in all tolerably good modern books on natives, we expect to find a full list or table of kinship terms, which includes all the data relative to it, and does not just pick out a few strange and anomalous relationships or expressions. In the investigation of kinship, the following up of one relation after another in concrete cases leads naturally to the construction of genealogical tables. Practised already by the best early writers, such as Munzinger, and, if I remember rightly, Kubary, this method has been developed to its fullest extent in the works of Dr. Rivers. Again, studying the concrete data of economic transactions, in order to trace the history of a valuable object, and to gauge the nature of its circulation, the principle of completeness and thoroughness would lead to construct tables of transactions, such as we find in the work of Professor Seligman.[4] It is in following

Professor Seligman's example in this matter that I was able to settle certain of the more difficult and detailed rules of the Kula. The method of reducing information, if possible, into charts or synoptic tables ought to be extended to the study of practically all aspects of native life. All types of economic transactions may be studied by following up connected, actual cases, and putting them into a synoptic chart; again, a table ought to be drawn up of all the gifts and presents customary in a given society, a table including the sociological, ceremonial, and economic definition of every item. Also, systems of magic, connected series of ceremonies, types of legal acts, all could be charted, allowing each entry to be synoptically defined under a number of headings. Besides this, of course, the genealogical census of every community, studied more in detail, extensive maps, plans and diagrams, illustrating ownership in garden land, hunting and fishing privileges, etc., serve as the more fundamental documents of ethnographic research.

A genealogy is nothing else but a synoptic chart of a number of connected relations of kinship. Its value as an instrument of research consists in that it allows the investigator to put questions which he formulates to himself *in abstracto*, but can put concretely to the native informant. As a document, its value consists in that it gives a number of authenticated data, presented in their natural grouping. A synoptic chart of magic fulfills the same function. As an instrument of research, I have used it in order to ascertain, for instance, the ideas about the nature of magical power. With a chart before me, I could easily and conveniently go over one item after the other, and note down the relevant practices and beliefs contained in each of them. The answer to my abstract problem could then be obtained by drawing a general inference from all the cases, and the procedure is illustrated in Chapters XVII and XVIII.[5] I cannot enter further into the discussion of this question, which would need further distinctions, such as between a chart of concrete, actual data, such as is a genealogy, and a

---

[4] For instance, the tables of circulation of the valuable axe blades, op. cit., pp. 531, 532.

[5] In this book, besides the adjoining Table, which does not strictly belong to the class of document of which I speak here, the reader will find only a few samples of synoptic tables, such as the list of Kula partners mentioned and analysed in Chapter XIII, Division II, the list of gifts and presents in Chapter VI, Division VI, not tabularised, only described; the synoptic data of a Kula expedition in Chapter XVI, and the table of Kula magic given in Chapter XVII. Here, I have not wanted to overload the account with charts, etc., preferring to reserve them till the full publication of my material.

chart summarising the outlines of a custom or belief, as a chart of a magical system would be.

Returning once more to the question of methodological candour, discussed previously in Division II I wish to point out here, that the procedure of concrete and tabularised presentation of data ought to be applied first to the Ethnographer's own credentials. That is, an Ethnographer, who wishes to be trusted, must show clearly and concisely, in a tabularised form, which are his own direct observations, and which the indirect information that form the bases of his account. The Table on the next page will serve as an example of this procedure and help the reader of this book to form an idea of the trustworthiness of any statement he is specially anxious to check. With the help of this Table and the many references scattered throughout the text, as to how, under what circumstances, and with what degree of accuracy I arrived at a given item of knowledge, there will, I hope remain no obscurity whatever as to the sources of the book.

To summarise the first, cardinal point of method, I may say each phenomenon ought to be studied through the broadest range possible of its concrete manifestations; each studied by an exhaustive survey of detailed examples. If possible, the results ought to be tabulated into some sort of synoptic chart, both to be used as an instrument of study, and to be presented as an ethnological document. With the help of such documents and such study of actualities the clear outline of the framework of the natives' culture in the widest sense of the word,

CHRONOLOGICAL LIST OF KULA EVENTS WITNESSED BY THE WRITER

First Expedition, August, 1914—March, 1915.

March, 1915. In the village of Dikoyas (Woodlark Island) a few ceremonial offerings seen. Preliminary information obtained.

Second Expedition, May, 1915—May, 1916.

June, 1915. A Kabigidoya visit arrives from Vakuta to Kiriwina. Its anchoring at Kavataria witnessed and the men seen at Omarakana, where information collected.

July, 1915. Several parties from Kitava land on the beach of Kaulukuba. The men examined in Omarakana. Much information collected in that period.

September, 1915. Unsuccessful attempt to sail to Kitava with To'uluwa, the chief of Omarakana.

October—November, 1915. Departure noticed of three expeditions from Kiriwina to Kitava. Each time To'uluwa brings home a haul of *mwali* (armshells).

November, 1915—*March*, 1916. Preparations for a big overseas expedition from Kiriwina to the Marshall Bennett Islands. Construction of a canoe; renovating of another; sail making in Omarakana; launching; *tasasoria* on the beach of Kaulukuba. At the same time, information is being obtained about these and the associated subjects. Some magical texts of canoe building and Kula magic obtained.

Third Expedition, October, 1917—October, 1918.

November, 1917—*December*, 1917. Inland Kula; some data obtained in Tukwaukwa.

December—February, 1918. Parties from Kitava arrive in Wawela. Collection of information about the *yoyova*. Magic and spells of Kaygau obtained.

March, 1918. Preparations in Sanaroa; preparations in the Amphletts; the Dobuan fleet arrives in the Amphletts. The *uvalaku* expedition from Dobu followed to Boyowa.

April, 1918. Their arrival; their reception in Sinaketa; the Kula transactions; the big intertribal gathering. Some magical formulae obtained.

May, 1918. Party from Kitava seen in Vakuta.

June, July, 1918. Information about Kula magic and customs checked and amplified in Omarakana, especially with regard to its Eastern branches.

August, September, 1918. Magical texts obtained in Sinaketa.

October, 1918. Information obtained from a number of natives in Dobu and Southern Massim district (examined in Samarai).

and the constitution of their society, can be presented. This method could be called *the method of statistic documentation by concrete evidence....*

Needless to add, in this respect, the scientific field work is far above even the best amateur productions. There is, however, one point in which the latter often excel. This is, in the presentation of intimate touches of native life, in bringing home to us these aspects of it with which one is made familiar only through being in close contact with the natives, one way or the other, for a long period of time. In certain results of scientific work—especially that which has been called "survey work"—we are given an excellent skeleton, so to speak, of the tribal constitution, but it lacks flesh and blood. We learn much about the framework of their society, but within it, we cannot perceive or imagine the realities of human life, the even flow of everyday events, the occasional ripples of excitement over a feast, or ceremony, or some singular occurrence. In working out the rules and regularities of native custom, and in obtaining a precise formula for them from the collection of data and native statements, we find that this very precision is foreign to real life, which never adheres rigidly to any rules. It must be supplemented by the observation of the manner in which a given custom is carried out, of the behaviour of the natives in obeying the rules so exactly formulated by the ethnographer, of the very exceptions which in sociological phenomena almost always occur.

If all the conclusions are solely based on the statements of informants, or deduced from objective documents, it is of course impossible to supplement them in actually observed data of real behaviour. And that is the reason why certain works of amateur residents of long standing, such as educated traders and planters, medical men and officials, and last, but not least, the few intelligent and unbiassed missionaries to whom Ethnography owes so much, surpass in plasticity and in vividness most of the purely scientific accounts. But if the specialised field worker can adopt the conditions of living described above, he is in a far better position to be really in touch with the natives than any other white resident. For none of them lives right in a native village, except for very short periods, and everyone has his own business, which takes up a considerable part of his time. Moreover, if, like a trader or a missionary or an official he enters into active relations with the native, if he has to transform or influence or make use of him, this makes a real, unbiassed, impartial observation impossible, and precludes all-round sincerity, at least in the case of the missionaries and officials.

Living in the village with no other business but to follow native life, one sees the customs, ceremonies and transactions over and over again, one has examples of their beliefs as they are actually lived through, and the full body and blood of actual native life fills out soon the skeleton of abstract constructions. That is the reason why, working under such conditions as previously described, the Ethnographer is enabled to add something essential to the bare outline of tribal constitution, and to supplement it by all the details of behaviour, setting and small incident. He is able in each case to state whether an act is public or private; how a public assembly behaves, and what it looks like; he can judge whether an event is ordinary or an exciting and singular one; whether natives bring to it a great deal of sincere and earnest spirit, or perform it in fun; whether they do it in a perfunctory manner, or with zeal and deliberation.

In other words, there is a series of phenomena of great importance which cannot possibly be recorded by questioning or computing documents, but have to be observed in their full actuality. Let us call them *the imponderabilia of actual life*. Here belong such things as the routine of a man's working day, the details of his care of the body, of the manner of taking food and preparing it; the tone of conversational and social life around the village fires, the existence of strong friendships or hostilities, and of passing sympathies and dislikes between people; the subtle yet unmistakable manner in which personal vanities and ambitions are reflected in the behaviour of the individual and in the emotional reactions of those who surround him. All these facts can and ought to be scientifically formulated and recorded, but it is necessary that this be done, not by a superficial registration of details, as is usually done by untrained observers, but with an effort at penetrating the mental attitude expressed in them. And that is the reason why the work of scientifically trained observers, once seriously applied to the study of this aspect, will, I believe, yield results of surpassing value. So far, it has been done only by amateurs, and therefore done, on the whole, indifferently.

Indeed, if we remember that these imponderable yet all important facts of actual life are part of the real substance of the social fabric, that in them are spun the innumerable threads which keep together the family, the clan, the village community, the tribe—their significance becomes clear. The more crystallised bonds of social grouping, such as the definite ritual, the economic and legal duties, the obligations, the ceremonial gifts and formal marks of regard, though equally important for the student, are certainly felt less strongly by the individual who has to fulfil them. Applying this to ourselves, we all know that "family life" means for us, first and foremost, the atmosphere of home, all the innumerable small acts and attentions in which are expressed the affection, the mutual interest, the little preferences, and the little antipathies which constitute intimacy. That we may inherit from this person, that we shall have to walk after the hearse of the other, though sociologically these facts belong to the definition of "family" and "family life," in personal perspective of what family truly is to us, they normally stand very much in the background.

Exactly the same applies to a native community, and if the Ethnographer wants to bring their real life home to his readers, he must on no account neglect this. Neither aspect, the intimate, as little as the legal, ought to be glossed over. Yet as a rule in ethnographic accounts we have not both but either the one or the other—and, so far, the intimate one has hardly ever been properly treated. In all social relations besides the family ties, even those between mere tribesmen and, beyond that, between hostile or friendly members of different tribes, meeting on any sort of social business, there is this intimate side, expressed by the typical details of intercourse, the tone of their behaviour in the presence of one another. This side is different from the definite, crystallised legal frame of the relationship, and it has to be studied and stated in its own right.

In the same way, in studying the conspicuous acts of tribal life, such as ceremonies, rites, festivities, etc., the details and tone of behaviour ought to be given, besides the bare outline of events. The importance of this may be exemplified by one instance. Much has been said and written about survival. Yet the survival character of an act is expressed in nothing so well as in the concomitant behaviour, in the way in which it is carried out. Take any example from our own culture, whether it be the pomp and pageantry of a state ceremony, or a picturesque custom kept up by street urchins, its "outline" will not tell you whether the rite flourishes still with full vigour in the hearts of those who perform it or assist at the performance or whether they regard it as almost a dead thing, kept alive for tradition's sake. But observe and fix the data of their behaviour, and at once the degree of vitality of the act will become clear. There is no doubt, from all points of sociological, or psychological analysis, and in any question of theory, the manner and type of behaviour observed in the performance of an act is of the highest importance. Indeed behaviour is a fact, a relevant fact, and one that can be recorded. And foolish indeed and short-sighted would be the man of science who would pass by a whole class of phenomena, ready to be garnered, and leave them to waste, even though he did not see at the moment to what theoretical use they might be put!

As to the actual method of observing and recording in field work these *imponderabilia of actual life and of typical behaviour*, there is no doubt that the personal equation of the observer comes in here more prominently, than in the collection of crystallised, ethnographic data. But here also the main endeavour must be to let facts speak for themselves. If in making a daily round of the village, certain small incidents, characteristic forms of taking food, of conversing, of doing work . . . are found occurring over and over again, they should be noted down at once. It is also important that this work of collecting and fixing impressions should begin early in the course of working out a district. Because certain subtle peculiarities, which make an impression as long as they are novel, cease to be noticed as soon as they become familiar. Others again can only be perceived with a better knowledge of the local conditions. An ethnographic diary, carried on systematically throughout the course of one's work in a district would be the ideal instrument for this sort of study. And if, side by side with the normal and typical, the ethnographer carefully notes the slight, or the more pronounced deviations from it, he will be able to indicate the two extremes within which the normal moves.

In observing ceremonies or other tribal events, . . . it is necessary, not only to note down those occurrences and details which are prescribed by tradition and custom to be the essential course of the act, but also the Ethnographer ought to record carefully and precisely, one after the other, the actions of the actors and of the spectators. Forgetting for a moment that he knows and understands the structure of this ceremony, the main dogmatic ideas underlying it, he might try to find himself only in the midst of an assembly of human beings, who behave seriously or jocularly, with earnest concentration or with bored frivolity, who are either in the same mood as he finds them every day, or else are screwed up to a high pitch of excitement, and so on and so on. With his attention constantly directed to this aspect of tribal life, with the constant endeavour to fix it, to express it in terms of actual fact, a good deal of reliable and expressive material finds its way into his notes. He will be able to "set" the act into its proper place in tribal life, that is to show whether it is exceptional or commonplace, one in which the natives behave ordinarily, or one in which their whole behaviour is transformed. And he will also be able to bring all this home to his readers in a clear, convincing manner.

Again, in this type of work it is good for the Ethnographer sometimes to put aside camera, note book and pencil, and to join in himself in what is going on. He can take part in the natives' games, he can follow them on their visits and walks, sit down and listen and share in their conversations. I am not certain if this is equally easy for everyone —perhaps the Slavonic nature is more plastic and more naturally savage than that of Western Europeans—but though the degree of success varies, the attempt is possible for everyone. Out of such plunges into the life of the natives—and I made them frequently not only for study's sake but because everyone needs human company—I have carried away a distinct feeling that their behaviour, their manner of being, in all sorts of tribal transactions, became more transparent and easily understandable than it had been before. All these methodological remarks, the reader will find again illustrated in the following chapters. . . .

Finally, let us pass to the third and last aim of scientific field work, to the last type of phenomenon which ought to be recorded in order to give a full and adequate picture of native culture. Besides the firm outline of tribal constitution and crystallised cultural items which form the skeleton, besides the data of daily life and ordinary behaviour, which are, so to speak, its flesh and blood, there is still to be recorded the spirit—the natives' views and opinions and utterances. For, in every act of tribal life, there is, first, the routine prescribed by custom and tradition, then there is the manner in which it is carried out, and lastly there is the commentary to it, contained in the natives' mind. A man who

submits to various customary obligations, who follows a traditional course of action, does it impelled by certain motives, to the accompaniment of certain feelings, guided by certain ideas. These ideas, feelings, and impulses are moulded and conditioned by the culture in which we find them, and are therefore an ethnic peculiarity of the given society. An attempt must be made therefore, to study and record them.

But is this possible? Are these subjective states not too elusive and shapeless? And, even granted that people usually do feel or think or experience certain psychological states in association with the performance of customary acts, the majority of them surely are not able to formulate these states, to put them into words. This latter point must certainly be granted, and it is perhaps the real Gordian knot in the study of the facts of social psychology. Without trying to cut or untie this knot, that is to solve the problem theoretically, or to enter further into the field of general methodology, I shall make directly for the question of practical means to overcome some of the difficulties involved.

First of all, it has to be laid down that we have to study here stereotyped manners of thinking and feeling. As sociologists, we are not interested in what A or B may feel *qua* individuals, in the accidental course of their own personal experiences— we are interested only in what they feel and think *qua* members of a given community. Now in this capacity, their mental states receive a certain stamp, become stereotyped by the institutions in which they live, by the influence of tradition and folk-lore, by the very vehicle of thought, that is by language. The social and cultural environment in which they move forces them to think and feel in a definite manner. Thus, a man who lives in a polyandrous community cannot experience the same feelings of jealousy, as a strict monogynist, though he might have the elements of them. A man who lives within the sphere of the Kula cannot become permanently and sentimentally attached to certain of his possessions, in spite of the fact that he values them most of all. These examples are crude, but better ones will be found in the text of this book.

So, the third commandment of field work runs: Find out the typical ways of thinking and feeling, corresponding to the institutions and culture of a given community, and formulate the results in the most convincing manner. What will be the method of procedure? The best ethnographical writers—

here again the Cambridge school with Haddon, Rivers, and Seligman rank first among English Ethnographers– have always tried to quote *verbatim* statements of crucial importance. They also adduce terms of native classification; sociological, psychological and industrial *termini technici*, and have rendered the verbal contour of native thought as precisely as possible. One step further in this line can be made by the Ethnographer, who acquires a knowledge of the native language and can use it as an instrument of inquiry. In working in the Kiriwinian language, I found still some difficulty in writing down the statement directly in translation which at first I used to do in the act of taking notes. The translation often robbed the text of all its significant characteristics—rubbed off all its points —so that gradually I was led to note down certain important phrases just as they were spoken, in the native tongue. As my knowledge of the language progressed, I put down more and more in Kiriwinian, till at last I found myself writing exclusively in that language, rapidly taking notes, word for word, of each statement. No sooner had I arrived at this point, than I recognised that I was thus acquiring at the same time an abundant linguistic material, and a series of ethnographic documents which ought to be reproduced as I had fixed them, besides being utilised in the writing up of my account.[6] This *corpus inscriptionum Kiriwiniensium* can be utilised, not only by myself, but by all those who, through their better penetration and ability of interpreting them, may find points which escape my attention, very much as the other *corpora* form the basis for the various interpretations of ancient and prehistoric cultures; only, these ethnographic inscriptions are all decipherable and clear, have been almost all translated fully and unambiguously, and have been provided with native cross-commentaries or *scholia* obtained from living sources.

No more need be said on this subject here, as later on a whole chapter . . . is devoted to it, and to its exemplification by several native texts. The *Corpus* will of course be published separately at a later date. . . .

Our considerations thus indicate that the goal of ethnographic field work must be approached through three avenues:

1. *The organisation of the tribe, and the anatomy of its culture* must be recorded in firm, clear outline. The method of *concrete, statistical documentation* is the means through which such an outline has to be given.

2. Within this frame, the *imponderabilia of actual life*, and the *type of behaviour* have to be filled in. They have to be collected through minute, detailed observations, in the form of some sort of ethnographic diary, made possible by close contact with native life.

3. A collection of ethnographic statements, characteristic narratives, typical utterances, items of folk-lore and magical formulae has to be given as a *corpus inscriptionum*, as documents of native mentality.

These three lines of approach lead to the final goal, of which an Ethnographer should never lose sight. This goal is, briefly, to grasp the native's point of view, his relation to life, to realise *his* vision of *his* world. We have to study man, and we must study what concerns him most intimately, that is, the hold which life has on him. In each culture, the values are slightly different; people aspire after different aims, follow different impulses, yearn after a different form of happiness. In each culture, we find different institutions in which man pursues his life-interest, different customs by which he satisfies his aspirations, different codes of law and morality which reward his virtues or punish his defections. To study the institutions, customs, and codes or to study the behaviour and mentality without the subjective desire of feeling by what these people live, of realising the substance of their happiness— is, in my opinion, to miss the greatest reward which we can hope to obtain from the study of man.

These generalities the reader will find illustrated in the following chapters. We shall see there the savage striving to satisfy certain aspirations, to attain his type of value, to follow his line of social ambition. We shall see him led on to perilous and difficult enterprises by a tradition of magical and heroical exploits, shall see him following the lure of his own romance. Perhaps as we read the account of these remote customs there may emerge a feeling of solidarity with the endeavours and ambitions of these natives. Perhaps man's mentality will be revealed to us, and brought near, along some lines which we never have followed before. Perhaps through realising human nature in a shape very distant and foreign to us, we shall have some light shed on our own. In this, and in this case only, we shall be justified in feeling that it has been worth our while to understand these natives, their institutions and customs, and that we have gathered some profit from the Kula.

URBAN ETHNOGRAPHY

Although in a very different place and time from Malinowski, Liebow in the following excerpt describing his field work with a group of young black men in Washington, D.C., is true to the spirit and technique of anthropological study. With a strong sense of the need to understand the total situation of the people he is with, with long periods of human contact over time, with an entering into their life with compassionate objectivity in grafting his research perspective onto a sympathetic human relationship, Liebow illustrates well the points made by Casagrande in the first excerpt of this section. His study (of which this selection is the appendix) gives meaning to a catch-phrase frequently heard these days: the "culture of poverty." It also, by example, helps define modern cultural anthropology as dealing with human behavior in all kinds of societies, not just the exotic or "developing." Liebow's work is a good example of what can be understood by the phrase "urban anthropology."

A FIELD EXPERIENCE IN RETROSPECT

ELLIOT LIEBOW

Robert read the book slowly and with feeling, pausing only occasionally to take a swig of gin and chase it quickly with some beer. Lonny listened quietly and watched with blinking eyes as Robert changed his voice for each of the characters, assuming a falsetto for Snow White. But my own interest started to wander, probably because I had already read the book and seen the movie.

Suddenly Robert raised his voice and startled me back into attention. I looked at Lonny—placid, eye-blinking Lonny—and at Ronald—a handkerchief around his head and a gold earring stuck in his left ear making him look like a storybook pirate—and wondered what the hell I was doing there with these two guys, drinking gin and beer and listening to *Snow White and the Seven Dwarfs*.

I thought back to the events leading up to this

situation. From this perspective, everything looked normal and reasonable. I retrieved my can of beer, sat back and listened to the rest of the story. Robert gave it a damn fine reading.

[Field Note, April 1962]

BACKGROUND

When I came to the Child Rearing Study Project on January 1, 1962, this NIMH-supported study of "Child Rearing Practices Among Low Income Families in the District of Columbia" was well into its third year. My job was to collect field material on low-income adult males to complement the data already secured through family interviews.

From the very beginning I felt comfortable with the prospect of working with lower-class Negroes. I was born and raised in Washington, D.C. My father and mother were both Jewish immigrants

Reprinted with permission of publisher. From Elliot Liebow, *Tally's Corner: A Study of Negro Streetcorner Men*, © 1967 by Little, Brown and Company (Inc.), Boston, pp. 232-56.

from Eastern Europe—my mother from Latvia, my father from Russia. My father was a grocer and we lived in rooms above or behind the various stores which he operated. All were in predominantly Negro neighborhoods.

School and playground were white, but all of our customers and most of the neighbors were Negroes. Among them and their children I had many acquaintances, several playmates and a few friends. The color line, retraced daily at school and playground and home, was always there; but so were my day-by-day contacts with Negro men, women and children in the store, on the street, and occasionally in their houses; watching a crap game in Sam's place; witnessing the Devil being exorcised from a woman writhing on the floor of a storefront church from my seat in the back row; shooting crap for pennies in a dark hallway; sitting with Benton on the curb, poking aimlessly at debris, waiting for something interesting to happen. It was not until I was seventeen and enlisted in the Marine Corps that I began to move in an almost exclusively white world.

PREPARING FOR THE FIELD

I spent the first week in familiarizing myself with the project and with the work that had already been done. I had several informal discussions with Dr. Hylan Lewis, the director of the project, and gradually gained a feeling for the kind of material that was wanted. Importantly, he laid down no hard-and-fast ground rules on the assumption that the job could best be done if I were free to feel my way around for a few weeks and discover for myself the techniques that were most congenial to me. His one prescription was that the work be securely anchored in the purposes of the project, remembering, too, that "Everything is grist for our mill." As I think back on this now, I see a clear connection between his instructions and his fondness for the quotation, "The scientific method is doing one's darndest with his brains, no holds barred."

Having partially digested the project literature, I told the director that I was ready to get started. He suggested a neighborhood that might be "a good place to get your feet wet." His instructions were: "Go out there and make like an anthropologist."

"Out there" was not at all like the Indian village of Winisk on Hudson Bay in which I had done field work. I was not at all sure how one "makes like an anthropologist" in this kind of "out there." Somewhat wistfully, perhaps, I thought how much neater things would be if anthropologists, as they had done in the early thirties, limited themselves to the study of "wholes," a tribe, a village, or some other social unit with distinct boundaries and small enough to be encompassed in its entirety by direct observation.

When I thought about just what I was going to do, I kept in mind the job Richard Slobodin had done for the Child Rearing Study in the summer of 1960.[1] As part of the effort to get at community as well as family influences in child rearing, the director had assigned Slobodin to "make like an anthropologist" in a one-block enclave in northwest Washington. It seemed to me that I could use his work as a model and, in the course of a year, produce several such studies, each covering a strategic part of the world of the low-income male. I thought of doing a neighborhood study, then moving on say, to a construction laborers' union, then a bootleg joint, and perhaps rounding these out with a series of genealogies and life histories. I was going to give myself about a month or so of poking around town, getting the feel of things, before committing myself to any firm plan of action.

IN THE FIELD

In taking up the director's suggestion that this would be "a good place to get your feet wet," I went in so deep that I was completely submerged and my plan to do three or four separate studies, each with its own neat, clean boundaries, dropped forever out of sight. My initial excursions into the street—to poke around, get the feel of things, and to lay out the lines of my field work—seldom carried me more than a block or two from the corner where I started. From the very first weeks or even days, I found myself in the middle of things; the principle lines of my field work were laid out, almost without my being aware of it. For the next year or so, and intermittently thereafter, my base of operations was the corner Carry-out across the street from my starting point.

The first time out, I had gone less than one short block when I noticed a commotion up the street.

---

[1] Richard Slobodin, " 'Upton Square': A Field Report and Commentary."

A man—Detective Wesley, I learned later— was dragging a kicking, screaming woman to a police call box. A small crowd had gathered on each of the four corners to watch. I approached two men and asked what the woman had done. Both were uncertain. The younger of the two said that he had heard two stories and proceeded to tell me both of them, concluding with the observation that he had known Detective Wesley for six or seven years and that he was "nobody to fool with."

I said that sometimes being a cop seems to do something to a man. This led to a discussion of policemen and each of us contributed personal experiences or anecdotes on the subject. After ten or fifteen minutes of this, the older man said goodbye and walked off. The younger man stayed on. Across the street from where we were standing was the Downtown Cafe. I suggested that we go in and have some coffee and he agreed. As we walked across the street he asked if I was a policeman. I told him no and explained that I was working on a study of family life in the city. There was no more discussion about who I was or why I was there. We sat at the bar for several hours talking over coffee.

I had not accomplished what I set out to do, but this was only the first day. And, anyway, when I wrote up this experience that evening, I felt that it presented a fairly good picture of this young man and that most of the material was to the point. Tomorrow, I decided, I would go back to my original plan—nothing had been lost.

But tomorrow never came. At nine the next morning, I headed down the same street. Four men were standing in a group in front of the Carry-out.

Three were winos, in their forties—all marked with old scars on face and neck, dressed shabbily, but sober. The fourth was a man of thirty-two or thirty-three, who looked as if he had just stepped out of a slick magazine advertisement. . . . One of the winos had a month-old puppy stuck in the front of his overcoat. Only the dog's head was exposed.

The group approached me and one of the older men said, "Isn't he a nice puppy?" I said yes, and began patting the dog. "He just bought him," one man said. "I wanted the female, too, to breed them," said the man holding the dog, "but that woman, she sold the female to her friend."

The puppy was whining. "Maybe it's hungry," said the older man, "let's get him some hamburger." "No man, he'll get worms from that stuff," said one of the others. I suggested milk and we all went into the Carry-out. I asked the waitress for a half pint of milk. The man asked for a saucer. "You can't feed him here," the waitress said, "the Health Department would close us up." She gave us a paper plate and the milk (paid for by me). We took the dog into a hallway next door. Everyone was pleased at how eagerly the puppy drank.

A man who had been in the Carry-out joined us in the hallway. "That's a shepherd, isn't he? Just what I want for my little boy." I said, "I wish I could get one for my little girl, but she's allergic to all animals, dust, and lots of things." "It's better that way," said one of the winos. "She'll outgrow it. But man, if you don't have that until you're full grown—man, look out." "Yes, that's right," the newcomer agreed. "I know a woman who got allergies after she was grown and she got bronica asthma with it."

The dog finished the milk. The owner put him back in his overcoat and I shook hands all around with the winos. We split up three ways. The winos went up the street, the well-dressed man down the street, and the newcomer—who turned out to be Tally Jackson—and I went into the Carry-out.

For more than four hours Tally and I lounged around in the Carry-out, talking, drinking coffee, watching people come in and go out, watching other hangers-on as they bantered with the waitresses, horsed around among themselves, or danced to the jukebox. Everyone knew Tally and some frequently sought out his attention. Tally sometimes participated in the banter but we were generally left undisturbed when we were talking. When I left at two o'clock, Tally and I were addressing each other by first names ("Elliot" was strange to him and we settled for "Ellix") and I was able to address the two waitresses by their first names without feeling uncomfortable. I had also learned to identify several other men by their first names or nicknames, had gotten hints on personal relationships, and had a biographical sketch (part of it untrue I learned later) of Tally.

Back on the street, I ended up at the Downtown Cafe, this time by way of the morning's now very drunk owner of the puppy, who was standing near the entrance. The puppy was our bond and we talked about him with an enthusiasm that perhaps neither of us felt. Later, the well-dressed man who had also been part of the puppy episode came in and joined me at the bar. Then, still drinking beer at the bar stool, I met two other men in quick succession. The first man had to leave shortly for his night-shift busboy job at the restaurant. The other was a surly man in his middle thirties who initiated the contact by taking the stool next to me and asking what kind of work I did, adding that he had seen me around the day before, watching Detective Wesley drag that woman across the street.

I told him briefly what my job was.

"Well, if you hang around here you'll see it all. Anything can happen and it does happen here. It can get rough and you can get your head knocked in. You'll be okay though, if you know one or two of the right people."

"That's good to know," I told him, guessing (and hoping) that he was one of the "right people." He left me with the impression that he was being friendly and, in a left-handed sort of way, was offering me his protection.

By the end of the second day I had met nine men, learned the names of several more, and spent many hours in close public association with several men, at least two of whom were well known. And perhaps most important of all, in my own mind I had partly sloughed off that feeling of being a stranger and achieved that minimum sense of "belonging" which alone permits an ease of manner and mind so essential in building personal relationships.

Over the next three or four weeks, I made several excursions into other neighborhoods and followed up at the Downtown Cafe and the Carry-out shop on an irregular basis, getting to know some of the people better and many others for the first time. Frequently I ate breakfast and lunch at the Carry-out and began putting occasional dimes in the jukebox and in the pinball machine. Ted Moore, who worked at a liquor store nearby and whom I had first met in the Carry-out while he was waiting for the store to open, regularly alternated with me in buying coffee and doughnuts in the morning. At the Downtown Cafe the man who told me that I'd be okay if I knew "one or two of the right people" publicly identified me as his friend. ("Sure I know him," he told another man in my presence. "We had a long talk the other day. He's my friend and he's okay, man, he's okay. At first I thought he was a cop, but he's no cop. He's okay.")

All in all, I felt I was making steady progress. There was still plenty of suspicion and mistrust, however. At least two men who hung around the Carry-out—one of them the local numbers man—had seen me dozens of times in close quarters, but they kept their distance and I kept mine. Once, accidentally, I caught the numbers man's eye as I walked in. We held the stare for three or four seconds and I nodded slightly but he wouldn't let go. I went on about my business, determined that I wasn't going to be stared down next time

and that he'd get no more nods from me unless he nodded first. As it turned out, I didn't have long to wait.

One mid-February day, I walked into the Carry-out.

. . . Tally was having a cup of coffee. "Look here," he said. "Where is this place?" Tally took out a sheet of paper from an envelope and handed it to me. It was a summons to appear as a witness for the defense in the case of the United States versus Lonny Reginald Small. A faint stamp indicated that Tally was to report to the United States District Court for the District of Columbia at 3rd and Pennsylvania Avenue, Northwest, at ten o'clock this morning. I read off the address. It was then 9:40. I suggested that Tally take a cab, but when Tally said he didn't have the money I offered to drive him down. He quickly accepted. On the way, Tally explained that Lonny was a friend of his. Lonny was being tried for murdering his wife last summer. "Lonny is a nice guy," he said. "He's one hundred percent."

Thus began a three-week odyssey into the world of Lonny Small, a young man of twenty-six who, according to the jury's subsequent verdict of "not guilty," had choked his wife to death accidentally. Upon his acquittal, Lonny was rearrested in the courthouse for a violation of probation (on a previous grand larceny conviction) in another jurisdiction. He waived extradition, was given a hearing, was released on an appearance bond, and after another hearing he was again placed on probation.

Almost imperceptibly, my association with Tally, and through him with Lonny, was projecting me into the role of a principal actor in Lonny's life. By being with Tally through the trial, I found that first Tally, then Lonny, were looking to me for leadership and, as in the question of waiving extradition, for decision making. Court officials, apparently taking their cues from Lonny, began looking to me as his spokesman.

The follow-up of Lonny, which took most of my time for at least the next two weeks, carried me into dozens of places and into contact with scores of people. Throughout this period I stayed in close touch with the project director, getting clearance for and weighing the possible consequences of my growing involvement with the authorities. I went to three different jails during this time, sat through one murder trial and two hearings in judges' chambers, testifying at one of them. I went to bondsmen's offices, to the United States Employment Service, to the Blessed Martin de Porres

Hostel (for homeless men) and into several private homes. I met policemen, judges, lawyers, bondsmen, probation officers, and one of Lonny's former employers. I talked with his friends and at least one enemy, his mother-in-law, whose daughter he had killed. I met in council several times with various members of his extended family (who accepted me, through Tally, as Lonny's friend, no questions asked) in their houses, and drove around with them to the houses of other members of the family trying to raise money for Lonny's bond.

Meanwhile, back at the Carry-out, where Tally and I were meeting regularly at night and where I tried to stop in during the day whenever possible, people I had never seen, or others I had seen but never spoken to, began coming up to me and asking, "Is Lonny out yet?" or "Did you raise his bail yet?" or simply, "How's it going?" Bumdoodle, the numbers man, one of those who had not known Lonny, was especially solicitous of Lonny's welfare. He, too, began calling me by my first name and, although I kept no record of it, I think it was at this time that he dropped all subterfuge in taking numbers in my presence and soon began taking bets from me.

By the middle of March, Tally and I were close friends ("up tight") and I was to let him know if I wanted or needed "anything, anytime." By April, the number of men whom I had come to know fairly well and their acceptance of me had reached the point at which I was free to go to the rooms or apartments where they lived or hung out, at almost any time, needing neither an excuse nor an explanation for doing so. Like other friends, I was there to pass the time, to hang around, to find out "what's happening."

I switched my day around to coincide with the day worker's leisure hours: from four in the afternoon until late at night, according to what was going on. Alone, or with one, two or half a dozen others, I went to poolrooms, to bars, or to somebody's room or apartment. Much of the time we just hung around the Carry-out, playing the pinball machine or standing on the corner watching the world go by. Regularly at five, I met my five "drinking buddies" when they came off from work and we went into a hallway for an hour or so of good drinking and easy talk.

Friday afternoon to Sunday night was especially exciting and productive. I'd go to Nancy's "place"

(apartment) where, at almost any hour, one could get liquor, listen to music, or engage in conversation. Or perhaps seven or eight of us would buy some beer and whiskey and go up to Tonk's apartment near the Carry-out where he lived with his wife. Occasionally, I'd pair up with one or two men and go to a party, a movie, or a crap game, which might be in almost any part of town. Sunday afternoon was an especially good time to pick up news or happenings of the preceding forty-eight hours. People were generally rested up from the night before, relaxed, and ready to fill one another in on events which involved the police, breakups of husband-wife relations and bed-and-board arrangements, drink-stimulated brawls, sex adventures, and parties they had witnessed, heard about, or participated in over Friday and Saturday.

By April most people seemed to be taking it for granted that I belonged in the area. At least two men did not trust me or like me, but by then I was too strongly entrenched for them to challenge successfully my right to be there, even had they chosen to do so. New people moved into the area and I found myself being regarded as an old-timer, sometimes being asked to corroborate events which predated my arrival.

Throughout this period, my field observations were focused on individuals: what they said, what they did, and the contexts in which they said them or did them. I sought them out and was sought out by them.

My field notes contain a record of what I saw when I looked at Tally, Richard, Sea Cat and the others. I have only a small notion—and one that I myself consider suspect—of what I saw when they looked at me.

Some things, however, are very clear. They saw, first of all, a white man. In my opinion, this brute fact of color, as they understood it in their experience and as I understood it in mine, irrevocably and absolutely relegated me to the status of outsider. I am not certain, but I have a hunch that they were more continuously aware of the color difference than I was. When four of us sat around a kitchen table, for example, I saw three Negroes; each of them saw two Negroes and a white man.

Sometimes, when the word "nigger" was being used easily and conversationally or when, standing on the corner with several men, one would have a few words with a white passerby and call him a "white mother-fucker," I used to play with the idea that maybe I wasn't as much of an outsider as I thought. Other events, and later readings of the field materials, have disabused me of this particular touch of vanity.

Whenever the fact of my being white was openly introduced, it pointed up the distance between me and the other person, even when the intent of introducing it was, I believe, to narrow that distance.

... All of us left Tally's room together. Tally grabbed my arm and pulled me aside near the storefront church and said, "I want to talk to you." With no further introduction, he looked me straight in the eye and started talking.

"I'm a liar. I been lying to you all along now and I want to set it straight, even if it means we can't be friends no more. I only lied to you about one thing. Everything else I told you is gospel truth but I did lie about one thing and that makes me a liar. I know that some white people think that if you catch a man in a lie one time you can't never trust him after that. And even if you feel that way about it I still got to tell you. You remember when you first come around here, I told you. ... Well, that was a lie. ... I didn't think nothing of it at first, but then you and me started going around together and when we started getting real tight, my conscience started whomping me. I kept looking for a place to tell you but it never seemed right. Then tonight . . . I knew this was the right time. I knew you were going to find out and I didn't want you to find out from somebody else. . . ."

Once I was with Richard in his hometown. It was his first visit in five years. We arrived in the middle of the night and had to leave before daybreak because Richard was wanted by the local police. We were in his grandmother's house. Besides Richard, there were his grandmother, his aunt, and two unrelated men, both long-time friends of Richard.

The group was discussing the possibility of Richard's coming home to stay and weighing the probable consequences. In the middle of the discussion, Richard interrupted and nodded at me. "Now Ellix here is white, as you can see, but he's one of my best friends. Him and me are real tight. You can say anything you want, right to his face. He's real nice." "Well," said his Aunt Pearl, "I always did say there are some nice white people."

Whether or not there is more to these citations than "Some of my best friends are . . ." or "Yes, but you're different," the wall between us remained, or better, the chain-link fence, since despite the barriers we were able to look at each other, walk alongside each other, talk and occasionally touch fingers. When two people stand up close to the fence on either side, without touching it, they can look through the interstices and forget that they are looking through a fence.

The disadvantage of being white was offset in part by the fact that, as an outsider, I was not a competitor. Thus, in the matter of skin color, I saw myself nowhere in the spectrum of black- to light-skinned (or "bright"); I was completely out of it, with no vested interest. It could be that this made it possible for some people to speak freely to me about skin color.

"You know, I'm the darkest one in my family. All my aunts, uncles, everybody is light-skinned and they were all down on me, except my grandmother. ... She'd do anything for me, maybe because she saw everyone else against me. ... All the time I was coming up, I kept hoping somebody would have a baby darker than me."

Looking at me, however, the people I came to know in the area probably saw more than a "white male adult." They saw or knew many other things as well, any one of which relegated me to outside status. Those with whom I was in regular contact knew, for example, that I was with them because it was my job to be with them, and they knew, according to their individual comprehension and my ability to communicate, just what my job was. They knew that I lived outside the area. They knew that I was a college graduate, or at least they associated an advanced education with the work I was doing. Moreover, it was apparent, certainly to me, that I was not fluent in their language. Thus, I was an outsider not only because of race, but also because of occupation, education, residence, and speech. The fact that I was Jewish came up only twice. Once, a man who worked but did not live in the area threw some Yiddish expressions at me because "I thought you looked Jewish." The other time was when I met a soldier in a local bootleg joint. We had been talking for some ten minutes or so when he asked me whether I was "Eyetalian." I told him I was Jewish. "That's just as good," he said. "I'm glad you're not white."

The fact that I was married and a father, and that I was bigger than average size—6'1", 185 pounds—probably didn't matter much, except as they entered incidentally into my personal relationship with one or another individual. Since the people I spent most of my time with ranged in age from twenty to the middle forties, I would guess that my age (thirty-seven) was not significant in itself.

On several different counts I was an outsider[2] but I also was a participant in a full sense of the word. The people I was observing knew that I was observing them, yet they allowed me to participate in their activities and take part in their lives to a degree that continues to surprise me. Some "exploited" me, not as an outsider but rather as one who, as a rule, had more resources than they did. When one of them came up with the resources—money or a car, for example—he too was "exploited" in the same way. I usually tried to limit money or other favors to what I thought each would have gotten from another friend had he the same resources as I. I tried to meet requests as best I could without becoming conspicuous. I was not always on the giving end and learned somewhat too slowly to accept food or let myself be treated to drinks even though I knew this would work a hardship on the giver.

When in the field, I participated as fully and as whole-mindedly as I could, limited only by my own sense of personal and professional propriety and by what I assumed to be the boundaries of acceptable behavior as seen by those I was with.

Occasionally, when I wanted to record a physical description of say, a neighborhood, an apartment, or a social event, I tried to be an observer only. In practice, I found it impossible to keep all traces of participation out of a straight observer role.

One Saturday night, with my observer role clearly in mind, I went to a dance at the Capitol Arena

where more than a thousand people were jammed together. I was the only white male, this was my first time at such an event, the music was so foreign to me that I picked out the wrong beat, and I was unable to identify several of the band instruments. I was, willy-nilly, an observer. But here are a few lines excerpted from the field observation:

> It was very hot, it was very noisy, it was very smelly, and it was all very exciting. It was impossible to remain simply an observer in a place like this, even for someone as phlegmatic as I. It was only a few minutes after Jackie Wilson started singing that I discovered that the noise wasn't nearly loud enough, the heat wasn't nearly hot enough, and the odor from more than a thousand closely packed people was not really strong enough at all. Like everyone else, I wanted more of everything.

Almost from the beginning, I adopted the dress and something of the speech of the people with whom I was in most frequent contact, as best I could without looking silly or feeling uncomfortable. I came close in dress (in warm weather, tee or sport shirt and khakis or other slacks) with almost no effort at all. My vocabulary and diction changed, but not radically. Cursing and using ungrammatical constructions at times—though they came easily —did not make any of my adaptations confusable with the speech of the street. Thus, while remaining conspicuous in speech and perhaps in dress, I had dulled some of the characteristics of my background. I probably made myself more accessible to others, and certainly more acceptable to myself. This last point was forcefully brought home to me one evening when, on my way to a professional meeting, I stopped off at the Carry-out in a suit and tie. My loss of ease made me clearly aware that the change in dress, speech, and general carriage was as important for its effect on me as it was for its effect on others.

In retrospect, it seems as if the degree to which one becomes a participant is as much a matter of perceiving oneself as a participant as it is of being accepted as a participant by others.

---

[2] From the outset, I had decided that I would never shoot crap, pool, or play cards for money, or bet money in any way (numbers excepted, since playing numbers is safely impersonal), and would meticulously avoid the slightest suspicion of a personal involvement with any woman. These self-imposed restrictions to some extent did underline my marginality. My explanation that I couldn't afford to chance a fight or bad feelings because of my job was usually accepted and I was generally excused from participating in these activities rather than excluded from them.

PART III

THE CULTURAL SHAPING OF BEHAVIOR

Let's start at the beginning, somewhere near the ground floor of what will become our conceptual structures. If as its "data-base" (that is, the empirical evidence it works with) cultural anthropology uses samples of human behavior, let us then look at some such examples. That is what the following selections do: give evidence of the diversity in various kinds of simple behavior when viewed in worldwide scope, and yet at the same time show the tendency toward standardization and patterning within any *particular* human group. They also show that the roots of cultural influence on the human being are very deep; indeed, both to be a human being in general and to belong to a specific human group in particular mean to be deeply shaped in action and thought by collective influences we will conceptualize as "culture." And, as will be seen in the examples, the aspects of human behavior that are thus influenced range from the "higher" conceptions in terms of which man relates to his world (such as language), to the most basic of man's other animalistic capacities: eating, loving, eliminating, and the others. There is something "real," then, to the cultural shaping and (at some levels) determining of behavior.

Thus, the main purpose of this section is, through specific examples of the extent and depth of the cultural structuring of behavior, to engender a working idea—a "first approximation"—of what culture "is" through seeing what it "does," to create that inchoate, diffuse *feeling* for the idea of something that has yet to be put into words; almost a definition by demonstration.

THE "HUMANITY" OF MAN'S BEHAVIOR

How "human" is human nature? Where does our "humanness" come from? Lay people and scholars alike used to consider that human beings acted as they do largely because it was ordained in their genes that they would do so—

71

that was the way nature built them. With the impact of the social sciences, and of anthropology in particular, however, the emphasis has shifted much more to the position that people are what their *experience* makes them, that there is, in other words, something beyond biology and genetics that shapes the character and behavior. (This is, of course, the familiar "nature-nurture controversy.") While the whole area of the biological base of human potential and capacity with respect to the "superorganic" determinants of behavior is a lively focus of scholarship these days (e.g., as in the field of ethology), there is no disputing the validity of the basic observation that many of the daily behavioral tasks of human living are shaped and created in their form (though perhaps not their necessity) by something beyond genetic programming. We will put a label on that "something" a little later on. For now, let us sample the variety of ways in which our "humanness" is expressed. Bates introduces this section of excerpts which sample the wide extent to which our being "human" depends upon our having grown up and continue to live in particular human groups which have particular ways of doing things, ways which become invested with emotion and value. Why invested with emotion and value? Because they are *our* ways, of course!

ON BEING HUMAN

MARSTON BATES

Placed on this isthmus of a middle state,
A Being darkly wise, and rudely great:
With too much knowledge for the Sceptic side,
With too much weakness for the Stoic's pride;
He hangs between; in doubt to act, or rest;
In doubt to deem himself a God, or Beast;
In doubt his Mind or Body to prefer . . .

ALEXANDER POPE,
Essay on Man

Every schoolday morning our son Glenn comes to the bedroom at a quarter to seven with cups of coffee. Nancy, obviously, has done a good job of raising our children—the oldest at home has the alarm clock, and they all take a certain amount of responsibility for keeping their parents in line. The coffee routine has now passed on through all four of them; and when Glenn goes away I don't know what we will do. Look after ourselves, I suppose.

I switch on the light and automatically look at my watch to check on Glenn's timing—we are all slaves of that damned clock. School, office, lecture, railway, dentist. They say it all started with the

monastery bells of the Middle Ages; but however it got started, Time now permeates every aspect of our civilization. The slavery starts at an early age: the schools, whatever else they do, manage to instill an acute dread of being tardy in most children. A few rebellious people manage to be tardy for most of their lives, despite the pressures; but we hardly regard them as models of conduct.

Anyway, I try to make some bright crack as I check on Glenn's timing, but it usually falls flat because neither of us feels very chipper before dawn. I reach for a cigarette—a deplorable habit, but again I am a slave—and start the slow process of pulling myself together to face the world for another day.

I have been sleeping on a bed. This seems perfectly natural to me. But if we take "natural" to mean doing what most people do, it is rather odd behavior. My guess would be that perhaps a quarter of the people of the world sleep on beds. I suspect that the commonest sleeping arrangement is matting that can be rolled up and stowed during the day—which is certainly practical from the point of view of space utilization. In warm climates the most

Reprinted with permission of author and publisher. From Marston Bates, *Gluttons and Libertines: Human Problems of Being Natural* (New York: Random House, 1967), pp. 3–17.

practical sleeping arrangement is the hammock—an invention of the American Indians. It is easily taken down if the space is needed; it is portable; it isolates the sleeper from creeping things on the ground; and it provides maximum ventilation. It takes getting used to; but so do most things.

The paraphernalia involved in Western sleeping become more peculiar when looked at in detail: springs, mattresses, sheets, blankets, pillows, pillowcases. Beds have a long history in the Graeco-Roman and Western worlds, but this total accumulation must be rather modern. Much of it I find puzzling. Our bed, for instance, has springs; but my wife has put a bedboard over them. Why not just have a board to start with? And then there are all of the rules for making up a bed, for covering it, for airing it. You could write a whole book about beds, and I suspect someone has.

Habitually I sleep naked. This seems to be rather aberrant behavior in our culture—or in most others. To be sure, I keep a dressing gown close at hand, just in case the house should catch on fire. But it appears that most men in the United States nowadays sleep either in pajamas (a word and custom of Hindu origin) or in underclothes (a particularly common habit with college students). A sociologist might study this, to see whether there is any relation between night clothing and geographical region, or median income, or level of education. I remember reading in the Kinsey report on the human male that nudity was an upper-class characteristic, which made me feel smug for a while.

Women, in my limited experience, cling to nightgowns, though they can sometimes be persuaded to take them off. Nightshirts for men became rare about a generation ago; I know a few people who still wear them—eccentrics, I suppose. It is curious how fashion penetrates even into the privacy of the bedroom. It may be, of course, that more women now wear pajamas than wear nightgowns—my figures on the subject are not really statistically significant.

I left myself smoking a cigarette and drinking a cup of coffee. I wish I could break that cigarette habit. Do you suppose anyone starts the morning in bed with a cigar or a pipe? It doesn't seem right, somehow. As for coffee—in England it would be tea—and mostly in the United States in a private home many people find it an absolute necessity to start the day with a cup of coffee.

Finally I get courage enough to crawl out from under the blanket into the world—or at least into the bathroom. Civilization does have advantages. I brush my teeth and exercise my gums just as my dentist has told me to—what a lot of trouble those teeth cause us! Then I shave. This is an ancient practice among some of the so-called "white" races which, along with the Australian blackfellows, are the only peoples with enough facial hair to bother with. It is said that the ancient Egyptians shaved off all body hair, but with us nowadays men limit the shaving process to the face. Our women shave their legs and their armpits, as I am reminded when I find my razor out of place. I cut myself, and I think that my wife will scold. She can't understand why, after some forty years of daily shaving, I haven't learned better. I don't understand either.

My morning routine has become quite fixed over the years: teeth, shave, shower. One summer at a conference I lived for a while in a dormitory and discovered that most of the people there took their baths either in the afternoon or evening. This came as a surprise—I had thought that taking a bath first thing in the morning was one of those basic laws of nature. I had realized, though, that men can be sharply divided into two groups: those that bathe before they shave and those that bathe after. The bath-first group believe that the preliminary soaping of the face helps soften the beard; the bath-afterward people (where I belong) find an economy of effort in using the shower to wash the shaving soap off their faces. But the subject of bath timing is apparently much more complicated than this.

Then I get dressed. What a long cultural history lies behind each action here! The males in our society wear "arctic type" fitted garments, an invention of the barbaric tribes of prehistoric northern Europe. Trousers, neatly preserved by the acid waters, have been dug up from Danish peat bogs. These trousers are convenient in cold weather, as any woman can tell you. The tropical draped garment, which carries over into the dress of our females, is more comfortable in hot weather. But comfort is a minor consideration in our clothing habits.

Each morning I have to face the problem of what to wear. I have lived much of my life in the tropics, and I hate the feeling of a tie around my neck and of leather shoes encasing my feet. But a professor is supposed to wear shoes, tie and coat. He is far less subject to convention than, say, a banker or a physician is; but there are limits if he doesn't want to be considered a crackpot. I want to play my role well enough to be accepted by the society in which I live, so most often (on days when I am due to lecture) I put on a tie and try to look respectable even though I feel like a fraud. My aim, as I phrase it to myself, is to be "a reasonable facsimile of a proper professor." But I don't know that I succeed very well.

Breakfast. "Glenn, you *must* finish your cereal." Eating soon after you get up is another of those fundamental laws of nature in the United States. In other parts of the world the fundamental laws of nature differ, but they are equally inexorable, whatever their form. Cereal, milk— whoever first had the idea of getting food by squeezing the udder of a cow or goat?— eggs, toast, fruit juice. In the South, grits come with the eggs automatically; at some line in Kentucky and Virginia these give way to hash-browned potatoes. To the west, grits disappear somewhere in Texas.

Thus in the matter of breakfast we have cultural diversity, geographical diversity, individual diversity. We conform with the common usage of our group in when we eat, what we eat, how we eat it. Sometimes, too, we diverge. I almost wrote "rebel" but such a strong word hardly seems appropriate for breakfast—though a child's reaction may be a real enough rebellion.

Quite unintentionally I have got into a curious situation in this breakfast matter. I have never been much given to eating, especially the first thing in the morning, and I solved the breakfast problem some years ago by the simple expedient of breaking two raw eggs into a glass of orange juice and drinking the mixture. The needed nutrients are present, with no time spent over the stove, no frying pan to clean—only a glass to rinse out. This seems to me eminently sensible. The rest of the household accepts my behavior, though no one has ever made any move to imitate.

For years I didn't have the courage to order this breakfast in a restaurant. Finally a friend who knew of my home habits persuaded me to try it: he pointed out that restaurants were supposed to serve people's needs, and why should I be afraid of what the waitress would think. This first try was in the French Quarter of New Orleans, and no eyebrows were raised. But when I gave the same order in cafés along the highway driving north, I met incredulity and reluctance. It turned out to be all right if I asked to have the eggs beaten in the juice

— I suppose because everyone knows about egg-nogs. I still haven't had the courage to order anything except an ordinary breakfast in the dining room of a proper hotel.

Such is the force of opinion governing human conduct even in a trivial detail. My conduct, at least. Then I stop and wonder whether I am peculiar. I suppose the average waitress in the average middle-class restaurant would definitely say "yes." On the waterfront they are used to the idea of raw eggs in beer, but they might think the orange juice odd. So whether I am peculiar or not depends on where I am, which opens up some large questions.

Everyone, really, is peculiar. Any biologist, used to studying the behavior of animals, becomes puzzled when he turns to man—and he is forced to the conclusion that the human animal as a species is peculiar. How did we get this way? And what does it mean?

We could say that human actions are never to be understood in purely biological terms. Like other animals, we have to eat—we need proteins, fats, carbohydrates, assorted vitamins and minerals. There is nothing unusual about these food requirements or about the way the human digestive system works. The process of metabolism with man, as with other animals, results in the accumulation of waste products which must be got rid of. The wastes take the form of urine and feces. The inner workings, then, are biological; but the outward actions, the modes of behavior, are something else again. Feces is just another word for shit—but see the problem?

I broke my leg a couple of years ago and learned many things in the slow process of recovery. The hospital immobilized me in traction and I remember, on one of the first mornings, that a nurse came in and asked "Have you had a B.M. yet?"

I was puzzled for a moment because they had been doing all sorts of odd things to me, and then asked her wonderingly, "But why on earth would they give me a basal metabolism?"

It turned out, of course, that B.M. meant "bowel movement." Somehow I had got through life without learning that particular circumlocution and it struck me as very odd—one of the many compromises with reality that have developed in the nursing situation. Because of our animal nature, we produce shit more or less regularly, but we dislike to admit this openly and we cannot talk about it with any equanimity. We would much rather pretend there was no such thing   stopping off in a "rest room" when the need arises—but in a hospital situation we are forced to be somewhat more direct.

Obviously I am skirting over a whole series of somewhat different problems here. There is the problem of action, of behavior; the problem of symbols, of words; the problem of relations between the sexes (I would have been able to talk much more directly with a male orderly); the problem of dealing with new situations (I eventually learned to cope both with bedpans and with nursing vocabulary). Yet all of these are but aspects, really, of the general human problem of being natural.

What does it mean, to be "natural"? Maybe it is natural for man to hide himself when excreting. Then maybe it is natural not only to hide the fact in the bushes, but also to gloss over the action with a deceptive kind of vocabulary. In many parts of the world the idea of decent and indecent actions is entangled with the use of decent and indecent words. One could argue that it is natural for man to treat actions and words as equivalent—at least it seems to be easy enough to start a fight by calling someone a bad name. If excretion, though unfortunately necessary, is naturally bad, one can see how the word for it naturally becomes bad too. But this still leaves puzzles.

"Natural" clearly means quite a number of different things, so that, when we start to talk about it, we can easily become lost in semantic problems. I checked the unabridged Oxford English Dictionary and found eighteen main definitions for "natural," each with a number of subheadings. For our present purposes, however, we can reduce these to three general ideas, which can be most readily distinguished in terms of their opposites. We can use "natural" as distinguished from "supernatural," "artificial" and "unnatural."

Natural and supernatural need concern us little. Our scientific civilization assumes that the world is orderly and not subject to capricious intervention and control by spirits. There are many cultures in which spirits are just as "real" as sharks or leopards—and a great deal more dangerous and more difficult to cope with. But in theory at least we treat the events of everyday life as the consequence of natural, rather than supernatural, forces.

Artificial is an easy word in some ways, more difficult in others. Essentially it means man-made. This is clear in the case of artifacts. An artificial rose is made from wax, glass, paper or what have

you, in imitation of nature. Yet, if we stop to think about it, the "natural" rose growing in our garden is also man-made the product of selection, hybridization and cultivation by man, and unlike anything that occurs in nature without human intervention. We recognize this rather vaguely when we talk about artificial hybrids or artificial selection, but we are, in general, reluctant to face the extent to which our environment has been altered by our own actions—the extent to which, in this sense, it is artificial.

If we use artificial to cover anything made or altered by man, the word really loses much of its usefulness. There is nothing natural left in the environments that most of us live in. To escape from an artificial world we have to go to the north woods of Canada, the forests of the upper Amazon, or the southwestern deserts. So much for the environment. But there is nothing natural left in human behavior, either: it is all governed or modified in varying degree by culture, tradition, opinion. We can hardly talk about artificial manners, for instance, because all manners are artificial; there is no natural man.

There may be a gain in the use of artificial in this very broad sense because we begin to see the extent to which human actions are the consequence of the human condition. We begin to see the hazards of trying to determine what is natural for man by studying apes or monkeys or white rats.

But if everything about man is artificial, if nothing is natural, does this mean that all human actions are unnatural? Clearly not, because we have shifted to another meaning of natural. Unnatural carries the idea of abnormal, unusual, strange. This doesn't help much: you can get into as much trouble with normal and abnormal as with natural and unnatural. We are involved with the cultural context in which all people live: what is unusual for some may be commonplace for others. For us it is unnatural to eat worms; for the Chinese, unnatural to drink milk. Sometimes I am driven to think that calling anything unnatural merely means that the speaker does not approve of it.

All of which sheds little light on the human problem of being natural. In the case of supernatural, most of us have no alternative to being natural during life, whatever may happen afterward. The sorcerers and magicians in our midst may think they escape this kind of naturalness, but the rest of us have come to view their claims dubiously. In the case of artificial, there seems to be no escape from artificiality into naturalness. Only in the case of natural versus unnatural do we have an apparent choice—which boils down to the question of whether or not to act in accord with the usual, the normal, of our particular culture, our way of life. We are faced with the problem of conformity, about which we in the West at least have lately become self-conscious.

One could argue that natural behavior is that usual to, or conforming with, human nature—but for that one needs a fairly definite concept of human nature. The anthropologists, with their descriptions of cultural relativism, and the psychologists, with their emphasis on individual learning and experience, have shown us that this is not easy. One comes to sympathize with the existentialist position that there is no such thing as human nature, that each man makes himself.

But if it is difficult to determine human nature, one can at least discuss the human condition, most easily in physical terms. Man is a mammal and a primate, which immediately defines many characteristics. He cannot spend his whole life swimming, like a dolphin; nor browse on grass, like a cow; nor scramble up a tree trunk unaided, like a squirrel or like some of his monkey relatives. He has an upright posture, with appropriately modified feet, legs and trunk, which makes him unique among the primates. His hands and arms, not needed for walking, are free for other functions, thus allowing him to develop his great ability at manipulating things. There are limits though: I have often wished, in situations such as cocktail parties, that I had a prehensile tail so that I could manage my drink, my canapé and my cigarette at the same time. A spider monkey would have no trouble.

Man has binocular vision, which enables him to judge distance well; and he can discriminate form and color. Many animals, however, have keener vision. Man's hearing is moderately good, but his sense of smell is quite poor. One could go on with such a list and describe the anatomical and physiological traits of the human animal with some accuracy, and in so doing one aspect of the human condition would be described. But how little this helps us in understanding ourselves! No matter how much care we devote to the study of the anatomy of the brain, we learn nothing about why "shit" is an indecent word for a necessary action; nothing about why men wear trousers and women skirts in our culture; nothing about food habits or

sex habits. Anatomy and physiology tell us nothing about shame, pride or modesty.

Our problem turns on the mind rather than the body: but how do we dissect the mind? It doesn't help much to say that body and mind are not separate entities, but simply different aspects of the physical organism. Maybe we should shift terms and talk, not about mind, but about self-consciousness or awareness. But we are still bogged down in words. How our awareness compares with that of a chimpanzee, a monkey or a dog, we do not know. Certainly we can find comparable expressions of emotions in animals and men, as Charles Darwin showed long ago. Perhaps from this we can infer comparable emotions, but it is difficult to find out about this because we cannot carry on discussions with other animals.

Certainly it is difficult to separate human actions, emotions and attitudes from the human habit of talking. It would be interesting to know how all of this got started. Did those ape-men living in South Africa a half a million years ago "talk" in some way comparable with ours? Did they listen to the advice of a wise old chief, and did they try to be faithful to their mates? Had they developed special ideas about food, sex and excretion—in other words, did they have cultural taboos? Which I suppose is asking how human they were. Their brains were only a little larger than those of modern chimpanzees: a cranial capacity of 450–550 cc., compared with 350–450 for the chimp and with 1200–1500 for modern man. But it is hard to know what this means in terms of behavior.

These Australopithecines—as the South African ape-men are properly called—were at least human enough to commit murder. Raymond Dart, in his book *Adventures with the Missing Link*, remarks on the jaw of an adolescent "which had been bashed in by a formidable blow from the front and delivered with great accuracy just to the left of the point of the jaw." Nothing of this sort happens in the case of squabbles among apes and monkeys, though they may be mean enough to each other when cooped up together in a zoo.

We have here direct evidence of a kind of behavior on the part of our remote evolutionary ancestors, though with no clue as to the meaning of the behavior; but even this much is rare. For the most part we have only bones and tools made of materials likely to survive—which tell us nothing about sex habits, or even skin color or body hair.

We have, in short, considerable evidence to help us in reconstructing the evolution of the human skeleton, but almost none to help us reconstruct the history of human behavior. Yet our striking peculiarities are in behavior, not in skeleton. We can get ideas about the possible background by watching living monkeys and apes; but man is so different that these inferences must be interpreted with great caution. For the most part we can only speculate about the history of human behavior, bolstering our speculations with whatever evidence we can find. This is no road to certainty; but speculation often is the impetus for scientific investigation, and it can be illuminating.

The outstanding peculiarity of man is the great control of custom, of culture, over behavior. This is obvious enough in the case of such things as food, sex and excretion, but it is far more pervasive. We can't even get out of breath "naturally." If we are late for an appointment we may tend to exaggerate our breathlessness to show how hard we were trying. On the other hand, people of my age try to suppress their panting, trying to hide the deterioration of age—or of too much smoking.

The effect of culture on behavior is not limited to actions; it influences all physiology in many ways. This shows up in the psychosomatic diseases—ulcers, dermatitis, asthma and a host of little-understood effects of "mind" on "body." This relationship is especially irritating when you know that a particular worry is causing a distressing physical effect like dermatitis—yet you can't escape the worry. Here is where psychotherapy or drugs, benign or otherwise, come in.

Then there is the curious human trait of blushing, whereby thoughts influence peripheral blood circulation. Here again we run into the perplexing problem of consciousness: you can't stop yourself from blushing by deciding not to. The possible origin and meaning of blushing fascinated Darwin, but neither he nor anyone else seems to have arrived at a satisfactory explanation of the phenomenon.

There is also the opposite and equally little understood process of influence of conscious thought on inner physiology, as in the exercises of Yoga. Apparently there is little a man can't do to his body if he puts his mind to it.

The human habit of hiding physiology brings up the corresponding habit of hiding anatomy. This of course depends on the development of clothing—a subject that fascinates me and that I want to explore in some detail later in this book. It would be interesting to know how the idea of covering parts of the body got started, but we shall probably never have direct evidence. It is quite likely that clothing started, not as protection against weather, nor as a dawning sense of modesty, but rather as one aspect of the general human tendency to tamper with appearance. The list of things that different peoples do to their bodies is both curious and impressive: cutting hair; chipping teeth; painting, tattooing and scarring skin; deforming the infant skull or feet; circumcising the penis; cutting or enlarging the clitoris; cutting holes in ears or nose to hang things from; draping objects around the neck or waist or arms or ankles. The motive among Ubangi women for adorning themselves with ridiculous lip plugs is no different from the motive of Western women who use make-up and hair curlers—or from that of men who endure haircuts, shaves and button-down-collar shirts.

Clothing probably derives from the habit of hanging things around the neck or waist, or perhaps from the habit of painting or scarring the skin. The advantage of an extra and artificial skin in bad weather would then be a later and accidental discovery. The concealing function of clothing is surely a secondary development and even in our society it is difficult to decide whether modesty or display is more important in the design of clothes: witness the bikinis, and the street-corner boys with their tight jeans.

I have not been able to think of any animal except man that ornaments itself by picking up additions for skin, fur or feathers. There is no argument about man's being a peculiar creature. But there is also no argument—among biologists at least—about his being an animal. The animal heritage is clear enough in anatomy and physiology—in the form of bones and muscles and guts; in the need for breathing and eating and excreting and copulating. But what of our heritage in behavior?

Human behavior has long formed the subject matter of a series of special sciences: psychology, anthropology, sociology, economics; probably history and political science should be added to the list. I can claim no special training in any of these subjects—though I once flunked a course in sociology. I am a biologist, and my special field as a research scientist has been mosquitoes and the diseases they transmit. But I am also a human being, and I have long been interested in watching other people and in trying to gain some understanding of myself. Somewhere, early, I came to feel that the behavior of the peoples of the Western world gave them no patent on the right way of living —no monopoly on either the satisfactions or the miseries available to our species.

Thus both the peculiarities of man as a species and the diversity in his ways of life fascinate me. It seems to me that diversity in itself is good; that there is no single "right way" for all people. I hope the reasoning behind my plea for diversity, for tolerance—and for the concomitant inhibition of destruction, which is so often intolerance will become clear as the book develops. The peculiarities of man and the diversity of his accepted customs show up in any aspect of his behavior that we stop to examine; but they seem clearest in relation to those two fundamental drives of all animals –food and sex.

FOOD

Although in any *particular* human group the range of what is eaten is selective, when we stand back and take mankind as a whole we see the enormous variety of things considered edible—materials that our own stomachs would probably instantly reject, such as rotted wood, clay, rotten bananas or human flesh, lice, and many more. Note that *our* stomachs might reject these as foods—but not the people who eat them. It is one thing to take the more distant perspective, as we do with the aid of Gillin's selection, and generalize about the range of things man (and this means any man) probably *could* learn to eat if he had the same exposure and experience as those in the group who actually do eat it. It is quite another thing to look at a given group and consider within that framework the emotional and value overtones to what is properly accepted as food. This is a good example of the well-known anthropological phrase, "culture relativism"—the notion that each item of behavior must be considered in its actual empirical context before it can be taken as a "culturally" acceptable practice. Furthermore, as Gillin notes, the simple cultural assumption of "three square meals a day" is by no means widespread. Why three? Why not one—or four, or five? Or no "meal" at all, but continual snacking?

VARIETY IN FOOD CUSTOMS

JOHN GILLIN

Let us examine a few more or less extreme examples of customary foodstuffs, taken at random from the literature. The Vedda of Ceylon eat no less than five kinds of rotted wood, usually garnished with honey, bark, leaves, and fruits.[1] Among some of the Guiana tribes, green-heart seeds, which are woody in consistency, were grated, soaked, and "mixed with rotted wood, pounded previously and sifted" at those times of the year when cassava bread was scarce.[2] A number of cases are on record from the sixteenth and seventeenth centuries of

Reprinted with permission of publisher. From John Gillin, "Custom and Range of Human Response," *Character and Personality*, 13 (1944), 121–31.
[1]Sarasin, P. and F. *Die Weddas von Ceylon und die sie umgebenden Völkerschaften*, Wiesbaden, 1893, vol. 1, pp. 401–409.

[2]Schomburgk, R. H. Diary of an ascent of the Rio Berbice. *J. Roy. geog. Soc.*, 1837, 7, 346; also Dance, Charles. *Chapters from a Guianese logbook*, Demerara, 1881, p. 177.

peoples who had formed the habit of eating small pebbles after each meal, and, to quote Gould and Pyle,[3] "It has frequently been stated that the peasants of Styria are in the habit of taking from two to five grains of arsenious acid daily for the purpose of improving the health, avoiding infections, and raising the whole tone of the body. It is a well-substantiated fact that the quantities taken habitually are quite sufficient to produce immediate death ordinarily."[4]

Clay- and earth-eating is customary among various peoples, sometimes, at least, motivated by an actively felt desire or drive. Among the Issa-Japura tribes of Amazonia (mainly the Boro and Witoto), for instance, the desire for clay, although regarded with disfavor in the culture, nevertheless is said to amount to an unconquerable craving, and if the clay cannot otherwise be obtained, it will be scraped from under the fireplace and eaten in secret. Possibly this is a response to a physiologic mineral need.[5] Schoolboys in Morocco eat potter's earth regularly before breakfast in the belief that they thereby learn their lessons better.[6] Dickens and Ford made a study of the widespread custom of clay-eating among the Negroes of Mississippi. The practice is also found among whites of this region, but is not so prevalent. By means of "hidden question" tests of statistical reliability, they found that 25 per cent of a random sample of 207 Negro school children had "eaten dirt" at least twice in a period of 16 days. Clay soils only were used, free from sand, and of a reddish brown color. "Reasons given for eating dirt were: it is good for you; tastes good, rather sour, like a lemon; helps women who are pregnant; and tastes good if put in the chimney and smoked first." The notion that people crave dirt is common. They get to the place where they feel that they must have clay to eat. . . . One hears, too, that dirt is carried long distances to people who can no longer get it themselves.[7] The authors conclude that "dirt eating is simply a culture trait like dipping snuff or smoking," although they think it may be related to an iron-deficient diet. More investigation is needed, because simply calling a practice a culture trait does not explain it.

Miss Hilda Hertz of Duke University has gathered some material on earth-eating among Negro informants in Durham, N. C. With her permission I quote a few passages from one of her informant's statements:

> It tastes good, but only if you can find good dirt. Around here [Durham, N. C.] I haven't had any good dirt. Good dirt is red clay and comes in big, large lumps. . . . Laundry starch tastes much like good dirt, but is not quite so good. A good many people eat it instead of dirt. I learned to eat dirt when I was very small. My mother eats it, but not my father. His family does not eat dirt, but my mother's family does.

Of ten North Carolina Negro earth-eaters who comprised Miss Hertz's informants, six habitually ate laundry starch as a substitute when dirt was unobtainable or when in fear of disapproval. At least three of this group seem to have developed a starch appetite which displaced their former dirt appetite. To date, samples of the dirt eaten by Miss Hertz's subjects have not been chemically analyzed, so that we are unable to discuss the possibility that the practice of eating it is a response to an innate "partial hunger." This may well be a factor in the custom, but the evidence seems to indicate that the important factor is the presence of an acquired appetite (acquired drive) developed through training or experience. The fact that the subject's mother comes from a family of "dirt-eaters," whereas her father does not and has not himself acquired the custom is significant. Also it is significant that starch-eating may displace earth-eating, for it is apparent that the chemical composition of laundry starch has nothing in common with that of red clay and presumably would not satisfy the same physiologic need. The similarity between the two substances seems to reside in the tactile sensation produced in the mouth, and one is led to believe that the craving, in such a case at least, is predominantly acquired rather than innate.

Clay-eating was also a well established trait among the ancient Peruvians. Here it may represent a trial-and-error cultural discovery based upon its medicinal value. Cobo reports also that "its powders, which are bland and loving, put on piles, are useful for drying them and consuming them, and mixed with vinegar and the sap of the *membrillo*

[3]Gould and Pyle, *op. cit.*, p. 413, quoting *Philos. Trans. Roy. Soc. London*, 1700.

[4]Gould and Pyle, *op. cit.*, p. 413.

[5]Whiffen, Thomas. *The Northwest Amazons*, London, 1915, pp. 124–125.

[6]Westermarck, Edward. *Ritual and belief in Morocco*, London, 1926, vol. 2, 600.

[7]Dickens, Dorothy, & Ford, Robert N. Geophagy (dirt eating) among Mississippi Negro school children. *Amer. social. Rev.*, 1942, 7, 65–69.

(quince tree) are used to stop bloody stools."[8] Lawson and Moon report that the modern Quechua Indians near Puno subsist mainly upon potatoes which are dipped before eating in an aqueous suspension of clay which they say "prevents souring of the stomach." They report that the clay is mostly kaolin, and remark that this substance is used pharmaceutically in modern medicine as a protective agent for gastric and intestinal mucosa and as a remedy for bacterial infection of the gut.[9] The chemical composition of this edible clay of the Peruvian highlands is given by Paz Soldán as: silica, 54.4 per cent; aluminum, 23.4 per cent; peroxide of iron, 6. per cent; lime, 2.8 per cent; magnesia, 1.58 per cent; potassium, magnesium, traces; water, 10.5 per cent.[10]

Earth-eating in one form or another has also been widely reported in the Amazonian and Guiana country.[11]

Judging by the number of societies which do so, it seems to be well established that members of the human species can be trained to tolerate and even to prefer putrefied food. It has been suggested that this may be a means of obtaining vitamins, as it is well known that the bacteria of putrefaction manufacture Vitamin B_1, for example. So long as toxin-producing organisms are not present in the putrefaction, no harm is done to the consumer. We may cite a few examples of the customary consumption of putrefied food.

The primitive Vedda of Ceylon "have . . . a decided preference for their game 'high'—if so mild a term can describe the exceedingly advanced condition."[12] The Lepchas of Sikkim "prefer their meat high, but not maggoty."[13] Certain tribes of the Northwest Coast savored a form of systematically rotted fish, among them the Tanaina, who "preserve silver salmon for winter use by burying them during August in a hole dug in the ground five or

six feet deep. . . . First, they put a layer of grass on the bottom of the hole, then a layer of silver salmon from which the viscera have been removed, then another layer of grass, then a layer of fish eggs, and again a layer of grass. . . . The fish become a little rotten but the eggs act as salt and the grass keeps them from freezing in a mass."[14] Referring to the North American Indians in general, an authoritative source says, "in many cases both animal and vegetable substances advanced toward putrefaction were preferred, as salmon eggs which were stored in sand, by the Alaskans, and immature corn in the ear which the Hurons are said to have soaked in water until it became putrid."[15] In Central America the Miskito and Sumu Indians of Nicaragua eat birds' eggs, "even when they are practically rotten."[16] These tribes also make two types of ensilage by burying green bananas or palm fruit, or sinking them in water. These products "have a very offensive odor, which may be smelled from a great distance," but nevertheless serve as staple foods during parts of the year.[17] The Eskimo are perhaps better known for their relish of decayed food products. The Polar Eskimo eat decayed birds, feathers, flesh, and all, which have been cached and prepared for this purpose;[18] and Stefansson says that the August catch of fish among the Central group with which he lived is "outright rotten" by the time it is eaten. He says that it is quite possible for white men to develop a desire for this mess and remarks of our society that "while it is good form to eat decayed milk products and decayed game, it is very bad form to eat decayed fish."[19] Among the Bemba of Africa "every item of a killed beast is devoured down to the ultimate entrail, in whatever state of decay. Small shreds of flesh are dried over the fire and lovingly stored in a corner of the owner's hut, whatever the smell."[20]

Although human groups may live on meat and/or fish alone or on a combination of meat and dairy products, it appears that there are no societies which subsist upon a starch diet alone, which is

[8]Cobo, Bernabé. *Historia del Nuevo Mundo*, Sevilla, 1890–95 (written about 1653), vol. 1, 243; see also Valdizán, Hermilio, & Maldonado, A. *La medicina popular Peruana*, Lima, 1922, vol. 2, 16–17.

[9]Lawson, A., & Moon, H. P. A clay adjunct to a potato dietary. *Nature*, 1928, 141, 40.

[10]Paz Soldán, J. L., in Raimondi, A., *El Perú*, Lima, 1904, vol. 4, 50.

[11]Gumilla, J. *Historia natural civil y geográfica de las naciones situadas en las riveras del Rio Orinoco*, Barcelona, 1791, p. 177; Crévaux, J. *Voyages en l'Amérique du Sud*, Paris, 1883, p. 287; de Goeje, C. H. Beiträge zur Völkerkunde von Surinam. *Int. Archiv. f. Ethnographie*, 1910, 19, 5; Koch-Grünberg, T. *Zwei Jahre unter den Indianern*, Berlin, 1910, vol. 2, 291.

[12]Bailey, J. An account of the wild tribes of the Veddas of Ceylon. *Trans. Ethnol. Soc. London*, 1863, n.s. 2, 288.

[13]Gorer, G. *Himalayan village*, London, 1938, p. 56.

[14]Osgood, C. The ethnography of the Tanaina. *Yale Univ. Publ. Anthrop.*, 1937, 16, 42.

[15]*Handbook of American Indians North of Mexico*. Smiths. Inst., Bur. Amer. Ethnol., Bull. 30, Washington, 1907, vol. 1, 467–468.

[16]Conzemius, Eduard. *Ethnographical survey of the Miskito and Sumu Indians of Honduras and Nicaragua*, Smiths. Inst., Bur. Amer. Ethnol., Bull. 106, Washington, 1932, p. 88.

[17]*Ibid.*, p. 91.

[18]Murdock, G. P. *Our primitive contemporaries*, New York, 1934, p. 199.

[19]Stefansson, V. Adventures in diet. *Harper's Magazine*, 1935, 171, 668–675.

[20]Richards, *op. cit.*, p. 57.

apparently a response to the human requirement for protein.[21] The researches of certain societies as to the edibility of various animal species have resulted in eating customs involving animals of a considerable variety. Let us briefly consider only insects, vermin, and reptiles. The Issa-Japura Indians eat monkeys (sometimes with the hair), frogs, iguanas, and head lice. With respect to the latter, "a scurf comb is a most important present, and to comb your neighbor's hair and eat the 'bag' an honour and a luxury. They will also eat the grubs of wasps and bees, and in fact any larvae."[22] According to Cobo, one of our most reliable informants on Peru of the Conquest period, the Indians there ate lice "as if they were grains of sesame or candied anis."[23] Lice, incidentally, were collected as a form of tribute. The Incas "obligated Indians who could not work at ordinary tasks because of age, infirmity, etc., so that they should not be lazy, to collect such lice as they found on themselves or other persons and to pay them as tribute; also Indians who had no other goods to pay."[24] The present writer has observed the eating of lice among the Barama River Caribs of British Guiana. Says Castner of the Indians of Alaska, "I noticed one old medicine man, without covering, catching mosquitoes and eating them. This they all do with the vermin they catch on each other's heads and bodies."[25] Among the Buganda of East Africa, "white ants are eaten alive or cooked. When eaten alive, the two wings are firmly grasped and the body is popped into the mouth. . . . When ants are to be cooked, they are put into the pot alive, cooked, taken out, put into a leaf bundle, then cooked again with matoke. . . . Served either whole . . . or else dried in the sun and then pounded and mixed with salt or butter . . . ."[26]

The people of the Lepcha village of Pantoong are reported to have been serpent eaters; they would stone a snake, cut off the head, and eat the body raw. Most Lepchas habitually eat dead domestic animals and carrion found in the forest, when avail-

able.[27] "Frogs were much appreciated by the Incas, for their delicate flesh; and in the towns where there were no live ones, they ate them dried."[28] At the present time, small lizards are hunted on the coast of Peru and eaten fresh or dried, not only by Indians but also by the Creoles. They may usually be obtained in dried bundles in the public markets.[29] A paste made from the eggs laid by a certain fly on the lakes is still extensively eaten in Mexico. . . .

From the point of view of species survival, the ability of man to obtain nourishment from so wide a variety of items and "to learn to like almost anything" has been a great advantage, for these abilities have enabled man to live in environments where more specialized animals starve. . . .

Hunger, or appetite associated with it, seems to be a drive which rises periodically, in our society at least, and which seemingly must be satisfied to some extent three times per day. Is this characteristic of the species? It is obvious, even in ordinary experience, that one can fast for various longer periods of time without permanent damage. How long can a human being be trained to withstand hunger "as a regular thing" and still continue to function as a member of society? In many circumstances, such as traveling and nomadic life, it would obviously be an advantage if men could develop the custom of eating, say, only once in three days, for thereby they could feed at established settlements and save the energy and inconvenience of carrying supplies with them. . . .

Except for specialists such as cargo carriers or in unusual circumstances, all societies of which I know seem to have patterns for feeding at least once a day. . . .

Within the 24-hour cycle, however, there is considerable cultural variability, even within the area of European civilization. Although each society prefers its own feeding schedule, it would be interesting to know what an optimum interval between feedings would be for the species. In North America the standard number of meals is three with an interval of from four to five hours between the first and second and from five to six hours between the second and third. Four meals per day was a standard in a number of peacetime European societies,

[21]Cf. notes 27 and 28, above; also Linton, Ralph. Crops, soils and culture in America. *The Maya and their neighbors*, New York, 1940, pp. 32–40.

[22]Whiffen, *op. cit.*, p. 130.

[23]*Op. cit.*, vol. 2, 278.

[24]Herrera, Antonio. *Historia general de los hechos de los castellanos en las islas y tierra firme del mar océano*, Madrid, 1728, Década V, Libro IV, p. 85.

[25]Castner, J. C. A story of hardship and suffering in Alaska, in *Compilation of narratives of explorations in Alaska*, Washington, 1900, pp. 686–709; quotation from p. 705.

[26]Anna, M. Notes on the preparation of food in Buganda. *Primitive man*, 1940, 26–28.

[27]Gorer, *op. cit.*, p. 56.

[28]Cobo, *op. cit.*, vol. 2, 140.

[29]Gillin, John. *Moche: a Peruvian coastal community*, Smithsonian Institution, Institute of Social Anthropology, Publ. 4, Washington, 1945, (in press).

e.g., England, which inserted afternoon tea and Germany, which inserted second breakfast into the three-meal schedule. In part of Scandinavia five and six meals per day were *de rigueur*. In each society individuals were trained "to feel hungry" at the appropriate feeding times.

Turning to preliterate cultures, we find a similar variety, although usually in the direction of fewer meals per day. For example, the Nama Hottentots of South Africa have "no fixed time for eating. Only the morning meal, taken after the cows have been milked and driven out to pasture, has a special name, *sobas*. The time and place of other meals are regulated according to circumstance; in camp by the return of the herds from pasture; on the march by the progress; on the hunt by a successful shot, and so on."[30] The Tupinamba would work in their gardens during the morning without breakfast, eating only one meal per day after they returned to the house, either about noon or later in the day.[31] One meal per day is also customary for the Tanala of Madagascar, although a few cold scraps left over from the day before may be eaten upon rising.[32] Among the Bemba, whose food customs have been so well studied by Richards, a single daily meal is the rule, and it occurs at very irregular times during the day, depending upon the type of work in prog-

ress. "Men and women are accustomed to go to their gardens in the early morning to do the bulk of their work on what we habitually describe as an 'empty stomach.' They return to the village about noon, when the whole community awaits the evening meal."[33] The concentration on a single daily meal in this pattern seems to require considerable training. Richards says that children are allowed to eat snacks all day long, and only as they approach adolescence do they succeed in emulating their elders. Among adults it is considered "undignified" to be eating at all hours of the day. Thus we seem to have the timing aspect of the eating customs operating on an acquired drive of prestige anxiety which overrides the hunger drive.

Other peoples eat two meals per day, for example, the Tiv, who eat at dusk and at noon,[34] and the Quechua of the Inca Empire.[35] The Mazai of East Africa take three meals per day: fresh milk in the early morning, a heavier meal about ten o'clock in the morning, and an evening meal.[36]

Perhaps these instances of varying meal schedules are sufficient to indicate something of the variety of the cultural control which is exerted over the hunger drive in the human species. We need more investigation of this subject if we are to be accurate in cultural planning in this field.

[30]Schapera, I. *The Khoisan peoples of South Africa*, London, 1930, p. 239.

[31]Soares de Souza, G. Tratado descriptivo do Brazil em 1587. *Rev. Inst. Hist. Geog. Braz.*, Rio de Janeiro, 1851, 14, 319.

[32]Linton, Ralph. The Tanala of Madagascar. *Field Mus. Nat. Hist., Anthr. Stud.*, 1933, 22 (1–334), 74; also Kardiner, A. *The individual and his society*, New York, 1939, p. 254.

[33]Richards, *op. cit.*, p. 72.

[34]Akiga. *Akiga's story: the Tiv tribe as seen by one of its members* (Rupert East, ed. and tr.), London, 1939, p. 147.

[35]Rowe, J. H. The Inca culture at the time of the Conquest. *Handbook of the Indians of South America* (J. H. Steward, ed.), Smiths. Inst., Bur. Amer. Ethnol., Washington (in press).

[36]Merker, F. *Die Masai*, Berlin, 1904, p. 32.

KISSING

Why did American movies dealing with love have to be censored before being shown in Japan? Wrong! It is because of the scenes of men and women kissing. Kissing is an extremely private act among the Japanese, and for it to be displayed so publicly is the ultimate in cultural bad taste. The pressing of one person's lips to another's isn't, then, a "natural" way of expressing affection (although it undoubtedly is built upon the pleasurable sensations involved in sucking, touching, brushing something with the lips). La Barre, in an article that comes soon, goes into the matter of kissing in some more detail; this excerpt by Pike serves to introduce the idea that what is taken in Western European culture as one of the basic forms of loving behavior between male and female (or some other combination of sexes!) is not "instinctive," but, on the contrary, has its roots in another part of nature.

THE NATURAL HISTORY OF A KISS

E. ROYSTON PIKE

What's so strange about a kiss? Surely kissing is one of the most natural things in the world, so natural indeed that we might almost ask, what are lips for if not for kissing? But this is what *we* think, and a whole lot of people think very differently. To them kissing is not at all natural. It is not something that everybody does, or would like to do. On the contrary, it is a deplorable habit, unnatural, unhygienic, bordering on the nasty and even definitely repulsive.

When we come to look into the matter, we shall find that there is a geographical distribution of kissing; and if some enterprising ethnologist were to prepare a "map of kissing" it would show a surprisingly large amount of blank space. Most of the so-called primitive races of mankind, such as the New Zealanders (Maoris), the Australian aborigines, the Papuans, Tahitians, and other South Sea Islanders, and the Esquimaux of the frozen north, were ignorant of kissing until they were taught the technique by the white men who appeared among them as voyagers and explorers, traders and missionaries. The Chinese have been wont to consider kissing as vulgar and all too suggestive of cannibalism, and, as we shall see in a moment, they have not been alone in this. The Japanese have no word for it in their vocabulary, and the practice is tabooed as utterly immodest and revolting, except of course among those who have made a point of adopting Western ways. But it is Africa which "has the sad distinction of being the largest non-kissing area in the world".

Such at least was the conclusion of the young English traveller Winwood Reade, and (to meet the objections of those who speak out of present-day experience) it should be explained that he was writing of a time when the natives of Equatorial Africa were still savages. The words are taken from his book *Savage Africa* (1863), in which he describes his travels in the then unknown "Gorilla country" of the Upper Gaboon in West Africa. Alone save for a few native attendants, he penetrated farther upcountry than a white man had

ever been before, and for some time he remained in a kind of honourable captivity as the guest of Quenqueza, the "king" of the Rembo tribesfolk. It was then that he met Ananga. She was beautiful —"full and finely moulded, hands and feet exquisitely small, complexion a deep warm colour, her eyes large and filled with a melancholy expression"—no wonder that, in one of those unguarded moments "in which the heart rises to the lips, and makes them do all sorts of silly things", he made to kiss her. . . .

Not on first meeting, of course, but when for weeks they had been for hours each day in one another's company. He had gone to Africa to study the gorilla in his native haunts, but he found "this pretty savage" a much more delicious study. At first she was timid, very timid, for she had never seen a white man before, but she tried to keep this from him lest she should hurt his feelings, "and I could read it only in her fluttering eyes and in her poor little heart, which used to throb so loudly when we were alone. I found her as chaste, as coquettish, and as full of innocent mischief, as a girl of sixteen would have been in England. In a little while I found myself becoming fond of her". So the thought came to him of a "new and innocent pleasure". To bestow a kiss upon lips which tremble with love for the first time—that (he reflected) was certainly an epoch in a man's existence; but just imagine what it must be to kiss one who has never conceived the possibility of such a thing, who has never dreamt that human lips could be applied to such a purpose! "And so, I kissed Ananga, the daughter of the king." And what happened? "She gave a shriek, and bounded from the house like a frightened fawn." What Winwood Reade had forgotten, or perhaps he had never realized, was that "this mode of salutation is utterly unknown in Western Africa. Ananga knew that the serpent moistens its victim with its lips before it begins its repast. All the tales of white cannibals which she had heard from infancy had returned to her. The poor child had thought that I was going to dine off her, and she had run for her life!"

Soon, however, it was "all's well that ends well". Ananga was pursued and brought back by Win-

Reprinted with permission of publisher. From E. Royston Pike, *The World's Strangest Customs* (London: Odhams Books. Ltd., 1966), pp. 11–19.

wood Reade's native interpreter. She was "panting and trembling, and her cheeks were wet with tears; but I explained to her that this was only a fashion of my country, and she offered her pouting lips in atonement of her folly".

Why was it, the young man mused, that these "poor benighted creatures", as he half-humorously calls them, "had never discovered our civilized method of endearment?" It was certainly not through any deficiency in their affection, or in their ability to show it. He had seen many a time the hunters returning to their village in the late afternoon, bringing with them the food they had gathered in the bush, and their womenfolk had hurried out to meet them and welcomed them as though they had been away for years, murmuring to them in baby language, calling them by their names of love, patting their breasts and laying arm upon arm, shaking their hands, caressing their faces and embracing them in every possible way—except with the lips. He sought an explanation, and all he could think of was that perhaps it was because African women have black lips ("though sometimes, but rarely, the under lip is red"), which hardly sounded very convincing.

Then like the cheerful young Englishman that he was, he went on to urge his lady-readers not "to despise the poor untutored African, or judge him too severely on account of an ignorance for which he is not to blame. He is ever willing to adopt the customs of a higher race". One day he had met a Negro in the Gaboon who had been converted to Christianity, and this man had assured him with honest pride that though the heathen did not know how to kiss, the Christians were becoming quite proficient in the art. Then on another occasion when visiting a village on the Grain Coast, a young Kruman, sitting with his wife in front of his hut, had called out to him as he went by, "Lookee, Massa, I sabby kiss!", and forthwith had suited the action to the word. But the lady "seemed to be much amused, and not altogether pleased with this novel application of the lips".

Dr. Johnson in his Dictionary defines a kiss as "a salute given by joining the lips", which may be accepted as the minimum of definition; a more intimate one is, "a prolonged pressing of mouth against mouth with slight intermittent movements". How and when did it all begin? In dictionaries of quotations we may find the pious wish, "May his soul be in heaven—he deserves it, I'm sure—who

was first the inventor of kissing." But there is no knowing who that man was, and it may well be (as naturalists have suggested) that kissing was not a human invention at all, but derives from such animal practices as a dog or cat rubbing its head against its master's knee, the intertwining of elephant trunks, the billing of birds, and the "caressing" strokes of insects' antennae. But if there *was* a man who first tried the experiment of pressing his lips against those of a pretty woman, we may be sure that he belonged to the Indo-European stream of race and culture.

In tracing the history of the kiss we are led back to ancient India. In the period of the Vedas, round about 2000 B.C., the Indians seem to have practised what is called the nose or sniff kiss, of which more later; but by about the time of the great Mahabharata epic (500 B.C.?) the salutation with the lips had become general. It was certainly well established when the ancient sage Vatsyayana composed his *Aphorisms on Love* (*Kama Sutra*), for amongst its twelve hundred and fifty verses are a number concerned with the technique of kissing with the lips. The best places for kissing are indicated, viz., the forehead, the eyes, the cheeks, the throat, the bosom, the breasts, the lips, and inside the mouth; and the different kinds of kiss are analysed according to their intensity and method of application, and it is further explained that there are different kinds of kisses for different parts of the body.

From India the practice is supposed to have spread westwards to Persia, Assyria, Syria, Greece, Italy, and by way of the channels of Roman influence throughout most of Europe. The Teutonic tribes on the borderlands of the Empire practised the mouth kiss, but it has been pointed out that there is no word for "kiss" in the Celtic tongues.

The Romans had different words for different kinds of kiss. The regular Latin word for a kiss was *osculum*, of which the primary meaning was "a little mouth" or "a sweet mouth". The osculum was not applied to the lips but to the face or cheek, and it came to be established as the kiss of friendship; in direct descent from it is the public embrace performed by French generals and politicians. Was this the kind of kiss that (so we are told by Plutarch) the Roman women, after they had burnt the ships which brought them from distant Troy, turned away the anger of their menfolk? We can hardly suppose so. Surely their endearments took the form of the mouth-to-mouth application, which is so much more tender and satisfying. But it would seem that a special word for this species of kiss did not make its appearance in the vocabulary until the last century B.C.

This was *basium*, and we are told that the young poet Catullus was the first and for some time the only writer to employ it to indicate something much more passionate than the osculum. This was, we may be sure, the kind of kiss that he applied to the lips of his beautiful but notoriously flighty mistress whom he calls Lesbia, although her name in real life was Clodia. Nor is there any reason to doubt that she liked them, if not quite so much as he did. "You ask how many kissings of you, Lesbia, are enough for me, and more than enough? As many as the grains of sand in the Libyan deserts, or as the stars that look down, in the silent watches of the night, on the stolen loves of men. If your Catullus, your mad Catullus, could kiss you with as many kisses as that, then perhaps this might be enough." Or as he put it in his most famous poem, that has been many times rendered into English, as by the young Coleridge:

A thousand kisses take and give!
Another thousand!—to the store
Add hundreds—then a thousand more!
And when they to a million mount,
Let confusion take the account—
That you, the number never knowing,
May continue, still bestowing. . .

From *basium* is derived the French *baiser*, as also the words for "kiss" in Italian, Spanish, and Portuguese. Some etymologists hold that it was also the parent of the old English word "buss", defined as a rude or playful kiss, a smack on the lips.

The Romans had a third kind of kiss, one that was given between the lips with the assistance of the tongue. This was *savium*, which meant originally "a mouth, or lips, puckered up to kiss". A diminutive of this was *saviolum*, "a sweet kiss", a word which Catullus employed in his verses; the transition from this to the kiss of passion was easy. Although Ovid seldom used the word, he was well acquainted with this sort of kiss, as every reader of his amatory poems will not need to be told; thus in Christopher Marlowe's translation of the *Amores* we read of a girl "who eagerly kissed me with her tongue", and of another who "in my lips her whole tongue hid, mine in hers she dips".

From the Romans the custom of kissing with the lips or mouth passed into the Middle Ages, when to be able to kiss nicely was a required accomplishment of a knight in the Courts of Love. Dante's description of the rapturous kissing of Paola and Francesca leads up to the Renaissance, when poet and playwright surrounded the kiss with all that speaks of romantic ecstasy. Nor were all the great practitioners of the art drawn from the warmer south; the custom was highly developed in England, so that we find Erasmus, the great Dutch humanist, expressing himself most favourably concerning the kissing powers and propensities of English womanhood. "The English girls are divinely pretty," he wrote in a letter to a friend on the Continent; "soft, pleasant, gentle, and charming as the Muses. They have one custom which cannot be too much admired. When you go anywhere on a visit all the girls kiss you. They kiss you when you arrive, they kiss you when you go away, and they kiss you again when you return. Go where you will, it is all kisses; and, my dear Faustus, if you had once tasted how soft and fragrant those lips are, you would wish to spend your whole life here."

One of the most persistent notes in the music of English poetry is the sound of the intimate contact of lips on lips, of mouth on mouth. Looking at it from the physiological angle, a kiss is what has been described as "a special case of tactile sensory pleasure". Of the senses involved (and there is more than one) the most important is touch. Nowhere is the sense of touch more highly developed than where the outer skin meets the inner skin or mucous membrane, and it is for this reason that the lips are one of the most erogenic areas in the body.

Another of the senses that may play a part is taste. The pioneer English anthropologist E. B. Tylor described a kiss as "salute by tasting", and it is on record that the lovers of Poppaea, the beautiful but licentious consort of the Emperor Nero, declared that her kisses had the flavour of wild berries. Closely connected with tasting is biting, and that refinement of it, suction with the closed lips. In one of his love-letters to Sophie de Monnier, Mirabeau writes, "I am kissing you and biting you all over: so enamoured am I of your creamy skin that I would cover it with bruises". In Italian there is an expression, "kissing with the teeth", which is a synonym for love-making. This form of kissing (if, indeed, it may be called that) is frequently met with in the literature of eroticism, but a specially charming illustration may be found in the "tender little idyll" that the young A. H. Savage Landor described in his book *Alone with the Hairy Ainu*.

In the course of his wanderings, on foot and on horseback, among these primitive people of the far north of Japan, he encountered many personable specimens, but there was one girl in particular, "the most lovely Ainu girl I had ever come across, and not nearly so hairy as most of them". When they sat together in the twilight she was a "perfect dream". He asked her to let him see the tattooing on her arm, and, rather to his surprise, the pretty maid took his hand in hers, clasped it tightly, and pressed it to her chest. "Then we wandered and wandered till it grew dark; we sat down, we chattered, we made love to each other." He would not have mentioned this small episode, he tells us, "if her ways of flirting had not been so extraordinary and funny. Loving and biting went together with her. She could not do the one without doing the other. As we sat on a stone in the semi-darkness she began by gently biting my fingers, without hurting me, as affectionate dogs often do their masters; she then bit my arms, then my shoulder, and when she had worked herself up into a passion she put her arms round my neck and bit my cheeks. It was undoubtedly a curious way of making love", and it was not until he "had been bitten all over, and was pretty tired of the new sensation", that she accompanied him back to the village. Kissing, as he understood the word, was apparently an unknown art to her.

Much more important than the gustatory is the olfactory element in kissing, even though there is next to nothing of it in the kisses given and taken in the Western world—probably because, as has been suggested, the sense of smell with us has become atrophied for want of use. Only rarely do we come across such a tribute as that of the old Roman poet Martial, here very prettily translated by an anonymous writer of the sixteenth century:

In winter chests like apples ripening. . .
As broken jars of Falerna wines to smell
Far off: or flowery gardens where bees dwell:
Perfumers' pots, burnt incense tossed on the air,
Chaplets new-fallen from rich perfumed hair. . .

Among primitive peoples, including all those mentioned above who do not kiss with the lips, the so-called "nose kiss" is the common form. Charles Darwin came across it among the Maoris of New Zealand. "The women on our first approach," he wrote, "began uttering something in a most dolorous voice; they then squatted themselves down and held up their faces; my companion (Mr. Bushby, the British Resident at Waimate) standing over them, one after another, placed the bridge of his nose at right angles to theirs, and commenced pressing. This lasted rather longer than a cordial handshake of the hand with us; and as we vary the force of the grasp of the hand in shaking, so do they in pressing. During the process they uttered comfortable little grunts, very much in the same manner as two pigs do, when rubbing against each other."

"Grunts", like a pair of affectionate pigs! "Comfortable" perhaps, but surely this is not the kind of thing that the Rose of Sharon burningly longed for when she implored her lover to "kiss me with the kisses of his mouth, for thy love is better than wine", or what Romeo proffered Juliet with the "two blushing pilgrims" of his lips, or what made Gretchen cling to Faust and ask for nothing better than that she, "faint with his kisses, should swoon and die!", or what Rabbie Burns bestowed on one of his Annies "that happy night Amang the rigs o' barley". No, not piggy grunts, not pressed noses, not amorous sniffings, but what Byron (who knew more than most men about this particular subject) described in a famous stanza of *Don Juan* as the action—

Where heart, and soul, and sense, in concert move,
And the blood's lava, and the pulse a blaze,
Each kiss a heart-quake. . .

TOILET HABITS

And how about toilet habits? Surely there is a "natural way" to defecate and urinate. This natural (that is, biological) act of getting rid of waste products from the body surely owes its form to man's structure and innate behavior potentials and not to a process of learning. For example, when urinating, women will squat or sit down and men stand. But again, not so. There is nothing in the architecture of the organism in respect to this particular function that dictates the posture we are accustomed to. But, surely then, is it universal that people will express a "natural" disgust with feces and urine, "offensive" substances, which the body must expel? If there is such an "instinctive" disgust, how does one explain the fact that, for example, the Eskimos (lacking soap) used to wash their hair and greasy faces with fresh urine? In the following selection (from a recent lively book), Rosebury, a noted bacteriologist, discusses variations in toilet habits through time and around the world.

TOILET TRAINING

THEODOR ROSEBURY

[Of latrines] their introduction cannot be ascribed to purely hygienic considerations, since many nations of comparatively high development have managed to get along without them; while on the other hand tribes in low stages of culture have resorted to them.

—J. G. Bourke, *Scatologic Rites of All Nations*

According to the British architect Lawrence Wright, in his book on the history of the flush toilet or water closet, the first patent for such a device was issued in 1775, and it was not until the bacteriologic era—between 1870 and 1900—that its use became common. No doubt dramatic experience with cholera and typhoid fever supplied the final push. The result has not been an unmixed blessing. What we have come with characteristic euphemism to call the bathroom or lavatory (in English inns the former label on a door may reveal nothing but a bathtub behind it) has achieved a place in our lives on which it would be interesting to have an ancient civilized perspective, say from Aristotle or Shakespeare. Some idea of what has happened to us may be suggested by three different exhibits: a satirical piece by anthropologist Horace Miner, a recent book simply called *The Bath Room* by architect Alexander Kira, and a current advertisement for "*Bijoux des Bains.*"

Professor Miner's piece is called "Body Ritual among the Nacirema" [*Amer. Anthropologist*, vol.

58, 503 7.] and purports to be an account of the strange customs of a people with "a highly developed market economy" who are quickly identified by spelling the tribe name backward. They spend much of their time in economic pursuits, but a large part in ritual activity, the focus of which

is the human body, the appearance and health of which loom as a dominant concern in the ethos of the people. While such a concern is certainly not unusual, its ceremonial aspects and associated philosophy are unique.

The fundamental belief underlying the whole system appears to be that the human body is ugly and that its natural tendency is to debility and disease. Incarcerated in such a body, man's only hope is to avert these characteristics through the use of the powerful influences of ritual and ceremony. Every household has one or more shrines devoted to this purpose. The more powerful individuals in the society have several shrines in their houses and, in fact, the opulence of a house is often referred to in terms of the number of such ritual centers it possesses. Most houses are of wattle and daub construction, but the shrine rooms of the more wealthy are walled with stone. Poorer families imitate the rich by applying pottery plaques to their shrine walls.

While each family has at least one such shrine, the rituals associated with it are not family ceremonies but are private and secret. The rites are normally only discussed with children, and then only during the period when they are being initiated into these mysteries . . .

Details follow of "a box or chest . . . built into the wall," in which "are kept charms and magical potions without which no native believes he could live"; of "medicine men" and "herbalists" who, having been "rewarded with substantial gifts" decide upon the contents of these potions and provide them; and of "holy-mouth-men" and the daily mouth-rite. This

> involves a practice which strikes the uninitiated stranger as revolting. It was reported to me that the ritual consists of inserting a small bundle of hog hairs into the mouth, along with certain magical powders, and then moving the bundle in a highly formalized series of gestures.

Descending from Professor Miner's Olympian perspective, we find Professor Kira down-to-earth. His book is touted on its flyleaf as "THE UNIQUE, FASCINATING AND SHOCKING STUDY OF AMERICA'S 'UNMENTIONABLE' ROOM." Subtitled "Criteria for Design," it turns out to be the report of extended research at Cornell University–sponsored jointly by the university's Agricultural Experiment Station and by a plumbing company [Bantam Books, N.Y., 1966]. The author is an architect, and his thesis is that bathroom furniture is archaic and urgently needs to be redesigned. He details careful investigations of persons engaged in the various bathroom activities, illustrated with drawings and photographs, the latter of women wearing bathing suits. He then proceeds to furnish detailed "Design Considerations for Cleansing" and similarly for defecation and urination. Figure 34 is a diagrammatic "plan view of sitting position on a conventional water closet" showing superimposed on the outline of a toilet seat an evidently bisexual figure and locating the positions over the seat opening respectively of the anus, the ischial tuberosities (bony foundations of the buttocks), and the female and male orifices, represented appropriately by the conventional symbols for Venus and Mars. The legs and feet are shown in two positions, the smaller feet of the inner or closer position being explained thus in the text:

> In sitting normally on a standard seat the weight is also borne by the back of the thighs. Women tend to be restricted by their clothing to sitting with their legs together and thus receive support all along the backs of the thighs. Men, on the other hand, as illustrated in Figure 34, sit with their legs spread apart and concentrate their weight at about the midpoint of the thighs.

Professor Kira affirms, apparently without question, the idea that a

> notion of total cleanness [sic] is a concept which appears to be basic to all peoples and to be generally valued in all cultures,

although he does observe in passing that

> in some countries it is still quite socially acceptable to smell of honest sweat.

But, he says,

> as physicians and anthropologists have pointed out, our various body odors are largely a carryover from primitive man, unnecessary in the present day.

Exhibit three depicts a flat metal box with cover raised enough to let a diamond bracelet, necklace, and ring spill out on a table. Attached to the box lid is a bejeweled set of faucet and two handles. The text speaks of a lady who has lots of diamonds, which her husband calls "hardware," jewels that spend more time in a vault than on the lady's person, especially when she is at home. It suggests that she could add facets of dazzle and brilliance to her home life by means of

> the sparkling elegance of beautiful faucets, like these in cut crystal, richly mounted in 24K gold plate. Elegant bathroom fixtures are as enduring as diamonds, yet cost far less (these are $216).

(I remember a remark made in a lecture by Professor Joseph MacFarland at the University of Pennsylvania when I was a student there. In speaking of dementia paralytica, also called general paralysis of the insane, a manifestation of neurosyphilis, he detailed among the symptoms certain delusions of grandeur that may show themselves, for example, by the sudden decision of a hitherto modest man to refurbish his bathroom in onyx and gold!)

Professor Kira builds on the assumption that "total cleanness" is desirable. He argues strongly and repeatedly that our cleanliest practices are not nearly good enough. Aside from the natural difference one would expect between a bacteriologist and an architect in interpretation of the phrase "total cleanness," it must be clear already, and will become more so, that I proceed on a different assumption. We have had a close look at the word "dirt" and have found it to mean several things, not all of which are evil. Professor Kira's word "total" seems to me inappropriate whether we observe it through a microscope or with the naked eye, or even with our noses.

I know of four books that concentrate actually or

symbolically on a single item of "bathroom" furniture, that miracle of modern plumbing by which civilizations are judged, the toilet bowl or water closet. One of these, which I have mentioned before, is Sir John Harington's *The Metamorphosis of Ajax*, an Elizabethan masterpiece in which is described, in an appropriate literary framework, what was probably the first proved instrument of this genus—or its reinvention (as we shall see) after a total eclipse during the Dark Ages. Two others are recent works. Reginald Reynolds' *Cleanliness and Godliness* was written in England during World War II. The author says he

> began this book to escape from a world that wearied me, and believing that the best part of man went down the drain . . .

Lawrence Wright's *Clean and Decent*, Viking Press, 1960, combines scholarship with plumbing technology. These three books are all lively and informative; but the fourth is in a class by itself.

The fourth book, which I have spoken of several times before, is the 496-page treatise *Scatologic Rites of All Nations*, compiled by Captain John G. Bourke, Third Cavalry, U.S.A., and published in 1891. On its title page appears the following descriptive matter and advice:

> A Dissertation upon the Employment of Excrementitious Remedial Agents in Religion, Therapeutics, Divination, Witchcraft, Love-Philtres, etc., in all Parts of the Globe. Based upon Original Notes and Personal Observations, and upon Compilation from over One Thousand Authorities. Not for General Perusal.

As I have already mentioned, Captain Bourke begins with a series of disclaimers that had me fooled at first. He intersperses his exposition with such editorial words as "horrible," "nastiness," "unseemingly," "lewd and vulgar," "disgusting," and others that suggest aversion to the whole enterprise. Early in the book he would have us believe that he is unequivocally on the angels' side, with this apology for the Puritans:

> The Puritan's horror of heathenish rites and superstitious vestiges had for its basis something above unreasoning fanaticism; he realized, if not through learned study, by an intuition which had all the force of genius, that every unmeaning practice, every rustic observance, which could not prove its title clear to a noble genealogy was a pagan survival, which conscience required him to tear up and destroy, root and branch.
> The Puritan may have made himself very much of

a burden and a nuisance to his neighbors before his self-imposed task was completed, yet it is worthy of remark and of praise that his mission was a most effectual one of wiping from the face of the earth innumerable vestiges of pre-Christian idolatry.

It was not until I worked my way further into this book that I took note of what looked like Bourke's cheek sticking out with his tongue behind it. As he warms to his subject he continues to throw in an occasional reminder of his piety and quotes others doing so with abandon; but most of the time he is detached in an eminently scientific way and seems to lose no chance to let versifiers and others give us the lighter side of his subject. . . .

Scatologic Rites is not an easily accessible book, and you may be unable to find it if you look for it, unless you have a specialist's credentials. I think we can assume that its rarity is not connected with any difficulty general readers would have in understanding it—even though it is a scholarly book—or even with a particularly widespread lack of interest in it. This would seem rather to be an aspect of our immediate problem: the book deals with a subject that has been carefully buried, and so it is itself kept guarded from the common view. But the reason for doing this, according to our working hypothesis, is sympathetic magic, which we are not afraid of. So let us take a good look at Bourke.

Put together with the rest of the exhibits, the good look will occupy the rest of this chapter and two more. Bourke gives us what Frazer left out. Much of it is remarkable, and the merely remarkable I need only transmit. But some of it is astonishing, and this I have undertaken to verify. Doing so seemed the more necessary because my two more recent sources omitted this material. Wright must have overlooked Bourke. Reynolds mentions one of his papers, but *Scatologic Rites* itself seems to have been sealed away from him in the British Museum, which was closed at the time to protect its treasures against German bombs.

Our immediate topic is the history of the privy.

Bourke tells us that certain Australian aborigines, as well as natives of the Marquesas in the South Pacific, and some American Indian tribes, observed the feline custom of burying their feces or covering them with earth. Their use for this purpose of a pointed stick or other digging instrument is similar to the practice of the ancient Jews and Turks. Harington [in *The Metamorphosis of Ajax*, 1596 (Columbia Univer. Press, 1962)] says:

every cat gives us an example (as housewifes tell us) to cover all our filthiness, & . . . to make your selfe, your gloves, and your clothes the more sweet, refuse not to follow the example of the Cat of the house . . .

The practice of the Jews is given in Deut. 23:

12. Thou shalt have a place also without the camp, whither thou shalt go forth abroad:
13. And thou shalt have a paddle upon thy weapon; and it shall be, when thou wilt ease thyself abroad, thou shalt dig therewith, and shalt turn back and cover that which cometh from thee . . .

Reynolds tells us that actual privies date as far back as Neolithic times [*Cleanliness and Godliness*, Doubleday, 1946]. The remains of such structures were dug up in the stone walls at Skara Brae in the Orkney Islands, with primitive stone-lined sewers running under the huts to the beach. Similar remains have been found in Cornwall and in the Gironde in France.

The remains of privies, usually fashioned out of masonry and provided with drains, some still functional when unearthed, *some even provided with flush devices*, have been dotted throughout Bronze Age cities going back to the third or fourth millennium B.C. Among the earliest were three privies left by the Sumerians at Tell Asmar in Iraq. Six were found at the palace of Sargon, dating from about 2400 B.C. Reynolds mentions that these had high seats, whereas those of the Orient were at floor level. (One assumes that the ancient Chinese, whose technology was well developed, had privies, but I have seen no description of them.) In the remains of the well-developed city of Mohenjo Daro in northwest India, which also dates from the third millennium B.C., were found bathrooms with masonry privies and drains made of flanged earthenware pipe. Other privies, sewers, and drains have been found in remains of ancient Egypt. A bathroom and lavatory and a well-preserved water closet were found at Tell el Amarna in Egypt, and also at Kahun, dating from the Second Dynasty (3400–2980 B.C.). Most of these were for nobles and priests, but some of those at Mohenjo Daro were in the poorest section, in the streets as well as the houses. The palace at Knossos in Crete contained very sophisticated water pipes, 2.5 feet long, nearly 1 inch thick, and slightly tapering toward one end. This superlative Minoan structure, dating back to about 1800 B.C., boasted bathrooms and a flushing water closet with a wooden seat.

The Greeks had hot and cold showers and tubs

(we know the latter from Diogenes and Archimedes) as well as privies, sewers, and aqueducts. Such things seemed to reach a peak and then decline among the later Romans, presumably with the advance of Christianity, and in the process the flush toilet evidently disappeared completely. But meanwhile the Romans built flushing latrines in Britain, their farthest outpost. Rome itself had nearly 1000 public baths, water being conveyed in lead pipes. The public latrines were social and convivial. Part of the reason for this custom was the conservation of the products for practical purposes, a separate matter to be considered later.

The Romans would have horrified Professor Kira, as they did Torquemada, whom Bourke calls "a Spanish author of high repute" and quotes regarding Romans and Egyptians as follows:

I assert that they used *to adore* . . . stinking and filthy privies and water-closets; and, what is viler and yet more abominable, what is an occasion for our tears and not to be borne with so much as mentioned by name, they adored the noise and wind of the stomach when it expels from itself any cold or flatulence; and other things of the same kind which . . . it would be a shame to name or describe.

Details of medieval and later history are contributed by Wright. The medieval word for privy was *garderobe*—a place to hang one's clothing— indicating that euphemism was already at work. In a plan of Southwall palace the privies radiated around a central shaft, facing outward onto a circular passage. Neighbors could converse with one another while decently out of sight. Where no stream or moat ran below, there might be a removable barrel, or a pit like one at Everswell in 1239:

What the cleaning of these pits meant is shown by an account of the work at Newgate Jail in 1281, when thirteen men took five nights to clear the "cloaca" . . . the men were paid three times the normal rate . . .

After the Black Death, which was attributed to everything imaginable except the rats and fleas that actually carried it, attempts were made everywhere to keep privies clean. About 1375 the cleaners were called *gongfermors*, who

seem to have become adapted to their horrid task, for an ancient story tells of one who complained, out of working hours, about the smell of a badly snuffed candle.

A parallel anecdote is quoted by Bourke with the date 1658:

A certain countryman at Antwerp . . . when he came into a shop of sweet smells, . . . began to faint, but one presently clapt some fresh smoking horse-dung under his nose and fetched him to again.

We are told by Wright that Leonardo da Vinci, in his proposal for Ten New Towns, aimed to

"distribute the masses of humanity, who live crowded together like herds of goats, filling their air with stench and spreading the seeds of plague and death." In these towns, the drainage of all private and public privies, and all garbage and street sweepings, were to be carried to the river by sewers (*via sotterane*). All the stairways in the tenement buildings were to be spiral, to prevent the insanitary use of stair landings. Leonardo invented a folding closet seat that "must turn round like the little window in monasteries, being brought back to its original position by a counterweight." . . . For Frances I at Ambrose Castle he proposed to install a number of water closets with flushing channels inside the walls, and ventilating shafts reaching up to the roof; and as people were apt to leave doors open, counterweights were to be fitted to close them automatically.

But like Leonardo's other inventions this was never actually built.

The Christians undermined hygiene, Reynolds complains. Sanitation was alien to their architecture, and the odor of sanctity was not always that of soap. He calls a chapter "The Ordure of Chivalry." The garderobes of the Tower of London, he says, were crude and too close to the banqueting hall. Latrines were so built as to permit of no ventilation. Even among the wealthy, the bottom layer of rushes on the floor "is undisturbed sometimes for twenty years, harbouring abominations not to be mentioned."

Harington provides testimony on this subject:

I found not only in mine own poor confused cottage, but even in the goodliest and stateliest pallaces of this realme . . . this same whorson sawcie stinke . . . great and well contrived houses . . . have vaults and secret passages . . . under ground, to convey away both the ordure and other noisome things . . . vents . . . drawing up the aire as a chimney doth smoke. By which it comes to passe manie times (specially if the wind stand at the mouth of the vaults) that what with fish-water coming from the kitchens, bloud and garbage of foul, washing of dishes, and the excrements of other houses joyned together, and all these in moyst weather stirred a little with some small streams of raine water. For as the proverbe is,

"Tis noted as the nature of a sinke,
Ever the more tis stird, the more to stink."

Before giving the details of his own invention, Sir John describes two earlier devices. First,

A close vault in the ground, widest in the bottome, and narrower upward, and to floor the same with hot lime and tarris [a rock used for mortar or cement] or some such dry paving as may keep out water and aire also . . .

He suggests that this device works so long as it is airless like a candle snuffer, hence unstirred; but "a crannie in the wall as big as a straw" spoils it. The second method is

either upon close or open vaults, so to place the sieges or seats as behind them rise tunnes [pipes, conduits, or chimney pots] of chimneys, to draw all the ill aires upwards . . .

This was the method used at Lincoln's Inn, and helped the neighborhood but not the privies themselves, especially when the wind was wrong.

Harington's water closet, which he diagrams and presents in full working detail, seems to have been duplicated, except for the one in his own "cottage," only at the Queen's palace at Richmond. It waited nearly two hundred years to be reinvented, and another century for general acceptance. That even the rich did not see the need for such a contrivance is shown by the practices that continued in the meantime.

By the early sixteenth century the "close stool" had begun to displace the garderobe, being, as Wright puts it, "cosier for the user but harder on the servants." Harington mentions an inventory item, "ffyve close stooles of black velvet quilted, with panns."

The enclosed chamber pot has generated a considerable literature, especially the practice that seems to have been universal at the time—what else was there to do?—of throwing its contents into the street at night through an upstairs window. Hogarth illustrates the procedure in his "Night," an engraving from the series *Four Times of the Day* (1738). Dryden, translating Juvenal, is evidently speaking of his own seventeenth-century London rather than of second-century Rome when he writes:

Return we to the dangers of the night;
And, first, behold our houses' dreadful height:
From whence come broken potsherds tumbling down;
And leaky ware, from garret windows thrown:
Well may they break our heads, and mark the
flinty stone.
'Tis want of sense to sup abroad too late;
Unless thou first hast settled thy estate.
As many fates attend thy steps to meet,
As there are waking windows in the street.
Bless the good gods, and think thy chance is rare
To have a pisspot only for thy share.

Bourke says there were no privies in Madrid in 1769, and the attempt by the king to introduce them, as well as sewers, "and to prohibit the throwing of human ordure out of windows after nightfall, as had been the custom, nearly precipitated a revolution." But in Paris there were royal ordinances as early as 1372 and again in 1395—doubtless inspired by the Black Death—against throwing ordure out of windows.

By 1738 we find Blondel, in France, speaking of *cabinets d'aisance à l'anglaise* or *lieux à soupape* (valve closets) as having originated in England; but they did not exist in London at the time. Wright mentions that at Windsor, Queen Anne had "a little place of Easement of marble with sluices of water to wash all down"; while a water closet reminiscent of Harington's is described in 1718 at Sir Francis Crew's house in Beddington in Surrey. But even after 1775, when Alexander Cummings took out a patent for a device with all the elements of a modern water closet, its acceptance came only slowly. One of the possible reasons is suggested by the drawing by Rowlandson, circa 1790, entitled "Work for the Plumber." It may have been harder to cope with bad plumbing than with none.

As late as 1858 "public conveniences" were still scarce and foul in London. Wright gives credit for winning the battle for better ones to George Jennings, about 1870; but the stranger abroad in an American city today may have legitimate grounds for complaint on this score. The modern flush toilet dates from about 1908, with improvements about 1935. But the outhouse and its Sears-Roebuck catalogue have not yet become obsolete.

There are reasons for believing that an accessory to the latrine has always been required by defecating human beings, although animals seem to get along quite well without it. The same accessory is less universally applied after urinating. Kira has words of glowing tribute for the bidet, which he thinks has acquired an evil reputation by association with an alleged sexual specialization. If not for this, he suggests, it might serve admirably toward his goal of total cleanness. In the absence of the bidet, we take for granted the use of paper. Men customarily limit its application to the anus. Kira recommends that they would do well to follow women in using it after urinating as well.

Means toward this end (indeed toward both ends) were not lacking before paper was available. The following passage is attributed by Bourke to Arminius Vambery (London, 1868):

> The manner of cleaning the body after an evacuation of any kind is defined by [Mohammedan] religious ritual. "The law commands 'Istinjah' (removal), 'Istinkah' (ablution), and 'Istibra' (drying)"—i.e., a small clod of earth is first used for the local cleansing, then water at least twice, and finally a piece of linen a yard in length. . . . In Turkey, Arabia, and Persia all are necessary, and pious men carry several clods of earth for the purpose in their turbans. "These acts of purification are also carried on quite publicly in the bazaars, from a desire to make a parade of their consistent piety." Vambery saw "a teacher give to his pupils, boys and girls, instruction in the handling of a clod of earth, and so forth, by way of experiment."

An earlier author, Tournefort (1718), is quoted as saying:

> Moslems urinate sitting down on the heels; for a spray of urine would make hair and clothes ceremonially impure. . . . After urinating, the Moslem wipes the os penis with one to three bits of stone, clay, or a handful of earth.

Mohammedans were evidently known also to drain the last drop of urine by touching the penis to a stone wall. Bourke mentions a practical joke played on them by Christians who put hot pepper on the wall. One assumes that the practice was looked upon as one of the pagan survivals which conscience required the Puritans "to tear up and destroy, root and branch."

Bourke cites Pinkerton (1814) as saying that, among the Chinese,

> it is usual for the princes, and even the people, to make water standing. Persons of dignity, as well as the vice-kings, and the principal officers, have gilded canes, a cubit long, which are bored through, and these they use as often as they make water, standing upright all the time; and by this means the tube carries the water to a good distance from them.

Bourke tells us that in Rome a bucket filled with salt water was placed in each public latrine, with a stick in it having a sponge tied to one end. With this instrument "the passer by cleansed his person, and then replaced the stick in the tub." Reynolds also speaks of this procedure and provides further details. After mentioning in passing *mempiria*, or balls of hay "which our medieval ancestors used [for] the final polish," he describes a medieval tool shaped like a hockey stick, and gives it as the source of the old phrase "to get hold of the wrong end of the stick." But in extenuation he emphasizes that "our horror of excrement . . . is really a very newfangled idea." He cites a story told by Sir Roger L'Estrange of King James I,

> that such was his absorption in this sport [hunting] that he would not leave the saddle even to relieve himself, so that his servants had a pretty mess to clean up at the day's end.

And since Sir Roger was an ardent royalist the story was not told to discredit the monarch.

Coming back to paper, Reynolds said of the wartime shortage:

> the day may soon come when we shall have to choose between a pound note and a petrol coupon, unless we go back to the Roman sponges or . . . mempiria.

He mentions an unnamed person who wrote to his enemy, "I have your letter before me, and it will soon be behind me"; and goes on to recommend a paper

> sufficiently thick but sufficiently pliable, glazed upon one side only and bearing, perhaps, some cheerful distich . . . to elevate the mind rather than to advertise the product or to proclaim each sheet to be the property of the Government or the Corporation of Margate.

As recently as 1962, when I was in London, I did indeed find the product in a public convenience marked, on every sheet, "Property of the British Empire." My good friend Dr. Max Pleasure, a dentist with a wit to match his name, now dead and much lamented, once wrote me from Israel, enclosing a sample of the local material, a very poor product indeed by lavish American standards, with the glaze on one side that Reynolds must accept as an irreducible minimum. Max had written on the glaze, his dental technology showing, "This side for polishing."

Nobody seems to have collected the international practices of today. Another old friend of mine could have done a good job of it if he had lived. Dr. Leon Buchbinder was an eminent bacteriologist and a longtime sufferer from ulcerative colitis. He became a collector of latrines, and in New York, and doubtless in many other places, he always knew the most direct path to a nearby one that met his standards. My own experience abroad is modest. At a *pension* on the Left Bank in Paris one private "bathroom" contained a bidet and a lavatory, and another provided a bathtub; the toilet was in the public hall, halfway between floors. In Moscow at the Hotel Ukraine the fixtures seemed to me somewhat overdone in splendor, especially the porcelain-and-nickel fittings over the tub for both regular and hand showers. Everything worked adequately but there was no shower curtain or other means of limiting the flood. By contrast the Hotel Malmen in Stockholm was elegant in its modernist simplicity; but a fixed glass panel in front of the shower restrained only a portion of the flood, and the toilet bowl dripped all night.

We think of our water-closet practices as universally, or at least as uniquely, civilized and correct. But customs vary surprisingly. Bourke tells us that Apache men in urinating always squat down, while women stand up; and similar reversals of our practice have been recorded in many other places. Montaigne mentions "people . . . where women piss standing, and men cowering." Dryden gives us these lines in his translation of Juvenal's sixth satire:

> Behold the strutting Amazonian whore!
> She stands in guard, with her right foot before;
> Her coat tucked up, and all her motions just,
> She stamps, and then cries, "Hah!" at every thrust.
> But laugh to see her, tired from many a bout,
> Call for the pot, and like a man piss out.

This posture seems to me strikingly similar to that shown widely today in women's magazines and elsewhere in advertisements for miniskirts.

Reynolds has compassion for male visitors in London accustomed to squatting and faced—or backed—in public conveniences with nothing but a vertical target.

Professor Miner's rule of sacred privacy is typically violated today in the lower ranks of the military and without duress by physicians. But at one time there was a grace in such matters that we have lost. It seems to have begun in Rome but came to be called "the French courtesy." Harington tells us of it:

> I have heard it serious told, that a great Magnifico of Venice, being ambassador in France, and hearing a Noble person was come to speak with him, made him stay till he had untyed his points; and when he was new set on his stoole, sent for the Noble man to come to him at that time; as a verie speciall favour.

GESTURE

In this, a now classic article, La Barre brings together a great many examples from the anthropological literature to show how much our basic motor behavior (expressions of affection, disgust, hostility, direction, and so on) is shaped by particular cultural models. Is there, for instance, a "natural" way to use the hands in indicating direction? Indeed, is it always the *hands* that are used in gestural indication of direction? As La Barre points out, in some human groups directional indication is given with the pursed lips and not with the hands. And further with the hands—the famous American anthropologist, Leslie Spier, once told of an experience he had in working among the Apache Indians. He had pinched his finger on a saddle girth and—as he had (culturally) learned to do—put it in his mouth to suck on it to relieve the pain—much to his Indian companion's astonishment. This was in no way a "natural" act. Or take the matter of applause to indicate approval—why don't we hiss, as some people do to convey the same meaning? But let La Barre continue with this overview of the many ways in which so much of what we have assumed to be basic "biological" behavior has a fundamental *cultural* dimension to it.

THE CULTURAL BASIS OF EMOTIONS AND GESTURES

WESTON LA BARRE

Psychologists have long concerned themselves with the physiological problems of emotion, as for example, whether the psychic state is prior to the physiological changes and causes them, or whether the conscious perception of the inner physiological changes in itself constitutes the "emotion." The physiologists also, notably Cannon, have described the various bodily concomitants of fear, pain, rage, and the like. Not much attention, however, has been directed toward another potential dimension of meaning in the field of emotions, that is to say the *cultural* dimension.

The anthropologist is wary of those who speak of an "instinctive" gesture on the part of a human being. One important reason is that a sensitivity to meanings which are culturally different from his own stereotypes may on occasion be crucial for the

anthropologist's own physical survival among at least some groups he studies, and he must at the very least be a student of this area of symbolism if he would avoid embarrassment.[1] He cannot safely rely upon his own culturally subjective understandings of emotional expression in his relations with persons of another tribe. The advisability and the value of a correct reading of any cultural symbolism whatsoever has alerted him to the possibility of culturally arbitrary, quasi-linguistic (that is, noninstinctual but learned and purely agreed-upon) meanings in the behavior he observes.

A rocking of the skull forward and backward upon its condyles, which rest on the atlas vertebra,

Reprinted with permission of publisher. From *Journal of Personality*, 16 (1947), 49–68.

[1]The notorious Massey murder in Hawaii arose from the fact that a native beach boy perhaps understandably mistook the Occidental "flirting" of a white woman for a *bona fide* sexual invitation. On the other hand, there are known cases which have ended in the death of American ethnographers who misread the cultural signs while in the field.

as an indication of affirmation and the rotation upon the axis vertebra for negation have so far been accepted as "natural" and "instinctive" gestures that one psychologist at least[2] has sought an explanation of the supposedly universal phenomenon in ascribing the motions of "yes" to the infant's seeking of the mother's breast, and "no" to its avoidance and refusal of the breast. This is ingenious, but it is arguing without one's host, since the phenomenon to be explained is by no means as widespread ethnologically, even among humans, as is mammalian behavior biologically.

Indeed, the Orient alone is rich in alternatives. Among the Ainu of northern Japan, for example, our particular head noddings are unknown:

the right hand is usually used in negation, passing from right to left and back in front of the chest; and both hands are gracefully brought up to the chest and gracefully waved downwards—palms upwards—in sign of affirmation.[3]

The Semang, pygmy Negroes of interior Malaya, thrust the head sharply forward for "yes" and cast the eyes down for "no."[4]

The Abyssinians say "no" by jerking the head to the right shoulder, and "yes" by throwing the head back and raising the eyebrows. The Dyaks of Borneo raise their eyebrows to mean "yes" and contract them slightly to mean "no." The Maori say "yes" by raising the head and chin; the Sicilians say "no" in exactly the same manner.[5]

A Bengali servant in Calcutta rocks his head rapidly in an arc from shoulder to shoulder, usually four times, in assent; in Delhi a Moslem boy throws his

head diagonally backward with a slight turning of the neck for the same purpose; and the Kandyan Singhalese bends the head diagonally forward toward the right, with an indescribably graceful turning in of the chin, often accompanying this with a cross-legged curtsey, arms partly crossed, palms upward—the whole performance extraordinarily beautiful and ingratiating. Indeed, did my own cultural difference not tell me it already, I would know that the Singhalese manner of receiving an object (with the right hand, the left palm supporting the right elbow) is not instinctive, for I have seen a Singhalese mother *teaching* her little boy to do this when I gave him a chunk of palm-tree sugar. I only regretted, later, that my own manners must have seemed boorish or subhuman, since I handed it to him with my right hand, instead of with both, as would any courteous Singhalese. Alas, if I had handed it to a little Moslem beggar in Sind or the Punjab with my *left* hand, he would probably have dashed the gift to the ground, spat, and called me by the name of an animal whose flesh he had been taught to dislike, but which I have not—for such use of the left hand would be insulting, since it is supposed to be confined to attending to personal functions, while the right hand is the only proper one for food.

Those persons with a passion for easy dominance, the professional dog-lovers, must often be exasperated at the stupidity of a dog which does not respond to so obvious a command as the pointed forefinger. The defense of man's best friend might be that this "instinctively" human gesture does not correspond to the kinaesthesias of a nonhanded animal. Nevertheless, even for an intelligent human baby, at the exact period when he is busily using the forefinger in exploring the world, "pointing" by an adult is an arbitrary, sublinguistic gesture which is not automatically understood and which must be *taught*. I am the less inclined to berate the obtuseness to the obvious of either dog or baby, because of an early field experience of my own. One day I asked a favorite informant of mine among the Kiowa, old Mary Buffalo, where something was in the *ramada* or willow-branch "shade" where we were working. It was clear she had heard me, for her eighty-eight-year-old ears were by no means deaf; but she kept on busying both hands with her work. I wondered at her rudeness and repeated the request several times, until finally with a puzzled exasperation which matched my own,

[2]E. B. Holt, *Animal drive and the learning process* (New York, 1931), p. 111, and personal conversations.
The idea is originally Darwin's, I believe (Charles Darwin, *The expression of the emotions in man and animals*, New York, 1873), but he himself pointed out that the lateral shake of the head is by no means universally the sign of negation. Holt has further noted the interesting point that in a surprising number of languages, quite unrelated to each other, the word for "mother" is a variant of the sound "ma." One can collect dozens of such instances, representing all the continents, which would seem to confirm his conjecture: the genuinely universal "sucking reflex" which brings the lips in approximation (m), plus the simplest of the simple open vowel sounds (a), are "recognized" by the mother as referring to her when the baby first pronounces them; hence they become the lexical designation of the maternal parent. Although this phenomenon becomes a linguistic one, it is only on some such physiological basis that one can explain the recurrence of the identical sound combinations in wholly unrelated languages referring to the same person, the mother. But there is no absolute semantic association involved: one baby boy I have observed used "mama" both to connote and to denote older persons of either sex.
[3]A. H. S. Landor, *Alone with the Hairy Ainu* (London, 1893), pp. 6, 233–234.
[4]W. W. Skeat and C. O. Blagden, *Pagan races of the Malay Peninsula* (London, 1906; 2 vols.).
[5]Otto Klineberg, *Race differences* (New York, 1935), p. 282.

she dropped her work and fetched it for me from in plain sight: she had been repeatedly pointing with her lips in approved American Indian fashion, as any Caucasian numbskull should have been able to see.

Some time afterward I asked a somewhat naïve question of a very great anthropologist, the late Edward Sapir: "Do other tribes cry and laugh as we do?" In appropriate response, Sapir himself laughed, but with an instant grasping of the point of the question: In which of these things are men alike everywhere, in which different? Where are the international boundaries between physiology and culture? What are the extremes of variability, and what are the scope and range of cultural differences in emotional and gestural expression? Probably one of the most learned linguists who have ever lived, Sapir was extremely sensitive to emotional and sublinguistic gesture—an area of deep illiteracy for most "Anglo-Saxon" Americans—and my present interest was founded on our conversation at that time.

Smiling, indeed, I have found may almost be mapped after the fashion of any other culture trait; and laughter is in some senses a geographic variable. On a map of the Southwest Pacific one could perhaps even draw lines between areas of "Papuan hilarity" and others where a Dobuan, Melanesian dourness reigned. In Africa, Gorer noted that

> laughter is used by the negro to express surprise, wonder, embarrassment and even discomfiture; it is not necessarily, or even often a sign of amusement; the significance given to "black laughter" is due to a mistake of supposing that similar symbols have identical meanings.[6]

Thus it is that even if the physiological behavior be present, its cultural and emotional functions may differ. Indeed, even within the same culture, the laughter of adolescent girls and the laughter of corporation presidents can be functionally different things; so too the laughter of an American Negro and that of the white he addresses.

The behaviorist Holt "physiologized" the smile as being ontogenetically the relaxation of the muscles of the face in a baby replete from nursing. Explanations of this order may well be the case, if the phenomenon of the smile is truly a physiological expression of generalized pleasure, which is caught up later in ever more complex conditioned reflexes. And yet, even in its basis here, I am not sure that

this is the whole story: for the "smile" of a child in its sleep is certainly in at least some cases the grimace of *pain* from colic, rather than the relaxation of pleasure. Other explanations such as that the smile is *phylogenetically* a snarl suffer from much the same *ad hoc* quality.

Klineberg writes:

> It is quite possible, however, that a smile or a laugh may have a different meaning for groups other than our own. Lafcadio Hearn has remarked that the Japanese smile is not necessarily a spontaneous expression of amusement, but a law of etiquette, elaborated and cultivated from early times. It is a silent language, often seemingly inexplicable to Europeans, and it may arouse violent anger in them as a consequence. The Japanese child is taught to smile as a social duty, just as he is taught to bow or prostrate himself; he must always show an appearance of happiness to avoid inflicting his sorrow upon his friends. The story is told of a woman servant who smilingly asked her mistress if she might go to her husband's funeral. Later she returned with his ashes in a vase and said, actually laughing, "Here is my husband." Her White mistress regarded her as a cynical creature; Hearn suggests that this may have been pure heroism.[7]

Many in fact of these motor habits in one culture are open to grave misunderstanding in another. The Copper Eskimo welcome strangers with a buffet on the head or shoulders with the fist, while the northwest Amazonians slap one another on the back in greeting. Polynesian men greet each other by embracing and rubbing each other's back; Spanish-American males greet one another by a stereotyped embrace, head over right shoulder of the partner, three pats on the back, head over reciprocal left shoulder, three more pats. In the Torres Straits islands "the old form of greeting was to bend slightly the fingers of the right hand, hook them with those of the person greeted, and then draw them away so as to scratch the palm of the hand; this is repeated several times."[8] The Ainu of Yezo have a peculiar greeting; on the occasion of a man meeting his sister, "The man held the woman's hands for a few seconds, then suddenly releasing his hold, grasped her by both ears and uttered the Aino cry. Then they stroked one another down the face and shoulders."[9] Kayan males

---

6Geoffrey Gorer, *Africa dances* (New York, 1935), p. 10.

7Lafcadio Hearn, The Japanese smile, in *Glimpses of unfamiliar Japan* (New York, 1894; 2 vols.), quoted in Klineberg, *op. cit.*
8*Report on the Cambridge expedition to the Torres Straits*, ed. A. C. Haddon (Cambridge, 1904; 5 vols.), IV, p. 306; Thomas Whiffen, *The North West Amazons* (London, 1905), p. 259.
9R. Hitchcock, The Ainos of Yezo, in *Papers on Japan*, pp. 464–465. See also Landor, *op. cit.*, pp. 6, 233–234.

in Borneo embrace or grasp each other by the fore-arm, while a host throws his arm over the shoulder of a guest and strokes him endearingly with the palm of his hand. When two Kurd males meet, "they grasp each other's right hand, which they simultaneously raise, and each kisses the hand of the other."[10] Among the Andaman Islanders of the Gulf of Bengal:

> When two friends or relatives meet who have been separated from each other for a few weeks or longer, they greet each other by sitting down, one on the lap of the other, with their arms around each other's necks, and weeping or wailing for two or three minutes till they are tired. Two brothers greet each other in this way, and so do father and son, mother and daughter, and husband and wife. When husband and wife meet, it is the man who sits in the lap of the woman. When two friends part from one another, one of them lifts up the hand of the other towards his mouth and gently blows on it.[11]

Some of these expressions of "joy" seem more lugu-brious than otherwise. One old voyager, John Turn-bull, writes as follows:

> The arrival of a ship brings them to the scene of action from far and near. Many of them meet at Matavai who have not seen each other for some length of time. The ceremony of these meetings is not without singularity; taking a shark's tooth, they strike it into their head and temples with great violence, so as to produce a copious bleeding; and this they will repeat, till they become clotted with blood and gore.

The honest mariner confesses to be nonplussed at this behavior.

> I cannot explain the origin of this custom, nor its analogy with what it is intended to express. It has no other meaning with them than to express the excess of their joy. By what construction it is considered symbolical of this emotion I do not understand.[12]

Quite possibly, then, the weeping of an American woman "because she is so happy" may merely indicate that the poverty of our gamut of physiological responses is such as to require using the same response for opposite meanings. Certainly weeping does obey social stereotypes in other cultures. Consider old Mary Buffalo at her brother's funeral: she wept in a frenzy, tore her hair, scratched her cheeks, and even tried to jump into the grave (being conveniently restrained from this by remoter relatives). I happened to know that she had not seen her brother for some time, and there was no particular love lost between them: she was merely carrying on the way a decent woman should among the Kiowa. Away from the grave, she was immediately chatting vivaciously about some other topic. Weeping is *used* differently among the Kiowa. Any stereotypes I may have had about the strong and silent American Indian, whose speech is limited to an infrequent "ugh" and whose stoicism to pain is limitless, were once rudely shattered in a public religious meeting. A great burly Wichita Indian who had come with me to a peyote meeting, after a word with the leader which I did not understand (it was probably permission to take his turn in a prayer) suddenly burst out blubbering with an abandon which no Occidental male adult would permit himself in public. In time I learned that this was a stereotyped approach to the supernatural powers, enthusiastic weeping to indicate that he was as powerless as a child, to invoke their pity, and to beseech their gift of medicine power. Everyone in the tipi understood this except me.

So much for the expression of emotion in one culture, which is open to serious misinterpretation in another: there is no "natural" language of emotional gesture. To return a moment to the earlier topic of emotional expression in greetings: West Africans in particular have developed highly the ritual gestures and language of greeting. What Gorer says of the Wolof would stand for many another tribe:

> The gestures and language of polite intercourse are stylized and graceful; a greeting is a formal litany of question and answer embracing everyone and everything connected with the two people meeting (the questions are merely formal and a dying person is stated to be in good health so as not to break the rhythm of the responses) and continuing for several minutes; women accompany it with a swaying movement of the body; with people to whom a special deference is due the formula is resumed several times during the conversation; saying goodbye is equally elaborate.[13]

---

[10]J. Perkins, Journal of a tour from Oroomish to Mosul, through the Koordish Mountains, and a visit to the ruins of Nineveh, *Journal of the American Oriental Society*, 1851, 2, 101; Charles Hose & William MacDougall, *The pagan tribes of Borneo* (London, 1912; 2 vols.), I, 124–125.

[11]A. R. Radcliffe-Brown, *The Andaman Islanders* (Cambridge, 1922), p. 117 and p. 74 n. 1.

[12]John Turnbull, *A voyage round the world* (London, 1813), pp. 301–302.

[13]Gorer, *op. cit.*, p. 38. Cf. Hollis, *The Masai, their language and folklore* (Oxford, 1905), pp. 284–287; E. Torday & T. A. Joyce, *Notes ethnographiques sur les peuples communément appelés Bakuba, ainsi que sur les peuplades apparentées, les Bushonga* (Brussels, 1910), pp. 233–234, 284, *et passim*. West Africans have developed the etiquette and protocol of greeting to a high degree, adjusting it to sex, age, relative rank, relationship degrees, and the like. Probably there is more than a trace of this ceremoniousness surviving in American Negro greetings in the South.

But here the sublinguistic gesture language has clearly emerged into pure formalisms of language which are quite plainly cultural.

The allegedly "instinctive" nature of such motor habits in personal relationships is difficult to maintain in the face of the fact that in many cases the same gesture means exactly opposite, or incommensurable things, in different cultures. Hissing in Japan is a polite deference to social superiors; the Basuto applaud by hissing, but in England hissing is rude and public disapprobation of an actor or a speaker. Spitting in very many parts of the world is a sign of utmost contempt; and yet among the Masai of Africa it is a sign of affection and benediction, while the spitting of an American Indian medicine man upon a patient is one of the kindly offices of the curer. Urination upon another (as in a famous case at the Sands Point, Long Island, country club, involving a congressman since assassinated) is a grave insult among Occidentals, but it is part of the transfer of power from an African medicine man in initiations and curing rituals. As for other opposite meanings, Western man stands up in the presence of a superior: the Fijians and the Tongans sit down. In some contexts we put on more clothes as a sign of respect; the Friendly Islanders take them off. The Toda of South India raise the open right hand to the face, with the thumb on the bridge of the nose, to express respect; a gesture almost identical among Europeans is an obscene expression of extreme disrespect. Placing to the tip of the nose the projecting knuckle of the right forefinger bent at the second joint was among the Maori of New Zealand a sign of friendship and often of protection;[14] but in eighteenth-century England the placing of the same forefinger to the right side of the nose expressed dubiousness about the intelligence and sanity of a speaker—much as does the twentieth-century clockwise motion of the forefinger above the right hemisphere of the head. The sticking out of the tongue among Europeans (often at the same time "making a face") is an insulting, almost obscene act of provocative challenge and mocking contempt for the adversary, so undignified as to be used only by children; so long as Maya writing remains undeciphered we do not know the meaning of the exposure of the tongue in some religious sculptures of the gods, but we can be sure it scarcely has the same significance as with us. In Bengali statues of the dread black mother goddess Kali, the tongue is protruded to signify great raging anger and shock; but the Chinese of the Sung dynasty protruded the tongue playfully to pretend to mock terror, as if to "make fun of" the ridiculous and unfeared anger of another person.[15] Modern Chinese, in South China at least, protrude the tongue for a moment and then retract it, to express embarrassment at a *faux pas*.

Kissing, as is well known, is in the Orient an act of private loveplay and arouses only disgust when indulged in publicly: in Japan it is necessary to censor out the major portion of love scenes in American-made movies for this reason. Correspondingly, some of the old *kagura* dances of the Japanese strike Occidentals as revoltingly overt obscenities, yet it is doubtful if they arouse this response in Japanese onlookers. Manchu kissing is purely a private sexual act, and though husband and wife or lovers might kiss each other, they would do it stealthily since it is shameful to do in public; yet Manchu mothers have the pattern of putting the penis of the baby boy into their mouths, a practice which probably shocks Westerners even more than kissing in public shocks the Manchu.[16] Tapuya men in South America kiss as a sign of peace, but men do not kiss women because the latter wear labrets or lip plugs. Nose-rubbing is Eskimo and Polynesian; and the Djuka Negroes of Surinam[17] show pleasure at a particularly interesting or amusing dance step by embracing the dancer and touching cheek to cheek, now on one side, now on the other—which is the identical attenuation of the "social kiss" between American women who do not wish to spoil each other's makeup.

In the language of gesture all over the world there are varying mixtures of the physiologically conditioned response and the purely cultural one, and it is frequently difficult to analyze out and segregate the two. The Chukchee of Siberia, for

[14]Klineberg, *op. cit.*, pp. 286–287, citing J. Lubbock, *Prehistoric times* (New York, 1872); E. Best, *The Maori* (Wellington [N. Z.], 1924; 2 vols.); R. H. Lowie, *Are we civilized?* (New York, 1929); and A. C. Hollis, *The Masai, their language and folklore* (Oxford, 1905), p. 315.

[15]*Chin P'ing Mei* (Shanghai, n. d.), Introduction by Arthur Waley. The sixteenth-century Chinese also had the expressions to act "with seven hands and eight feet" for awkwardness, and "to sweat two handfuls of anxiety."
[16]S. M. Shirokogoreff, *Social organization of the Manchus* (Extra Vol. III, North China Branch, Royal Asiatic Society, Shanghai, 1924), pp. 122–123.
[17]M. C. Kahn, Notes on the Saraimaccaner Bush Negroes of Dutch Guiana, *Amer. Anthrop.*, 1929, 31, 473.

example, have a phenomenal quickness to anger, which they express by showing the teeth and growling like an animal—yet man's snout has long ceased being functionally useful in offensive or defensive biting as it has phylogenetically and continuously retreated from effective prognathism. But this behavior reappears again and again: the Malayan pagans, for example, raise the lip over the canine tooth when sneering and jeering. Is this instinctual reflex or mere motor habit? The Tasmanians stamped rapidly on the ground to express surprise or pleasure; Occidentals beat the palms of the hands together for the same purpose ordinarily, but in some rowdier contexts this is accompanied by whistling and a similar stamping of the feet. Europeans "snort" with contempt; and the non-Mohammedan primitives of interior Malaya express disgust with a sudden expiration of the breath. In this particular instance, it is difficult to rid oneself of the notion that this is a consciously controlled act, to be sure, but nevertheless at least a "symbolic sneeze" based upon a purely physiological reflex which does rid the nostrils of irritating matter. The favorite gesture of contempt of the Menomini Indians of Wisconsin—raising the clenched fist palm down up to the level of the mouth, then bringing it swiftly downwards, throwing forth the thumb and first two fingers—would seem to be based on the same "instinctual" notion of rejection.

However, American Indian gestures soon pass over into the undisputedly linguistic area, as when two old men of different tribes who do not know a word of each other's spoken language, sit side by side and tell each other improper stories in the complex and highly articulate intertribal sign language of the Plains. These conventionalized gestures of the Plains sign language must of course be learned as a language is learned, for they are a kind of kinaesthetic ideograph, resembling written Chinese. The written Chinese may be "read" in the Japanese and the Korean and any number of mutually unintelligible spoken Chinese dialects; similarly, the sign language may be "read" in Comanche, in Cheyenne, or in Pawnee, all of which belong to different language families. The primitive Australian sign language was evidently of the conventionalized Plains type also, for it reproduced words, not mere letters (since of course they had no written language), but unfortunately little is known in detail of its mechanisms.

Like the writing of the Chinese, Occidental man has a number of ideographs, but they are sublinguistic and primarily *signs to action* or *expressions of action*. Thus, in the standard symbolism of cartoons, a "balloon" encircling print has signified *speaking* since at least the eighteenth century. Interestingly, in a Maya painting on a vase from Guatemala of pre-Columbian times, we have the same speech "balloons" enclosing ideographs representing what a chief and his vassal are saying, though what that is we do not know.[18] In Toltec frescoes speech is symbolized by foliated or noded crooks or scrolls, sometimes double, proceeding out of the mouths of human figures, although *what* is said is not indicated.[19] In the later Aztec codices written on wild fig-bark paper, speech is conventionalized by one or more little scrolls like miniature curled ostrich feathers coming out of the mouths of human beings, while motion or walking is indicated by footprints leading to where the person is now standing in the picture.[20] In American cartoons the same simple idea of footprints is also used. The ideograph of "sawing wood" indicates the action of *snoring* or *sleeping*. A light bulb with radial lines means that a "bright idea" has just occurred in the mind of the character above whose head it is written. While even children learn in time to understand these signs in context, no one would maintain that the electric-light "sign" could naturally be understood by an individual from another tribe than our own. Birds singing, a spiral, or a five-pointed star means unconsciousness or semiconsciousness through concussion. A dotted line, if curved, indicates the past trajectory of a moving object; if straight and from eye to object, the action of seeing. None of these visual aids to understanding are part of objective nature. Sweat drops symbolize surprise or dumfounding, although the physiology of this sign is thoroughly implausible. And]%!*/-#?°?[& very often says the unspeakable, quite as ? signifies query and ! surprise.

Many languages have *spoken* punctuation marks, which English grievously lacks. On the other hand, the speakers of English have a few *phonetic* "ideographs," at least two of which invite to action. An imitation of a kiss, loudly performed, summons a dog, if that dog understands this much of English. A bilateral clucking of the tongue adjures a horse

---

[18]George C. Vaillant, *The Aztecs of Mexico* (Garden City, N. Y., 1941), plate 7, top.
[19]*Ibid.*, plate 24.
[20]*Ibid.*, plates 42, 57, 61.

to "giddyap," i.e., to commence moving or to move more smartly; and in some parts of the country at least, it has a secondary semantic employment in summoning barnyard fowl to their feeding. The dental-alveolar repeated clicking of the tongue, on the other hand, is not a symbolic ideophone to action, but a *moral comment* upon action, a strongly critical disapprobation largely confined in use to elderly females preoccupied with such moral commentary. These symbolic ideophones are used in no other way in our language; but in African Bushman and Hottentot languages, of course, these three sounds plus two others phonetically classified as "clicks" (as opposed to sonants like b, d, g, z and surds like p, t, k, s, etc.) are regularly employed in words like any other consonants. It is nonsense to suppose that dogs, horses, or chickens are equipped for "instinctive" understanding or response to these human-made sounds, as much as that speakers of English have an instinctive understanding of Hottentot and Bushman. Certainly the sounds used in the Lake Titicaca plateau to handle llamas are entirely different.[21]

Sublinguistic "language" can take a number of related forms. Among the Neolithic population of the Canary Islands there was a curious auxiliary "language" of conventionalized whistles, signals which could be understood at greater distances than mere spoken speech. On four bugle tones, differently configured, we can similarly order soldiers to such various actions as arising, assembling, eating, lowering a flag, and burying the dead. The drum language of West Africa, however, is more strictly linguistic than bugle calls. Many West African languages are tonemic, that is, they have pitch-accent somewhat like Chinese or Navaho. Drum language, therefore, by reproducing not only the rhythm but also the tonal configurations of familiar phrases and sentences, is able to send messages of high semantic sophistication and complexity, as easily recognizable as our "Star-Spangled Banner" sung with rhythm and melody, but without words. The Kru send battle signals on multiple-pitched horns, but these are not conventional tunes like our bugle calls, but fully articulated

sentences and phrases whose tonemic patterns they reproduce on an instrument other than the human vocal cords. The Morse and International telegraph codes and Boy Scout and Navy flag communication (either with hand semaphores or with strings of variously shaped and colored flags) are of course mere auditory or visual alphabets, tied down except for very minor conventionalized abbreviations to the *spelling* of a given language. (The advantages of a phonetic script, however, are very evident when it comes to sending messages via a Morselike code for Chinese, which is written in ideographs which have different phonetic pronunciations in different dialects; Japanese has some advantage in this situation over Chinese in that its ideographs are already cumbrously paralleled in *katakana* and *hiragana* writing, which is quasiphonetic.) Deaf-and-dumb language, if it is the mere spelling of words, is similarly bound to an alphabet; but as it becomes highly conventionalized it approaches the international supralinguistic nature of the Plains Indian sign language. Of this order are the symbols of mathematics, the conventionalizations on maps for topography, the symbol language for expressing meteorological happenings on weather maps, and international flag signals for weather. Modern musical notation is similarly international: a supralinguistic system which orders in great detail what to do, and with what intensity, rhythm, tempo, timbre, and manner. Possibly the international nature of musical notation was influenced by the fact that medieval neume notation arose at a time when Latin was an international lingua franca, and also by the international nature of late feudal culture, rather than being an internationally-agreed-upon consensus of scientific symbolism. Based on the principles of musical notation, there have been several experimental attempts to construct an international system of dance notation, with signs to designate the position and motions of all parts of the body, with diacritical modifications to indicate tempo and the like. But while the motions of the classical ballet are highly stereotyped, they are semantically meaningless (unlike *natya* dancing in India and Ceylon, and Chinese and other Asiatic theatrics), so that this dance notation is mere *orders to action* like musical notation, with no other semantic content. Western dancing as an art form must appear insipid in its semantic emptiness to an Oriental who is used to articulate literary *meaning* in his dance forms. This is not to

---

[21]Weston La Barre, *The Aymara Indians of the Lake Titicaca Plateau*, Memoir 68, Amer. Anthrop. Assn. (Menasha, Wisconsin, 1947). All the tribes of the Provincia Oriental of Ecuador had the "cluck of satisfaction" (Alfred Simpson, *Travels in the wilds of Ecuador and exploration of the Putumayo River*, 1886, p. 94), which among the tribes of the Issa-Japura rivers is a "sign of assent and pleasure" (Whiffen, *op. cit.*, p. 249).

deny, however, that Occidental kinaesthetic language *may* be heavily imbued with great subtleties of meaning: the pantomime of the early Charlie Chaplin achieved at least a pan-European understanding and appreciation, while the implicit conventionalizations and stereotypes of Mickey Mouse (a psychiatrically most interesting figure!) are achieving currently an intercontinental recognition and enjoyment.

If all these various ways of *talking* be generously conceded to be purely cultural behavior, surely *walking*—although learned—is a purely physiological phenomenon since it is undeniably a panhuman trait which has brought about far-reaching functional and morphological changes in man as an animal. Perhaps it is, basically. And yet, there would seem to be clear evidence of cultural conditioning here. There is a distinct contrast in the gait of the Shans of Burma versus that of the hill people: the Kachins and the Palaungs keep time to each step by swinging the arms from side to side in front of the body in semicircular movements, but the Shans swing their arms in a straight line and do not bring the arms in front of the body. Experts among the American missionaries can detect the Shan from the Palaung and the Kachin, even though they are dressed in the same kinds of garment, purely from observing their respective gaits, and as surely as the character in a Mark Twain story detected a boy in girl's clothes by throwing a rat-chunker in his lap (the boy closed his legs, whereas a girl would spread her skirt). If an American Indian and an adult American male stride with discernible mechanical differences which may be imputed to the kinds of shoes worn and the varying hardness of the ground in woods or city, the argument will not convince those who know— but would find it hard to describe—that the Singhalese and the Chinese simply and unquestionably just do walk differently, even when both are barefooted. Amazonian tribes show marked sexual contrasts in their styles of walking: men place one foot directly in front of the other, toes straight forward, while women walk in a rather stilted, pigeon-toed fashion, the toes turned inward at an angle of some thirty degrees: it is regarded as a sign of power if the muscles of the thighs are made to come in contact with each other in walking. To pick a more familiar example, it is probable that a great many persons would agree with Sapir's contention that there does exist a peculiarly East European Jewish gait—a kind of kyphotic Ashkenazim shuffle or trudge—which is lost by the very first generation brought up in this country, and which, moreover, may not be observed in the Sephardic Jews of the Iberian Peninsula. Similar evidence comes from a recent news article: "Vienna boasts that it has civilized the Russians . . . has taught them how to walk like Europeans (some Russians from the steppes had a curious gait, left arm and left foot swinging forward at the same time)."[22] The last parenthesis plays havoc with behavioristic notions concerning allegedly quadrupedal engrams behind our "normal" way of walking!

It is very clear that the would-be "natural" and "instinctive" gestures of actors change both culturally and historically. The back-of-the-hand-to-the-forehead and sideways-stagger of the early silent films to express intense emotion is expressed nowadays, for example, by making the already expressionless compulsive sullen mask of the actress one shade still more flat: the former technique of exaggerated pantomime is no doubt related to the limitations of the silent film, the latter to the fact that even a raised eyebrow may travel six feet in the modern close-up. The "deathless acting" of the immortal Bernhardt, witnessed now in ancient movies, is scarcely more dated than the middle-Garbo style, and hardly more artificially stylized than Hepburn's or Crawford's. Indeed, for whatever reason, Bernhardt herself is reported to have fainted upon viewing her own acting in an early movie of *Camille*.[23] There are undoubtedly both fashions and individual styles in acting, just as there are in painting and in music composition and performance, and all are surely far removed from the instinctual gesture. The fact that each contemporary audience can receive the communication of the actor's gestures is a false argument concerning the "naturalness" of that gesture: behavior of the order of the "linguistic" (communication in terms of culturally agreed-upon arbitrary symbols) goes far beyond the purely verbal and the spoken.

That this is true can be decisively proved by a

---

[22]Paula Hoffman, Twilight in the Heldenplatz, *Time*, June 9, 1947, 49:23, 31. A related kind of motor habit—which is of course conscious—was that of the Plains Indian men who wore the buffalo robe "gathered . . . about the person in a way that emphasized their action or the expression of emotion" (*Handbook of American Indians north of Mexico*, Bulletin 30, Bureau Amer. Ethnol., Washington, D. C., 1907–1910; 2 vols.). For the Amazonians, see Whiffen, *op. cit.*, p. 271.
[23]Maurice Bardèche and Robert Brasillach, *The history of motion pictures* (New York, 1938), p. 130.

glance at Oriental theatrics. Chinese acting is full of stylized gestures which "mean" to the audience that the actor is stepping over the threshold into a house, mounting a horse, or the like; and these conventionalizations are just as stereotyped as the colors of the acting masks which indicate the formalized personalities of the stock characters, villains or heroes or supernaturals. In Tamil movies made in South India, the audience is quickly informed as to who is the villain and who the hero by the fact that the former wears Europeanized clothing, whereas the latter wears the native *dhoti*. But this is elementary: for the intricate *natya* dancing of India, the postural dance dramas of Bali, and the sacred *hula* of Polynesia are all telling articulated stories in detailed gestural language. That one is himself illiterate in this language, while even the child or the ignorant countryman sitting beside one on the ground has an avid and understanding enjoyment of the tableau, leaves no doubt in the mind that this *is* a gestural language and that there *are* sublinguistic kinaesthetic symbolisms of an arbitrary but learnable kind.

Hindu movies are extraordinarily difficult for the Occidental man to follow and to comprehend, not only because he must be fortified with much reading and knowledge to recognize mythological themes and such stereotypes as the *deus-ex-machina* appearance of Hanuman the monkey-god, but also because Americans are characteristically illiterate in the area of gesture language. The kinaesthetic "business" of even accomplished and imaginative stage actors like Sir Laurence Olivier and Ethel Barrymore is limited by the rudimentary comprehension of their audiences. Americans watch enthusiastically the muscular skills of an athlete in *doing* something, but they display a proud muckerism toward the dance as an art form which attempts to *mean* something. There are exceptions to this illiteracy, of course, notably among some psychiatrists and some ethnologists. Dr. H. S. Sullivan, for example, is known to many for his acute understanding of the postural tonuses of his patients. Another psychiatrist, Dr. E. J. Kempf, evidences in the copious illustrations of his "Psychopathology" a highly cultivated sense of the kinaesthetic language of tonuses in painting and sculpture, and can undoubtedly discover a great deal about a patient merely by glancing at him. The linguist, Dr. Stanley Newman, has a preternatural skill in recognizing psychiatric syndromes through the in-

dividual styles of tempo, stress, and intonation.[24] The gifted cartoonist, Mr. William Steig, has produced, in *The Lonely Ones*, highly sophisticated and authentic drawings of the postures and tonuses of schizophrenia, depression, mania, paranoia, hysteria, and in fact the whole gamut of psychiatric syndromes. Among anthropologists, Dr. W. H. Sheldon is peculiarly sensitive and alert to the emotional and temperamental significance of constitutional tonuses.[25] I believe that it is by no means entirely an illusion that an experienced teacher can come into a classroom of new students and predict with some accuracy the probable quality of individual scholastic accomplishment—even as judged by other professors—by distinguishing the unreachable, unteachable *Apperceptions masse*-less sprawl of one student, from the edge-of-the-seat starved avidity and intentness of another. Likewise, an experienced lecturer can become acutely aware of the body language of his listeners and respond to it appropriately until the room fairly dances with communication and counter-communication, head-noddings, and the tenseness of listeners soon to be prodded into public speech.

The "body language" of speakers in face-to-face conversation may often be seen to subserve the purposes of outright linguistic communication. The peoples of Mediterranean origin have developed this to a high degree. In Argentina,[26] for example, the gesture language of the hands is called "ademanes" or "with the hands." Often the signs are in

[24]Stanley S. Newman, Personal symbolism in language patterns, *Psychiatry*, 1939, 2, 177–184; Cultural and psychological features in English intonation, *Trans. N. Y. Acad. Sci.*, 1944, ser. II, 7, 45–54; (with Vera G. Mather), Analysis of spoken language of patients with affective disorders, *Amer. J. Psychiat.*, 1938, 94, 913–942; Further experiments in phonetic symbolism, *Amer. J. Psychol.*, 1933, 45, 53–57; Behavior patterns in linguistic structure, a case history, in *Language, culture and personality, Essays in honor of Edward Sapir* (Menasha, Wis., 1931), pp. 94–106. The Witoto and Bororo have a curious motor habit: "When an Indian talks he sits down—no conversation is ever carried on when the speakers are standing unless it is a serious difference of opinion under discussion; nor, when he speaks, does the Indian look at the person addressed, any more than the latter watches the speaker. Both look at some outside objects. This is the attitude also of the Indian when addressing more than one listener, so that he appears to be talking to some one not visibly present." A story-teller turns his back on the listener and talks to the wall of the hut (Whiffen, *op. cit.*, p. 254).

[25]W. H. Sheldon, *The varieties of temperament* (New York & London, 1942). The argument of one variety of athletosome or somatotonic scientist that Sheldon is unable or unconcerned to muscle his findings into manageable, manipulable statistical forms wherewith to bludgeon and compel the belief of the unperceiving, is of course peculiarly irrelevant. The psychiatrist soaked in clinical experience is similarly helpless in his didactic relations with a public which either has not, or cannot, or will not see what he has repeatedly observed clinically.

[26]Arthur Daniels, Hand-made repartee, New York *Times*, October 5, 1941.

no need of language accompaniment: "What a crowd!" is stated by forming the fingers into a tight cluster and shaking them before you at eye level; "Do you take me for a sucker?" is asked by touching just beneath the eye with a finger, accompanying this with appropriate facial expressions of jeering or reproach as the case might be; and "I haven't the faintest idea" is indicated by stroking beneath the chin with the back of the palm. One Argentine gentleman, reflecting the common notion that *ademanes* have the same vulgarity and undignified nature as slang—appropriate only for youngsters or lower-class folk—nevertheless, within five minutes of this statement, had himself twirled an imaginary moustache ("How swell!") and stroked one hand over the other, nodding his head wisely ("Ah ha! there's hanky-panky going on there somewhere!"). Argentine gesture-language is nearly as automatic and unconscious as spoken language itself, for when one attempts to collect a "vocabulary" of *ademanes*, the Argentine has to stop and think of situations first which recall the *ademanes* that "naturally" follow. The naturalness of at least one of these might be disputed by Americans, for the American hand-gesture meaning "go away" (palm out and vertical), elbow somewhat bent, arm extended vigorously as the palm is bent to a face-downward horizontal position, somewhat as a base-ball is thrown and in a manner which could be rationalized as a threatened or symbolic blow or projectile-hurling) is the same which in Buenos Aires would serve to summon half the waiters in a restaurant, since it means exactly the opposite, "Come here!" When the Argentines use the word "mañana" in the familiar sense of the distant and improbable future, they accompany the word by moving the hand forward, palm down, and extending the fingers lackadaisically—a motion which is kinaesthetically and semantically related perhaps to the Argentine "come here!" since this symbolically *brings*, while "mañana" *pushes off*. Kissing the bunched fingertips, raising them from the mouth and turning the head with rolled or closed eyes, means "Wonderful! Magnificent!," basically per-haps as a comment or allusion to a lady, but in many remotely derived senses as well. "Wonder-ful!" may also be expressed by shaking one of the hands smartly so that the fingers make an audible clacking sound, similar to the snapping of the fingers, but much louder. But this gesture may signify pain as well as enjoyment, for if one steps

on an Argentine's toes, he may shake his fingers as well as saying "Ai yai!" for "ouch!" The same gesture, furthermore, can be one of impatience, "Get a move on!" Were one to define this gesture semantically, then, in a lexicon of *ademanes*, it would have to be classified as a nondescript inten-sificative adverb whose predication is indicated by the context. In fast repartee an Argentine, even though he may not be able to get a word in edge-wise, can make caustic and devastating critiques of the speaker and his opinions, solely through the subtle, timed use of *ademanes*.

A study of conventional gesture languages (in-cluding even those obscene ones of the *mano cor-nuta*, the thumbed nose, the *mano fica*, the thumb-nail snapped out from the point of the canine tooth, and so forth,[27] as well as those more articulated ones of the Oriental dance dramas), a study of the body language of constitutional types (the uncor-ticated, spinal-reflex spontaneity and *legato* feline quality of the musclebound athletosome, his body knit into rubbery bouncing tonuses even in repose; the collapsed colloid quality of the epicurean vis-cerotonic whose tensest tonus is at best no more than that of the chorion holding the yolk advan-tageously centered in the albumen of an egg, or the muscle habituated into a tendon supporting a flitch of bacon; and the multiple-vectored, tangled-string-iness of the complex "high-strung" cerebrotonic, whose conceptual alternatives and nuances of con-trol are so intricately involved in his cortex as to inhibit action), and the study of psychiatric types (the Egyptian-statue grandeur and hauteur of the paranoiac's pose; the catatonic who offers his motor control to the outsider because he has withdrawn his own executive ego into an inner, autistic cere-bral world and has left no one at the switch-

---

[27]The only place I have seen this discussed recently is in an article by Sandor Feldman, The blessing of the Kohenites, *American Imago*, 1941, 2, 315–318. In the same periodical is an exquisitely sensitive interpretation of one person's interpretation of the signs of the zodiac in terms of positions and tonuses of the human body (Doris Webster, The origin of the signs of the zodiac, *ibid.*, 1940, 1, 31–47). Other papers, of the few which could be cited with relevance to the present problem, would include: Macdonald Critchley, *The language of gesture* (New York, 1939); G. W. Allport and P. E. Vernon, *Studies in expressive movement* (New York, 1933); F. C. Hayes, Should we have a dictionary of gestures? *Southern Folk-Lore Quarterly*, 1940, 4, 239–245; Felix Deutsch, Analysis of postural behavior, *Psychoanal. Quart.*, 1947, 16, 195–213; Paul Schilder, *The image and appearance of the human body*, Psyche Monographs (London, 1935); Th. Pear, Suggested parallels between speaking and clothing, *Acta Psychol.*, Hague, 1935, 1, 191–201; J. C. Flugel, On the mental attitude to present-day clothing, *Brit. J. med. Psychol.*, 1929, 9, 97; La Meri, *Gesture language of the Hindu dance* (New York, c. 1940); Rudolf von Laban, *Laban's dance notations* (New York, c. 1928).

board; the impermanent, varying, puppet-on-a-string, spastic tonuses of the compulsive neurotic which picture myotonically his ambivalence, his rigidities, and his perfectionism; the broken-lute despair of the depressive; and the distractable, *staccato*, canine, benzedrine-muscledness of the manic)—all might offer us new insights into psychology, psychiatry, ethnology and linguistics alike.

DRESS

And what about clothing and adornment—are these common features of human life subject to the dictation of other than biologically-programmed patterns? Considerably, and in the following excerpt Hoebel illustrates how variously the human body is draped, shaped, covered, uncovered, painted, pinched, shaved, trimmed, cut, punctured, stretched, and what not, in order to conform to current and customary social expectation. Hoebel's reference to the widespread practice of hair straightening and kink-removing among American Negroes is, of course, dated comment, from a time preceding the current popularity of "natural" or "Afro" hair styles among American blacks. Similarly, given the time of the book's publication, he does not comment upon the "hippy" style of dress and personal adornment among youth and its symbolic meaning, its intended "signal" status in conveying to the viewer a message commenting on perceived social reality (such as the "Establishment"). But even that omission, in a passage written only a relatively few years ago, can be taken to illustrate another point: how much such activity as draping the body with textiles can get swept up into another domain in human behavior, that of meaning and symbolic function—in short, the problem of the relation of clothing to its social and cultural context.

CLOTHING AND ORNAMENT

E. ADAMSON HOEBEL

Man is a rebel against nature. He is prone to accept few things as they come. In all matters it is his irrepressible belief that by his tinkering he can improve upon them. His instrument is culture.

In all times and climes, man undertakes to effect what he vainly believes are improvements upon his bodily appearance. His sartorial accomplishments, both primitive and civilized, are wonderful if not always beautiful to behold. The time and effort that has gone into painting, pricking, scarring, puncturing, and otherwise mutilating and deforming the

human body for aesthetic and status reasons is beyond all calculation. We shall leave it to sociologists and economists to conjure up their guesses as to how many billion dollars are spent per year on clothes and cosmetics in this most advanced of civilizations. Suffice it that in the critical year of 1947 one of the burning American issues was whether the American woman would or would not take on a "new look." As if there could have been any doubt about it!

The Naked Savage. People who wear little or no clothing are no contradiction to what has just been said. Be man ever so unclothed, he is never unadorned. If he wears not so much as a G-string, he

Reprinted with permission of publisher. From E. Adamson Hoebel, *Man in the Primitive World: An Introduction to Anthropology* (New York: McGraw-Hill Book Co., Inc., 1949), pp. 150–60.

certainly sports a nose, ear, or lip plug, or bears his tattoos or scarifications, or paints his face, or curls his hair or cuts it off, or blackens his teeth, or knocks them out, or perhaps merely files them to a point.

The sense of modesty is merely a habit, no instinct. The discomfiture that is felt when one's sense of modesty is disturbed is a diffused neurophysiological upset of a large part of the nervous and organic system, shock-stimulated by a behavior situation that contrasts sharply with those to which a person has been intensely habituated. And of course, there is more than the element of mere habit in the total situation. There has also been a strong ideational indoctrination that penalties, social or supernatural, accompany any departure from the habituated pattern. Apprehension of dire consequences contributes much of the tone of fear and anxiety that colors the feelings of immodesty.

To this day, old-timers among Comanche males feel acutely uncomfortable and indecent if they thoughtlessly go out without a G-string, even though fully clothed in American store pants and shirt.

A favored tale among anthropologists is that of Baron von Nordenskiold, who in his Amazonian travels undertook to purchase the facial plugs of a Botocudo[1] woman, who stood all unabashed in customary nudity before him. Only irresistible offers of trade goods at long last tempted her to remove and hand over her labrets. When thus stripped of her proper raiment, she fled in shame and confusion into the jungle. After all, the close identification between the Botocudo as a person and the *botocudo* as a plug is such that to become unplugged is most un-Botocudo.

Such circumstances make it perfectly clear that the use of clothing does not rise out of any innate sense of modesty, but that modesty results from customary habits of clothing or ornamentation of the body and its parts.

Among primitive peoples the use or nonuse of clothing is more or less functional, although not wholly so. People who dwell in the tropical rain forests tend to get along with a minimum of cloth-ing. This is true in Africa, the Americas, and Oceania. Generally, however, the men wear some sort of a pubic covering, a suspensory or supporter. It is hardly necessary to seek magical reasons for the widespread use of this device, as was done by the early anthropologist Waitz,[2] and after him by Sumner.[3] It is a practical device that lends physical comfort. Notions of mystic shielding of the male sex organ from evil influences, if they exist, are more likely to be secondary developments. Certainly, the conspicuous coverings of gleaming shells, gourds, bark, hide, cloth, or grass do not serve to divert attention but rather to attract it.

An alternative to the rigid sheath is a small apron of leather, grass, or cloth worn in front, or fore and aft, or between the legs and about the waist. Such a garment is frequently worn by women as well as men. It is the basic, and often the only, bit of clothing for most primitive peoples.

When warmth is needed, something more must be added. Most races of mankind are so relatively hairless as to need artificial insulation. Hence, we rob the animals of their hairy covering—skin and all. The trapper flays the beast and prepares the hide, the tailor shapes it, and the lady of fashion slips the skins of animals over her own when she makes her winter excursions. Wool coverings are also produced at the expense of animals, but not necessarily by lethal methods.

Shoshoneans weave rabbitskin robes, as did the early prehistoric Basket Makers. African Bushmen provide themselves with skin cloaks. The Yahgan of Tierra del Fuego wore a small sealskin, sea-otter, or fox cape as the sole protection against a nasty subantarctic climate—except for a small pubic covering worn by women. The Ona of the same area and the nearby Tehuelche . . . sported longer and larger capes. The Tasmanians wore no proper cloak, but the men were given to draping and tying sundry strips of fur around their shoulders and limbs. For the most part, the Tasmanians smeared themselves with grease and red ochre as proof against cold, as did also the Fuegians. The Central Australians, like the Tasmanians, deviate from the norm of collectors and gatherers who live in the temperate zone in that they have no cloaks. They seem never to have hit upon the idea of wearing skin for clothing. For the men a conspicuous pubic

---

[1]"The *Botocudo* owe their name to the large cylindrical wooden plugs worn by men and women alike in the ear lobes and lower lips. These cylinders, of light wood (*Chorisia ventricosa*), were 3 to 4 inches (7.6 to 10 cm.) in diameter and 1 inch (2.5 cm.) thick. The ears were perforated at the age of 7 or 8, the lips a few years later." A. Metraux, "The Botocudo," in *Handbook of the Indians of South America*, Vol. 1, p. 534.

[2]F. T. Waitz, *Anthropologie der Naturvölker*, Vol. 6, pp. 575–576.
[3]W. G. Sumner, *Folkways*, pp. 432, 456.

tassel suspended from a belt of human hair plus arm bands of twisted fur suffice. A woman is dressed if she has a string of beads around her neck.

When we turn our attention once again to South America, we find that the fur mantle is worn by Patagonians and Indians of the Gran Chaco in inclement weather. The famous woven wool ponchos of the Andean Indians are undoubtedly a cultural elaboration of this more primitive covering.

In North America, the buffalo-hide robe of the Plains Indians was also a form of cape, a large one, later to be replaced by the trader's blanket, which is to this day the symbol of the conservative Indian, the "blanket Indian," who clings to the old ways. Even in rugged Northeastern Woodlands the draped robe was the chief item of winter clothing, besides leggings and moccasins. In the Southeastern states the natives went naked except for a loin cloth. When cold did sweep down from the north, they, too, cast on a loose robe or cape of fur.

The Tailored Man. Tailoring, it may be seen from our remarks, was not one of the more widely esteemed human arts. Most of mankind, including such sophisticates as the Greeks and Romans and the late Mahatma Gandhi, have done quite well without it. The feature that is unique about tailoring is that by means of sewing, clothing may be made more or less to fit the human frame. The very idea of tailoring is "fit," and "well-tailored" means more fit rather than less. In temperate and arctic climates it is functionally advantageous to have tailored clothes. The insulating efficiency of clothing is greatly enhanced by the closed, tubular effect of the tailored garment, which gives little room for the play of chilly breezes upon the body. In the tropical rain forest or torrid desert the very advantages of tailored clothing become its disadvantages.

Two factors, therefore, have combined to limit the pre-Columbian distribution of tailored clothing to Europe, northern Asia, and the northern half of North America: (1) selective adjustment to climatic factors; and (2) the fact that tailoring is an advanced technique, which the lowly Fuegians, who certainly could have used warm garments,[4] were incapable of inventing for themselves.

That cultural improvements are not *ipso facto*

beneficial is incidentally demonstrated in the debilitating effect of the introduction of European clothing among the Yahgan, of whom Cooper writes:

> The clothing of the Yahgan seems to us utterly inadequate, given the climatic conditions—temperatures commonly around and well below freezing point in winter, high winds, frequent snow, hail, sleet, and cold rain—but in view of the seeming role played in their decline by introduced European clothing and their relative good health prior thereto, perhaps their clothing was reasonably well-adapted to the environment.

In this case, we would observe that it is not so much that their clothing was reasonably well adapted (which it was not) as that they were physiologically reasonably well adapted to a *specific* environmental situation. The adjustment was more biological than cultural. The introduction of tailored European clothing was a cultural modification that so altered the total environment of the Yahgans as to disturb disastrously the biological balance between them and their physical world. Inexorable extinction apparently stalks them.

This, of course, has been a common consequence of culture contact when very primitive peoples find their environment drastically unsettled by incursive elements emanating from a suddenly presented, unlike, and higher culture.

To return to the problem of the distribution of tailored clothing, it originally was made among the arctic and subarctic peoples of Siberia and North America and the ancient Chinese. The distribution in North America, as Wissler pointed out,[5] was coterminous with the distribution of caribou; in Asia the association was coterminous with the reindeer. Although the Northwest Coast Indians could easily have adopted the tailoring technique (they did sew boxes together), they did not do so. The northern bison hunters of the Plains did, however, make loosely tailored shirts and dresses of the modified poncho type.

Real tailoring is done by the Eskimos and Indians of the Canadian woods. Coats are fitted with genuine sleeves and necks. Eskimo garments with the fur turned in and the outer skin dyed and decorated are not only functional but aesthetic.

The diffusion of tailoring in prehistoric times raises several unsolved problems. Did it spread

---

[4]J. M. Cooper, "The Yahgan" in *Handbook of South American Indians*, Vol. 1, p. 87.

[5]C. Wissler, *The American Indian*, p. 62.

from the ancient civilization of China to the Siberian barbarians, thence east and west? Or did the primitive skin workers of north Asia develop it, whence it came to the Chinese?

The westward diffusion into Europe proper did not occur until a number of centuries after the conquests of Caesar. And finally, since the bursting of the confines of Europe in modern times, when tailored clothing became the symbol of the European conqueror, human creatures in all parts of the world have now enclosed their bodies in suits and dresses. The lovely tapa sarong of the Polynesian has given way to the missionary's Mother Hubbard. But lo, our parents having "civilized" the Polynesian out of the sarong, we moderns have taken its charms for our own.

Shoes and Hats. A properly dressed American woman never goes to church or afternoon tea without shoes and hat. The upper and nether extremities must be covered. Shoes and hats, like tailored clothing, may be functional—or mere status symbols.

Among primitives footgear is more common than headgear. The status functions of headgear can be served readily enough by hairdos. The protective functions of hats are also notably less important than the protective function of shoes.

Here again, the physical environment is an important factor in influencing the adoption or non-adoption of an element of material culture.

The problem of fabricating a foot covering that will stand up under the wet rot of the tropical jungle is practically insoluble. Even our best efforts with all the resources of science were not very satisfactory in the South Pacific campaigns of the Second World War. Jungle primitives prefer to go barefoot. An unshod foot dries more quickly and comfortably than one encased in a soaking and muddy moccasin. For this reason the highly sophisticated Indians of the Northwest Coast rain forest went barefoot, even in southern Alaska.

The simplest footgear is a piece of hide folded about the foot. When tailored, it becomes a moccasin of the type made famous by North American Indians. Further development of this form produces the boot. The so-called "Arctic boot" is an adjunct of true tailoring. This is not at all surprising, since anyone skilled enough in cutting and sewing to make a boot is *ipso facto* skilled enough to tailor clothing, and vice versa. Further, the same climatic circumstances that lend to tailored clothes their functional value act likewise with respect to boots.

People who have to plod around in snow and cold find high tops more comfortable. Who enjoys walking through snowdrifts in oxfords? However, we have learned in anthropology not to expect that necessity necessarily mothers invention. The Indians of the North American boreal forests (the Canadian woodlands), who make tailored clothing and are confronted with heavy snows, make moccasins instead of boots, in spite of the fact that the more northerly of these Indians have contact with boot-wearing Eskimos. The boot of the Eskimos, worn from Greenland to Alaska, was undoubtedly borrowed from the Siberian herders and hunters. It is quite definitely an Asiatic trait.

The high, thigh-length, Cavalier-style riding boot of the Tehuelche Indians of the Patagonia pampas (whence comes its name, "the Patagonian boot") is apparently a post-Columbian adoption. The early, horseless "foot Tehuelche" wore a kind of moccasin stuffed with straw.[6] Because of its association with the horse, a post-Columbian acquisition, the Patagonian boot is hardly to be considered an independent primitive invention. But it is interesting to note that similar boots were not adopted in the Amazon, where the natives still prefer to go barefoot, or in the Andean region where the prehistoric sandal holds sway.

The sandal is the other type of primitive footgear that finds great favor. In its simplest form it is a piece of leather roughly fitted to the sole and held firm by thongs passing over the foot.

Basketry-type sandals with woven fiber soles were very popular with prehistoric Southwestern Basket-Maker Indians. Wissler noted that "in eastern North America moccasins were discarded when walking in the rain, in wet grass, or upon moist ground."[7] This was also true of the Incas with their rawhide-soled sandals, which would go soft and feel squishy when wet, then become hard and out of shape when dried. Wissler cites a correlation between the sandal and textile clothing in both the Old World and the New.[8] This correlation is most probably an indirect one. It is not that weaving gives rise to the use of sandals, but rather that each is an aspect of sedentary life; ergo, of higher primitive culture as such.

The Hairdo. Concern with the coiffure is one of

---

[6] J. M. Cooper, "The Patagonian and Pampean Hunters" in *Handbook of South American Indians*, Vol. 1, p. 144.
[7] Wissler, *op. cit.*, p. 65.
[8] *Ibid.*, p. 64.

the most intense interests of mankind. We know not when the earliest prehistoric men and women first began to play with the cranial hair. Archaeological evidence from the Upper Paleolithic in Europe decisively demonstrates that Cro-Magnon man and his contemporaries laid great emphasis upon the female hairdo. In the Aurignacian statuette of the Venus of Willendorf . . . no facial features were carved by the artist. To him there was no interest in a pretty face. But the pattern of the hair style is meticulously incised.

This trait of the Venus of Willendorf in the Aurignacian epoch, 30,000 to 40,000 years ago, were not a mere accident but a strong feature of the culture, for a similar degree of care was lavished upon the hair pattern of the female head from the *Grotte du Pape* at Brassempouy.

All recent primitives, from those of the lowest cultures to the highest, treat the hair. Add to this the fact that all civilized people do likewise, and we see that here is another universal trait in human culture.

The trimming and arrangement of the hair is not merely a matter of decoration and ornamentation; in culture after culture, it serves to symbolize social position. The most basic status represented in the treatment of the hair is that of sex. Males and females within any given society almost without exception have different ways of fixing the hair. With us the symbolism is so strong that short-haired women are considered mannish and long-haired men effeminate.

Less universally, hair styles are used to indicate age status. Omaha Indian boys had their heads shaved close, with isolated tufts of hair left here and there. Men wore either their full head of hair lying loose, or they shaved it off, except for a continuous roach along the sagittal line. Likewise, it used to be that young girls in our society wore their hair down, until after adolescence they were privileged to put it up. Today rigid custom is weakened, but the flavor of the symbolism remains. Matrons strive for "that girlish look" by wearing their hair in a long bob, while teen-agers put on sophisticated airs with the upsweep. It is all very confusing to the bewildered male, who is the intended victim of these tactical subterfuges.

Among the Omahas the shaved head of the boys indicated more than just age status, for the patterns of the remaining tufts were different for the boys of each clan. "The cutting of the hair was done, it was said, in order to impress on the mind of a child, as in an object lesson, the gentes [patrilineal clan] to which a playmate belonged."[9] This selfsame practice is widespread among Sudanese West Africans. There the pates of children are divided into patterns of diamonds and squares formed by parting the hair and gathering it into tightly tied tufts. In Africa, the various patterns indicate different social affiliations. In America, some of the styles can frequently be seen on small Negro children, but among American Negroes, who have long since lost all vestiges of African clan organization, the practice apparently[10] expresses no more than a style convention that is but a survival of the old practice. A definitely New World symbolism has arisen among American Negroes in the matter of hair form. The passion for hair-straightening and kink-removing compounds among American Negroes reflects an identification of nonkinky hair with the social status of Caucasians.

The varieties of hair decoration are so multifarious the world over that it is not possible to attempt a distributional summary here. Mention should be made of the localized Melanesian custom, particularly in New Ireland, of bleaching out black hair to a reddish orange with lime. This phenomenon confounded any number of American G.I.'s when they were first confronted with it in the South Pacific.

A closing comment on this subject would reemphasize the vital significance of the relation between hair treatment and formal social position. What is the meaning of the colloquialism, "They really let their hair down and had a good time?" Do we actually let down our hair? Only figuratively. What is let down are the customary restraints that keep us within our more cautiously preserved social roles. Let-down hair is ordinarily hidden from the public view, as is also the "uncensored" personality.

Cosmetics and Jewelry. Americans spend an estimated 700 million dollars on cosmetics in a normal year.[11] It is not the primitive but the universal man in us that accounts for this seeming extravagance. Viewed from the apex of a lofty aesthetics, cosmetic aesthetics seem basely barbaric. Lotions, pastes, powders, pigments, and synthetic essences to alter the texture, color, feel, and smell of the external surfaces of the human body are neither primitive

---

[9]A. C. Fletcher and F. LaFlesche, *The Omaha Tribe* (Bureau of American Ethnology, Annual Report 27, 1911), p. 198.
[10]There has been no investigation into the possible functional significances of hair arrangements in American Negro children.
[11]J. Gunther, *Inside U.S.A.*, p. xii.

nor civilized. They are only the universal cultural responses to the basic human need for favorable response. They are designed to heighten the stimulus intensity of the physical presence of one person upon the touch, smell, sight, and perhaps taste of others. The others are usually of the opposite sex, but not exclusively so. If personality is the social stimulus value of an individual, then cosmetics intensify personality.

Rouge is the most common cosmetic for two reasons: (1) red ochre (iron oxide) occurs in many places and is readily procurable; and (2) red is the primary color with the longest wavelength perceptible to the human eye, the color with the greatest natural stimulus value. When mixed with grease, it may be harmlessly applied to the human body. Yellow, black, blue, and white are the other favored colors.

Body painting among primitive peoples is for the most part limited to special occasions. Such occasions are, of course, usually ritual and ceremonial. They are events out of the ordinary, and painting changes the individual from an ordinary person to a man of distinction. War paint is usually linked to magical potency and serves less to frighten the enemy than to bolster the faint heart of its wearer. Thus, much of primitive cosmetic practice takes on symbolic values.

The trouble with paint and cosmetics, as every woman knows, is that its application is not lasting. The solution hit upon by many peoples is tattooing.

In North America, light tattooing runs from the Eskimos down the West Coast and into South America. The two high centers of the art, however, were Polynesia and Japan. Curiously, the status associations of tattooing in Polynesia and the civilized world are just reversed. With us soldiers and sailors in the lower ranks, longshoremen, and unskilled laborers are the persons who usually get themselves tattooed. For persons of higher status, it is definitely *déclassé*. But within the lower classes it serves as a symbol of masculinity and toughness. In Polynesia, the higher the social status, the fuller the tattooing. It extended over face, body, and limbs; in some overenthusiastic cases even to the tongue. The process was long-drawn-out and painful, but socially rewarding.

The technique of tattooing is to puncture the skin with needles carrying an indelible dye—usually carbon black. This posed a problem for Negroes and the Australian Blackfellows. No white dye for tattooing was ever discovered by them. The solution hit upon in Africa and Australia is to incise the skin instead of puncturing it. Then by rubbing ashes, grit, or other irritants into the wounds scar tissue can be encouraged to form, so that a series of raised lumps remain in a permanent visible pattern.

In Central Australia cicatrization or *scarification*, as the process is called, is a part of the adolescent initiatory rites for boys. The patterns are simply parallel rows of lines on the chest and back, but they are absolutely necessary to manhood. So important are they as symbols of manhood that individuals voluntarily repeat the operations in later life to keep their scars large and fresh.

In Africa, scarification among the Congo Bantus is also part of the initiatory rite or follows after. The designs are in some instances elaborate geometric patterns. : . .

German corps (fraternity) students and university men give great kudos to dueling scars. Reputedly they have great sex appeal. A wound that does not fester and leave a glaring scar is a dead loss. So important are the duel-born scarifications that German impostors have been known to slash themselves with a razor and rub in salt to leave the impression that they, too, bear the scars of honor.

Decorative Deformations and Mutilations. Tattooing and scarification are only superficial ornamental embellishments impressed upon the body. Piercing of the nasal septum, the lips, or ears so that sundry bones, feathers, shell, wood, or metal ornaments may be shoved through them extends from the most primitive to highly civilized peoples. The invention of the screw and spring clip has only recently obviated the need for ear puncturing among our own ladies, who find the functionally atrophied external ear a convenient appendage from which to dangle pretty baubles.

Incas, in South America, and Bagandas, among others in Africa, gradually extend the ear lobes to receive thin disks as much as 6 to 8 inches in diameter. Inca nobility wore disks of gold. Baganda women, with their huge lip labrets, are familiar to all circus sideshow visitors.

Separation of the cervical vertebrae and extension of the neck in ringed brass collars by Burmese women is another familiar distortion.

Cranial deformation was much esteemed as a mark of beauty by various Northwest American Indian tribes (*viz.*, the Flatheads of Idaho) and also by the Incas and other Andean peoples, who bound a flat board against the frontal region of the head of a baby in the cradleboard in order to produce a recessed forehead and a high, peaked occipital. Binding with cloth to produce long heads was also practiced.

Circumcision and subincision are not so much mutilations for ornamentation as they are mystical and status operations. The one is the removal of the foreskin of the penis; the other a slitting of the skin and urethra along the length of the male sex organ. Among the Central Australians they symbolize masculinity in a male-dominated and ideologically masculine society; like scarification, the operations (often fatal) are performed without anesthesia and with flint knives on adolescent boys as a part of initiation into manhood. Most African tribes also circumcise at adolescence, and for similar reasons.

Filing or knocking out of incisor teeth occurs in scattered distribution from Australia up through Melanesia and Indonesia, and over into Africa. Prehistoric Europeans and American Indians spared themselves this mark of distinction. Of all the decorative blemishes imposed by man upon himself this is perhaps the most foolish. Scarification, tattooing, and circumcision may be painful, but except as they cause death through infection, they do not inhibit the healthy functioning of the body. The deliberate destruction of the teeth does just that.

Yet, as has been shown throughout this discussion, what is lost physically is gained socially. Mind triumphs over matter. No matter if the psychic satisfactions are not rational. The need that is met is elemental. The fashion and jewelry industries, the cosmetic manufacturers and purveyors, the beauticians, all may rest secure that their services have a future—as long as all mankind's.

PAIN

In the last section Hoebel mentioned practices found in many parts of the world where the human body is subjected to what we can call "cosmetic mutilation" (an example is the current popularity among American females of pierced ear lobes). Usually such operations cause considerable pain—but this is "acceptable" pain, pain which is submitted to voluntarily because the person wants to be "in style" and cannot be so without the associated experience of pain. I note this simply because the sensation of pain, another basic biological reaction of the organism, is like other processes of human living noted in this section in that it is not entirely its own master. It, too, or at least its *expression*, is programmed by something other than the physiological and neurological dimensions involved in it. When, how much, to what extent, and in what manner to express (to "show") pain are *learned* behavior patterns and, being shared in a human group, are therefore some of the basic stuff of what we will later call "culture." In the following brief article, Christopherson discusses the interrelation between pain as a physical sensation and the cultural structuring of the response to it. In his article he refers to a now classic study done by Zborowski on differential pain responses among several American ethnic groups that might be of further interest to you.

SOCIOCULTURAL CORRELATES OF PAIN RESPONSE

VICTOR A. CHRISTOPHERSON

Pain is a highly subjective sensation and it cannot be seen, felt or denied by any other than the one

who reports it. We all know what it is, for it is a near universal experience, and it is almost always a nuisance to everyone concerned. On the other hand, pain is probably as vital to the health and

Reprinted with permission of publisher. From *Social Science*, vol. 46. no. 1 (January 1971), 33–37.

welfare of an individual as his daily bread. Some pain warns of disease and injury; however, other pain is apparently useless and pernicious—that which accompanies trigeminal neuralgia, for example. Inasmuch as pain is too frequently instrumental in patient behavior and so often a point of contact between the nurse and patient, all effort made to comprehend pain and its implications should be time profitably spent.

Pain is a difficult and elusive concept when it comes to definition, and attempts to evolve standard and adequate concepts go back many years. The word "pain" is derived from the Latin *poena* which means punishment. Aristotle considered pain an emotion which was the opposite of pleasure. More recent definitions are grounded more soundly in science perhaps, but it would be difficult to improve much on the Aristotelian concept.

Pain response is a secondary or derivative phenomenon as opposed to the primary sensation of pain per se. The response, however, may be more significant than the sensation, for it colors and affects the way the sufferer relates to his world. When different individuals suffer the apparent same degree and kind of tissue damage or noxious stimuli, the most casual observation reveals differences in response. The question has been raised as to what it is to which the individuals are responding. Does a certain amount of tissue damage "feel" different to different individuals, or do individuals respond differently to the same feeling?

LEARNING FACTORS IN PAIN RESPONSE

Without consideration of physiological determinants of differential pain response, there is ample grist for the mill with regard to determinants of a learning type. Learning approaches to pain response and pain management might succeed not only in providing a basis for greater insight into patient behavior, but the learning approach might provide the nurse with tools which have a more permanent impact than any analgesic. At the present time, however, learned responses to pain sensation represent an area somewhat less well developed than such areas of pain study as physiology of pain, classification of pain, and relief of pain.

That cultural patterning can affect and possibly reverse what is considered common and appropriate pain response is indicated by the widely read anthropological novel by Ruesch entitled *Top of the World*. The culture of the Polar Eskimo described

in this book encourages laughter as the most acceptable response to pain.

Keele cites the French surgeon René Leriche's observations of Russian Cossacks in World War I.[1] The surgeon, by invitation of some Russian officers, dislocated the joints of the hands and feet of Cossack soldiers without an anesthetic and without complaint from the men.

Pain is undoubtedly influenced by a number of variables in addition to tissue damage. E. G. Poser[2] suggests ethnic origin as one of the possible sources of response variation. Mark Zborowski's[3] study is perhaps the best known and most frequently cited study relating sociocultural background to pain responses. He compared pain responses of Jewish, Italian, Irish, and old Americans. The last group consisted of individuals who were predominantly of Anglo stock, and who had lived in the United States a number of generations. Other studies of sociocultural variables were carried out by Sternbach and Tursky,[4] Sherman and Robbillard,[5] and Lambert, Libman, and Poser.[6] In each case it appeared that the ways in which people responded to pain had been influenced by their backgrounds and previous experience—in effect, pain response is a learned response.

SITUATIONAL DETERMINANTS

In some situations, response to tissue damage and presumably pain seems to transcend national and subcultural patterns in favor of cogent situational determinants. Beecher's well-known studies of seriously wounded soldiers in a combat zone hospital *vis-à-vis* male civilians who had undergone major surgery revealed sharp differences in response to comparable tissue damage.[7] Beecher attributed the difference in response to the significance of the wound to the men in question. The soldier perceived his wound as a blessing. It enabled him to escape the battlefield and leave with honor. It was his ticket out. The civilian, on the other hand, perceived his wound as a calamity. It was painful and disabling. Only one fifth of the postoperative patients refused medication for the relief of pain, whereas two thirds of the wounded soldiers refused medication.

Another example, well known to nurses, of the influence of context or situational determinants was the common observation during World War II concerning the bravery of soldiers suffering from severe wounds. In contrast, they were observed to respond emotionally to the point sometimes of tears over the unwelcome prospect of daily antibiotic injections.

It is all well and good to learn about the Polar Eskimos or the soldiers of World War II, but once the concept or principle has been established, it is important to make application in one's own area of operation. Consequently, the author undertook a study comparing pain response of the three dominant ethnic groups in southern Arizona, namely, Mexican Americans, Anglos, and Papago Indians.

ETHNIC COMPARISONS

There were a number of very significant differences in pain response found on the part of all three groups when considered in relation to one another. The nurse who works with Mexican-American patients could scarcely afford to ignore or remain ignorant of the pain orientation of this subculture. Pain, for example, may have a meaning to the person involved which has little or no bearing on the medical or prognostic implications from the Anglo point of view. Even among the dominant culture groups, it may be that much of the reported pain is not so important as the patient thinks it is; it may, however, be a good deal more important than the nurse or physician thinks it is.

An excellent reference to help the nurse appreciate and understand the significance of the differences between the Anglo and Mexican-American pain cultures would be *Cultural Differences and Medical Care* by Lyle Saunders.[8] A few points made by Saunders that provide an excellent backdrop for our findings in differential pain response are the following recurring behavioral responses on the part of the Spanish-speaking patients:[9]

1. Delay in seeking medical aid.
2. Failure to keep appointments.
3. Ignoring dietary recommendations, particularly those that apply to the feeding of infants.
4. Failure to follow instructions.
5. Resistance to suggestions for hospitalization.
6. Resistance to sanatorium treatment for TB.
7. Leaving institutions against medical advice.
8. Failure to obtain prenatal care.
9. Resistance to surgery.
10. Failure of communication in history taking.

Underlying these problems are a number of areas in which the perceptions and points of view developed by Spanish-speaking and Anglo cultural bases may be in sharp opposition. Illustrative of these areas are the following contrasts in cultural perspective:

1. *Anglo:* disease and pain result from known, predictable, and frequently controllable causes.

Spanish-speaking: disease and pain are manifestations of the will of God, of fate, of the actions of enemies, of punishment for moral deviations, or of the whimsicalities of chance. There is not much that one could or should do to avoid or prevent these things.

2. *Anglo:* a person may be ill regardless of how he feels.

Spanish-speaking: illness is a matter of subjective feeling. A person is not ill if he feels well.

3. *Anglo:* the presence of disease requires surrendering the patient to professional healers who, for his own good, may require that he be separated from his family during the treatment process.

Spanish-speaking: the presence of disease requires that the family surround the patient ever more closely than usual and that the role of the healer, if one is consulted, be subordinated to that of the family group.

4. *Anglo:* one should be alert to future possibilities of present conditions and take steps to avoid undesirable consequences.

Spanish-speaking: the future is nebulous and distant; one will do well to cope with problems of the present.

5. *Anglo:* contagion can be transmitted by anyone.

Spanish-speaking: one cannot inadvertently harm someone he loves.

The characterizations are but a small portion indeed of the considerable amount of available information to assist the nurse in successful interaction with Spanish-speaking Americans. Inasmuch as the Papago Indians are much less acculturated with respect to the dominant Anglo society than are the Mexican Americans, their pain response might be expected to vary more considerably from the Anglo norms. The investigation proved this to be the case.

The several Papago Indian reservations are very near Tucson and together occupy an area of almost 3,000,000 acres. In spite of their geographical proximity to major population centers, the Papagos' concepts of health, disease, and significance of pain are far removed from the norms of middle-class

America. An inquiry into the pain responses of the Papago is a venture into another world. The Papago world is served by principles of causality that are not only completely foreign and naive from the Anglo view, but they are determinative of a great many phenomena of ceremonial and everyday life that come into conflict with the educational objectives and health goals established by the dominant culture.

Dreaming of a certain animal, crossing its track, or showing some form of disrespect can bring about a disease or painful condition. In the event the Papago suffering a painful condition is unable to obtain relief from a fetich with magical curative properties, help from a shaman or medicine man may be sought. When the Papago feels himself to be "out of harmony" with the established order of things, he expects to be sick or have some misfortune befall him. Much of the medicine man's success is due to his bringing the person back into harmonious relation with his environment. As such, the shaman's medicine is highly charged with a practical psychology.

From the Anglo point of view, the Papago's response to pain is stoical indeed. Keeping in mind, however, that an individual's behavior is a product of his assumptions, attitudes, and knowledge, the inference that a Papago responds better or less well to pain than the Anglo is an oversimplification. One contributory factor is that the Papago simply does not know about, and consequently does not consider, available alternatives to pain. The examples of pain response we discussed with the physician and nurses at the Papago Indian Hospital, at Sells, Arizona, led one of the nurses to comment, "We have learned from experience that when a Papago complains of pain or requests medication, such requests should receive prompt attention, for he is usually in serious trouble." . . .

In addition to the cultural determinants of pain response, there are the idiosyncratic factors which influence each individual within a general cultural or learning situation. Much of the idiosyncratic response to pain appears to hinge upon the individual's self-concept—how he sees himself. An orthopedic surgeon recently related to the author many examples of the remarkably short recovery periods of university athletes to major and painful surgery resulting from athletic injuries. He said, referring to the athletes, "The image they have of

themselves simply does not include or permit physical disability or incapacity. They are usually up making passes at the nurses when most people would still be stretched out flat, feeling sorry for themselves."[10]

Understanding the role that learning and cultural influences have with regard to how the individual responds to pain, and then applying some of the learning techniques now being utilized in elementary psychology classes should help maximize the effectiveness of all attempts to deal with what is perhaps the most distressing and universal symptom of mankind, pain.

NOTES

The investigation upon which this discussion was based was supported in part by a research grant, No. 1390, from the Vocational Rehabilitation Administration, Department of Health, Education, and Welfare, Washington, and in part by The Agricultural Experiment Station, The University of Arizona, Tucson, Arizona (Agricultural Experiment Station Journal Paper No. 1683).

1. K. D. Keele, "Pain: Past and Present," *Yale Review*, September 1959, pp. 43–50.

2. E. G. Poser, "Some Psycho-Social Determinants of Pain Tolerance," presented at the XVI International Congress of Psychology, Washington, 1963.

3. Mark Zborowski, "Cultural Components in Response to Pain," *The Journal of Social Issues*, No. 4, 1952, pp. 16–30.

4. Richard A. Sternbach and B. Tursky, "Ethnic Differences Among Housewives in Psychophysical and Skin Potential Responses to Electric Shock," *Psychophysiology*, January 1965, pp. 241–246.

5. E. C. Sherman and E. Robillard, "Sensitivity to Pain in the Aged," *Canadian Medical Association Journal*, October 29, 1960, pp. 944–947.

6. W. E. Lambert et al., "The Effect of Increased Salience of a Membership Group on Pain Tolerance," *Journal of Personality*, September 1960, pp. 350–357.

7. H. K. Beecher, "Pain in Men Wounded in Battle," *Annals of Surgery*, January 1946, pp. 95–105; "Relationship of Significance of Wound to the Pain Experience," *Journal of the American Medical Association*, August 25, 1956, pp. 1609–1613.

8. Lyle Saunders, *Cultural Differences and Medical Care*, New York: Russell Sage Foundation, 1954.

9. These two sets of points were made by Saunders in a conference address at The University of Arizona in 1961.

10. Charles Bechtol, Department of Orthopedic Surgery, University of California at Los Angeles.

SPACE

As with every other animal, man's life occurs in space and through time. But these are not neutral properties; they are given meaning and value for the human species. "Space," as an abstract concept from the world of theoretical physics, becomes in the study of man's life an idea affecting both forms and dynamics of group life as well as individual behavior. How deeply perceptions and use of space are built into the person is quickly seen, as a simple example, by an American traveler in Britain who starts to cross a street—the hesitant look in both directions for oncoming traffic, the almost constant decisions whether to walk down the sidewalk on the right or left side against the flow of other people—these betray a long period of largely unconscious training in a different framework for behavior in space. An even more dramatic and complicated "experiment" of this kind was evident in Sweden, when a few years ago the nation shifted from left-handed driving patterns to the much more widespread right-handed pattern. Not only were individual driving habits involved in this change-over, but also implicated were all the paraphernalia associated with the driving pattern (such as road signs, traffic lights, exit doors on busses, etc.).

In the excerpt that follows, Edward Hall, an anthropologist who has long been interested in the cultural structuring of some of these fundamental dimensions of man's behavior, offers cogent and yet familiar examples of this point. Space, like so much else in life, is given pattern, form, and structure by the value framework man brings into the situation.

SPACE SPEAKS

EDWARD T. HALL

Every living thing has a physical boundary that separates it from its external environment. Beginning with the bacteria and the simple cell and ending with man, every organism has a detectable limit which marks where it begins and ends. A short distance up the phylogenetic scale, however, another, non-physical boundary appears that exists outside the physical one. This new boundary is harder to delimit than the first but is just as real. We call this the "organism's territory." The act of laying claim to and defending a territory is termed territoriality.

Reprinted with permission of Doubleday and Co., Inc. From Edward T. Hall, *The Silent Language.* Copyright © 1959 by Edward T. Hall, pp. 146–64.

It is territoriality with which this chapter is most concerned. In man, it becomes highly elaborated, as well as being very greatly differentiated from culture to culture.

Anyone who has had experience with dogs, particularly in a rural setting such as on ranches and farms, is familiar with the way in which the dog handles space. In the first place, the dog knows the limits of his master's "yard" and will defend it against encroachment. There are also certain places where he sleeps: a spot next to the fireplace, a spot in the kitchen, or one in the dining room if he is allowed there. In short, a dog has fixed points to which he returns time after time depending upon the occasion. One can also observe that dogs create zones around them. Depending upon his relationship to the dog and the zone he is in, a trespasser can evoke different behavior when he crosses the invisible lines which are meaningful to the dog.

This is particularly noticeable in females with puppies. A mother who has a new litter in a little-used barn will claim the barn as her territory. When the door opens she may make a slight movement or stirring in one corner. Nothing else may happen as the intruder moves ten or fifteen feet into the barn. Then the dog may raise her head or get up, circle about, and lie down as another invisible boundary is crossed. One can tell about where the line is by withdrawing and watching when her head goes down. As additional lines are crossed, there will be other signals, a thumping of the tail, a low moan or a growl.

One can observe comparable behavior in other vertebrates—fish, birds, and mammals. Birds have well-developed territoriality, areas which they defend as their own and which they return to year after year. To those who have seen a robin come back to the same nest each year this will come as no surprise. Seals, dolphin, and whales are known to use the same breeding grounds. Individual seals have been known to come back to the same rock year after year.

Man has developed his territoriality to an almost unbelievable extent. Yet we treat space somewhat as we treat sex. It is there but we don't talk about it. And if we do, we certainly are not expected to get technical or serious about it. The man of the house is always somewhat apologetic about "his chair." How many people have had the experience of coming into a room, seeing a big comfortable chair and heading for it, only to pull themselves up short, or pause and turn to the man and say, "Oh, was I about to sit in your chair?" The reply, of course, is usually polite. Imagine the effect if the host were to give vent to his true feelings and say, "Hell, yes, you're sitting in my chair, and I don't like anybody sitting in my chair!" For some unknown reason, our culture has tended to play down or cause us to repress and dissociate the feelings we have about space. We relegate it to the informal and are likely to feel guilty whenever we find ourselves getting angry because someone has taken our place.

Territoriality is established so rapidly that even the second session in a series of lectures is sufficient to find a significant proportion of most audiences back in the same seats. What's more, if one has been sitting in a particular seat and someone else occupies it, one can notice a fleeting irritation. There is the remnant of an old urge to throw out the interloper. The interloper knows this too, because he will turn around or look up and say, "Have I got your seat?" at which point you lie and say, "Oh no, I was going to move anyway."

Once while talking on this subject to a group of Americans who were going overseas, one very nice, exceedingly mild-mannered woman raised her hand and said, "You mean it's natural for me to feel irritated when another woman takes over my kitchen?" Answer: "Not only is it natural, but most American women have very strong feelings about their kitchens. Even a mother can't come in and wash the dishes in her daughter's kitchen without annoying her. The kitchen is the place where 'who will dominate' is settled. All women know this, and some can even talk about it. Daughters who can't keep control of their kitchen will be forever under the thumb of any woman who can move into this area."

The questioner continued: "You know that makes me feel so relieved. I have three older sisters and a mother, and every time they come to town they march right into the kitchen and take over. I want to tell them to stay out of my kitchen, that they have their own kitchens and this is my kitchen, but I always thought I was having unkind thoughts about my mother and sisters, thoughts I wasn't supposed to have. This relieves me so much, because now I know I was right."

Father's shop is, of course, another sacred territory and best kept that way. The same applies to his study, if he has one.

As one travels abroad and examines the ways in which space is handled, startling variations are discovered—differences which we react to vigorously. Since none of us is taught to look at space as isolated from other associations, feelings cued by the handling of space are often attributed to something else. In growing up people learn literally thousands of spatial cues, all of which have their own meaning in their own context. These cues "release" responses already established in much the same way as Pavlov's bells started his dogs salivating. Just how accurate a spatial memory is has never been completely tested. There are indications, however, that it is exceedingly persistent.

Literally thousands of experiences teach us unconsciously that space communicates. Yet this fact would probably never have been brought to the level of consciousness if it had not been realized that space is organized differently in each culture. The associations and feelings that are released in a member of one culture almost invariably mean something else in the next. When we say that some foreigners are "pushy," all this means is that their handling of space releases this association in our minds.

What gets overlooked is that the response is there *in toto* and has been there all along. There is no point in well-meaning people feeling guilty because they get angry when a foreigner presents them with a spatial cue that releases anger or aggression. The main thing is to know what is happening and try to find out which cue was responsible. The next step is to discover, if possible, whether the person really intended to release this particular feeling or whether he intended to engender a different reaction.

Uncovering the specific cues in a foreign culture is a painstaking and laborious process. Usually it is easier for the newcomer to listen to the observations of old-timers and then test these observations against his own experience. At first he may hear, "You're going to have a hard time getting used to the way these people crowd you. Why, when you are trying to buy a theater ticket, instead of standing in line and waiting their turn they all try to reach in and get their money to the ticket seller at once. It's just terrible the way you have to push and shove just to keep your place. Why, the last time I got to the ticket window of the theater and poked my head up to the opening, there were five arms and hands reaching over my shoulder waving money." Or he may hear the following: "It's as much as your life is worth to ride the streetcars. They're worse than our subways. What's more, these people don't seem to mind it at all." Some of this stems from the fact that, as Americans we have a pattern which discourages touching, except in moments of intimacy. When we ride on a streetcar or crowded elevator we will "hold ourselves in," having been taught from early childhood to avoid bodily contact with strangers. Abroad, it's confusing when conflicting feelings are being released at the same time. Our

senses are bombarded by a strange language, different smells, and gestures, as well as a host of signs and symbols.

However, the fact that those who have been in a foreign country for some time talk about these things provides the newcomer with advance warning. Getting over a spatial accent is just as important, sometimes more so, than eliminating a spoken one. Advice to the newcomer might be: Watch where people stand, and don't back up. You will feel funny doing it, but it's amazing how much difference it makes in people's attitudes toward you.

HOW DIFFERENT CULTURES USE SPACE

Several years ago a magazine published a map of the United States as the average New Yorker sees it. The details of New York were quite clear and the suburbs to the north were also accurately shown. Hollywood appeared in some detail while the space in between New York and Hollywood was almost a total blank. Places like Phoenix, Albuquerque, the Grand Canyon, and Taos, New Mexico, were all crowded into a hopeless jumble. It was easy to see that the average New Yorker knew little and cared less for what went on in the rest of the country. To the geographer the map was a distortion of the worst kind. Yet to the student of culture it was surprisingly accurate. It showed the informal images that many people have of the rest of the country.

As a graduate student I lived in New York, and my landlord was a first-generation American of European extraction who had lived in New York all his life. At the end of the academic year as I was leaving, the landlord came down to watch me load my car. When I said goodby, he remarked, "Well, one of these Sunday afternoons I put my family in the car and we drive out to New Mexico and see you."

The map and the landlord's comment illustrate how Americans treat space as highly personalized. We visualize the relationship between places we know by personal experience. Places which we haven't been to and with which we are not personally identified tend to remain confused.

Traditionally American space begins with "a place." It is one of the oldest sets, comparable to, but not quite the same as, the Spanish *lugar*. The reader will have no difficulty thinking up ways in which place is used: "He found a place in her heart," "He has a place in the mountains," "I am tired of this place," and so on. Those who have children know how difficult it is to get across to them the whole concept of place—like Washington, or Boston, or Philadelphia, and so on. An American child requires between six and seven years before he has begun to master the basic concepts of place. Our culture provides for a great variety of places, including different classes of places.

Contrasted with the Middle East, our system is characterized by fine gradations as one moves from one space category to the next. In the world of the Arab there are villages and cities. That is about all. Most non-nomadic Arabs think of themselves as villagers. The actual villages are of varying population, from a few families up to several thousands.

The smallest place category in the United States is not covered by a term like hamlet, village, or town. It is immediately recognizable as a territorial entity, nevertheless, because such places are always named. They are areas with no recognizable center where a number of families live—like Dogpatch of the funny papers.

Our Dogpatches present the basic American pattern in uncomplicated form. They have scattered residences with no concentration of buildings in one spot. Like time, place with us is diffused, so that you never quite know where its center is. Beyond this the naming of place categories begins with the "crossroads store" or "corner" and continues with the "small shopping center," the "county seat," the "small town," "large town," "metropolitan center," "city," and "metropolis." Like much of the rest of our culture, including the social ranking system, there are no clear gradations as one moves from one category to the next. The "points" are of varying sizes, and there are no linguistic cues indicating the size of the place we are talking about. The United States, New Mexico, Albuquerque, Pecos are all said the same way and used the same way in sentences. The child who is learning the language has no way of distinguishing one space category from another by listening to others talk.

The miracle is that children eventually are able to sort out and pin down the different space terms from the meager cues provided by others. Try telling a five-year-old the difference between where you live in the suburbs and the town where your wife goes to shop. It will be a frustrating task, since the child, at that age, only comprehends where *he* lives.

His room, his house, his place at the table are the places that are learned early.

The reason most Americans have difficulty in school with geography or geometry stems from the fact that space as an informal cultural system is different from space as it is technically elaborated by classroom geography and mathematics. It must be said in fairness to ourselves that other cultures have similar problems. Only the very perceptive adult realizes that there is anything really difficult for the child to learn about space. In reality, he has to take what is literally a spatial blur and isolate the significant points that adults talk about. Sometimes adults are unnecessarily impatient with children because they don't catch on. People do not realize that the child has heard older people talking about different places and is trying to figure out, from what he hears, the difference between this place and that. In this regard it should be pointed out that the first clues which suggest to children that one thing is different from another come from shifts in tone of voice which direct attention in very subtle but important ways. Speaking a fully developed language as we do, it is hard to remember that there was a time when we could not speak at all and when the whole communicative process was carried on by means of variations in the voice tone. This early language is lost to consciousness and functions out of awareness, so that we tend to forget the very great role it plays in the learning process.

To continue our analysis of the way a child learns about space, let us turn to his conception of a road. At first a road is whatever he happens to be driving on. This doesn't mean that he can't tell when you take a wrong turn. He can, and often will even correct a mistake which is made. It only means that he has not yet broken the road down into its components and that he makes the distinction between this road and that road in just the same way that he learns to distinguish between the phoneme *d* and the phoneme *b* in initial position in the spoken language.

Using roads for cross-cultural contrast, the reader will recall that Paris, being an old city as well as a French city, has a street-naming system that puzzles most Americans. Street names shift as one progresses. Take Rue St.-Honoré, for example, which becomes Rue du Faubourg St.-Honoré, Avenue des Ternes, and Avenue du Roule. A child growing up in Paris, however, has no more difficulty learning his system than one of our children learning ours. We teach ours to watch the intersections and the directions and that when something happens— that is, when there is a change of course at one of these points—you can expect the name to change. In Paris the child learns that as he passes certain landmarks—like buildings that are well known, or statues—the name of the street changes.

It is interesting and informative to watch very young children as they learn their culture. They quickly pick up the fact that we have names for some things and not for others. First, they identify the whole object or the set— a room, for instance; then they begin to fixate on certain other discrete objects like books, ashtrays, letter openers, tables, and pencils. By so doing they accomplish two things. First, they find out how far down the scale they have to go in identifying things. Second, they learn what are the isolates and patterns for handling space and object nomenclature. First children are often better subjects than second children, because, having learned the hard way, the first one will teach the second one without involving the parents.

The child will ask, "What's this?" pointing to a pencil. You reply, "A pencil." The child is not satisfied and says, "No, this," pointing to the shaft of the pencil and making clear that she meant the shaft. So you say, "Oh, that's the shaft of the pencil." Then the child moves her finger one quarter inch and says, "What's this?" and you say, "The shaft." This process is repeated and you say, "That's still the shaft; and this is the shaft, and this is the shaft. It's all the shaft of the pencil. This is the shaft, this is the point, and this is the eraser, and this is the little tin thing that holds the eraser on." Then she may point to the eraser, and you discover that she is still trying to find out where the dividing lines are. She manages to worm out the fact that the eraser has a top and sides but no more. She also learns that there is no way to tell the difference between one side and the next and that no labels are pinned on parts of the point, even though distinctions are made between the lead and the rest of the pencil. She may glean from this that materials make a difference some of the time and some of the time they do not. Areas where things begin and end are apt to be important, while the points in between are often ignored.

The significance of all this would undoubtedly have escaped me if it hadn't been for an experience on the atoll of Truk. In a rather detailed series of studies in technology I had progressed to the point of having to obtain the nomenclature of the canoe and the wooden food bowl. At this point it was necessary for me to go through what children go through—that is, point to various parts after I thought I had the pattern and ask if I had the name right. As I soon discovered, their system of carving up microspace was radically different from our own. The Trukese treat open spaces, without dividing lines (as we know them), as completely distinct. Each area has a name. On the other hand, they have not developed a nomenclature for the edges of objects as elaborately as Westerners have done. The reader has only to think of rims and cups and the number of different ways in which these can be referred to. There is the rim itself. It can be square or round or elliptical in cross section; straight, flared, or curved inward; plain or decorated, and wavy or straight. This doesn't mean that the Trukese don't elaborate rims. They do; it just means that we have ways of talking about what we do and not as many ways of talking about what happens to an open area as they do. The Trukese separate parts which we think of as being "built in" to the object.

A certain decoration or carving at either end of a canoe-shaped food bowl is thought of as being separate or distinct from the rim in which it has been carved. It has an essence of its own. Along the keel of the canoe the carving, called the *chunefatch*, has characteristics with which it endows the canoe. The canoe is one thing, the chunefatch something else. Open spaces without obvious markers on the side of the bowl have names. Such distinctions in the dividing up of space make the settling of land claims unbelievably complicated in these islands. Trees, for instance, are considered separate from the soil out of which they grow. One man may own the trees, another the soil below.

Benjamin Whorf, describing how Hopi concepts of space are reflected in the language, mentions the absence of terms for interior three-dimensional spaces, such as words for room, chamber, hall, passage, interior, cell, crypt, cellar, attic, loft, and vault. This does not alter the fact that the Hopi have multi-room dwellings and even use the rooms for special purposes such as storage, grinding corn, and the like.

Whorf also notes the fact that it is impossible for the Hopi to add a possessive pronoun to the word for room and that in the Hopi scheme of things a room in the strict sense of the word is not a noun and does not act like a noun.

Since there is a wealth of data on how strongly the Hopi feel about holding onto things which are theirs, one has to rule out the possessive factor in Whorf's reference to their inability to say "my room." It's just that their language is different. One might be led to assume by this that the Hopi would then lack a sense of territoriality. Again, nothing could be farther from the truth. They just use and conceive of space differently. We work from points and along lines. They apparently do not. While seemingly inconsequential, these differences caused innumerable headaches to the white supervisors who used to run the Hopi reservation in the first part of this century.

I will never forget driving over to one of the villages at the end of a mesa and discovering that someone was building a house in the middle of the road. It later developed that the culprit (in my eyes) was a man I had known for some time. I said, "Paul, why are you building your house in the middle of the road? There are lots of good places on either side of the road. This way people have to knock the bottoms out of their cars driving around on the rocks to get to the village." His reply was short and to the point: "I know, but it's my right." He did have a right to a certain area laid down long before there was a road. The fact that the road had been used for many years meant nothing to him. Use and disuse of space in our terms had nothing to do with his ideas of possession.

SPACE AS A FACTOR IN CULTURE CONTACT

Whenever an American moves overseas, he suffers from a condition known as "culture shock." Culture shock is simply a removal or distortion of many of the familiar cues one encounters at home and the substitution for them of other cues which are strange. A good deal of what occurs in the organization and use of space provides important leads as to the specific cues responsible for culture shock.

The Latin house is often built around a patio that is next to the sidewalk but hidden from outsiders behind a wall. It is not easy to describe the degree to which small architectural differences such as this affect outsiders. American Point Four technicians living in Latin America used to complain that they felt "left out" of things, that they were "shut off." Others kept wondering what was going on "behind those walls." In the United States, on the other hand, propinquity is the basis of a good many relationships. To us the neighbor is actually quite close. Being a neighbor endows one with certain rights and privileges, also responsibilities. You can borrow things, including food and drink, but you also have to take your neighbor to the hospital in an emergency. In this regard he has almost as much claim on you as a cousin. For these and other reasons the American tries to pick his neighborhood carefully, because he knows that he is going to be thrown into intimate contact with people. We do not understand why it is that when we live next to people abroad the sharing of adjacent space does not always conform to our own pattern. In France and England, for instance, the relations between neighbors are apt to be cooler than in the United States. Mere propinquity does not tie people together. In England neighbor children do not play as they do in our neighborhoods. When they do play, arrangements are sometimes made a month in advance as though they were coming from the other side of town!

Another example has to do with the arrangement of offices. In this case one notices great contrast between ourselves and the French. Part of our over-all pattern in the United States is to take a given amount of space and divide it up equally. When a new person is added in an office, almost everyone will move his desk so that the newcomer will have his share of the space. This may mean moving from positions that have been occupied for a long time and away from favorite views from the window. The point is that the office force will make its own adjustments voluntarily. In fact, it is a signal that they have acknowledged the presence of the new person when they start rearranging the furniture. Until this has happened, the boss can be sure that the new person has not been integrated into the group.

Given a large enough room, Americans will distribute themselves around the walls, leaving the center open for group activities such as conferences. That is, the center belongs to the group and is often marked off by a table or some object placed there both to use and save the space. Lacking a conference table, members will move their chairs away from their desks to form a "huddle" in the middle. The pattern of moving from one's place to huddle is symbolized in our language by such ex-pressions as, "I had to take a new position on that point," or "The position of the office on this point is . . ."

The French, by contrast, do not make way for each other in the unspoken, taken-for-granted way that we do. They do not divide up the space with a new colleague. Instead they may grudgingly give him a small desk in a dark corner looking toward the wall. This action speaks eloquently to Ameri-cans who have found themselves working for the French. We feel that not to "make a place" accents status differences. If the rearrangement which says, "Now we admit you to the group, and you are going to stay," fails to take place, Americans are likely to feel perilously insecure. In French offices the key figure is the man in the middle, who has his fingers on everything so that all runs smoothly. There is a centralized control. The French educa-tional system runs from the middle, so that all students all over France take the same class at the same time.

It has already been mentioned that ordering is an important element in American patterns. As a general rule, whenever services are involved we feel that people should queue up in order of arrival. This reflects the basic equalitarianism of our cul-ture. In cultures where a class system or its rem-nants exist, such ordinality may not exist. That is, where society assigns rank for certain purposes, or wherever ranking is involved, the handling of space will reflect this.

To us it is regarded as a democratic virtue for people to be served without reference to the rank they hold in their occupational group. The rich and poor alike are accorded equal opportunity to buy and be waited upon in the order of arrival. In a line at the theater Mrs. Gotrocks is no better than anyone else. However, apart from the English, whose queueing patterns we share, many Europeans are likely to look upon standing in line as a viola-tion of their individuality. I am reminded of a Pole who reacted this way. He characterized Americans as sheep, and the mere thought of such passiveness was likely to set him off crashing into a line at what-ever point he pleased. Such people can't stand the idea of being held down by group conformity as if they were an automaton. Americans watching the Pole thought he was "pushy." He didn't bother to hide the fact that he thought we were much too subdued. He used to say, "What does it matter if

there is a little confusion and some people get served before others?"

FORMAL SPACE PATTERNS

Depending upon the culture in question, the formal patterning of space can take on varying degrees of importance and complexity. In America, for ex-ample, no one direction takes precedence over another except in a technical or utilitarian sense. In other cultures one quickly discovers that some directions are sacred or preferred. Navajo doors must face east, the mosques of the Moslems must be oriented toward Mecca, the sacred rivers of India flow south. Americans pay attention to direc-tion in a technical sense, but formally and in-formally they have no preference. Since our space is largely laid out by technical people, houses, towns, and main arteries are usually oriented ac-cording to one of the points of the compass. The same applies to roads and main highways when the topography allows, as it does in the flat expanses of Indiana and Kansas. This technical patterning allows us to locate places by co-ordinates (a point on the line). "He lives at 1321 K Street, N.W." tells us that he lives in the northwest part of town in the thirteenth block west of the line dividing the town into east-west halves and eleven blocks north of the line dividing the town into north-south halves, on the left side of the street, about one quarter of the way up the block.

In the country we will say, "Go out of town ten miles west on Highway 66 until you get to the first paved road turning north. Turn right on that road and go seven miles. It's the second farm on your left. You can't miss it."

Our concept of space makes use of the edges of things. If there aren't any edges, we make them by creating artificial lines (five miles west and two miles north). Space is treated in terms of a co-ordinate system. In contrast, the Japanese and many other people work within areas. They name "spaces" and distinguish between one space and the next or parts of a space. To us a space is empty—one gets into it by intersecting it with lines.

A technical pattern which may have grown out of an informal base is that of positional value or ranking. We have canonized the idea of the posi-tional value in almost every aspect of our lives, so much so that even children four years old are fully aware of its implications and are apt to fight with each other as to who will be first.

In addition to positional value, the American pattern emphasizes equality and standardization of the segments which are used for measuring space or into which space is divided, be it a ruler or a suburban subdivision. We like our components to be standard and equal. American city blocks tend to have uniform dimensions whereas towns in many other parts of the world are laid out with unequal blocks. This suggests that it was no accident that mass production, made possible by the standardization of parts, had its origins in the United States. There are those who would argue that there are compelling technological reasons for both mass production and parts standardization. However, an examination of actual practice indicates that Europeans have produced automobiles in the past —and very good ones too—in which the cylinders were all of different sizes. The difference in dimensions was not great, of course, a matter of a very few thousandths of an inch. This, however, was enough to cause the car to make noise and use too much oil if it was repaired by an American mechanic unfamiliar with the European patterns that lack the uniformity isolate.

Japan, too, has a passion for uniformity, though it is somewhat different from ours. All mats (*tatami*) on the floors of Japanese houses and all windows, doors, and panels are usually of identical dimensions in a given district. In newspaper advertisements of houses for sale or rent the dimensions are usually given in terms of the number of mats of a specific area. Despite this example of uniformity, the Japanese differ from us in a way which can have considerable economic results. In one case, for example, they manufactured a very large order of electronic parts according to rigid specifications which they were quite able to meet. When the product arrived in the United States, it was discovered that there were differences between various batches of these parts. The customer subsequently discovered that while the whole internal process of manufacture had been controlled, the Japanese had failed to standardize their gauges! It is no accident that in the United States there is a Bureau of Standards. Much of the success of this country's technical skill and productivity, which we are trying to pass on to other nations, rests on these and similar unstated patterns.

HOW SPACE COMMUNICATES

Spatial changes give a tone to a communication, accent it, and at times even override the spoken word. The flow and shift of distance between people as they interact with each other is part and parcel of the communication process. The normal conversational distance between strangers illustrates how important are the dynamics of space interaction. If a person gets too close, the reaction is instantaneous and automatic—the other person backs up. And if he gets too close again, back we go again. I have observed an American backing up the entire length of a long corridor while a foreigner whom he considers pushy tries to catch up with him. This scene has been enacted thousands and thousands of times—one person trying to increase the distance in order to be at ease, while the other tries to decrease it for the same reason, neither one being aware of what was going on. We have here an example of the tremendous depth to which culture can condition behavior.

One thing that does confuse us and gets in the way of understanding cultural differences is that there are times in our own culture when people are either distant or pushy in their use of space. We, therefore, simply associate the foreigner with the familiar; namely those people who have acted in such a way that our attention was drawn to their actions. The error is in jumping to the conclusion that the foreigner feels the same way the American does even though his overt acts are identical.

This was all suddenly brought into focus one time when I had the good fortune to be visited by a very distinguished and learned man who had been for many years a top-ranking diplomat representing a foreign country. After meeting him a number of times, I had become impressed with his extraordinary sensitivity to the small details of behavior that are so significant in the interaction process. Dr. X. was interested in some of the work several of us were doing at the time and asked permission to attend one of my lectures. He came to the front of the class at the end of the lecture to talk over a number of points made in the preceding hour. While talking he became quite involved in the implications of the lecture as well as what he was saying. We started out facing each other and as he talked I became dimly aware that he was standing a little too close and that I was beginning to back up. Fortunately I was able to suppress my first impulse and remain stationary because there was nothing to communicate aggression in his behavior except the conversational distance. His voice was eager, his manner intent, the set of his body communicated only interest and eagerness to talk. It also came to me in a flash that someone who had been so successful in the old school of diplomacy could not possibly let himself communicate something offensive to the other person except outside of his highly trained awareness.

By experimenting I was able to observe that as I moved away slightly, there was an associated shift in the pattern of interaction. He had more trouble expressing himself. If I shifted to where I felt comfortable (about twenty-one inches), he looked somewhat puzzled and hurt, almost as though he were saying: "Why is he acting that way? Here I am doing everything I can to talk to him in a friendly manner and he suddenly withdraws. Have I done anything wrong? Said something that I shouldn't?" Having ascertained that distance had a direct effect on his conversation, I stood my ground, letting him set the distance.

Not only is a vocal message qualified by the handling of distance, but the substance of a conversation can often demand special handling of space. There are certain things which are difficult to talk about unless one is within the proper conversational zone.

Not long ago I received a present of some seeds and chemicals along with the information that if I planted the seeds the chemicals would make them grow. Knowing little about hydroponics except that the plants should be suspended above the fluid in which chemicals are dissolved, I set out to find a suitable flowerpot. At every flower shop I was met with incredulity and forced to go through a routine involving a detailed explanation of just what it was I wanted and how hydroponics worked.

My ignorance of both hydroponics and florist shops made me feel somewhat ill at ease, so that I did not communicate in the manner that I use when I am speaking on a familiar subject in a familiar setting. The role that distance plays in a communication situation was brought home to me when I entered a shop in which the floor was filled with benches spaced at about twenty-inch intervals. On the other side of the benches was the female proprietor of the shop. As I entered, she craned her neck as though to reach over the benches, raised her voice slightly to bring it up to the proper level, and said, "What was it you wanted?" I tried once. "What I'm looking for is a *hydroponic* flowerpot." "What kind of flowerpot?" still with the neck

craned. At this point I found myself climbing over benches in an effort to close up the space. It was simply impossible for me to talk about such a subject in a setting of this sort at a distance of fifteen feet. It wasn't until I got to within three feet that I was able to speak with some degree of comfort.

Another example is one that will be familiar to millions of civilians who served in the Army during World War II. The Army, in its need to get technical about matters that are usually handled informally, made a mistake in the regulations on distance required for reporting to a superior officer. Everyone knows that the relationship between officers and men has certain elements which require distance and impersonality. This applied to officers of different ranks when they were in command relationship to each other. Instructions for reporting to a superior officer were that the junior officer was to proceed up to a point three paces in front of the officer's desk, stop, salute, and state his rank, his name, and his business: "Lieutenant X, reporting as ordered, sir." Now, what cultural norms does this procedure violate, and what does it communicate? It violates the conventions for the use of space. The distance is too great, by at least two feet, and does not fit the situation. The normal speaking distance for business matters, where impersonality is involved at the beginning of the conversation, is five and a half to eight feet. The distance required by the army regulations borders on the edge of what we would call "far." It evokes an automatic response to shout. . . . There are, of course, many subjects which it is almost impossible to talk about at this distance, and individual army officers recognize this by putting soldiers and junior officers at ease, asking them to sit down or permitting them to come closer. However, the first impression was that the Army was doing things the hard way.

For Americans the following shifts in the voice are associated with specific ranges of distances:

1. *Very close* (3 in. to 6 in.) — Soft whisper; top secret
2. *Close* (8 in. to 12 in.) — Audible whisper; very confidential
3. *Near* (12 in. to 20 in.) — Indoors, soft voice; outdoors, full voice; confidential
4. *Neutral* (20 in. to 36 in.) — Soft voice, low volume; personal subject matter

5. *Neutral* (4½ ft. to 5 ft.)	Full voice; information of non-personal matter
6. *Public Distance* (5½ ft. to 8 ft.)	Full voice; with slight overloudness; public information for others to hear
7. *Across the room* (8 ft. to 20 ft.)	Loud voice; talking to a group
8. *Stretching the limits of distance*	20 ft. to 24 ft. indoors; up to 100 ft. outdoors; hailing distance, departures

In Latin America the interaction distance is much less than it is in the United States. Indeed, people cannot talk comfortably with one another unless they are very close to the distance that evokes either sexual or hostile feelings in the North American. The result is that when they move close, we withdraw and back away. As a consequence, they think we are distant and cold, withdrawn and unfriendly. We, on the other hand, are constantly accusing them of breathing down our necks, crowding us, and spraying our faces.

Americans who have spent some time in Latin America without learning these space considerations make other adaptations, like barricading themselves behind their desks, using chairs and typewriter tables to keep the Latin American at what is to us a comfortable distance. The result is that the Latin American may even climb over the obstacles until he has achieved a distance at which he can comfortably talk.

TIME

We continue with Edward Hall, an excerpt from his widely read and easily available book on the press of culture on behavior. This time he is speaking of that other fundamental concept in scientific conceptions of the world, time. Again, for human behavior in social life it is not a neutral or "objective" quality inherent in nature, but a standardized way of seeing the world that has affect and value dimensions. Take, for example, the idea of uniform time zones. The "passage" of the sun "around" the world (which we say when viewed from our geocentric perspective) is continuous, is a gradient; the sun does not shine for one hour on one spot, then suddenly move over to another, like some object rolling down a stairway. But for many reasons, it has become not only convenient but necessary for man to *impose* a *dis*continuous order and standard framework on this natural process (in other words, to apply a cultural framework of standardized agreements and understanding onto a natural flow of events). In the United States, the idea of "artificially" making time in a given region uniform came to the fore in the last century, when railway travel and coordination of schedules was impossible unless there *was* agreement that, for example, the 3:06 eastbound Blazer would wait on the side track until the 2:59 westbound Whiz had gone its way on the main track. And yet, coordination of such schedules could occur *only if* everyone concerned was using the same basic time frame—only if the conductors' watches were, in fact, operating on "Eastern" (or whatever) Standard time. But such agreement is imposed on nature—it is not, in its details, given by nature. How many people still say, when the time for shifting to "daylight saving time" from "standard" time occurs, that they won't conform—after all, nobody has a right to tinker with "God's Time"! On the international scene, when (in the 1880's) proposals were being put forth for dividing the entire world into standard zones and Greenwich, England, was being discussed as the prime meridian, or the fundamental starting point for all standardized measures of time, the French delegates to the international conference strenuously objected. After all, Paris, certainly no place in England, was the center of the world!

THE VOICES OF TIME

EDWARD T. HALL

People of the Western world, particularly Americans, tend to think of time as something fixed in nature, something around us and from which we cannot escape; an ever-present part of the environment, just like the air we breathe. That it might be experienced in any other way seems unnatural and strange, a feeling which is rarely modified even when we begin to discover how really differently it is handled by some other people. Within the West itself certain cultures rank time much lower in overall importance than we do. In Latin America, for example, where time is treated rather cavalierly, one commonly hears the expression, "Our time or your time?" "*Hora americana, hora mejicana?*"

As a rule, Americans think of time as a road or a ribbon stretching into the future, along which one progresses. The road has segments or compartments which are to be kept discrete ("one thing at a time"). People who cannot schedule time are looked down upon as impractical. In at least some parts of Latin America, the North American (their term for us) finds himself annoyed when he has made an appointment with somebody, only to find a lot of other things going on at the same time. An old friend of mine of Spanish cultural heritage used to run his business according to the "Latino" system. This meant that up to fifteen people were in his office at one time. Business which might have been finished in a quarter of an hour sometimes took a whole day. He realized, of course, that the Anglo-Americans were disturbed by this and used to make some allowance for them, a dispensation which meant that they spent only an hour or so in his office when they planned on a few minutes.

The American concept of the discreteness of time and the necessity for scheduling was at variance with this amiable and seemingly confusing Latin system. However, if my friend had adhered to the American system he would have destroyed a vital part of his prosperity. People who came to do business with him also came to find out things and to visit each other. The ten to fifteen Spanish-Americans and Indians who used to sit around the office (among whom I later found myself after I had learned to relax a little) played their own part in a particular type of communications network.

Not only do we Americans segment and schedule time, but we look ahead and are oriented almost entirely toward the future. We like new things and are preoccupied with change. We want to know how to overcome resistance to change. In fact, scientific theories and even some pseudo-scientific ones, which incorporate a striking theory of change, are often given special attention.

Time with us is handled much like a material; we earn it, spend it, save it, waste it. To us it is somewhat immoral to have two things going on at the same time. In Latin America it is not uncommon for one man to have a number of simultaneous jobs which he either carries on from one desk or which he moves between, spending a small amount of time on each.

While we look to the future, our view of it is limited. The future to us is the foreseeable future, not the future of the South Asian that may involve centuries. Indeed, our perspective is so short as to inhibit the operation of a good many practical projects, such as sixty- and one-hundred-year conservation works requiring public support and public funds. Anyone who has worked in industry or in the government of the United States has heard

Reprinted with permission of publisher. From Edward T. Hall, *The Silent Language* (New York: Premier Book, Fawcett World Library, 1959), pp. 19–29.

the following: "Gentlemen, this is for the long term! Five or ten years."

For us a "long time" can be almost anything—ten or twenty years, two or three months, a few weeks, or even a couple of days. The South Asian, however, feels that it is perfectly realistic to think of a "long time" in terms of thousands of years or even an endless period. A colleague once described their conceptualization of time as follows: "Time is like a museum with endless corridors and alcoves. You, the viewer, are walking through the museum in the dark, holding a light to each scene as you pass it. God is the curator of the museum, and only He knows all that is in it. One lifetime represents one alcove."

The American's view of the future is linked to a view of the past, for tradition plays an equally limited part in American culture. As a whole, we push it aside or leave it to a few souls who are interested in the past for very special reasons. There are, of course, a few pockets, such as New England and the South, where tradition is emphasized. But in the realm of business, which is the dominant model of United States life, tradition is equated with *experience*, and experience is thought of as being very close to if not synonymous with know-how. Know-how is one of our prized possessions, so that when we look backward it is rarely to take pleasure in the past itself but usually to calculate the know-how, to assess the prognosis for success in the future.

Promptness is also valued highly in American life. If people are not prompt, it is often taken either as an insult or as an indication that they are not quite responsible. There are those, of a psychological bent, who would say that we are obsessed with time. They can point to individuals in American culture who are literally time-ridden. And even the rest of us feel very strongly about time because we have been taught to take it so seriously. We have stressed this aspect of culture and developed it to a point unequaled anywhere in the world, except, perhaps, in Switzerland and north Germany. Many people criticize our obsessional handling of time. They attribute ulcers and hypertension to the pressure engendered by such a system. Perhaps they are right.

SOME OTHER CONCEPTS OF TIME

Even within the very borders of the United States there are people who handle time in a way which is almost incomprehensible to those who have not made a major effort to understand it. The Pueblo Indians, for example, who live in the Southwest, have a sense of time which is at complete variance with the clock-bound habits of the ordinary American citizen. For the Pueblos events begin when the time is ripe and no sooner.

I can still remember a Christmas dance I attended some twenty-five years ago at one of the pueblos near the Rio Grande. I had to travel over bumpy roads for forty-five miles to get there. At seven thousand feet the ordeal of winter cold at one o'clock in the morning is almost unbearable. Shivering in the still darkness of the pueblo, I kept searching for a clue as to when the dance would begin.

Outside everything was impenetrably quiet. Occasionally there was the muffled beat of a deep pueblo drum, the opening of a door, or the piercing of the night's darkness with a shaft of light. In the church where the dance was to take place a few white townsfolk were huddled together on a balcony, groping for some clue which would suggest how much longer they were going to suffer. "Last year I heard they started at ten o'clock." "They can't start until the priest comes." "There is no way of telling when they will start." All this punctuated by chattering teeth and the stamping of feet to keep up circulation.

Suddenly an Indian opened the door, entered, and poked up the fire in the stove. Everyone nudged his neighbor: "Maybe they are going to begin now." Another hour passed. Another Indian came in from outside, walked across the nave of the church, and disappeared through another door. "Certainly now they will begin. After all, it's almost two o'clock." Someone guessed that they were just being ornery in the hope that the white men would go away. Another had a friend in the pueblo and went to his house to ask when the dance would begin. Nobody knew. Suddenly, when the whites were almost exhausted, there burst upon the night the deep sounds of the drums, rattles, and low male voices singing. Without warning the dance had begun.

After years of performances such as this, no white man in his right mind will hazard a guess as to when one of these ceremonial dances will begin. Those of us who have learned now know that the dance doesn't start at a particular time. It is geared to no schedule. It starts when "things" are ready!

As I pointed out, the white civilized Westerner has a shallow view of the future compared to the Oriental. Yet set beside the Navajo Indians of northern Arizona, he seems a model of long-term patience. The Navajo and the European-American have been trying to adjust their concepts of time for almost a hundred years. So far they have not done too well. To the old-time Navajo time is like space —only the here and now is quite real. The future has little reality to it.

An old friend of mine reared with the Navajo expressed it this way: "You know how the Navajo love horses and how much they love to gamble and bet on horse races. Well, if you were to say to a Navajo, 'My friend, you know my quarter horse that won all the races at Flagstaff last Fourth of July?' that Navajo would eagerly say 'yes, yes,' he knew the horse; and if you were to say, 'In the fall I am going to give you that horse,' the Navajo's face would fall and he would turn around and walk away. On the other hand, if you were to say to him, 'Do you see that old bag of bones I just rode up on? That old hay-bellied mare with the knock-knees and pigeon toes, with the bridle that's falling apart and the saddle that's worn out? You can have that horse, my friend, it's yours. Take it, ride it away now.' Then the Navajo would beam and shake your hand and jump on his new horse and ride away. Of the two, only the immediate gift has reality; a promise of future benefits is not even worth thinking about."

In the early days of the range control and soil conservation programs it was almost impossible to convince the Navajo that there was anything to be gained from giving up their beloved sheep for benefits which could be enjoyed ten or twenty years in the future. Once I was engaged in the supervision of the construction of small earth dams and like everyone else had little success at first in convincing Navajo workmen that they should work hard and build the dam quickly, so that there would be more dams and more water for the sheep. The argument that they could have one dam or ten, depending on how hard they worked, conveyed nothing. It wasn't until I learned to translate our behavior into their terms that they produced as we knew they could.

The solution came about in this way. I had been discussing the problem with a friend, Lorenzo Hubbell, who had lived on the reservation all of his life. When there were difficulties I used to find it helpful to unburden myself to him. Somewhere in his re-

marks there was always a key to the underlying patterns of Navajo life. As we talked I learned that the Navajo understood and respected a bargain. I had some inkling of this when I noticed how unsettled the Indians became when they were permitted to fall down on the job they had agreed to do. In particular they seemed to be apprehensive lest they be asked to repay an unfulfilled obligation at some future time. I decided to sit down with the Navajo crew and talk to them about the work. It was quite useless to argue about the future advantages which would accrue from working hard; linear reasoning and logic were meaningless. They did respond, however, when I indicated that the government was giving them money to get out of debt, providing jobs near their families, and giving them water for their sheep. I stressed the fact that in exchange for this, they must work eight hours every day. This was presented as a bargain. Following my clarification the work progressed satisfactorily.

One of my Indian workmen inadvertently provided another example of the cultural conflict centering around time. His name was "Little Sunday." He was small, wiry, and winning. Since it is not polite to ask the Navajo about their names or even to ask them what their name is, it was necessary to inquire of others how he came to be named "Little Sunday." The explanation was a revealing one.

In the early days of the white traders the Indians had considerable difficulty getting used to the fact that we Europeans divided time into strange and unnatural periods instead of having a "natural" succession of days which began with the new moon and ended with the old. They were particularly perplexed by the notion of the week introduced by the traders and the missionaries. Imagine a Navajo Indian living some forty or fifty miles from a trading store that is a hundred miles north of the railroad deciding that he needs flour and maybe a little lard for bread. He thinks about the flour and the lard, and he thinks about his friends and the fun he will have trading, or maybe he wonders if the trader will give him credit or how much money he can get for the hide he has. After riding horseback for a day and a half to two days he reaches the store all ready to trade. The store is locked up tight. There are a couple of other Navajo Indians camped in the hogan built by the trader. They say the trader is inside but he won't trade because it's Sunday. They bang on his door and he tells them, "Go away, it's Sunday," and the Navajo says, "But

I came from way up on Black Mesa, and I am hungry. I need some food." What can the trader do? Soon he opens the store and then all the Navajo pour in. One of the most frequent and insistent Sunday visitors was a man who earned for himself the sobriquet "Big Sunday." "Little Sunday," it turns out, ran a close second.

The Sioux Indians provide us with another interesting example of the differing views toward time. Not so long ago a man who was introduced as the superintendent of the Sioux came to my office. I learned that he had been born on the reservation and was a product of both Indian and white cultures, having earned his A.B. at one of the Ivy League colleges.

During a long and fascinating account of the many problems which his tribe was having in adjusting to our way of life, he suddenly remarked: "What would you think of a people who had no word for time? My people have no word for 'late' or for 'waiting,' for that matter. They don't know what it is to wait or to be late." He then continued, "I decided that until they could tell time and knew what time was they could never adjust themselves to white culture. So I set about to teach them time. There wasn't a clock that was running in any of the reservation classrooms. So I first bought some decent clocks. Then I made the school buses start on time, and if an Indian was two minutes late that was just too bad. The bus started at eight forty-two and he had to be there."

He was right, of course. The Sioux could not adjust to European ways until they had learned the meaning of time. The superintendent's methods may have sounded a bit extreme, but they were about the only ones that would work. The idea of starting the buses off and making the drivers hold to a rigid schedule was a stroke of genius; much kinder to the Indian, who could better afford to miss a bus on the reservation than lose a job in town because he was late.

There is, in fact, no other way to teach time to people who handle it as differently from us as the Sioux. The quickest way is to get very technical about it and to make it mean something. Later on these people can learn the informal variations, but until they have experienced and then mastered our type of time they will never adjust to our culture.

Thousands of miles away from the reservations of the American Indian we come to another way of handling time which is apt to be completely un-

settling to the unprepared visitor. The inhabitants of the atoll of Truk in the Southwest Pacific treat time in a fashion that has complicated life for themselves as well as for others, since it poses special problems not only for their civil and military governors and the anthropologists recording their life but for their own chiefs as well.

Time does not heal on Truk! Past events stack up, placing an ever-increasing burden on the Trukese and weighing heavily on the present. They are, in fact, treated as though they had just occurred. This was borne out by something which happened shortly after the American occupation of the atoll at the end of World War II.

A villager arrived all out of breath at the military government headquarters. He said that a murder had been committed in the village and that the murderer was running around loose. Quite naturally the military government officer became alarmed. He was about to dispatch M.P.s to arrest the culprit when he remembered that someone had warned him about acting precipitously when dealing with "natives." A little inquiry turned up the fact that the victim had been "fooling around" with the murderer's wife. Still more inquiry of a routine type, designed to establish the place and date of the crime, revealed that the murder had not occurred a few hours or even days ago, as one might expect, but seventeen years before. The murderer had been running around loose in the village all this time.

A further example of how time does not heal on Truk is that of a land dispute that started with the German occupation in the 1890s, was carried on down through the Japanese occupation, and was still current and acrimonious when the Americans arrived in 1946.

Prior to Missionary Moses' arrival on Uman in 1867 life on Truk was characterized by violent and bloody warfare. Villages, instead of being built on the shore where life was a little easier, were placed on the sides of mountains where they could be better protected. Attacks would come without notice and often without apparent provocation. Or a fight might start if a man stole a coconut from a tree that was not his or waylaid a woman and took advantage of her. Years later someone would start thinking about the wrong and decide that it still had not been righted. A village would be attacked again in the middle of the night.

When charges were brought against a chief for things he had done to his people, every little slight, every minor graft would be listed; nothing would be forgotten. Damages would be asked for everything. It seemed preposterous to us Americans, particularly when we looked at the lists of charges. "How could a chief be so corrupt?" "How could people remember so much?"

Though the Truk islanders carry the accumulated burden of time past on their shoulders, they show an almost total inability to grasp the notion that two events can take place at the same time when they are any distance apart. When the Japanese occupied Truk at the end of World War I they took Artie Moses, chief of the island of Uman, to Tokyo. Artie was made to send a wireless message back to his people as a demonstration of the wizardry of Japanese technology. His family refused to believe that he had sent it, that he had said anything at all, though they knew he was in Tokyo. Places at a distance are very real to them, but people who are away are very much away, and any interaction with them is unthinkable.

An entirely different handling of time is reported by the anthropologist Paul Bohannan for the Tiv, a primitive people who live in Nigeria. Like the Navajo, they point to the sun to indicate a general time of day, and they also observe the movement of the moon as it waxes and wanes. What is different is the way they use and experience time. For the Tiv, time is like a capsule. There is a time for visiting, for cooking, or for working; and when one is in one of these times, one does not shift to another.

The Tiv equivalent of the week lasts five to seven days. It is not tied into periodic natural events, such as the phases of the moon. The day of the week is named after the things which are being sold in the nearest "market." If we had the equivalent, Monday would be "automobiles" in Washington, D.C., "furniture" in Baltimore, and "yard goods" in New York. Each of these might be followed by the days for appliances, liquor, and diamonds in the respective cities. This would mean that as you traveled about, the day of the week would keep changing, depending on where you were.

A requisite of our own temporal system is that the components must add up: Sixty seconds have to equal one minute, sixty minutes one hour. The American is perplexed by people who do not do this. The African specialist Henri Alexandre Junod, reporting on the Thonga, tells of a medicine man who had memorized a seventy-year chronology and

could detail the events of each and every year in sequence. Yet this same man spoke of the period he had memorized as an "era" which he computed at "four months and eight hundred years' duration." The usual reaction to this story and others like it is that the man was primitive, like a child, and did not understand what he was saying, because how could seventy years possibly be the same as eight hundred? As students of culture we can no longer dismiss other conceptualizations of reality by saying that they are childlike. We must go much deeper. In the case of the Thonga it seems that a "chronology" is one thing and an "era" something else quite different, and there is no relation between the two in operational terms.

If these distinctions between European-American time and other conceptions of time seem to draw too heavily on primitive peoples, let me mention two other examples—from cultures which are as civilized, if not as industrialized, as our own. In comparing the United States with Iran and Afghanistan very great differences in the handling of time appear. The American attitude toward appointments is an example. Once while in Tehran I had an opportunity to observe some young Iranians making plans for a party. After plans were made to pick up everyone at appointed times and places everything began to fall apart. People would leave messages that they were unable to take so-and-so or were going somewhere else, knowing full well that the person who had been given the message couldn't possibly deliver it. One girl was left stranded on a street corner, and no one seemed to be concerned about it. One of my informants explained that he himself had had many similar experiences. Once he had made eleven appointments to meet a friend. Each time one of them failed to show up. The twelfth time they swore they would both be there, that nothing would interfere. The friend failed to arrive. After waiting for forty-five minutes my informant phoned his friend and found him still at home. The following conversation is an approximation of what took place:

"Is that you, Abdul?" "Yes." "Why aren't you here? I thought we were to meet for sure." "Oh, but it was raining," said Abdul with a sort of whining intonation that is very common in Parsi.

If present appointments are treated rather cavalierly, the past in Iran takes on a very great importance. People look back on what they feel are the wonders of the past and the great ages of Persian culture. Yet the future seems to have little reality or certainty to it. Businessmen have been known to invest hundreds of thousands of dollars in factories of various sorts without making the slightest plan as to how to use them. A complete woolen mill was bought and shipped to Tehran before the buyer had raised enough money to erect it, to buy supplies, or even to train personnel. When American teams of technicians came to help Iran's economy they constantly had to cope with what seemed to them an almost total lack of planning.

Moving east from Iran to Afghanistan, one gets farther afield from American time concepts. A few years ago in Kabul a man appeared, looking for his brother. He asked all the merchants of the market place if they had seen his brother and told them where he was staying in case his brother arrived and wanted to find him. The next year he was back and repeated the performance. By this time one of the members of the American embassy had heard about his inquiries and asked if he had found his brother. The man answered that he and his brother had agreed to meet in Kabul, but neither of them had said what year.

LANGUAGE

Let us continue the line of thought opened up by Hall's passages dealing with the shaping of our actions and ideas by a framework larger than our own immediate learning experiences. The following article by Benjamin Lee Whorf is one of a series of writings by him that have been very influential in raising questions about how much we observe in the world and pay attention to follows from the language we learn to use. Language—a system of words (symbols) representing ideas or concepts—is primarily a group thing, an essential part of culture; anyone with his "private" language cannot communicate with anyone else. Whorf's argument—that the language we learn shapes the reality we see—may not be universally accepted in its radical implications, but his writings have been stimulating and provocative enough that much research still continues on aspects of this problem, often termed "psycholinguistics." One of Whorf's major points is that our language shapes our reality in ways that are by no means conscious; in fact, so much below the levels of awareness that we learn to take the assumptions embedded in language as "natural," as the "way the world is," and rarely question them. In the development of this view Whorf was strongly influenced by Edward Sapir, who in the excerpt following this one continues that point.

SCIENCE AND LINGUISTICS

BENJAMIN LEE WHORF

Every normal person in the world, past infancy in years, can and does talk. By virtue of that fact, every person—civilized or uncivilized—carries through life certain naive but deeply rooted ideas about talking and its relation to thinking. Because of their firm connection with speech habits that have become unconscious and automatic, these notions tend to be rather intolerant of opposition. They are by no means entirely personal and haphazard; their basis is definitely systematic, so that we are justified in calling them a system of natural

Reprinted with permission of publisher. From *The Technology Review*, vol. 42, no. 6 (April 1940), 229–31, 247–48.

logic a term that seems to me preferable to the term common sense, often used for the same thing.

According to natural logic, the fact that every person has talked fluently since infancy makes every man his own authority on the process by which he formulates and communicates. He has merely to consult a common substratum of logic or reason which he and everyone else are supposed to possess. Natural logic says that talking is merely an incidental process concerned strictly with communication, not with formulation of ideas. Talking, or the use of language, is supposed only to "express" what is essentially already formulated nonlinguistically. Formulation is an independent process, called thought or thinking, and is supposed to be largely indifferent to the nature of particular languages. Languages have grammars, which are assumed to be merely norms of conventional and social correctness, but the use of language is supposed to be guided not so much by them as by correct, rational, or intelligent *thinking*.

Thought, in this view, does not depend on grammar but on laws of logic or reason which are supposed to be the same for all observers of the universe—to represent a rationale in the universe that can be "found" independently by all intelligent observers, whether they speak Chinese or Choctaw. In our own culture, the formulations of mathematics and of formal logic have acquired the reputation of dealing with this order of things, i.e., with the realm and laws of pure thought. Natural logic holds that different languages are essentially parallel methods for expressing this one-and-the-same rationale of thought and, hence, differ really in but minor ways which may seem important only because they are seen at close range. It holds that mathematics, symbolic logic, philosophy, and so on, are systems contrasted with language which deal directly with this realm of thought, not that they are themselves specialized extensions of language. The attitude of natural logic is well shown in an old quip about a German grammarian who devoted his whole life to the study of the dative case. From the point of view of natural logic, the dative case and grammar in general are an extremely minor issue. A different attitude is said to have been held by the ancient Arabians: Two princes, so the story goes, quarreled over the honor of putting on the shoes of the most learned grammarian of the realm; whereupon their father, the caliph, is said to have remarked that it was the glory of his king-

dom that great grammarians were honored even above kings.

The familiar saying that the exception proves the rule contains a good deal of wisdom, though from the standpoint of formal logic it became an absurdity as soon as "prove" no longer meant "put on trial." The old saw began to be profound psychology from the time it ceased to have standing in logic. What it might well suggest to us today is that if a rule has absolutely no exceptions, it is not recognized as a rule or as anything else; it is then part of the background of experience of which we tend to remain unconscious. Never having experienced anything in contrast to it, we cannot isolate it and formulate it as a rule until we so enlarge our experience and expand our base of reference that we encounter an interruption of its regularity. The situation is somewhat analogous to that of not missing the water till the well runs dry, or not realizing that we need air till we are choking.

For instance, if a race of people had the physiological defect of being able to see only the color blue, they would hardly be able to formulate the rule that they saw only blue. The term blue would convey no meaning to them, their language would lack color terms, and their words denoting their various sensations of blue would answer to, and translate, our words light, dark, white, black, and so on, not our word blue. In order to formulate the rule or norm of seeing only blue, they would need exceptional moments in which they saw other colors. The phenomenon of gravitation forms a rule without exceptions; needless to say, the untutored person is utterly unaware of any law of gravitation, for it would never enter his head to conceive of a universe in which bodies behaved otherwise than they do at the earth's surface. Like the color blue with our hypothetical race, the law of gravitation is a part of the untutored individual's background, not something he isolates from that background. The law could not be formulated until bodies that always fell were seen in terms of a wider astronomical world in which bodies moved in orbits or went this way and that.

Similarly, whenever we turn our heads, the image of the scene passes across our retinas exactly as it would if the scene turned around us. But this effect is background, and we do not recognize it; we do not see a room turn around us but are conscious only of having turned our heads in a stationary room. If we observe critically while turning the head or eyes quickly, we shall see, no motion it is true, yet a blurring of the scene between two clear views. Normally we are quite unconscious of this continual blurring but seem to be looking about in an unblurred world. Whenever we walk past a tree or house, its image on the retina changes just as if the tree or house were turning on an axis; yet we do not see trees or houses turn as we travel about at ordinary speeds. Sometimes ill-fitting glasses will reveal queer movements in the scene as we look about, but normally we do not see the relative motion of the environment when we move; our psychic make-up is somehow adjusted to disregard whole realms of phenomena that are so all-pervasive as to be irrelevant to our daily lives and needs.

Natural logic contains two fallacies: First, it does not see that the phenomena of a language are to its own speakers largely of a background character and so are outside the critical consciousness and control of the speaker who is expounding natural logic. Hence, when anyone, as a natural logician, is talking about reason, logic, and the laws of correct thinking, he is apt to be simply marching in step with purely grammatical facts that have somewhat of a background character in his own language or family of languages but are by no means universal in all languages and in no sense a common substratum of reason. Second, natural logic confuses agreement about subject matter, attained through use of language, with knowledge of the linguistic process by which agreement is attained, i.e., with the province of the despised (and to its notion superfluous) grammarian. Two fluent speakers, of English let us say, quickly reach a point of assent about the subject matter of their speech; they agree about what their language refers to. One of them, A, can give directions that will be carried out by the other, B, to A's complete satisfaction. Because they thus understand each other so perfectly, A and B, as natural logicians, suppose they must of course know how it is all done. They think, e.g., that it is simply a matter of choosing words to express thoughts. If you ask A to explain how he got B's agreement so readily, he will simply repeat to you, with more or less elaboration or abbreviation, what he said to B. He has no notion of the process involved. The amazingly complex system of linguistic patterns and classifications which A and B must have in common before they can adjust to each other at all, is all background to A and B.

These background phenomena are the province of the grammarian—or of the linguist, to give him his more modern name as a scientist. The word linguist in common, and especially newspaper, parlance means something entirely different, namely, a person who can quickly attain agreement about subject matter with different people speaking a number of different languages. Such a person is better termed a polyglot or a multilingual. Scientific linguists have long understood that ability to speak a language fluently does not necessarily confer a linguistic knowledge of it, i.e., understanding of its background phenomena and its systematic processes and structure, any more than ability to play a good game of billiards confers or requires any knowledge of the laws of mechanics that operate upon the billiard table.

The situation here is not unlike that in any other field of science. All real scientists have their eyes primarily on background phenomena that cut very little ice, as such, in our daily lives; and yet their studies have a way of bringing out a close relation between these unsuspected realms of fact and such decidedly foreground activities as transporting goods, preparing food, treating the sick, or growing potatoes, which in time may become very much modified simply because of pure scientific investigation in no way concerned with these brute matters themselves. Linguistics is in quite similar case; the background phenomena with which it deals are involved in all our foreground activities of talking and of reaching agreement, in all reasoning and arguing of cases, in all law, arbitration, conciliation, contracts, treaties, public opinion, weighing of scientific theories, formulation of scientific results. Whenever agreement or assent is arrived at in human affairs, and whether or not mathematics or other specialized symbolisms are made part of the procedure, *this agreement is reached by linguistic processes, or else it is not reached.*

As we have seen, an overt knowledge of the linguistic processes by which agreement is attained is not necessary to reaching some sort of agreement, but it is certainly no bar thereto; the more complicated and difficult the matter, the more such knowledge is a distinct aid, till the point may be reached —I suspect the modern world has about arrived at it—when the knowledge becomes not only an aid but a necessity. The situation may be likened to that of navigation. Every boat that sails is in the lap of planetary forces; yet a boy can pilot his small craft around a harbor without benefit of geography, astronomy, mathematics, or international politics. To the captain of an ocean liner, however, some knowledge of all these subjects is essential.

When linguists became able to examine critically and scientifically a large number of languages of widely different patterns, their base of reference was expanded; they experienced an interruption of phenomena hitherto held universal, and a whole new order of significances came into their ken. It was found that the background linguistic system (in other words, the grammar) of each language is not merely a reproducing instrument for voicing ideas but rather is itself the shaper of ideas, the program and guide for the individual's mental activity, for his analysis of impressions, for his synthesis of his mental stock in trade. Formulation of ideas is not an independent process, strictly rational in the old sense, but is part of a particular grammar and differs, from slightly to greatly, as between different grammars. We dissect nature along lines laid down by our native languages. The categories and types that we isolate from the world of phenomena we do not find there because they stare every observer in the face; on the contrary, the world is presented in a kaleidoscopic flux of impressions which has to be organized by our minds—and this means largely by the linguistic systems in our minds. We cut nature up, organize it into concepts, and ascribe significances as we do, largely because we are parties to an agreement to organize it in this way—an agreement that holds throughout our speech community and is codified in the patterns of our language. The agreement is, of course, an implicit and unstated one, *but its terms are absolutely obligatory;* we cannot talk at all except by subscribing to the organization and classification of data which the agreement decrees.

This fact is very significant for modern science, for it means that no individual is free to describe nature with absolute impartiality but is constrained to certain modes of interpretation even while he thinks himself most free. The person most nearly free in such respects would be a linguist familiar with very many widely different linguistic systems. As yet no linguist even is in any such position. We are thus introduced to a new principle of relativity, which holds that all observers are not led by the same physical evidence to the same picture of the universe, unless their linguistic backgrounds are similar, or can in some way be calibrated.

This rather startling conclusion is not so apparent if we compare only our modern European languages, with perhaps Latin and Greek thrown in for good measure. Among these tongues there is a unanimity of major pattern which at first seems to bear out natural logic. But this unanimity exists only because these tongues are all Indo-European dialects cut to the same basic plan, being historically transmitted from what was long ago one speech community; because the modern dialects have long shared in building up a common culture; and because much of this culture, on the more intellectual side, is derived from the linguistic backgrounds of Latin and Greek. Thus this group of languages satisfies the special case of the clause beginning "unless" in the statement of the linguistic relativity principle at the end of the preceding paragraph. From this condition follows the unanimity of description of the world in the community of modern scientists. But it must be emphasized that "all modern Indo-European-speaking observers" is not the same thing as "all observers." That modern Chinese or Turkish scientists describe the world in the same terms as Western scientists means, of course, only that they have taken over bodily the entire Western system of rationalizations, not that they have corroborated that system from their native posts of observation.

When Semitic, Chinese, Tibetan, or African languages are contrasted with our own, the divergence in analysis of the world becomes more apparent; and when we bring in the native languages of the Americas, where speech communities for many millenniums have gone their ways independently of each other and of the Old World, the fact that languages dissect nature in many different ways becomes patent. The relativity of all conceptual systems, ours included, and their dependence upon language stand revealed. That American Indians speaking only their native tongues are never called upon to act as scientific observers is in no wise to the point. To exclude the evidence which their languages offer as to what the human mind can do is like expecting botanists to study nothing but food plants and hothouse-roses and then tell us what the plant world is like!

Let us consider a few examples. In English we divide most of our words into two classes, which have different grammatical and logical properties. Class 1 we call nouns, e.g., "house," "man"; Class 2, verbs, e.g., "hit," "run." Many words of one class can act secondarily as of the other class, e.g., "a hit," "a run," or "to man" the boat, but on the primary level the division between the classes is absolute. Our language thus gives us a bipolar division of nature. But nature herself is not thus polarized. If it be said that strike, turn, run, are verbs because they denote temporary or short-lasting events, i.e., actions, why then is fist a noun? It also is a temporary event. Why are lightning, spark, wave, eddy, pulsation, flame, storm, phase, cycle, spasm, noise, emotion, nouns? They are temporary events. If man and house are nouns because they are long-lasting and stable events, i.e., things, what then are keep, adhere, extend, project, continue, persist, grow, dwell, and so on, doing among the verbs? If it be objected that possess, adhere, are verbs because they are stable relationships rather than stable percepts, why then should equilibrium, pressure, current, peace, group, nation, society, tribe, sister, or any kinship term, be among the nouns? It will be found that an "event" to *us* means "what our language classes as a verb" or something analogized therefrom. And it will be found that it is not possible to define event, thing, object, relationship, and so on, from nature, but that to define them always involves a circuitous return to the grammatical categories of the definer's language.

In the Hopi language, lightning, wave, flame, meteor, puff of smoke, pulsation, are verbs—events of necessarily brief duration cannot be anything but verbs. Cloud and storm are at about the lower limit of duration for nouns. Hopi, you see, actually has a classification of events (or linguistic isolates) by duration type, something strange to our modes of thought. On the other hand, in Nootka, a language of Vancouver Island, all words seem to us to be verbs, but really there are no Classes 1 and 2; we have, as it were, a monistic view of nature that gives us only one class of word for all kinds of events. "A house occurs" or "it houses" is the way of saying "house," exactly like "a flame occurs" or "it burns." These terms seem to us like verbs because they are inflected for durational and temporal nuances, so that the suffixes of the word for house event make it mean long-lasting house, temporary house, future house, house that used to be, what started out to be a house, and so on.

Hopi has a noun that covers every thing or being that flies, with the exception of birds, which class is denoted by another noun. The former noun may be said to denote the class (FC–B)—flying class minus bird. The Hopi actually call insect, airplane, and aviator all by the same word, and feel no difficulty about it. The situation, of course, decides any possible confusion among very disparate members of a broad linguistic class, such as this class (FC–B). This class seems to us too large and inclusive, but so would our class "snow" to an Eskimo. We have the same word for falling snow, snow on the ground, snow packed hard like ice, slushy snow, wind-driven flying snow—whatever the situation may be. To an Eskimo, this all-inclusive word would be almost unthinkable; he would say that falling snow, slushy snow, and so on, are sensuously and operationally different, different things to contend with; he uses different words for them and for other kinds of snow. The Aztecs go even farther than we in the opposite direction, with cold, ice, and snow all represented by the same basic word with different terminations; ice is the noun form; cold, the adjectival form; and for snow, "ice mist."

What surprises most is to find that various grand generalizations of the Western world, such as time, velocity, and matter, are not essential to the construction of a consistent picture of the universe. The psychic experiences that we class under these headings are, of course, not destroyed; rather, categories derived from other kinds of experiences take over the rulership of the cosmology and seem to function just as well. Hopi may be called a timeless language. It recognizes psychological time, which is much like Bergson's "duration," but this "time" is quite unlike the mathematical time, T, used by our physicists. Among the peculiar properties of Hopi time are that it varies with each observer, does not permit of simultaneity, and has zero dimensions, i.e., it cannot be given a number greater than one. The Hopi do not say, "I stayed five days," but "I left on the fifth day." A word referring to this kind of time, like the word day, can have no plural. . . .

Hopi grammar, by means of its forms called aspects and modes, also makes it easy to distinguish between momentary, continued, and repeated occurrences, and to indicate the actual sequence of reported events. Thus the universe can be described without recourse to a concept of dimensional time. How would a physics constructed along these lines work, with no T (time) in its equations? Perfectly, as far as I can see, though of course it would require different ideology and perhaps different mathematics. Of course V (velocity) would have to go too. The Hopi language has no word really equivalent to our "speed" or "rapid." What translates these terms is usually a word meaning intense or very, accompanying any verb of motion. Here is a clew to the nature of our new physics. We may have to introduce a new term I, intensity. Every thing and event will have an I, whether we regard the thing or event as moving or as just enduring or being. Perhaps the I of an electric charge will turn out to be its voltage, or potential. We shall use clocks to measure some intensities, or, rather, some *relative* intensities, for the absolute intensity of anything will be meaningless. Our old friend acceleration will still be there but doubtless under a new name. We shall perhaps call it V, meaning not velocity but variation. Perhaps all growths and accumulations will be regarded as V's. We should not have the concept of rate in the temporal sense, since, like velocity, rate introduces a mathematical and linguistic time. Of course we know that all measurements are ratios, but the measurements of intensities made by comparison with the standard intensity of a clock or a planet we do not treat as ratios, any more than we so treat a distance made by comparison with a yardstick.

A scientist from another culture that used time and velocity would have great difficulty in getting us to understand these concepts. We should talk about the intensity of a chemical reaction; he would speak of its velocity or its rate, which words we should at first think were simply words for intensity in his language. Likewise, he at first would think that intensity was simply our own word for velocity. At first we should agree, later we should begin to disagree, and it might dawn upon both sides that different systems of rationalization were being used. He would find it very hard to make us understand what he really meant by velocity of a chemical reaction. We should have no words that would fit. He would try to explain it by likening it to a running horse, to the difference between a good horse and a lazy horse. We should try to show him, with a

superior laugh, that his analogy also was a matter of different intensities, aside from which there was little similarity between a horse and a chemical reaction in a beaker. We should point out that a running horse is moving relative to the ground, whereas the material in the beaker is at rest.

One significant contribution to science from the linguistic point of view may be the greater development of our sense of perspective. We shall no longer be able to see a few recent dialects of the Indo-European family, and the rationalizing techniques elaborated from their patterns, as the apex of the evolution of the human mind; nor their present wide spread as due to any survival from fitness or to anything but a few events of history—events that could be called fortunate only from the parochial point of view of the favored parties. They, and our own thought processes with them, can no longer be envisioned as spanning the gamut of reason and knowledge but only as one constellation in a galactic expanse. A fair realization of the incredible degree of diversity of linguistic system that ranges over the globe leaves one with an inescapable feeling that the human spirit is inconceivably old; that the few thousand years of history covered by our written records are no more than the thickness of a pencil mark on the scale that measures our past experience on this planet; that the events of these recent millenniums spell nothing in any evolutionary wise, that the race has taken no sudden spurt, achieved no commanding synthesis during recent millenniums, but has only played a little with a few of the linguistic formulations and views of nature bequeathed from an inexpressibly longer past. Yet neither this feeling nor the sense of precarious dependence of all we know upon linguistic tools which themselves are largely unknown need be discouraging to science but should, rather, foster that humility which accompanies the true scientific spirit, and thus forbid that arrogance of the mind which hinders real scientific curiosity and detachment.

UNCONSCIOUS PATTERNING

In these few pages, Sapir does two things. First, he talks more about how deeply a cultural system influences our behavior. He thus summarizes the main point of this entire section—that, in its broad outlines, our distinctive ways of behavior in various human groups are the product not only of genetically-given patterns, but also of other aspects of group life, such as idea systems, value systems, and symbol systems. And for the most part we are not fully aware of how much of our behavior is thus patterned and structured.

The second point he makes serves as a transition from this section of the book to the next; he reiterates the crucial idea of *levels* of *phenomena* and *levels* of *analysis*. When we talk of "the individual" and "the group" we are talking of such levels—not of antithetical "things." Without a full understanding of what these ideas basically mean in regard to the abstractions we make from our observations, any student in the behavioral or social sciences will get off on a fundamentally wrong foot. Is there such a thing as "social behavior" distinctly different from "individual" behavior? Or if there is a difference, where does such difference lie—in the events of nature themselves, or in our way of perceiving and *con*ceiving such events? It is into this critical area of thought and understanding that Sapir's excerpt introduces us, and which the next section of the book takes up in more detail—the area of the *conceptualization* of culture.

THE UNCONSCIOUS PATTERNING OF BEHAVIOR IN SOCIETY

EDWARD SAPIR

We may seem to be guilty of a paradox when we speak of the unconscious in reference to social activity. Doubtful as is the usefulness of this concept when we confine ourselves to the behavior of the individual, it may seem to be worse than doubtful when we leave the kinds of behavior that are strictly individual and deal with those more complex kinds of activity which, rightly or wrongly, are supposed to be carried on, not by individuals as such, but by the associations of human beings that constitute society. It may be argued that society has no more of an unconscious than it has hands or legs.

I propose to show, however, that the paradox is a real one only if the term "social behavior" is understood in the very literal sense of behavior referred to groups of human beings which act as such, regardless of the mentalities of the individuals which compose the groups. To such a mystical group alone can a mysterious "social unconsciousness" be ascribed. But as we are very far from believing that such groups really exist, we may be

able to persuade ourselves that no more especial kind of unconsciousness need be imputed to social behavior than is needed to understand the behavior of the individual himself. We shall be on much safer ground if we take it for granted that all human behavior involves essentially the same types of mental functioning, as well conscious as unconscious, and that the term "social" is no more exclusive of the concept "unconscious" than is the term "individual," for the very simple reason that the terms "social" and "individual" are contrastive in only a limited sense. We will assume that any kind of psychology that explains the behavior of the individual also explains the behavior of society in so far as the psychological point of view is applicable to and sufficient for the study of social behavior. It is true that for certain purposes it is very useful to look away entirely from the individual and to think of socialized behavior as though it were carried on by certain larger entities which transcend the psycho-physical organism. But this viewpoint implicitly demands the abandonment of the psychological approach to the explanation of human conduct in society.

It will be clear from what we have said that we

Reprinted from *The Unconscious: A Symposium,* Ethel S. Drummer, ed. (New York: Knopf, 1927), pp. 114–24.

do not find the essential difference between individual and social behavior to lie in the psychology of the behavior itself. Strictly speaking, each kind of behavior is individual, the difference in terminology being entirely due to a difference in the point of view. If our attention is focused on the actual, theoretically measurable behavior of a given individual at a given time and place, we call it "individual behavior," no matter what the physiological or psychological nature of that behavior may be. If, on the other hand, we prefer to eliminate certain aspects of such individual behavior from our consideration and to hold on only to those respects in which it corresponds to certain norms of conduct which have been developed by human beings in association with one another and which tend to perpetuate themselves by tradition, we speak of "social behavior." In other words, social behavior is merely the sum or, better, arrangement of such aspects of individual behavior as are referred to culture patterns that have their proper context, not in the spatial and temporal continuities of biological behavior, but in historical sequences that are imputed to actual behavior by a principle of selection.

We have thus defined the difference between individual and social behavior, not in terms of kind or essence, but in terms of organization. To say that the human being behaves individually at one moment and socially at another is as absurd as to declare that matter follows the laws of chemistry at a certain time and succumbs to the supposedly different laws of atomic physics at another, for matter is always obeying certain mechanical laws which are at one and the same time both physical and chemical according to the manner in which we choose to define its organization. In dealing with human beings, we simply find it more convenient for certain purposes to refer a given act to the psycho-physical organism itself. In other cases the interest happens to lie in continuities that go beyond the individual organism and its functioning, so that a bit of conduct that is objectively no more and no less individual than the first is interpreted in terms of the non-individual patterns that constitute social behavior or cultural behavior.

It would be a useful exercise to force ourselves to see any given human act from both of these points of view and to try to convince ourselves in this way that it is futile to classify human acts as such as having an inherently individual or social significance. It is true that there are a great many organismal functions that it is difficult to think of in social terms, but I think that even here the social point of view may often be applied with success. Few social students are interested, for instance, in the exact manner in which a given individual breathes. Yet it is not to be doubted that our breathing habits are largely conditioned by factors conventionally classified as social. There are polite and impolite ways of breathing. There are special attitudes which seem to characterize whole societies that undoubtedly condition the breathing habits of the individuals who make up these societies. Ordinarily the characteristic rhythm of breathing of a given individual is looked upon as a matter for strictly individual definition. But if, for one reason or another, the emphasis shifts to the consideration of a certain manner of breathing as due to good form or social tradition or some other principle that is usually given a social context, then the whole subject of breathing at once ceases to be a merely individual concern and takes on the appearance of a social pattern. Thus, the regularized breathing of the Hindu Yogi, the subdued breathing of those who are in the presence of a recently deceased companion laid away in a coffin and surrounded by all the ritual of funeral observances, the style of breathing which one learns from an operatic singer who gives lessons on the proper control of the voice, are, each and every one of them, capable of isolation as socialized modes of conduct that have a definite place in the history of human culture, though they are obviously not a whit less facts of individual behavior than the most casual and normal style of breathing, such as one rarely imagines to have other than purely individual implications. Strange as it may seem at first blush, there is no hard and fast line of division as to class of behavior between a given style of breathing, *provided that it be socially interpreted*, and a religious doctrine or a form of political administration. This is not to say that it may not be infinitely more useful to apply the social mode of analysis of human conduct to certain cases and the individual mode of analysis to others. But we do maintain that such differences of analysis are merely imposed by the nature of the interest of the observer and are not inherent in the phenomena themselves.

All cultural behavior is patterned. This is merely a way of saying that many things that an individual does and thinks and feels may be looked upon not merely from the standpoint of the forms of behavior that are proper to himself as a biological organism but from the standpoint of a generalized mode of conduct that is imputed to society rather than to the individual, though the personal genesis of conduct is of precisely the same nature, whether we choose to call the conduct individual or social. It is impossible to say what an individual is doing unless we have tacitly accepted the essentially arbitrary modes of interpretation that social tradition is constantly suggesting to us from the very moment of our birth. Let anyone who doubts this try the experiment of making a painstaking report of the actions of a group of natives engaged in some form of activity, say religious, to which he has not the cultural key. If he is a skillful writer, he may succeed in giving a picturesque account of what he sees and hears, or thinks he sees and hears, but the chances of his being able to give a relation of what happens in terms that would be intelligible and acceptable to the natives themselves are practically nil. He will be guilty of all manner of distortion. His emphasis will be constantly askew. He will find interesting what the natives take for granted as a casual kind of behavior worthy of no particular comment, and he will utterly fail to observe the crucial turning points in the course of action that give formal significance to the whole in the minds of those who do possess the key to its understanding. This patterning or formal analysis of behavior is to a surprising degree dependent on the mode of apprehension which has been established by the tradition of the group. Forms and significances which seem obvious to an outsider will be denied outright by those who carry out the patterns; outlines and implications that are perfectly clear to these may be absent to the eye of the onlooker. It is the failure to understand the necessity of grasping the native patterning which is responsible for so much unimaginative and misconceiving description of procedures that we have not been brought up with. It becomes actually possible to interpret as base what is inspired by the noblest and even holiest of motives, and to see altruism or beauty where nothing of the kind is either felt or intended.

Ordinarily a cultural pattern is to be defined both in terms of function and of form, the two concepts being inseparably intertwined in practice, however convenient it may be to dissociate them in theory. Many functions of behavior are primary in the sense that an individual organic need, such as the satisfaction of hunger, is being fulfilled, but often the functional side of behavior is either entirely transformed or, at the least, takes on a new increment of significance. In this way new functional interpretations are constantly being developed for forms set by tradition. Often the true functions of behavior are unknown and a merely rationalized function may be imputed to it. Because of the readiness with which forms of human conduct lose or modify their original functions or take on entirely new ones, it becomes necessary to see social behavior from a formal as well as from a functional point of view, and we shall not consider any kind of human behavior as understood if we can merely give or think we can give, an answer to the question "For what purpose is this being done?" We shall have also to know what is the precise manner and articulation of the doing.

Now it is a commonplace of observation that the reasoning intelligence seeks to attach itself rather to the functions than to the forms of conduct. For every thousand individuals who can tell with some show of reason why they sing or use words in connected speech or handle money, there is barely one who can adequately define the essential outlines of these modes of behavior. No doubt certain forms will be imputed to such behavior if attention is drawn to it, but experience shows that the forms discovered may be very seriously at variance with those actually followed and discoverable on closer study. In other words, the patterns of social behavior are not necessarily discovered by simple observation, though they may be adhered to with tyrannical consistency in the actual conduct of life. If we can show that normal human beings, both in confessedly social behavior and often in supposedly individual behavior, are reacting in accordance with deep-seated cultural patterns, and if, further, we can show that these patterns are not so much known as felt, not so much capable of conscious description as of naïve practice, then we have the right to speak of the "unconscious patterning of behavior in society." The unconscious nature of this patterning consists not in some mysterious function of a racial or social mind reflected in the minds of the individual members of society, but merely in a typical unawareness on the part of the individual of outlines and demarcations and significances of conduct which he is all the time implicitly following. Jung's "racial unconscious" is neither an intelligible nor a necessary concept. It introduces more difficulties than it solves, while we have all we need for the psychological understanding of social behavior in the facts of individual psychology.

Why are the forms of social behavior not adequately known by the normal individual? How is it that we can speak, if only metaphorically, of a social unconscious? I believe that the answer to this question rests in the fact that the relations between the elements of experience which serve to give them their form and significance are more powerfully "felt" or "intuited" than consciously perceived. It is a matter of common knowledge that it is relatively easy to fix the attention on some arbitrarily selected element of experience, such as a sensation or an emotion, but that it is far from easy to become conscious of the exact place which such an element holds in the total constellations of behavior. It is easy for an Australian native, for instance, to say by what kinship term he calls so and so or whether or not he may undertake such and such relations with a given individual. It is exceedingly difficult for him to give a general rule of which these specific examples of behavior are but illustrations, though all the while he acts as though the rule were perfectly well known to him. *In a sense it is well known to him.* But this knowledge is not capable of conscious manipulation in terms of word symbols. It is, rather, a very delicately nuanced feeling of subtle relations, both experienced and possible. To this kind of knowledge may

be applied the term "intuition," which, when so defined, need have no mystic connotations whatever. It is strange how frequently one has the illusion of free knowledge, in the light of which one may manipulate conduct at will, only to discover in the test that one is being impelled by strict loyalty to forms of behavior that one can feel with the utmost nicety but can state only in the vaguest and most approximate fashion. It would seem that we act all the more securely for our unawareness of the patterns that control us. It may well be that, owing to the limitations of the conscious life, any attempt to subject even the higher forms of social behavior to purely conscious control must result in disaster. Perhaps there is a far-reaching moral in the fact that even a child may speak the most difficult language with idiomatic ease but that it takes an unusually analytical type of mind to define the mere elements of that incredibly subtle linguistic mechanism which is but a plaything of the child's unconscious. Is it not possible that the contemporary mind, in its restless attempt to drag all the forms of behavior into consciousness and to apply the results of its fragmentary or experimental analysis to the guidance of conduct, is really throwing away a greater wealth for the sake of a lesser and more dazzling one? It is almost as though a misguided enthusiast exchanged his thousands of dollars of accumulated credit at the bank for a few glittering coins of manifest, though little, worth.

PART IV

THE CONCEPTUALIZATION OF CULTURE

We have seen the variety found in patterned human behavior around the world, even such behavior as might be thought of as most "biological" in its genesis and expression. But can the matter be left at that? Can we do anything further with these diverse observations?

We come now to a hard but essential part in the process of knowing— translating descriptions of observed "customary" events into *ideas* or concepts dealing with those events, with the grouping of those events into classes, and with the interrelations of those classes with other classes of events. We are concerned, let's remember, with the concept of culture, that is, with drawing some conclusions and inferences from the patterned behavior we have seen as to the existence of "something" located somewhere in nature to which we might put the *word* "culture" referring to the *concept* of culture. We will do so if it is *useful* to do so, if there seem to be recurring events or systems in empirical events that we can more conveniently group together and thus label than deal with in isolation from each other. The purpose of the following series of readings is, then, to work toward at least a "first approximation" understanding of *a* concept of culture, a kind of conception of culture increasingly widely used by American anthropologists. In this section we will be interested in both the process of inference by which we come to recognize an example of a cultural dimension, as well as in what seem to be the essential features or characteristics of that concept. Subsequent sections of readings will enlarge the perspective and framework within which those events abstracted as "cultural processes" will be seen to operate.

WHAT WE START WITH

In the following pages Homans gets us off on the formidable task of *conceptualization*—of rising from looking at a series of events occurring in nature, to the level of working ideas in our minds about those events. As he says, this is a difficult job, one beset with all kinds of dead ends, loose notions, and slippages between words (concepts) and the things they refer to. But it is an essential operation; we can't go any further in the study of "culture" until the fundamental operations of the mind by which we will reach some agreement on what we mean are laid out. Homans, starting with simple steps, reveals the developing of working ideas (conceptualization) as a *process* by which we work back and forth between ideas and observations. He starts, as we did in Part III, with observations of behavior, of people doing and saying things. He shows the kinds of mental and semantic operations that a behavioral scientist goes through in order to be able to say to someone else what kinds of observations in nature he is referring to when he uses a particular term or concept. This is often called "operationalism," and because of its fundamental importance for all of what follows in this reader the next three selections are also concerned with what it means.

Homans says that he will start his book by developing several basic concepts and later on using them in combination to analyze several problems in human social behavior. The concepts, as you will see, are fundamental in one form or another to all the social and behavioral sciences: he starts with "custom," which we can think of simply as descriptive patterns or regularities in human behavior; he then takes up "activity" (very similar to the notion of sheer behavior itself); then "interaction" (the fundamental concept for all more complicated ideas of social relationships and social structures); and finally "sentiment" (a concept having some similarities to concepts such as "value" and "belief"). I mention these three latter concepts not so much because they will all turn out to be important in the rest of this reader (although they will do that), but to show an example of the relationship between basic observations of behavior and the abstracting from that behavior of certain recurrent patterns or themes that are gathered together under the umbrella of a particular word (which represents a concept). Homans thus gives us, in a simplified way, an overview of the process of *conceptualization* which will be the central theme of this section.

I am not bothered, and I hope you won't be, by the fact that Homans is apparently speaking to sociologists in these pages. I am sure that he would not mind his words being used to educate all kinds of students in understanding human social behavior. Indeed, although this is not the place to dwell any further on it, there are many areas of overlap in methods, concepts, and research problems between the fields of anthropology and sociology. And common to both the sociologist and anthropologist who study organized human social life, some such concepts as Homans introduces here are commonly used as basic tools of the trade, no matter by what word or words they may be called.

THE ELEMENTS OF BEHAVIOR

GEORGE C. HOMANS

This chapter is a tough one, perhaps the toughest in the book, but we had better know the worst at once. It tries to do two things at the same time. First, it tries to show how the kinds of generalization we

From *The Human Group* by George C. Homans, © 1950 by Harcourt Brace Jovanovich, Inc., N.Y., and reprinted with their permission.

shall be interested in are reached: how we go from simple descriptions of social events to uniformities in the behavior of a limited number of persons and groups and finally to generalizations that may apply to all groups. Second, it tries to define the words, or concepts, that will come into these highest generalizations. As we shall see, the two jobs mesh with one another and must be carried on together.

One of the big problems of sociology, as of all social science, is semantic: the problem of the relation between the words used and the observations made. The meanings of words are usually given by definitions, but the trouble with definitions, as one of the first great semanticists, Lord Bacon, pointed out, is that "the definitions themselves consist of words, and those words beget others: so that it is necessary to recur to individual instances, and those in due series and order."[1] Bacon meant that the end of the chain of words must be anchored in an act something like the one by which a mother teaches her child the meaning of the word *cow:* she points at the beast and says the word. Acts of this kind are not available to us. We are not in the open air watching a group in action, and we cannot learn the meaning of sociological concepts by having someone point to various items in the behavior of the group and, as he does so, name the concepts. But we can do the next best thing. We can take the descriptions of group behavior made by good observers, persons who, unlike themselves, have been watching groups in the open air; we can point to certain things they saw and give these things names. The names are the concepts.

Our work presupposes the direct observation of human behavior. It does not for the most part deal with what men write in answer to a questionnaire or what they say when a research assistant has his foot in the door. It deals with what men say and do on the ordinary occasions of ordinary life. This kind of fact is surprisingly hard to collect; it demands an observer who is not himself so much a part of the situation that he cannot view it with a fresh eye, and one who does not, by the mere fact of his presence, change what would otherwise be said and done. Anthropologists who live with the tribes they study and who back up their lengthy questionings of native informants with firsthand observations of daily life collect this kind of material, and so do a few sociologists who study groups and communities in our own society. Our work relies on theirs. Some social scientists find this kind of material hard and unsatisfying to work with: it can seldom be converted into statistics and always leaves unanswered many interesting questions—and they shy away from it. Nevertheless it is the stuff of everyday existence, and we start with it here.

EVENTS IN THE SINGLE GROUP

We are going to begin with a description of everyday social events in a society not our own. The world is a stage, and one of its many scenes opens:

The room is low and rectangular. The left wall is filled by a door, closed, and a big stone fireplace, fitted for cooking. Chairs and benches are set around the fireplace. Against the back wall a table stands, and to the right of the table a colored picture hangs over a cabinet containing a small figure. The right wall is taken up by a dresser, full of kitchen gear and crockery, on one side of which is a door and on the other a staircase leading upstairs. Through a window over the table a yard, with a cart in it, is seen in dim light.

A woman opens the door, right, and comes into the room. She goes to the fireplace, rakes together the ashes on the hearth, some of them still alive, puts on new fuel, and rekindles the blaze. Then she fills a kettle with water and hangs it on a hook over the fire. When it boils, she makes tea; meanwhile she lays out dishes, cutlery, bread, and milk on the table, and gets ready to cook eggs.

A middle-aged man and two younger ones enter, exchange a few words with the woman, pull up chairs, sit down at the table, and begin to eat. The woman herself does not sit, but stands by, ready to bring up more food and drink if the men ask for them. When the men have eaten, the older one says to the younger ones, "Well, we'd better be off." They go out.

By this time a girl has joined the woman in the room, but not until the men have left do the two sit down for their meal. Before they have finished, crying is heard outside, right. The woman leaves and later returns carrying a young child in her arms. She fondles and comforts it, then feeds it in its turn.

She turns to the girl, who is already washing the dishes, with a remark about making butter. . . .[2]

We need not go on. This scene, or something much like it, has been enacted millions of times in the history of mankind, and it shows, of course, a farm family beginning a working day. It is not an American farm family, though families of this sort were common not so long ago in America and survive in some places still. It is a countryman's family in the southwest of Ireland. Farm families, differing from this one in some outward appearances, but perhaps not very different in essentials, have for centuries formed the foundations of society in Europe, the Near East, India, China, and much of the Americas. This social unit is characteristic of many of the countries that have the largest popula-

[1]F. Bacon, *Novum Organum,* Bk. I, aphorism lix.

[2]Adapted from C. M. Arensberg and S. T. Kimball, *Family and Community in Ireland,* 35.

tions. Only in recent years and in a few places have we begun to see the appearance of a new kind of family. The old-fashioned farm family—if we may call it that—is still the commonest of human groups.

The scene is familiar. We begin and end with the familiar and are lucky to be able to do so, but the important point at the moment is not the familiarity of the scene. It is rather that a scene like this is part of the raw material of sociology: a description of a series of *events*, in each of which at one particular place and time a person did certain things, in certain physical surroundings, perhaps with certain implements and together with certain other persons. All science begins with process, the flux of things, the passing scene. Generalization must be true to events. We forget their vividness at our peril. And how refreshing they are! "Here," we can say, "is one kind of certainty. No matter how we interpret them, and no matter how far they fall short of telling the whole story, these things, at least these things, *happened*."

There can be little interpretation of, generalization from, single events. We can learn much—and it is good discipline, too— from trying merely to report, that is, from trying to describe human behavior in words altogether flat, simply descriptive, devoid of interpretation. In any strict sense, it cannot be done. Any noun implies some context; even a word like *table* implies something about the use of a physical object. But in the effort to leave out at least the higher levels of meaning, we can discover how much meaning we regularly put into our descriptions. Perhaps we shall see how easy it is to commit ourselves to an interpretation before we know what we are doing.

Our description of the farm family beginning the day is just such a flat description as a playwright might write in setting the opening scene of his play. The meaning unfolds only as the action of the play develops. Thus the older woman is not called the mother of the family, nor the man the father. "Mother" and "father" assume a certain scheme of social relationships, and from the single scene we cannot be sure that we are dealing with that kind of scheme. It is better to begin with distinctions like those between man and woman, youth and age. In the same way, the cabinet is not called a shrine. If we had called it that, we should have been assuming something that the single scene cannot tell us. Nevertheless, there are items in the description that might be remembered, should he run across them

again, by anyone anxious to build up a picture of the relationships between the members of the family. For instance, the older man gives orders to the two younger ones or at least gives the signal to go out and begin the day's work. The woman likewise points out to the girl the job—making butter— that the two of them will do in the course of the day. Both women wait for the men to finish eating before they sit down themselves. The older woman comforts and plays with the baby. And so on. An observer builds up his picture of social relationships from repeated events like these.

CUSTOM

The next stage in the analysis of human behavior— and it always implies the first—is reached when we recognize simple recurrences in events, recurrences at different intervals. To go back to our farm family, we note that almost every day the men go out to work in the fields; that every year, at about the same season, they dig potatoes; that in this work the father directs the activities of the sons. The women do the chores around the house but do not work in the fields; so long as there is a youngster in the house, the mother feeds it, goes to it when it cries, comforts and protects it. And so on. The behavior of the members of a group is a symphony, a symphony that may have discords. There are different voices— as the wood winds are a voice in a symphony—each with its themes, which come in at different intervals, sometimes quietly, sometimes loudly, sometimes in the foreground, sometimes in the background. Often there is a conductor who is himself a voice, and there are recurrences in the group of voices, in the movement as a whole. Like lazy listeners, we who are at the symphony never hear all the voices and all their harmonies. We hear only the ones we are interested in hearing.

These recurrences in social behavior, when recognized as recurrences, are called customs. For the moment we are simply going to accept custom as a fact, giving notice at the same time that the fact raises an important question, which will be considered in a later chapter. We mention the question now only to show we are aware of it. Some students of society are inclined to take the recurrences in the behavior of a group for granted. They are interested in the details of particular customs, but not in custom itself as an aspect of group life. Other students go further, as Edmund Burke did years ago, and see custom as useful, even necessary. Men cannot plan for the future without relying on the massive regularities of expected behavior. Yet when everything intelligent has been said about the usefulness of custom, one more profound question remains: What makes custom customary? For the brute fact is that customs do change. In view of the constantly varied forces playing on society, it is amazing that anything can be recognized as persistent. The recurrences are miracles, not commonplaces; and miracles, if they happen often, are just the things we should study most closely. As soon as we do, we find that nothing is more defenseless than a custom, alone. Not single customs, but systems of customs, survive. Anthropologists used to talk about the "tyranny of custom" as if custom were a mold pressing social organization into a shape. This view is misleading. Custom is not something outside of, and apart from, social organization but is implicit in organization. These are large generalizations. We state them now, but only in a much later chapter shall we try to back them up. By that time we hope to have the tools to do the job.

The usual descriptions of groups consist of statements of custom, that is, recurrences in human behavior at different places or at different intervals. "The Irish countrymen live on isolated farms." . . . "The men of a Tikopia village commonly put out to sea together when they go fishing." The books and articles that are our sources, that we must work with, are full of such remarks. But we must never forget, having a lively sense of the shifting sands on which we build, that statements of custom, if they are worth anything, are founded on repeated observations of individual events in single scenes. With this in mind, let us return to the Irish farm family, and now study a description of the relationships between its members, particularly father, mother, and son. The description is a statement of custom: a summary of the recurrences in many single scenes like the one with which this chapter opened.

The growing child ordinarily sees his father as owner and principal worker of the farm. When the whole family group of father, mother, children, and whatever other relatives may be living with them, works in concert, as at the potato planting, the turf cutting, and the haymaking, it is the father who directs the group's activities, himself doing the heavy tasks. . . .

In his earliest childhood, of course, the mother looms larger in the child's consciousness than the father. The child's first duties, as soon as he can

speak and walk, are to run on petty errands to neighbors and near-by "friends." Soon he is taking his father's meals to him in the fields or going on errands to the nearest shop. Until he is seven and has gone through First Communion, his place is in the house with the women, and his labor is of very little importance. After First Communion, at six or seven, he begins to be thrown more with his elder brothers, and comes to do small chores which bring him more and more into contact with his father and with the other men of the neighborhood . . . But not till he passes Confirmation and leaves school (generally at the same time) does he take on full men's work. Even then, as he becomes adult and takes on more and more of the heavy tasks of the farm work, he never escapes his father's direction, until his father dies or makes over the farm to him at his marriage . . .

It goes without saying that the father exercises his control over the whole activity of the "boy." It is by no means confined to their work together. Indeed, the father is the court of last resort, which dispenses punishment for deviations from the norm of conduct in all spheres. Within the bounds of custom and law he has full power to exercise discipline. Corporal punishment is not a thing of the past in Ireland, and, especially in the intermediate stages of the child's development, from seven to puberty, it gets full play.

It is during those years that the characteristic relationship between father and son is developed in rural communities. The son has suffered a remove from the previous almost exclusive control of its mother, in which an affective content of sympathy and indulgence was predominant, and is brought into contact for the first time with the father and older men. But the transfer is not completed. There is a hiatus in his development through the years of school when his participation in men's work and his relationship with his father has little chance of developing into an effective partnership. A real union of interests does not take place until after Confirmation and school-leaving, when for the first time his exclusive contacts and his entire day-to-day activity, particularly in farm work, will be with his father and the older men.

This fact colors greatly the relationship of father and son, as far as affective content goes. There is none of the close companionship and intimate sympathy which characterizes, at least ideally, the relationship in other groups. Where such exists, it is a matter for surprised comment to the small farmers. In its place there is developed, necessarily perhaps, a marked respect, expressing itself in the tabooing of many actions, such as smoking, drinking, and physical contact of any sort, which can be readily observed in any small farm family. Coupled with this is the life-long subordination . . . which is never relaxed even in the one sphere in which farmer father and son can develop an intense community of interest – farm work. Nothing prevents the development of great mutual pride, the boy in his experienced and skillful mentor, tutor, and captain in work, and the man in a worthy and skillful successor and fellow workman, but on the other hand everything within the behavior developed in the relationship militates against the growth of close mutual sympathy. As a result, the antagonisms inherent in such a situation often break through very strongly when conflicts arise . . .

On the other hand, the relationship of mother and son has a very different content. Like that between father and son, it is the product of years of development. It is marked, too, by a similar retention of subordinate status on the part of the son. In farm work the boy is subject to the commands of his mother even when, fully adult, he has passed over exclusively to men's work. . . . But within the scope of such a subordination there is a quite different affective history. The relationship is the first and earliest into which a child enters. It is very close, intimate, and all-embracing for the first years of life; only gradually does the experience of the child expand to include brothers, sisters, and last, the older male members of the household.

Until seven, the child of either sex is the constant companion of its mother. If the family is numerous an elder child, usually a sister, may take over much of the mother's role, but the mother is always near-by. As the woman works in the house or fields, the child is kept by her side. In the house it usually sits in a crib by the fire or plays about on the floor, but always within sight and sound. It learns its speech from its mother, amid a flood of constant endearments, admonitions, and encouragements. The woman's work never separates her from the child. Custom imposes no restraints or interruptions in her solicitude. She looks after its comforts, gives it food, dresses it, etc. She constantly exercises restraints and controls over it, teaching it day by day in a thousand situations the elements of prudery, modesty and good conduct.

The controls she exercises are of a different kind from those of the father. She is both guide and companion. Her authority most often makes itself felt through praise, persuasion, and endearment. Only when a grave breach of discipline demands a restraining power greater than hers, or when an appeal to ultimate authority is needed, does the father begin to play his role. Especially in the years before puberty, the farm father enters the child's cognizance as a disciplinary force. The barriers of authority, respect, extra-household interests, and the imperatives of duty rather than of encouragement make it difficult for any intimacy to develop.

Even after Confirmation the child's relationship to his mother is not materially weakened. He becomes confirmed, it is true, in a masculine scorn for feminine interests and pursuits, but he can and must still look for protection to his mother against a too-arbitrary exercise of his father's power. In family disputes the mother takes a diplomatic, conciliatory role. From her intermediary position she can call upon the strongest ties between herself and her sons to restore rifts in parental authority and filial submission.

Throughout the years of the son's full activity in the farm economy under the father's headship, the mother still remains the source of comfort and the preparer of food and is still infinitely solicitous of his welfare. It is only at marriage that the bond is broken . . . If the child must leave the farm for other walks of life, the closest possible relationship is still maintained. When one goes home, it is to see one's mother. There is always an attempt to carry on a correspondence. In exile, the bond lingers as a profound sentimental nostalgia.[3]

Before we go on to our main purpose, we must get some preliminaries out of the way. This passage describes a relationship between three persons, not the conventional triangle of a love story but the triangle that has father, mother, and son at its corners. The pattern of the relationship is clearly marked—which is a reason why we chose a description of an Irish family and not one of an American family. The latter is more familiar to us but its pattern is not so easily characterized. In the Irish family the relationship between mother and son is one of warm affection, the relationship between father and son is one of admiration mixed with respect. Moreover, these relationships are not peculiar to Ireland: it is interesting how often the pattern repeats itself in farm families, and indeed in other families, all over the world. Nor are these relationships inevitable. It is not simply "natural" that a son should love his mother, though we all like to think it is. He loves his mother because the repeated, thousand-times-repeated, events in which the two are brought together are of a certain kind. From earliest childhood she cares for him; but change her behavior and the emotion would change too. In like manner, the son's feeling for the father is colored by the father's control over him in the many-times-repeated events of farm work. Nor, to go a step further, are the two series of events—the events determining these mother-son and father-son relationships—isolated from the rest of the world. Instead they are related to the division of labor and assignment of authority in a going farm enterprise, surviving in an environment.

We shall not be misled by the use of the words "the child," "his mother," and "his father" in the singular. These are shorthand for "children," "mothers," and "fathers." An anthropologist would say that the passages quoted above tell us some of the customs of Irish countrymen, a statistician that they may perhaps express some kind of average in

---

[3]Reprinted by permission of the publishers from Conrad Maynadier Arensberg and Solon Toothaker Kimball, *Family and Community in Ireland*, Cambridge, Mass.: Harvard University Press, 1940, pp. 51–60.

the behavior of a certain number of groups—Irish farm families—over a certain span of time. The statistician might find fault with the passages for not letting him know the relation between the "sample" and the "universe," that is, the relation between the number of groups directly observed and the larger number for whose behavior the average is supposed to hold good. He might also find fault with the passages for giving us no idea of the number of groups—there must be a few—whose behavior deviates in some degree from the average. He might say that the statements are by implication quantitative but that they do not let an outsider make any judgment of their quantitative reliability. His criticisms are good, and they can be answered only by raising new questions: How much more effort, in men, time, and money, would be needed to get the kind of data he wants? Given a limited supply of all three, how far would getting his kind of data interfere with getting a wider, though admittedly less reliable, coverage of group behavior? These are questions not of scientific morality but of strategy and, in the broad sense, economics: getting the most for one's money. They themselves beg for quantitative answers. And we might finally ask the different and more searching question: How far does the craving to get the kind of data a statistician considers reliable lead social scientists to take up questions for which this kind of data can easily be secured instead of questions that are interesting for other reasons? To which the statistician might reply: If we are not getting what I want, are we getting anything on which we can found a science? We should keep these questions in mind, for much of the material we shall be working with is not of the kind the statistician wants.

DEFINITION OF CONCEPTS

Let us go back over our work so far. We began with a flat description of events within a single group; then we went on to a statement of the customs of an unspecified but limited number of groups: the families of Irish countrymen. The next step is a long one; in fact it will take up the rest of this book. We shall set up some hypotheses—and they will remain hypotheses because we shall only set them up, not prove them—that may sum up a few aspects of social behavior in an unlimited number of groups all over the world. There is no use saying now what these hypotheses are; we shall find out soon enough, and one move in particular we must make before

we can formulate any hypotheses of high generalization, such as ours will be. We must define a few of the concepts that come into them. Though we cannot do so by pointing at objects and saying the concept, we can take the next best step. We can examine a passage like the one above, point out certain words in it, ask ourselves whether the aspects of social behavior to which the words refer have anything in common, and then, if they do, give a name to this common element. The name is the concept. We might have written a passage of our own for this purpose, but anyone can solve a problem if he sets it up himself. It is much more convincing to use someone else's passage, as we have done.

ACTIVITY

Let us look, then, at certain words and phrases in this passage, and first, perhaps, at words like these: *potato planting, turf cutting, haymaking, corporal punishment, smoking, drinking, gives food, dresses, looks after, plays, sits, walks, speaks, talks, First Communion, Confirmation.* In the passage we can pick out many more such words, and also some of greater generality, like *work* and *activity.* Let us agree that they have something in common, without committing ourselves on the question whether this something is important. They all refer to things that people do: work on the physical environment, with implements, and with other persons. If we want to be precise, we can say that all these words and phrases refer in the end to movements of the muscles of men, even though the importance of some of the movements, like talk and ceremonies, depends on their symbolic meaning. We shall speak of the characteristic they have in common as an *element* of social behavior, and we shall give it a name, as a mere ticket. It might be called *action,* if *action* had not been given a more general meaning, or *work,* if *work* did not have a special meaning in the physical sciences and may yet have an analogous one in sociology. Instead of either of these, we shall call it *activity,* and use it, in much the same way that it is used in everyday speech, as an analytical concept for the study of social groups.

We call activity an element, not implying that it is some ultimate, indivisible atom of behavior. It is no more than one of the classes into which we choose to divide something that might be divided in other, and less crude, ways. In fact we call it an element just because the vagueness of that word gives us room to move around in. Above all we must realize that activity is not a variable like temperature in physics: it cannot be given a single series of numerical values. Instead, a number of aspects of activity might be measured. We are sometimes able to measure the *output* or rate of production of certain kinds of activity, for instance, factory work, and sometimes the *efficiency* of activity, the relation of input to output. We might even be able to assign an index to the degree of *similarity* of one activity to another. And so on. These are true variables, at least in possibility, though we could not give them numerical values in every piece of research. In later chapters we shall have to make sure, when we speak of activity, which particular variable we have in mind.

INTERACTION

Going back now to the passage we are working with, let us look at expressions like these: the boy is *thrown with* his elder brothers; he comes more and more *into contact with* his father; he never *escapes from* his father's direction; he *participates* in the men's work; he is a *companion* of his mother; he goes to *see* his mother, and so on. The element that these phrases have in common is more or less mixed with other things, for in our language one word seldom states one clear idea. For instance, what does the word *see* mean in the phrase "going to see someone"? Yet there is a common element, and it seems to be some notion of sheer interaction between persons, apart from the particular activities in which they interact. When we refer to the fact that some unit of activity of one man follows, or, if we like the word better, is stimulated by some unit of activity of another, aside from any question of what these units may be, then we are referring to *interaction*. We shall speak of interaction as an element of social behavior and use it as an analytical concept in the chapters that follow.

We may find it hard to think consistently of interaction as separate from the other elements of behavior, but we shall have to do so in this book, and the fact is that in our everyday thinking we often keep it separate without realizing as much. When we say "Tom got in touch with Harry," or "Tom contacted Harry," or "Tom was an associate of Harry's," we are not talking about the particular words they said to one another or the particular activities they both took part in. Instead we are talking about the sheer fact of contact, of associa-

tion. Perhaps the simplest example of interaction, though we should find it complex enough if we studied it carefully, is two men at opposite ends of a saw, sawing a log. When we say that the two are interacting, we are not referring to the fact that both are sawing: in our language, sawing is an *activity*, but to the fact that the push of one man on the saw is followed by the push of the other. In this example, the interaction does not involve words. More often interaction takes place through verbal or other symbolic communication. But when in the armed forces men talk about the chain of command, or in a business ask what officers report to what other ones, they are still talking about channels of communication—the chains of interaction—rather than the communications themselves or the activities that demand communications.

Just as several variables are included under the concept of activity, so several are included under interaction. We can study the *frequency* of interaction: the number of times a day or a year one man interacts with another or the members of a group interact with one another. We can measure the ratio between the amount of time one man is active, for instance, talking, and the *duration* of his interlocutor's activity. Or we can study the *order* of interaction: Who originates action? Where does a chain of interactions start and where does it go? If Tom makes a suggestion to Dick, does Dick pass it on to Harry?[4] Once again, we shall have to make sure from time to time that we are talking about one variable under interaction and not another. Our observations of this element can often be rather precise and definite, which gives them infinite charm for persons of a certain temperament.

When we called the first of our elements *activity*, we may have been using the obvious and appropriate word. But in calling the second element *interaction*, are we not needlessly using a strange word when a familiar one is on hand? Why not speak of *communication* rather than *interaction*? Our answer is: The word *communication* is neither general enough in one sense nor specific enough in another. When people think of communication, they think of communication in words, but here we are including under interaction both verbal and nonverbal communication. What is more, the word *communication*

---

[4] For a systematic discussion of interaction as an element of social behavior, see E. D. Chapple, with the collaboration of C. M. Arensberg, *Measuring Human Relations* (Genetic Psychology Monographs, Vol. 22 (1940)).

is used in several different ways in everyday speech. It may mean the content of the message, signal, or "communication" being transmitted, or the process of transmission itself, as when people speak of "methods of communication," or to the sheer fact, aside from content or process of transmission, that one person has communicated with another. Only to the last of these three do we give the name of interaction, and the unfamiliarity of the word may underline the fact that its meaning is specific. Nevertheless we shall, from time to time, when there is no risk of confusion, use the word *communication* in place of *interaction*, so that our language will not sound hopelessly foreign.

SENTIMENT

Now let us go back to our passage again and consider another set of words and phrases: *sentiments of affection, affective content of sympathy and indulgence, intimate sympathy, respect, pride, antagonism, affective history, scorn, sentimental nostalgia*. To these we shall arbitrarily add others, such as *hunger*, and *thirst*, that might easily have come into the passage. What can we say these words have in common? Perhaps the most we can say, and it may not be very much, is that they all refer to internal states of the human body. Laymen and professional psychologists call these states by various names: drives, emotions, feelings, affective states, sentiments, attitudes. Here we shall call them all *sentiments*, largely because that word has been used in a less specialized sense than some of the others, and we shall speak of *sentiment* as an element of social behavior.

Notice the full range of things we propose to call sentiments. They run all the way from fear, hunger, and thirst, to such probably far more complicated psychological states as liking or disliking for individuals, approval or disapproval of their actions. We are lumping together under this word some psychological states that psychologists would certainly keep separate. Our employment of the concept *sentiment* can only be justified by what we do with it, so that at the moment all we can ask is indulgence for our failure in orthodoxy.

We must now consider a question that may not seem important but that has come up again and again, in one form or another, ever since the behaviorists first raised it. We can *see* activities and interactions. But if sentiments are internal states of the body, can we see them in the same way? It is

true that a person may say he feels hungry or likes someone, and that in everyday life, if we are dealing with him, we take account of what he has to say about his own feelings. But scientists may be forgiven for believing that subjective judgments are treacherous things to work with. They are not reliable; we cannot tell whether two persons would reach the same judgment under the same circumstances, and reliability is the rock on which science is built. Some scientists even believe that they can reach important generalizations, in psychology and sociology, without paying any attention whatever to subjective judgments; and they would ask us whether there is anything we can point to as sentiment that has not already been included under activity and interaction. Can it be independently observed? Perhaps in some animals the more violent sentiments can be so observed. In a dog or cat, pain, hunger, fear, and rage are marked by measurable changes in the body, particularly in the glands of internal secretion.[5] We assume that this is also true of human beings, but few of the necessary measurements can easily be made. For mild sentiments such as friendliness, and these are the ones we shall be working with most often here, we are not sure how far the bodily changes occur at all. The James-Lange theory that a sentiment and a set of visceral changes are one and the same thing cannot be driven too far. On an occasion that might conceivably have called for emotion, the undamaged human being reacts so as to cut down the amount of visceral change taking place. The body mobilizes for action, if that is appropriate, and reduces the merely emotional changes.

Science is perfectly ready to take leave of common sense, but only for a clear and present gain. Lacking more precise methods for observing sentiments, since the biological methods can only be used in special circumstances, have we anything to gain by giving up everyday practice? Have we not rather a good deal to lose? And what is everyday practice? In deciding what sentiments a person is feeling, we take notice of slight, evanescent tones of his voice, expressions of his face, movements of his hands, ways of carrying his body, and we take notice of these things as parts of a whole in which the context of any one sign is furnished by all the others. The signs may be slight in that

---

[5] See W. B. Cannon, *Bodily Changes in Pain, Hunger, Fear, and Rage*.

the physical change from one whole to another is not great, but they are not slight so long as we have learned to discriminate between wholes and assign them different meanings. And that is what we do. From these wholes we infer the existence of internal states of the human body and call then anger, irritation, sympathy, respect, pride, and so forth. Above all, we infer the existence of sentiments from what men say about what they feel and from the echo that their words find in our own feelings. We can recognize in ourselves what they are talking about. All those who have probed the secrets of the human heart have known how misleading and ambiguous these indications can sometimes be, how a man can talk love and mean hate, or mean both together, without being aware of what he is doing. Yet we act on our inferences, on our diagnoses of the sentiments of other people, and we do not always act ineffectively. In this book we are trying to learn how the elements of our everyday social experience are related to one another. Leaving out a part of that experience—and sentiment is a part—would be reasonable only if we had a better kind of observation to take its place. Some sciences have something better; ours does not yet.

We may end with a practical argument. This book is, in one of its intentions, an effort to bring out the generalizations implicit in modern field studies of human groups. If the men who made the studies felt that they could infer and give names to such things as sentiments of affection, respect, pride, and antagonism, we shall see what we can do with their inferences, remembering always that a more advanced theory than ours may have to wait for more precise and reliable observations. No theory can be more sophisticated than the facts with which it deals.

Under the element of *sentiment*, several different kinds of studies can and have been made. Perhaps the best-known ones are carried on by the public opinion pollsters and attitude scalers using questionnaires they get people to answer. Especially when they try to find out the *number* of persons that approve or disapprove of, like or dislike, a proposal for action or a candidate for public office, they are studying at least one variable under this element. Often they go further and try to discover not only how many persons approve or disapprove but the *conviction* with which they do so: whether they

are sure they are right, feel somewhat less sure, or remain undecided. The pollsters may also try to find out the *intensity* of the sentiments concerned: a man may disapprove of something intellectually and yet not feel strongly about it. His emotions may not have been deeply aroused. . . .

SUMMARY

To use the language of the sciences, our *conceptual scheme* consists, so far, of *persons* and three elements of their behavior: *activity, interaction,* and *sentiment.* We shall add other concepts as we go along; these we begin with. Using these concepts, we shall try to reach analytical hypotheses describing the behavior of persons in groups. These hypotheses are a third level in the process of generalization. At the risk of repetition, let us take an example from the material we have just been studying. The first level consists of descriptions of individual events. Thus, on a certain day in a certain farm in County Clare, Mary Shaughnessy took up her little son, fed him, and fondled him. The second level consists of descriptions of the average behavior of a limited number of persons in a limited area over a limited span of time. Thus, among the Irish countrymen the women's work never separates them from their children, and custom imposes no restraints or interruptions on their solicitude. The third level consists of descriptions of behavior that may, we hope, apply to many groups, and to persons in many kinds of relationship to one another, not necessarily mothers and sons. Thus, the greater the interaction between two persons, the greater, in general, the sentiments of affection they feel for one another. This last kind of description is an analytical hypothesis. We must not worry yet about whether it is true. That question comes up later; at the moment we are only illustrating what we mean. If, moreover, it does turn out to be true, it will be true only as one of a series, or system, of such expressions, each of which qualifies the others, but again this is not a question that need disturb us now.

When all is said and done, let us not delude ourselves. This classification of the elements of behavior is old and crude, both. The concepts, sentiment, activity, and interaction, are close to common-sense ideas. They have all been used by social scientists before, though not all together. And there are many other ways of breaking group life down into its elements, other classifications and cross classifications far more subtle than this. We may have to elaborate on this one as the work progresses. It is not the last word but the first.

USEFULNESS OF THE CONCEPTS

The real question is not whether the classification is old and crude but whether it is useful, and this can hardly be settled now. It can hardly be found either useful or useless before it is used. Here, as at a play, we must practice what Coleridge called "the willing suspension of disbelief." However skeptical we may be as to its worth, we can still take the scheme on trial and give it a chance to show what it can do.

Even if this particular breakdown or classification does not turn out to be useful, experience seems to show that some classification is immeasurably better than no classification at all. It can at least serve as a check-off list. In making a study of a group, or in reading a description of one, a classification will help us decide whether a minimum of important facts has been gathered. It serves as a filing cabinet or set of pigeonholes where data can collect until they are needed. It may also help us stick to the subject. In sociology we tend to wander all over our material; we never quite know what we are talking about at any particular moment. The reason is not that we are incompetent, but that we have no device for fixing our attention. Any classification, no matter how crude, provided only it is used regularly, forces us to take up one thing at a time and consider systematically the relations of that thing to others. This is one of the roads that leads to generalization.

So much for classification in general. A classification of this particular kind may help us to extensionalize, that is, to go behind the big words and phrases so common in this field to the actual observations to which they refer. We do not want to get rid of the big words but to give them underpinnings, to show their relation, through concepts of a lower degree of abstraction, to the things we see and hear in human behavior. Interaction, sentiment, and activity are such low-order concepts.

There seem to be two kinds of sociologist, both contributing much, both running into difficulties. We may call them the pedestrians and the intuitives. Take first the pedestrian. Sociology, with the other social sciences, has completed a large number of researches, scrupulous in method, thorough in exe-

cution, and illuminating in results. Yet it is often true that something is lacking. It is curious how often one reaches the end of a good, stubborn, down-to-earth research report, crammed with common sense, and finds the author floundering when, not a moment before, he was sure of his ground. If you will examine what has happened, you will discover that, when he tried to state his conclusions in the most general terms, these terms suddenly could not bear the weight put upon them.

Take now the intuitive. He has judgments on the evils of the present social order that we feel sure are great with meaning, yet the meaning never quite comes to light—once more because the medium used, the language, breaks down under the strain. Here is an example; a sociologist writes: "No society can function as a society unless it gives the individual member social status and function, and unless the decisive social power is legitimate power. The former establishes the basic frame of social life: the purpose and meaning of society. The latter shapes the space within the frame: it makes society concrete and creates its institutions. If the individual is not given social status and function, there can be no society but only a mass of social atoms flying through space without aim or purpose."[6] We feel that this man is saying something important and something forgotten by most students of our fearful ills. Yet the truth is that he uses a lot of big words like "social status and function," "the purpose and meaning of social life," "power," and "the basic frame of social life" which are left wholly unrelated to observed fact.

The "pedestrian" does not get through from fact to adequate generalization; the "intuitive" does not get through from generalization to adequate fact. For the former, the conclusions, as he states them, tend to hold good only within the imposed limits of his research. For the latter, his intuitions, however suggestive, tend to remain just intuitions, of which there have been millions in human history. You cannot *do* anything with them. Neither man contributes to a growing body of social theory, summing up much work. Yet without such a theory neither individual research nor individual intuition can issue in wise social action. A science, like an army, cannot advance unless it keeps its lines of communication clear   the lines of communication

---

6P. F. Drucker. *The Future of Industrial Man*, 25.

between its words and its facts. To this problem our present method is addressed.

Finally, a classification of this kind may help us out of a dilemma that seems to threaten a science like anthropology. On the one hand, some of the students of culture—the "design for living" of a society—emphasize "cultural relativity" so far that each culture, tribal or national, becomes a unique entity, inherently different from all others. In one sense each culture is indeed unique, and certainly this emphasis has been necessary and useful, but carried far enough it almost implies that the differences between cultures are matters of kind, not of degree, and that there are no common elements in which cultures differ by amounts that might be measured, however crudely. On the other hand, some students have been trying to discover what specific institutions appear in every society, and they have found very few. Something that can be recognized as marriage—a man and at least one woman living together—is almost the only one, and even this is somewhat ambiguous, as some of the circumstances surrounding marriage itself, for instance, the rules governing the choice of marriage partner, vary greatly from society to society. Not that marriage is a small matter—far from it. But to say that marriage is the only institution all societies have in common is a little like saying that the only things we can be sure of are death and taxes. It does not take us very far. In comparing groups, do we have to choose between radical difference and commonplace similarity?

Some of the natural sciences have been able to avoid this dilemma, largely because their problems have been simpler than those of the social sciences. For instance, a mixture of fruit juice, liquor, and ice in a cocktail shaker is a very different thing, looked at in one way, from a mixture of hot air and gasoline in an automobile engine cylinder.

Superficially they seem to have only two traits in common: both are mixtures and both exist in enclosed spaces. In the study of cultures, anthropology has hardly gone beyond this kind of comparison. But in the science of thermodynamics, the liquid and the hot gas find a new and different kind of similarity and difference. On the one hand, some aspects of the behavior of both can be described in terms of the same three variables: pressure, temperature, and volume. On the other hand, the two differ in the values, and in the rates of change of the values, of these three variables, as also in some constants characteristic of water, fruit juice, air, and gasoline. The liquid and the hot gas are alike in that the same kinds of measurement can be applied to both; they differ in the values that these measurements take. Similarity is no longer superficial, nor difference radical. Anthropology and sociology have not reached this stage of sophistication, and perhaps they never will, but they certainly never will if they fail to recognize the kind of logical problem they face. Pressure, temperature, and volume are true analytical concepts. Activity, interaction, and sentiment, though we may call them analytical concepts, are not quite the same kind of thing. Let us be clear about that. But they may be steps in the direction of such things.

Now we are ready to go to work. We have laid out the job and our conceptual tools. Remember what our procedure is to be. We are going to study cases: descriptions of the behavior of particular groups. First, each case will be stated in ordinary literary language; it will simply be reported. Then an analysis will be made of the case, using the concepts defined so far. With each new case, moreover, the analysis will develop in complexity, and new concepts will be added as the need for them arises. In this way, the relationship between fact and theory should be clear at every step.

WORDS AS TOOLS

The points Homans made in the last selection are basic and worth spending more time with. In this excerpt from a widely read book by the semanticist S. I. Hayakawa, we see in somewhat more general terms the relation between words used and the things they represent. To understand this process is important, for practically all of what we know we conceive of and certainly speak or write by using words. (Recall the selection by B. L. Whorf in the last section?) Certainly for most of the behavioral or social sciences, we are forced to use *words* (instead of, for example, mathematical symbols) to represent our conceptualizations from observable events. It is, therefore, very important to have a clear understanding of words as tools, to know their uses as well as their liabilities and the dangers inherent in their misapplication (such as mistaking the word for the process or thing represented, like "love"). It is often the case that much of the apparent disagreement in anthropology and the other social sciences comes about not so much because of differences in findings, as differences in the empirical uses of the terms employed. As we will see shortly, the central term of anthropology, "culture," is particularly subject to widely different meanings—that is, people use the word "culture" to tie the *concept* of "culture" to many different kinds of empirical events.

Hayakawa thus traces out the process of assigning a word as a symbol for a certain portion of the changing events we see around us; as did Bronowski in Part I, he shows the pragmatic need to group some of these events together as "classes" of things and to apply a label to that class. But he also shows something else that is of first importance in understanding "culture" (or "society," for that matter) and relating it to the ongoing stream of behavior: the process of abstraction and what this means both for using words and for understanding how nature is organized. Particularly for avoiding the confusions of language usage that lead people to argue about things at different levels of abstraction, Hayakawa's discussion is extremely important. For example, how to cut short those sometimes endless discussions about the relation between the "person" and the "society."

HOW WE KNOW WHAT WE KNOW

S. I. HAYAKAWA

The crucial point to be considered in a study of language behavior is the relationship between language and reality, between words and not-words. Except as we understand this relationship, we run the grave risk of straining the delicate connection between words and facts, of permitting our words to go wild, and so of creating for ourselves fabrications of fantasy and delusion.—WENDELL JOHNSON

BESSIE, THE COW

The universe is in a perpetual state of flux. The stars are growing, cooling, exploding. The earth itself is not unchanging; mountains are being worn away, rivers are altering their channels, valleys are

deepening. All life is also a process of change, through birth, growth, decay, and death. Even what we used to call "inert matter"—chairs and tables and stones—is not inert, as we now know, for, at the submicroscopic level, it is a whirl of electrons. If a table looks today very much as it did yesterday or as it did a hundred years ago, it is not because it has not changed, but because the changes have been too minute for our coarse perceptions. To modern science there is no "solid matter." If matter looks "solid" to us, it does so only because its motion is too rapid or too minute to be felt. It is "solid" only in the sense that a rapidly rotating color chart is "white" or a rapidly spinning top is "standing still." Our senses are extremely limited, so that we constantly have to use instruments, such as microscopes, telescopes, speedometers, stethoscopes, and seismographs, to detect and record occurrences which our senses are not able to record directly. The way in which we happen to see and feel things is the result of the peculiarities of our nervous systems. There are "sights" we cannot see, and, as even children know today with their high-frequency dog whistles, "sounds" that we cannot hear. It is absurd, therefore, to imagine that we ever perceive anything "as it really is."

Inadequate as our senses are, with the help of instruments they tell us a great deal. The discovery of microörganisms with the use of the microscope has given us a measure of control over bacteria; we cannot see, hear, or feel electromagnetic waves, but we can create and transform them to useful purpose. Most of our conquest of the external world, in engineering, in chemistry, and in medicine, is due to our use of mechanical contrivances of one kind or another to increase the capacity of our nervous systems. In modern life, our unaided senses are not half enough to get us about in the world. We cannot even obey speed laws or compute our gas and electric bills without mechanical aids to perception.

To return, then, to the relations between words and what they stand for, let us say that there is before us "Bessie," a cow. Bessie is a living organism, constantly changing, constantly ingesting food and air, transforming it, getting rid of it again. Her blood is circulating, her nerves are sending messages. Viewed microscopically, she is a mass of variegated corpuscles, cells, and bacterial organisms; viewed from the point of view of modern physics, she is a perpetual dance of electrons. What she is in her entirety, we can never know; even if we could at any precise moment say what she was, at the next moment she would have changed enough so that our description would no longer be accurate. It is impossible to say completely what Bessie or anything else really *is*. Bessie is not a static "object," but a dynamic process.

The Bessie that we experience, however, is something else again. We experience only a small fraction of the total Bessie: the lights and shadows of her exterior, her motions, her general configuration, the noises she makes, and the sensations she presents to our sense of touch. *And because of our previous experience, we observe resemblances in her to certain other animals to which, in the past, we have applied the word "cow."*

THE PROCESS OF ABSTRACTING

The "object" of our experience, then, is not the "thing in itself," but *an interaction between our nervous systems (with all their imperfections) and something outside them.* Bessie is unique—there is nothing else in the universe exactly like her in all respects. But we automatically *abstract* or select from the process-Bessie those features of hers in which she resembles other animals of like shape, functions, and habits, and we *classify* her as "cow."

When we say, then, that "Bessie is a cow," we are only noting the process-Bessie's resemblances to other "cows" and *ignoring differences.* What is more, we are leaping a huge chasm: from the dynamic process-Bessie, a whirl of electro-chemico-neural eventfulness, to a relatively static "idea," "concept," or *word,* "cow." In this connection, the reader is referred to the diagram entitled "The Abstraction Ladder," which he will find on page 153.[1]

As the diagram illustrates, the "object" we see is an abstraction of the lowest level; but it is still an abstraction, since it leaves out characteristics of the process that is the real Bessie. The *word* "Bessie" (cow_1) is the lowest *verbal* level of abstraction, leaving out further characteristics—the differences between Bessie yesterday and Bessie today, between Bessie today and Bessie tomorrow—and selecting only the similarities. The word "cow" selects only the similarities between Bessie (cow_1), Daisy (cow_2), Rosie (cow_3), and so on, and therefore leaves out still more about Bessie. The word "livestock" selects or abstracts only the features that Bessie has in common with pigs, chickens, goats, and sheep. The term "farm asset" abstracts only the features Bessie has in common with barns, fences, livestock, furniture, generating plants, and tractors, and is therefore on a very high level of abstraction.

Our concern here with the process of abstracting may seem strange since the study of language is all too often restricted to matters of pronunciation, spelling, vocabulary, grammar, and sentence structure. The methods by which composition and oratory are taught in old-fashioned school systems seem to be largely responsible for this widespread notion that the way to study words is to concentrate one's attention exclusively on words.

---

[1]The "Abstraction Ladder" is based on "The Structural Differential," a diagram originated by Alfred Korzybski to explain the process of abstracting. For a fuller explanation both of the diagram and of the process it illustrates, see his *Science and Sanity: An Introduction to Non-Aristotelian Systems and General Semantics* (1933), especially Chapter 25.

ABSTRACTION LADDER

Start reading from the bottom *UP*

8. "wealth"

8. The word "wealth" is at an extremely high level of abstraction, omitting *almost* all reference to the characteristics of Bessie.

7. "asset"

7. When Bessie is referred to as an "asset," still more of her characteristics are left out.

6. "farm assets"

6. When Bessie is included among "farm assets," reference is made only to what she has in common with all other salable items on the farm.

5. "livestock"

5. When Bessie is referred to as "livestock," only those characteristics she has in common with pigs, chickens, goats, etc., are referred to.

4. "cow"

4. The word "cow" stands for the characteristics we have abstracted as common to cow_1, cow_2, cow_3 . . . cow_n. Characteristics peculiar to specific cows are left out.

3. "Bessie"

3. The word "Bessie" (cow_1) is the *name* we give to the object of perception of level 2. The name *is not* the object; it merely *stands for* the object and omits reference to many of the characteristics of the object.

2.

2. The cow we perceive is not the word, but the object of experience, that which our nervous system abstracts (selects) from the totality that constitutes the process-cow. Many of the characteristics of the process-cow are left out.

1. The cow known to science ultimately consists of atoms, electrons, etc., according to present-day scientific inference. Characteristics (represented by circles) are infinite at this level and ever-changing. This is the *process level.*

But as we know from everyday experience, learning language is not simply a matter of learning words; it is a matter of correctly relating our words to the things and happenings for which they stand. We learn the language of baseball by playing or watching the game *and studying what goes on*. It is not enough for a child to learn to *say* "cookie" or "dog"; he must be able to use these words in their proper relationship to nonverbal cookies and nonverbal dogs before we can grant that he is learning the language. As Wendell Johnson has said, "The study of language begins properly with a study of what language is about."

Once we begin to concern ourselves with what language is about, we are at once thrown into a consideration of how the human nervous system works. When we call Beau (the Boston terrier), Pedro (the chihuahua), Snuffles (the English bulldog), and Shane (the Irish wolfhound)—creatures that differ greatly in size, shape, appearance, and behavior—by the same name, "dog," our nervous system has obviously gone to work *abstracting* what is common to them all, ignoring for the time being the differences among them.

WHY WE MUST ABSTRACT

This process of abstracting, of leaving characteristics out, is an indispensable convenience. To illustrate by still another example, suppose that we live in an isolated village of four families, each owning a house. A's house is referred to as *maga;* B's house is *biyo;* C's is *kata*, and D's is *pelel*. This is quite satisfactory for ordinary purposes of communication in the village, unless a discussion arises about building a new house—a spare one, let us say. We cannot refer to the projected house by any one of the four words we have for the existing houses, since each of these has too specific a meaning. We must find a *general* term, at a higher level of abstraction, that means "something that has certain characteristics in common with *maga, biyo, kata*, and *pelel*, and yet is not A's, B's, C's, or D's." Since this is much too complicated to say each time, an *abbreviation* must be invented. So we choose the noise, *house*. Out of such needs do our words come—they are a form of shorthand. The invention of a new abstraction is a great step forward, since it *makes discussion possible*—as, in this case, not only the discussion of a fifth house, but of all future houses we may build or see in our travels or dream about.

A producer of educational films once remarked to the writer that it is impossible to make a shot of "work." You can shoot Joe hoeing potatoes, Frank greasing a car, Bill spraying paint on a barn, but never just "work." "Work," too, is a shorthand term, standing, at a higher level of abstraction, for a characteristic that a multitude of activities, from dishwashing to navigation to running an advertising agency to governing a nation, have in common. The special meaning that "work" has in physics is also clearly derived from abstracting the common characteristics of many different kinds of work. ("A transference of energy from one body to another, resulting in the motion or displacement of the body acted upon, in the direction of the acting force and against resistance." Funk and Wagnalls' *Standard College Dictionary*.)

The indispensability of this process of abstracting can again be illustrated by what we do when we "calculate." The word "calculate" originates from the Latin word *calculus*, meaning "pebble," and derives its present meaning from such ancient practices as putting a pebble into a box for each sheep as it left the fold, so that one could tell, by checking the sheep returning at night against the pebbles, whether any had been lost. Primitive as this example of calculation is, it will serve to show why mathematics works. Each pebble is, in this example, an abstraction representing the "oneness" of each sheep—its numerical value. And because we are abstracting from extensional events on clearly understood and uniform principles, the numerical facts about the pebbles are also, barring unforeseen circumstances, numerical facts about the sheep. Our x's and y's and other mathematical symbols are abstractions made from numerical abstractions, and are therefore abstractions of still higher level. And they are useful in predicting occurrences and in getting work done because, since they are abstractions properly and uniformly made from starting points in the extensional world, the relations revealed by the symbols will be, again barring unforeseen circumstances, relations existing in the extensional world.

ON DEFINITIONS

Definitions, contrary to popular opinion, tell us nothing about things. They only describe people's linguistic habits; that is, they tell us what noises people make under what conditions. Definitions should be understood as *statements about language*.

House. This word, at the next higher level of abstraction, can be substituted for the more cumbersome expression, "Something that has characteristics in common with Bill's bungalow, Jordan's cottage, Mrs. Smith's guest home, Dr. Jones's mansion. . . ."

Red. A feature that rubies, roses, ripe tomatoes, robins' breasts, uncooked beef, and lipsticks have in common is abstracted, and this word expresses that abstraction.

Kangaroo. Where the biologist would say "herbivorous mammal, a marsupial of the family Macropodidae," ordinary people say "kangaroo."

Now it will be observed that while the definitions of "house" and "red" given here point *down* the abstraction ladder (see the charts) to *lower* levels of abstraction, the definition of "kangaroo" remains at the same level. That is to say, in the case of "house," we could if necessary go and *look* at Bill's bungalow, Jordan's cottage, Mrs. Smith's guest home, and Dr. Jones's mansion, and figure out for ourselves what features they seem to have in common; in this way, we might begin to understand under what conditions to use the word "house." But all we know about "kangaroo" from the above is that where some people say one thing, other people say another. That is, when we stay at the *same* level of abstraction in giving a definition, we do not give any information, unless, of course, the listener or reader is already sufficiently familiar with the defining words to work himself down the abstraction ladder. Dictionaries, in order to save space, have to assume in many cases such familiarity with the language on the part of the reader. But where the assumption is unwarranted, definitions at the same level of abstraction are worse than useless. Looking up "indifference" in some cheap pocket dictionaries, we find it defined as "apathy"; we look up "apathy" and find it defined as "indifference."

Even more useless, however, are the definitions that go *up* the abstraction ladder to higher levels of abstraction—the kind most of us tend to make automatically. Try the following experiment on an unsuspecting friend:

"What is meant by the word *red?*"
"It's a color."
"What's a *color?*"
"Why, it's a quality things have."
"What's a *quality?*"
"Say, what are you trying to do, anyway?"

You have pushed him into the clouds. He is lost.

If, on the other hand, we habitually go *down* the abstraction ladder to *lower* levels of abstraction

when we are asked the meaning of a word, we are less likely to get lost in verbal mazes; we will tend to "have our feet on the ground" and know what we are talking about. This habit displays itself in an answer such as this:

"What is meant by the word *red?*"
"Well, the next time you see some cars stopped at an intersection, look at the traffic light facing them. Also, you might go to the fire department and see how their trucks are painted."

"LET'S DEFINE OUR TERMS"

An extremely widespread instance of an unrealistic (and ultimately superstitious) attitude toward definitions is found in the common academic prescription, "Let's define our terms so that we shall all know what we are talking about." As we have already seen in Chapter 4, the fact that a golfer, for example, cannot define golfing terms is no indication that he cannot understand and use them. Conversely, the fact that a man can define a large number of words is no guarantee that he knows what objects or operations they stand for in concrete situations. Having defined a word, people often believe that some kind of understanding has been established, ignoring the fact that the words in the definition often conceal even more serious confusions and ambiguities than the word defined. If we happen to discover this fact and try to remedy matters by defining the defining words, and then, finding ourselves still confused, we go on to define the words in the definitions of the defining words, and so on, we quickly find ourselves in a hopeless snarl. The only way to avoid this snarl is to keep definitions to a minimum and to point to extensional levels wherever necessary; in writing and speaking, this means giving specific examples of what we are talking about.

OPERATIONAL DEFINITIONS

Another way to keep extensional levels in mind, when definitions are called for, is to use what physicist P. W. Bridgman called "operational definitions." As he says,

To find the length of an object, we have to perform certain physical operations. The concept of length is therefore fixed when the operations by which length is measured are fixed. . . . In general, we mean by any concept nothing more than a set of operations; *the concept is synonymous with the corresponding set of operations.*[2]

---

[2]*The Logic of Modern Physics* (1927), p. 5.

The operational definition, then, as Anatol Rapoport explains, is one that tells you "*what to do and what to observe* in order to bring the thing defined or its effects within the range of one's experience." He gives the following simple example of how to define "weight": go to a railroad station or drugstore, look for a scale, stand on it, put in a penny, read the number at which the pointer comes to rest. *That* is your weight. But supposing different scales give different readings? Then your weight can be said to be within the range of, say, 140 to 145 pounds. With more accurate scales you might get closer readings, such as 142 pounds plus-or-minus one. But there is no "property" called weight that exists apart from the operations measuring it. As Rapoport says, "If the only way we can be aware of the amount of weight is by means of the scale, then the very definition of weight has to be in terms of the scale."[3]

Such, then, is the scientific, or "operational," point of view towards definition—one that attempts rigidly to exclude non-extensional, non-sense statements. We can extend this idea from science to the problems of everyday life and thought. Just as there is no such thing as "length" apart from the operations by which length is measured, just as there is no "weight" apart from the operations by which weight is determined, there is likewise no "democracy" apart from the sum-total of democratic *practices*, such as universal franchise, freedom of speech, equality before the law, and so on. Similarly, there is no such thing as "brotherhood" apart from brotherly behavior, nor "charity" apart from charitable actions.

The operational point of view does much to keep our words meaningful. When people say things like, "Let's have no more of *progressive* methods in our schools," "Let's get back to *sound business principles* in running our county government," "Let's try to do the *Christian* thing," "Let's put father back as head of the family," we are entitled to ask, "what do you mean—*extensionally speaking?* To ask this question often—of ourselves as well as of others—is to do our bit towards reducing the vast amount of non-sense that is written, spoken, and shouted in this incredibly garrulous world.

The best examples in everyday life of operational definitions are to be found in cookbooks, which

[3]*Operational Philosophy* (1953), p. 25.

describe the *operations* by means of which the entity defined may be extensionally experienced. Thus: "*Steak Diane.* Slice tenderloin beef very thin and give it a few whacks with a meat mallet to flatten it even more; sprinkle with salt and pepper to taste. Have your pan very hot. . . ." (*The Sunset Cook Book*.) Writers and speakers would do well to study cookbooks occasionally to increase the clarity and verifiability of their utterances.

CHASING ONESELF IN VERBAL CIRCLES

In other words, the kind of "thinking" we must be extremely wary of is that which *never* leaves the higher verbal levels of abstraction, the kind that never points *down* the abstraction ladder to lower levels of abstraction and from there to the extensional world:

"What do you mean by *democracy?*"
"Democracy means the preservation of human rights."
"What do you mean by *rights?*"
"By rights I mean those privileges God grants to all of us—I mean man's inherent privileges."
"Such as?"
"Liberty, for example."
"What do you mean by *liberty?*"
"Religious and political freedom."
"And what does that mean?"
"Religious and political freedom is what we enjoy under a democracy."

Of course it is possible to talk meaningfully about democracy, as Jefferson and Lincoln have done, as Frederick Jackson Turner does in *The Frontier in American History* (1950), as Karl R. Popper does in *The Open Society and Its Enemies* (1950), as T. V. Smith and Eduard Lindeman do in *The Democratic Way of Life* (1939)—to name only the first examples that come to mind. The trouble with speakers who never leave the higher levels of abstraction is not only that their audiences fail to notice when they are saying something and when they are not; but also that they themselves lose their ability to discriminate. Never coming down to earth, they frequently chase themselves around in verbal circles, unaware that they are making meaningless noises.

This is by no means to say that we must never make extensionally meaningless noises. When we use directive language, when we talk about the future, when we utter ritual language or engage in social conversation, we often make utterances that have no extensional verifiability. It must not be overlooked that our highest ratiocinative and imaginative powers are derived from the fact that symbols *are* independent of things symbolized, so that we are free not only to go quickly from low to extremely high levels of abstraction (from "canned peas" to "groceries" to "commodities" to "national wealth") and to manipulate symbols even when the things they stand for cannot be so manipulated ("If all the freight cars in the country were hooked up to each other in one long line . . ."), but we are also free to manufacture symbols at will even if they stand only for abstractions made from other abstractions and not for anything in the extensional world. Mathematicians, for example, often play with symbols that have no extensional content, just to find out what can be done with them; this is called "pure mathematics." And pure mathematics is far from being a useless pastime, because mathematical systems that are elaborated with no extensional applications in mind often prove to be applicable later in useful and unforeseen ways. But when mathematicians deal with extensionally meaningless symbols, they usually know what they are doing. *We* likewise must know what we are doing.

Nevertheless, all of us (including mathematicians), when we speak the language of everyday life, often make meaningless noises without knowing that we are doing so. We have already seen what confusions this can lead to. The fundamental purpose of the abstraction ladder, as shown in both this chapter and the next, is to make us aware of the process of abstracting.

THE DISTRUST OF ABSTRACTIONS

We may, using our abstraction ladder, allocate statements as well as words to differing levels of abstraction. "Mrs. Levin makes good potato pancakes" may be regarded as a statement at a fairly low level of abstraction, although, to be sure, it leaves out many elements, such as (1) the meaning of "goodness" in potato pancakes, and (2) the infrequent occasions when her pancakes fail to turn out well. "Mrs. Levin is a good cook," is a statement at a higher level of abstraction, covering Mrs. Levin's skill not only with potato pancakes, but also with roasts, pickles, noodles, strudels, and so on, nevertheless omitting *specific* mention of what she can accomplish. "Chicago women are good cooks," is a statement at a still higher level of abstraction; it can be made (if at all) only from ob-

servation of the cooking of a statistically significant number of Chicago women. "The culinary art has reached a high state in America," would be a still more highly abstract statement and, if made at all, would have to be based not only on observation of the Mrs. Levins of Chicago, New York, San Francisco, Denver, Albuquerque, and Chattanooga, but also on observation of the quality of meals served in hotels and restaurants, the quality of training in high school and college departments of home economics, the quality of writings on culinary art in American books and magazines, and many other relevant factors.

Unfortunately, though understandably, there is a tendency in our times to speak with contempt of "mere abstractions." The ability to climb to higher and higher levels of abstraction is a distinctively human trait, without which none of our philosophical or scientific insights would be possible. In order to have a science of chemistry, one *has* to be able to think of "H_2O," leaving out of consideration for the time being the wetness of water, the hardness of ice, the pearliness of dew, and the other extensional characteristics of H_2O at the objective level. In order to have a study called "ethics," one has to be able to think of what elements in ethical behavior have in common under different conditions and in different civilizations; one has to abstract that which is common to the behavior of the ethical carpenter, the ethical politician, the ethical businessman, and the ethical soldier—and that which is common to the laws of conduct of the Buddhist, the Orthodox Jew, the Confucian, and the Christian. Thinking that is most abstract can also be that which is most generally useful. The famous injunction of Jesus, "And as ye would that men should do to you, do ye also to them likewise," is, from this point of view, a brilliant generalization of more particular directives—a generalization at so high a level of abstraction that it appears to be applicable to all men in all cultures.

But high-level abstractions acquire a bad reputation because they are so often used, consciously or unconsciously, to confuse and befuddle people. A grab among competing powers for oil resources may be spoken of as "protecting the integrity of small nations." (Remember Japan's "Greater East Asia Co-prosperity Sphere"?) An unwillingness to pay social security taxes may be spoken of as "maintaining the system of free enterprise." Depriving the Negro of his vote in violation of the

Constitution of the United States may be spoken of as "preserving states' rights." The consequence of this free, and often irresponsible, use of high-level abstractions in public controversy and special pleading is that a significant portion of the population has grown cynical about *all* abstractions.

But, as the abstraction ladder has shown, *all we know are abstractions.* What you know about the chair you are sitting in is an abstraction from the totality of that chair. When you eat white bread, you cannot tell by the taste whether or not it has been "enriched by vitamin B" as it says on the wrapper; you simply have to trust that the process (from which the words "vitamin B" are abstracted) is actually there. What you know about your wife—even if she has been your wife for thirty years—is again an abstraction. Distrusting all abstractions simply does not make sense.

The test of abstractions then is not whether they are "high-" or "low-level" abstractions, but *whether*

they are referrable to lower levels. If one makes a statement about "culinary arts in America," one should be able to refer the statement down the abstraction ladder to particulars of American restaurants, American domestic science, American techniques of food preservation, down to Mrs. Levin in her kitchen. If one makes a statement about "civil rights in Wisconsin," one should know something about national, state, and local statutes; one should also know something about the behavior of policemen, magistrates, judges, academic authorities, hotel managers, and the general public in Wisconsin, all of whose acts and whose decisions affect that minimum of decent treatment in the courts, in politics, and in society that we call "civil rights." A preacher, a professor, a journalist, or politician whose high-level abstractions can systematically and surely be referred to lower-level abstractions is not only talking, he is saying something. As *Time* would say, no windbag, he.

ANTHROPOLOGICAL CONSTRUCTS

Keesing continues discussion of what Hayakawa was talking about—the need for conceptualization, for devising abstract "constructs" of what we see in nature if we are to handle and try to understand some of the interrelation of events. In this case, however, he is speaking of some of these basic matters using examples and words more directly related to our concern with "culture" as an idea, a construct, showing some of the possible relations between this word and the range and variety of observations of actual behavior that lies behind such use. In his example, he talks of a distinction often found in anthropological analyses of culture, for example, the distinction between "ideal" or normative culture and the "real" or "behavioral" culture; and the distinction (representing different levels of abstraction and inference) between "overt" (or "explicit") culture and "covert" (or "implicit") culture.

THE ABSTRACT OR "CONSTRUCT" NATURE OF ANTHROPOLOGICAL CONCEPTS

FELIX M. KEESING

One of the crucial yet difficult hurdles to surmount in understanding the scientific analysis of behavior is to grasp the nature of generalization in this field.

From *Cultural Anthropology: The Science of Custom* by Felix M. Keesing, © 1958 by Felix M. Keesing. Adapted and reprinted by permission of Holt, Rinehart and Winston, Inc.

Early cultural anthropologists, like other social scientists, developed the habit of describing customs as though they had an existence independent of the individuals concerned with them. The rule, say, that a husband should avoid his mother-in-law, or that a person should show deference in the presence of a person of superior rank, appears for the culture and group concerned to have a solid reality. Some have even spoken of culture as being a *superorganic* heritage with its own laws or processes capable of being studied apart from the individuals who carry it in their learned experience.

Numbers of later theorists, however, have worried over this habit of mind. Scientific generalizations about "culture," "society," "personality," and "character" are, they insist, "abstracted" or "constructed" from the behavior of individuals. "A culture," for example, seen in its totality, is such a construct; so, too, is "the modal personality" characteristic of that culture. A "trait" is also a construct, though of much less generality. In this sense they are classifying concepts, just as with so many other scientific terms, e.g., atom, molecule, species, galaxy.

Furthermore, following up a view now prevalent in discussions of the philosophy and method of science called *operationalism*, they say that concepts and constructs have meaning only in terms of the "operations" which enter into their definition—the instrumental and symbolic procedures which are employed in establishing them. The implications of this important line of thought are (a) that culture does not have any independent existence apart from the repetitive similar behavior of individuals, or in the case of material culture the similar single artifacts they make; "society" does not exist apart from the individuals who are participating in a form of organization; "personality" relates only to the similar characteristics of individuals; and (b) that as anthropological and other social science "operations" become progressively more controlled and precise, the concepts and constructs will become correspondingly more valid.

Theorists following up this viewpoint attacked with vigor any tendencies to consider culture to be an independent or superorganic phenomenon. To attribute any separate existence to cultural constructs is to fall into the error of "reification," that is, making real things out of scientific abstractions. A few anthropologists became so unhappy with careless "reifying" in the language dealing with culture that they even proposed abolition of the term "culture" itself. It is quite difficult, in fact, to talk about culture without implying that it has a reified, or superorganic, existence apart from scientific generalization. A field worker easily writes that "such-and-such a culture moved to this or that

area," or that "this culture met that culture," or that "one culture stood firm when others were changing." In reality, it was individuals-trained-in-similar-behavior who were moving, meeting, being conservative. But culture continues to be an indispensable concept simply because regularities in individual behavior can be generalized for scientific purposes in this way. The same is true of other broad operating concepts such as society and personality.

For many types of problem, indeed, it is possible to deal with cultural generalizations as though culture has an existence of its own, apart from individuals. Differing patterns of behavior may be traced historically and geographically. The symbols which are shared by a cultural group may be isolated and examined, as in language or art. This is done in everyday life as well as in science: a humorous story, perhaps in differing versions, goes the rounds, a hero is widely extolled, a wedding is compared with other weddings.

The issues here can be made clearer if one considers the everyday generalizing tendencies in language. We see, on the streets, a "terrier" here, a "dachshund" there, a "poodle" still farther along; then we generalize in the term "a dog" or just the category "dog." The category "dog," useful as it is, has no real existence, but is a kind of *abstraction*, or *construct* of this class of mammals of which we can see, hear, touch, sometimes smell, and might if we wished (as is the custom in some cultures) taste, individual specimens. Or we may apply the same reasoning in a further discussion of one of the cases cited above, that of the Ainu arrow, as follows:

Q. Are all these Ainu ceremonial arrows going to be exactly alike?

AA. No. . . . No two persons making them could shape them exactly the same. . . . Each one would be a little different. . . .

Q. Then how can I know this one is an average or a normal type of arrow?

A. It must have some essential features which all ceremonial arrows should share.

Q. But there would be differences?

AA. Yes, but they would all vary around the same type. . . . They would need to approximate to the same shape. . . . All would need to have about the same length of tip. . . . All would need to have a notch so they could be shot by a bow. . . . They would have to be of projectile shape and balance.

Q. What you are implying is that, within whatever *range of variation* is possible or permitted in this recognized *class* of objects, there is likely to be a *modal* or central tendency, a highest frequency pattern, to which all such arrows approximate. What do these statements mean?

A. Can I ask a question? How, then, can we know that the arrow you're showing us is an average one—or fits closely the mode?

Q. Well, you can't merely from this one case. If you aren't prepared to take my word, what could you do about it?

AA. Look at a number of them. . . . See what the range of variation can be. . . . Strike a kind of average. . . . Use statistics.

Q. Who has had a statistics course? What is an "average"?

A. The average is the *mean*, as where all arrow lengths are added up and divided by the number of arrows. Then there is the *median*, the middle point at which half of the series fall on one side and half on the other. These are different measures from the mode which is the highest frequency.

Q. Good. Let's try another approach. Is the modal arrow type the same as the "normal" or the "ideal" arrow?

A. (*After long pause.*) The arrow makers, I suppose, must have had some ideal kind of arrow, one which would be the best or perfect form.

Q. Would you expect many arrows to approximate to such perfect form?

AA. No. I think that only the best arrow maker could get near to that ideal. Others might make good, or pretty good, or just poor arrows. . . . The people would have a standard as to what good and bad arrows are. . . . I think what you are getting at is that the mode in the case of the arrow may be quite a bit different from the ideal.

Q. It's getting clear that where in the case of modality we are talking of highest frequency tendencies, in the case of what is counted *ideal*, or the *norm*, we are dealing with a measure or standard of expectation, of value. The maker cannot deviate too much from this normative standard without criticism and disapproval of his fellows. How, then, would you go about establishing the norm in Ainu arrows?

A. Ask the best-informed people? . . . Watch the arrow maker who is counted the best work-

man. . . . Find out what brings approval and disapproval.

Q. How would we relate the terms "mode" and "norm" to a more general concept we have used already; that of "pattern"?

A. Could we say that a certain custom will have a modal pattern and a normative pattern?

Q. Then what would be the relation of the two?

A. They could be quite a lot different, or they could be just about the same. That is, people could all obey a custom if it is important enough. . . . Wouldn't that have to be studied for every separate item of custom?

Q. Do we ever see, or touch, a "pattern" of behavior?

A. No. It is really a kind of scientific generalization.

Q. Yes. The pattern of a custom, as described scientifically, is really an *abstraction* or *construct* from numerous individual cases. In the case of the Ainu arrow it is a class of artifacts, but it could equally well be an action sequence of behavior by individuals trained to value that mode or norm.

A. How can we tell when such a pattern is rightly located and described?

Q. The anthropologist does not depend on one case or on a few cases—or if he has to he should say so. Being a participant-observer over a long period, he locates a whole number of cases wherever possible. He gets from this the sense of repetition, and of what is essential and basic to the item of behavior. Ideally he would record sample case after sample case until he had adequate knowledge of the range, and also of the mode in a statistically valid sense. But the complexities of behavior patterns, and in some matters a lack of frequent practice, or of practice easily open to observation—the Ainu bear ceremony is a case of infrequent occurrence—make this nearly always a matter of the anthropologist's judgment and his integrity in field work rather than of exact numerical counting. What kinds of customs would you say are easiest to record in terms of very fixed and exact patterns?

AA. Those that are very rigidly fixed as habits? . . . Those you can't break without severe punishment, like incest or killing. . . .

Q. Certainly an anthropologist, recording in our own society the rules on killing one's fellows or engaging in forbidden sex relations among relatives (incest) would judge from his comparative experience that he could put the item down confidently in his field notebook as both modal and normative without expecting much range of deviation. Conforming to such rules has very high frequency in its patterning, and the abstractions or scientific constructs involved have very high predictability value. What kinds of behavior would you expect to be least patterned and so least predictable?

A. Perhaps the making of ordinary arrows—the Ainu could make them of various shapes and sizes.

Q. Perhaps so. But the likelihood is that arrows must have a reasonably similar form, based on principles of aerodynamics.

A. Perhaps some custom in which the people have very free choice, and where they don't have to conform?

Q. What might be an example, in our own culture, of low frequency in patterning, or to put it another way, of a great range of permissible variation?

AA. Your choice of sports. . . . Joining in a crowd to watch a fire. . . .

Q. Good. In every system of life, or culture, there are customs which have low pattern frequency and minor normative value, hence little predictability, as regards individual behavior. Here the abstractions or constructs which the anthropologist makes should certainly indicate the individual range as well as whatever mode or norm can be discerned.

The steps taken by the anthropologist in "constructing" or "abstracting" whatever regularities or patterns are evident in behavior are brought out clearly in this exchange. Like any other observer, he sees, hears, feels, smells, or tastes specific items of experience, associated with specific artifacts or persons: innovative or habitual acts of individuals, and communicative acts between individuals. From these, with the best linguistic, statistical, and other controls his field work allows, he builds up *classes* of artifacts and of behavior. Partly this step can be based on actual words used by the people themselves in classifying experience, e.g., "We [Menomini] are related to totemic animals"; "Candles are used in church." But partly it may emerge from scientific frames of reference of which the people may be totally unaware, e.g., "religion

among northeast Asian peoples such as the Ainu emphasizes close relations of men with animals such as the bear." In turn for each *class* of behavior he makes the effort to sample the *range* and establish the *mode* and *norm*.

It is possible, now, to add a series of further propositions about culture, which arise particularly when account is being taken of the "operations" which enter into scientific generalization. First, constructs or generalized statements about culture can stress its normative aspect. From this viewpoint, the concept is concerned with norms of behavior which represent what have been variously called expectations (or expectancies), values, goals, ideals, designs for living. Humans are inveterate rule makers. The society presents to the individual what he *should* do, the behaviors which are counted *normal*, correct, desirable, in its particular cultural tradition. In turn, the actual behavior of the individual is likely to approximate to these norms, especially to the extent they are "valued," or affectively (emotionally) charged as being "good," held up as conative (action) goals and cognitive (thought) ideals as being "right," backed up by compulsions or "sanctions" as being "expected," "lawful." For some behaviors the ideal may be a perfect standard out of ordinary reach, e.g., never breaking traffic laws. So far as individual behaviors deviate in a marked degree from these normative patterns the person concerned is thought of as progressively more *abnormal*, i.e., unconventional, Bohemian, queer, bad, criminal, even insane. . . . Beyond is the realm of "unthinkable" behavior—though, indeed, such behavior may be a norm in another culture, e.g., the marriage of a brother to a sister. Anthropologists may therefore speak of the *normative culture*, or sometimes the *ideal culture*.

Again, constructs or generalized statements about culture can stress its modal aspect. The actual behaviors of individuals tend to cluster according to a trend or mode. No two individuals reproduce exactly the same artifact or action sequence, nor does the same individual at different times: a range of at least minor variation shows. But in any group or "population" and in any class or "universe" of behavior there is likely to be a high frequency or central tendency, and sometimes more than one, within the total range of individual conduct involved. As regards the class of behavior "handshake" in our society, there are broadly modal features, e.g., grasping of right hands, an up-and-down

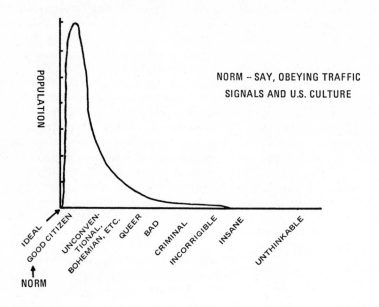

Cultural Norm: an Example

Cultural Mode: an Example

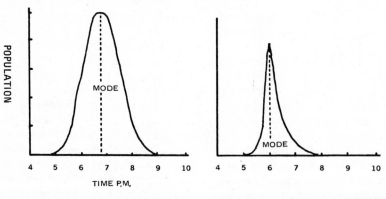

motion, an etiquette context. But there are also *polymodal* tendencies, as with the polite handshake between strangers, the double handclasp of warm friends, the secret pressures of fraternity brothers. In turn, these latter greeting behaviors can be regarded as modal to such more limited classes of etiquette. Some anthropologists have called the actual behavior of individuals within a cultural tradition the *real culture*, or the *behavioral culture*. This real or behavioral culture, with its different extent and directions of variation, has its most patterned manifestations in the *modal* constructs which an anthropologist works out as subject to greatest regularity and hence statistically typical.

In a very homogeneous and stable culture, the norms and modes of behavior tend to correspond closely. People are likely to do with greatest frequency what they are expected to do. But discrepancies presumably occur in all cultures, and they certainly do in our own. The cultural shoe, so to speak, will always pinch somewhere. As indicated above, some ideals or goals, such as those relative to the perfect citizen, the infallible leader, or the successful magician, may be set so high that few approximate to the expected behaviors. Individuals tend to lag and dodge those rules which chafe them as requiring great effort, interfering with personal tastes, or otherwise making heavy demands.

This discrepancy becomes exaggerated when customs are changing, or when a social group aligns itself on different sides of an issue. A frequently cited example is the former prohibition law in the United States, which many people felt free to break. The modes of practical behavior certainly stood statistically far from the norms represented in the Volstead Act. It would be more accurate, however, to say that public opinion clustered around two opposing norms, pro- and anti-prohibition, and modes of behavior tended to cluster accordingly at two widely separated zones. In a variegated and changing cultural milieu the contrasts between what are traditionally the ideal cultural patterns and the real behavior patterns are often very great.

Normative constructs relating to a given culture are likely to have their counterpart in well-formulated verbal statements which the people themselves make about their way of life; modal constructs tend to be scientific abstractions. The anthropologist, listening to admonitions by elders and parents, probing what different individuals say about their beliefs and activities, gets into his notebook statement after statement of what a person is assumed to do, or should do—whether they do it or not. An informant nearly always talks initially about the cultural norms rather than about individual or even modal behaviors. For this reason, normative patterns tend to be what various social scientists have called overt, explicit, manifest, or "conscious." They are part of the established symbol system of the culture, emerging especially in language terms and statements. By contrast, modal patterns are more likely to be covert, implicit, latent, or "unconscious"—or at least, even if the people concerned make assertions about what is "most frequently done" or "common practice," a careful field check is considered essential if at all feasible. For both types of record, however, the anthropologist's written report is almost always dominated by statements which are scientific constructs, even if interspersed with illustrative cases from specific behavior.

The distinction made here between the overt (explicit, manifest, and so on) and the covert (implicit, latent, and so on) has had considerable vogue in recent behavioral science literature. It goes back in anthropology to the 1930's, when an earlier preoccupation with externals of behavior and artifacts was being enriched by admitting study of motivation, function, and integration to the scientific frame of reference. Where the former could be seen, heard, and otherwise observed at the sensory level, the latter were regarded as inferential constructs formulated through an exercise of insight or judgment, and so were considered to be covert or implicit rather than overt or explicit. Culture then divided easily into *overt (explicit) culture* and *covert (implicit) culture*.

The operation of these terms, however, is more complicated than appears at first sight. The covert culture category, for example, had readily assignable to it the "unconscious patterning" of behavior, premise and value systems, functions and configurations. But what may be unconscious in behavioral habit for an individual most of the time may emerge to consciousness when some crisis occurs or alternative choices present themselves. Moreover, premises, values, and other motivational and integrational tendencies in behavior which a people share are usually (or even perhaps in a measure always) capable of being expressed in verbalized form by words and phrases in their language. The anthropologist constructs the proposition, for example, that the world view of the Zuni Indians of the American Southwest judges the world to be good rather than evil; but a Zuni mother probably often states to her child various equivalents of the English statement: "The world is good." A Zuni priest, too, may convey this theme in prayer and other ritual. The so-called covert or implicit level of culture tends therefore to dwindle as a category when the explicit symbolic reference system of language is taken into account. Our own tradition, for example, has run strongly to crystallizing in abstract words and in clear-cut scientific, philosophical, and other statements what is so often spoken of as the covert in culture. We also have a plentiful store of proverbs, tales, political and legal statements, religious tenets, and other linguistic devices with which to administer in appropriate situations the motivational and evaluational sets of our culture both to children and to adults.

A category still remains, however, where the distinction between overt and covert constructs appears to be capable of valid use. What a people themselves recognize and make explicit about their culture is not necessarily all that an intellectually curious person, and especially an observer using a scientific frame of reference, can abstract from the behavior concerned. An anthropologist analyzing, for example, the character structure or value system inherent in a particular cultural tradition can try after refinements of generalization beyond what the traditional symbolism of the language milieu concerned have reached. Faced by Benedict's penetrating study of Japanese culture and personality, *The Chrysanthemum and the Sword* (1946), Japanese anthropologists and other social scientists have

been critically reviewing both her work and their own national behavior system to see how closely her model fits. . . . The recent tendency, following this line of thought, is to speak of the overt, explicit, or manifest in a cultural system as covering all that the people concerned actually have recognized and formulated in their tradition. The covert, implicit, or latent then comprises whatever understandings can be won through scientific observation and analysis.

These statements about abstraction and generalization relating to culture could be matched with similar analyses relating to society, personality, and character. For further understanding the following exercises might be undertaken:

1. Locate and analyze a normative pattern widely accepted in contemporary society.
2. Locate and analyze a case where the real behavior shows wide variation. How far can modal tendencies be traced?
3. What would be an example of the covert (implicit, and so on) as relating to our own culture?

In sum, scientific generalizations about behavior necessitate the formulation and control of constructs or abstractions. They enable us to view behavior in a schematic or summary fashion. On the one hand, the Scylla of superorganic assumptions or reification must be avoided. On the other hand, the Charybdis of labeling all constructs "unreal" has its dangers. Cultural constructs, whether formulated as generalized statements in the language of the people being studied, or by the scientist through his sharpened intellectual operations, certainly have whatever "overt" substance we may be prepared to grant to formulated symbols.

OPERATIONAL DEFINITIONS

Finally, to tie down this process of "operationalization" of several concepts you will read much about in the social sciences, a passage from A. F. C. Wallace, one of the leaders in the "culture and personality" field of inquiry. Central to most research problems in that field is a clear understanding of the use of words and concepts relating to individual behavior, on the one hand, and social and cultural systems, on the other. This involves, for one thing, showing the kinds of observations a researcher is tying his word or concept to, and, for another, locating any given concept (such as "personality structure") on a ladder of abstraction that leads from behavior ascribable to a single individual to behavior said to be common to everyone in a group. The scheme Wallace outlines here (developed from an idea suggested by Theodore Graves) offers a concrete example, using as content the kinds of observations of behavior very familiar to cultural anthropologists. The specific kinds of inferences Wallace draws are offered, of course, only as teaching examples of the *process* of relating one's words and concepts to portions of observable reality.

OPERATIONAL DISCRIMINATIONS AMONG CONCEPTS

A. F. C. WALLACE

The most celebrated definition of culture is Tylor's:

Culture . . . is that complex whole which includes knowledge, belief, art, morals, law, custom, and any other capabilities and habits acquired by man as a member of society.

If the word "personality" is substituted for "culture" in the above sentence and the phrase "the individual" for "man," it will serve as a passable definition of personality as well. But there are, of course, other definitions of varying levels of abstractness, each one emphasizing those dimensions of observation which are most appealing to its author. The writer, for instance, in a probabilistic mood, suggested that culture be defined as:

. . . those ways of behavior or techniques of solving problems which, being more frequently and more closely approximated than other ways, can be said to have a high probability of use by individual members of society.

Personality, in this context, would be simply:

. . . those ways of behavior or techniques of solving problems which have a high probability of use by one individual.

Usually the author of any such a definition has in mind some kind of observation by which individual cultures or personalities are recognized, bounded, and properly described. The ethnographer may have in mind, when he gives a definition of culture, a long sequence of operations, beginning with learning the language, taking photographs, talking to people, watching what goes on and trying it himself, and fifteen years later ending up with intricate comparative analysis of recorded data by the use of some specific schema, based on a particular theoretical position. An archaeologist has in mind ecological parameters, digging, certain types of durable material remains, classification, labelling, and analysis by an equally specific but different schema. A psychoanalyst, when he thinks of "personality," has in mind the characteristic individual shape of psychodynamic structures whose elements are oedipal conflicts, castration anxieties, imagos, mechanisms of defense, and so forth; while the clinical psychologist, describing personality structure from Rorschach test data, is visualizing a bar graph, based on frequencies of such phenomena as allusions to color, line, texture, perspective, and movement, and is inferring such characteristics as introversion, stereotypy, imaginativeness, and self-control. Thus, there is no one concept of culture, nor a single concept of personality, which is universally agreed upon and is universally useful.

We do not propose to list here a set of definitions of the words "culture" and "personality," and then, by some suitable criteria, to select the best. Nor shall we offer new definitions. The student should realize that dozens, if not hundreds, of respectable definitions exist. Most of them, unfortunately, are ontological definitions: that is to say, they assert that culture *is* such and such, or that personality *is* one thing or another. And ontological definitions are the bane of science. They postulate Platonic essences, states of being in a realm of absolutes, about which argument may rage endlessly without any resolution but that of authority. Discussion of such definitions is sterile, as Hume

Reprinted with permission of publisher. From A. F. C. Wallace, *Culture and Personality* (New York: Random House, 1961), pp. 6–15.

pointed out long ago, when in his *Enquiry Concerning Human Understanding* (1748, Sect. XII, Part 3) he made the famous assertion:

> If we take in our hand any volume . . . let us ask, *Does it contain any abstract reasoning concerning quantity or number?* No. *Does it contain any experimental reasoning concerning matter of fact and existence?* No. Commit it then to the flames: for it can contain nothing but sophistry and illusion.

The more profitable procedure is to regard the words "culture" and "personality" as the names for indefinitely large numbers of different empirical operations. All of the operations under the rubric "culture" have in common certain broad and general features, and similarly with those referrable to "personality." An examination of textbooks and symposia concerning human personality will reveal, for instance, that a number of theories of personality dynamics and a bewildering variety of observational techniques are employed by dozens of authorities: projective tests, depth interviews, questionnaires, life histories, laboratory experiments, verbalized introspection, and so forth, on an infinitude of subject matters. And on these data various distinctive and stylized abstractive manipulations are performed, the results of which are treated as descriptive of various traits, forces, factors, vectors, structures, and so on, in many different arrangements. Similarly, with materials on culture: informant interviews, participant observation, film strips and photographs, tape-recorded texts, published literature, censuses, maps, material objects, and so on, are collected, and then subjected to various abstractive and analytical procedures, the products whereof are regarded as constituting an ethnographic description. Obviously, whatever culture "is" and whatever personality "is," the empirical operations by which they are described vary, depending on both the observer and the situation of his observations.

It is possible, however, to discriminate between these two words, and others relevant to this area of inquiry, and to describe their relationship in terms of certain of their operational characteristics. Three dimensions are of particular relevance: the number of persons observed, directly or indirectly; the number of kinds of behavior observed; and the level of abstraction achieved by various analytic and synthetic operations. All three dimensions of variation, furthermore, are to be considered under

a constant condition; namely, that the observations are made of individuals within the boundaries of a specified population at a given time. The semantic relationships can best be represented in tabular form. First, we shall consider only the first two dimensions, of number of individuals and number of behavioral categories observed, allowing level of abstraction to vary. Table I represents the operational differentiation of several terms (some of them to be further defined later in the text) by number of individuals and by number of behavioral categories.

The contents of Table I (and the meaning of the expression "equivalence structure") can perhaps best be illuminated by a series of nine illustrations, corresponding to the nine cells of the table:

CELL 1. We observe that an old American Indian man, who lives alone in a small house on a reservation where we are staying, whenever he leaves the house (to walk to the general store, or to visit relatives, or for whatever reason) props a stick of wood against the lockless door. On being asked why he does this, he says, "It is a sign to people that I am away and that they should not enter." Without any further information about this type of behavior, we temporarily regard it as a personal *habit*.

CELL 2. On further inquiry, we find that a dozen of our acquaintances on this reservation follow the same practice when they leave the house empty: they prop a stick of wood, or a broom, against the door. They all say, on inquiry, that it is a sign of the occupant's temporary absence and of his wish that no one enter. Some aver that almost everyone on the reservation does this. We conclude that putting a stick against the door is a *custom* in this community, regularly followed by many persons when they leave a dwelling temporarily empty. Comparing notes later with another anthropologist, we learn that the same custom is practiced on a number of reservations in the area, and we begin to refer to it as a *culture trait* with an unknown distribution.

CELL 3. Although we are unable to make inquiry in every household in the community, we are told by some of our informants that almost everyone on the reservation props a stick against the door when leaving the house. We consider that it is likely that this custom is also a cultural *universal* on this reservation, but hesitate to make the claim categorically because of the difficulty and expense of even the attempt to demonstrate universality in the field.

CELL 4. Our curiosity is now piqued. We come from a city in which the custom is to lock all doors and windows when the house is empty and, if the absence is to be lengthy, to leave some sign (such as a burning light or the absence of accumulated mail) that the house is occupied. The rationale usually given for doing this is the prevention of theft and vandalism. We note that the Indian custom draws

TABLE 1

CULTURE-AND-PERSONALITY TERMINOLOGY DIFFERENTIATED BY NUMBERS OF
INDIVIDUALS AND OF BEHAVIOR CATEGORIES OBSERVED

1. When one has observed
    one individual in a group,
    many individuals in a group,
    all individuals in a group,

2. and the behavior observed is, in the language of this investigation, of
    one category (i.e., a particular class of act, or sequence of acts, consistently performed in a class of situations),
    many categories, arranged in an equivalence structure,
    all those categories which exist in some equivalence structure,

3. then, depending on the abstractive operations, the statement of the observations will be a description of a . . .

NUMBER OF BEHAVIOR CATEGORIES

	ONE CATEGORY	TWO OR MORE CATEGORIES	ALL CATEGORIES
ONE	habit, response, behavior potential, etc. 1	character trait, motive, complex, value, syndrome, etc. 4	mazeway, personality, psycho-biological system, etc. 7
TWO OR MORE	culture trait, custom, role, alternative, speciality, etc. 2	relationship, institution, ritual, theme, etc. 5	sub-culture, status per-sonality, etc. 8
ALL	culture trait, custom, role, theme, universal, etc. 3	relationship, institution, ritual, theme, focus, etc. 6	pattern, configuration, culture, national character, modal personality, etc. 9

(left axis label: NUMBER OF INDIVIDUALS)

attention to the owner's absence, rather than conceals it, and that the leaning stick of wood constitutes no barrier to entry, since the door is not locked. Several speculations occur to us: First of all, we feel sure that the absent owner is confident that his neighbors will not enter his house when a stick is propped against the door; in other words, that he conceives of the two types of behavior as being equivalent, and therefore expects that his house will be left alone if he plays the stick-propping role. Secondly, we suspect that any Indian who "stick-props" will probably display certain other behaviors as well, which have in common a quality of confidence that explicit requests will be honored. Our interest in this possibility leads us to go back to our earlier informant, whose habit of stick propping had first led us to the subject. We interview him at some length, not only on stick-propping, but on matters related to confidence in the granting of wishes, and learn that he does indeed regard personal requests, both to him and from him, as carrying an expectation of fulfillment. He makes requests of us, once we get to know him, for transportation, for errands, for legal advice, and for gifts of food, tobacco, and even money. On the other hand, he freely accedes to our wishes that he spend time as an informant without pay, accompanies us in order to introduce us to others, shares his own limited resources without stint. We feel that, at least in contrast to most whites whom we know, he has a characterological *trait* of expectation of wish-granting, whether he be the wisher or the grantor.

CELL 5. Indeed, as we come to know many people

on the reservation, we find that this wish-granting expectancy trait is so common that we can call it a *theme* in the culture. We now observe that on several occasions, when we have gone with one or another of our informants to visit a house where someone can give us certain information, our guide will not bother to knock on a door against which a stick is propped, nor will he enter in order to look for or await the occupants. We are told, several times, "You don't go into a house when a stick is propped against the door." We conclude that stick-propping and house-avoidance behaviors constitute, for many pairs of persons, complementary roles; the two behaviors are equivalent in the logician's sense that whenever, but only when. person *A* plays role *a*, person *B* will play role *b*. We begin to refer to this equivalence structure as an *institution*.

CELL 6. Inasmuch as we suspect, although we cannot demonstrate, that the complementary stick-propping and house-avoidance behaviors are universals, and inasmuch as this institution is only one expression of a more general theme of expectancy of wish-granting, we feel that we may now be dealing with an area of cultural *focus*. This hypothesized focus would fall on the development and maintenance of institutions which express the theme of expectancy of wish-granting. The pursuit of this hypothesis leads us to consider that wishes expressed in dreams are, indeed, historically known to have been the source of a number of cultural innovations, as for instance the cultural reforms sponsored by a religious prophet in the previous century. We observe also that many religio-medical secret societies, and even major political institutions, in myth are asserted to have originated in dreams or dreamlike wishes.

CELL 7. Because we are now on good terms with the old man, we ask him whether he will tell us the story of his life, recount some of his dreams, and be a subject for several tests, including the Rorschach and the TAT. Although he displays some discomfort, particularly about recounting dreams (which we expected), he feels that he must grant our wish. The indelicacy of asking for dreams he excuses on the grounds that we are whites, and white people have different customs; hence, telling us his dreams is "not the same thing" as telling a neighbor. We thus obtain a large body of psychological materials. The produc of their analysis we regard as a description of the structure of his *personality*, since the statements made in this description are abstractions which we consider to be relevant to virtually all areas of his behavior.

CELL 9. In addition to working with the old man, we have been obtaining similar, if less extensive, projective test data from a large number of persons on the reservation. Furthermore, we have, with the help of several excellent informants and of our own day-by-day observation, been filling in the content categories of the *Outline of Cultural Materials*. These large bodies of data we do not analyze carefully in the field, but on our return to the University we work with them and produce, from the projective test data, a description of the *modal personality structure* of the population and, from the ethnographic data, a sketch of the *culture*.

CELL 8. One probable source of error in any general attribution to all members of the society of the modal personality description, derived by the procedures outlined for Cell 9, is the existence of sex, age, and other social differentials in the sample. Wishing to avoid the possibility of an unwary reader's attributing the modal personality type to sub-groups where personality norms actually differ significantly from the modal type, we construct separate modal types for males and females, for children, active adults, and inactive ("old") adults, and for the two major ethnic groups which compose the population (approximately one-third of the tribe are sixth-generation immigrant refugees from another culture area). This refinement of the analysis reveals that there are indeed significant differences among the modal types constructed for age, sex, and ethnic sub-groups within the population, and between some of these sub-types and the general type. This discovery of distinctive *status personalities*, which correspond roughly with the *sub-cultures* of distinctive social sub-groups, does not invalidate the modal personality type characteristic of the population as a whole, of course, since its definition involved specification of its relative frequency within the population. But it makes possible much more exact understanding of the interpersonal dynamics of the society than dependence on knowledge of the general modal type would permit.

CONCEPTS OF CULTURE

Perhaps enough has been said up to this point about the process of conceptualization and the different kinds of ideas it can lead to that we can take a look now at the central concept we are concerned with: "culture." The following article by Kluckhohn and Kelly presents, in a dialogue fashion, the many meanings that have been given to the concept and the diverse ways the word has been used, not only in anthropological discourse but also in the common language (indeed, this is one of the difficulties with the word). The purpose of introducing this article at this point is to underscore how widely and various can be the meanings—and, against a background of the preceding several selections, the importance of your having an idea how to adjust for a diversity of meanings: by insisting on knowing how the term is "operationalized," by what observable events or by what things you shall know it.

A second purpose for the article at this point is to introduce discussion of some of the most important and critical aspects of the kind of usage of the concept that is becoming common in the behavioral sciences: the notion that culture, in its formation and expression, is intricately tied in with symbols and symbol systems; and this, in turn, is interlocked with a system of values and beliefs. In the dialogue that introduces these ideas, you will be reminded of the purpose of some of the material presented in Part I, that is, "culture" (as preferred ways of doing things) channels and shapes into particular behavioral forms many of our most basic biological drives and needs, as well as activities not so directly tied to such drives.

In this overview of the wide-ranging ways the concept is used another theme is also evident: "culture" is a concept at the group level of analysis, not at the level of the individual; it is a property of *social* life in the first instance, and only secondarily (through socialization) of the individual person. This point is tricky, and one that we will spend more time with later. But it is important at this stage of the game to keep in mind that, even though we are now taking an overview of varying concepts of culture, they all are agreed on one thing· the cultural dimension to human life is rooted in social learning and social existence. The "individual" is only a subset of that larger system, and while not all his learned experience is "cultural," all "culture" is based on the learned (and communicated) experience of numerous individuals comprising a given group. But, as I say, more on this point later. For now keep it in mind that we are moving further and further away from single individuals and are speaking of a property of *group life* when we speak of "culture." Later in more detail we will take up the differentiation between concepts of "culture" and such concepts as "society."

THE CONCEPT OF CULTURE

CLYDE KLUCKHOHN and WILLIAM H. KELLY

THE LAWYER: At the last meeting of this little discussion group of ours, we got into quite an argument about "culture" as a technical term in anthropology—exactly what anthropologists mean by it and whether it is any use or not. The big dictionaries and even the anthropological books here in the

Reprinted with permission of publisher. From *The Science of Man in the World Crisis*, ed. Ralph Linton (New York: Columbia University Press, 1949), pp. 78–106.

club library didn't help us out very much. We did gather that the anthropological conception, like all the other scientific and popular usages, carries with it an implication of human interference, of something being added to, or altered from, a state of nature. But we found ourselves wishing that we could ask questions which might clear up points which were sidestepped or simply not discussed by these formal statements. We therefore prevailed upon you gentlemen to come here and let us put you on the spot.

THE HISTORIAN: Was I right in insisting last time that the anthropologist's conception of culture is much more inclusive than the historian's?

FIRST ANTHROPOLOGIST: Yes, to anthropologists a humble cooking pot is as much a cultural product as is a Beethoven sonata.

THE BUSINESSMAN: I am relieved to hear that. For my wife a person who has culture is a person who can talk about Debussy, T. S. Eliot, Picasso, and those people.

THE LAWYER: Do anthropologists apply the term "culture" to our civilization? Isn't there a difference between "culture" and "civilization"?

SECOND ANTHROPOLOGIST: To most anthropologists, a civilization is simply a special type of a culture, namely, a complex or "high" culture. More specifically, a civilization is—as the derivation of the word itself suggests—the culture of a people who live in cities. People who have lived in cities have invariably possessed a somewhat complex way of life, and have almost always had a written language.

THIRD ANTHROPOLOGIST: Perhaps it would also be well to state for the record that anthropologists have never followed another distinction which certain sociologists have made between culture and civilization. This usage discriminates between "civilization" as comprising the sum total of human "means" and "culture" as constituting the collectivity of human "ends."

FIRST ANTHROPOLOGIST: Many educated people seem to have the notion that "culture" applies only to exotic ways of life or to societies where relative simplicity and relative homogeneity prevail. Some sophisticated missionaries, for example, will use the anthropological conception in discussing the special modes of living of South Sea Islanders, but seem amazed at the idea that it could be applied equally to the inhabitants of New York City. And social workers in New York City will talk about the "culture" of a colorful and well-knit immigrant group, but boggle at utilizing the concept toward understanding the behavior of staff members in the social service agency itself.

THE ECONOMIST: A moment ago you used the term "society." This brings me to a point which I have found confusing in certain recent more or less popular writings of anthropologists. Sometimes the terms "culture" and "society" seem to have been used almost as synonyms.

FIRST ANTHROPOLOGIST: There would be fairly general agreement in our profession that this is undesirable. The usage which has attained almost complete acceptance among us can be put simply, though not altogether precisely, as follows: A "society" refers to a group of people who have learned to work together; a "culture" refers to the distinctive ways of life of such a group of people.

THE PHILOSOPHER: In my language, then, "a culture" is an abstraction, whereas "a society" is not?

THIRD ANTHROPOLOGIST: That is certainly correct in the sense that you can see the individuals who make up a society, while you never see "culture." However, the statement must not be made to imply that the processes of inference and abstraction are not involved in many of the specific problems of deciding where one society leaves off and another begins. Some anthropologists assert that such problems can always be resolved by sufficiently detailed observation of the frequencies with which human beings in a defined territory interact. This is doubtless a valid operation by which to decide what individuals constitute "a society," but we should be deluding ourselves if we pretended that reasoning were not as necessary as observation to the delimitation of a society.

SECOND ANTHROPOLOGIST: I can't agree with your first statement that culture is never observed directly. What does an anthropologist actually do when he is working in the field? Yes, he sees the human organisms who make up a society. He sees not only them, but also their behavior. He likewise sees the objects they have made and all of the alterations which they produced in their natural environment. What the anthropologist does is to record the distinctive ways of behaving which he sees and those results of behavior which are also characteristic. These constitute the culture of the group.

THIRD ANTHROPOLOGIST: There is no doubt that you have rightly described what anthropologists actually do in the field. But those recordings which you have mentioned I would prefer to consider as the anthropologist's raw data. Both "society" and "culture" are conceptual constructs. In each case, although in importantly different ways, the anthropologist has added to or subtracted from what he actually saw. Both the society and the culture which he portrays are conceptual models—not firsthand recordings of all he observed.

THE PSYCHOLOGIST: Let me see if I can translate into my own lingo. Culture means the totality of social habits.

FIRST ANTHROPOLOGIST: "Habit" is too neutral a term. It would be more exact to say "socially valued habits," for a group is never affectively indifferent to its culture.

THE PSYCHOLOGIST: I suppose that branch of psychology which is most intimately related to "culture" is what we today call "learning theory." Wouldn't you agree that the transmission of culture can be understood only in so far as learning and teaching are understood?

FIRST ANTHROPOLOGIST: Yes, inasmuch as all human beings of whatever "races" seem to have about the same nervous systems and biological equipment generally, we would anticipate that the basic processes of learning are very similar if not identical among all groups. We therefore look to the psychologist to inform us about the laws of learning. On the other hand, we can show that *what* is learned, from whom learning takes place, and when the learning of certain skills usually occurs, varies according to culture. Also, I should like to point out that there is one danger in speaking of culture as being "taught." "Teaching" is not limited, as in the popular sense, to conscious instruction. Individuals learn—"absorb" more nearly suggests, in nontechnical language, the process—much of their culture through imitation of both the "matched-dependent" and "copying" types. Take, for example, those gestures and expressive movements ("motor habits") which are observed as characteristic of certain groups. Every anthropologist regards these as cultural phenomena, and yet only in dancing schools, armies, and the like is explicit instruction as to posture, and so forth, given.

THE PSYCHOLOGIST: If I am not mistaken, C. S. Ford has defined culture as consisting of "traditional ways of solving problems" or "learned problem solutions."

THIRD ANTHROPOLOGIST: It is true that any culture is, among other things, a set of techniques for adjusting both to the external environment and to other men. In so far as Ford's statement points to this fact, it is helpful, but it will not do as a synoptic

definition. For cultures create problems as well as solving them. If the lore of a people states that frogs are dangerous creatures, or that it is not safe to go about at night because of were-animals or ghosts, threats are posed which do not arise out of the inexorable facts of the external world. This is why all "functional" definitions of culture tend to be unsatisfactory: they disregard the fact that cultures create needs as well as provide a means of fulfilling them.

THE PSYCHIATRIST: In fact, my profession has always tended to think of culture as something which was repressive to the "natural" nature of man, as something which produced needless neuroses by demands and thwartings during the process of molding individuals into shapes uncongenial to their native temperament.

THIRD ANTHROPOLOGIST: This seems to us to be another half-truth. Culture is *both* fulfilling and frustrating.

FOURTH ANTHROPOLOGIST: I have held my peace, but at this point I really must protest. Where is this "culture" which you talk about as doing this and that? If anthropology is to become a natural science, it must deal only in empirical and observable entities. In spite of the fact that most archeologists, ethnologists, and social anthropologists still feel that "culture" is their master concept, I maintain we would get further if we stuck to human interaction with other humans and with the natural environment. You can see those things, but has any of you ever seen "culture"?

FIRST ANTHROPOLOGIST: I freely admit that to say "culture" does something is an inexact or metaphorical way of speaking. But this is merely a convenient shorthand expression in place of the long-winded though admittedly more precise "the human representatives of the group which share this culture do thus and so." As for "seeing": your admired natural scientists have never seen "gravity" or "evolution." And yet they find the introduction of these concepts indispensable for making the facts intelligible and for predicting them. "Culture" is an abstract generalizing concept, as essential to the understanding and prediction of events in the human world as is gravity to the understanding and prediction of events in the physical world.

SECOND ANTHROPOLOGIST: I accept and use the concept "culture," but I shy away from these high abstractions. I think it is better to stick to a more traditional definition, such as: "Culture is that complex whole which includes artifacts, beliefs, art, all the other habits acquired by man as a member of society, and all products of human activity as determined by these habits."

FIRST ANTHROPOLOGIST: That is all right as a descriptive statement of what students of culture investigate. But as a definition I find it awkward. The enumeration is incomplete, and experience shows that in definitions by enumeration those elements which are not explicitly stated tend to be forgotten even though they be implied. You, for example, have not even mentioned language.

THIRD ANTHROPOLOGIST: I would file two other objections. First, the definition is too intellectualistic. One gets no hint that people are other than affectively neutral toward their culture. This is just a list of culture content. Except, possibly, for the single word "whole," there is no indication that culture has organization as well as content.

THE ECONOMIST: How about "social heredity" as a brief abstract definition of culture?

THIRD ANTHROPOLOGIST: This definition has been widely current and has been of much utility in drawing attention to the fact that human beings have a social as well as a biological heritage. The principal drawbacks to this conception of culture are that it implies too great stability of culture and too passive a role on the part of man. It suggests that man gets his culture as he gets his genes—without effort and without resistance. It tends too much to make us think of the human being as what Dollard has called "the passive porter of a cultural tradition." Men are, as Simmons has recently reminded us, not only the carriers and the creatures of culture—they are also creators and manipulators of culture. "Social heredity" suggests too much of the dead weight of tradition.

THE PSYCHIATRIST: Yes, culture is not merely a "given." Really, in a strictly literal sense, it is not a "given" at all—it is only available. Indeed, Ortega y Gasset has defined culture as "that which is sought." The phrase "social legacy" perhaps avoids some of these difficulties, but even this is hardly satisfactory. One wants a definition which points to the fact that the irreducible datum of the social scientist is the individual and his behavior. From the angle of individual psychology, no definition

of culture is adequate which does not make us aware of the active role of the individual as regards his culture and of the fact that he has an impulse life.

THE BUSINESSMAN: Much of what has been said was mildly diverting as an exhibition in logical adroitness, but frankly I still don't altogether see why anybody bothers about "culture" at all.

FIRST ANTHROPOLOGIST: Well, one of the interesting things about human beings is that they try to understand themselves and their own behavior. While this has been particularly true of Europeans in recent times, there is no group which has not developed a scheme or schemes to explain man's actions. I would claim that the concept of culture is essential to such understanding.

SECOND ANTHROPOLOGIST: I would phrase the case a little differently. Science is concerned with all observable phenomena, including man himself and his behavior. "Culture" is a convenient descriptive category for organizing our objective reports on human behavior.

THE PHILOSOPHER: It strikes me that the last two statements contain the key to much of our apparent disagreement. For some anthropologists "culture" is primarily a descriptive concept; for others it is primarily an explanatory concept. So-called "definitions" are always constructed from a point of view—which is all too often left unstated. Not all definitions are substantive (that is, "descriptive"). Nor is "explanatory" the only other alternative. Some of the definitions which have been partially stated or implied have been "functional"; others may be characterized as epistemological—that is, they have been intended to point toward the type of phenomena from which we gain our knowledge of "culture." There is also the point that some definitions look toward the actions of the individual as the starting point of all assertions, whereas others, while perhaps admitting these as ultimate referents, depart from abstractions attributable to groups. However, the distinction between "explanatory" and "descriptive" seems to be most central.

"CULTURE" AS AN EXPLANATORY CONCEPT

THIRD ANTHROPOLOGIST: *By "culture" we mean those historically created selective processes which channel men's reactions both to internal and to external stimuli.*

SECOND ANTHROPOLOGIST: That is certainly an "analytical abstraction" all right.

THIRD ANTHROPOLIGIST: That is precisely the idea: that with this concept certain aspects of the concrete phenomena may be analyzed out, and thus whole events may be better "explained" and predicted.

FIRST ANTHROPOLOGIST: Very neat. And it seems to me to cover the ground. It avoids the difficulty lurking in those many definitions of culture which employ the phrase "acquired by man as a member of society." That phrase seems to suggest that "culture" as an explanatory concept refers *only* to dimensions of the behavior of individuals resultant upon their membership in a particular society (either through birth or through later affiliation). But "culture" also helps us to understand such processes as "diffusion," "culture contact," "acculturation."

THIRD ANTHROPOLOGIST: Yes, culture as an explanatory concept is useful alike in analyzing actions of individuals (whether treated as individuals or as groups) and in elucidating geographical distributions of artifacts or forms of behavior and historical sequences.

FIRST ANTHROPOLOGIST: One could perhaps rephrase your definition along substantive lines by saying that by culture we mean those historically created definitions of the situation which individuals tend to acquire by virtue of participation in or contact with groups which tend to share ways of life which are in some respects distinctive.

FOURTH ANTHROPOLOGIST: Even I find some merit in the explanatory definition proposed. You at least make some concession to a behavioristic approach when you speak of "reactions" and "stimuli."

THIRD ANTHROPOLOGIST: Naturally I would agree that any concept or proposition in social science must be ultimately referable back to human behavior. Even when we deal with distribution of "culture traits," we must not forget that we are dealing with products of human hands, with traces left by human activity.

FOURTH ANTHROPOLOGIST: But why did you find it necessary to include "*internal* stimuli"?

THIRD ANTHROPOLOGIST: When a man eats, he is reacting to an internal "drive," namely, hunger contractions consequent upon the lowering of blood sugar and so forth, but his precise reaction to these internal stimuli cannot be predicted by physiological knowledge alone. Whether a healthy adult tends to "feel hungry" twice, three times, or four times a day and the hours at which these "feelings" tend to recur is a question of culture. *What* he eats is of course limited by sheer objective availability, but is also partly regulated by culture. It is a biological fact that some types of berries are poisonous, but it is a cultural fact that, a few generations ago, most Americans considered tomatoes to be poisonous and refused to eat them. On the other hand, milk, which we regard as a healthful and pleasing food, is regarded by certain peoples of the earth as either dangerous or disgusting. Such selective, discriminative use of the environment is characteristically cultural. In a still more general sense, too, the process of eating is channeled by culture. Whether a man eats to live, lives to eat, or eats and lives is partly individual idiosyncrasy, but there are also marked correlations of individual tendencies along these lines with cultural groups.

SECOND ANTHROPOLOGIST: Why do you use the word "reaction" instead of more straightforward "action"?

THIRD ANTHROPOLOGIST: Because "reaction" comes nearer to conveying the feeling tone which is associated with all selective designs for living.

FOURTH ANTHROPOLOGIST: I am partially convinced, but I must once more come back to my question: Why did you introduce this unseen "culture"?

THIRD ANTHROPOLOGIST: There is no human being, if he be even a few weeks old, who reacts completely freshly to any stimulus situation. Very few human responses indeed can be explained entirely through even the most complete knowledge of the individual biological equipment, private experience up to that point, and the objective facts of the given situation.

FOURTH ANTHROPOLOGIST: But where does "culture" come from? You seem to invoke it as a kind of *deus ex machina*.

THIRD ANTHROPOLOGIST: Culture is, as it were, the precipitate of history. It includes those aspects of the past which, usually in altered form, live on in the present. In more than one sense "history is a sieve."

BIOLOGIST: Do you mean that culture consists of those ways of meeting situations which prove to have survival value?

THIRD ANTHROPOLOGIST: This is a large and important part of the truth. The process of culture may well be regarded as something added to man's innate biological capacities; it provides instruments which enlarge or may even substitute for biological functions and which to a limited degree compensate for biological limitations—as in insuring that the biological fact of death does not always mean that what the dead individual has learned is lost to humanity.

Nevertheless, I believe this to be a dangerously misleading formulation unless it is properly explained and qualified. In the first place, as Linton and others have documented, it is an observed fact that most groups elaborate certain aspects of their culture far beyond maximal relative utility or survival value. In other words, not all culture is adaptive—in the sense of promoting sheer physical survival. At times indeed it does exactly the opposite. We must bring in the concept of adjustment (that is, lowering of tension) as well as that of adaptation. In the second place, aspects of culture which once directly promoted survival may persist even after they have ceased to have survival value. An analysis of contemporary Navaho culture will disclose many features which cannot possibly be construed as adaptations to the total environment in which Navahos now find themselves. However, it is altogether likely that these represent survivals, with modifications which have occurred during the centuries, of cultural forms which were adaptive in one or another environment in which certain ancestors of the contemporary Navaho lived prior to entering the Southwest.

FIRST ANTHROPOLOGIST: In other words, you are saying that no way of reacting is taken over by the group unless it has direct adaptive or adjustive value for individuals as such (or as constituting a group) at the time the design for living becomes cultural.

THIRD ANTHROPOLOGIST: Right. The main point is that, as Boas so often insisted, we cannot account for complex historical changes by any simple formula. While many patterned ways of reacting unquestionably represent almost inevitable responses to an external environment in which the group lives or once lived, there are certainly also many cases where the inexorable conditions of action merely limit the possibility of response rather than eventually compelling one and only one mode of adaptation. These "choices" are probably themselves determined—if we make our theoretical system wide enough to encompass all possible types of factors. But, within the more usual frame of reference, they are the "accidents of history."

Let me give an example or two. In a society where the chief really has great power, one particular chief happens to be born with an endocrine imbalance which brings about certain (to that group) unusual idiosyncrasies in personality. By virtue of his position, he is able to bring about certain modifications in the way of life of his group (say, in religion) which are congenial to his "temperament." It may be argued, and it may be true, that no amount of authority could insure the persistence of such alterations unless they somehow had adjustive or adaptive value for more than a single individual. I do not believe that the empirical evidence bearing on this problem has been sufficiently analyzed to permit a definite answer to the question. But what is certain is that such a circumstance has been known to be followed by relatively temporary or relatively enduring changes in group designs for living—sometimes primarily in the form of strong "reaction formations." The fact of the chief's position and all that was consequent upon it is not an accident from the point of view of the theoretical systems usually employed in analyzing such steps. The unusual temperament is, however, due to an "accident of the genetic process."

Or, suppose that in the same group a chief dies as a relatively young man, leaving an infant as his heir. This has been observed to result in a marked crystallization of two factions around two rival older relatives, each of whom has about an equally valid claim to act as "regent." Through these circumstances a complete and lasting splitting off of two groups has been observed to take place. Each group thereafter has pursued its own separate destiny, and the end result is the formation of two distinguishable variants of what was at one time a more or less homogeneous culture. Now, to be sure, it is likely that the original factional lines had their bases in "economic," demographic, or other "external" conditions. Yet, had it not been for the "accidental" death of the one chief in his early maturity, the society might have indefinitely continued intact as an equilibrium of opposed tendencies. In short, the form and the mesh of the "sieve which is history" must be seen and shaped not only by the total "environment" at any given point in time but also by individual "psychological" and "accidental" factors.

FIRST ANTHROPOLOGIST: Could we then say that culture includes all those ways of feeling, thinking, and acting which are not inevitable as a result of human biological equipment and process and (or) objective external situations?

THIRD ANTHROPOLOGIST: My objection to that definition would be: first, that this defines culture as a "residual category"—which is logically undesirable; second, I believe it is better to mention explicitly the time dimension as indicated by the phrase "historically created."

FIRST ANTHROPOLOGIST: This suggests also the cumulative nature of culture.

THIRD ANTHROPOLOGIST: Yes, provided we remember that in another sense culture is not exactly "cumulative." Culture at any given time-point has likewise the property of uniqueness. That is why it is absolutely essential to include the word "selective" in any definition.

THE LAWYER: I can see that there has been a selection of possible modes of behavior and that these selections then may become established in a group, but aren't you overemphasizing this aspect? It seems to me that in common sense terms if we understand human nature, and if we then make our interpretation in the light of the concrete situation at hand, we get along very well.

FIRST ANTHROPOLOGIST: No, if you will look beyond the records of our own time and place you will find that the matter is not so simple. There are certain recurrent and inevitable human problems, and the ways in which man can meet them are limited by his biological equipment and by certain facts of the external world. Anthropologists have perhaps in recent years been too much preoccupied with the diversity found upon the earth and have neglected the basic similarities. But apart from these important but very general resemblances, the conception of one single, unchanging "human nature" is a reassuring fiction of folklore. When it comes to details, there are "human natures." For example, old age is a situation to which all human beings who live long enough must adjust. But we find that in some human societies the old, regardless of their particular achievements, are entitled to respect and even to authority. In other societies, we find that the old, again regardless of individual differences,

are ordinarily treated with relative indifference or active contempt. In still other societies, whether or not an aged person is treated with deference or with neglect seems to depend on his own past history rather than upon his period of life. Thus we see that though age is a biological fact it is always culturally defined. This fact of the plasticity of "human nature" is the widest and the most certain induction which anthropologists can derive from the cross-cultural record.

The precise *forms* which biological and social processes take are myriad, and these *forms* are cultural. Let us take an instance where, as so often, biological and social facts are intertwined. In many human groups which have been described, the physically weak have been, almost without qualification, at a disadvantage. In some groups, however, it has been observed that there have been effective deterrents against the strong taking advantage of the weak. Bullying has been punished by social disapproval and hence has actually been relatively rare. In a few societies, there is a tendency to give privileged positions to the physically weak or to certain types of the physically weak.

Just as sociobiological situations or purely social situations can be stylized, so also some purely biological situations may be stylized. Take vomiting, for example. Vomiting is a biological event and it can be produced by causes which are solely biological. But in other cases, although individual differences in neurological equipment and in previous experience play their part, the event sequence which would lead up to vomiting could never be predicted purely on the basis of biological knowledge. For instance, Americans who have eaten rattlesnake have been known to vomit upon being told what they had been fed. Since rattlesnake meat is perfectly nutritious, the vomiting is produced by some extrabiological factor.

Similar illustrations could be given for other biological processes, such as weeping and fainting. These biological processes are also caught in a cultural web, as it were. Here is a particularly telling example. The newborn infant excretes whenever tensions in bladder and colon reach a certain level of intensity. Before long, however, biological rhythms have surrendered to superimposed designs which are not directly derived from the facts of biology. Most adult human beings in normal health defecate only once or at most twice during a day. This tends to occur within rather fixed hours and, in many human groups, only at certain designated places and under defined conditions as to who else may (should) or may (should) not be present. So interesting and so vital is the interrelation of the biological and the cultural dimensions of human behavior that some anthropologists feel the study of these connections to be the differential feature of anthropology.

THE PSYCHOLOGIST: Isn't this just a kind of "conditioning"?

THE BIOLOGIST: Yes, couldn't we call it simply "environmental conditioning"?

FIRST ANTHROPOLOGIST: A very special sort of conditioning. No group deliberately sets out to train its children to vomit under certain circumstances. This result, rather, is a kind of incidental by-product of a style of life or of some aspect of such a style of life.

THIRD ANTHROPOLOGIST: The naïve—and very powerful—view is that we have individual organisms (they can be seen) and that they exist in an external world (which can also be seen and described). This is the view which "common-sense" takes, and it is very hard to shake oneself out of this apparently sensible formula. But it simply won't cover the facts, the awareness of the external environment is too highly selective for that. Put down various groups of adults who have been trained in different social traditions in the same desert island. What they see in their surroundings will not be identical at all. Nor will, of course, the techniques by which they endeavor to adjust themselves to the surroundings. Between culturalized men and their environment there exists, as it were, a screen which is intangible and invisible but none the less real. This screen is "culture."

THE PSYCHOLOGIST: In trying to understand a single concrete act on the part of an individual I have found it helpful to ask these questions:

1. What are the innate endowments and limitations of the individual?

2. What has his total experience been prior to the act we are studying?

3. What is his immediate situation?

FIRST ANTHROPOLOGIST: No one of these variables can be elucidated in a completely satisfactory manner without introducing the concept "culture."

1. Except in the case of newborn babies and of individuals born with clear-cut structural or func-tional abnormalities we can observe "innate endowments" only as modified by cultural training. In a hospital in New Mexico where Zuni Indian, Navaho Indian, and white American babies are born it is possible to classify the newly arrived infants as hyperactive, average, and hypoactive. Some babies from each "racial" group will fall into each category, though a higher proportion of the white babies will fall into the hyperactive class. But if a Navaho baby, a Zuni baby, and a white baby— all classified as about equally hyperactive at birth— are again observed at the age of two years, the Zuni baby—*as compared with the white child*—will no longer seem given to quick and restless activity, though he may seem so as compared with other Zunis of the same age. The Navaho child is likely to fall in between as contrasted with the Zuni and the white though he will probably still seem hyperactive if seen against the standard of a series of Navaho youngsters.

2. The sheer factual description of the individual's experience doesn't get us very far. His interpretation of these events is indispensable, and this will be made, at least in part, in terms of norms current in his group. Losing a mother tends to mean one thing in one society, quite a different thing in another society.

3. Naturally, the immediate situation as well as past experience is reacted to, not in purely rational or objective fashion but in terms of the situation as meaningfully defined by the participant. Almost no human situations are viewed in ways which are altogether a consequence of the individual's experience. Culture is—among other things—a set of ready-made definitions of the situation which each participant only slightly retailors in his own idiomatic way.

THE BIOLOGIST: May we get back to some examples?

THIRD ANTHROPOLOGIST: If we are to begin at the beginning we start off, I suppose, with the basic observation of the diversity of human behavior.

A few years ago a young man of American parentage but who had been reared in a Chinese family from infancy on, paid his first visit to America. Reporters commented not only upon his apparently complete bewilderment in the American way of lift, but also upon the fact that his walk, arm and hand movements, and facial expression were "Chinese—not American." They insisted that one had to fix one's attention upon his blond hair and blue eyes to convince oneself that he was of white stock at all. Here the point is that an individual's acts and attitudes not only failed to resemble those of his own close relatives in this country but that they resembled those of all members of an alien physical group and contrasted with those of all members of his own physical group.

To take a less dramatic but better-known illustration, a third generation Italian, unless he has been reared in the Italian colony of a large American city, shows "social habits" which resemble those of "Old Americans" much more closely than they do those of residents of Italy. The influence of the various domestic and geographical environments in which these Italian-Americans grew up was not so powerful but that we can recognize common tendencies in all of them which ally them to other "Americans."

The variations and similarities which obtain between groups of human beings must also both be clarified. Groups of the same strain of physical heredity show great differences in behavioral norms and groups of unquestionably different strains show great similarities. It has been remarked by many observers in the Japanese relocation centers that Japanese who have been born and brought up in this country, especially those who were reared apart from any large colony of Japanese, resemble their white neighbors in all behavioral characteristics much more closely than they do their own Japanese relatives who had been educated in Japan and then immigrated to this country.

THE PSYCHOLOGIST: This proves that human beings can learn from each other—and we knew that already. What proof is there that if all white Americans were wiped out the Japanese-American wouldn't eventually revert to designs for living highly similar to those characteristics of the Japanese of Japan?

THIRD ANTHROPOLOGIST: Obviously, there can be no certain answer to such a hypothetical question. But note carefully that the concept of culture as I have phrased it in no way denies the possible importance of innate factors. It does not assert the patent absurdity that the behavior of all Japanese (of Japan) or the behavior of all white Americans is minutely identical. It says merely that the behavior of each group though showing much individual variation still shows certain common tendencies within the one group which contrast sharply with those within the other group. Since the common tendencies of the American group are also to a perceptible degree exhibited by large numbers of individuals of Japanese racial stock—although it is not claimed that their behavior shows precisely the same modalities as the white Americans—it is argued that these shared trends may be attributed to the presence and influence of communicable designs for living.

THE ECONOMIST: Perhaps if Japan were depopulated and colonized by white Americans these would, within a certain number of generations, develop social definitions of the situation which would hardly be distinguishable from those characteristic of the Japanese today.

THIRD ANTHROPOLOGIST: The natural environments of the United States are very various, and yet the Americans of the arid Southwest and of rainy Oregon still behave in ways which are easily distinguishable from inhabitants of the Australian desert on the one hand and from those of verdant England on the other.

Tribes like the Pueblo and Navaho, living in substantially identical natural and biological environments, still manifest very different ways of life. The English who live in the Hudson Bay region and those who live in British Somaliland still share common designs for living. It is true, of course, that the different natural environments are responsible for observable alterations. But the striking fact is that, in spite of the tremendous environmental differences, shared designs for living still persist.

The inhabitants of two not widely separated villages in New Mexico, Ramah and Fence Lake, are both of the so-called "Old American" physical stock. Almost certainly a physical anthropologist would say they represented random samples from the same physical population. The rocky tablelands, the annual rainfall and its distribution, the flora and fauna surrounding the two villages hardly show perceptible variations. The density of population and the distance from a main highway is almost exactly the same in the two cases. Nevertheless, even the casual visitor immediately notices distinctions. There are characteristic differences in dress; the style of the houses is different; there is a saloon in one town and not in the other. A completion of this catalog would conclusively demonstrate that very different patterns of life prevail in the two settlements. Why? Primarily because the two villages represent variants of the general Anglo-American social traditions. They have slightly different cultures.

THE PHILOSOPHER: There are two questions upon which I must pin you down. The first is: where is the locus of culture—in society or in the individual?

THIRD ANTHROPOLOGIST: Asking the question that way poses a false dilemma. Remember that "culture" is an abstraction. Hence culture as a concrete, observable entity does not exist anywhere—unless you wish to say that it exists in the "minds" of the men who make the abstractions. The objects and events from which we make our abstractions do have an observable existence. But culture is like a map. Just as a map isn't the territory but an abstract representation of the territory so also a culture is an abstract description of trends toward uniformity in the words, acts, and artifacts of human groups. The data, then, from which we come to know culture are not derived from an abstraction such as "society" but from direct observable behavior and behavioral products. Note, however, that "culture" may be said to be "supraindividual" in at least two nonmystical, perfectly empirical senses:

1. Objects as well as individuals manifest culture.
2. The continuity of culture never depends upon the continued existence of any particular individuals.

THE PHILOSOPHER: Very good. Now my second question: Can "culture" ever be said to be the cause of anything?

THIRD ANTHROPOLOGIST: Not in any very strict or exact way of speaking. In the first place, I would always question the advisability of using the term "cause" in any social science theory. Too much of a unidirectional force is implied. Rather I should use "determinant" with its connotation of interdependence of the relevant forces. But even to say "culture determines" is a very inaxact and elliptical way of speaking, justified perhaps in certain circumstances by the convenience of brevity. Inexact, however, it is, because no concrete phenomenon is ever completely and solely determined by culture. Sometimes, to be sure, culture may be the "strategic factor"—that is, the crucial element that determines that a given act tends to be differently carried out in one group than in another or that the fact is somehow not what we would anticipate from a knowledge of the physical and biological

forces operative. But "cultural determinism" in any simple or literal sense is as objectionable as any other class of unilateral determinism such as "geographical determinism" or "economic determinism."

Although, in the concrete, the influence of culture is always mediated by men or artifacts, one is nevertheless justified in speaking of culture as *a* determinant of events when a discussion is being carried on at a high level of abstraction—provided the degree of abstraction is not lost sight of. The point may become clearer from an analogy—though all analogies (including this one!) are dangerous. Suppose a man who has a plague which is thought to be due to a postulated but unseen virus enters a city and infects the population. What "causes" the epidemic—the man or the virus? Clearly, either answer is equally correct depending upon the conceptual system within which one is working. We should be too close to reifying an abstraction if we said that, in similar fashion, either men or things can become "hosts" to culture. Also, this metaphor, like the definition of culture as "social heredity" implies too passive a relationship between men and culture—as if culture were a bacteria acquired entirely casually and unknowingly by contact. And yet the simile remains tantalizing. One may even point out that it is less misleading than "social heredity," for genes are acquired in fixed and immutable form—once and for all—at birth, whereas bacteria change with the host and in time, though a given species remains recognizable in spite of this variation according to different hosts.

THE PHILOSOPHER: Could you relate what you have just said to the arguments over the proposition of Spengler, Sorokin, and others that cultures have their own independent laws of growth and decay?

THIRD ANTHROPOLOGIST: If what I have said is correct, anthropologists have probably been too hasty in their rejections of these theories. The theories you mention have, to greater or lesser degree, been phrased unfortunately so that condemnations of them as "mystical" or "metaphysical" can be given superficial plausibility. But an anthropologist who really wishes to understand these interpretations can "translate" them into his own conceptual scheme so that, if the levels of abstraction be kept straight, they seem to merit partial acceptance or at least careful reëxamination.

For, while no culture is "superorganic" in the

sense that it would continue to "exist" after all the human beings who shared it had died and all the nonhuman manifestations of that culture had been destroyed, still a culture that is a going concern has properties which exhibit some independence from the other forces with which the culture is in interaction. One of the diagnostic features of a culture is its selectivity. Most specific needs can be satisfied in a wide variety of ways but "the culture selects" only one or a very few of the organically and physically possible modes. "The culture selects" is, to be sure, a metaphorical way of speaking. The *original* choice was necessarily made by an individual and then followed by other individuals (or it wouldn't have become culture). But from the angle of those individuals who later learn this bit of culture the existence of this element in a design for living has the *effect* of a selection which was not made by these human beings as a reaction to their own particular situation but was rather a choice made by individuals long gone but which still tends to bind our contemporary actors.

Such a selective awareness of the natural environment, such a stereotyped interpretation of man's place in the world is not merely inclusive; by implication it also excludes other possible alternatives. Because of the "strain toward consistency" in cultures such inclusions and exclusions are meaningful far beyond the specific activity which is overtly involved. Just as the "choice" of an individual at a crucial epoch commits him in certain directions for the rest of his life, so the original bents, trends, "interests" which become established in the designs for living of a newly formed society tend to channel a culture in some directions as opposed to others. Subsequent variations in the culture—both those which arise internally and those which are a response to contact with other cultures or to changes in the natural environment—are not random. In some sense, at least, there is probably "cultural orthogenesis" as well as biological orthogenesis.

THE LAWYER: Now I only wonder how you are going to make the transition from "culture" to "a culture." No physicist speaks of "a gravity."

FIRST ANTHROPOLOGIST: Surely when the physicist "explains" the falling of certain concrete bodies at a given time and place he must—if he is to be precise as to details—get beyond the general principle of "gravity." He must describe the particular field of gravity which affected those bodies at just that time. Similarly "a culture" is just a convenient short expression for "a special field of that force known as culture."

"CULTURE" AS A DESCRIPTIVE CONCEPT

THE PHYSICIAN: Can we say that culture in general as a descriptive concept means the accumulated treasury of human creation: books, paintings, buildings, and the like; the knowledge of ways of adjusting to our surroundings, both human and physical; language, customs, and systems of etiquette, ethics, religion, and morals that have been built up through the ages?

FIRST ANTHROPOLOGIST: In referring to culture as "a storehouse of adjustive responses" and as a human creation you strike notes upon which we would all now agree. But the objections to an enumerative definition and to a definition which lists, in part, concrete phenomena are serious.

SECOND ANTHROPOLOGIST: Yes, I also now fully share the view that, even at a descriptive level, culture must be considered as an abstraction. Even a "culture trait" is, in a sense, an "ideal type." Take, for instance, the alarm clock. No two are ever exactly alike: some are large, some are small; some work perfectly and others don't; some are shiny and some are painted in soft colors. If we examine minutely enough several which have just been produced by the same factory, we should find that even these show small differences.

THE BUSINESSMAN: Let me take this idea a little further. A bank is a general term applying to all the specific institutions that conduct certain types of financial transactions. Doesn't culture, then, as a descriptive concept mean the sum of all such generalizations?

FIRST ANTHROPOLOGIST: I would prefer to say "a summation of all the ideas for standardized types of behavior."

THIRD ANTHROPOLOGIST: The notion of defining culture, in a descriptive sense, as a set of blueprints for action in the widest sense (including feeling, of course) is very attractive. And it is probably perfectly sound, provided that it is clearly realized that such a statement is made from the standpoint of the observer, the student of culture, rather than from that of the participant in culture. For the participant much of culture is unverbalized and probably in a still wider sense implicit.

THE PSYCHIATRIST: I agree. I have always protested against such statements as "culture consists of ideas" because we know well from comparative psychiatry that there is also such a thing as "culturally standardized unreason."

FIRST ANTHROPOLOGIST: Yes, while a great deal of culture is cognitive and is cognitively transmitted, the place of feeling bulks enormously.

THE ECONOMIST: Perhaps we need three categories: rational, irrational, and nonrational.

THIRD ANTHROPOLOGIST: Quite. In Pareto's jargon, some of culture is "logical," some is "illogical," but probably the highest proportion is "nonlogical."

FOURTH ANTHROPOLOGIST: May we then give the following substantive definition: *By culture we mean all those historically created designs for living, explicit and implicit, rational, irrational, and nonrational, which exist at any given time as potential guides for the behavior of men.*

THE LAWYER: I have only one question: Why is it necessary to say "at any given time"?

FOURTH ANTHROPOLOGIST: Because culture is constantly being created and lost. No definition must suggest that culture is static or completely stable.

SECOND ANTHROPOLOGIST: Does "designs for living" mean that you intend the concept to include only "theory"—that is, the ways in which things ought to be done or felt?

FOURTH ANTHROPOLOGIST: No, "design" denotes both "theory" and "practice." In our own professional jargon "design" is meant to designate both "behavioral patterns" and "ideal patterns." Remember that culture is always a conceptual construct. The anthropologist not only observes that people say (or otherwise indicate) that they have certain standards for behavior, violations of which are punished by great or small sanctions; he equally notes that even disapproved behavior systems tend to fall into certain modalities. From the observer's standpoint it is as if people were unconsciously adhering to certain "blueprints" or "designs" also for conduct which is prohibited or indifferent from the standpoint of shared "moral" norms.

THE LAWYER: May we have a definition of "a culture," in the descriptive sense?

FIRST ANTHROPOLOGIST: *A culture is a historically derived system of explicit and implicit designs for living, which tends to be shared by all or specially designated members of a group.*

THIRD ANTHROPOLOGIST: That satisfies me. The word "system" does a lot of work in that definition. It suggests abstraction. It directly implies that a culture is organized, that it is selective.

THE PSYCHOLOGIST: I like the word "tends." Some of us have in the past felt cheated because we have been assured that studying a culture would give us the common ground against which various personality figures emerged. Our own investigations along this line seem to indicate that it was misleading to depict any single background as being in any literal sense "common" to all members of any group.

FIRST ANTHROPOLOGIST: Yes, just as "tends" reminds us that no individual thinks, feels, or acts precisely as the "design" indicates that he will or should, so also "specially designated" is a reminder that not all of the "blueprints" which constitute a culture are meant to apply to each and every individual. There are sex differentials, age differentials, class differentials, prestige differentials, and so on.

THIRD ANTHROPOLOGIST: It seems to me that you have enunciated two related but separate propositions. It is important that we should not mix them. First, there is the proposition that the sharing is tendency rather than fact. As L. K. Frank puts it, what we can actually observe is the "idiomatic version of each personality's utilization of cultural patterns." And he goes on to make a useful analogy something along these lines:

> We can abstract the regularities and uniformities and likewise observe the personality distortions and skewings, as we have learned to observe the statistical regularities of a gas but also recognize and acknowledge the irregular and non-conforming behavior of individual molecules of that gas.

Second, there is the proposition of the compartmentalization and segmentation of a culture. While each individual's utilization of pattern is idiomatic, some sets of patterns are always felt as appropriate for certain categories of individuals. A background of culture is to be regarded as approximately constant—not for every individual in all groups which have some continuity and functional wholeness, but rather for those who occupy the same set of statuses or perform about the same roles within the total group.

FIRST ANTHROPOLOGIST: Correct. But this important fact must not obscure another fact of equal or greater significance. At least in those groups which have some historical continuity and which are generally designated as "societies," all individuals tend to share common interpretations of the external world and man's place in it. To some degree every individual is affected by this common "view of life." A culture is made up of overt patterned ways of behaving, feeling, and reacting. But it also includes a characteristic set of unstated premises or hypotheses which vary greatly in different societies. Thus one group unconsciously assumes that every chain of actions has a goal and that when this goal is reached tension will be reduced or disappear. To another group, thinking based upon this assumption is meaningless: they see life not as a series of purposive sequences but as made up of experiences which are satisfying in and of themselves, rather than as means to ends.

THE PHILOSOPHER: Are you saying that each culture is integrated about certain dominant interests and in accord with certain postulates and assumptions?

THIRD ANTHROPOLOGIST: Probably very few cultures indeed can be regarded as completely integrated systems. Most cultures, like most personalities, can be regarded as equilibria of opposed tendencies. But even in cultures which do not approach complete integration one may detect certain recurrent themes in a variety of specific contexts.

THE PSYCHOLOGIST: Are you talking about what some anthropologists have called the "absolute logics," of a people or about what others refer to as "the logic of the sentiments."

THIRD ANTHROPOLOGIST: Both. Every people not only has a sentiment structure which is to some degree unique but also a more or less coherent body of distinctive presuppositions about the world. This last is really a borderland between reason and feeling. Perhaps in a certain ultimate sense the "logic" of all peoples is the same. But their premises are certainly different.

THE PHILOSOPHER: Do you mean the conscious, the stated premises—what a logician would call the "postulates"—or the unstated premises or "assumptions"?

THIRD ANTHROPOLOGIST: Both. Certainly some of the most critical premises of any culture are often unstated, even by the intellectuals of the group.

Likewise the basic categories of "thinking" are implicit, save, perhaps, to a tiny minority in rationally sophisticated societies like our own.

FOURTH ANTHROPOLOGIST: If the premises and the system of categories are unconscious, how are they transmitted?

FIRST ANTHROPOLOGIST: Mainly, probably, through the language. Especially the morphology of a language preserves the unformulated philosophy of the group. For example, Dorothy Lee has shown that among the Trobriand Islanders "the sequence of events does not automatically fall into the mold of causal or telic relationship." Because of the mold which grammar imposes upon their "thinking" these people find certain types of communication with Europeans difficult since Europeans almost inevitably talk in causal terms."

The very morphology of any language inevitably begs far-reaching questions of metaphysics and of values. A language is not merely an instrument for communication and for rousing the emotions. Every language is also a device for categorizing experience. The continuum of experience can be sliced very differently. We tend all too easily to assume that the distinctions which Indo-European languages (or our own particular language) force us to make are given by the world of nature. As a matter of fact, comparative linguistics shows very plainly that any speech demands unconscious conceptual selection on the part of its speaker. No human organism can respond to all the kaleidoscopic stimuli which impinge upon it from the external world. What we notice, what we talk about, what we feel as important is in some part a function of our linguistic patterns. Because these linguistic habits tend to remain as unquestioned "background phenomena," each people tends to take its fundamental categories, its unstated basic premises for granted. It is assumed that others will "think the same way," for "it's only human nature." When others face the same body of data but come to different conclusions, it is seldom thought that they might be proceeding from different premises. Rather, it is inferred that they are "stupid" or "illogical" or "obstinate."

FOURTH ANTHROPOLOGIST: How does it happen that different people have different systems of categories?

FIRST ANTHROPOLOGIST: A language is one aspect of a culture. Therefore, we must refer to the "accidents of history" and to all the other forces which we mentioned as producing the forms of culture. Each individual tends to classify his experiences along the lines laid down by the grammar to which he is habituated, but the grammar itself is a cultural product. Dorothy Lee has made this point very well:

> True enough, the thought of the individual must run along its grooves; but these grooves, themselves, are a heritage from individuals who laid them down in an unconscious effort to express their attitudes toward the world. Grammar contains in crystalized form the accumulated and accumulating experience, the Weltanschauung of a people.

THIRD ANTHROPOLOGIST: There is perhaps also another angle to the perpetuation of cultural organization, particularly at the implicit level. This is the culturally prescribed system of child training. If all adults have been subjected to about the same deprivations and frustrations during socialization, they tend to see life in somewhat the same terms. Roheim says, "The dominant idea of a culture may be an addiction but it is always a system formation that can be explained on the basis of the infantile situation." Margaret Mead deals with the relation of "infantile traumas" to the one or more focal points in each culture under the conception of "plot in culture."

FOURTH ANTHROPOLOGIST: Although partially won over, I am still unhappy about this term "implicit culture."

THIRD ANTHROPOLOGIST: A conception of this order is made necessary by certain eminently practical considerations. It is well documented that programs of the British Colonial services or of our own Indian service which have been carefully thought through for their continuity with the cultural inventory and with the overt cultural patterns, nevertheless fail to work out. Intensive investigation also does not reveal any flaws in the set-up at the technological level. The program is sabotaged by resistance which must be imputed to the manner in which the members of the group have been conditioned by *implicit* designs for living to think and feel in ways which were unexpected to the administrator.

FIRST ANTHROPOLOGIST: Students of culture change are also agreed that the way in which a group accepts, rejects, or readapts borrowed elements cannot be fully understood in terms of direct and ex-

plicit functions. The process is also related to the cultural structure, including those portions of it which are implicit. Even after the content of the culture of a group of American Indians has become completely European, its way of life still somehow retains a distinctive flavor, as if the "container" remained "aboriginal."

THIRD ANTHROPOLOGIST: We would freely admit that conceptual instruments which are objective enough and precise enough to deal with the patterning of implicit culture are only beginning to be evolved. The importance of tacit cultural premises and categories is probably obvious enough. But the sheer statement of the presence and absence of these (and of all other features of culture, whether implicit or explicit) is not enough. The full significance of any single element in a cultural design will be seen only when that element is viewed in the total matrix of its relationship to other elements and indeed to other designs. Naturally, this includes accent or emphasis, as well as position. Accent is manifested sometimes through frequency, sometimes through intensity. The indispensable importance of these questions of arrangement and emphasis may be driven home by an analogy. Take a musical chord made up of three notes. If we are told that the three notes in question are A, B, and G, we receive information which is fundamental. But it alone will not enable us to predict the type of sensation which the playing of this chord is likely to evoke in us or in other specified visitors. We need many different sorts of relationship data. Are the notes to be played in that or some other order? What duration will each receive? How will the emphasis, if any, be distributed? We also need, of course, to know whether the cord will be played in the key of C or in the key of B-flat minor, and whether the instrument is to be a piano or an accordion.[1]

THE UTILITY OF THE CONCEPT "CULTURE" IN ITS VARIOUS SENSES

THE BUSINESSMAN: I'd like to interject a practical question: What good is this concept so far as the contemporary world is concerned? What can you do with it?

---

[1] Limitations of space necessitated shortening the final typescript draft of this paper by one third. In addition to the elimination of certain technical refinements, the authors were obliged to omit two topics which they consider essential to a complete treatment of the subject: The distinction between the "social" and the "cultural" and the place of symbols in a consideration of culture theory.

FIRST ANTHROPOLOGIST: First and foremost I would insist that its use lies in the aid the concept gives to man's endless quest to understand himself and his own behavior. For example, this relatively new idea makes some of the questions which trouble one of the most learned and acute thinkers of our age, Reinhold Niebuhr, seem pseudo-problems. In his recent book *The Nature and Destiny of Man* he argues that the universally human sense of guilt or shame and man's capacity for self-judgment necessitates the assumption of supernatural forces. But these facts are susceptible of self-consistent and relatively simple "explanation" in purely naturalistic terms through the concept of culture. Social life among humans never occurs without a system of "conventional understandings" which are transmitted more or less intact from generation to generation. Any individual is familiar with some of these and they constitute a set of standards against which he judges himself. To the extent that he fails to conform he experiences discomfort, because the intimate conditioning of infancy and childhood put great pressure on him to internalize these norms, and his unconscious tendency is to associate withdrawal of love and protection or active punishment with deviation.

This and other issues which have puzzled philosophers and scientists for countless generations become fully or partially understandable by means of this fresh conceptual instrument. But if your interest is in action rather than thought, the principal claim which can be made for culture is that it helps us enormously toward predicting human behavior. One of the reasons that such prediction has not been very successful thus far has been that it has been carried out, for the most part, on the naïve assumption of a minutely homogenous "human nature." In the framework of this assumption all human thinking proceeds from the same premises; all human beings are motivated by the same needs and goals. But in the cultural framework we see that, while the ultimate logic of all peoples may be the same (and thus communication and understanding are possible), the thought processes depart from radically different premises—especially unconscious or unstated premises. But those who have the cultural outlook are more likely to look beneath the surface and bring the culturally determined premises to the light of day. This may well not bring about immediate agreement and harmony, but it will at least facilitate a more ra-

tional approach to the problem of "international understanding." and to diminish friction between groups within a nation.

The conception of culture also encourages paying attention to the more concrete aspects of ways of life other than our own. It suggests, for example, the usefulness of knowledge of alien "customs" if we wish to predict how a foreign people will behave in a certain situation and of respect for these same customs if we wish to get along with that foreign people.

A culture is not only a reticulum of patterned means for satisfying needs but equally a network of stylized goals for individual and group achievement. If we need to predict human action we must not assume that the effective motivations in all human groups are the same. Even the primary drives, like hunger and sex, though biological "givens," are subtly modified and channeled by culture. What kind of food, what type of sexual experience will be most striven after cannot be predicted through biological knowledge alone. There exists for every human group "secondary drives." Among us, for example, the "need" for cars or radios often goads individuals even harder than that for sexual satisfaction.

Every culture is also a structure of expectancies. If we know a culture, we know what various classes of individuals within it expect from each other— and from outsiders of various categories. We know what types of activity are held to be inherently gratifying.

SECOND ANTHROPOLOGIST: One great contribution is that of providing some persons with some detachment from the conscious and unconscious emotional values of their own culture. The phrase "some detachment" must be emphasized. An individual who viewed the designs for living of his group with complete detachment would almost certainly be disoriented and unhappy. But I can prefer (that is, feel affectively attached to) American manners while at the same time perceiving certain graces in English manners which are lacking or more grossly expressed in ours. Thus while unwilling to forget that I am an American and hence with no desire to ape English drawing room behaviors, I can still derive a lively pleasure from association with English people on "social" occasions. Whereas if I have no detachment, if I am utterly provincial, I am likely to regard English manners as utterly ridiculous, uncouth, perhaps even immoral. With that attitude I shall certainly not get on well with the English and I am likely to resent bitterly any modification of our manners in the English or any other direction. Such attitudes clearly do not make for international understanding, friendship, and coöperation. They equally make for a too rigid social structure. Anthropological documents and anthropological teachings are valuable, therefore, in that they tend to emancipate individuals from a too perfervid allegiance to every item in the cultural inventory. The person who has been exposed to the anthropological perspective by incongruity is more likely, on the one hand, to "live and let live" both within his own society and in his dealings with members of other societies; on the other hand, he will probably be more flexible in regard to needful changes in social organization to meet changed technological structure and changed economies.

THIRD ANTHROPOLOGIST: In a way, I would say that the most important implication of "culture" for action is the profound truth (so frequently overlooked by every sort of "social planners") that you can never start with a clean slate so far as human beings are concerned. No human being or group of human beings can ever freshly see the world in which they move. Every human is born into a world defined by already existing cultural patterns. Just as an individual who has lost his memory is no longer "normal," so the idea that at any point in its history a society can become completely emancipated from its past culture is inconceivable. This is the source of the tragic failure of the Weimar constitution in Germany. Seen in detached context, it was an admirable document. But it failed miserably in actual life, partly because it provided for no continuity with existent designs for acting, feeling, and thinking.

Finally, as the word "design" in our definitions implies, every culture has organization as well as content. This fact carries with it the highly practical warning to administrators and lawmakers that a "custom" which it is desired to abolish or modify cannot be isolated. Any change may have repercussions in areas of behavior where they are least expected.

While serious anthropologists disavow all messianic pretensions and make no claim that "culture" is any "philosopher's stone" which will end all problems, nevertheless the explanatory concept

does carry an overtone of legitimate hope to troubled men. If the Germans and the Japanese are as they have been mainly because of their genes, the outlook is an almost hopeless one, but if their propensities for cruelty and aggrandizement are primarily the result of situational factors ("economic" pressures and so on) and their cultures, then something can be done about it.

BIBLIOGRAPHIC NOTE

We have thought it inappropriate to burden this paper with detailed documentation. But the principal sources which have directly influenced our thinking follow.

Bidney, David, "On the Philosophy of Culture in the Social Sciences," *Journal of Philosophy*, XXXIX (1942), 449–57; "On the Concept of Culture and Some Cultural Fallacies," *American Anthropologist*, XLVI (1944), 30–45.

Blumenthal, Albert, "A New Definition of Culture," *American Anthropologist*, XLII (1940), 571–86.

Dollard, John, "Culture, Society, Impulse and Socialization," *American Journal of Sociology*, XLV (1939), 50–63.

Ford, C. S., "Culture and Human Behavior," *Scientific Monthly*, LV (1942), 546–57.

Frank, L. K., "Man's Multidimensional Environment," *Scientific Monthly*, LVI (1943), 344–57.

Lee, Dorothy, "Conceptual Implications of an Indian Language," *Philosophy of Science*, V, No. 1 (Jan., 1938); "A Primitive System of Values," *Philosophy of Science*, VII, No. 3 (July, 1940).

Linton, Ralph, *The Study of Man* (New York, 1936); "Culture, Society and the Individual," *Journal of Abnormal and Social Psychology*, XXXV (1938), 425–36; *Acculturation in Seven American Indian Tribes* (New York, 1940).

Malinowski, B., "Culture," *Encyclopedia of the Social Sciences*, IV (1931), 621–45; "Man's Culture and Man's Behavior," *Sigma Xi Quarterly*, XXIX (1941), 182–96; XXX (1942), 66–78.

Miller, Neal E., and John Dollard, *Social Learning and Imitation* (New Haven, Conn., 1941).

Murdock, G. P., "The Science of Culture," *American Anthropologist*, XXXIV (1932), 200–215.

Redfield, Robert, *The Folk Culture of Yucatan* (Chicago, 1941).

Roheim, Geza, *The Origin and Function of Culture* (Nervous and Mental Disease Monograph Series, No. 69, New York, 1943).

Sapir, Edward, "Culture, Genuine and Spurious," *American Journal of Sociology*, XXIX (1924), 401–29.

Simmons, Leo, *Sun Chief* (New Haven, Conn., 1942).

ANTHROPOLOGY AND ITS USE OF "CULTURE"

With this excerpt from Keesing, we turn to a briefer and more pointed discussion of anthropological uses of the word and concept "culture." With the particular concrete examples he uses, Keesing introduces the idea that the concept is *expandable* and *contractable*. Any given item of behavior, large or small, is potentially (at least) analyzable as having a cultural dimension; the concept should therefore be considered and used in dynamic, flexible fashion, and not be taken as a rigidly-bounded, boxed-in kind of idea applicable only to the behavior of entire "societies," or only "groups" of any stipulated size. There can be—and *is*—for example, a "cultural" dimension in the patterned behavior of families. This can be seen in the area of food habits, for one thing. Although most families might well conform to type for what "most" American families consider fit for human consumption (not including, for instance, rattlesnake meat or witchetty grubs in the normal diet), still, there are variations in content, styles of cooking, variety and rigidity in patterning, and so forth. Such variations, insofar as they constitute repeated patterns having value overtones within each family group, can be considered as a "cultural" dimension to social behavior at that level of organization. How many quarrels have started, for example, by a newly-married husband offering the comment that his *mother* didn't used to cook eggs like that?

Keesing ends on a note that we will take up in more detail with the next set of excerpts: a cultural dimension to human life adds a *symbolic* dimension, a realm of meaning ascribed to objective realities, which is different from that for other animal species. Man's world, the milieu in which he ". . . lives, moves, and has his being," is greatly (but not, of course, exclusively) a world in which a plane of meaning overlies and interpenetrates that of fact. Conceived in this way, "culture" might be considered (as suggested in the introduction) as the assignment of value to fact.

ANTHROPOLOGICAL USE OF THE TERM "CULTURE"

FELIX M. KEESING

What is the meaning of this central concept with which anthropologists approach behavior and custom?

Nineteenth-century anthropologists, casting around for a term to cover all of human custom, fixed upon the term "culture." From anthropology the concept has spread to other social sciences so that such collateral students of human behavior as the psychologist and sociologist use it today in this sense.

Some confusion arises between this technical use of the term "culture" and a more popular usage. We may be accustomed to saying: "He is a cultured person," or "She has culture." We mean that the individual is accomplished in the arts or social graces. Culture is often used, too, in this sense by writers in the humanities. The scientific use, once

From *Cultural Anthropology: The Science of Custom* by Felix M. Keesing, © 1958 by Felix M. Keesing. Adapted and reprinted by permission of Holt, Rinehart and Winston, Inc.

mastered, approaches more fully the original meaning of the word, which is derived from the Latin verb *colere* ("to cultivate or instruct") and the noun *cultus* ("cultivation or training"). Culture in its broadest sense is cultivated behavior, that is, the totality of man's learned, accumulated experience which is socially transmitted, or more briefly, behavior acquired through social learning.

This seems simple and matter of fact enough. Actually there are numerous problems connected with the scientific use or "operation" of this term, as with so many other scientific concepts. The major ones will appear as the story of cultural study is unfolded. Some hints of them may be gained by sampling some of the definitions of culture given by various theorists:

> That complex whole which includes knowledge, belief, art, morals, law, custom, and any other capabilities and habits acquired by man as a member of society.—Tylor (1871)
>
> The sum total of the knowledge, attitudes and habitual behavior patterns shared and transmitted by the members of a particular society.—Linton (1940)
>
> [All the] historically created designs for living, explicit and implicit, rational, irrational, and non-rational, which exist at any given time as potential guides for the behavior of men.—Kluckhohn and Kelly (1945)
>
> The mass of learned and transmitted motor reactions, habits, techniques, ideas, and values—and the behavior they induce.—Kroeber (1948)
>
> The man-made part of the environment.—Herskovits (1955)

Kroeber and Kluckhohn (1952) have uncovered over one hundred and sixty different delineations of the term "culture" by anthropologists and others.

An initial difficulty in the study of culture is that for the most part we are not in the habit of analyzing deliberately the customs which shape our behavior. It is a tenet of cultural anthropology that culture tends to be unconscious. This comes out most clearly, perhaps, in the phase of learned, cultural behavior we call language. We are trained to the special set of speech and other signals, and to their meanings, which is our "native tongue," without being particularly conscious that it has a grammar, or repetitive regularities of structure. We learn grammar painfully and self-consciously in school, or in tackling a "foreign" language and forget it easily, without impairing our speech habits. It is significant that the first anthropological theorist to bring out clearly the *unconscious patterning*

of cultural behavior was Edward Sapir, a specialist in linguistics (in the late 1920's).

It is no accident that anthropologists were the first social scientists to develop clearly the concept of "culture." Dealing as they did with customs over the world which often were in startling contrast to their own, they developed habits of viewing human behavior objectively, self-consciously. The beginner in anthropology can share this advantage, in being presented with differences in custom. By getting into the habit of looking at "patterns of culture" (the title of Ruth Benedict's widely known book) among American Indians, African tribesmen, and other overseas peoples, it becomes possible to bring into consciousness our own culture. It could be said here that some students, having this experience for the first time, find it quite new and even shocking. But, like taking a cold shower, it feels fine after a while, and certainly makes for intellectual vigor.

Ahead of theoretical discussion, some "experiments" may easily be devised to give awareness of the characteristics of culture and of ways in which it can be studied. In the cases chosen here, the experiments will be reported in the form of a typical class dialogue between instructor and students.

EXAMPLE 1. A MENOMINI INDIAN GRAVE MARKER

Q. (*Questioner.*) Here is an item of culture, such as you might see in a museum or by visiting the people from whom it comes. What would you say it is?

AA. (*Answers.*) A land marker. . . . Something used in a religious ceremony. . . . The sign on a house to show the owner. . . . A totem post. . . .

Q. What led you to make such identifications? You were obviously inferring from previous knowledge.

A. Why are those marks in red paint?

A. It must be something out of the ordinary.

Q. Would you think it is, or was, something important to the people?

A. Yes. They wouldn't have gone to such trouble if it were just something to use and throw away.

Q. Have a guess as to some of those markings.

AA. First I'd like to note that the sharpened end has been in the ground. It must be a marker to tell something. . . . Isn't that an animal? It looks to me like a bear. Why is it upside down?... The man might have been dead.... Was it a grave marker?

Q. Yes. Do you think the people were agriculturalists?

A. No. I think they were mainly hunters. Perhaps that's the totem of the owner—or the person who was buried.

Q. You've been reading some anthropology, evidently. They hunted, but had minor gardening. Why should there be six crosses?

A. He may have been an important person to have so many.

Q. Good guess. Among this people, a funeral ceremony involved summoning the spirits of at least four dead people to act as attendants on a four-day journey to the spirit land. They were summoned by persons who had killed them in fighting.

A. I'd say he may have been a chief.

Q. Yes, he was. What kinds of *values* do you think people in this culture put a premium on? What made a person important?

AA. I'd say being a brave warrior.... And being a good hunter.... They had very definite beliefs about the dead.... They counted that men were related to animals....

Q. You will note that our discussion centered first on ethnographic description of the object. Then we began to dig deeper. We saw that it is part of a *pattern*, though subject to variation: the number of crosses, for example, or the type of animal totem. We then asked: What does this *do*, or, to put it more technically, what is its *function* in this culture? We also glanced at its relation to the dominant values, premises, goals, of this culture, or, as some say in technical language, the *configurations* that give the culture its *integration* or total *character*. We didn't ask some other possible questions: for example, What is its *origin* (we would have to go to myth and folklore for what the people had to say on this, and to archaeology, if it were a less perishable object, to see what could be scientifically traced); or again, What is its *distribution*, among neighboring peoples and otherwise?

EXAMPLE 2. A CEREMONIAL ARROW USED IN THE AINU "BEAR FEAST"

Q. What's this?

AA. An arrow.... A dart....

Q. You're doing a dangerous thing, reading something from our culture into an item from another culture.

A. But I can't think of anything it could be but a projectile because it has that sort of form.

Q. O.K. Look at this point. What could it kill?

AA. It couldn't kill a large animal.... Perhaps it was used for birds.... Did it have poison on it? (No, the tip is clean.)

A. That ornamentation and piece of red cloth indicate that it was not an ordinary arrow. Perhaps it was shot in a ceremony, just to wound, as in a bullfight.

Q. You're warm. Would a person take the trouble to carve an arrow unless it was something important—or, as we could say. had symbolic meaning? What would you guess about the people's livelihood or economic base?

A. I'd say they were hunters. If it was to kill or wound an animal in a ceremony it must have been very important to them—perhaps their main food. Were they Eskimos?

A. Not in my opinion. Eskimos use bone and ivory, and have hardly any wood.

A. But couldn't that be why it was important? Wood was valuable.

Q. You're off on an interesting discussion of habitat-culture relations, but actually it's a red herring.

A. The black-and-white designs on the arrow are geometric and rather conventionalized. Did they do much wood carving?

Q. If you looked up this people in the *Encyclopaedia Britannica* you'd see a picture showing that they made similar designs on their ceremonial clothing. Actually these people are in north Japan.

A. They must be the Ainu. They hunted bears.

Q. Yes. The outstanding public ritual of the Ainu is the so-called "Bear Feast." These ceremonial arrows were shot into the bear which was the centerpiece of this religious ceremony. The bear would probably have been reared for such an occasion from a cub, and an understanding of the long-drawn-out killing and feasting would take us into a world of meanings and values far different from our own.

A. Didn't they think it cruel?

Q. I'm afraid what people think is "cruel," and also what is "good" and "right," vary widely from culture to culture. The Ainu would doubtless be amazed and resentful if you were to question his ethics here. If an Ainu came to an American community he would be correspondingly shocked and repelled by some of our everyday actions: for example, the idea of men and women dancing in pairs closely embraced.

EXAMPLE 3. A CANDLESTICK AND CANDLE

Q. Here is something from our own culture.

A. A candle.

Q. Yes. You recognized its *form* immediately. What is its *function* in our culture?

A. It gives light.

Q. Well, that's its immediate *use*. What is its *meaning*, and especially its *function* in terms of the wider concerns of our life?

AA. We don't use it much for ordinary lighting now. . . . It's used on the dinner table as a decoration. . . . That's a red candle; it's one of the symbols for Christmas. If it had been yellow, I'd take it to be a Halloween or Thanksgiving candle. . . .

Q. What else?

A. It's used in church. Especially the Catholic churches burn candles. I guess to understand that, we'd have to make a study of the Christian religion and its origins.

Q. Can *function* change and *form* remain?

A. Of course. Candles once were used for lighting everywhere.

Q. Not exactly everywhere. Watch out that your statement is scientifically exact. Just where candles were used and not used would be a matter of studying the *diffusion* of this particular item of culture after its *invention*. At any given time it would have a specific *distribution* among cultures over the earth.

A. Can form change while function remains the same?

Q. We're going to have to discuss what we mean by "form." Obviously it has in it elements of regularity, of pattern, of structure, like the materials and shape of this candle and its holder. What do you think about the answer to your question?

A. Well, at any rate, candles can be made in many shapes and sizes, and the stores are always coming out with new forms.

Q. Do you see church candles changing as much as, say, those given as gifts for Christmas?

A. No. I guess religion is a pretty conservative part of any culture.

Q. You've offered there a good if broad hypothesis on cultural stability such as a student in social anthropology might develop as a problem area in research by testing its accuracy and reliability in different cultures under dynamic conditions. The circumstances under which people change, or resist change, in their cultural behavior is one of the interests of social anthropologists today.

EXAMPLE 4. AN AFTERNOON TEA

Q. So far we've been talking primarily about material objects, or, as anthropologists call them, "artifacts." Let's try briefly an analysis of an action sequence in which a group of people is engaged. Give me a brief formal description of what we call in our culture an "afternoon tea."

AA. It is held between lunch and dinner. . . . Tea is poured into cups for each person. . . . There are usually cookies, and other light food. . . . Sometimes it is very elaborate, with decorations and lots of food. Specially chosen people pour the tea. There may be important guests. . . .

Q. All right. We can all bring to mind a pretty clear picture of the main elements: people together in the afternoon, distribution of tea and food for those who want it. How would we go about digging into its significance?

AA. (*Rather prolonged silence.*)

Q. Are the people there because they are hungry?

AA. (*Laughter.*) Often they're ladies dieting. . . . The food may be largely for show. . . . Men often think tea's a sissy drink. . . . It's a kind of social occasion. . . .

Q. What about the people who are there?

AA. Some put in an appearance because it's the thing to do. . . . They are friends of the hostess. . . . They may want to show off their clothes. . . .

Q. I think I sense a kind of giggly amusement among you. That often happens when we start analyzing our own culture for the first time in an objective, scientific way. We find that our customs are snarled up in emotional tensions, and these *affects* tend to show when we start probing. But an Eskimo anthropologist, if there were one, would look at our afternoon tea ceremony or our death usages quite dispassionately. If I were to be asking you what our customs and attitudes are about death and funerals you would undoubtedly show some other, and perhaps individually varying, types of affective accompaniment. By the way, would it help in this case to ask who was *not* invited to tea?

A. In some cases it certainly would! In Washington, D.C., the people who were not invited to one of the big political or diplomatic teas would certainly take it as an indication that they were officially nobodies.

Q. How would you put this scientifically?

A. (*After some hesitation.*) I'd say that one of the functions of such an important tea was to define *social status.*

A. I was going to say that it is a kind of public display of social relations.

Q. It certainly could be that. In such a case, the Eskimo anthropologist might have a special eye out to see if any individual or individuals get special service, such as the first cup, or is otherwise the center of attention. Anything else?

A. When some of my friends get together for tea, all the news and gossip of the neighborhood go the round.

Q. Good. . . .

A. (*Interrupting.*) In my home town, the minister probably drinks more tea than anyone else; he can't exactly refuse when visiting around.

Q. What about the origins and backgrounds of tea drinking?

AA. The tea ceremony of Japan. . . . The China trade. . . . The Boston tea party. . . . The advertisements to "taste tea and see." . . .

Q. So you see, all these same essential problems of cultural analysis are there: questions of origins and history, of distribution, of the contribution the item makes to cultural integration, of form and function, of stability and change. The Eskimo anthropologist might perhaps begin his report on the afternoon tea custom something like this: "A widely prevalent ceremony, that of tea drinking in the afternoon, is one of the behavioral patterns connected particularly with social integration and status recognition. . . ."

The context of custom to which the general concept of *culture* is applied should be apparent enough from these examples. It is also clear that

in each case a particular customary tradition, that is, *a culture*, was being dealt with. Out of such materials a series of general propositions may be drawn relating to "culture," to "a culture," and to the constituent elements of cultural behavior. These can challenge our thought at this stage, and will be what much of the analysis in later chapters will be about. In the case of each proposition, reference will be made to the examples above to show what is meant.

Culture is concerned with actions, ideas, and artifacts which individuals in the tradition concerned learn, share, and value. Mainly it is delineated in the form of generalized statements about behavior. The minimal significant elements or components of custom which can be isolated within cultural behavior are called by some anthropologists *traits* of culture. The putting of an animal totem on a gravestick is a trait of Menomini culture, pouring tea into a cup is one shared by both Westerners and Asians. Isolating such units of custom is basic to all cultural analysis. Those using the term "trait" may in turn call a group of associated elements a *trait-complex*, e.g., the Ainu bear feast, an afternoon tea. Others have preferred to speak of such an organized system of group behavior as an *institution*. These terms will be discussed more fully later.

Culture can be studied as a historical phenomenon. Its elements originate through *innovation*, spread through *diffusion*, and otherwise have a specific chronological story, e.g., the association of candles with religion. More widely, questions concerning the origin, growth, and differentiation of culture throughout human history can be faced.

Culture can be studied as a regional phenomenon. Its elements have, at any one time, a given geographic or locality *distribution*, e.g., the regional spread of ceremonial tea drinking. Here, the wider viewpoint involves cultural phenomena throughout the whole world.

Culture tends to be patterned. It involves repeating similar approved behavior, so that it has a recognizable *form* or *structure*. To the extent that individuals fit their behavior over time to the approved pattern, the culture remains *stable*, e.g., the number of crosses on a gravestick appropriate to an important person. Moreover, underlying all cultures, we have already noted, is a general or universal patterning, as expressed in categories such as economic activity, religion, art, and language.

The patterning of culture will be a major theme of the text as a whole.

Elements of culture have a function. They *do* something, have *meaning*, for the people concerned, within the total context of their culture, e.g., afternoon tea and social status. To understand any element of culture both form and function must be explored. Important anthropological theory will be seen as gathering around the concept of function. . . .

A culture, looked at as a whole, tends to be integrated. It has what were called *configurations*, or more or less consistent premises, values, goals, which give it unity, e.g., the meanings of the Ainu bear feast. Study of the integrating factors of culture is a major concern of contemporary social anthropology. . . .

A culture is subject to change, and indeed always tends to be more or less on the move. Individual behaviors vary, innovations occur, even basic configurations may change, e.g., modifications in form and function of candles. . . .

The concept of "a culture" is most valid to the extent that the local way of life is a well-defined, homogeneous, and stable one. In their traditional settings the Menomini Indians and the Ainu of Japan had very distinctive "cultures" in this sense. These peoples had well-defined cultural solutions worked out over generations to meet virtually every problem which might arise, i.e., their cultures were highly *patterned*, or *structured*, in terms of regularities of behavior which were learned and transmitted from generation to generation.

The same is true to a point in our own cultural traditions, as witness candles and afternoon teas. We wear clothes, eat three main meals a day, sleep in beds, play games according to rules. Yet Western "civilization" sprawls out in many cultural variations, shaped by differences in language, nationality, religion, class, occupation, and other factors. In later discussion of "national character" the question will be raised as to how far what is thought of as the American, English, French, or any other comparable way of life has enough unity to be called "a culture." Anthropologists, it can be said here, do recognize a distinctive American culture, with numbers of basic elements of action and value which are shared by all persons trained to this tradition. But even when we talk of an American culture as a whole it is also clear that it encompasses many varying traditions, e.g., New England, the deep South, the rural Midwest, "Café Society," the Pennsylvania Dutch. American culture is also undergoing many rapid changes.

The scientific "operations," as they were called earlier, which go into measuring and otherwise defining "culture" under such diversified and dynamic conditions are necessarily more complex. Instead of "a culture" with clear-cut patterns, we are here dealing with "a culture" in the sense of a broadly common or continuing tradition but with less sharp and consistent patterning and with multiple internal variations. Some anthropologists have called any clearly distinguishable set of subpatterns within a culture a *subculture*. Others have recently been using, as a more general term to cover any significant and organized body of cultural behavior, the concept of *a cultural system*.

By a "system" is meant here a group of interrelated elements treated as a whole. System theory, it can be noted, is currently one of the most important unifying areas of thought in science, and in knowledge more generally, entering into such diversified fields as mathematics, physics, biology, the behavioral sciences, and philosophy. The system that is American culture, for example, has within it numerous more specific cultural systems which may become significant for study according to the problems under investigation, e.g., a given community, a factory, Hollywood. American culture, too, is one of a considerable number of cultural systems comprehended within the larger cultural milieu of "Western culture," or "Western civilization," and still more generally within what we shall see Redfield calling the "great traditions."

Among the most distinctive cultural systems, to use this nimble concept further, are the highly structured types of learned behavior associated with language (signal-meaning systems, especially speech), political affiliation (as with citizenship or nationality), and religion (involving focal beliefs and values). As we examine them later, we shall see that these facets or aspects of culture have their own very distinctive distributions in human societies. In small isolated groups they tend to march closely with "a culture." Yet even here they may have very different boundaries, e.g., much the same cultural tradition, say, a buffalo hunting way of life among North American Indians of the Plains, can be carried in different languages; the Ghost Dance faith, a nineteenth-century religious movement among North American Indians, could win adherents in many different Indian tribes. In more complex traditions, the cultural whole may include multiple linguistic, citizenship, and belief systems, and these in turn may be diffused more or less widely over a series of rather distinctive cultural groups. Europe, for example, in addition to having French, Italian, German, and other traditions, divides into considerably different zonings on the basis of spoken language, of nationality, and of religion. Indeed, all other cultural components, such as economic or artistic traditions, also have their own distributions in particular systems which can be isolated for study, as will be seen later.

Two groups with different cultures, coming into contact, are in a situation where one may take over cultural elements from the other—or more usually where each has elements "diffused" from the other. Where contact and diffusion occur with some continuity, the transfer process is called *acculturation*. Everywhere along the world's frontiers today, formerly isolated groups are undergoing such acculturation through contact with the modern West. Cultural reformulation of this kind, old in human history, will be seen as taking many forms. . . . Though in the United States acculturation is seen most fully at work among American Indian and other minority peoples who are adjusting to the European-oriented milieu of American life, we are well aware that the American tradition also includes some minor acculturation to such traditions, as witness the wearing of moccasins or eating Chinese or Mexican food.

Culture is a "continuum." This further proposition about culture in general recognizes the fact that cultural traditions have accumulated without any break in continuity. Cultural elements, once invented, pass by learning from individual to individual. They must be shared from one generation to another, and by living members of the group concerned. Any break in the learning chain would lead to their disappearance. Broadly considered, all of human culture from its beginnings has a continuity in trained human minds.

This concept was particularly stressed by Linton. He points out (1936) that the cultural continuum extends from "the beginning of human existence to the present." Cultures have variously crossed and recrossed, fused and divided; elements have been added here and lost there. A culture seen at any point in the continuum is the result of "all the changes and vicissitudes" of the past, and has in it the potential for continuing change.

Culture is "symbolic." It is a series of artifacts or man-made objects and of personal motivations and actions to which *meanings* are attached. By definition, a "symbol" is some form or fixed sensory sign to which some fixed meaning has been arbitrarily assigned. As the signs are signaled between persons trained to know the form and meaning they have in the cultural tradition concerned, these individuals share common understandings. A person outside that culture may see material objects or overt behaviors, as the visitor would in watching, say, a Pueblo Indian ceremony, or hear the signs in spoken language. But unless he knows their meanings they are incomprehensible. He takes great risks in guessing from his own cultural meanings, though he may occasionally infer a general answer where the significance is associated closely with the form or sign, as witness the Ainu arrow. A culture, looked at from this sign-meaning aspect, is sometimes referred to as a *symbol system*.

SYMBOL

The following several selections take up a subject that is crucial to any understanding of human life and behavior: the nature and function of symbols and of man's (apparently) unique capacity for the formulation and handling of a symbolic dimension to his experience. The first excerpt is from a book by a German philosopher, Ernst Cassirer, whose name is practically synonymous with modern discussions of the role of symbolism in human life. In this brief excerpt he sets the framework for the other selections that follow: namely, that human existence cannot be comprehended without starting from the awareness that the distinctive feature of man's world is that it is a *symbolic world*, a world of superimposed meanings that are formed and communicated by symbols. Man acts and lives ". . . in a new *dimension* of reality." It is this new dimension of reality which, as we will see, is the cornerstone of the cultural dimension, or the cultural system in organized human social life.

A CLUE TO THE NATURE OF MAN: THE SYMBOL

ERNST CASSIRER

The biologist Johannes von Uexküll has written a book in which he undertakes a critical revision of the principles of biology. Biology, according to Uexküll, is a natural science which has to be developed by the usual empirical methods—the methods of observation and experimentation. Biological thought, on the other hand, does not belong to the same type as physical or chemical thought. Uexküll is a resolute champion of vitalism; he is a defender of the principle of the autonomy of life. Life is an ultimate and self-dependent reality. It cannot be described or explained in terms of physics or chemistry. From this point of view Uexküll evolves a new general scheme of biological research. As a philosopher he is an idealist or phenomenalist. But his phenomenalism is not based upon metaphysical or epistemological considerations; it is founded rather on empirical principles. As he points out, it would be a very naïve sort of dogmatism to assume that there exists an absolute reality of things which is the same for all living beings. Reality is not a unique and homogeneous thing; it is immensely diversified, having as many different schemes and patterns as there are different organisms. Every organism is, so to speak, a monadic being. It has a world of its own because it has an experience of its own. The phenomena that we find in the life of a certain biological species are not transferable to any other species. The experiences—and therefore the realities —of two different organisms are incommensurable with one another. In the world of a fly, says Uexküll, we find only "fly things"; in the world of a sea urchin we find only "sea urchin things."

From this general presupposition Uexküll de-velops a very ingenious and original scheme of the biological world. Wishing to avoid all psychological interpretations, he follows an entirely objective or behavioristic method. The only clue to animal life, he maintains, is given us in the facts of comparative anatomy. If we know the anatomical structure of an animal species, we possess all the necessary data for reconstructing its special mode of experience. A careful study of the structure of the animal body, of the number, the quality, and the distribution of the various sense organs, and the conditions of the nervous system, gives us a perfect image of the inner and outer world of the organism. Uexküll began his investigations with a study of the lowest organisms; he extended them gradually to all the forms of organic life. In a certain sense he refuses to speak of lower or higher forms of life. Life is perfect everywhere; it is the same in the smallest as in the largest circle. Every organism, even the lowest, is not only in a vague sense adapted to (*angepasst*) but entirely fitted into (*eingepasst*) its environment. According to its anatomical structure it possesses a certain *Merknetz* and a certain *Wirknetz*—a receptor system and an effector system. Without the coöperation and equilibrium of these two systems the organism could not survive. The receptor system by which a biological species receives outward stimuli and the effector system by which it reacts to them are in all cases closely interwoven. They are links in one and the same chain which is described by Uexküll as the *functional circle (Funktionskreis)* of the animal.[1]

I cannot enter here upon a discussion of Uexküll's biological principles. I have merely referred to his concepts and terminology in order to pose a gen-

Reprinted with permission of publisher. From Ernst Cassirer, *An Essay on Man: An Introduction to a Philosophy of Human Culture*, © 1944 by Yale University Press, New Haven, pp. 23–26.

[1] See Johannes von Uexküll, *Theoretische Biologie* (2d ed. Berlin, 1938); *Umwelt und Innenwelt der Tiere* (1909; 2d ed. Berlin, 1921).

eral question. Is it possible to make use of the scheme proposed by Uexküll for a description and characterization of the *human world?* Obviously this world forms no exception to those biological rules which govern the life of all the other organisms. Yet in the human world we find a new characteristic which appears to be the distinctive mark of human life. The functional circle of man is not only quantitively enlarged; it has also undergone a qualitative change. Man has, as it were, discovered a new method of adapting himself to his environment. Between the receptor system and the effector system, which are to be found in all animal species, we find in man a third link which we may describe as the *symbolic system.* This new acquisition transforms the whole of human life. As compared with the other animals man lives not merely in a broader reality; he lives, so to speak, in a new *dimension* of reality. There is an unmistakable difference between organic reactions and human responses. In the first case a direct and immediate answer is given to an outward stimulus; in the second case the answer is delayed. It is interrupted and retarded by a slow and complicated process of thought. At first sight such a delay may appear to be a very questionable gain. Many philosophers have warned man against this pretended progress. "L'homme qui médite," says Rousseau, "est un animal dépravé": it is not an improvement but a deterioration of human nature to exceed the boundaries of organic life.

Yet there is no remedy against this reversal of the natural order. Man cannot escape from his own achievement. He cannot but adopt the conditions of his own life. No longer in a merely physical universe, man lives in a symbolic universe. Language, myth, art, and religion are parts of this universe. They are the varied threads which weave the symbolic net, the tangled web of human experience. All human progress in thought and experience refines upon and strengthens this net. No longer can man confront reality immediately; he cannot see it, as it were, face to face. Physical reality seems to recede in proportion as man's symbolic activity advances. Instead of dealing with the things themselves man is in a sense constantly conversing with himself. He has so enveloped himself in linguistic forms, in artistic images, in mythical symbols or religious rites that he cannot see or know anything except by the interposition of this artificial medium.

His situation is the same in the theoretical as in the practical sphere. Even here man does not live in a world of hard facts, or according to his immediate needs and desires. He lives rather in the midst of imaginary emotions, in hopes and fears, in illusions and disillusions, in his fantasies and dreams. "What disturbs and alarms man," said Epictetus, "are not the things, but his opinions and fancies about the things."

From the point of view at which we have just arrived we may correct and enlarge the classical definition of man. In spite of all the efforts of modern irrationalism this definition of man as an *animal rationale* has not lost its force. Rationality is indeed an inherent feature of all human activities. Mythology itself is not simply a crude mass of superstitions or gross delusions. It is not merely chaotic, for it possesses a systematic or conceptual form.[2] But, on the other hand, it would be impossible to characterize the structure of myth as rational. Language has often been identified with reason, or with the very source of reason. But it is easy to see that this definition fails to cover the whole field. It is a *pars pro toto;* it offers us a part for the whole. For side by side with conceptual language there is an emotional language; side by side with logical or scientific language there is a language of poetic imagination. Primarily language does not express thoughts or ideas, but feelings and affections. And even a religion "within the limits of pure reason" as conceived and worked out by Kant is no more than a mere abstraction. It conveys only the ideal shape, only the shadow, of what a genuine and concrete religious life is. The great thinkers who have defined man as an *animal rationale* were not empiricists, nor did they ever intend to give an empirical account of human nature. By this definition they were expressing rather a fundamental moral imperative. Reason is a very inadequate term with which to comprehend the forms of man's cultural life in all their richness and variety. But all these forms are symbolic forms. Hence, instead of defining man as an *animal rationale,* we should define him as an *animal symbolicum.* By so doing we can designate his specific difference, and we can understand the new way open to man—the way to civilization.

_____
[2] See Cassirer, *Die Begriffsform im mythischen Denken* (Leipzig, 1921).

THE SYMBOLIC PROCESS

We return again to Hayakawa, with a selection from his book, *Language in Thought and Action*. In this passage he lays out what is involved in symbolizing as a process, of its nature and its role in human behavior, of the highly arbitrary form that any given symbol may take with reference to different kinds of "reality" (something illustrated in Part III in discussions of the cultural structuring of gestures, for example), and of not only the widespread but the many different kinds of symbols in human life. Hayakawa's basic theme, one which any student of human life must get clear, is that of the difference between the word (or any other symbol—be it flag, clothing style, gesture, posture, or what not) and the empirical event with which it is linked in a relationship of meaning. It is not that there is *no* relationship of any kind between the symbol and the thing symbolized—for in usage there commonly develops very strong emotional associations and connotative meanings; it is just that there is very little direct or compulsory direction given by the objective event as to what form its symbolization might take. That is one reason the understanding of culture is beset with misinterpretations until the system of meanings, symbolically expressed, is decoded. It is like an alphabet, which structures reality; but many alphabets, each having different symbols and different arrangements of those symbols, may do the job of symbolizing sounds equally well. Man's symbol systems therefore play, as it were, a shadow drama, with shifting scenes imposed over the background of empirical events.

SYMBOLS

S. I. HAYAKAWA

This basic need, which certainly is obvious only in man, is the need of symbolization. The symbol-making function is one of man's primary activities, like eating, looking, or moving about. It is the fundamental process of the mind, and goes on all the time.
—SUSANNE K. LANGER

Man's achievements rest upon the use of symbols.
—ALFRED KORZYBSKI

THE SYMBOLIC PROCESS

Animals struggle with each other for food or for leadership, but they do not, like human beings, struggle with each other for things that *stand for* food or leadership: such things as our paper, symbols of wealth (money, bonds, titles), badges of rank to wear on our clothes, or low-number license plates, supposed by some people to stand for social precedence. For animals, the relationship in which

Reprinted with permission of author and publisher from S. I. Hayakawa, *Language in Thought and Action* (New York: Harcourt, Brace and World, Inc., 1964), pp. 23–32.

one thing *stands for* something else does not appear to exist except in very rudimentary form.[1]

The process by means of which human beings can arbitrarily make certain things *stand for* other things may be called the *symbolic process*. When-

[1]One investigator, J. B. Wolfe, trained chimpanzees to put poker chips into an especially constructed vending machine ("chimpomat") which supplied grapes, bananas, and other food. The chimpanzees proved to be able to distinguish chips of different "values" (1 grape, 2 grapes, zero, and so on) and also proved to be willing to work for them if the rewards were fairly immediate. They tended, however, to stop work as they accumulated more chips. Their "money system" was definitely limited to rudimentary and immediate transactions. See Robert M. Yerkes' *Chimpanzees: A Laboratory Colony* (1943).

Other examples of animals successfully learning to react meaningfully to things-that-stand-for-other-things can readily be offered, but as a general rule these animal reactions are extremely simple and limited when contrasted with human possibilities in this direction. For example, it appears likely that a chimpanzee might be taught to drive a simplified car, but there would be one thing wrong with its driving: its reactions are such that if a red light showed when it was halfway across a street, it would stop in the middle of the crossing, while, if a green light showed when another car was stalled in its path, it would go ahead regardless of consequences. In other words, so far as such a chimpanzee would be concerned, the red light could hardly be said to *stand for* stop; it *is* stop.

ever two or more human beings can communicate with each other, they can, by agreement, make anything stand for anything. For example, here are two symbols:

$$X \qquad Y$$

We can agree to let X stand for buttons and Y stand for bows; then we can freely change our agreement and let X stand for the Chicago White Sox and Y for the Cincinnati Reds; or let X stand for Chaucer and Y for Shakespeare, X for North Korea, and Y for South Korea. *We are, as human beings, uniquely free to manufacture and manipulate and assign values to our symbols as we please.* Indeed, we can go further by making symbols that stand for symbols. If necessary we can, for instance, let the symbol M stand for all the X's in the above example (buttons, White Sox, Chaucer, North Korea) and let N stand for all the Y's (bows, Cincinnati Reds, Shakespeare, South Korea). Then we can make another symbol, T, stand for M and N, which would be an instance of a symbol of symbols of symbols. This freedom to create symbols of *any* assigned value and to create *symbols that stand for symbols* is essential to what we call the symbolic process.

Everywhere we turn, we see the symbolic process at work. Feathers worn on the head or stripes on the sleeve can be made to stand for military rank; cowrie shells or rings of brass or pieces of paper can stand for wealth; crossed sticks can stand for a set of religious beliefs; buttons, elks' teeth, ribbons, special styles of ornamental haircutting or tattooing, can stand for social affiliations. The symbolic process permeates human life at the most primitive and the most civilized levels alike. Warriors, medicine men, policemen, doormen, nurses, cardinals, and kings wear costumes that symbolize their occupations. American Indians collected scalps, college students collect membership keys in honorary societies, to symbolize victories in their respective fields. There are few things that men do or want to do, possess or want to possess, that have not, in addition to their mechanical or biological value, a symbolic value.

All fashionable clothes, as Thorstein Veblen has pointed out in his *Theory of the Leisure Class* (1899), are highly symbolic: materials, cut, and ornament are dictated only to a slight degree by considerations of warmth, comfort, or practicability. The more we dress up in fine clothes, the more we restrict our freedom of action. But by means of delicate embroideries, easily soiled fabrics, starched shirts, high heels, long and pointed fingernails, and other such sacrifices of comfort, the wealthy classes manage to symbolize, among other things, the fact that they don't have to work for a living. On the other hand, the not-so-wealthy, by imitating these symbols of wealth, symbolize their conviction that, even if they do work for a living, they are just as good as anybody else.

With the changes in American life since Veblen's time, many changes have taken place in our ways of symbolizing social status. Except for evening and party wear, fashionable clothes nowadays are often designed for outdoor life and therefore stress comfort, informality, and, above all, freedom from the conventions of business life—hence the gaily colored sports shirts for men and capri pants for women.

In Veblen's time a deeply tanned skin was indicative of a life spent in farming and other outdoor labor, and women in those days went to a great deal of trouble shielding themselves from the sun with parasols, wide hats, and long sleeves. Today, however, a pale skin is indicative of confinement in offices and factories, while a deeply tanned skin suggests a life of leisure—of trips to Florida, Sun Valley, and Hawaii. Hence, a sun-blackened skin, once considered ugly because it symbolized work, is now considered beautiful because it symbolizes leisure. "The idea is," as Stanton Delaplane said in the San Francisco *Chronicle*, "to turn a color which, if you were born with it, would make it extremely difficult to get into major hotels." And pallid people in New York, Chicago, and Toronto who cannot afford midwinter trips to the West Indies find comfort in browning themselves with drugstore tanning solutions.

Food, too, is highly symbolic. Religious dietary regulations, such as those of the Catholics, Jews, and Mohammedans, are observed in order to symbolize adherence to one's religion. Specific foods are used to symbolize specific festivals and observances in almost every country—for example, cherry pie on George Washington's birthday; haggis on Burns' Nicht. And eating together has been a highly symbolic act throughout all of man's known history: "companion" means one with whom you share your bread.

The white Southerner's apparently illogical attitude toward Negroes can also be accounted for on symbolic grounds. People from outside the South often find it difficult to understand how many white Southerners accept close physical contact with Negro servants and yet become extremely upset at the idea of sitting beside Negroes in restaurants or buses. The attitude of the Southerner rests on the fact that the ministrations of a Negro servant—even personal care, such as nursing—have the symbolic implication of social inequality; while admission of Negroes to buses, restaurants, and non-segregated schools has the symbolic implication of social equality.

We select our furniture to serve as visible symbols of our taste, wealth, and social position. We often choose our residences on the basis of a feeling that it "looks well" to have a "good address." We trade in perfectly good cars for later models, not always to get better transportation, but to give evidence to the community that we can afford it.[2]

Such complicated and apparently unnecessary behavior leads philosophers, both amateur and professional, to ask over and over again, "Why can't human beings live simply and naturally?" Often the complexity of human life makes us look enviously at the relative simplicity of such lives as dogs and cats lead. But the symbolic process, which makes possible the absurdities of human conduct, also makes possible language and therefore all the human achievements dependent upon language. The fact that more things can go wrong with motor-cars than with wheelbarrows is no reason for going back to wheelbarrows. Similarly, the fact that the symbolic process makes complicated follies possible is no reason for wanting to return to a cat-and-dog existence. A better solution is to understand the symbolic process so that instead of being its victims we become, to some degree at least, its masters.

LANGUAGE AS SYMBOLISM

Of all forms of symbolism, language is the most highly developed, most subtle, and most complicated. It has been pointed out that human beings, by agreement, can make anything stand for anything. Now, human beings have agreed, in the

course of centuries of mutual dependency, to let the various noises that they can produce with their lungs, throats, tongues, teeth, and lips systematically stand for specified happenings in their nervous systems. We call that system of agreements *language*. For example, we who speak English have been so trained that, when our nervous systems register the presence of a certain kind of animal, we may make the following noise: "There's a cat." Anyone hearing us expects to find that, by looking in the same direction, he will experience a similar event in his nervous system—one that will lead him to make an almost identical noise. Again, we have been so trained that when we are conscious of wanting food, we make the noise "I'm hungry."

There is, as has been said, *no necessary connection between the symbol and that which is symbolized.* Just as men can wear yachting costumes without ever having been near a yacht, so they can make the noise "I'm hungry" without being hungry. Furthermore, just as social rank can be symbolized by feathers in the hair, by tattooing on the breast, by gold ornaments on the watch chain, or by a thousand different devices according to the culture we live in, so the fact of being hungry can be symbolized by a thousand different noises according to the culture we live in: "*J'ai faim*," or "*Es hungert mich*," or "*Ho appetito*," or "*Hara ga hetta*," and so on.

However obvious these facts may appear at first glance, they are actually not so obvious as they seem except when we take special pains to think about the subject. Symbols and things symbolized are independent of each other; nevertheless, we all have a way of feeling as if, and sometimes acting as if, there were necessary connections. For example, there is the vague sense we all have that foreign languages are inherently absurd: foreigners have such funny names for things, and why can't they call things by their right names? This feeling exhibits itself most strongly in those tourists who seem to believe that they can make the natives of any country understand English if they shout loud enough. Like the little boy who was reported to have said, "Pigs are called pigs because they are such dirty animals," they feel that the symbol is inherently connected in some way with the thing symbolized. Then there are the people who feel that since snakes are "nasty, slimy creatures" (incidentally, snakes are *not* slimy), the word "snake" is a *nasty, slimy word.*

[2]The writer once had an eight-year-old car in good running condition. A friend of his, a repairman who knew the condition of the car, kept urging him to trade it for a new model. "But why?" the writer asked. "The old car's in fine shape still." The repairman answered scornfully, "Yeah, but what the hell. All you've got is transportation."

Recently, the term "transportation car" has begun to appear in advertisements; for example, " '48 Dodge Runs perfectly good; transportation car. Leaving, must sell. $100." (Classified section of the *Pali Press*, Kailua, Hawaii.) Apparently it means a car that has no symbolic or prestige value and is good only for getting you there and bringing you back a miserable kind of vehicle indeed!

THE PITFALLS OF DRAMA

Naïveté regarding the symbolic process extends to symbols other than words, of course. In the case of drama (stage, movies, television), there appear to be people in almost every audience who never quite fully realize that a play is a set of fictional, symbolic representations. An actor is one who symbolizes other people, real or imagined. In a movie some years ago, Fredric March enacted with great skill the role of a drunkard. Florence Eldridge (Mrs. March) reports that for a long time thereafter she got letters of advice and sympathy from women who said that they too were married to alcoholics. Also some years ago it was reported that when Edward G. Robinson, who used to play gangster roles with extraordinary vividness, visited Chicago, local hoodlums would telephone him at his hotel to pay their professional respects.

One is reminded of the actor, playing the role of a villain in a traveling theatrical troupe, who, at a particularly tense moment in the play, was shot by an excited cowpuncher in the audience. But this kind of confusion does not seem to be confined to unsophisticated theatergoers. In recent times, Paul Muni, after playing the part of Clarence Darrow in *Inherit the Wind*, was invited to address the American Bar Association; Ralph Bellamy, after playing the role of Franklin D. Roosevelt in *Sunrise at Campobello*, was invited by several colleges to speak on Roosevelt. Also, there are those astonishing patriots who rushed to the recruiting offices to help defend the nation when, on October 30, 1938, the United States was "invaded" by an "army from Mars" in a radio dramatization.[3]

THE WORD IS NOT THE THING

The above, however, are only the more striking examples of confused attitudes toward words and symbols. There would be little point in mentioning them if we were *uniformly and permanently aware* of the independence of symbols from things symbolized, as all human beings, in the writer's opinion, *can be* and *should be*. But we are not. Most of us have, in some area or other of our thinking, improper habits of evaluation. For this, society itself is often to blame: most societies systematically encourage, concerning certain topics, the habitual

confusion of symbols with things symbolized. For example, if a Japanese schoolhouse caught on fire, it used to be obligatory in the days of emperor-worship to try to rescue the emperor's *picture* (there was one in every schoolhouse), even at the risk of one's life. (If you got burned to death, you were posthumously ennobled.) In our society, we are encouraged to go into debt in order that we may display, as symbols of prosperity, shiny new automobiles. Strangely enough, the possession of shiny automobiles even under these conditions makes their "owners" *feel* prosperous. In all civilized societies (and probably in many primitive ones as well), the symbols of piety, of civic virtue, or of patriotism are often prized above actual piety, civic virtue, or patriotism. In one way or another, we are all like the brilliant student who cheats on his exams in order to make Phi Beta Kappa; it is so much more important to have the symbol than the things it stands for.

The habitual confusion of symbols with things symbolized, whether on the part of individuals or societies, is serious enough at all levels of culture to provide a perennial human problem.[4] But with the rise of modern communications systems, the problem of confusing verbal symbols with realities assumes peculiar urgency. We are constantly being talked at, by teachers, preachers, salesmen, public-relations counsels, government agencies, and moving-picture sound tracks. The cries of the hawkers of soft drinks, detergents, and laxatives pursue us into our homes, thanks to radio and television—and in some houses the sets are never turned off from morning to night. The mailman brings direct-mail advertising. Billboards confront us on the highway, and we even take portable radios with us to the seashore.

We live in an environment shaped and largely created by hitherto unparalleled semantic influences: mass-circulation newspapers and magazines which are given to reflecting, in a shocking number of cases, the weird prejudices and obsessions of their publishers and owners; radio programs, both local and network, almost completely dominated by commercial motives; public-relations counsels who are simply highly paid craftsmen in the art of manipulating and reshaping our semantic environment in ways favorable to their clients. It is

[3]See Hadley Cantril's *The Invasion from Mars* (1940); also John Houseman's "The Men from Mars," *Harper's* (December 1948).

[4]The charge against the Pharisees, it will be remembered, was that they were obsessively concerned with the symbols of piety at the expense of an adequate concern with its spirit.

an exciting environment, but fraught with danger: it is only a slight exaggeration to say that Hitler conquered Austria by radio. Today, the full resources of advertising agencies, public-relations counsels, radio, television, and slanted news stories are brought to bear in order to influence our decisions in election campaigns, especially in years of presidential elections.

Citizens of a modern society need, therefore, more than that ordinary "common sense" which was defined by Stuart Chase as that which tells you that the world is flat. They need to be systematically aware of the powers and limitations of symbols, especially words, if they are to guard against being driven into complete bewilderment by the complexity of their semantic environment. The first of the principles governing symbols is this: The symbol is NOT the thing symbolized; the word is NOT the thing; the map is NOT the territory it stands for.

MAPS AND TERRITORIES

There is a sense in which we all live in two worlds. First, we live in the world of happenings which we know at first hand. This is an extremely small world, consisting only of that continuum of the things that we have actually seen, felt, or heard—the flow of events constantly passing before our senses. So far as this world of personal experience is concerned, Africa, South America, Asia, Washington, New York, or Los Angeles do not exist if we have never been to these places. Jomo Kenyetta is only a name if we have never seen him. When we ask ourselves how much we know at first hand, we discover that we know very little indeed.

Most of our knowledge, acquired from parents, friends, schools, newspapers, books, conversation, speeches, and television, is received *verbally*. All our knowledge of history, for example, comes to us only in words. The only proof we have that the Battle of Waterloo ever took place is that we have had reports to that effect. These reports are not given us by people who saw it happen, but are based on other reports: reports of reports of reports, which go back ultimately to the first-hand reports given by people who did see it happening. It is through reports, then, and through reports of reports, that we receive most knowledge: about government, about what is happening in Korea, about what picture is showing at the downtown theater—in fact, about anything that we do not know through direct experience.

Let us call this world that comes to us through words the *verbal world*, as opposed to the world we know or are capable of knowing through our own experience, which we shall call the *extensional world*. (The reason for the choice of the word "extensional" will become clear later.) The human being, like any other creature, begins to make his acquaintance with the extensional world from infancy. Unlike other creatures, however, he begins to receive, as soon as he can learn to understand, reports, reports of reports, reports of reports of reports. In addition he receives inferences made from reports, inferences made from other inferences, and so on. By the time a child is a few years old, has gone to school and to Sunday school, and has made a few friends, he has accumulated a considerable amount of second- and third-hand information about morals, geography, history, nature, people, games—all of which information together constitutes his verbal world.

Now, to use the famous metaphor introduced by Alfred Korzybski in his *Science and Sanity* (1933), this verbal world ought to stand in relation to the extensional world as a *map* does to the *territory* it is supposed to represent. If a child grows to adulthood with a verbal world in his head which corresponds fairly closely to the extensional world that he finds around him in his widening experience, he is in relatively small danger of being shocked or hurt by what he finds, because his verbal world has told him what, more or less, to expect. He is prepared for life. If, however, he grows up with a false map in his head—that is, with a head crammed with error and superstition—he will constantly be running into trouble, wasting his efforts, and acting like a fool. He will not be adjusted to the world as it is; he may, if the lack of adjustment is serious, end up in a mental hospital.

Some of the follies we commit because of false maps in our heads are so commonplace that we do not even think of them as remarkable. There are those who protect themselves from accidents by carrying a rabbit's foot. Some refuse to sleep on the thirteenth floor of hotels—a situation so common that most big hotels, even in the capitals of our scientific culture, skip "13" in numbering their floors. Some plan their lives on the basis of astrological predictions. Some play fifty-to-one shots on the basis of dream books. Some hope to make their teeth whiter by changing their brand of tooth paste. All such people are living in verbal worlds that bear little, if any, resemblance to the extensional world.

Now, no matter how beautiful a map may be, it is useless to a traveler unless it accurately shows the relationship of places to each other, the structure of the territory. If we draw, for example, a big dent in the outline of a lake for, let us say, artistic reasons, the map is worthless. But if we are just drawing maps for fun without paying any attention to the structure of the region, there is nothing in the world to prevent us from putting in all the extra curlicues and twists we want in the lakes, rivers, and roads. No harm will be done *unless someone tries to plan a trip by such a map.*

Similarly, by means of imaginary or false reports, or by false inferences from good reports, or by mere rhetorical exercises, we can manufacture at will, with language, "maps" which have no reference to the extensional world. Here again no harm will be done unless someone makes the mistake of regarding such "maps" as representing real territories.

We all inherit a great deal of useless knowledge, and a great deal of misinformation and error (maps that were formerly thought to be accurate), so that there is always a portion of what we have been told that must be discarded. But the cultural heritage of our civilization that is transmitted to us—our socially pooled knowledge, both scientific and humane—has been valued principally because we have believed that it gives us accurate maps of experience. The analogy of verbal worlds to maps is an important one and will be referred to frequently throughout this book. It should be noticed at this point, however, that there are two ways of getting false maps of the world into our heads: first, by having them given to us; second, by creating them ourselves when we misread the true maps given to us.

SYMBOLS IN HUMAN BEHAVIOR

The following paper by Leslie White, like his earlier one on "Science is *Sciencing*," is widely known. And for good reason—for it presents in clear, lucid style a point of fundamental relevance for anyone studying the social or behavioral sciences. White reiterates some of the points already made in the excerpts by Cassirer and Hayakawa, and made in passing reference by many of the other writers whose work has been included in this reader. But White goes further and places his discussion of symbols and their role in human life at the center of any consideration of the nature of culture, with a discussion relating to the nature of the gap between the qualities and dynamics of man's life and those of other animals, even his closest relatives in the primate world. White also introduces discussion of the difference between "signs" and "symbols," with the former playing an important role in associative learning for many animals (again, including man), but with the latter—symbols, reflecting congeries of meanings and values—being the property only of man. Symbols, then, or more properly the symbolizing *process*, is at the heart of the cultural process.

THE SYMBOL: THE ORIGIN AND BASIS OF HUMAN BEHAVIOR

LESLIE A. WHITE

I

In July, 1939, a celebration was held at Leland Stanford University to commemorate the hundredth

anniversary of the discovery that the cell is the basic unit of all living tissue. Today we are beginning to realize and to appreciate the fact that the symbol is the basic unit of all human behavior and civilization.

All human behavior originates in the use of sym-

Reprinted with permission of publisher. From *Philosophy of Science*, vol. 7 (1940), 451–63.

bols. It was the symbol which transformed our anthropoid ancestors into men and made them human. All civilizations have been generated, and are perpetuated, only by the use of symbols. It is the symbol which transforms an infant of homo sapiens into a human being; deaf mutes who grow up without the use of symbols are not human beings. All human behavior consists of, or is dependent upon, the use of symbols. Human behavior is symbolic behavior; symbolic behavior is human behavior. The symbol is the universe of humanity.

II

The great Darwin declared that "there is no fundamental difference between man and the higher mammals in their mental faculties," that the difference between them consists "solely in his [man's] almost infinitely larger power of associating together the most diversified sounds and ideas," (Ch. III, *The Descent of Man*). Thus the difference between the mind of man and that of other mammals is merely one of degree, and it is not "fundamental."

Essentially the same views are held by many present day students of human behavior. Professor Ralph Linton, an anthropologist, writes in *The Study of Man:*[1] "The differences between men and animals in all these [behavior] respects are enormous, but they seem to be differences in quantity rather than in quality," (p. 79; the same idea is also expressed on p. 68). "Human and animal behavior can be shown to have so much in common," Professor Linton observes, "that the gap [between them] ceases to be of great importance," (p. 60). Dr. Alexander Goldenweiser, likewise an anthropologist, believes that "In point of sheer psychology, mind as such, man is after all no more than a talented animal" and "that the difference between the mentality here displayed [by a horse and a chimpanzee] and that of man is merely one of degree."[2]

That there are numerous and impressive similarities between the behavior of man and that of ape is fairly obvious; it is quite possible that even chimpanzees in zoos have noted and appreciated them. Fairly apparent, too, are man's behavioral similarities to many other kinds of animals. Almost as obvious, but not easy to define, is a difference in behavior which distinguishes man from all other

living creatures. I say 'obvious' because it is quite apparent to the common man that the non-human animals with which he is familiar do not and cannot enter, and participate in, the world in which he, as a human being, lives. It is impossible for a dog, horse, bird, or even an ape, ever to have *any* understanding of the meaning of the sign of the cross to a Christian, or of the fact that black (white among the Chinese) is the color of mourning. But when the scholar attempts to *define* the mental difference between animal and man he sometimes encounters difficulties which he cannot surmount and, therefore, ends up by saying that the difference is merely one of degree: man has a bigger mind, "larger power of association," wider range of activities, etc.[3]

There is a *fundamental* difference between the mind of man and the mind of non-man. This difference is one of kind, not one of degree. And the gap between the two types is of the greatest importance —at least to the science of comparative behavior. Man uses symbols; no other creature does. A creature either uses symbols or he does not; there are no intermediate stages.

III

A symbol is a thing the value or meaning of which is bestowed upon it by those who use it. I say 'thing' because a symbol may have any kind of physical form; it may have the form of a material object, a color, a sound, an odor, a motion of an object, a taste.

The meaning, or value, of a symbol is in no instance derived from or determined by properties intrinsic in its physical form: the color appropriate to mourning may be yellow, green, or any other color; purple need not be the color of royalty; among the Manchu rulers of China it was yellow.

[1] New York, 1936.
[2] *Anthropology*, p. 39; New York, 1937.

[3] We have a good example of this in the distinguished physiologist, Anton J. Carlson. After taking note of "man's present achievements in science, in the arts (including oratory), in political and social institutions," and noting "at the same time the apparent paucity of such behavior in other animals," he, as a common man "is tempted to conclude that in these capacities, at least, man has a qualitative superiority over other mammals," ("The Dynamics of Living Processes," in *The Nature of the World and Man*, H. H. Newman, ed., p. 477; Chicago, 1926). But, since, as a scientist, Professor Carlson cannot *define* this qualitative difference between man and other animals, since as a physiologist he cannot explain it, he refuses to admit it. ". . . the physiologist does not accept the great development of articulate speech in man as something qualitatively new; . . ." (p. 478) and suggests helplessly that some day we may find some new "building stone," an "additional lipoid, phosphatid, or potassium ion," in the human brain which will explain it, and concludes by saying that the difference between the mind of man and that of non-man is "probably only one of degree," (*op. cit.*, pp. 478–79).

The meaning of the word 'see' is not intrinsic in its phonetic (or pictorial) properties. "Biting one's thumb at"[4] someone might mean anything. The meanings of symbols are derived from and determined by the organisms who use them; meaning is bestowed by human organisms upon physical forms which thereupon become symbols.[5]

All symbols must have a physical form otherwise they could not enter our experience.[6] But the meaning of a symbol cannot be perceived by the senses. One cannot tell by looking at an x in an algebraic equation what it stands for; one cannot ascertain with the ears alone the symbolic value of the phonetic compound $si;$ one cannot tell merely by weighing a pig how much gold he will exchange for; one cannot tell from the wave length of a color whether it stands for courage or cowardice, "stop" or "go"; nor can one discover the spirit in a fetish by any amount of physical or chemical examination. The meaning of a symbol can be communicated only by symbolic means, usually by articulate speech.

But a thing which in one context is a symbol is, in another context, not a symbol but a sign. Thus, a word is a symbol only when one is concerned with the distinction between its meaning and its physical form. This distinction *must* be made when one bestows value upon a sound-combination or when a previously bestowed value is discovered for the first time; it *may* be made at other times for certain purposes. But after value has been bestowed upon, or discovered in, a word, its meaning becomes identified, in use, with its physical form. The word then functions as a sign,[7] rather than as a symbol. Its meaning is then perceived with the senses. This fact that a thing may be both symbol (in one con-

text) and non-symbol (in another context) has led to some confusion and misunderstanding.

Thus Darwin says: "That which distinguishes man from the lower animals is not the understanding of articulate sounds, for as everyone knows, dogs understand many words and sentences," (Ch. III, *The Descent of Man*).

It is perfectly true, of course, that dogs, apes,[8] horses, birds, and perhaps creatures even lower in the evolutionary scale, can be taught to respond in a specific way to a vocal command. But it does not follow that no difference exists between the meaning of "words and sentences" to a man and to a dog. Words are both signs and symbols to man; they are merely signs to a dog. Let us analyze the situation of vocal stimulus and response.

A dog may be taught to roll over at the command "Roll over!" A man may be taught to stop at the command "Halt!" The fact that a dog can be taught to roll over in Chinese, or that he can be taught to "go fetch" at the command "roll over" (and, of course, the same is true for a man) shows that there is no necessary and invariable relationship between a particular sound combination and a specific reaction to it. The dog or the man can be taught to respond in a certain manner to *any* arbitrarily selected combination of sounds, for example, a group of nonsense syllables, coined for the occasion. On the other hand, any one of a great number and variety of responses may become evocable by a given stimulus. Thus, so far as the *origin* of the relationship between vocal stimulus and response is concerned, the nature of the relationship, i.e., the meaning of the stimulus, is not determined by properties intrinsic in the stimulus.

But, once the relationship has been established between vocal stimulus and response, the meaning of the stimulus becomes *identified with the sounds;* it is then *as if* the meaning were intrinsic in the sounds themselves. Thus, 'halt' does not have the same meaning as 'hilt' or 'malt.' A dog may be conditioned to respond in a certain way to a sound of a given wave length. Sufficiently alter the pitch of the sound and the response will cease to be forthcoming. The meaning of the stimulus has become identified with its physical form; its value is perceived with the senses.

---

[4] "Do you bite your thumb at us, sir?" *Romeo and Juliet*, Act I, Sc. I.

[5] "Now since sounds have no natural connection with our ideas, but have all their signification from the arbitrary imposition of men . . . ," John Locke, *Essay Concerning the Human Understanding*, Bk. III, ch. 9.

"When *I* use . . . [a] word, it means just what I choose it to mean," said Humpty Dumpty to Alice. (*Through the Looking Glass*).

[6] This statement is valid regardless of our theory of experiencing. Even the exponents of "Extra-Sensory Perception," who have challenged Locke's dictum that "the knowledge of the existence of any other thing [besides ourselves and God] we can have only by sensation," (Bk. 4, ch. II, *Essay Concerning the Human Understanding*,) have been obliged to work with physical rather than ethereal forms.

[7] A *sign* is a physical form whose function is to indicate some other object, quality, or event. The meaning of a sign may be intrinsic, inseparable from its physical form and nature, as in the case of the height of a column of mercury as an indication of temperature; or, it may be merely identified with its physical form, as in the case of a hurricane signal displayed by a weather bureau. But in either case, the meaning of the sign is perceived with the senses.

---

[8] "Surprising as it may seem, it was very clear during the first few months that the ape was considerably superior to the child in responding to human words," W. N. and L. A. Kellogg, *The Ape and the Child*, (New York, 1933).

Thus we see that in *establishing* a relationship between a stimulus and a response the properties intrinsic in the stimulus do not determine the nature of the response. But, *after the relationship has been established* the meaning of the stimulus is *as if* it were *inherent* in its physical form. It does not make any difference what phonetic combination we select to evoke the response of terminating self-locomotion. We may teach a dog, horse, or man to stop at any vocal command we care to choose or devise. But once the relationship has been established between sound and response, the meaning of the stimulus becomes identified with its physical form and is, therefore, perceivable with the senses.

So far we have discovered no difference between the dog and the man; they appear to be exactly alike. And so they are as far as we have gone. But we have not told the whole story yet. No difference between dog and man is discoverable so far as learning to respond appropriately to a vocal stimulus is concerned. But we must not let an impressive similarity conceal an important difference. A porpoise is not yet a fish.

The man differs from the dog—and all other creatures—in that *he can and does play an active role in determining what value the vocal stimulus is to have, and the dog cannot.* As John Locke has aptly put it, "All sounds [i.e., in language] . . . have their signification from the arbitrary imposition of men." The dog does not and cannot play an active part in determining the value of the vocal stimulus. Whether he is to roll over or go fetch at a given stimulus, or whether the stimulus for roll over be one combination of sounds or another is a matter in which the dog has nothing whatever to "say." He plays a purely passive role and can do nothing else. He learns the meaning of a vocal command just as his salivary glands may learn to respond to the sound of a bell. But man plays an active role and thus becomes a creator: Let *x* equal three pounds of coal and it does equal three pounds of coal; let removal of the hat in a house of worship indicate respect and it becomes so. This creative faculty, that of freely, actively, and arbitrarily bestowing value upon things, is one of the most commonplace as well as *the* most important characteristic of man. Children employ it freely in their play: "Let's pretend that this rock is a wolf."

The difference between the behavior of man and other animals then, is that the lower animals may receive new values, may acquire new meanings, but they cannot create and bestow them. Only man can do this. To use a crude analogy, lower animals are like a person who has only the receiving apparatus for wireless messages: He can receive messages but cannot send them. Man can do both. And this difference is one of kind, not of degree: a creature can either "arbitrarily impose signification," to use Locke's phrase, can either create and bestow values, or he cannot. There are no intermediate stages.[9] This difference may appear slight, but, as a carpenter once told William James in discussing differences between men, "it's very important." All *human* existence depends upon it and it alone.

The confusion regarding the nature of words and their significance to men and the lower animals is not hard to understand. It arises, first of all, from a failure to distinguish between the two quite different contexts in which words function. The statements, "The meaning of a word[10] cannot be perceived with the senses," and "The meaning of a word can be perceived with the senses," though contradictory, are nevertheless equally true. In the *symbol* context the meaning cannot be perceived with the senses; in the *sign* context it can. This is confusing enough. But the situation has been made worse by using the words 'symbol' and 'sign' to label, not the *different contexts*, but *one and the same thing:* the word. Thus a word is a symbol *and* a sign, two different things. It is like saying that a vase is a *doli* and a *kana*—two different things—because it may function in two contexts, esthetic and commercial.[11]

That which is a *symbol* in the context of origination becomes a *sign* in use thereafter. Things may be either signs or symbols to man; they can be only signs to other creatures.

IV

Very little indeed is known of the organic basis of the symbolic faculty: we know next to nothing of the neurology of symbolizing.[12] And very few

---

[9] Professor Linton speaks of "the faintest foreshadowings of language . . . at the animal level," (*op. cit.*, p. 74). But precisely what these "faintest foreshadowings" are he does not say.

[10] What we have to say here would, of course, apply equally well to gestures (e.g., the "sign of the cross," a salute), a color, a material object, etc.

[11] Like a word, the value of a vase may be perceived by the senses or imperceptible to them depending upon the context in which it is regarded. In an esthetic context its value is perceived with the senses. In the commercial context this is impossible; we must be *told* its value—in terms of price.

[12] Cf. "A Neurologist Makes Up His Mind," by C. Judson Herrick, *Scientific Monthly*, August, 1939. Professor Herrick is a distinguished one of a not too large number of scientists who are interested in the structural basis of symbol using.

scientists—anatomists, neurologists, physical anthropologists—appear to be interested in the problem. Some, in fact, seem to be unaware of the existence of such a problem. The duty and task of giving an account of the organic basis of symbolizing does not fall within the province of the sociologist or the cultural anthropologist. On the contrary, he should scrupulously exclude it as irrelevant to his problems and interests; to introduce it would bring only confusion. It is enough for the sociologist or cultural anthropologist to take the ability to use symbols, possessed by man alone, as given. The use to which he puts this fact is in no way affected by his, or even the anatomist's, inability to describe the symbolic process in neurological terms. However, it is well for the social scientist to be acquainted with the little that neurologists and anatomists do know about the structural basis of "symboling." We, therefore, review briefly the chief relevant facts here.

The anatomist has not been able to discover why men can use symbols and apes cannot. So far as is known the only difference between the brain of man and the brain of an ape is a quantitative one: ". . . man has no new kinds of brain cells or brain cell connections," (A. J. Carlson, *op. cit.*). Nor does man, as distinguished from other animals, possess a specialized "symbol-mechanism." The so-called speech areas of the brain should not be identified with symbolizing. These areas are associated with the muscles of the tongue, larynx, etc. But symbolizing is not dependent upon these organs. One may symbolize with the fingers, the feet, or with any part of the body that can be moved at will.[13]

To be sure, the symbolic faculty was brought into existence by the natural processes of organic evolution. And we may reasonably believe that the focal point, if not the locus, of this faculty is in the brain, especially the forebrain. Man's brain is much larger than that of an ape, both absolutely and relatively.[14] And the forebrain especially is large in man as compared with ape. Now in many situations we know that quantitative changes give rise to qualitative differences. Water is transformed into steam by additional quantities of heat. Additional power and speed lift the taxi-ing airplane from the ground and transform terrestrial locomotion into flight. The difference between wood alcohol and grain alcohol is a qualitative expression of a quantitative difference in the proportions of carbon and hydrogen. Thus a marked growth in size of the brain in man may have brought forth a *new kind* of function.

V

All culture (civilization) depends upon the symbol. It was the exercise of the symbolic faculty that brought culture into existence and it is the use of symbols that makes the perpetuation of culture possible. Without the symbol there would be no culture, and man would be merely an animal, not a human being.

Articulate speech is the most important form of symbolic expression. Remove speech from culture and what would remain? Let us see.

Without articulate speech we would have no *human* social organization. Families we might have, but this form of organization is not peculiar to man; it is not *per se, human*. But we would have no prohibitions of incest, no rules prescribing exogamy and endogamy, polygamy or monogamy. How could marriage with a cross cousin be prescribed, marriage with a parallel cousin proscribed, without articulate speech? How could rules which

[13]The misconception that speech is dependent upon the so-called (but mis-called) organs of speech, and, furthermore, that man alone has organs suitable for speech, is not uncommon even today. Thus Professor L. L. Bernard lists "The fourth great organic asset of man is his vocal apparatus, also characteristic of him alone." (*Introduction to Sociology*, J. Davis and H. E. Barnes, eds., p. 399; New York, 1927).

The great apes have the mechanism necessary for the production of articulate sounds: "It seemingly is well established that the motor mechanism of voice in this ape [chimpanzee] is adequate not only to the production of a considerable variety of sounds, but also to definite articulations similar to those of man," R. M. and A. W. Yerkes, *The Great Apes*, p. 301 (New Haven, 1929). Also: "All of the anthropoid apes are vocally and muscularly equipped so that they could have an articulate language if they possessed the requisite intelligence," E. A. Hooton, *Up From the Ape*, p. 167 (New York, 1931).

Furthermore, the mere production of articulate sounds would not be symbolizing any more than the mere "understanding of words and sentences" (Darwin) is. John Locke made this clear two and a half centuries ago: "Man, therefore had by nature his organs so fashioned, as to be *fit to frame articulate sounds*, which we call words. But this was not enough to produce language; for parrots,

and several other birds, will be taught to make articulate sounds distinct enough, which yet, by no means, are capable of language. Besides articulate sounds, therefore, it was farther necessary, that he should be *able to use these sounds as signs of internal conceptions*; and to make them stand as marks for the ideas within his own mind, whereby they might be made known to others. . . ," Book III, Ch. I, Secs. 2, *Essay Concerning the Human Understanding*.

And J. F. Blumenbach, a century later, declared in his *On the Natural Variety of Mankind*, "That speech is the work of reason alone, appears from this, that other animals, although they have nearly the same organs of voice as man, are entirely destitute of it," (quoted by R. M. and A. W. Yerkes, *op. cit.*, p. 23).

[14]Man's brain is about two and one-half times as large as that of a gorilla. "The human brain is about 1/50 of the entire body weight, while that of a gorilla varies from 1/150 to 1/200 part of that weight," (Hooton, *op. cit.*, p. 153).

prohibit plural mates possessed simultaneously but permit them if possessed one at a time, exist without speech?

Without speech we would have no political, economic, ecclesiastic, or military organization; no codes of etiquette or ethics; no laws; no science, theology, or literature; no games or music, except on an ape level. Rituals and ceremonial paraphernalia would be meaningless without articulate speech. Indeed, without articulate speech we would be all but toolless: we would have only the occasional and insignificant use of the tool such as we find today among the higher apes, for it was articulate speech that transformed the nonprogressive tool-using of the ape into the progressive, cumulative tool-using of man, the human being.

In short, without symbolic communication in some form, we would have no culture. "In the Word was the beginning" of culture—and its perpetuation also.[15]

To be sure, with all his culture man is still an animal and strives for the same ends that all other living creatures strive for: the preservation of the individual and the perpetuation of the race. In concrete terms these ends are food, shelter from the elements, defense from enemies, health, and offspring. The fact that man strives for these ends just as all other animals do has, no doubt, led many to declare that there is "no fundamental difference between the behavior of man and of other creatures." But man does differ, not in *ends* but in *means*. Man's means are cultural means: culture is simply the human animal's way of living. And, since these means, culture, are dependent upon a faculty possessed by man alone, the ability to use symbols, the difference between the behavior of man and of all other creatures is not merely great, but basic and fundamental.

VI

The behavior of man is of two distinct kinds: symbolic and nonsymbolic. Man yawns, stretches, coughs, scratches himself, cries out in pain, shrinks with fear, "bristles" with anger, and so on. Nonsymbolic behavior of this sort is not peculiar to man; he shares it not only with the other primates but with many other animal species as well. But man communicates with his fellows with articulate speech, uses amulets, confesses sins, makes laws, observes codes of etiquette, explains his dreams, classifies his relatives in designated categories, and so on. This kind of behavior is unique; only man is capable of it; it is peculiar to man because it consists of, or is dependent upon, the use of symbols. The nonsymbolic behavior of man is the behavior of man the animal; the symbolic behavior is that of man the human being.[16] It is the symbol which has transformed man from a mere animal to a human animal.

As it was the symbol that made mankind human, so it is with each member of the race. A baby is not a human being so far as his behavior is concerned. Until the infant acquires speech there is nothing to distinguish his behavior qualitatively from that of a young ape.[17] The baby becomes a human being when and as he learns to use symbols. Only by means of speech can the baby enter and take part in the human affairs of mankind. The questions we asked previously may be repeated now. How is the growing child to know of such things as families, etiquette, morals, law, science, philosophy, religion, commerce, and so on, without speech? The rare cases of children who grew up without symbols because of deafness and blindness, such as those of Laura Bridgman, Helen Keller and Marie Heurtin, are instructive.[18] Until they "got the idea" of symbolic communication they were not human beings, but animals, they did not participate in behavior which is peculiar to human beings. They were "in" human society as dogs are, but they were not *of*

---

[15]"On the whole, however, it would seem that language and culture rest, in a way which is not fully understood, on the same set of faculties . . . ," A. L. Kroeber, *Anthropology*, p. 108, (New York, 1923). It is hoped that this essay will make this matter more "fully understood."

[16]It is for this reason that observations and experiments with apes, rats, etc., can tell us nothing about human behavior. They can tell us how ape-like or rat-like man is, but they throw no light upon human behavior because the behavior of apes, rats, etc., is nonsymbolic.

The title of the late George A. Dorsey's best seller, *Why We Behave Like Human Beings*, was misleading for the same reason. This interesting book told us much about vertebrate, mammalian, primate, and even man-animal behavior, but virtually nothing about symbolic, i.e., human, behavior. But we are glad to add, in justice to Dorsey, that his chapter on the function of speech in culture, (Ch. II) in *Man's Own Show: Civilization* (New York, 1931), is probably the best discussion of this subject that we know of in anthropological literature.

[17]In their fascinating account of their experiment with a baby chimpanzee, kept for nine months in their home and treated as their infant son was treated, Professor and Mrs. Kellogg speak of the "humanization" of the little ape: "She may thus be said to have become 'more humanized' than the human subject . . ." (p. 315).

This is misleading. What the experiment showed so strikingly was *how like an ape* a child of homo sapiens is *before he learns to talk*. The boy even employed the ape's "food bark"! The experiment also demonstrated the ape's utter inability to learn to talk, which means an inability to become humanized at all.

[18]The reader will find a resume of the more significant facts of these cases in W. I. Thomas, *Primitive Behavior*, pp. 50–54, 776–777 (New York, 1937).

human society. And, although the present writer is exceedingly skeptical of the reports of the so-called "wolf children," "feral men," etc., we may note that they are described, almost without exception, as without speech, "beastly," and "inhuman."

VII

Summary. The natural processes of organic evolution brought into existence in man, and man alone, a new and distinctive ability: the ability to use symbols. The most important form of symbolic expression is articulate speech. Articulate speech means communication of ideas; communication means preservation—tradition—and preservation means accumulation and progress. The emergence of the organic faculty of symbol-using has resulted in the genesis of a new order of phenomena: a superorganic, or cultural, order. All civilizations are born of, and are perpetuated by, the use of symbols. A culture, or civilization, is but a particular kind of form (symbolic) which the biologic, life-perpetuating activities of a particular animal, man, assume.

Human behavior is symbolic behavior; if it is not symbolic, it is not human. The infant of the genus homo becomes a human being only as he is introduced into and participates in that superorganic order of phenomena which is culture. And the key to this world and the means of participation in it is—the symbol.

SYMBOLS AND VALUES

In this next excerpt, Dorothy Lee carries a little further the argument that White made. Whereas White was saying that symbols, with their constituent meanings, are *imposed* on reality, Lee is saying that, in the context of life, symbols have a much more organic relationship with the events they symbolize; they *infuse* reality with meaning and are not easily disentangled from the perceived event itself. The perceived object or event in its relation to human life, the person, and the symbol which apprehends it are all interrelated in a coherent whole, a "field" of articulating elements which are seen as "elements" only upon analysis. For the person, the value representing the event and its value implications are taken as they come—as the fabric of experience itself. In moments of great personal crisis, for example, such as (in, perhaps, older days) the soldier dying to save the regimental flag from violation, the psychological unity of the act is comprised of widely disparate "objective" elements: a tattered piece of cloth, an assemblage of individual persons, and a vague sense of a remembered heroic past. But so surcharged with emotion and value is every element that they combine into an organic whole—this is the kind of interrelation among the elements of symbol, value, and empirical events comprising organized human social life that Lee is stressing in her article. It presents a cogent and concrete discussion of the idea that the central core of "culture" is one of meaning and values, which is included as the excerpt that follows hers, one by Clyde Kluckhohn and A. L. Kroeber.

SYMBOLIZATION AND VALUE

DOROTHY D. LEE

I

In Western thought, a symbol is usually something which "represents," which "fits." We "apply" such symbols, as for example, when we "apply" words to things or names to persons; and these symbols then "stand for" the things to which they have been "applied." We even speak of "inventing" symbols; and our social scientists, worried over this age which has lost its values, speak of the need to "create" new symbols, so as to impart value to a meaningless life. This conception of the symbol as something distinct from and applicable to, is possible because of a mode of thinking according to which it is possible and desirable to abstract elements from a total situation, and to separate idea or form from substance. This conception is not a common one outside the province of Western civilization; and in many other cultures, it is inconceivable to make such a split. Here the symbol— the personal name, the picture, the emblem, the word—is an inextricable component of that which, to Western thinking, it represents. And indeed there is a widely held theory to the effect that this conception is due to an inability to abstract, that it is the mark of a low stage in the development of the mind, apparently resting in the assumption that when human beings are able to abstract, they do so. Yet the most recent scientific thought, the most highly "developed," rejects abstraction as impossible. According to the field theory, elements are considered as incapable of retaining their identity once removed from the field.

The thesis of this essay is that the symbol is in fact a part of a whole, a component of a field which also contains the so-called *thing*, as well as the process of symbolizing, and the apprehending individual. In this view, the concept of the symbol is close to the original meaning of the word in Greek. The *symbol*, the broken off part of the coin given to the parting friend, is not a separate ele-ment, but carries with it wherever it goes the whole coin in which it has participated, as well as the situation of hospitality during which the coin was broken in half; and when it is finally matched with the remaining half, the whole has value because the symbol has conveyed—not created or applied or evoked—this value. According to the view presented here, symbols are a part of the process whereby the experienced world, the world of perception and concept, is created out of the world of physical reality, the so-called given, the undifferentiated mass, or energy or set of relations.[1]

The system of symbolization, by means of which the individual punctuates, categorizes, shapes this physical reality, transforming it into the world of sensory perception and concept, is implicit in a variety of behavioral patterns within a culture. Language may be called such a system of symbols or acts of symbolization. It is not a system of names for passively sensed objects and relations already existing in the outer world; but neither does it fit experience into predetermined molds. It is a creative process, in which the individual has an agentive function; it is part of a field, which contains, in addition, the world of physical reality, the sensing and thinking individual, and the experienced reality. In this way, each word, each grammatical formation, is not an empty label to be applied; it has meaning, not because meaning has been arbitrarily assigned to it, but because it contains the meaning of the concrete situations in which it participates and has participated, and which it has helped create. With participation in situations the meaning of the symbol increases; and when the situation contains value, the symbol itself contains and conveys value. We have societies which proceed on this assumption, and systematically increase the value content of their symbols.

A discussion of language as a system through which the individual transforms physical reality

Reprinted with permission of publisher. From *Symbols and Values: An Initial Study*, Thirteenth Symposium of the Conference on Science, Philosophy and Religion, eds. Lyman Bryson, Louis Finkelstein, R. M. MacIver, and Richard McKeon, © 1954 by Harper and Brothers, New York, pp. 73-85.

[1]Underlying the discussion of the symbol in this essay, is my own stand that there exists a physical reality, containing man but independent of man's experience. It is beyond my power of philosophical reasoning, as well as beyond the scope of this essay, to expound or define this stand.

into experienced reality will clarify what I mean. By language, I do not mean only oral or written expression, but the entire system of codification underlying all verbal expression.

According to the classical view, the word is not the *thing*. This object that I hold in my hand is independent of the label I give it. It *is* not a pencil; I only assign to it the name pencil. What *it is*, is assumed to be independent of what *I call it*. Pencil is only a sound complex, a word for the reality, the *thing*. But the sound aspect of "pencil" is only one aspect of it. When I call this "pencil," I also classify it, as a substantive, a noun; I separate it as other than the fingers it elongates. Is it a *thing* before I call it a pencil? If it is not, then I am not "applying" a name to an already existing thing. This physical reality, this formless mass of energy, or set of relations, is delimited, is given form and substance, becomes the *thing* pencil, only through my calling it a pencil. In naming it, I give it recognition and a status in the categories of experienced reality. Calling it a pencil is the symbolic process through which I have created it; so that its name, or rather its naming, is a necessary part of itself, without which it is not this *thing*. And, conversely, its name cannot be separated from it as a self-contained element, it has no independent existence as symbol to be applied to an already existing *thing*. A Maidu Indian, for example, would probably have given no recognition to, or would not have delimited this reality into, the pencil as object; instead, he would have perceived the specific act of the hand—in this case the act of pointing with a pencil—and would have expressed this by means of a suffix which, attached to the verb, "to point," means: to-point-with-a-long-thin-instrument (such as a pencil, or a straight pipe, or a cigarette, or a stick). There is no reference to substance or to an object in this suffix. What is a pencil to me is a qualification or an attribute of an act for him, and belongs to a class with cigarettes and other objects of this shape only in so far as they elongate the hand making such an act possible. If this can be called a *thing*, then the symbolic process has at any rate helped create different *things* out of the physical reality.

I would say, therefore, that the classical *this* is not the *thing*, but the reality itself. At the point where it is a *thing*, it has already been made into a thing. The word and the thing are not discrete elements to be related by the speaker; they are

interdependent, incapable of existence apart from and without the act of the individual.

Again, when we teach our children the proper use of singular and plural, we assume that we are teaching them the proper verbal symbols for already existing singularity and plurality. But in this respect also, we find a difference in other cultures. There is evidence that the Wintu Indians recognize or perceive first of all humanity, human-being-ness, and only secondarily the delimited person. They make no distinction between singular and plural, and a cardinal number is never used with this generic, primary form of the word. They individuate, however, making a particular out of the original generic form of the word; out of *nop*[2]— deermeat or venison—they derive *nopum*—(a) deer; out of *se*—handness, hand—they derive *semum* —finger. Yet here also, unless the Wintu chooses to use a separate word meaning one or several or giving the definite number, there is nothing to show whether the word refers to singular or plural; *nopum* may be one or many individual deer; *semum* may be one or several fingers. When the Wintu want to show that two or more individuals are involved in the same situation, they do not use the *and* to express connection. They will say, "Mary we gathered wood," not: "Mary and I . . ."; "Coyote they mutually-grandmothered dwelled", not: "Coyote and his grandmother dwelled." *We* and *they* are primary; the specific, the singular, is derivative, and seems to be used only by way of clarification. That this is the way they perceive, the *thing* they create, is suggested by the fact that when they are referring to individuals who do not participate in the same situation already, that is, when they bring two individuals together in their statement, they do use the *and;* for example, "Shell *and* Fly (unrelated and living in different villages) each had a son." I find no instance, however, when the *and* is used to connect relatives, or individuals who are intimately connected, to put it in our terms.

The Wintu share this characteristic with many other cultures. Raymond Firth, reporting on the Tikopia of the South Pacific, has to explain c n occurrences and terms of speech which are to ly unacceptable to Western minds. There was one such occasion during a ceremonial cycle, when he

---

[2]In accordance with the non-technical character of this paper, special phonetic symbols are avoided.

saw several women assembled in a house. He asked a friend what the women were doing there, and received the answer: "The Atua Fafine (the chief Goddess) it is she." For all his efforts, it is impossible for him to make this sound logical and acceptable to people who know that ten women are plural; to people who learn from early childhood that the singular comes first, before the plural; who, when they decline and conjugate start from one and going on to many, who soon learn that one plus one equals two, and later learn to speak of the one and the many, implying the distinction and the hierarchy even when they are questioning it.

When we try to translate terms such as brother and sister into non-Indo-European languages, we become aware of the share which our linguistic categories have in creating the *thing*, the so-called referent of the word. Take the word for brother, for example. In English, its referent is a "male considered in his relation to another having the same parents." Is the individual to whom I apply this word the *thing*? If the word, "brother," merely "stands for" an already existing *thing*, then I should be able to translate this word successfully into other languages. Only the sound complex will vary; the referent will remain the same. But when I try to translate this word into Wintu, I find that, in the perceived world of these people there is no such *thing*. I need three words for this one referent, and one of these words has in addition reference to something which I recognize as a different *thing*. I need to say *labei*—"Male considered in relation to a younger male having the same parents," or *liekut* —"male considered in relation to an older male ...''; or I must say *soh*—"male or female considered in relation to an individual of opposite sex having the same parents." If my word, "brother," refers to a given, a thing existing irrespective of me and my naming, then the Wintu and the Turks and the Andamanese and a large number of other societies perceive falsely; but how can I prove that I am right and all these others are wrong?

There is further the question of relations; are these found in nature and does the relational word then merely refer to an already existing relation? According to Western thought, these objects are *on* the table; the word, "on," refers to the present relationship between objects and table. Yet a Wintu who saw this might very well say, "The table lumps-severally." At any rate, he does say, "The hill

lumps," when I would have said, "There is a house on the hill," or "a rock on the hill"; and he says, "The hill lumps-severally," when I would have said, "People have spread their blankets over the bushes to sun them." In the face of this it is difficult to maintain that the *thing*, the perceived, is the same in the two cases. In one case, through the process of symbolization, two disparate objects and a relation are created; in another, a continuity.

I do not mean to imply by all this that communication is impossible. Ethnographers in the field have found it possible and even easy to explain what they mean by the word, "brother," and to understand what their informants meant by their terms for individuals having the same parents. What this implies, however, is that, for true communication, we cannot assume as a matter of course that our classifications are the same for people of all cultures; that translation is merely the substitution of one sound-complex for another. Once we are aware that the basis of classification is not a universal one, we can find out whether our different words do name the same thing, and if they do not, we can qualify our word. With such qualification, the English term can be understood; but I doubt whether, without repeated usage in relevant situations, this word will convey immediately, for the new user, the same *thing* which it does for the English-speaking ethnographer.

II

Before I continue with the discussion of the symbol, I should be clear that, to my mind, nothing of what I have said applies to the metaphor. Only when the symbol is defined as something which is made to stand for something else can the two be thought of as similar. There is further the strong possibility that, whereas symbolization is a universal process, the existence of metaphors is limited to those cultures where the definition of the self is that of something discrete and other to everything else. In cultures where the self is not conceived of as entirely disparate from the other, the word which seems to us to be a metaphor is probably only a means of pointing out the participation of one thing in another. When a rejected Wintu lover sings a song calling his love a grizzly bear, he seems of course, to be speaking metaphorically. Yet perhaps he is reminding her that she *is* to some extent grizzly bear. Certainly, in the myths it is impossible to tell at what point Grizzly Bear is a bear, and at what point she is a woman—and, in fact, the question seems irrelevant in that context. Grosbeak turns easily into Grasshopper, Coyote becomes many coyotes; so to call a grasshopper a bird, or a deer a herd, would not be to use a metaphor. Participation of self in what is for us the other is so much a matter of course, that the Wintu speak of a man who is menstruating (in respect of) his wife, or is ill (in respect of) his son. Again, when the Trobriand garden magician says:

Thy head taytu is the millipede shooting along
Thy leaves are the millipede shooting along. . . .
(and)
The yam lifts, it-is-a-bushhen-nest-lifting
The yam lifts, it-is-an-earthoven-lifting. . . .

I believe he is not speaking metaphorically, but is either imparting these qualities as ingredients into the yam, or reminding the yam that it in fact partakes of millipedeness, bushhenness, etc. At least, such an explanation is in keeping with Trobriand thought as we know it.

I believe, however, that is is often true in Western society as well. Those of us who do not conceive of the self as disparate, such as our poets, for example, are probably speaking symbolically when they appear to be using metaphors.

The application of metaphor is a process whereby an already existing symbol or *thing* is made to stand for another already existing symbol or thing. Thus it differs fundamentally from the creative process of symbolization.

III

I have tried to establish that the symbol is not a thing, but that it is rather a point in a creative process, that of symbolization, whereby the physical reality is transformed into the *thing*, the experienced reality; that the symbol conveys the meaning of the situation in which it participates, and has no existence and no meaning apart from this situation. When we study societies other than our own, we find that the cultural behavior can often be understood only on the assumption that here, in fact, symbols are regarded as being, rather than standing for, the *thing*. For example, according to Wilson who writes the section on Egypt in *Before Philosophy*, the priest in ancient Egypt, the symbol of the God, actually *was* God; so that when he was hon-

ored or insulted, the God was affected directly through the symbol, not indirectly through a representative. Wilson calls this principle of the participation of the symbol in the *thing*, the principle of consubstantiation. Because of this principle, he holds, it was possible to put small models of loaves of bread into a tomb and know that the dead was eating actual bread. Among primitive societies, we have the Trobrianders, among whom the garden magician performs a magical act in the village garden before every secular agricultural act on the part of the rest of the village group. He works on one standard plot, and only in one corner of this; yet, when he rubs the small corner with his handful of weeds, talking to it persuasively, he is treating the entire village garden. All the garden land has been persuaded to produce good yams.

The Tiv of Nigeria furnish a case where a large group of people perceived the *thing* in its symbol. The case is related by Akiga, a Tiv with a Western education, who was skeptical of the reports of magical killings which he had heard. At one time he heard that his father had killed and flayed one of his (Akiga's) many sisters, and given her skin to her brother to wear on the occasion of a special ceremonial dance. Akiga went to the dance to see what would happen, and there he saw his brother dancing, holding a woman's filter and his father's pipe. The following day, the people who had gone to the dance were full of the story of how Hilehaan had danced in his sister's skin. They were not trying to deceive anyone; they were talking among themselves, discussing the important event they had witnessed. They had obviously perceived the-skin-of-Hilehaan's-sister (in the filter) who-had-been-flayed-by-her-father (in the father's pipe). Only the Western minded Akiga saw just a filter and a pipe.

In Western civilization, the difference in the conception of the symbol as representing or as participating, constitutes one of the main differences of doctrine between the Catholic Church and most of the Protestant sects. The question at issue is whether, at communion, the bread *represents* the flesh of Christ, or *is* the flesh of Christ.

When "primitives" are said to be incapable of distinguishing the word from the *thing*, or to confuse an object with its name, I suspect that what we have is rather the recognition of this participation of the symbol in the *thing*. When we reflect on our own use of words, we find that with us also, words do more than designate; they have more or less meaning, according to the situations in our personal lives in which they have participated. For example, when I teach, I can use terms for the function of evacuation and for sexual activity freely, so long as I confine myself to Latin words. Otherwise there is discomfort and emotional tension. This does not mean that the Latin terms do not carry the situation in which they have participated. They do; but what they convey is the passage in the textbook, or the paragraph in the dictionary; and these are eminently appropriate to the classroom. When I use the word, "micturition," it carries with it, perhaps, a number of defining words, but not the concrete act. Anglo-Saxon terms for sexual activity would heighten the emotional atmosphere and be very disturbing in the classroom. But not so the Latin terms; they may have participated in love-making in the experience of the Romans, but nobody makes love in Latin nowadays.

This is true also of the words for death or dying. Those of us who have experienced death tend to avoid the symbolizing word in speaking of these situations, because the word conveys the unbearable situation. The need for a term is filled then by a number of substitute terms, such as "passed away," or by differently phrased sentences which avoid the charged word. Yet none of us feels the urge to do this when speaking of people we have not loved. Julius Caesar died; he did not pass away.

IV

The symbol thus gets its meaning through participation in the concrete situation; and it grows in meaning, and even changes in meaning, with each participation. Before it functions in individual experience, it holds no meaning. To the child who hears a word for the first time, the word contains the meaning of the situation in which he hears it, including the mother's tone of voice, her gestures and facial expression. To someone learning the use of a word from a dictionary or from a classroom definition, the word holds only whatever value is present in this situation; probably none. But once the individual uses the newly learned word, once a concrete situation is experienced through the agency of the word, the word contains the value of this symbolized situation. So the symbol, in this case the word, is a thing in process, containing and conveying the value which has become embodied

in it, and communicating it in so far as there is community of experience between speaker and hearer.

When I choose a name for my child, for example, I may only choose it because it sounds well with the surname. Perhaps the first time I use the name, I am actually only "applying" it to my newborn daughter. But from this time on, the name is not just a set of syllables, an empty designation. From now on it contains Anna-ness; it is a name not to be taken in vain. This is an attitude which we have officially about the name of God. Yet we do take God's name in vain, and in situations where we would not welcome his presence, apparently firm in our belief that the name does not convey the *thing*.

Those of us who are concerned with the meaningless life of our industrial society speak of the need for introducing value through creating new symbols. But symbols in themselves have no value, and they cannot convey value to a situation. Only after they have participated in a situation can they have value, and then only in so far as the situation itself holds value.

V

In conclusion, I shall speak about the Bella Coola of British Columbia whose culture is based upon the definition of the symbol as I have presented it here, and who proceed deliberately and carefully to incorporate value in their symbols through having them participate in situations which they imbue with value for this purpose.

Among the Bella Coola, an individual is not complete without a name. He has no definition, no validity, no status without a name. He cannot become a chief, or a hunter, or a carpenter without the necessary symbolic ingredient. The names are embodied in family myths, and carry with them certain prerogatives with which they become imbued at the special mythical occurrence during which they originated. Names do not "stand for." When they have become duly validated and belong to a person as the symbolic component, they can be loaned over a period of time, or rented out, or given away as a gift; and now the name is no more part of the man to whom it had belonged up to now. At death, a man's names die with him. They are now in the burial ground, empty of value.

An infant lacks value as well as validity and

social place at birth. If he is the child of a slave, he has minus value, unless this has been "washed away" in the womb through a special ceremonial giftgiving. When a child is born, a family name is resurrected to be given to the newborn. But the name at this time is "as nothing." It is weak; and the prerogatives it contains cannot be validly assumed. It is necessary to give validity to the act of giving the name, and to infuse value into the name.

For the Bella Coola, the process of validation of this introduction of the symbolic component consists of displaying the whole situation—the name with the embodied prerogatives and the myth from which they derive—in a structured public situation; and in this display, in the singing of the song which the prerogative contains, in the recounting of that portion of the myth in which it is embedded, the symbol participates in the situation. But, for the symbol to acquire value, the situation must have value; and the Bella Coola proceed to imbue the situation with value. The creation of value consists of giving a gift; and the value created is exactly equal to the value of the gift. When a name is given to a child, or assumed by an adult, and thereafter whenever any of its ingredients are publicly displayed, gifts are given away. As the gift is given, it is "emptied" of value; it "becomes nothing." Its value "flows away" into the name which is being publicly displayed. The gifts make the name "bright," "strong," "heavy," "firm," "clear," "upright"; and the strengthening of the name is the strengthening of the individual, so no clear distinction is made between the two. Occasions for strengthening a name or for assuming a new name, and particularly of those which carry with them the prerogative of a special seat, require the accumulation of large amounts of property, and often include a number of specific ceremonials—such as the dance of the returned dead—and necessitate the invitation of widely scattered guests, so that the display may be sufficiently public. Eventually, as the occasions increase in extent, as a man's wife "drags across" enough names—prerogatives properly validated—and as enough other gifts have been given away to "shield him from the fire," to "make him strong and heavy as he moves about the earth," to "make his seat soft," to "shore him up so he does not wobble," the occasions become extensive enough to be potlatches. After giving four potlatches, a man has accumulated enough value inside himself

to be considered a chief; now "he is so strong, he can go where he will." In all this, it is never clear whether reference is made to the symbolic component or to the whole individual, the *thing*.[3]

The exercise of a craft or a profession is the display of a prerogative, and must always be validated; and with each such display, the value of the prerogative is increased. A man can have the physical skill of hunting, the knowledge and judgment necessary, but he cannot be effective, he cannot be a hunter without the duly validated symbolic component. On the other hand, as the prerogative is strengthened through repeated display, it may become eventually stronger than the rest of the man, than, for example, his (material) knowledge. This was particularly the case of the profession of warrior. Those who had the prerogative of being warriors, had to kill upon request—without fee, since this was the display of the prerogative McIlwraith tells the story of one such warrior, who was sick of killing, yet could not stop, as his prerogative had become too strong for him through his repeated killings. In the end, he retired into a cave one winter, and his dead body was found there the following spring; this was the only way he could stop killing.

A precisely formulated case of creating value is found in the so-called coppers of the Bella Coola. These are thin pieces of copper of a special shape and size, which are displayed at public occasions, and eventually are destroyed to "make bone" for a returned dead relative. A copper, whose recognized value is known as three hundred dollars is broken in two, or thrown into the fire; its value flows out of it and into the dead. Now the copper, which a minute ago was full of value, is completely empty of value.

Presently the owner of the copper picks it up and gives it to a poor man, who cleans and straightens

<hr />

[3]It should be made clear here that, for value to be accumulated in the name, no return gifts must be given. To do so would be a deliberate act of destruction. However, other gifts are in fact also given by the individual, increasing his prestige, his non-symbolic aspect. Such gifts do not "become nothing." The giving of such a gift diminishes the recipient by as much as it increases the giver. If the gift is not returned, the recipient remains diminished in being; if an equal gift is returned, he recovers only his original stature. It is to his interest then, not only to return the gift, but to exceed the received gift as much as he can, even to double it. When he does so, the original giver becomes diminished, and proceeds to give a larger gift, as soon as he can do so. These are not validating gifts, and need not form a part of the potlatch, though they usually do so; and they are clearly distinguished from those gifts whose value "flows away" into the symbol.

and repairs it and sells it to a chief for perhaps twenty dollars which can be spent only for acquiring food to be given away publicly. That is, the twenty dollars are given away as a gift to infuse value into the copper, which now contains value to the degree of twenty dollars. The chief now proceeds to increase the value of the copper. Perhaps he gives it a name with the appropriate public display; and gives away fifty dollars to validate the display. He next invites guests, displays the copper, has it passed from hand to hand—has it fully participate in the event—and gives away gifts to the amount of eighty dollars. He does this gradually, for all growth is a matter of time. He cannot merely assign a value to it; nor can he infuse value into it all at once. Eventually, when enough value has been imbued, so that the copper can function at a dance of the returned dead, the owner flings it in the fire, and again it is emptied of its value.

The white traders quickly spotted the importance of the coppers, and before long had flooded the market with them. They thought of them naturally as having value, or as representing value; perhaps as analogous to our paper money. But the coppers neither had nor lacked value in themselves. They were symbols only in the sense in which the symbol has been presented here; they acquired and conveyed only the value inherent in the situation in which they participated. No one wanted to buy a copper unless he was ready to go through the long and expensive procedure of infusing it with value. So the flood of coppers brought no inflation; the value of coppers neither could rise nor fall, through such manipulation. Being true symbols, they could acquire valid existence and value only through participation in meaningful situations.

BIBLIOGRAPHY

Roland B. Dixon, "Maidu," *Handbook of American Indian Languages*, edited by Franz Boas, Washington, 1911, bulletin 40, part I.

Akiga's Story, the Tiv tribe as seen by one of its members, translated and annotated by Rupert East, Oxford University Press, London, 1939.

Raymond Firth, *The Work of the Gods in Tikopia*, Lund, Humphries & Co., Ltd., London, 1940, 2 vols.

Dorothy D. Lee, "Linguistic Reflection of Wintu Thought," *International Journal of American Linguistics*, 1944, X, pp. 181–187.

"Notes on the Conception of the Self Among the Wintu Indians," *Journal of Abnormal and Social Psychology*, 1950, XLV, pp. 538–543.

"Being and Value in a Primitive Culture," *Journal of Philosophy*, 1949, XLVI, pp. 401–415.

T. F. McIlwraith, *The Bella Coola Indians*, The University of Toronto Press, Toronto, 1948, 2 vols.

Bronislaw Malinowski, *Coral Gardens and Their Magic*, American Book Co., New York, 1935, 2 vols.

John A. Wilson, "Egypt," *The Intellectual Adventure of Ancient Man*, Henri Frankfort and others, The University of Chicago Press, Chicago, 1946.

CULTURE AS VALUES

This excerpt is from a monograph that is an important milestone in the analysis of the meanings of the word and concept, "culture." Following an inventory of the many different usages of the word, Kluckhohn and Kroeber, outstanding world figures in anthropology, discuss the several dimensions of meaning involved in its various applications. They present also their preferred (because it is the most profitable and useful) conception. A central strand in such a conception is that culture is a framework or system of meaning which, the product of a collective past, is imposed upon an oncoming social reality. Culture "programs," as it were, much of individual and social behavior; it gives the standards and criteria by which objective reality is accorded significance and value, or, on the other hand, considered irrelevant and devoid of substance. In this conception, "culture" is seen not as "custom" itself, not the actual patterned behavior; but as the standards, the bases of comparison, the framework of preferences and orientations by which behavior and events in nature are judged.

SIGNIFICANCE AND VALUES

A. L. KROEBER and CLYDE KLUCKHOHN

We come now to those properties of culture which seem most distinctive of it and most important: its significance and its values. Perhaps we should have said "significance or values," for the two are difficult to keep separated and perhaps constitute no more than somewhat different aspects of the same thing.

First of all, significance does not mean merely ends. It is not teleological in the traditional sense. Significance and values are of the essence of the organization of culture. It is true that human endeavor is directed toward ends; but those ends are shaped by the values of culture; and the values are felt as intrinsic, not as means. And the values are variable and relative, not predetermined and eternal, though certain universals of human biology and of human social life appear to have brought about a few constants or near-constants that cut across cultural differences. Also the values are part of nature, not outside it. They are the products of men, of men having bodies and living in societies, and are the structural essence of the culture of these societies of men. Finally, values and significances are "intangibles" which are "subjective" in that they can be internally experienced, but are also objective in their expressions, embodiments, or results.

Psychology deals with individual minds, and most values are the products of social living, become part of cultures, and are transmitted along with the rest of culture. It is true that each new or changed value takes its concrete origin (as do all aspects of culture) in the psychological processes of some particular individual. It is also true that each individual holds his own idiosyncratic form of the various cultural values he has internalized. Such matters are proper subjects of investigation for the psychologist, but values in general have a predominantly historical and sociocultural dimension. Psychology deals mainly with processes or mechanisms, and values are mental content. The processes by which individuals acquire, reject, or modify values are questions for psychological enquiry—or for collaboration between psychologists and anthropologists or sociologists. The main trend, however, is evidenced by the fact that social psychology, that bridge between psychology and sociology, recognizes a correspondence between values and attitudes, but has for the most part concerned itself, as social psychology, only with the attitudes and has abstracted from the values; much as individual psychology investigates the process of learning but not knowledge, that which is learned.

Values are primarily social and cultural: social in scope, parts of culture in substance and form. There are individual variants of cultural values and also certain highly personal goals and standards developed in the vicissitudes of private experience and reinforced by rewards in using them. But these latter are not ordinarily called values, and they must in any case be discriminated from collective values. Or, the place of a value in the lives of some persons may be quite different from that in the cultural scheme. Thus day-dreaming or autoerotic practices may come to acquire high value for an individual while being ignored, ridiculed, or condemned socioculturally. These statements must not be construed as implying that values have a substantive existence outside of individual minds, or that a collective mind containing them has any such substantive existence. The locus or place of residence of values or anything else cultural is in individual persons and nowhere else. But a value becomes a group value, as a habit becomes a custom or individuals a society, only with collective participation.

This collective quality of values accounts for their frequent anonymity, their seeming the spontaneous result of mass movement, as in morals, fashion responses, speech. Though the very first inception of any value or new part thereof must take place in an individual mind, nevertheless this attachment is mostly lost very quickly as socialization gets under way, and in many values has been long since forgotten. The strength of the value is, however, not impaired by this forgetting, but rather increased. The collectivization may also tend to decrease overt, explicit awareness of the value itself.

Reprinted with permission of publisher. From *Culture: A Critical Review of Concepts and Definitions*, Papers of the Peabody Museum of American Archaeology and Ethnology, Harvard University, vol. 47, no. 1 (1952), 171–74.

It maintains its hold and strength, but covertly, as an implicit a priori, as a non-rational folkway, as a "configuration" rather than a "pattern" in Kluck-hohn's 1941 distinction. This means in turn that functioning with relation to the value or standard becomes automatic, as in correct speech; or compulsive as in manners and fashion; or endowed with high-potential emotional charge as often in morals and religion; in any event, not fully conscious and not fully rational or self-interested.

Values are important in that they provide foci for patterns of organization for the material of cultures. They give significance to our understanding of cultures. In fact values provide the only basis for the fully intelligible comprehension of culture, because the actual organization of all cultures is primarily in terms of their values. This becomes apparent as soon as one attempts to present the picture of a culture without reference to its values. The account becomes an unstructured, meaningless assemblage of items having relation to one another only through coexistence in locality and moment—an assemblage that might as profitably be arranged alphabetically as in any other order; a mere laundry list.

Equally revealing of the signifiance of values is an attempt to present the description of one culture through the medium of the value patterns of another. In such a presentation, the two cultures will of course come out alike in structure. But since some of the content of the culture being described will not fit the model of the other culture, it will either have to be omitted from the description, or it will stultify this model by not fitting it, or it will be distorted in order to make it seem to fit. This is exactly what happened while newly discovered languages were being described in terms of Latin grammar.

For the same reason one need not take too seriously the criticism sometimes made of ethnographers that they do not sufficiently distinguish the ideal culture from the actual culture of a society: that they should specify what exists only ideally, at all points specify the numbers of their witnesses, the personalities of their informants, and so on. These rules of technical procedure are sound enough, but they lose sight of the main issue, which is not validation of detail but sound conception of basic structure. This basic structure, and with it the significant functioning, are much more nearly given by the so-called ideal culture than by the actual

one. This actual culture can indeed be so over-documented that the values and patterns are buried. It might even be said without undue exaggeration that—adequate information being assumed as available—the description of the ideal culture has more significance than the actual, if a choice has to be made. If the picture of the ideal culture is materially unsound or concocted, it will automatically raise doubts. But if the picture of the actual culture makes no point or meaning, it may be hard to inject more meaning from the statistical or personalized data available. In short, the "ideal" version of a culture is what gives orientation to the "actual" version.

Another way of saying this is that in the collection of information on a culture, the inquirer must proceed with empathy in order to perceive the cardinal values as points of crystallization. Of course this does not mean that inquiry should begin and end with empathy. Evidence and analysis of evidence are indispensable. But the very selection of evidence that will be significant is dependent on insight exercised during the process of evidence-collecting. What corresponds in whole-culture studies to the "hypothesis tested by evidence" in the experimental sciences is precisely a successful recognition of the value-laden patterns through which the culture is organized.

Values and significances are of course intangibles, viewed subjectively; but they find objective expression in observable forms of culture and their relations—or if one prefer to put it so, in patterned behavior and products of behavior.

It is this subjective side of values that led to their being long tabooed as improper for consideration by natural science. Instead, they were relegated to a special set of intellectual activities called "the humanities," included in the "spiritual science" of the Germans. Values were believed to be eternal because they were God-given, or divinely inspired; or at least discovered by that soul-part of man which partakes somewhat of divinity, as his body and other bodies and the tangibles of the world do not. A new and struggling science, as little advanced beyond physics, astronomy, anatomy, and the rudiments of physiology as Western science still was only two centuries ago, might cheerfully concede this reservation of the remote and unexplored territory of values to the philosophers and the theologians and limit itself to what it could treat mechanistically. But a science of total nature cannot permanently cede anything which it can deal with by any of its procedures of analysis of phenomena and interpretation of evidence. The phenomena of culture are "as phenomenal" as those of physical or vital existence. And if it is true that values provide the organizing relations of culture, they must certainly be included in the investigation of culture.

"CULTURE" AS ORIENTATION: AN EXAMPLE

For the last several excerpts we have been considering a particular kind of use of the word and concept, "culture"—that which emphasizes culture as an abstract framework of standards for choice that man in social life brings to the situation. Such a framework, which is one of value and belief, is inherently tied in with man's capacities for the symbolic process, for visualizing, formulating, and creating a world of events and objects that is superimposed over the world "objectively" seen and is compelling in its influence on behavior. But culture conceived in this way as a system of symbols representing emotion-laden values and beliefs—a pattern of preferred choice among alternative kinds of behavior, which acts as something of a "program" for social reality (to use the computer metaphor)—is an abstract notion. Let's tie it down with a selection that illustrates this kind of meaning for the concept of culture. The following excerpt is from an essay by Geertz, who deals with a particular institutional segment of human social life, religion. But the kind of use he makes of "culture as a symbol system" can easily be extended to other institutional areas, such as politics, kinship, or the economic sphere. Remember now that we are considering the *cultural dimension* (or cultural *system*) as one part of an ongoing concrete reality, that is, religion as comprising a belief-and-value system embedded in social relationships. I make this point now because in a moment we will turn to more consideration of the cultural system as one interlocking part of a *socio*cultural system. For now, however, let us get from Geertz a sense of how pervasive and directive a cultural system can be, as seen with the content of religious symbols and religious conceptions.

RELIGION AS A CULTURAL SYSTEM

CLIFFORD GEERTZ

The term 'culture' has by now acquired a certain aura of ill-repute in social anthropological circles because of the multiplicity of its referents and the studied vagueness with which it has all too often been invoked. (Though why it should suffer more for these reasons than 'social structure' or 'personality' is something I do not entirely understand.) In any case, the culture concept to which I adhere has neither multiple referents nor, so far as I can see, any unusual ambiguity: it denotes an historically transmitted pattern of meanings embodied in symbols, a system of inherited conceptions expressed in symbolic forms by means of which men com-

Reprinted with permission of publisher. From *Anthropological Approaches to the Study of Religion*, ed. Michael Banton, © 1966 by Tavistock Press, London.

municate, perpetuate, and develop their knowledge about and attitudes toward life. Of course, terms such as 'meaning', 'symbol', and 'conception' cry out for explication. But that is precisely where the widening, the broadening, and the expanding come in. If Langer (1962, p. 55) is right that 'the concept of meaning, in all its varieties, is the dominant philosophical concept of our time', that 'sign, symbol, denotation, signification, communication . . . are our [intellectual] stock in trade', it is perhaps time that social anthropology, and particularly that part of it concerned with the study of religion, became aware of the fact. . . . As we are to deal with meaning, let us begin with a paradigm: viz. that sacred symbols function to synthesize a people's ethos the tone, character, and quality of their life, its moral and aesthetic style and mood—and their world-view—the picture they have of the way things in sheer actuality are, their most comprehensive ideas of order (Geertz, 1958). In religious belief and practice a group's ethos is rendered intellectually reasonable by being shown to represent a way of life ideally adapted to the actual state of affairs the world-view describes, while the world-view is rendered emotionally convincing by being presented as an image of an actual state of affairs peculiarly well arranged to accommodate such a way of life. This confrontation and mutual confirmation has two fundamental effects. On the one hand, it objectivizes moral and aesthetic preferences by depicting them as the imposed conditions of life implicit in a world with a particular structure, as mere common sense given the unalterable shape of reality. On the other, it supports these received beliefs about the world's body by invoking deeply felt moral and aesthetic sentiments as experiential evidence for their truth. Religious symbols formulate a basic congruence between a particular style of life and a specific (if, most often, implicit) metaphysic, and in so doing sustain each with the borrowed authority of the other.

Phrasing aside, this much may perhaps be granted. The notion that religion tunes human actions to an envisaged cosmic order and projects images of cosmic order onto the plane of human experience is hardly novel. But it is hardly investigated either, so that we have very little idea of how, in empirical terms, this particular miracle is accomplished. We just know that it is done, annually, weekly, daily, for some people almost hourly; and we have an enormous ethnographic literature to

demonstrate it. But the theoretical framework which would enable us to provide an analytic account of it, an account of the sort we can provide for lineage segmentation, political succession, labor exchange, or the socialization of the child, does not exist.

Let us, therefore, reduce our paradigm to a definition, for, although it is notorious that definitions establish nothing, in themselves they do, if they are carefully enough constructed, provide a useful orientation, or reorientation, of thought, such that an extended unpacking of them can be an effective way of developing and controlling a novel line of inquiry. They have the useful virtue of explicitness: they commit themselves in a way discursive prose, which, in this field especially, is always liable to substitute rhetoric for argument, does not. Without further ado, then, a *religion* is:

> (1) a system of symbols which acts to (2) establish powerful, pervasive, and long-lasting moods and motivations in men by (3) formulating conceptions of a general order of existence and (4) clothing these conceptions with such an aura of factuality that (5) the moods and motivations seem uniquely realistic.

1. *a system of symbols which acts to . . .*

Such a tremendous weight is being put on the term 'symbol' here that our first move must be to decide with some precision what we are going to mean by it. This is no easy task, for, rather like 'culture', 'symbol' has been used to refer to a great variety of things, often a number of them at the same time. In some hands it is used for anything which signifies something else to someone: dark clouds are the symbolic precursors of an oncoming rain. In others it is used only for explicitly conventional signs of one sort or another: a red flag is a symbol of danger, a white of surrender. In others it is confined to something which expresses in an oblique and figurative manner that which cannot be stated in a direct and literal one, so that there are symbols in poetry but not in science, and symbolic logic is misnamed. In yet others, however (Langer, 1953, 1960, 1962), it is used for any object, act, event, quality, or relation which serves as a vehicle for a conception—the conception is the symbol's 'meaning'—and that is the approach I shall follow here. The number 6, written, imagined, laid out as a row of stones, or even punched into the program tapes of a computer is a symbol. But so also is the Cross, talked about, visualized, shaped worriedly in air or fondly fingered at the neck, the expanse of painted canvas called 'Guernica' or the bit of painted stone called a churinga, the word 'reality' or even the morpheme '-ing.' They are all symbols, or at least symbolic elements, because they are tangible formulations of notions, abstractions from experience fixed in perceptible forms, concrete embodiments of ideas, attitudes, judgements, longings, or beliefs. To undertake the study of cultural activity—activity in which symbolism forms the positive content—is thus not to abandon social analysis for a Platonic cave of shadows, to enter into a mentalistic world of introspective psychology or, worse, speculative philosophy, and wander there forever in a haze of 'Cognitions', 'Affections', 'Conations', and other elusive entities. Cultural acts, the construction, apprehension, and utilization of symbolic forms, are social events like any other; they are as public as marriage and as observable as agriculture.

They are not, however, exactly the same thing; or, more precisely, the symbolic dimension of social events is, like the psychological, itself theoretically abstractable from those events as empirical totalities. There is still, to paraphrase a remark of Kenneth Burke's (1941, p. 9), a difference between building a house and drawing up a plan for building a house, and reading a poem about having children by marriage is not quite the same thing as having children by marriage. Even though the building of the house may proceed under the guidance of the plan or—a less likely occurrence—the having of children may be motivated by a reading of the poem, there is something to be said for not confusing our traffic with symbols with our traffic with objects or human beings, for these latter are not in themselves symbols, however often they may function as such.[1] No matter how deeply interfused the cultural, the social, and the psychological may be in the everyday life of houses, farms, poems, and marriages, it is useful to distinguish them in analysis, and, so doing, to isolate the generic traits of each against the normalized background of the other two (Parsons & Shils, 1951).

So far as culture patterns, i.e. systems or complexes of symbols, are concerned, the generic trait which is of first importance for us here is that they are extrinsic sources of information (Geertz, 1964a). By 'extrinsic', I mean only that—unlike genes, for example—they lie outside the boundaries of the individual organism as such in that intersubjective world of common understandings into which all human individuals are born, in which they pursue their separate careers, and which they leave persisting behind them after they die (Schutz, 1962). By 'sources of information', I mean only that—like genes—they provide a blueprint or template in terms of which processes external to themselves can be given a definite form (Horowitz, 1956). As the order of bases in a strand of DNA forms a coded program, a set of instructions, or a recipe, for the synthesization of the structurally complex proteins which shape organic functioning, so culture patterns provide such programs for the institution of the social and psychological processes which shape public behavior. Though the sort of information and the mode of its transmission are vastly different in the two cases, this comparison of gene and symbol is more than a strained analogy of the familiar 'social heredity' sort. It is actually a substantial relationship, for it is precisely the fact that genetically programmed processes are so highly generalized in men, as compared with lower animals; that culturally programmed ones are so important, only because human behavior is so loosely determined by intrinsic sources of information that extrinsic sources are so vital (Geertz, 1962). To build a dam a beaver needs only an appropriate site and the proper materials—his mode of procedure is shaped by his physiology. But man, whose genes are silent on the building trades, needs also a conception of what it is to build a dam, a conception he can get only from some symbolic source—a blueprint, a textbook, or a string of speech by someone who already knows how dams are built, or, of course, from manipulating graphic or linguistic elements in such a way as to attain for himself a conception of what dams are and how they are built.

This point is sometimes put in the form of an argument that cultural patterns are 'models', that they are sets of symbols whose relations to one another 'model' relations among entities, processes or what-have-you in physical, organic, social, or psychological systems by 'paralleling', 'imitating', or 'simulating' them (Craik, 1952). The term 'model' has, however, two senses—an 'of' sense and a 'for' sense—and though these are but aspects of the same basic concept they are very much worth distinguishing for analytic purposes. In the first, what is stressed is the manipulation of symbol structures so as to bring them, more or less closely, into parallel with the pre-established non-symbolic system, as when we grasp how dams work by developing a theory of hydraulics or constructing a flow chart. The theory or chart models physical relationships in such a way—i.e. by expressing their structure in synoptic form—as to render them apprehensible: it is a model *of* 'reality'. In the second, what is stressed is the manipulation of the non-symbolic systems in terms of the relationships expressed in the symbolic, as when we construct a dam according to the specifications implied in an hydraulic theory or the conclusions drawn from a flow chart. Here, the theory is a model under whose guidance physical relationships are organized: it is a model *for* 'reality'. For psychological and social systems, and for cultural models that we would not ordinarily refer to as 'theories', but rather as 'doctrines', 'melodies', or 'rites', the case is in no way different. Unlike genes, and other non-symbolic information sources, which are only models *for*, not models *of*, culture patterns have an intrinsic double aspect: they give meaning, i.e. objective conceptual form, to social and psychological reality both by shaping themselves to it and by shaping it to themselves.

It is, in fact, this double aspect which sets true symbols off from other sorts of significative forms. Models *for* are found, as the gene example suggests, through the whole order of nature, for wherever there is a communication of pattern such programs are, in simple logic, required. Among animals, imprint learning is perhaps the most striking example, because what such learning involves is the automatic presentation of an appropriate sequence of behavior by a model animal in the presence of a learning animal which serves, equally automatically, to call out and stabilize a certain set of responses genetically built into the learning animal (Lorenz, 1952). The communicative dance of two bees, one of which has found nectar and the other of which seeks it, is another, somewhat different, more complexly coded example (von Frisch, 1962). Craik (1952) has even suggested that the thin trickle of water which first finds its way down from a mountain spring to the sea and smooths a little channel for the greater volume of water that follows after it plays a sort of model *for* function. But models *of*—linguistic, graphic, mechanical, natural, etc. processes which function not to provide sources of information in terms of which other processes can be patterned, but to represent those patterned processes as such, to express their structure in an alternative medium—are much rarer and may perhaps be confined, among living animals, to

man. The perception of the structural congruence between one set of processes, activities, relations, entities, etc. and another set for which it acts as a program, so that the program can be taken as a representation, or conception—a symbol—of the programmed, is the essence of human thought. The inter-transposability of models *for* and models *of* which symbolic formulation makes possible is the distinctive characteristic of our mentality.

2. . . . *to establish powerful, pervasive, and long-lasting moods and motivations in men by . . .*

So far as religious symbols and symbol systems are concerned this inter-transposability is clear. The endurance, courage, independence, perseverance, and passionate willfulness in which the vision quest practices the Plains Indian are the same flamboyant virtues by which he attempts to live: while achieving a sense of revelation he stabilizes a sense of direction (Lowie, 1924). The consciousness of defaulted obligation, secreted guilt, and, when a confession is obtained, public shame in which Manus' seance rehearses him are the same sentiments that underlie the sort of duty ethic by which his property-conscious society is maintained: the gaining of an absolution involves the forging of a conscience (Fortune, 1935). And the same self-discipline which rewards a Javanese mystic staring fixedly into the flame of a lamp with what he takes to be an intimation of divinity drills him in that rigorous control of emotional expression which is necessary to a man who would follow a quietistic style of life (Geertz, 1960). Whether one sees the conception of a personal guardian spirit, a family tutelary or an immanent God as synoptic formulations of the character of reality or as templates for producing reality with such a character seems largely arbitrary, a matter of which aspect, the model *of* or model *for*, one wants for the moment to bring into focus. The concrete symbols involved—one or another mythological figure materializing in the wilderness, the skull of the deceased household head hanging censoriously in the rafters, or a disembodied 'voice in the stillness' soundlessly chanting enigmatic classical poetry—point in either direction. They both express the world's climate and shape it.

They shape it by inducing in the worshipper a certain distinctive set of dispositions (tendencies, capacities, propensities, skills, habits, liabilities, pronenesses) which lend a chronic character to the flow of his activity and the quality of his experience.

A disposition describes not an activity or an occurrence but a probability of an activity being performed or an occurrence occurring in certain circumstances: 'When a cow is said to be a ruminant, or a man is said to be a cigarette-smoker, it is not being said that the cow is ruminating now or that the man is smoking now. To be a ruminant is to tend to ruminate from time to time, and to be a cigarette-smoker is to be in the habit of smoking cigarettes' (Ryle, 1949, p. 117). Similarly, to be pious is not to be performing something we would call an act of piety, but to be liable to perform such acts. So, too, with the Plains Indian's bravura, the Manus' compunctiousness, or the Javanese's quietism which, in their contexts, form the substance of piety. The virtue of this sort of view of what are usually called 'mental traits' or, if the Cartesianism is unavowed, 'psychological forces' (both unobjectionable enough terms in themselves) is that it gets them out of any dim and inaccessible realm of private sensation into that same well-lit world of observables in which reside the brittleness of glass, the inflammability of paper, and, to return to the metaphor, the dampness of England.

So far as religious activities are concerned (and learning a myth by heart is as much a religious activity as detaching one's finger at the knuckle), two somewhat different sorts of disposition are induced by them: moods and motivations.

A motivation is a persisting tendency, a chronic inclination to perform certain sorts of act and experience certain sorts of feeling in certain sorts of situation, the 'sorts' being commonly very heterogenous and rather ill-defined classes in all three cases. . . .

As a motive, 'flamboyant courage' consists in such enduring propensities as to fast in the wilderness, to conduct solitary raids on enemy camps, and to thrill to the thought of counting coup. 'Moral circumspection' consists in such ingrained tendencies as to honor onerous promises, to confess secret sins in the face of severe public disapproval, and to feel guilty when vague and generalized accusations are made at seances. And 'dispassionate tranquility' consists in such persistent inclinations as to maintain one's poise come hell or high water, to experience distaste in the presence of even moderate emotional displays, and to indulge in contentless contemplations of featureless objects. Motives are thus neither acts (i.e. intentional behaviors) nor feelings, but liabilities to perform particular classes of act or have particular classes of feeling. And when we say that a man is religious, i.e. motivated by religion, this is at least part—though only part—of what we mean.

Another part of what we mean is that he has, when properly stimulated, a susceptibility to fall into certain moods, moods we sometimes lump together under such covering terms as 'reverential', 'solemn', or 'worshipful'. Such generalized rubrics actually conceal, however, the enormous empirical variousness of the dispositions involved, and, in fact, tend to assimilate them to the unusually grave tone of most of our own religious life. The moods that sacred symbols induce, at different times and in different places, range from exultation to melancholy, from self-confidence to self-pity, from an incorrigible playfulness to a bland listlessness—to say nothing of the erogenous power of so many of the world's myths and rituals. No more than there is a single sort of motivation one can call piety is there a single sort of mood one can call worshipful.

The major difference between moods and motivations is that where the latter are, so to speak, vectorial qualities, the former are merely scalar. Motives have a directional cast, they describe a certain overall course, gravitate toward certain, usually temporary, consummations. But moods vary only as to intensity: they go nowhere. They spring from certain circumstances but they are responsive to no ends. Like fogs, they just settle and lift; like scents, suffuse and evaporate. When present they are totalistic: if one is sad everything and everybody seems dreary; if one is gay, everything and everybody seems splendid. Thus, though a man can be vain, brave, willful and independent at the same time, he can't very well be playful and listless, or exultant and melancholy, at the same time (Ryle, 1949, p. 99). Further, where motives persist for more or less extended periods of time, moods merely recur with greater or lesser frequency, coming and going for what are often quite unfathomable reasons. But perhaps the most important difference, so far as we are concerned, between moods and motivations is that motivations are 'made meaningful' with reference to the ends toward which they are conceived to conduce, whereas moods are 'made meaningful' with reference to the conditions from which they are conceived to spring. We interpret motives in terms of their consummations, but we interpret moods in terms of their sources. We say that a person is industrious because he wishes to succeed, we say that a person is worried because he is conscious of the hanging threat of nuclear holocaust. And this is no less the case when the interpretations invoked are ultimate. Charity becomes Christian charity when it is enclosed in a conception of God's purposes; optimism is Christian optimism when it is grounded in a particular conception of God's nature. The assiduity of the Navaho finds its rationale in a belief that, since 'reality' operates mechanically, it is coercible; their chronic fearfulness finds its rationale in a conviction that, however 'reality' operates, it is both enormously powerful and terribly dangerous (Kluckhohn, 1949).

3. . . . by formulating conceptions of a general order of existence and . . .

That the symbols or symbol systems which induce and define dispositions we set off as religious and those which place those dispositions in a cosmic framework are the same symbols ought to occasion no surprise. For what else do we mean by saying that a particular mood of awe is religious and not secular except that it springs from entertaining a conception of all-pervading vitality like mana and not from a visit to the Grand Canyon? Or that a particular case of asceticism is an example of a religious motivation except that it is directed toward the achievement of an unconditioned end like nirvana and not a conditioned one like weight-reduction? If sacred symbols did not at one and the same time induce dispositions in human beings and formulate, however obliquely, inarticulately, or unsystematically, general ideas of order, then the empirical differentia of religious activity or religious experience would not exist. A man can indeed be said to be 'religious' about golf, but not merely if he pursues it with passion and plays it on Sundays: he must also see it as symbolic of some transcendent truths. And the pubescent boy gazing soulfully into the eyes of the pubescent girl in a William Steig cartoon and murmuring, 'There is something about you, Ethel, which gives me a sort of religious feeling', is, like most adolescents, confused. What any particular religion affirms about the fundamental nature of reality may be obscure, shallow, or, all too often, perverse, but it must, if it is not to consist of the mere collection of received practices and conventional sentiments we usually refer to as moralism, affirm something. If one were to essay a

minimal definition of religion today it would perhaps not be Tylor's famous 'belief in spiritual beings', to which Goody (1961), wearied of theoretical subtleties, has lately urged us to return, but rather what Salvador de Madariaga has called 'the relatively modest dogma that God is not mad'.

Usually, of course, religions affirm very much more than this: we believe, as James (1904, Vol. 2, p. 299) remarked, all that we can and would believe everything if we only could. The thing we seem least able to tolerate is a threat to our powers of conception, a suggestion that our ability to create, grasp, and use symbols may fail us, for were this to happen we would be more helpless, as I have already pointed out, than the beavers. The extreme generality, diffuseness, and variability of man's innate (i.e. genetically programmed) response capacities means that without the assistance of cultural patterns he would be functionally incomplete, not merely a talented ape who had, like some underprivileged child, unfortunately been prevented from realizing his full potentialities, but a kind of formless monster with neither sense of direction nor power of self-control, a choas of spasmodic impulses and vague emotions (Geertz, 1962). Man depends upon symbols and symbol systems with a dependence so great as to be decisive for his creatural viability and, as a result, his sensitivity to even the remotest indication that they may prove unable to cope with one or another aspect of experience raises within him the gravest sort of anxiety. . . .

There are at least three points where chaos—a tumult of events which lack not just interpretations but *interpretability*—threatens to break in upon man: at the limits of his analytic capacities, at the limits of his powers of endurance, and at the limits of his moral insight. Bafflement, suffering, and a sense of intractable ethical paradox are all, if they become intense enough or are sustained long enough, radical challenges to the proposition that life is comprehensible and that we can, by taking thought, orient ourselves effectively within it—challenges with which any religion, however 'primitive', which hopes to persist must attempt somehow to cope.

Of the three issues, it is the first which has been least investigated by modern social anthropologists (though Evans-Pritchard's (1937) classic discussion of why granaries fall on some Azande and not on others, is a notable exception). Even to consider people's religious beliefs as attempts to bring anomalous events or experiences—death, dreams, mental fugues, volcanic eruptions, or marital infidelity—within the circle of the at least potentially explicable seems to smack of Tyloreanism or worse. But it does appear to be a fact that at least some men—in all probability, most men—are unable to leave unclarified problems of analysis merely unclarified, just to look at the stranger features of the world's landscape in dumb astonishment or bland apathy without trying to develop, however fantastic, inconsistent, or simple-minded, some notions as to how such features might be reconciled with the more ordinary deliverances of experience. Any chronic failure of one's explanatory apparatus, the complex of received culture patterns (common sense, science, philosophical speculation, myth) one has for mapping the empirical world, to explain things which cry out for explanation tends to lead to a deep disquiet—a tendency rather more widespread and a disquiet rather deeper than we have sometimes supposed since the pseudo-science view of religious belief was, quite rightfully, deposed. After all, even that high priest of heroic atheism, Lord Russell, once remarked that although the problem of the existence of God had never bothered him, the ambiguity of certain mathematical axioms had threatened to unhinge his mind. And Einstein's profound dissatisfaction with quantum mechanics was based on a—surely religious—inability to believe that, as he put it, God plays dice with the universe.

But this quest for lucidity and the rush of metaphysical anxiety that occurs when empirical phenomena threaten to remain intransigently opaque is found on much humbler intellectual levels. Certainly, I was struck in my own work, much more than I had at all expected to be, by the degree to which my more animistically inclined informants behaved like true Tyloreans. They seemed to be constantly using their beliefs to 'explain' phenomena; or, more accurately, to convince themselves that the phenomena were explainable within the accepted scheme of things, for they commonly had only a minimal attachment to the particular soul possession, emotional disequilibrium, taboo infringement, or bewitchment hypothesis they advanced and were all too ready to abandon it for some other, in the same genre, which struck them

as more plausible given the facts of the case. What they were *not* ready to do was abandon it for no other hypothesis at all; to leave events to themselves.

And what is more, they adopted this nervous cognitive stance with respect to phenomena which had no immediate practical bearing on their own lives, or for that matter on anyone's. When a peculiarly shaped, rather large toadstool grew up in a carpenter's house in the short space of a few days (or, some said, a few hours), people came from miles around to see it, and everyone had some sort of explanation—some animist, some animatist, some not quite either—for it. Yet it would be hard to argue that the toadstool had any social value in Radcliffe-Brown's (1952) sense, or was connected in any way with anything which did and for which it could have been standing proxy, like the Andaman cicada. Toadstools play about the same role in Javanese life as they do in ours and in the ordinary course of things Javanese have about as much interest in them as we do. It was just that this one was 'odd', 'strange', 'uncanny'—*aneh*. And the odd, strange, and uncanny simply must be accounted for—or, again, the conviction that it *could be accounted* for sustained. One does not shrug off a toadstool which grows five times as fast as a toadstool has any right to grow. In the broadest sense the 'strange' toadstool did have implications, and critical ones, for those who heard about it. It threatened their most general ability to understand the world, raised the uncomfortable question of whether the beliefs which they held about nature were workable, the standards of truth they used valid.

Nor is this to argue that it is only, or even mainly, sudden eruptions of extraordinary events which engender in man the disquieting sense that his cognitive resources may prove unavailing or that this intuition appears only in its acute form. More commonly it is a persistent, constantly re-experienced difficulty in grasping certain aspects of nature, self, and society, in bringing certain elusive phenomena within the sphere of culturally formulatable fact, which renders man chronically uneasy and toward which a more equable flow of diagnostic symbols is consequently directed. It is what lies beyond a relatively fixed frontier of accredited knowledge that, looming as a constant background to the daily round of practical life, sets ordinary human experience in a permanent context of metaphysical concern and raises the dim, back-of-the-mind suspicion that one may be adrift in an absurd world. . . .

The second experiential challenge in whose face the meaningfulness of a particular pattern of life threatens to dissolve into a chaos of thingless names and nameless things—the problem of suffering—has been rather more investigated, or at least described, mainly because of the great amount of attention given in works on tribal religion to what are perhaps its two main loci: illness and mourning. Yet for all the fascinated interest in the emotional aura that surrounds these extreme situations, there has been, with a few exceptions such as Lienhardt's recent (1961, pp. 151ff) discussion of Dinka divining, little conceptual advance over the sort of crude confidence-type theory set forth by Malinowski: viz. that religion helps one to endure 'situations of emotional stress' by 'open[ing] up escapes from such situations and such impasses as offer no empirical way out except by ritual and belief into the domain of the supernatural' (1948, p. 67). The inadequacy of this 'theology of optimism', as Nadel (1957) rather drily called it, is, of course, radical. Over its career religion has probably disturbed men as much as it has cheered them; forced them into a head-on, unblinking confrontation of the fact that they are born to trouble as often as it has enabled them to avoid such a confrontation by projecting them into sort of infantile fairy-tale world where—Malinowski again (1948, p. 67)—'hope cannot fail nor desire deceive'. With the possible exception of Christian Science, there are few if any religious traditions, 'great' or 'little', in which the proposition that life hurts is not strenuously affirmed and in some it is virtually glorified. . . .

As a religious problem, the problem of suffering is, paradoxically, not how to avoid suffering but how to suffer, how to make of physical pain, personal loss, worldly defeat, or the helpless contemplation of others' agony something bearable, supportable—something, as we say, sufferable. It was in this effort that the Ba-Ila woman—perhaps necessarily, perhaps not—failed and, literally not knowing how to feel about what had happened to her, how to suffer, perished in confusion and despair. Where the more intellective aspects of what Weber called the Problem of Meaning are a matter affirming the ultimate explicability of experience, the more affective aspects are a matter of affirming its ultimate sufferableness. As religion on one side

anchors the power of our symbolic resources for formulating analytic ideas in an authoritative conception of the overall shape of reality, so on another side it anchors the power of our, also symbolic, resources for expressing emotions—moods, sentiments, passions, affections, feelings—in a similar conception of its pervasive tenor, its inherent tone and temper. For those able to embrace them, and for so long as they are able to embrace them, religious symbols provide a cosmic guarantee not only for their ability to comprehend the world, but also, comprehending it, to give a precision to their feeling, a definition to their emotions which enables them, morosely or joyfully, grimly or cavalierly, to endure it.

Consider in this light the well-known Navaho curing rites usually referred to as 'sings' (Kluckhohn & Leighton, 1946; Reichard, 1950). A sing—the Navaho have about sixty different ones for different purposes, but virtually all of them are dedicated to removing some sort of physical or mental illness—is a kind of religious psychodrama in which there are three main actors: the 'singer' or curer, the patient, and, as a kind of antiphonal chorus, the patient's family and friends. The structure of all the sings, the drama's plot, is quite similar. There are three main acts: a purification of the patient and audience; a statement, by means of repetitive chants and ritual manipulations, of the wish to restore well-being ('harmony') in the patient; an identification of the patient with the Holy People and his consequent 'cure'. The purification rites involved forced sweating, induced vomiting, etc. to expel the sickness from the patient physically. The chants, which are numberless, consist mainly of simple optative phrases ('may the patient be well', 'I am getting better all over', etc.). And, finally, the identification of the patient with the Holy People, and thus with cosmic order generally, is accomplished through the agency of a sand painting depicting the Holy People in one or another appropriate mythic setting. The singer places the patient on the painting, touching the feet, hands, knees, shoulders, breast, back, and head of the divine figures and then the corresponding parts of the patient, performing thus what is essentially a communion rite between the patient and the Holy People, a bodily identification of the human and the divine (Reichard, 1950). This is the climax of the sing: the whole curing process may be likened, Reichard says, to a spiritual osmosis in which the illness in man and the power of the deity penetrate the ceremonial membrane in both directions, the former being neutralized by the latter. Sickness seeps out in the sweat, vomit, and other purification rites; health seeps in as the Navaho patient touches, through the medium of the singer, the sacred sand painting. Clearly, the symbolism of the sing focuses upon the problem of human suffering and attempts to cope with it by placing it in a meaningful context, providing a mode of action through which it can be expressed, being expressed understood, and being understood, endured. The sustaining effect of the sing (and since the commonest disease is tuberculosis, it can in most cases be only sustaining), rests ultimately on its ability to give the stricken person a vocabulary in terms of which to grasp the nature of his distress and relate it to the wider world. Like a calvary, a recitation of Buddha's emergence from his father's palace or a performance of *Oedipus Tyrannos* in other religious traditions, a sing is mainly concerned with the presentation of a specific and concrete image of truly human, and so endurable, suffering powerful enough to resist the challenge of emotional meaninglessness raised by the existence of intense and unremovable brute pain.

The problem of suffering passes easily into the problem of evil, for if suffering is severe enough it usually, though not always, seems morally undeserved as well, at least to the sufferer. But they are not, however, exactly the same thing—a fact I think Weber, too influenced by the biases of a monotheistic tradition in which, as the various aspects of human experience must be conceived to proceed from a single, voluntaristic source, man's pain reflects directly on God's goodness, did not fully recognize in his generalization of the dilemmas of Christian theodicy Eastward. For where the problem of suffering is concerned with threats to our ability to put our 'undisciplined squads of emotion' into some sort of soldierly order, the problem of evil is concerned with threats to our ability to make sound moral judgements. What is involved in the problem of evil is not the adequacy of our symbolic resources to govern our affective life, but the adequacy of those resources to provide a workable set of ethical criteria, normative guides to govern our action. The vexation here is the gap between things as they are and as they ought to be if our conceptions of right and wrong make sense, the gap between what we deem various individuals deserve

and what we see that they get—a phenomenon summed up in that profound quatrain:

> The rain falls on the just
> And on the unjust fella;
> But mainly upon the just,
> Because the unjust has the just's umbrella.

Or if this seems too flippant an expression of an issue that, in somewhat different form, animates the Book of Job and the *Baghavad Gita*, the following classical Javanese poem, known, sung, and repeatedly quoted in Java by virtually everyone over the age of six, puts the point—the discrepancy between moral prescriptions and material rewards, the seeming inconsistency of 'is' and 'ought'— rather more elegantly:

> We have lived to see a time without order
> In which everyone is confused in his mind.
> One cannot bear to join in the madness,
> But if he does not do so
> He will not share in the spoils,
> And will starve as a result.
> Yes, God; wrong is wrong:
> Happy are those who forget,
> Happier yet those who remember and have
>   deep insight.

Nor is it necessary to be theologically self-conscious to be religiously sophisticated. The concern with intractable ethical paradox, the disquieting sense that one's moral insight is inadequate to one's moral experience, is as alive on the level of so-called 'primitive' religion as it is on that of the so-called 'civilized'. The set of notions about 'division in the world' that Lienhardt describes (1961, pp. 28–55) for the Dinka is a useful case in point. Like so many peoples, the Dinka believe that the sky, where 'Divinity' is located, and earth, where man dwells, were at one time contiguous, the sky lying just above the earth and being connected to it by a rope, so that men could move at will between the two realms. There was no death and the first man and woman were permitted but a single grain of millet a day, which was all that they at that time required. One day, the woman—of course—decided, out of greed, to plant more than the permitted grain of millet and in her avid haste and industry accidently struck Divinity with the handle of the hoe. Offended, he severed the rope, withdrew into the distant sky of today, and left man to labor for his food, to suffer sickness and death, and to experience separation from the source of his being, his Creator. Yet the meaning of this strangely familiar story to the Dinka is, as indeed is Genesis to Jews and Christians, not homiletic but descriptive. . . .

Thus the problem of evil, or perhaps one should say the problem *about* evil, is in essence the same sort of problem of or about bafflement and the problem of or about suffering. The strange opacity of certain empirical events, the dumb senselessness of intense or inexorable pain, and the enigmatic unaccountability of gross iniquity all raise the uncomfortable suspicion that perhaps the world, and hence man's life in the world, has no genuine order at all—no empirical regularity, no emotional form, no moral coherence. And the religious response to this suspicion is in each case the same: the formulation, by means of symbols, of an image of such a genuine order of the world which will account for, and even celebrate, the perceived ambiguities, puzzles, and paradoxes in human experience. The effort is not to deny the undeniable—that there are unexplained events, that life hurts, or that rain falls upon the just—but to deny that there are inexplicable events, that life is unendurable, and that justice is a mirage. The principles which constitute the moral order may indeed often elude men, as Lienhardt puts it, in the same way as fully satisfactory explanations of anomalous events or effective forms for the expression of feeling often elude them. What is important, to a religious man at least, is that this elusiveness be accounted for, that it be not the result of the fact that there are no such principles, explanations, or forms, that life is absurd and the attempt to make moral, intellectual or emotional sense out of experience is bootless. The Dinka can admit, in fact insist upon, the moral ambiguities and contradictions of life as they live it because these ambiguities and contradictions are seen not as ultimate, but as the 'rational', 'natural', 'logical' (one may choose one's own adjective here, for none of them is truly adequate) outcome of the moral structure of reality which the myth of the withdrawn 'Divinity' depicts, or as Lienhardt says, 'images'.

The Problem of Meaning in each of its intergrading aspects (how these aspects in fact intergrade in each particular case, what sort of interplay there is between the sense of analytic, emotional, and moral impotence, seems to me one of the outstanding, and except for Weber untouched, problems for comparative research in this whole field) is a matter of affirming, or at least recognizing, the inescapability of ignorance, pain, and injustice on the human plane while simultaneously denying that these irrationalities are characteristic of the world as a whole. And it is in terms of religious symbolism, a symbolism relating man's sphere of existence to a wider sphere within which it is conceived to rest, that both the affirmation and the denial are made.[2]

4. *. . . and clothing those conceptions with such an aura of factuality that . . .*

There arises here, however, a profounder question: how is it that this denial comes to be believed? how is it that the religious man moves from a troubled perception of experienced disorder to a more or less settled conviction of fundamental order? just what does 'belief' mean in a religious context? Of all the problems surrounding attempts to conduct anthropological analysis of religion this is the one that has perhaps been most troublesome and therefore the most often avoided, usually by relegating it to psychology, that raffish outcast discipline to which social anthropologists are forever consigning phenomena they are unable to deal with within the framework of a denatured Durkheimianism. But the problem will not go away, it is not 'merely' psychological (nothing social is), and no anthropological theory of religion which fails to attack it is worthy of the name. We have been trying to stage Hamlet without the Prince quite long enough.

It seems to me that it is best to begin any approach to this issue with frank recognition that religious belief involves not a Baconian induction from everyday experience—for then we should all be agnostics—but rather a prior acceptance of authority which transforms that experience. The existence of bafflement, pain, and moral paradox—of The Problem of Meaning—is one of the things that drive men toward belief in gods, devils, spirits, totemic principles, or the spiritual efficacy of cannibalism (an enfolding sense of beauty or a dazzling perception of power are others), but it is not the basis upon which those beliefs rest, but rather their most important field of application. . . .

In tribal religions authority lies in the persuasive power of traditional imagery; in mystical ones in the apodictic force of supersensible experience; in charismatic ones in the hypnotic attraction of an extraordinary personality. But the priority of the acceptance of an authoritative criterion in religious matters over the revelation which is conceived to flow from that acceptance is not less complete than in scriptural or hieratic ones. The basic axiom underlying what we may perhaps call 'the religious perspective' is everywhere the same: he who would know must first believe.

But to speak of 'the religious perspective' is, by implication, to speak of one perspective among others. A perspective is a mode of seeing, in that extended sense of 'see' in which it means 'discern', 'apprehend', 'understand', or 'grasp'. It is a particular way of looking at life, a particular manner of construing the world, as when we speak of an historical perspective, a scientific perspective, an aesthetic perspective, a common-sense perspective, or even the bizarre perspective embodied in dreams and in hallucinations.[3] The question then comes down to, first, what is 'the religious perspective' generically considered, as differentiated from other perspectives; and second, how do men come to adopt it.

If we place the religious perspective against the background of three of the other major perspectives in terms of which men construe the world—the common-sensical, the scientific, and the aesthetic—its special character emerges more sharply. What distinguishes common sense as a mode of 'seeing' is, as Schutz (1962) has pointed out, a simple acceptance of the world, its objects, and its processes as being just what they seem to be—what is sometimes called naïve realism—and the pragmatic motive, the wish to act upon that world so as to bend it to one's practical purposes, to master it, or so far as that proves impossible, to adjust to it. The world of everyday life, itself, of course, a cultural product, for it is framed in terms of the symbolic conceptions of 'stubborn fact' handed down from generation to generation, is the established scene and given object of our actions. Like Mt. Everest it is just there and the thing to do with it, if one feels the need to do anything with it at all, is to climb it. In the scientific perspective it is precisely this givenness which disappears (Schutz, 1962). Deliberate doubt and systematic inquiry, the suspension of the pragmatic motive in favor of disinterested observation, the attempt to analyze the world in terms of formal concepts whose relationship to the informal conceptions of common sense become increasingly problematic—there are the hallmarks of the attempt to grasp the world scientifically. And as for the aesthetic perspective, which

under the rubric of 'the aesthetic attitude' has been perhaps most exquisitely examined, it involves a different sort of suspension of naïve realism and practical interest, in that instead of questioning the credentials of everyday experience that experience is merely ignored in favor of an eager dwelling upon appearances, an engrossment in surfaces, an absorption in things, as we say, 'in themselves': 'The function of artistic illusion is not "make-believe" . . . but the very opposite, disengagement from belief— the contemplation of sensory qualities without their usual meanings of "here's that chair", "That's my telephone" . . . etc. The knowledge that what is before us has no practical significance in the world is what enables us to give attention to its appearance as such' (Langer, 1957, p. 49). And like the common-sensical and the scientific (or the historical, the philosophical, and the autistic), this perspective, this 'way of seeing' is not the product of some mysterious Cartesian chemistry, but is induced, mediated, and in fact created by means of symbols. It is the artist's skill which can produce those curious quasi-objects—poems, dramas, sculptures, symphonies— which, dissociating themselves from the solid world of common sense, take on the special sort of eloquence only sheer appearances can achieve.

The religious perspective differs from the common-sensical in that, as already pointed out, it moves beyond the realities of everyday life to wider ones which correct and complete them, and its defining concern is not action upon those wider realities but acceptance of them, faith in them. It differs from the scientific perspective in that it questions the realities of everyday life not out of an institutionalized scepticism which dissolves the world's givenness into a swirl of probabilistic hypotheses, but in terms of what it takes to be wider, non-hypothetical truths. Rather than detachment, its watchword is commitment; rather than analysis, encounter. And it differs from art in that instead of effecting a disengagement from the whole question of factuality, deliberately manufacturing an air of semblance and illusion, it deepens the concern with fact and seeks to create an aura of utter actuality. It is this sense of the 'really real' upon which the religious perspective rests and which the symbolic activities of religion as a cultural system are devoted to producing, intensifying, and, so far as possible, rendering inviolable by the discordant revelations of secular experience. It is, again, the imbuing of a certain specific complex of symbols—of the metaphysic they formulate and the style of life they recommend—with a persuasive authority which, from an analytic point of view is the essence of religious action.

Which brings us, at length, to ritual. For it is in ritual—i.e. consecrated behavior—that this conviction that religious conceptions are veridical and that religious directives are sound is somehow generated. It is in some sort of ceremonial form—even if that form be hardly more than the recitation of a myth, the consultation of an oracle, or the decoration of a grave—that the moods and motivations which sacred symbols induce in men and the general conceptions of the order of existence which they formulate for men meet and reinforce one another. In a ritual, the world as lived and the world as imagined, fused under the agency of a single set of symbolic forms, turn out to be the same world, producing thus that idiosyncratic transformation in one's sense of reality to which Santayana refers. . . . Whatever role divine intervention may or may not play in the creation of faith—and it is not the business of the scientist to pronounce upon such matters one way or the other—it is, primarily at least, out of the context of concrete acts of religious observance that religious conviction emerges on the human plane.

However, though any religious ritual, no matter how apparently automatic or conventional (if it is truly automatic or merely conventional it is not religious), involves this symbolic fusion of ethos and world-view, it is mainly certain more elaborate and usually more public ones, ones in which a broad range of moods and motivations on the one hand and of metaphysical conceptions on the other are caught up, which shape the spiritual consciousness of a people. Employing a useful term introduced by Singer (1955), we may call these full-blown ceremonies 'cultural performances' and note that they represent not only the point at which the dispositional and conceptual aspects of religious life converge for the believer, but also the point at which the interaction between them can be most readily examined by the detached observer. . . .

Of course, all cultural performances are not religious performances, and the line between those that are and artistic, or even political ones, is often not so easy to draw in practice, for, like social forms, symbolic forms can serve multiple purposes. But the point is that, paraphrasing slightly, Indians

—'and perhaps all peoples'—seem to think of their religion 'as encapsulated in these discrete performances which they [can] exhibit to visitors and to themselves' (Singer, 1955). The mode of exhibition is however radically different for the two sorts of witness, a fact seemingly overlooked by those who would argue that 'religion is a form of human art' (Firth, 1951, p. 250). Where for 'visitors' religious performances can, in the nature of the case, only be presentations of a particular religious perspective, and thus aesthetically appreciated or scientifically dissected, for participants they are in addition enactments, materializations, realizations of it—not only models *of* what they believe, but also models *for* the believing of it. In these plastic dramas men attain their faith as they portray it.

As a case in point, let me take a spectacularly theatrical cultural performance from Bali—that in which a terrible witch called Rangda engages in a ritual combat with an endearing monster called Barong.[4] Usually, but not inevitably presented on the occasion of a death temple celebration, the drama consists of a masked dance in which the witch—depicted as a wasted old widow, prostitute, and eater of infants—comes to spread plague and death upon the land and is opposed by the monster—depicted as a kind of cross between a clumsy bear, a silly puppy, and a strutting Chinese dragon. Rangda, danced by a single male, is a hideous figure. Her eyes bulge from her forehead like swollen boils. Her teeth become tusks curving up over her cheeks and fangs protruding down over her chin. Her yellowed hair falls down around her in a matted tangle. Her breasts are dry and pendulous dugs edged with hair, between which hang, like so many sausages, strings of colored entrails. Her long red tongue is a stream of fire. And as she dances she splays her dead-white hands, from which protrude ten-inch claw-like fingernails, out in front of her and utters unnerving shrieks of metallic laughter. Barong, danced by two men fore-and-aft in vaudeville horse fashion, is another matter. His shaggy sheepdog coat is hung with gold and mica ornaments that glitter in the half-light. He is adorned with flowers, sashes, feathers, mirrors, and a comical beard made from human hair. And though, a demon too, his eyes also pop and he snaps his fanged jaws with seemly fierceness when faced with Rangda or other affronts to his dignity, the cluster of tinkling bells which hang from his absurdly arching tail somehow contrives to take most of the edge off his fearfulness. If Rangda is a satanic image, Barong is a farcical one, and their clash is a clash (an inconclusive one) between the malignant and the ludicrous.

This odd counterpoint of implacable malice and low comedy pervades the whole performance. Rangda, clutching her magical white cloth, moves around in a slow stagger, now pausing immobile in thought or uncertainty, now lurching suddenly forward. The moment of her entry (one sees those terrible long-nailed hands first as she emerges through the split gateway at the top of a short flight of stone stairs) is one of terrific tension when it seems, to a 'visitor' at least, that everyone is about to break and run in panic. She herself seems insane with fear and hatred as she screams deprecations at Barong amid the wild clanging of the gamelan. She may in fact go amok. I have myself seen Rangdas hurl themselves headlong into the gamelan or run frantically about in total confusion, being subdued and reoriented only by the combined force of a half-dozen spectators; and one hears many tales of amok Rangdas holding a whole village in terror for hours and of impersonators becoming permanently deranged by their experiences. But Barong, though he is charged with the same mana-like sacred power (*sakti* in Balinese) as Rangda, and his impersonators are also entranced, seems to have very great difficulty in being serious. He frolics with his retinue of demons (who add to the gaiety by indelicate pranks of their own), lies down on a metallaphone while it is being played or beats on a drum with his legs, moves in one direction in his front half and another in his rear or bends his segmented body into foolish contortions, brushes flies from his body or sniffs aromas in the air, and generally prances about in paroxysms of narcissistic vanity. The contrast is not absolute, for Rangda is sometimes momentarily comic as when she pretends to polish the mirrors on Barong's coat, and Barong becomes rather more serious after Rangda appears, nervously clacking his jaws at her and ultimately attacking her directly. Nor are the humorous and the horrible always kept rigidly separated, as in that strange scene in one section of the cycle in which several minor witches (disciples of Rangda) toss the corpse of a stillborn child around to the wild amusement of the audience; or another, no less strange, in which the sight of a pregnant woman alternating hysterically between tears and laughter while being knocked

about by a group of grave-diggers, seems for some reason excruciatingly funny. The twin themes of horror and hilarity find their purest expression in the two protagonists and their endless, indecisive struggle for dominance, but they are woven with deliberate intricacy through the whole texture of the drama. They—or rather the relations between them—are what it is about.

It is unnecessary to attempt a thoroughgoing description of a Rangda-Barong performance here. Such performances vary widely in detail, consist of several not too closely integrated parts, and in any case are so complex in structure as to defy easy summary. For our purposes, the main point to be stressed is that the drama is, for the Balinese, not merely a spectacle to be watched but a ritual to be enacted. There is no aesthetic distance here separating actors from audience and placing the depicted events in an unenterable world of illusion, and by the time a full-scale Rangda-Barong encounter has been concluded a majority, often nearly all, of the members of the group sponsoring it will have become caught up in it not just imaginatively but bodily. In one of Belo's examples (1960, pp. 159–168) I count upwards of seventy-five people—men, women, and children—taking part in the activity at some point or other, and thirty to forty participants is in no way unusual. As a performance, the drama is like a high mass not like a presentation of *Murder in the Cathedral:* it is a drawing near, not a standing back.

In part, this entry into the body of the ritual takes place through the agency of the various supporting roles contained in it—minor witches, demons, various sorts of legendary and mythical figures—which selected villagers enact. But mostly it takes place through the agency of an extraordinarily developed capacity for psychological dissociation on the part of a very large segment of the population. A Rangda-Barong struggle is inevitably marked by anywhere from three or four to several dozen spectators becoming possessed by one or another demon, falling into violent trances 'like firecrackers going off one after the other' (Belo, 1960), and, snatching up krisses, rushing to join the fray. Mass trance, spreading like a panic, projects the individual Balinese out of the commonplace world in which he usually lives into that most uncommonplace one in which Rangda and Barong live. To become entranced is, for the Balinese, to cross a threshold into another order of existence—the word for trance is *nadi*, from *dadi*, often translated 'to become' but which might be even more simply rendered as 'to be'. And even those who, for whatever reasons, do not make this spiritual crossing are caught up in the proceedings, for it is they who must keep the frenzied activities of the entranced from getting out of hand by the application of physical restraint if they are ordinary men, by the sprinkling of holy water and the chanting of spells if they are priests. At its height a Rangda-Barong rite hovers, or at least seems to hover, on the brink of mass amok with the diminishing band of the unentranced striving desperately (and, it seems almost always successfully) to control the growing band of the entranced.

In its standard form—if it can be said to have a standard form—the performance begins with an appearance of Barong, prancing and preening, as a general prophylactic against what is to follow. Then may come various mythic scenes relating the story—not always precisely the same one—upon which the performance is based—until finally Barong and then Rangda appear. Their battle begins. Barong drives Rangda back toward the gate of the death temple. But he has not the power to expel her completely and he is in turn driven back toward the village. At length, when it seems as though Rangda will finally prevail, a number of entranced men rise, krisses in hand, and rush to support Barong. But as they approach Rangda (who has turned her back in meditation), she wheels upon them and, waving her *sakti* white cloth, leaves them comatose on the ground. Rangda then hastily retires (or is carried) to the temple, where she herself collapses, hidden from the aroused crowd which, my informants said, would kill her were it to see her in a helpless state. The Barong moves among the kris dancers and wakens them by snapping his jaws at them or nuzzling them with his beard. As they return, still entranced, to 'consciousness', they are enraged by the disappearance of Rangda, and unable to attack her they turn their krisses (harmlessly because they are entranced) against their own chests in frustration. Usually sheer pandemonium breaks out at this point with members of the crowd, of both sexes, falling into trance all around the courtyard and rushing out to stab themselves, wrestle with one another, devour live chicks or excrement, wallow convulsively in the mud, and so on, while the non-entranced attempt to relieve them of their krisses and keep them at least minimally in order. In time, the trancers sink, one by one, into coma from which they are aroused by the priests' holy water and the great battle is over—once more a complete stand-off. Rangda has not been conquered, but neither has she conquered.

One place to search for the meaning of this ritual is in the collection of myths, tales, and explicit beliefs which it supposedly enacts. However, not only are these various and variable—for some people Rangda is an incarnation of Durga, Siva's malignant consort, for others she is Queen Mahendradatta, a figure from a court legend set in eleventh century Java, for yet others, the spiritual leader of witches as the Brahmana Priest is the spiritual leader of men; and notions of who (or 'what') Barong is are equally diverse and even vaguer—but they seem to play only a secondary role in the Balinese' preception of the drama. It is in the direct encounter with the two figures in the context of the actual performance that the villager comes to know them as, so far as he is concerned, genuine realities. They are, then, not representations of anything, but presences. And when the villagers go into trance they become—*nadi*—themselves part of the realm in which those presences exist. To ask, as I once did, a man who has *been* Rangda whether he thinks she is real is to leave oneself open to the suspicion of idiocy.

The acceptance of authority that underlies the religious prespective that the ritual embodies thus flows from the enactment of the ritual itself. By inducing a set of moods and motivations—an ethos—and defining an image of cosmic order—a worldview—by means of a single set of symbols, the performance makes the model *for* and model *of* aspects of religious belief mere transpositions of one another. Rangda evokes fear (as well as hatred, disgust, cruelty, horror, and, though I have not been able to treat the sexual aspects of the performance here, lust); but she also depicts it. . . .

And on his side Barong not only induces laughter, he incarnates the Balinese version of the comic spirit—a distinctive combination of playfulness, exhibitionism, and extravagant love of elegance which, along with fear, is perhaps the dominant motive in their life. The constantly recurring struggle of Rangda and Barong to an inevitable draw is thus—for the believing Balinese—both the formulation of a general religious conception and the authoritative experience which justifies, even compels, its acceptance.

5. . . . that the moods and motivations seem uniquely realistic

But no one, not even a saint, lives in the world religious symbols formulate all of the time, and the majority of men live in it only at moments. The everyday world of common-sense objects and practical acts is, as Schutz (1962, pp. 226ff.) says, the paramount reality in human experience—paramount in the sense that it is the world in which we are most solidly rooted, whose inherent actuality we can hardly question (however much we may question certain portions of it), and from whose pressures and requirements we can least escape. A man, even large groups of men, may be aesthetically insensitive, religiously unconcerned, and unequipped to pursue formal scientific analysis, but he cannot be completely lacking in common sense and survive. The dispositions which religious rituals induce thus have their most important impact—from a human point of view—outside the boundaries of the ritual itself as they reflect back to color the individual's conception of the established world of bare fact. The peculiar tone that marks the Plains vision quest, the Manus confession, or the Javanese mystical exercise pervades areas of the life of these peoples far beyond the immediately religious, impressing upon them a distinctive style in the sense both of a dominant mood and a characteristic movement. The interweaving of the malignant and the comic, which the Rangda-Barong combat depicts, animates a very wide range of everyday Balinese behavior, much of which, like the ritual itself, has an air of candid fear narrowly contained by obsessive playfulness. Religion is sociologically interesting not because, as vulgar positivism would have it (Leach, 1954, pp. 10ff.), it describes the social order (which, in so far as it does, it does not only very obliquely but very incompletely), but because, like environment, political power, wealth, jural obligation, personal affection, and a sense of beauty, it shapes it.

The movement back and forth between the religious perspective and the common-sense perspective is actually one of the more obvious empirical occurrences on the social scene, though, again, one of the most neglected by social anthropologists, virtually all of whom have seen it happen countless times. Religious belief has usually been presented as an homogeneous characteristic of an individual, like his place of residence, his occupational role, his kinship position, and so on. But religious belief in the midst of ritual, where it engulfs the total person, transporting him, so far as he is concerned, into another mode of existence, and religious belief as the pale, remembered reflection of that experience in the midst of everyday life are not precisely the same thing, and the failure to realize this has led to some confusion, most especially in connection with the so-called 'primitive mentality' problem. Much of the difficulty between Lévy-Bruhl (1926) and Malinowski (1948) on the nature of 'native thought', for example, arises from a lack of full recognition of this distinction; for where the French philosopher was concerned with the view of reality savages adopted when taking a specifically religious perspective, the Polish-English ethnographer was concerned with that which they adopted when taking a strictly common-sense one. Both perhaps vaguely sensed that they were not talking about exactly the same thing, but where they went astray was in failing to give a specific accounting of the way in which these two forms of 'thought' —or, as I would rather say, these two modes of symbolic formulation—interacted, so that where Lévy-Bruhl's savages tended to live, despite his postludial disclaimers, in a world composed entirely of mystical encounters, Malinowski's tended to live, despite his stress on the functional importance of religion, in a world composed entirely of practical actions. They became reductionists (an idealist is as much of a reductionist as a materialist) in spite of themselves because they failed to see man as moving more or less easily, and very frequently, between radically contrasting ways of looking at the world, ways which are not continuous with one another but separated by cultural gaps across which Kierkegaardian leaps must be made in both directions. . . .

The recognition and exploration of the qualitative difference—an empirical, not a transcendental difference—between religion pure and religion applied, between an encounter with the supposedly 'really real' and a viewing of ordinary experience in light of what that encounter seems to reveal, will, therefore, take us further toward an understanding of what a Bororo means when he says 'I am a parakeet', or a Christian when he says 'I am a sinner', than either a theory of primitive mysticism in which the commonplace world disappears into a cloud of curious ideas or of a primitive pragmatism in which religion disintegrates into a collection of useful fictions. The parakeet example, which I take from Percy (1961), is a good one. For, as he points out, it is unsatisfactory to say either that the Bororo thinks he is literally a parakeet (for he does not try to mate with other parakeets), that his statement is false or nonsense (for, clearly, he is not offering—or at least not only offering—the sort of class-membership argument which can be confirmed or refuted as, say, 'I am a Bororo' can be confirmed or refuted), or yet again that it is false scientifically but true mythically (because that leads immediately to the pragmatic fiction notion which, as it denies the accolade of truth to 'myth' in the very act of bestowing it, is internally self-contradictory). More coherently it would seem to be necessary to see the sentence as having a different sense in the context of the 'finite province of meaning' which makes up the religious perspective and of that which makes up the common-sensical. In the religious, our Bororo is 'really' a 'parakeet', and given the proper ritual context might well 'mate' with other 'parakeets'—with metaphysical ones like himself not commonplace ones such as those which fly bodily about in ordinary trees. In the common-sensical perspective he is a parakeet in the sense—I assume—that he belongs to a clan whose members regard the parakeet as their totem, a membership from which, given the fundamental nature of reality as the religious perspective reveals it, certain moral and practical consequences flow. A man who says he is a parakeet is, if he says it in normal conversation, saying that, as myth and ritual demonstrate, he is shot through with parakeetness and that this religious fact has some crucial social implications—we parakeets must stick together, not marry one another, not eat mundane parakeets, and so on, for to do otherwise is to act against the grain of the whole universe. It is this placing of proximate acts in ultimate contexts that makes religion, frequently at least, socially so powerful. It alters, often radically, the whole landscape presented to common sense, alters it in such a way that the moods and motivations induced by religious practice seem themselves supremely practical, the only sensible ones to adopt given the way things 'really' are.

Having ritually 'lept' (the image is perhaps a bit too athletic for the actual facts—'slipped' might be more accurate) into the framework of meaning which religious conceptions define and, the ritual ended, returned again to the common-sense world, a man is—unless, as sometimes happens, the experience fails to register—changed. And as he is changed so also is the common-sense world, for it is now seen as but the partial form of a wider reality which corrects and completes it. But this correction and completion is not, as some students of 'comparative religion' (e.g. Campbell, 1949, pp. 236–237) would have it, everywhere the same in content. The nature of the bias religion gives to ordinary life varies with the religion involved, with the particular dispositions induced in the believer by the specific conceptions of cosmic order he has come to accept. On the level of the 'great' religions, organic distinctiveness is usually recognized, at times insisted upon to the point of zealotry. But even at its simplest folk and tribal levels—where the individuality of religious traditions has so often been dissolved into such desiccated types as 'animism', 'animatism', 'totemism', 'shamanism', 'ancestor worship', and all the other insipid categories by means of which ethnographers of religion devitalize their data—the idiosyncratic character of how various groups of men behave because of what they believe they have experienced is clear. A tranquil Javanese would be no more at home in guilt-ridden Manus than an activist Crow would be in passionless Java. And for all the witches and ritual clowns in the world, Rangda and Barong are not generalized but thoroughly singular figurations of fear and gaiety. What men believe is as various as what they are—a proposition that holds with equal force when it is inverted.

It is this particularity of the impact of religious systems upon social systems (and upon personality systems) which renders general assessments of the value of religion in either moral or functional terms impossible. The sorts of moods and motivations which characterize a man who has just come from an Aztec human sacrifice are rather different from those of one who has just put off his Kachina mask. Even within the same society, which one 'learns' about the essential pattern of life from a sorcery rite and from a commensual meal will have rather diverse effects on social and psychological functioning. One of the main methodological problems in writing about religion scientifically is to put aside at once the tone of the village atheist and that of the village preacher, as well as their more sophisticated equivalents, so that the social and psychological implications of particular religious beliefs can emerge in a clear and neutral light. And when that is done, overall questions about whether religion is 'good' or 'bad', 'functional' or 'dysfunctional', 'ego strengthening' or 'anxiety producing' disappear like the chimeras they are, and one is left with particular evaluations, assessments, and diagnoses in particular cases. There remain, of course, the hardly unimportant questions of whether this or that religious assertion is true, this or that religious experience genuine, or whether true religious assertions and genuine religious experiences are possible at all. But such questions cannot even be asked, much less answered, within the self-imposed limitations of the scientific perspective. . . .

For an anthropologist, the importance of religion lies in its capacity to serve, for an individual or for a group, as a source of general, yet distinctive conceptions of the world, the self, and the relations between them, on the one hand—its model *of* aspect —and of rooted, no less distinctive 'mental' dispositions—its model *for* aspect—on the other. From these cultural functions flow, in turn, its social and psychological ones.

Religious concepts spread beyond their specifically metaphysical contexts to provide a framework of general ideas in terms of which a wide range of experience—intellectual, emotional, moral—can be given meaningful form. The Christian sees the Nazi movement against the background of The Fall which, though it does not, in a causal sense, explain it, places it in a moral, a cognitive, even an affective sense. An Azande sees the collapse of a granary upon a friend or relative against the background of a concrete and rather special notion of witchcraft and thus avoids the philosophical dilemmas as well as the psychological stress of indeterminism. A Javanese finds in the borrowed and reworked concept of *rasa* ('sense-taste-feeling-meaning') a means by which to 'see' choreographic, gustatory, emotional, and political phenomena in a new light. A synopsis of cosmic order, a set of religious beliefs, is also a gloss upon the mundane world of social relationships and psychological events. It renders them graspable.

But more than gloss, such beliefs are also a template. They do not merely interpret social and psychological processes in cosmic terms—in which

case they would be philosophical, not religious— but they shape them. In the doctrine of original sin is embedded also a recommended attitude toward life, a recurring mood, and a persisting set of motivations. The Zande learns from witchcraft conceptions not just to understand apparent 'accidents' as not accidents at all, but to react to these spurious accidents with hatred for the agent who caused them and to proceed against him with appropriate resolution. *Rasa*, in addition to being a concept of truth, beauty, and goodness, is also a preferred mode of experiencing, a kind of affectless detachment, a variety of bland aloofness, an unshakeable calm. The moods and motivations a religious orientation produces cast a derivative, lunar light over the solid features of a people's secular life.

The tracing of the social and psychological role of religion is thus not so much a matter of finding correlations between specific ritual acts and specific secular social ties—though these correlations do, of course, exist and are very worth continued investigation, especially if we can contrive something novel to say about them. More, it is a matter of understanding how it is that men's notions, however implicit, of the 'really real' and the dispositions these notions induce in them, color their sense of the reasonable, the practical, the humane, and the moral. How far they do so (for in many societies religion's effects seem quite circumscribed, in others completely pervasive); how deeply they do so (for some men, and groups of men, seem to wear their religion lightly so far as the secular world goes, while others seem to apply their faith to each occasion, no matter how trivial); and how effectively they do so (for the width of the gap between what religion recommends and what people actually do is most variable cross-culturally)—all these are crucial issues in the comparative sociology and psychology of religion. Even the degree to which religious systems themselves are developed seems to vary extremely widely, and not merely on a simple evolutionary basis. In one society, the level of elaboration of symbolic formulations of ultimate actuality may reach extraordinary degrees of complexity and systematic articulation; in another, no less developed socially, such formulations may remain primitive in the true sense, hardly more than congeries of fragmentary by-beliefs and isolated images, of sacred reflexes and spiritual pictographs. One need only think of the Australians and the Bushmen, the Toradja and the Alorese, the Hopi and the Apache, the Hindus and the Romans, or even the Italians and the Poles, to see that degree of religious articulateness is not a constant even as between societies of similar complexity.

The anthropological study of religion is therefore a two-stage operation: first, an analysis of the system of meanings embodied in the symbols which make up the religion proper, and, second, the relating of these systems to social-structural and psychological processes. My dissatisfaction with so much of contemporary social anthropological work in religion is not that it concerns itself with the second stage, but that it neglects the first, and in so doing takes for granted what most needs to be elucidated. To discuss the role of ancestor worship in regulating political succession, of sacrificial feasts in defining kinship obligations, of spirit worship in scheduling agricultural practices, of divination in reinforcing social control, or of initiation rites in propelling personality maturation are in no sense unimportant endeavors, and I am not recommending they be abandoned for the kind of jejune cabalism into which symbolic analysis of exotic faiths can so easily fall. But to attempt them with but the most general, common-sense view of what ancestor worship, animal sacrifice, spirit worship, divination, or initiation rites are as religious patterns seems to me not particularly promising. Only when we have a theoretical analysis of symbolic action comparable in sophistication to that we now have for social and psychological action, will we be able to cope effectively with those aspects of social and psychological life in which religion (or art, or science, or ideology) plays a determinant role.

NOTES

1. The reverse mistake, especially common among neo-Kantians such as Cassirer (1953–57), of taking symbols to be identical with, or 'constitutive of', their referents is equally pernicious. 'One can point to the moon with one's finger,' some, probably well-invented, Zen Master is supposed to have said, 'but to take one's finger for the moon is to be a fool.'

2. This is *not*, however, to say that everyone in every society does this; for as the immortal Don Marquis once remarked, you don't have to have a soul unless you really want one. The oft-heard generalization (e.g. Kluckhohn, 1953) that religion is a human universal embodies a confusion between the probably true (though on present evidence unprovable) proposition that there is no human society in which cultural patterns that we can, under the present definition or one like it, call religious are totally lacking, and the surely untrue proposition that all men in all

societies are, in any meaningful sense of the term, religious. But if the anthropological study of religious commitment is underdeveloped, the anthropological study of religious non-commitment is non-existent. The anthropology of religion will have come of age when some more subtle Malinowski writes a book called 'Belief and Unbelief (or even "Faith and Hypocrisy") in a Savage Society'.

3. The term 'attitude' as in 'aesthetic attitude' (Bell, 1914) or 'natural attitude' (Schutz, 1962; the phrase is originally Husserl's) is another, perhaps more common term for what I have here called 'perspective'. But I have avoided it because of its strong subjectivist connotations, its tendency to place the stress upon a supposed inner state of an actor rather than on a certain sort of relation—a symbolically mediated one —between an actor and a situation. This is not to say, of course, that a phenomenological analysis of religious experience, if cast in inter-subjective, non-transcendental, genuinely scientific terms (see Percy, 1958) is not essential to a full understanding of religious belief, but merely that that is not the focus of my concern here. 'Outlook', 'frame of reference', 'frame of mind', 'orientation', 'stance', 'mental set', etc. are other terms sometimes employed, depending upon whether the analyst wishes to stress the social, psychological, or cultural aspects of the matter.

4. The Rangda-Barong complex has been extensively described and analysed by a series of unusually gifted ethnographers (Belo, 1949, 1960; deZoete & Spies, 1938; Bateson & Mead, 1942; Covarrubias, 1937) and I will make no attempt to present it here in more than schematic form. Much of my interpretation of the complex rests on personal observations made in Bali during 1957–1958 (see Geertz, 1964b).

REFERENCES

BATESON, G., 1958. *Naven*. Stanford: Stanford University Press, 2nd ed.

BATESON, G. & MEAD, M. 1942. *Balinese Character*. New York: N.Y. Academy of Sciences.

BELL, C. 1914. *Art*. London: Chatto & Windus.

BELO, J. 1949. *Bali: Rangda and Barong*. New York: J. J. Augustin.

—— 1960. *Trance in Bali*. New York: Columbia University Press.

BURKE, K. 1941. *The Philosophy of Literary Form*. n.p.: Louisiana State University Press.

CAMPBELL, J. 1949. *The Hero with a Thousand Faces*. New York: Pantheon.

CASSIRER, E. 1953–57. *The Philosophy of Symbolic Forms* (trans. R. Mannheim). New Haven: Yale University Press. 3 vols.

COVARRUBIAS, M. 1937. *The Island of Bali*. New York: Knopf.

CRAIK, K. 1952. *The Nature of Explanation*. Cambridge: Cambridge University Press.

EVANS-PRITCHARD, E. E. 1937. *Witchcraft, Oracles and Magic Among the Azande*. Oxford: Clarendon Press.

FIRTH, R. 1951. *Elements of Social Organization*. London: Watts; New York: Philosophical Library.

FORTUNE, R. F. 1935. *Manus Religion*. Philadelphia: American Philosophical Society.

VON FRISCH, K. 1962. Dialects in the Language of the Bees. *Scientific American*, August.

GEERTZ, C. 1958. Ethos, World-View and the Analysis of Sacred Symbols. *Antioch Review*, Winter (1957–58): 421–437.

—— 1960. *The Religion of Java*. Glencoe, Ill.: The Free Press.

—— 1962. The Growth of Culture and the Evolution of Mind. In J. Scher (ed.), *Theories of the Mind*. New York: The Free Press, pp. 713–740.

—— 1964a. Ideology as a Cultural System. In D. Apter (ed.), *Ideology of Discontent*. New York: The Free Press.

—— 1964b. 'Internal Conversion' in Contemporary Bali. In J. Bastin & R. Roolvink (eds.), *Malayan and Indonesian Studies*, Oxford: Oxford University Press, pp. 282–302.

GOODY, J. 1961. Religion and Ritual: The Definition Problem. *British Journal of Sociology* 12: 143–164.

HOROWITZ, N. H. 1956. The Gene. *Scientific American*, February.

JAMES, WILLIAM. 1904. *The Principles of Psychology*. New York: Henry Holt, 2 vols.

JANOWITZ, M. 1963. Anthropology and the Social Sciences. *Current Anthropology* 4: 139, 146–154.

KLUCKHOHN, C. 1949. The Philosophy of the Navaho Indians. In F. S. C. Northrop (ed.), *Ideological Differences and World Order*. New Haven: Yale University Press, pp. 356–384.

—— 1953. Universal Categories of Culture. In A. L. Kroeber (ed.), *Anthropology Today*. Chicago: University of Chicago Press, pp. 507–523.

KLUCKHOHN, C. & LEIGHTON, D. 1946. *The Navaho*. Cambridge, Mass.: Harvard University Press.

LANGER, S. 1953. *Feeling and Form*. New York: Scribner's.

—— 1960. *Philosophy in a New Key*. Fourth Edition. Cambridge, Mass.: Harvard University Press.

—— 1962. *Philosophical Sketches*. Baltimore: Johns Hopkins.

LEACH, E. R. 1954. *Political Systems of Highland Burma*. London: Bell; Cambridge, Mass.: Harvard University Press.

LÉVY-BRUHL, L. 1926. *How Natives Think*. New York: Knopf.

LIENHARDT, G. 1961. *Divinity and Experience*. Oxford: Clarendon Press.

LORENZ, K. 1952. *King Solomon's Ring*. London: Methuen.

LOWIE, R. H. 1924. *Primitive Religion*. New York: Boni and Liveright.

MACINTYRE, A. 1957. The Logical Status of Religious Belief. In A. MacIntyre (ed.), *Metaphysical Beliefs*. London: SCM Press, pp. 167–211.

MALINOWSKI, B. 1948. *Magic, Science and Religion*. Boston: Beacon Press.

NADEL, S. F. 1957. Malinowski on Magic and Religion. In R. Firth (ed.), *Man and Culture*. London: Routledge & Kegan Paul, pp. 189–208.

PARSONS, T. & SHILS, E. 1951. *Toward a General Theory of Action*. Cambridge, Mass.: Harvard University Press.

PERCY, W. 1958. Symbol, Consciousness and Intersubjectivity. *Journal of Philosophy* 15: 631–641.

—— 1961. The Symbolic Structure of Interpersonal Process. *Psychiatry* 24: 39–52.

RADCLIFFE-BROWN, A. R. 1952. *Structure and Function in Primitive Society*. Glencoe, Ill.: Free Press.

RADIN, P. 1957. *Primitive Man as a Philosopher*. New York: Dover.

REICHARD, G. 1950. *Navaho Religion*. New York: Pantheon, 2 vols.

RYLE, G. 1949. *The Concept of Mind*. London: Hutchinson; New York: Barnes & Noble.

SANTAYANA, G. 1905–1906. *Reason in Religion*. Vol. 2 of *The Life of Reason, or The Phases of Human Progress*. London: Constable; New York: Scribner's.

SCHUTZ, A. 1962. *The Problem of Social Reality* (vol. I of *Collected Papers*). The Hague: Martinus Nijhoff.

SINGER, M. 1955. The Cultural Pattern of Indian Civilization. *Far Eastern Quarterly* 15: 23–36.

—— 1958. The Great Tradition in a Metropolitan Center: Madras. In M. Singer (ed.), *Traditional India*. Philadelphia: American Folklore Society, pp. 140–82.

SMITH, C. W. & DALE, A. M. 1920. *The Ila-Speaking Peoples of Northern Rhodesia*. London: Macmillan.

DE ZOETE, B. & SPIES, W. 1938. *Dance and Drama in Bali*. London: Faber & Faber.

CULTURE, SYMBOLS, AND SOCIETY

This excerpt from a book by Ross continues some of the points made by Geertz and others in preceding selections. It talks of shared—and communicated—*meanings* as being the "glue" that holds an assembly of persons together, that, in effect, makes or creates out of an assemblage of "persons" what we call a "society." To talk of values and beliefs as the core of human culture is to talk also of a social reality in which they are embedded in daily behavior. It is, in other words, to talk of a cultural system as providing one dimension of a more comprehensive system that includes another kind of dimension as well, that of social relationships and interlocking group and institutional activities. It is to these general kinds of questions that Ross turns our attention: "culture" as values symbolically communicated in a social field. At this point, then, we have seen something of the general character of the concept of culture, of the indispensability of *symbolism* to that concept of culture, and of the entwining of values and beliefs with symbolism. We are now putting all these together with a *social dimension* of organized human life and setting the stage for the next section of readings.

COMMUNICATION, SYMBOLS, AND SOCIETY

RALPH ROSS

Communication is a subject larger than precise meaning and literal exposition. It includes other uses of language, and nonlinguistic communication —gesture, ritual, symbol, action, art, and religion— in so far as they have communicable meaning. In dealing with this aspect of communication, its relations to man and society are all-important. Man can be defined as a symbol-using animal at least as well as he can be defined in any other way; and social relationships can be traced effectively on the basis of the network of symbols and communications in society.

Communication is more than meaning, for it is *meaning* that is communicated. Meaning may be private, imparted to no one; but communication implies at least two minds. An identical meaning may be communicated in several different ways: by speech, writing, or gesture, for example. *Communication is a process in which meaning is conveyed. It is also purposive: it is an intended provoking of response.* If I see dark clouds in the sky I may expect rain, and it is this I refer to when I say that I know the meaning of dark clouds. When I think of dark clouds as meaning something, I am treating them as a "sign" I am interpreting. But I have not received a communication because no one intended

to provoke a response by placing the clouds before my eyes.

Communication is always social. It contains three elements, one of which has an important corollary: (1) a person who communicates, (2) the signs by which he communicates, and (3) a person who interprets the signs. The communicator need not be present, or even alive. Dead authors and artists communicate. The signs must be present to the interpreting mind, although they need not be present in fact. They may be only remembered, as the first chapter of a book is when one is in the middle, or the first movement as a symphony nears its close.

The corollary is implied by the third element. To be able to interpret a sign one must know the conventional system within which the signs have their meaning. One must know English in order to understand an English sentence. To an Eskimo visiting one of our cities for the first time, a green light at an intersection may have no meaning, or it may not have the meaning intended by the highway commission; one must understand the system of traffic signals in order to interpret a green light successfully. In the same way, one must be familiar with the principles of Chinese music in order to grasp the meaning of a Chinese musical composition; one must understand the system of Japanese flower arrangements in order to know what is intended by the flowers set in a Japanese room.

With this corollary, what seemed simple and

From *Symbols and Civilization* by Ralph Ross, © 1957, 1962 by Harcourt Brace Jovanovich, Inc., New York, and reprinted with their permission.

straightforward becomes complex and devious. The conventional meaning system may be one that gives systematic rules for interpreting signs. Traffic signals and mathematics do so, mathematics less successfully because there are cases of context altering meaning even in mathematics. But a language, especially a language spoken by a civilized nation, is subject to all the difficulties we discussed under the heading of scientific language, and many more. Both language and art have implicit in them the presuppositions of the culture from which they come. Their use reveals much of the intellectual history of that culture and the psychology of the people who compose it. Language and art, in turn, help make that history and that psychology what they are. We will try to explain these perhaps cryptic statements.

Community and *communication* are words which show an immediate similarity. They emphasize commonness, togetherness. People gather or live *together* for certain purposes, and they *share* meanings and attitudes; the first presupposes the second, for without communication there is no comminity. Community depends on shared experience and emotion, and communication enters into and clarifies the sharing. Forms of communication like art and religion and language are themselves shared by a community,[1] and each of them contains and conveys ideas, attitudes, perspectives, and evaluations which are deeply rooted in the history of the community.

Language shows the differences in cultural ideas most clearly. Malinowski insisted that no dictionary translation into English of the speech of Trobriand Islanders would give their meaning, because their language carried traditional ideas unfamiliar to people outside their culture. So a seemingly simple description of arrival in a canoe carried in its very syntax and its metaphors a great weight of competitive boasting. "We paddle in place; we turn, we see our companion," may sound like description, but for the Trobrianders the emphasis is on being in front, being able to paddle faster than others.

The syntax of modern English expresses many deep-rooted ideas of Western civilization and makes it difficult to say untraditional things. The way in which English expresses the idea of the self in terms of ownership is a case in point. I *have* a body; I *have* a mind; I *have* a soul. Then who am I who has all these things? I may be thought to be one or another of them, or all three in combination. The syntax, however, makes it sound as if I were none of them, but something else, and what else could I be? This confusion is due to a traditional metaphysic of substance and attributes, according to which things referred to by nouns or substantives are somehow substantial, while their attributes, or properties, or qualities, are not. Of course, "body," "mind," and "soul" are ordinarily substantives but they are used as if they were attributes, or properties, of "I" in the instance above.

As we learn our language, we acquire the cultural ideas with which it is freighted without conscious realization that we are doing so. To take a different kind of example: God, obviously not endowed by Christianity with sexual qualities, is always "He." His Son is born of a woman and God is referred to as the Father. The images of a patriarchal society thus color our religious attitudes through the very language which conveys them.

Language and civilization grow together. As other aspects of the civilization develop, its language, whose structure already expresses an earlier age, must be wrestled with and sometimes altered in order to express new thought properly. But new thought does not grow apart from language; new thinking and new ways of speaking go together. One way of expressing new ideas, especially abstract ones, without wrenching the language from its customary uses, is to use metaphors based on more familiar notions, thus assimilating the new ideas into the older linguistic and intellectual habits.[2] Some ideas of physics, for example, were so difficult for even physicists of past centuries to understand, that they immediately acquired metaphoric statement. How would one say in literal English what is conveyed by "bodies attract and repel each other," which sounds for all the world like human affection and aversion?

In contrast there is the difficulty faced by a thoroughly literal man with scientific training when he tries to understand the humbler uses of language. These have their meaning defined by the human behavior of which they are part, not just by the words that are uttered. "Blood is thicker than water" is not intended as a biological truth. Let

---

[1] Art and religion, as we shall contend, are not only forms of communication; they have aspects of creation and feeling which are individual and can be thought of in themselves.

[2] See pp. 22–25.

us first distinguish three different situations, all of which are meaningful, so that we can isolate the "humbler" expressions and see their value. (1) A man carrying a pail of water under whose weight he is stooped and straining shows the observer that the pail is heavy. (2) If the same man utters the statement "This is heavy," we have that information without watching him. (3) If he is a scientist, he may make an exact statement, "This pail of water weighs fifty-seven and a half pounds." There is an enormous gain in the scientific quality of communication.

Is this gain without loss? No; much has been lost. The more exact statement, which specifies the weight, has lost the idea that it is a hardship to carry this pail of water, an idea that was conveyed by the first statement. And even the first statement has lost the *quality* of hardship that we feel when we see this man carrying this pail over this ground. Battlefield communiques are more "scientific" than firsthand descriptions by soldiers and they convey specific information about a battle more effectively, but there is a loss as well as a gain in this advance in accuracy. For when the *experience* of battle is *reproduced* in literature, as it is in *War and Peace*, *The Charterhouse of Parma*, and *The Red Badge of Courage*, more is kept of the meanings and power of experience than can be found in statistical tables of Napoleon's campaigns or of the American Civil War.

The statement "This is heavy" is an example of a "humble" use of language. It is imprecise—for we don't know how heavy it is—and perhaps querulous. The hardship of carrying the pail of water is not stated; if we did not know what the situation was we would not know that the man who carried the pail was complaining. If he had been discussing a brick of solid gold the statement "This is heavy" might imply happiness if he were the owner, or envy if he were not.

Many "humble" uses of language may be thought of as non-cognitive, in the sense that the words alone do not convey the meaning of their use. That meaning is in the situation as a whole and the words, though central to the situation, cannot be disconnected from it and still retain their function. Here we are thinking of the use of words in attention-getting, reassuring, sharing, dedicating, and things of that sort. We often use a person's name at the beginning of a sentence addressed to him, to make sure that he listens to what we say. Some-

times we utter whole sentences merely to make him aware of our presence and so to assure ourselves of our importance, perhaps even of our existence. "What a nice day," we may say, just to get attention, to be recognized. At other times we speak in order to give another person assurance that we are aware of his presence, saying perhaps the same thing that called his attention to us. Again, we reassure him by saying any of a variety of things which shed no light on the matter which has led us to speak. We say, "Everything will be all right," or "There, there," or "Don't worry about a thing." By expressions like "My, my," or "Did you see that?" or "Isn't it wonderful?" we show that we are sharing an experience and often increase the pleasure in another person's experience, and in our own, by emphasizing the fact that we are undergoing it at the same time.

What we have been saying about language should show its wonders as well as the difficulties of using it for thought. But the wonders far outweigh the difficulties. In fact, the difficulties are only the problems of mastering language for the service of thought. Without language, man is scarcely human and thought only rudimentary.

Man is not the only creature capable of co-operation with his fellows for the sake of shared ends, but he is the only creature who has culture. Some "higher" animals co-operate in a rudimentary way and, under laboratory conditions, have been trained to co-operate even more. It is in insect societies, however, that co-operation is at its height in the nonhuman world. The ant, the termite, and the bee are endowed with instinct which results in highly social behavior. The ant and the bee communicate sufficiently so that one member of the heap or hive can direct the others to food. The dance of the bee seems even to communicate an estimate of the direction and distance of the food that has been found. Nonhuman animals, other than insects, do not seem able to communicate with such exactness; but they are able, by vocalizations of different kinds, to express emotion and to attract the attention of their fellows. This often results in behavior directed to their needs or wants.

The ant communicates by touch and the bee by movement in space. Animals gesture as well as make sounds. One has only to watch a chimpanzee in the zoo to see a stance of hostility or a movement of conciliation (terms for human behavior, to be sure, but metaphorically descriptive enough). Yet communication among "higher" animals is scarcely greater than among the social insects—if, indeed, it is as great. And although there are herds and packs of animals, there is nothing in the animal world below the level of man that remotely resembles insect societies in complexity of organization. The reason seems to be that societies may exist on the basis of instinct or of language. Insects have the former and men the latter, and other animals do not have enough of either.

More instinct-directed behavior is found in creatures who are lower in the evolutionary scale. A rough rule is that the higher the intelligence of the species, the less its instinct. There are wasps that fight the much larger tarantula spider, sting him in a spot the size of a pin point, which paralyzes him, and carry him off to a nest where they deposit their eggs, leaving the living flesh for the larvae to feed on. And a wasp separated from her fellows at birth and confronted with a tarantula for the first time behaves in the same way. The sea exhibits countless instances of marvelously developed instinct. Grunions lay their eggs in the sand just as the tide is receding. The adults get back to sea, leaving the eggs to mature in the sun-warmed sand until the returning tides rupture the eggs and carry out to sea the baby fish which emerge from them. European eels swim some three thousand miles from their fresh-water homes in rivers and streams to the Sargasso Sea, where they reproduce and die, leaving their young to return to fresh water, a trip taking as much as three years, where they live until sexual maturity and then repeat the cycle.

Either man has no instincts at all, or we do not know what they are. His chief internal equipment for survival is the brain and central nervous system; his chief external equipment is his hands. Brain and hands create tools which are a much extended and variable external equipment. Other animals are limited to the equipment they carry with them as parts of their bodies: fangs and claws, tusks, paws for digging, quills or shells for protection. These alter slowly in the course of evolution but they cannot, like tools, be discarded or created at will.

In addition to brain and hands, man's equipment for survival includes those organs, like the larynx, which make it possible for man to live socially. Man has not survived, as the lion has, individually, in isolated families or small herds. Man is able to talk, and speech makes possible co-operative undertakings which protect him from his enemies, shelter

him from the elements, and lead to the creation, the transmission, and the alteration of culture.

Only man has a developed, or verbal, language, so it is only man who can learn things precisely and store them in memory in all their essentials. Language is a necessary condition for the existence of culture, for what is learned by one man is transmitted to others; and what is wanted for co-operative undertakings of any complexity can be expressed in words. Then the organization of a society and the things it has learned can be transmitted to the next generation, thus continuing the culture that has been created. Language manages what nature cannot: the transmission of acquired characteristics. Each generation adds to the store of culture, or changes what it has inherited, making culture cumulative. Growth and change give man a history, and, properly speaking, he is the only creature who has a history.

Finally, language contributes inestimably to man's sheer physical survival, not only by giving him knowledge acquired by others at his own time or in the past, but also because language is needed for co-operation to meet novel situations. Instinct alone allows the insect to cope excellently with a limited number of situations that are invariant, or nearly so; language may be used to guide behavior in new ways in the face of the unexpected.

There are other forms of communication which, as we shall see, store and transmit knowledge, hold a society together, and direct conduct. But it is doubtful whether these would even exist if man had no language. And surely only language can communicate precisely the abstract ideas of science and philosophy or the practical wants and concerns fulfilled in industry, trade, and the countless minutiae of life.

In the life of the child, language often has a part contrary to the one it plays in the development of civilization. In civilization, verbalization and conceptualization often take place *after* the event. Religious ritual is explained by the theology that follows it, political action is studied and its principles *subsequently* formulated, Aristotle's rules for the drama are written when the great age of Greek tragedy is past. The child, however, is often taught the word *before* he knows its referent, and may even be able to repeat sentences whose meanings emerge only in later life.

We cannot specify exactly the part that language plays in socialization, but we can be confident that it is a very large part. Socialization not only makes a person a member of the culture, but it also makes him fully a human being. Apart from society, man does not even exhibit potentiality for living in the most rudimentary culture. We cannot be sure precisely how much the humanness of man depends on language, but there is a good deal of evidence that without it man is scarcely recognizable as human, and that language is probably necessary for all higher cultural accomplishments.

There have been many reports of the survival of children who were lost at a tender age in uninhabited places. Only a few of the reports are credible, but these describe their subjects in very much the same way. Strange man-like creatures found in isolated regions in the Middle Ages, children presumably raised by wolves, and the few feral men reported more recently are regularly described as savage, unintelligent by human standards, and exhibiting more characteristics of other animals than of man. In some instances the children never can learn to speak or write or to take their places as ordinary members of society. When found, they usually go about on all fours, are savage to men, and prefer raw meat. Occasionally one of them lives for some years in captivity and acquires a few of the habits of the culture, including even a simple vocabulary. There is great theoretical importance in reports of feral children (and in the case cited below) because the decisiveness of the role of language in socializing children is one of the hypotheses on which social scientists can scarcely experiment.

In the past it was believed that behavior is learned to a great extent by imitation. But the occasional case of the child raised in the company of one or more adults who do not speak indicates that the special factor of language may be more significant for socialization than had been assumed. This is evident in the story of Isabella.[3] In brief, the sociologist Kingsley Davis studied a girl called Isabella who had lived the first six and a half years of her life in a single room with her deaf-mute mother. She rarely saw the rest of the family and in consequence had learned no language; she and her mother communicated solely by means of gestures. When Isabella was found and brought into society she showed some of the characteristics of the feral

child; according to Professor Davis, "Her behavior towards strangers, especially men, was almost that of a wild animal, manifesting much fear and hostility. In lieu of speech she made only a strange croaking sound. In many ways she acted like an infant."

Although there seemed no hope for Isabella, she was trained intensively, at first with almost no success. It took one week to get Isabella even to attempt vocalization. Yet little more than two months later she was putting sentences together, and sixteen months after that she had a vocabulary of nearly two thousand words and was, of course, reading and writing. Her I.Q. had trebled in a year and a half and she was well on the way to catching up with children of her own chronological age.

Since the chief lack in Isabella's socialization up to six and a half years of age was language, one should be entitled to conclude tentatively that it is the absence of language in the environments of feral children that accounts for much of their seeming nonhumanity. In other words, language is a *necessary* condition for *rudimentary* socialization. Yet language alone does not bring a child up to the average level of his society; it is not a *sufficient* condition for *average* socialization. This is evidenced by studies of children in remote, relatively unchanging areas, children who were raised normally on the spoken word and were given ordinary education. One such study, of isolated mountain children,[4] shows that their average I.Q. is less than the average of children in ordinary small towns. It is important, however, to note that whereas the scores of the mountain children on intelligence tests were consistently a little below average for the nation, Isabella's score was almost zero. This is a measure, perhaps, of the part language plays in socialization.

In its simplest definition, a symbol is a conventional sign. A sign represents, or signifies; it conveys a meaning. Signs may be either natural or conventional. The meaning of natural signs is *discovered*, for they are part of the causal connections of nature. When litmus turns red in a solution, the color is a sign of the presence of acid. The meaning of conventional signs or symbols, however, is fixed by use and agreement; they are arbitrarily chosen, in that they have no causal connection with what they represent. All words are symbols although not

[3]Kingsley Davis, "Final Note on a Case of Extreme Isolation," *American Journal of Sociology*, Vol. 52, 1947, p. 432.

[4]Mandel Sherman and Cora B. Key, "The Intelligence of Isolated Mountain Children," *Child Development*, Vol. 3, 1932.

all symbols are words. And words have no direct efficacy to alter things; their power is indirect, through their effect on men.

In some forms of magic, symbols were thought to have power over things, but often their power was only over intelligences, spirits, or demons who accomplished the ends desired. Faust's power lay in his temporary control of Mephistopheles. On the other hand, when words have direct control over things, either those "things" are animate and intelligent or the "words" are mere uttered sounds—not symbols at all—functioning as natural phenomena, perhaps as vibrations in the air. When Ali Baba opened the door of the thieves' cave by pronouncing "Open Sesame," that was magic, and either the door is "animate" or the sounds he uttered would have to activate the mechanism the way the beam does a photoelectric cell.

A is a natural sign of *B* if *A* is evidence that *B* will occur. But a natural sign need not be a natural phenomenon; it may be an artifact. Rails are as much a natural sign of the existence of a train as dark clouds are of rain. Even symbols may be treated as natural signs, in so far as their *existence* or *use*, not just their meaning, is evidence of something. If a language has twelve words which are synonyms for "house" and no words for "home," we may infer several things about the culture which produced that language. When a man makes a mistake in speech he may be revealing something about himself that would not have been shown by the correct statement. The psychiatrist A. A. Brill reported an incident that amused Sigmund Freud. At a dinner to help launch Theodore Roosevelt's candidacy for president and to honor his "square deal," an ungenerous host served only sandwiches and lemonade. One of the hungry guests said to the host, "You may say what you please about Teddy, but there is one thing— he can always be relied on; he always gives you a square meal."

Symbols, we have said, require an interpreter who knows something of the system by virtue of which the symbol has meaning. Natural signs require an interpreter who knows a theory, or general law, in terms of which the sign is an index of the existence of something else. To interpret dark clouds to mean rain or red litmus paper to mean an acid solution, one must know something general about the connection between clouds and rainfall or litmus and acid. Without symbols there are no scientific laws, and without scientific laws there are

no natural signs. So there is a dependence even of natural signs on language.

Because symbols are arbitrary, in that any symbol we agree on will carry the meaning we give it, we may be tempted to infer that no symbol is a better sign than any other. But we should be wrong. It makes no difference that we use the word "horse" for a particular beast of burden instead of any other word we could invent, but it made an enormous difference to the development of mathematics that Roman numerals were replaced by Arabic. Simplicity and flexibility are virtues in a system of symbols. Regular prefixes and suffixes which can be used with many words make it easier to create and understand new meanings.

Although most people in our own culture know that words are arbitrary and are not parts of the things they signify, they often belie this knowledge by their behavior. It is expected that the act of love will be described only in technical terms in the classroom, the drawing room, and the lecture hall. So too with excretion. And death is often described in euphemism: "He passed away." It is as if Anglo-Saxon words are part of the thing described, while Latin roots preserve a distance.

There are three chief ways of using words: to express the feelings of their user, to arouse a response in the hearer or reader, and to stand for a referent. These are the expressive, evocative, and referential functions of language. Much of the time words are used in all three ways at once, but usually one or another function is emphasized. Expressive and evocative elements are almost always present, and when there is reference as well, it affects expression and evocation. Exclamations are almost exclusively expressive. "Damn!" or "Oh, God!" may be uttered even when one is alone, and are clearly not intended to have a referent. Commands are basically evocative. So are sales talks, which are aimed at a response— purchase— and which describe a commodity only in order to stimulate the response. Directions given to a stranger are referential and are quite neutral as expression or evocation. We do not care whether he goes to this or another destination, but we try to use words to describe a route accurately. Scientific writing at its best strongly emphasizes the referential, whereas literary art is a combination of the expressive, evocative, and referential, and neglects any one of these functions at its peril.

Only when language is referential can its meaning

be gathered by attending to language alone. When language is expressive or evocative its meaning depends in good part on the circumstances in which it is uttered. "Look out" is usually a warning of danger, but the words alone do not convey the full meaning of the speaker, which may be "duck," "jump," or "stand still." It all depends on the kind of danger confronting the hearer or the speaker's interpretation of that danger.

Sometimes the word "symbolism" is used in a special way, to describe a kind of art in which the key symbols have not only their ordinary referents but also a larger significance. In the first canto of the *Inferno*, for example, Dante speaks of his encounter with a leopard, a lion, and a she-wolf. The names of these beasts refer to the beasts themselves, but they also signify pleasure, ambition, and avarice. Thus they are "symbols" in a special sense, not just as all words are symbols, but in having a secondary, indirect reference for which the interpreter needs additional knowledge. Perhaps the basic point about this use of "symbol" is that the word has its ordinary single referent and that referent in turn is thought of as a symbol with still another referent. Dante (actually his translator) uses the word "lion" to stand for the lion, an animal, but the beast himself is a symbol of ambition. This is not ambiguity, for the word does not have two unrelated meanings; it means ambition *because* it means lion.[5] It is such a chain of reference which perhaps characterizes the important social symbols, like the flag. But this is only one point about a complicated matter which is still obscure.

Action, too, can be symbolic. In so far as an act accomplishes something directly, brings about an end, it is functional. But many acts are performed for the sake of their meanings—whether or not the acts affect anything materially—and so are essentially symbolic. Ritual is symbolic in that it is an expression of meaning, although it may also be thought to bring about specific ends. Ceremony

and etiquette are symbolic: the hat is removed or the knee bent as a sign of respect. The individual to whom the ceremony is addressed is usually thought of in his status, not his person. Soldiers are taught that they salute the rank, not the man; and it is the Queen, not Elizabeth, to whom the lady at court curtseys. Etiquette is a symbolism of rank and prestige, as well as a way of regulating social intercourse.

Symbols, then, may be words, things, or actions. They are conventional signs which can be interpreted properly only by knowing their socially determined meanings. And those meanings are not decided explicitly at conventions of lexicographers. They develop out of the needs and uses of each society. They reflect the experiences of the people by the objects and relations they symbolize, and the values of the culture by the emphases they provide.

Symbols often have meanings in addition to their ordinary ones which do not appear on the level of consciousness but emerge in dream and fantasy. Under hypnosis or the influence of truth serums people do not merely reveal things they previously refused to divulge; they also reveal things of which they were not consciously aware. A hypnotized patient may remember where he lost something. In addition, things become symbols, take on meanings not consciously attributed to them. Some of these symbols, like snakes and birds, are so widespread that a number of people believe them to be universal among men, not limited to particular cultures. It still seems unlikely, however, that isolated peoples who live in climates with neither snakes nor birds would use them as symbols of any kind, conscious or unconscious. Within our own culture, in any event, there have been some provocative experiments on communication of dream symbols. Farber and Fisher, for example, worked with people under hypnosis.[6]

. . . They described to Subject *A* under hypnosis a painful "experience," and then asked him to dream about this implanted "experience." The subject thereupon reported a dreamlike, disguised reproduction of the "experience," transposed into more or less classical symbols, almost as if this naïve individual had read a dictionary of dream symbolism. Then the experimenters showed Subject *A*'s hypnotic dream to

---

[5]There is a current literary use of "symbol" which should be noted. A symbol in a poem may be thought of as in great part referring to other symbols in the same poem instead of to anything outside the poem, although of course the meaning of each symbol, like that of any word, comes from outside the poem. This is, in its internal relations, like mathematical symbols which refer to other mathematical symbols rather than to the external world, or like musical phrases whose meaning is found within the composition itself.

There is still another technical use of "symbol" that is important. Traditionally, art historians have used "symbol" to mean particular emblems, like the thunderbolts of Jupiter or the wheel of Catherine, which constitute a sort of code in which thunderbolts or wheels mean Jupiter or Catherine.

[6]Described by Dr. Lawrence S. Kubie, "Communication Between Sane and Insane: Hypnosis," *Cybernetics*, Transactions of the Eighth Conference, Josiah Macy, Jr., Foundation, 1952, p. 96.

Subject *B* while under hypnosis, and asked Subject *B* under hypnosis what the dream of Subject *A* had meant. Thereupon Subject *B* translated the dream of Subject *A* back into the essence of the unpleasant story which had originally been told to Subject *A*.

That is more than a trick. It is a very important experiment which has been repeated often enough to make us sure that one human being can on a dissociated level translate accurately the symbolic representations of the unconscious content of thought and feeling of another human being, thus exposing and uncovering repressed experiences which the other has had in the past. This is a critical and conclusive demonstration of the power and specificity of unconscious psychological processes, and of their importance in the communications which pass between men.

Our responses to the symbols of nation, family, religion, and love—to mention a few of the things most important to our lives—probably have an unconscious as well as a conscious element. Behavior in response to the use of these symbols is often more extreme than their conscious meanings would warrant. We may risk or even sacrifice our lives when a purely "rational" attitude would lead us to neither. "To give one's life for a belief," wrote Anatole France, "is a high price to pay for a conjecture." The translation of "belief" into "conjecture" retains much of the conscious and referential meaning of the word "belief," but it loses the deep emotions it evokes and the layers of meaning. Such translation in terms of reference alone is necessary for science and exact thought, but insufficient for the social function of a symbol, that of welding individual men together to make a community. Social symbols bind us to one another in society and allow us to share the attitudes, emotions, and values that make social groups cohesive. Such symbols may be objects like the flag, the cross or crescent, the eagle, the hammer and sickle; or they may be formalized action of the sort we call ritual.

The wealth of meaning that is associated with the symbol of the cross is more like the ambiguous meanings of an artistic symbol than the single use of a sign in science. In ancient Rome the cross was an instrument of torture and death; the meaning lingers as we associate the cross with the passion of Christ. Christ's passion generalized means suffering, moral goodness, and redemption, and the cross stands for these, too, as well as for Christendom itself, which presumably accepts those meanings. When we place a cross atop a building we may intend only to mark the building as a church, yet all the associated meanings may be evoked at once in the spectator.

Ritual action has the same richness of ambiguity and evokes intensity of emotion in the same way as objects that are social symbols. The ceremony of the mass—which has, of course, specific religious meanings—and the salute to the flag permit us to share the deep emotional commitments which are the cement of society. Secular rituals share with religious ceremony the elements of celebration, dedication, and consecration, which we will discuss in connection with religion. It is not so much the precise content of the rituals or the theoretical meaning we might assign to them that works this spell, but a generalized and often vague feeling that accompanies them. We may, in a given ritual, dedicate ourselves to the service of our country, and the idea of what we are doing may move us emotionally, but the familiarity of the ritual, the others who perform it at the same time, the feeling that we are connected with something larger than ourselves, that we are accepted, that we have a place where we belong—these concomitants of ritual are in some ways the most important things about them.

It is reported that a schoolteacher, listening attentively to a child recite the "pledge of allegiance," heard the familiar words in slightly altered form: "I pledge my legions to the flag, and the Republicans for which it stands; one nation invisible, with liberals and justice for all." Obviously the children who recite this garbled pledge have no clear idea of what they are saying. Yet the emotional charge, what we just called the concomitants of ritual, is probably not impaired—or at most impaired only slightly—and the purpose of the pledge is fairly well realized.

Various traditions in the Western world would have to treat what has just been said as essentially irrational. The kind of thinking that is involved in classical economics and in much of utilitarianism is, for the most part, a calculation of advantage. Advantage, in these intellectual frameworks, is individual, and what is "reasonable" is the attainment of individual advantage with the maximum of efficiency. Of course, it was also believed by classical economists that what is economically good for one will benefit all, and by utilitarians that the ultimate good is that of the greatest number. But the calculation of advantage for one or for the greatest number was still in terms of dollars and cents or quantities of pleasure. These doctrines are so much a part of us that young people, in periods of adolescent rebellion against the conventions among which they live, often regard the ordinary symbolism and ritual of their society as benighted. So they ask why we continue such forms as the funeral service and the marriage ceremony, implying that they are "useless," a word which in the tradition of utilitarianism is virtually a synonym of "irrational."

After all, why should we not bury the dead quickly and hygienically, marry and divorce merely by recording our intentions, try to live as "rationally" as possible? The answer is that, apart from their purely religious significance, funeral rites and symbols reaffirm each man's place in society, in the family, in friendship, and in love. They commemorate his existence, the particulars of his life, and the gap he leaves in the lives of others. A man is not a machine and is not replaceable in every detail by any other man; each man is unique and this uniqueness, too, is commemorated. Society expresses in the funeral its interest in each of its members and its continuance in its surviving members. It affirms both the death of a man and his continuance, in memory and influence, in his family, his friends, his society itself.

Classical epic and tragedy offer vivid examples of the social importance of one man's death. Homer's *Iliad* ends with the funeral rites of Hector, leader of the Trojan forces, heir to the throne. Why did Homer not conclude his epic with Hector's death? Because the funeral exhibits the meaning of that death to Troy, to Greece, to future ages. Hector was the great champion of his people. While he lived, Troy survived. His death meant the destruction of Troy, the end of all her greatness, the return of the Greek kings to their own lands, even a new direction for civilization.

Hamlet, too, does not close with the death of the Prince. There is a symbolic soldier's funeral and an oration by Hamlet's successor, Fortinbras. The meaning of Hamlet's life is stated and his virtues extolled. It is not just *a* prince who died, but *this* prince, and his death deprived his country of his gifts— rich gifts, for he had been "the glass of fashion and the mould of form," and "was likely, had he been put on [the throne], to have proved most royally."

The protagonist of classical tragedy was the king, the prince, the hero. His death was important to his community as a whole. But the life of even the humblest member of society makes a difference to some few others and so, in a way, to his society. By commemorating his life and his death in appropriate rite and symbol, we give "meaning" to our own lives and deaths, an importance that is never for ourselves alone. The "meaning" of a man's life and of his death is not only in himself, but also in his relations to others as individuals, and in his place and role in society. As John Donne said, "No man is an *Iland*, intire of itselfe; every man is a peece of the *Continent*, a part of the *maine;* if a *Clod* bee washed away by the *Sea, Europe* is the lesse, as well as if a *Promontorie* were, as well as if a *Mannor* of thy *friends* or of *thine owne* were; any mans *death* diminishes *me*, because I am involved in *Mankinde;* And therefore never send to know for whom the *bell* tolls; It tolls for *thee*."[7]

Is it "reasonable," then, to eliminate the funeral service? Obviously not. The calculation of our own advantage that would impel us to dispose of the human dead like so much waste matter would yield, on a larger and *more reasonable* calculation, great disadvantage. It would impoverish our lives and destroy much of their significance. It is not "reasonable" to judge every action by its consequence for direct personal advantage; nor is it "reasonable" to approve ritual and symbolic action only because *enlightened* self-interest finds greater advantage in preserving society than in attaining personal ends in opposition to society. If we act out of enlightened self-interest alone we will have destroyed the emotional and traditional base of society.[8]

For some intellectual purposes it is useful to treat every human action as a choice or decision based on a calculation of advantage. The study of economics has profited by such treatment. But we should never forget that this is only a way of stating things that helps us perform particular intellectual tasks; it is not an adequate description of the nature of man. To be sure, man may find living in society advantageous, but the man who comes to that conclusion is one who has been raised in society, not in the "state of nature." Any man may prefer one type of society to another, but his judgment is al-

7"Devotion XVII."
8Of course, when rites are performed by rote or cheapened by extraneous sentiment, they become shoddy and hollow. After witnessing such rites, a spectator may turn from them in disgust and conclude that all rites for he may see no better ones are mere superstition.

ready conditioned by the society that has made him what he is. Santayana says wisely, "It is in the subsoil of uniformity, of tradition, of dire necessity that human welfare is rooted, together with wisdom and unaffected art, and the flowers of culture that do not draw their sap from that soil are only paper flowers."

The bonds of society are the shared symbols, rituals, values, and beliefs of its members, and it is in these that the "meaning" of the society is contained. Bonds may restrain, like the chains on a slave, or they may sustain, like the climber's rope. Social bonds do both. They contain us within the limits of social approval, yet they provide the ways in which we develop our lives and our cultures. There is an analogy here to the forms of art. The sonnet limits its author severely, yet it can give his work incisiveness and power. Personal freedom yields little of value outside a social order and tradition; it can in fact be guaranteed only in a political and social order, and the value of individual differences, of choice and free intelligence, and the arts and sciences which they nurture, are dependent on shared ritual, symbol, and emotion. Out social roots are often forgotten because they are firmly embedded and raise no practical problem. If we forget them overlong, we may uproot them, and with them, ourselves.

PART V

CULTURE AND
THE SOCIOCULTURAL LEVEL OF EVENTS

If considered as we have just done, culture as a system of values symbolically formulated and transmitted does not stand alone in the flow of reality. Such a system requires the agency of a human group if it is to be transmitted from one generation to another; conversely, from the point of view of the organization of a human group, there is needed some degree of fundamental agreement upon standards, rules, values in terms of which relations among members of the group will be regulated and sanctioned. Thus there is a complementary and reciprocal relationship between "culture" (conceived as an abstracted system of values governing behavior) and the specific patterns of interpersonal relations among members of a given group that embody and give life to those values. It is for this reason that we must introduce some readings that deal with relations between those two very familiar terms that by and large tend to represent different sets of events in observable reality—or at least different kinds of abstractions or emphases from the flow of social reality: *culture* and *society*. As will be clear in the readings also, we are self-consciously now trying to think in terms of a "levels" framework, the kind of framework of hierarchical levels of phenomena (or systems and sub-systems) first introduced by White and here carried forward by other writers. And, because of the close intertwining of human society with human culture, that level on which anthropologists and sociologists both stand (no matter where they may wander on that level in pursuit of their preferred conceptualizations) is usually termed the *group* level of events, or the *sociocultural* level.

LEVELS OF PHENOMENA

Recall how Leslie White, in his article, "Science is *Sciencing*," spoke of "levels" of events in nature and how we must recognize that when we are trying to analyze phenomena at one level we must use concepts appropriate to that level. We have been talking about the concept of culture, and have

245

spoken of it as a product of *group* experience, of collective social life. And in the last two excerpts we have come closer to the discussion of the relationship between culture, conceived as a symbol system expressing values, and a social system. It is now time, therefore, to give more explicit attention to that idea of the *group* level of events, the *social* level of phenomena. In the case of human societies, however, because their very existence depends upon and is highly structured by culture, many behavioral scientists refer to this level as a *sociocultural* level, and this is what I will do here. "Culture" and "society" are to be seen as two systems, each analyzable in its own right, but in reality interpenetrating and mutually influencing each other. They are *dimensions* of the ongoing organized behavior of a collection of human beings.

The following excerpt is from a statement by a biologist, Alex Novikoff. It presents the basic idea of "integrative" levels of phenomena, such as cell, organism, society, and so forth, in which each "lower" level participates as an element in the "higher" or more comprehensive level, and in which the phenomena of the higher levels must be conceptualized in terms appropriate to those levels and not reduced to principles of organization appropriate to lower levels. In terms of what we are concerned with in this reader, for example, this means that the organizing principles of what we call "society" are not to be found in the depth psychology of the individual human being. Some features of that are involved, of course; but there is something more also included—and that something more is the concept of the social relationship. Because this is such an important point for the social sciences, we will follow this excerpt by Novikoff with another dealing with the same idea.

THE CONCEPT OF INTEGRATIVE LEVELS AND BIOLOGY

ALEX B. NOVIKOFF

The concept of integrative levels of organization is a general description of the evolution of matter through successive and higher orders of complexity and integration. It views the development of matter, from the cosmological changes resulting in the formation of the earth to the social changes in society, as continuous because it is never-ending, and as discontinuous because it passes though a series of different levels of organization—physical, chemical, biological and sociological.

In the continual evolution of matter, new levels of complexity are superimposed on the individual units by the organization and integration of these units into a single system. What were wholes on one level become parts on a higher one. Each level of organization possesses unique properties of structure and behavior which, though dependent on the properties of the constituent elements, appear only when these elements are combined in the new system. Knowledge of the laws of the lower level is necessary for a full understanding of the higher level; yet the unique properties of phenomena at the higher level can not be predicted, *a priori*, from the laws of the lower level. The laws describing the *unique* properties of each level are qualitatively distinct, and their discovery requires methods of research and analysis appropriate to

Reprinted with permission of publisher. From *Science*, 101 (March 2, 1945), 209–15.

the particular level. These laws express the new organizing relationships, *i.e.*, the reciprocal relationships of elementary units to each other and to the unit system as a whole.

The concept of integrative levels recognizes as equally essential for the purpose of scientific analysis both the isolation of parts of a whole and their integration into the structure of the whole. It neither reduces phenomena of a higher level to those of a lower one, as in mechanism, nor describes the higher level in vague non-material terms which are but substitutes for understanding, as in vitalism. Unlike other "holistic" theories, it never leaves the firm ground of material reality. Integration does not imply, as Lillie has recently maintained, "special vital factors"[1] or "something of the mental or psychic."[2] Both parts and wholes are material entities, and integration results from the interaction of the parts, as a consequence of their properties. The concept points the need to study the organizational interrelationships of parts and whole. This full recognition of both units and whole leads to a more adequate understanding of the whole.

The different levels of matter, while distinct, are not completely delimited from each other. No boundary in nature is fixed and no category airtight. "Mesoforms" are found at the transition point of one level of organization to the next. Between the highest level of organization of nonliving, the crystal, and the lowest level of unicellular organisms are protein para-crystals, the viruses, with some of the internal structure and behavior of living substance. Between the single-cell organism and the multicellular organism are the colonial organisms. Yet the absence of rigid demarcation between two levels does not make the difference between them any less clear or fundamental. Mesoforms, "the more clearly we understand them, will all the more clearly serve to bring out the essentially new elements of (the) higher order."[3]

There is both continuity and discontinuity in the evolution of the universe; and consideration of one to the exclusion of the other acts to retard the development of biological and sociological sciences. Knowledge of the general qualities of development common to all levels of organization of matter will aid in the analysis and description of the concrete attributes of each level. But it can not be a substitute for such analysis or for the determination of the qualitative uniqueness of each level and the characteristic laws which govern it.

PHYSICO-CHEMICAL AND BIOLOGICAL LEVELS

The concept of integrative levels does not regard living organisms as machines made of a multitude of discrete parts (physico-chemical units), removable like pistons of an engine and capable of description without regard to the system from which they are removed. Its approach is one which biochemists are adopting more and more: living cells present problems not to be encountered in the test-tube or flask. The structural pattern of the cell plays a decisive role in many of the chemical reactions which constitute metabolism. The ordering, as well as speed, of the chemical reactions in the cell are largely the result of the distribution and activity of colloidal enzymes. Korr[4] has indicated that even simple colloidal systems "represent a much higher level of integration . . . and that, because of the quantitative and qualitative modification which interfaces and their molecular groupings impose, there emerge new classes of phenomena for which there are no analogies in homogeneous systems, and which, therefore, require new sets of rules." Commoner[5] has discussed the increased dependence of enzyme function on structural factors in the living cell. The degree of dependence of a particular enzyme system on protoplasmic structure or physico-chemical organization can be revealed by changes in this structure, both natural and experimentally produced.

It has been the great contribution of the "organicists" that they have demonstrated the error of the mechanistic reduction of the biological organism to the physico-chemical. It is therefore unfortunate that "organicism" has been marred by non-material concepts. Organicists fail to picture the "whole" as developing through the integration of individual units of matter into a single system; they omit a discussion of the organizing relationships of the parts. They try to describe the behavior of the organism solely in terms of the higher level, the whole. As a result, the impression is created that no material basis exists for the part-whole relation.

Almost all the text-book definitions of physiology reduce phenomena of living matter, a highly com-

[1] Ralph S. Lillie, *The American Naturalist*, 72: 414, 1938.
[2] Ralph S. Lillie, *Philosophy of Science*, 7: 327, 1940.
[3] Joseph Needham, *The Modern Quarterly* (London) 1: 30: 1938.

[4] Irvin Korr, *Cold Spring Harbor Symposia*, 7: 74, 1939.
[5] Barry Commoner, *Quarterly Review of Biology*, 17: 46, 1942.

plex and integrated system, to the level of free molecules and atoms. Certainly chemical and physical form are operative in cells, yet defining physiology as "the physics and chemistry of life processes" overlooks the fact that the cell organization imposes a new and higher order on physico-chemical change, and the tissues, organs, organ-systems and organism impose; higher order on cell activity. Physiology rightly concerns itself also with the activities of the higher orders: cellular organization and function as well as chemistry and physics in the narrow sense; the tissue organ, organ-system as well as the cell. No matter how complete our knowledge of the chemistry and physics of living systems becomes in the future, living substance must still be recognized as matter on a higher level, with new, unique properties which have emerged on combination of the lower-level units. When molecules become part of a highly integrated system, protoplasm, it is important to know the properties of the molecules, but protoplasmic behavior needs description in terms and laws which have a meaning for molecules, in specifically biological terms and laws.

BIOLOGICAL LEVELS

Within the biological level, there are a series of other integrative levels.

I

In the multicellullar organism there is a hierarchy of levels—cells, tissues, organs, organ-systems and organism. Viewed in terms of integrative levels, Heilbrunn's assertion that "general physiology thus becomes cellular physiology" and that "the ultimate mechanism responsible for any form of vital activity lies inherent in the individual cells"[6] is one-sided. A full understanding of the organism is not possible without complete knowledge of the activities of its cells. But knowledge of "the individual cells" does not exhaust the problems of organism physiology, for the activity of the individual cell is greatly influenced by the products of activity of other cells in tissue organ, organ-system and organism.

The inadequacy of a cell concept in which the cell is considered an independent unit of activity is clear from the work of experimental embryologists. The embryo is not a collection of unrelated portions developing independently of each other; on the

contrary, the development of any cell is dependent not only on its own constitution but also on the nature of the surrounding materials outside the egg or produced in adjacent cells of the embryo. If ectoderm cells which normally form belly skin were removed from a salamander embryo and transplanted over the mouth organizer of a frog embryo, they would develop into salamander structures—of the mouth; they would form teeth and not belly skin.

Similarly, in the adult organism, plant or animal, the behavior of a cell is influenced by the activity of other cells of the body. Thus, the hormone, auxin, produced in the apical cells of a plant, will cause the elongation of stem cells, inhibit the growth of cells of lateral buds, influence the course of differentiation of root cells and stimulate the growth of cambium cells. Chiefly through such hormones, the cells of the plant body are integrated into an organism. In animals, the activity of cells is under the integrating influence of nerve impulses, hormones and other cell products like carbon dioxide. Activity of cells of the salivary glands is dependent upon stimulation by nerve impulses begun elsewhere in the body. The behavior of uterine cells depends not only on its own constitution, but also on hormones produced by cells of pituitary and ovary. Carbon dioxide produced by muscle cells in the legs will influence the behavior of the respiratory center cells in the medulla.

Just as cells do not exist in isolation in the organism, neither do organs or organ-systems. Thus, the functioning of the heart (the rate and force of its beat) is not unrelated to the pressure of the blood in the aorta and carotid arteries, the diameter of the arterioles or the amount of blood returning through the veins; nor is the circulatory system unaffected by or without effects on the nervous, endocrine, muscular or respiratory systems. Coghill,[7] using embryos, and Lashley[8] and Goldstein,[9] studying adult animals and men, have demonstrated the weakness of an atomistic approach to the activity of the nervous system and have emphasized that it functions as an integrated whole.

II

Populations constitute a distinct level of integration, higher than that of the individual organism.

---

[6]L. V. Heilbrunn. "An Outline of General Physiology," pp. 3, 4. Philadelphia, 1943.

[7]G. E. Coghill, SCIENCE, 78: 131, 1933.
[8]K. S. Lashley, "Brain Mechanisms and Intelligence," Chicago 1929.
[9]Kurt Goldstein, "The Organism." New York, 1939.

Schneirla, in his excellent studies on the interrelations between individual behavior of the army-ant and the population unit or colony, stresses this point. "Any social organization represents a qualitatively new emergent level not equivalent to that which might be attained through a mere summation of the properties of its constituent individuals."[10a] It is solely the reactions of the individual ant which are responsible for the highly organized mass behavior; yet "strictly speaking, the Eciton worker has no behavior pattern outside the social sphere."[10b]

Dobzhansky, in his authoritative work on population genetics, similarly described populations as higher levels of integration. The fate of a newly-arisen genetic variant depends not alone on its effect on the individual organism but also upon the "dynamic regularities of the physiology of populations." Thus, it is the effective size of a population which may determine whether a useless or even deleterious mutant will, through chance recombinations, become incorporated into the constitution of the group. The smaller this population size the less effective is selective pressure in evolution. Dobzhansky emphasizes that evolutionary changes are changes in the genetic constitution of groups—of populations. Through natural selection, migration, and isolation, biological groups are produced whose genetic structure is molded in relation to the environment. The laws of population genetics which describe these evolutionary changes are on a higher level than those of the genetics of the individual. "The rules governing the genetic structure of a population are, nevertheless, distinct from those governing the genetics of individuals, just as rules of sociology are distinct from physiological ones, although they are in fact merely integrated forms of the latter."[10c]

The concept of integrative levels stresses the need to study living organisms at all levels—cells, tissues, organs, organ-systems, organisms and populations. It is not "organicist"; always the reciprocal relationship of elementary units to each other and to the unit system as a whole must be studied. It is not mechanistic; the detailed methods of study at higher levels will include not only some used at lower levels but new methods peculiar to the higher levels; the laws of one level will be expressed differently from those of the others.

BIOLOGICAL AND SOCIAL LEVELS

According to the concept of integrative levels, man's social relationships represent a new level, higher than that of his biological make-up. Man's behavior differs from that of other animals because of his possession of body structures, notably, the highly developed nervous system, which make thought and speech possible and whose functioning is profoundly affected by social or cultural influences. Man possesses a unique head and hand, and is able to confront nature not only with his body but with tools devised and wielded by him. The crude tools of primitives give way to the more complex technology characteristic of modern society. As the technological forces change, the social and economic relations of men change, and, with them, man's behavior. Socio-economic or cultural forces thus come to dominate biological factors in directing man's actions.

In a penetrating analysis of Sigmund Freud's failure to recognize the inseparability of the biological and the cultural forces which determine man's behavior, Barlett writes,

> The biological organism, by its existence in society, has become a "new biological species." . . . The biological organism is transformed; it no longer exists as a biological phenomenon, strictly speaking. Under the influence of society, the biological has become the psychological. New laws of motion have come into being which are neither biological nor sociological, but the subject of study of a different science, psychology.[10d]

The concept of integrative levels, as it stresses the need to study the interrelationships between the biological and sociological, emphasizes the fact that the two constitute two distinct levels. Blurring this distinction leads to anthropomorphism and to mystical, often dangerous, statements about society.

Anthropomorphism—endowing animals, and even plants, with human attributes, psychical and social—transports the higher level (social) bodily into the lower level (biological). In doing so, it presents a wholly erroneous picture of the animal. The aspects of behavior common to man and animals are studied in comparative psychology, just as comparative cytology studies the uniformity of structure of diverse cells and comparative biochemistry

---

10(a) T. C. Schneirla, *Psychological Review*, 48: 465, 1941; (b) *idem, The Journal of Comparative Psychology*, 29: 447, 1940; (c) Theodosius Dobzhansky, "Genetics and the Origin of Species," p. 11. New York, 1941; (d) Francis H. Bartlett, "Sigmund Freud," p. 80. London, 1938.

the fundamental chemical changes common to all cells and organisms. Often, the significance of certain aspects of man's behavior (*e.g.*, instincts) can be illuminated by studies on lower animals where the problem may be analyzed more directly. And in the anthropoid apes, it is possible to investigate the beginning of reflective thought and of social influences on behavior.

Yet the study of animal behavior can not be a substitute for the study of man's behavior. As we establish the likenesses in behavior of animals and men, we must simultaneously investigate the fundamental qualitative differences between them. Except in certain pathological conditions, man's behavior is as unique as the organs which he, alone of all animals, possesses; thought, speech, labor are impossible without a highly developed brain and a hand. It is his unique biological constitution which makes possible the development of truly social relations among men. Many investigators studying the integrated animal populations, the so-called societies of animals, appear to have overlooked the fact that animal societies never rise above the biological level, that only man's society is truly sociological.

Any one who has tried to teach biological change to college students knows the barriers to learning which have been created by the identification of animals with men throughout the student's lifetime. Every phenomenon is approached by them in terms of human experience. There is no time scale other than the clock, calendar or century. Yet important biological change can be expressed only in a "non-human" time scale. For each living organism travels at two enormously different speeds of life.[11] The comparatively rapid one is easy to comprehend because the changes can be observed; the birth, growth and death of the body, the movement of the plant on the window sill, and even the less obvious chemical changes of cells and organisms. But only the end results of changes over many thousands of centuries can be seen in the diverse plants and animals, each almost perfectly adapted to its environment. A species, in high-speed terms, is constant; but in low-speed terms, it is changing.

Thinking in high-speed terms of these low-speed phenomena leads almost inevitably to teleological conceptions, ascribing these phenomena to a divine purpose in nature. The terrestrial mammal has no

gills because the air, containing little water, would dry out the exposed soft tissues; the earthworm has no eyes because it has no need for them, buried as it is in the ground. Such teleological reasoning is carried over even to changes which are directly observable. The heart beats in order to bring food-laden blood to all cells of the organism. The leaf bends to the light in order to intercept more energy for photosynthesis. There is no awareness that ascribing such purposive behavior to the heart or the plant imparts the ability to reason and to look into the future, in one case to a small individual part of the organism, and, in the other, to an organism which lacks a nervous system let alone a brain!

The history of biology demonstrates that teleology explains nothing, and, worse still, hampers the search for explanations and causes. You do not study the causal development of eyes in worms if you believe their absence in earthworms is explained by the statement that underground worms need none. Nor do you trouble to analyze the causes of cardiac muscle contraction or the distribution of plant growth hormones if it suffices to say that the heart beats to pump blood and the leaf bends to get light. You do not study the causes of evolution or the explanation of mutual adaptation of organism and environment if you assert, as Gerard has recently, that the "selection or creation of these particular mechanisms" is volitional or purposive.[12] Only when purpose was excluded from descriptions of all biological activity except rational behavior of human beings, could biological problems be properly formulated and analyzed. . . .

CONCLUSION

The concept of integrative levels describes the progress of evolution of the inanimate, animate and social worlds. It maintains that such progress is the result of forces which differ in each level and which can properly be described only by laws which are unique for each level. Since higher level phenomena always include phenomena at lower levels, one can not fully understand the higher levels without an understanding of the lower level phenomena as well. But a knowledge of the lower levels does not enable us to predict, *a priori*, what will occur at a higher level. Although some may have validity for the higher level, laws of a lower level are inade-

[11]Henry Collier, "An Interpretation of Biology," Chapter 5. London, 1938.

[12]Ralph W. Gerard, "Organic Freedom," p. 425; "Freedom, Its Meaning," edited by R. N. Anshen. New York, 1940, *Scientific Monthly*, 50: 349, 1940.

quate to describe the higher level. The laws unique to the higher level can be discovered by approaches appropriate to the particular level; to do otherwise is invalid scientifically and, in some instances, dangerous socially.

By stressing the material interrelationships of parts and whole and the qualitative uniqueness of each level of integration, the concept is of genuine help to biologists. Its dialectical approach avoids "organicism," "fatalism" and mechanical "atomism," and helps attain a fuller understanding of such problems as the interrelations of cellular structure and metabolism, of cell and organism in ontogeny and in adult physiology, of individual and population biologies, of biological and social factors in the development of man's behavior; and the mechanisms responsible for organic evolution. By avoiding teleology, the concept aids the search for causes of biological phenomena.

The concept of integrative levels indicates to research biologists the crucial aspects of their problems, the solution of which puts the known facts into proper perspective by revealing the decisive element, the element imparting the uniqueness to the phenomena under study. It emphasizes the importance of studying the "mesoforms," matter at the point of transition from one level of organization to the next, so as to deepen our understanding of the unique qualities of the higher level. For example, it would indicate that an intensive study of the transition region between the chemical and biological levels, between protein and protoplasm, will help reveal the organizing relations unique to living matter and fundamental to vital activities.

As biologists become more familiar with the concept, a greater number will recognize its value both as an aid in the understanding of biological data already accumulated and as a reliable guide for research. Such recognition of its value will, however, be delayed by any presentation which creates the erroneous impression that it is metaphysical, teleological or mystical. This article has pointed to shortcomings in the presentation of the concept in some recent biological literature, with the hope that this may help make future references to the concept more reliable.

LEVELS OF ANALYSIS

S. F. Nadel was one of the most productive and stimulating of modern social (or "sociocultural") anthropologists. The pages that follow are taken from his book, *The Foundations of Social Anthropology*, which ranges over many of the philosophical, methodological, and substantive problems of the field. Included is the point we have just been considering—the "part-whole" relationship problem (or, in this particular instance, the "individual" and the environing social group of which he is a part). It is an idiom very similar to modern "general systems" theory. Some of the language and concepts he uses will already be familiar from White, Novikoff, Hayakawa, and other writers whose works you have seen earlier. As Nadel tries to point out, it does little good toward understanding relations among events if a retreat to the simplifying artificiality, ". . . it is *nothing but* . . ." is used when approaching a complex social fact. He sees social reality as comprised of reciprocal, "feedback" kinds of processes between levels of events; there is both a "social" aspect as well as a "psychophysical" aspect to every "social fact." (And in his "social" aspect he would probably be including what I have called the *cultural* dimension of group life.) In any case, Nadel's excerpt, following that of Novikoff, will help establish the general idea of "emergent" levels of phenomena, without which an understanding of many issues in the social and behavioral sciences will remain confused.

THE HIERARCHY OF SCIENCES

S. F. NADEL

Empirical science is arranged, fortuitously or otherwise, in a hierarchy of disciplines each representing a level of analysis, which proceeds to a certain point and no further. Social enquiry has its place in that hierarchy, being placed above psychology, which in turn is placed above physiology, chemistry, and physics.[1] In this general hierarchy the analytical levels stand in the relationship of progressive inclusiveness so that any phenomenon taken to define a unit on one level may be broken down to components which are the unit phenomena on the next lower level. In every phenomenon visible on the higher level, then, phenomena open to a lower-level analysis must be implicit, and all formulations of unit phenomena on the higher level constitute a 'shorthand' as compared with the 'longhand' of lower-level analysis. Furthermore, any statement of the regularities discovered on the higher level must 'bracket' regularities discovered or discoverable on the lower level; these are taken for granted and assumed to be established (at least potentially) by that deeper-going analysis. I have used the word 'must', for all this is indeed a basic postulate of our understanding. We cannot conceive of the kind of nature in which, say, physical laws would be inapplicable to chemical processes or the bloodstream of the organism would not obey the laws governing the behaviour of fluids.

In the natural sciences this seems to be all. Their field of observation is homogeneous and only conveniently divided between different disciplines, each of which merely defines the level of complexity in the phenomena to which, by common agreement, analysis is to penetrate. The human sciences, too, appear at first sight to embrace a homogeneous field, divided fortuitously and conveniently into different levels of analysis: man is the same whether he is studied by sociology, psychology or physiology, and reveals different aspects of his being only in conformity with the agreed depth of analysis.

Thus every social fact, that is, every human action in respect of other humans is, *at any given moment*, a complex of psychological processes (by which I mean mental events, such as seeing, hearing, thinking, desiring), physiological processes (movements, muscle-tensions, innervations), and innumerable other processes discoverable on yet deeper levels of analysis, and can be broken down to these events and processes. It is merely convenient to handle the phenomena and their relations, on a given level, in the less completely analyzed form and to frame them in the corresponding 'shorthand' concepts. Economy alone would forbid the breaking-up of, say, 'marriage' or 'war' into their mental and physiological components; the description of any social fact would fill volumes if it had to be expressed in the longhand of the more complete analysis. Yet 'marriage' and 'war' *are* all these implicit facts, and nothing really new. In applying the more far-reaching analysis we merely *repeat*, in more detailed and copious language, all that can be discovered in the less fully analyzed phenomena.[2] Thus it has been said that 'mind' is only a 'short-cut expression' for physiological observations;[3] and that the concepts referring to social behaviour only summarize the facts open to the lower-level analysis of psychology.[4]

Now if this were all, the step to a lower level of analysis would not help us to understand the problems encountered on the higher level. More precisely, such a step would widen our knowledge, but only in the sense of unfolding the 'inside' of any phenomenon we study. If we were to name the regularities discovered in social enquiry (e.g. the interdependence of war and economic factors) in terms of psychology or physiology, we should indeed be 'diagnosing' independently established

---

Reprinted with permission. From S. F. Nadel, *The Foundations of Social Anthropology* (Glencoe: The Free Press, 1951), pp. 209–19.

[1] For the purpose of this argument we will consider this hierarchy in a simplified form, disregarding specialized disciplines which either occupy the same level though pursuing different interests (e.g. biology as compared with physiology), or represent additional, intermediate levels (e.g. biochemistry).

[2] A perfect model of this three-level approach will be found in E. C. Tolman (1938b). He chooses, in fact, the same example, marriage, to show how the sociological data of 'group conduct' (i.e. the institution 'marriage') can be broken down to the psychological data of individual behaviour ('X going to the wedding'), and these in turn to physiological activities, neural and biochemical processes, etc. Tolman, however, emphasizes that the psychological data 'are not in a final sense independent and absolute'; rather are they always immersed in a 'field' constituted by the 'culture pattern', i.e. by data definable only on the sociological level (p. 235). This view essentially accords with the one developed further on.

[3] C. C. Pratt (1939), p. 26.

[4] F. W. H. Rivers (1926), p. 14.

facts—the efficacy of feelings, acts of volition, thoughts, or of muscular strain, locomotion, and of the processes of metabolism. But 'independently established' would only mean 'studied by different methods'. We should discover no causes, only correlates, and no hidden machines driving the things we first perceived, but only the things themselves, looked at, as it were, from underneath.

Obviously, this is not true, or not entirely true. The criteria of scientific convenience and economy cannot therefore exhaust the relations between the levels of analysis in the human sciences. I propose to show that the analogy with the natural sciences breaks down on closer inspection for three reasons. It breaks down, first, because in the human sciences the transition from level to level involves what I propose to call a 'phenomenal regression'; secondly, because social and psychological phenomena are incapable of completely independent definition; and thirdly, because social and psychological phenomena also 'interact' (to use for the moment the conventional phraseology). It is this last fact which turns the hierarchy of levels into true causal relations between the levels.

(1) Each level of analysis has its own 'current character of importance' (to borrow Whitehead's phrase). By this I mean that the phenomenal complexes—the complexes of facts given to our experience—are, on any given level, important and interesting as such. The relations that can be pursued between facts of the given phenomenal complexity have their peculiar relevance, which cannot simply be replaced by that of relations discovered on a different level of analysis. In progressive analysis precisely this occurs. The phenomenal properties of facts given on one level disappear on the next lower level. The peculiar qualities of solids or liquids are no longer visible when chemistry is replaced by physics; the irritation of nerve ends is no longer itself, but something else, when the physiologist hands over to the biochemist. This phenomenal regression matters little in the natural sciences, which reduce the qualities of phenomena to mere 'pointer-readings' on indicators and the whole phenomenal world to one of pure measurement.[5] In the human sciences, which remain attached to the phenomenal side of things, it matters a great deal. Man is still the same for the physiologist, psychologist, and anthropologist. But the fact that man's

fears, considered physiologically, become something else, or that his culture and society, broken down to psycho-physical processes, disappear as phenomenal entities, means that the subject matter of these disciplines itself disappears. Thus, between one level of analysis and the next there is a break, a relevant discontinuity—not merely a conventional and fortuitous division. In the field of human phenomena therefore the hierarchy of sciences appears broken up into a series of separate and self-contained disciplines. We now understand why the transition from one to the other appears to be more than merely a deepening of analysis; it gives at least the illusion of stepping into another order of existence, governed by regularities peculiar to it and only there established.

(2) At the same time, the current character of importance of any given level may spread to the other levels. Although I know that in any social action certain mental events are implicit I may be interested in rendering them explicit. In the simplest case this is only a question of the extent to which general knowledge concerning these implicit events can be taken for granted and tacitly assumed. Clearly, I shall not bother to mention the knowledge concerning vision, hearing, or memory which psychologists have accumulated, nor the physiologist's knowledge of muscle tensions and innervations, though all these processes must operate in the movements and perceptions which go to make up any social action. But occasionally this specialist knowledge requires to be expressed in so many words or at least referred to, as it were, in a footnote. For certain social actions have the result (intended or not) of producing or utilizing particular mental states or physiological processes. Think of religious cults or dances inducing mental dissociation and hysteria, of alleged cures of disease, customary ways of securing physical fitness, and the like. As a student of society I wish to be reassured that I have correctly diagnosed these phenomena, which are not really my field; perhaps, too, I wish to learn more about them since this amplified knowledge might lead me to relevant connections I should otherwise overlook. This sort of situation poses no problem of method but only bears on practical considerations. Nor is it peculiar to the human sciences; the study of electric currents in nerve-physiology or of the surface tension of liquids in chemistry represents the same amplification of knowledge in terms of lower-level analysis.

---

[5] Sir Arthur Eddington (1928), p. 252.

But in the human sciences this amplification is more pervasive and is entailed in the very definition of our subject matter. For in any statement about social events we must *name* at least one species of the implicit lower-level events. We cannot define action except as intended behaviour, and hence must specifically refer to the mental functions underlying or carrying the intention—the desires, aims, motives, and so forth. But let me emphasize that this reference is descriptive, not explanatory; we do not establish a novel and causal relation between a specific action and the intention carrying it, but merely amplify our statement that such-and-such is an 'action' by indicating that, with deeper analysis, we should find in it intentions (as well as other mental events).[6]

(3) Yet it surely also makes sense to say that social facts exist and arise *because* the actors have had certain intentions or felt the efficacy of certain mental events, and that they have intentions and other mental events *because* certain social facts happen to exist. The social fact thus entails psychological (or psycho-physical) processes not only as part of its texture but also as something that exists outside and apart from it, namely, as its cause or antecedent and as its effect or consequent. It is a matter of common agreement that the social field is pervaded throughout by relations of this causal and circular kind. In other words, we take it for granted that social facts are not merely the 'outside' to which psycho-physical facts are the 'inside', but that the two also affect and condition each other, that is, 'interact'.

In accepting this co-existence of implicitness and interaction we are faced with certain logical difficulties. For we predicate some mutual influence between a datum visible on one level of analysis and the same datum analyzed more deeply; between a 'shorthand' standing for certain phenomena and the phenomena themselves. This sounds paradoxical; and, indeed, in natural science this would mean, for example, that the chemical properties of a fluid interact with the molecular structure underlying the chemical properties; or that the irritation of nerve ends influences, and is influenced by, the biochemical processes which are the 'long

hand' for the physiological data. This is obviously nonsense. But, in the human field, precisely this is true. (The old controversy over psycho-physical interaction proves that in psychology such propositions are not nonsensical.) In sociology and anthropology, as I have presumed, no one will quarrel with the assumption that social facts 'act' upon mental facts and *vice versa*.

The paradox is resolved when we realize that we do not arbitrarily adopt the 'shorthand' which is the social fact, but that it is forced upon us, upon our way of perceiving and understanding, by the organization of the data themselves. The unity for which the 'shorthand' stands—marriage, the family, a ceremonial, a legal procedure, or whatever the mode of action may be—is phenomenally there; it palpably attaches to the combination of psycho-physical elements—the sensations, thoughts, motions, and the like—which make up the given mode of action. Call this phenomenal unity a 'pattern', or a recognizable 'type' of action, or—more correctly—a 'norm'; for we always understand this combination of diverse elements to be of a required kind, that is, to exemplify a rule of conduct. Furthermore, this combination of elements is effective *as a whole*; it exercises its peculiar influence upon the same elements not so combined or organized—upon other sensations, thoughts, motions in the environment, and is in turn subject to the influences coming from them. For a convenient illustration we may contrast the actors in any mode of action, say, a ceremonial or legal procedure, with the spectators or onlookers, with a public of some kind. While the sensations, thoughts, and motions of the actors would combine to make up the unitary phenomenon, the particular ceremonial or legal procedure, the spectators would react to the phenomenon as such, and under the influence of its occurrence, with their own, separate sensations, thoughts, and motions. But this is too simplified a picture. The reactions of a public also form part of the total social fact as we, the observers, understand it; while each actor, apart from contributing to the make-up of the social fact, also sees it as such a total combination, made up of the behaviour of all other actors and exemplifying a norm of conduct; indeed his own sensations, thoughts, and motions are reactions to that totality, that is, thoughts about the ceremonial or procedure, likes and dislikes with regard to its rules, intentions

---

[6]As we shall see. this analysis does not completely reduce social facts to mental events; for the latter always contain an implicit reference to 'objects', some of which are again social facts, i.e. the results of social actions or such actions themselves (see below. pp. 291 ff.).

to join in or to keep away, and so forth.[7] The valid distinction between 'actions' and 'reactions' lies elsewhere. For the behaviour of any individual involved in the efficacy of a social fact, whether as onlooker or participant, can be of two kinds. It may only occur under the influence of, and be absorbed in, the normal course of events, simply falling within the given 'pattern', 'type,' or 'norm'; alternatively, his behaviour may relevantly influence the course of events, affecting its end results, or the particular form it takes, or even the future validity of the 'norm'; so that his sensations, thoughts, and motions will add some novel feature to the combination of psycho-physical processes as it now eventuates.

The organization of psycho-physical processes into that phenomenal unit we call a social fact thus has at any moment, and for any organism involved in it, an 'outside' and an 'inside', whose frontiers may move at any subsequent moment. More generally speaking, the combination of psycho-physical processes which is the social fact has a past and a future. It shapes its own future whenever it eventuates; for though it is produced in a particular form at a point in time, its effectiveness lasts beyond this point. And it has a past when it cannot yet have occurred in this particular form, or cannot have occurred at all; for at some stage this combination has been produced for a first time, that is, has been created. It is produced and created by individuals out of their psycho-physical resources; but these individuals and others must be conceived of as existing both before and after that stage, so that at any given moment they (or their psycho-physical processes) are both creative of social facts and subject to their effectiveness. Social facts are unthinkable without this genetic or, in the widest sense, historical aspect. Once we grasp this, we also grasp the final consequence, that something that is not yet a social fact, but only an event in a mind or organism, can become that repetitive, patterned, standardized complex of events in numerous minds and organisms which we call a mode of action or a social fact, and can

go on involving more minds in its effectiveness. Thus, though the social fact is made up of psycho-physical processes it can also be understood to result from them and to initiate or cause such processes, as though it were a thing extraneous to them.

For this process of 'becoming' which underlies all social and psychological 'interaction' certain scholars have found the name *emergence*. By this is meant a 'novelty of behaviour arising from the specific . . . organization of a number of elements, whether inorganic, organic, or mental, which thereby constitute a whole, as distinguished from their mere sum, or resultant'.[8] Emergence is thus a 'synthetic event'; it is 'creative of real novelty, of some new quality or property of a type that did not exist before the emergence'; and this 'new quality or property has causal efficiency, (making) a difference to the further course of events'.[9] 'Emergence' so understood seems to hold good in the whole field of organic life and evolution; these implications I will not venture to discuss. But I would hold, with the defenders of 'emergent evolution', that social facts are 'emergents' from the orders of things which we call psychological and organic. To the relation of *implicitness* between the phenomena analyzed on different levels we must thus add this other relation, of *emergence* from level to level.

Let me stress that there is nothing fictitious or metaphysical, nor purely metaphorical, about emergent properties in the field of social phenomena. Nor are they unfamiliar. A thought or experience expressed, a gesture performed, in so far as they subsequently influence other events in the environment of thought and action, are instances of rudimentary emergence. A book in which thoughts are perpetuated, a lasting monument or work of art, a code of law or morals, or an act of authority accepted or resented by others, are emergents in the full sense of the word. If we call such things and events 'social' or 'cultural', and not psycho-physical, we do so precisely because they possess the peculiar efficacy of emergents.

We must, however, enlarge a little upon the conditions necessary for emergence to take place. I have said that something that is an event in a mind or organism at one moment may, at the next, be-

---

[7]Max Weber similarly pointed out that the 'empirical reality' of any social fact includes both the numerous actions, intentions, and 'actual relationships' of the individuals concerned, and certain ideas *about* the obtaining norms of behaviour present in varying degrees of clarity in the actors' minds. While the 'conceptualization' of the social fact, carried out by the student of the society, must always rest on a synthesis of both these aspects (see 1904, pp. 71-4).

[8]W. M. Wheeler (1928), p. 14.
[9]W. McDougall (1934), pp. 120-1, *et passim*. Similar statements will be found in the writings of Lloyd Morgan and C. D. Broad. See also Talcott Parson (1937), p. 749.

come a social fact. Now, this is possible only under two conditions: first, the mental and organic events materializing in the action of an individual must be capable of being *experienced by others*; and secondly, this experiencing by others must *once more evoke action*. Expressed differently, the mental event-become-action must add to the environment of objects in which all experiences and actions take place. We assume therefore that, once the initial action materializes, it is there to be perceived, remembered, perhaps felt, and responded to; it thus, in some measure, delimits the random experiences of others, and hence their random behaviour, providing 'objects' for the former and models, goals, or constraints for the latter. If the objects and models endure, and if they are uniformly responded to, the resulting novel combination of events in many minds and organisms is the social fact 'emerged'. Yet no mental or organic event occurs in a vacuum. Any 'initial' mental event I posit can be such an event only in a relative sense; so far as my empirical knowledge goes, it must already have occurred in a given environment of objects, models, goals, and constraints. The mental event, then, which materializes in novel action must also, at some preceding moment, have been provoked or shaped by the experiencing of a given environment. This is little better than a truism; if a book has been written which changes the outlook and behaviour of other people, or a person acts in some novel way which serves others as model or warning, the writer or actor has clearly himself been influenced by the books or actions of others; and as he adds to the environment, so this 'addition' of his is in some measure also a response to the pre-existing environment. Stated more generally, the 'initial' mental event *causes* social action to run a novel course, and the modes of social action existing at any moment *cause* mental events to be of a certain kind. This circular relationship can be expressed in the following diagram:

This double causality is not, of course, complete or rigid. For not all mental events materialize in action, or in actions of sufficient magnitude and novelty to add significantly to the environment; nor does the environment of pre-existing modes of action fully and uniformly delimit the random experiences and responses of the individuals within it. If this were so, the two forms of causality would cancel out; for the former would lead to a world re-made in every action and the latter to a world where no novel action ever takes place. In reality, there is some permanence and some novelty in this world of ours. Can we at least say this: If we knew all the conditions under which mental events materialize in novel actions, as well as all the conditions under which 'objects' in the environment evoke mental events of a uniform kind, we should know the machinery which, ultimately, moves our world? It is doubtful if we can say as much, for we cannot exclude some randomness that evades any statement in terms of conditions and their effects. Even so, this 'machinery' exists and is analyzable, if only incompletely; it exists in the psycho-physical make-up of man and the regularities governing it.

In any closed system, in any culture or society free from outside influences, this knowledge must, if you like, lead us in a circle; but to resolve it we need not go back to hypothetical beginnings.[10] The circle is resolved by the principle of emergence, which is as continuous as the existence of society and culture. Sometimes, as we have seen, the circle appears broken up into conspicuous beginnings—whenever mental events materialize in actions capable of significantly altering the environment. I shall later speak of this kind of emergence as of the *genesis* of social facts. More often, the emergence is not fully creative, but, as it were, re-

[10]Goldenweiser calls the relationship between culture and the individual mind, whereby one springs from the other, yet is also determined by it, 'superficially paradoxical', adding that, if our knowledge were 'infinitely expanded', it would finally derive culture from the individual mind (1933, p. 59).

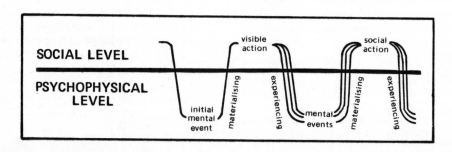

creative or repetitive, peopling the environment with permanent and familiar models, goals, and constraints of behaviour. As I shall try to show, this 'repetitive' emergence of social from psycho-physical facts accounts for the *linkage* of social facts. Whether emergence is one or the other, it exhibits that novel relation between the different levels of analysis to which I referred before. Once more we draw this lesson: In the human sciences the transition from one to the other assumes the significance of a step into a different order of existence. And now this is more than an illusion; for the different order fully means different, 'independently established' facts and their regularities which, viewed from the higher level, must appear both as causal determinants and as 'hidden mechanisms'.

"CULTURE" AND "SOCIETY"

A few pages from Keesing now to bring Nadel's and Novikoff's discussion down to more concrete terms. He takes up two of the central terms in all the social sciences, "culture" and "society," and shows how these have been given differential importance (as well as somewhat different meanings) in the hands of anthropologists and sociologists. By now the multiplicity of meanings for many of the basic terms in the social sciences will have become familiar to you, so that is nothing new. The main point to be understood here, however, is that one of the most common usages assigns "society" as a word and concept to the pattern of *relations* among persons interacting with each other over time in somewhat predictable patterns, while "culture" is given the conceptual status of a framework governing much of that standardized behavior. In their genesis, both terms have their roots in the socio-cultural level of events; a given human society is a "sociocultural system," with some analysts preferring to use the concept of culture as the point of entry into understanding that total system, while for others the concept of the structure of social relationships is the preferred point of entry.

THE RELATION OF CULTURE TO "SOCIETY"

FELIX M. KEESING

What does the anthropologist mean by "society"?

"Society" has been developed as a key concept primarily by sociologists. Anthropologists have tended to use rather the concept of a "cultural group" or an "ethnic group," that is, a population culturally distinctive or ethnologically more or less unique. Yet some, especially British social anthropologists, will be seen as making "society" as central a term in analyzing group behavior as the anthropologically older term "culture."

Society was defined above as the aggregation of individuals in organized populations or groups. Put most simply, "culture" puts the focus on the customs of a people; "society" puts it upon the people who are practicing the customs. As Linton states it, a society is "a permanent collection of human beings"; the "institutions by which they live together" are their culture. Geertz, summarizing a rich stream of thought by sociologists and social anthropologists in the Harvard University Department of Social Relations on the significance of these concepts, says of culture and society, or social structure:

From *Cultural Anthropology: The Science of Custom* by Felix M. Keesing, © 1958 by Felix M. Keesing. Adapted and reprinted by permission of Holt, Rinehart and Winston, Inc.

Culture is the fabric of meaning in terms of which human beings interpret their experience and guide their action; social structure is the form that action takes, the actually existing network of social relations. Culture and social structure are then but different abstractions from the same phenomena [1957, pp. 33–34].

The essential relation between these concepts leads to the frequent use of a conjoined form "sociocultural" as applied to group behavior.

Culture could not exist without people conditioned to it, and transmitting it to their descendants: without "society." But can "society" exist without culture? For example, do not other animals besides man aggregate in organized groups? Again, are there not forms of human social behavior where learned and patterned custom has little or no part, as in mob or panic behavior?

Some scientists use the term "society" to apply to organized populations of animals other than man. The "social" insects, for example, such as bees and ants, often have very complicated types of aggregation. Many animals run in herds, or whatever else we may call their groups, and have orderly "family" life, a hierarchy of leadership, and other systems of organization. While some small margin of learning may be involved, such behavior is essentially triggered by inborn, genetically controlled mechanisms. Culture is non-existent, or merely foreshadowed, at nonhuman organic levels. . . . As used here, society is far wider in scope than culture.

To avoid confusion, many social scientists prefer to limit the term "society" to culturally shaped human populations. They may substitute such terms as "sociality" or "aggregation" when speaking of animals other than man. The distinction between culture and society then becomes easier to "operate" in analyzing behavior. Whatever the usage, however, it is clear that "social organization" among humans is overwhelmingly based on learned and well-established patterns of conduct, that is, on culture, e.g., marriage and family customs, community organization, rank and class, government. Only in the extreme stress of crisis or sudden new experience are the tried habit patterns likely to break down into spontaneous, random, or minimally structured behaviors of individuals and groups, as in the cited cases of panic or mob action. Nearly always, however, a cultural pattern asserts itself, as in following a certain type of leader, or in some circumstances carrying out a lynching. Such informal types of collective behavior have been studied more by sociologists than by anthropologists.

"A society" refers correspondingly to a specific and usually localized population with distinctive customary ways of aggregation. It will consist of a definable number of individuals, whether large or small, with given age and sex patterns, birth and death rates, community distribution of settlement pattern, degree of mobility, and other characteristics which have an intimate relation, as will be seen, to the culture concerned. For a tiny Pacific island such a social group may consist of a few dozen or a few hundred persons, plus perhaps in local eyes numerous spirits and ghosts capable of interacting with the living. At the other extreme is what some social philosophers have called "the Great Society" characteristic of modern civilization.

Would "a society," then, be coterminus with "a culture"? This would be most likely to be so in an isolated, homogeneous, and stable group, as in a small island community. The picture which the anthropologist brings back from most of the remoter zones of the world, however, is of a number of little societies (sometimes single communities) which may share a fairly common regional or localized culture, including closely similar social patterns, yet which are politically independent and more or less constantly feuding and warring with one another, e.g., the African Bantu, the Polynesian islanders. . . . By contrast, most of the large societies are multicultural: the United States, seen as a total society, has a vast network of social relationships which include American Indian tribes, Chinatowns, Spanish-American villages, overseas students from many countries. The world's frontier communities, too, as with ports and towns in underdeveloped countries, are likely to have indigenous and immigrant groups of culturally varying backgrounds more or less interdependent and integrated into what is often called a *plural society*. Obviously, in these latter more diversified population groups the concept of "a society" becomes less sharply meaningful than in the small homogeneous group: they tend to be a composite of many *subsocieties* or *social systems*, and they are likely to have many ties outward to other populations and systems.

Anthropologists usually speak of any ethnic group as having a *social organization* as one aspect of its culture. By a social organization they mean the sum of the customs or culturally transmitted behaviors relating to community aggregation, age, sex, family, friendship, leadership, class, and other group ties. . . . The more formally patterned or institutionalized arrangements through which a group or population becomes integrated to form a society are called by some its *social structure*. An anthropologist may also use the term *social system* in this general sense; but it may be better to employ it, as was done with "cultural system" to refer in more mobile fashion to any type or level of organized group behavior significant for the problem he is studying, e.g., the social system of a factory or hospital, or a kin group or class, of a nation or civilization.

Anthropologists also use increasingly a more general social science concept of *interpersonal* relations to refer to the totality of social links among individuals making up such a group. Some stress a similar general concept of *interaction*, i.e., the play of interpersonal relations, based, of course, almost wholly on culturally shaped habits.

CULTURAL DIMENSION

Clyde Kluckhohn was one of the leaders in the development of a general theory of human social behavior. One of his distinctive themes, expressed in many publications and on many classroom occasions, was that of viewing a *cultural dimension* as part of—but not the whole—a more encompassing system of elements involved in human group life. Taking any concrete set of observable acts, he sees a framework of "levels" or dimensions as the appropriate analytic approach; and rejecting a disciplinary imperialism of any kind (including his own), he carries a bit further than did Keesing the necessity for conceptualizing a specifically *cultural* dimension in relation to the totality of behavioral activities in a human group.

THE CULTURAL AND THE SOCIAL DIMENSIONS

CLYDE KLUCKHOHN

Let us have no "cheap and easy monism" in social science. The conceptual scheme of unified social science can never be securely integrated about *any* single master abstraction. The physical anthropologists are right to demand attention to the biological dimension. The social anthropologists are correct in insisting that the study of culture (to the neglect of social interaction) leads to impressionistic and "metaphysical" descriptions of social behavior which have a much more "literary" than "scientific" flavor. The emphasis of ethnologists upon

geographic and ecological milieu has also its utterly legitimate side—provided only and always that this dimension again is not taken as "the main" or "*the* basic" part of the total picture. When we turn our interest from analytical abstractions like "culture" to the concrete acts from which, after all, any empirical social science must take its ultimate departure, we see that our conceptual scheme must be a manifold embracing four dimensions, no one of which dare be regarded as universally primary. When we closely scrutinize human action, analyzing and comparing acts of human beings which have occurred at different times and places but which appear to subserve similar adjustive and adaptive results, we find that while any given act is a whole, a unit in the concrete, there are nevertheless four

From Clyde Kluckhohn, "Comments on 'The Problem of Communication Between Cultures Seen as Integrated Wholes' by C. J. Friedrich," in *Approaches to National Unity*, L. Bryson et al. eds., © 1945 by Conf. on Science, Philosophy, and Religion, Inc. Reprinted by permission of Harper and Row, Inc.

analytically isolable dimensions to most human deeds (including, of course, verbal deeds). Blindness to any one of these is apt to result in a false over-simplification of the forces determining an act or a series of acts, in a squeezing out of one or more factors which are absolutely essential to a complete comprehension of human action and especially to the prediction of how some or most of the individuals constituting a defined group will behave under particular circumstances.

The first isolable dimension (biological) arises out of the fact that human beings are organisms. Because of differing genes possessed by various individuals (or present in differing frequencies in populations) and also because of the ways in which organisms have been modified as a result of their experiences (such as diseases, nutrition, accidents involving loss of limbs or other capacities, etc.), human action inevitably has certain potentialities and limitations which are biologically defined. The second dimension (impersonal environmental) arises out of the fact that human beings must adjust to certain impersonal forces (such as gravity and weather) and objects (including both "natural" phenomena, like mountains or rivers, and man-made artifacts). The presence or absence of such impersonal forces in any given human situation again supplies both opportunities for and constraints upon human action.

The third abstraction (social) arises out of the fact that human beings must adjust to other human beings as well as to impersonal forces and objects. To some extent these adjustments are implemented and limited only by the presence or absence of other human beings in specified numbers, at particular points, and of specified age, sex, size, and intelligence, relative to the actors whose action is being "explained." Insofar as the human environment of action does not go beyond such inevitables of the interaction of human beings with each other, it may be called "the social environment." It is imperative, however, to isolate a fourth dimension (the cultural) before we can adequately deal with the total environment of human action. This fourth abstraction arises from the observed fact that any given human interaction can take place in a variety of ways so far as the limitations and facilitations of the biological and impersonal environmental conditions are concerned. Some human interactions, indeed, do seem to be subject only to the constraints supplied by the field of biological and physical

forces. Such interactions may be designated as "social" without further qualification. However, careful observations of the words and deeds of human beings make it certain that many of their acts are not a consequence simply of physical and biological potentialities and limitations. If the latter were the case, the possible variations within a defined field of biological and physical forces would be random. But they most definitely are not random. The variations within different human groups which have some historical continuity tend beyond all possible doubt to cluster around certain norms. These norms are demonstrably different as between groups which have different historical continuities. These observed stylizations of action which are characteristic of human groups are the basis for isolating the fourth, or cultural, dimension to action.

The concrete social (*i.e.*, interactive) behavior observed among human beings must in most cases be assumed to be the combined product of biological and cultural "forces." Often, then, the "social" and the "cultural" are inextricably intermingled in observable acts. However, some social acts are not culturally patterned. This is one reason for including a distinct "social" dimension. Another arises out of one certainly valid aspect of Durkheim's position. If we postulate that all ongoing human behavior must be in some sense adaptive and/or adjustive, we must posit social collectivities as the referents of some behavior systems, for these cannot be "explained" as meeting needs (biological or "psychological") of isolated human organisms. In other words, "society," like "culture," is an "emergent" with properties not altogether derivable from a summation of even the fullest kind of knowledge of the parts. Indeed—to go back to the framework of "determination"—it seems likely that culture itself may be altered by social as well as by biological and natural environmental forces. A plurality of individuals (of such and such numbers, etc.) continuously interacting together, produces something new which is a resultant not merely of previously existing cultural patterns and a given impersonal environmental situation but also of the sheer fact of social interaction. Suppose that two random samples of, say, 5000 and 500 persons from a society possessing a relatively homogeneous culture are set down on islands of identical ecological environment (but of areas varying proportionately with the sizes of the two groups). After a few generations (or a shorter interval) one could anticipate that two quite distinct cultures would have evolved —partly as a result of "historical accidents" but also as accommodations to the contrasting number of actual and potential face-to-face relationships. Patterns for human adjustment which were suitable to a society of 500 would not work equally well in the society of 5000 and vice versa. Thus we must regard the environment of interaction (abstracted from the cultural patterning which prevails in it) as one of the determiners of alterations in the system of designs for living (culture).

CULTURE AND THE SOCIAL SYSTEM

Finally, following are two excerpts that summarize the several which have just discussed culture as one of two interlocking systems in a "sociocultural" system that is a given human society. The short statement by Kroeber and Parsons represents a coming together of two of the outstanding figures in American social science over the past generation (for Kroeber, even longer). The points they make are by now familiar to you, but their language is succinct and the distinctions they attempt to draw are important in sorting out preferred conceptual usages for common words employed. In addition they give some level of understanding to how these "master" concepts relate to the *disciplines* and university departments which, to the beginning student, are the most immediately familiar aspects of the social or behavioral sciences.

THE CONCEPTS OF CULTURE AND OF SOCIAL SYSTEM

A. L. KROEBER and TALCOTT PARSONS

There seems to have been a good deal of confusion among anthropologists and sociologists about the concepts of *culture* and *society* (or, *social system*). A lack of consensus—between and within disciplines—has made for semantic confusion as to what data are subsumed under these terms; but, more important, the lack has impeded theoretical advance as to their interrelation.

There are still some anthropologists and sociologists who do not even consider the distinction necessary on the ground that all phenomena of human behavior are sociocultural, with both societal and cultural aspects at the same time. But even where they recognize the distinction, which can be said now to be a commonplace, they tend to assume determinative primacy for the set of phenomena in which they are more interested.

Sociologists tend to see all cultural systems as a sort of outgrowth or spontaneous development, derivative from social systems. Anthropologists are more given to being holistic and therefore often begin with total systems of culture and then proceed to subsume social structure as merely a part of culture. ("Social anthropology" perhaps represents a secession within anthropology that inclines to prefer the sociological assumption.)

Our objective in the present joint statement is to point out, so far as methodological primacy is concerned, that, either of these assumptions is a preferential *a priori* and cannot be validated in today's state of knowledge. Separating cultural from societal aspects is not a classifying of concrete and empirically discrete sets of phenomena. They are distinct systems in that they abstract or select two analytically distinct sets of components from the same concrete phenomena. Statements made about relationships within a cultural pattern are thus of

Reprinted with permission of publisher. From *American Sociological Review*, vol. 23, no. 5 (1958), 582–83.

a different order from those within a system of societal relationships. Neither can be directly reduced to terms of the other; that is to say, the order of relationships within one is independent from that in the other. Careful attention to this independence greatly increases the power of analytical precision. In sum, we feel that the analytical discrimination should be consistently maintained without prejudice to the question of which is more "important," "correct" or "fundamental," if indeed such questions turn out to be meaningful at all.

It is possible to trace historically two successive analytical distinctions that have increased this analytical precision. It might be suggested that the first differentiation was a division of subject-matter broadly along the lines of the heredity-environment distinction. In English-speaking countries, at least, the most important reference point is the biologically oriented thinking of the generation following the publication of Darwin's *Origin of Species*. Here the social scientists were concerned with defining a sphere of investigation that could not be treated as simply biological in the then current meaning of that concept. Tylor's concept of culture and Spencer's of the social as superorganic were important attempts to formulate such a sphere. Thus the organism was assigned to the biological sciences and culture-society (as yet more or less undifferentiated) assigned to the sociocultural sciences.

In the formative period of both disciplines, then, culture and society were used with relatively little difference of meaning in most works of major influence. In the anthropological tradition, Tylor and Boas used culture to designate that aspect of total human social behavior (including its symbolic and meaningful products) that was independent of the genetic constitutions and biological characteristics of organisms. The ideas of continuity, creation, accumulation, and transmission of culture independent of biological heredity were the key ones. On the sociological side, Comte and Spencer, and Weber and Durkheim spoke of society as meaning essentially the same thing that Tylor meant by culture.

For a considerable period this condensed concept of culture-and-society was maintained, with differentiation between anthropology and sociology being carried out not conceptually but operationally. Anthropologists tended to confine their studies to nonliterate societies and sociologists concerned themselves with literate ones (especially their own.)

It did not seem necessary to go much further. Now we believe that knowledge and interests have become sufficiently differentiated so that further distinctions need to be made and stabilized in the routine usage of the relevant professional groups. Such a need has been foreshadowed in the practice of many anthropologists in speaking of social organization as one major segment or branch of culture, and of some sociologists in discriminating such categories as values, ideologies, science, and art from social structure.

In this way a second analytical distinction has taken (or is taking) shape. We suggest that it is useful to define the concept *culture* for most usages more narrowly than has been generally the case in the American anthropological tradition, restricting its reference to transmitted and created content and patterns of values, ideas, and other symbolic-meaningful systems as factors in the shaping of human behavior and the artifacts produced through behavior. On the other hand, we suggest that the term *society*—or more generally, *social system*—be used to designate the specifically relational system of interaction among individuals and collectivities. To speak of a "member of a culture" should be understood as an ellipsis meaning a "member of the society of culture X." One indication of the independence of the two is the existence of highly organized insect societies with at best a minimal rudimentary component of culture in our present narrower sense.

Parenthetically we may note that a similar analytical distinction has begun to emerge with reference to the older concept of the organism, on the other side of the division outlined above by which the social sciences came to be differentiated from the biological. Where the term organism was once used to designate both biological and psychological aspects, it has recently come to be increasingly important to discriminate a specifically psychological component from the merely biological. Thus the term personality is being widely used as an appropriate or favored term expressive of the distinction.

To speak, then, of the analytical independence between culture and social system is, of course, not to say that the two systems are not related, or that various approaches to the analysis of the relationship may not be used. It is often profitable to hold constant either cultural or societal aspects of the same concrete phenomena while addressing attention to the other. Provided that the analytical distinction between them is maintained, it is therefore idle to quarrel over the rightness of either approach. Important work has been prosecuted under both of them. It will undoubtedly be most profitable to develop both lines of thinking and to judge them by how much each increases understanding. Secondly, however, building on the more precise knowledge thus gained, we may in time expect to learn in which area each type of conceptualization is the more applicable and productive. By some such procedure, we should improve our position for increasing understanding of the relations between the two, so that we will not have to hold either constant when it is more fruitful not to do so.

We therefore propose a truce to quarreling over whether culture is best understood from the perspective of society or society from that of culture. As in the famous case of heredity "versus" environment, it is no longer a question of how important each is, but of how each *works* and how they are interwoven with each other. The traditional perspectives of anthropology and sociology should merge into a temporary condominium leading to a differentiated but ultimately collaborative attack on problems in intermediate areas with which both are concerned.

PUTTING IT ALL TOGETHER

Finally, we put it all together—what it takes to make a human "society" go. What are the *system requirements* of human social life? In this article, the early product of several eminent social scientists, a number of themes and elements already discussed separately are brought together. We started with a discussion of the concept of culture, looked at it apart from a social context, then tied it in with notions of social structure and social relationship. With this article we go even a bit further and begin to throw out ties to such areas as personality development (with the question of why and how there occurs continuity in social forms and value frameworks) and to such areas as the relationship of society to the geographic and physical environment. With reference to the latter point, the article serves as a good bridge to the discussion of another of the sets of encompassing relationships that we must consider when looking at culture as a process: distinctive patterns of orientation toward and exploitation of the physical environment—"culture" as part of an "ecosystem," to which we will turn after this article by Aberle and his colleagues.

THE FUNCTIONAL PREREQUISITES OF A SOCIETY

D. F. ABERLE, A. K. COHEN, A. K. DAVIS, M. J. LEVY, JR., F. X. SUTTON

A comparative social science requires a generalized system of concepts which will enable the scientific observer to compare and contrast large bodies of concretely different social phenomena in consistent terms. A promising step in furthering the development[1] of systematic social analysis is a tentative formulation of the functional prerequisites of a society. Functional prerequisites refer broadly to the things that must get done in any society if it is

Reprinted with permission of author and University of Chicago Press. From *Ethics*, 60 (January 1960), 100–111.

[1]Already well under way. Cf. Talcott Parsons, "The Position of Sociological Theory," *American Sociological Review*, XIII (1948), 156–64, and the references cited therein, esp. the "Discussion" by Robert K. Merton, *ibid.*, pp. 164–68.

to continue as a going concern, i.e., the generalized conditions necessary for the maintenance of the system concerned. The specific structural arrangements for meeting the functional prerequisites differ, of course, from one society to another and, in the course of time, change in any given society.[2]

This paper offers (1) a definition of a society on the most general level; (2) a statement of four generalized conditions, the complete realization of any one of which would terminate the existence of a society as defined; (3) a list of the functional prerequisites of a society. It seeks to justify the inclusion of each prerequisite by the demonstration that in its hypothetical absence the society could not survive, since at least one of the four conditions terminating a society would occur. There is no reason to believe that the list of functional prerequisites offered here is definitive. It is subject to revision with the growth of general theory and with experience in its application to concrete situations.

Any formulation of functional prerequisites depends for its categories on the theory of action employed. Our theory of action uses the concept of an actor whose orientation to his situation is threefold: cognitive, affective, and goal-directed. The actor is an abstraction from the total human being. Many of the qualities of the human being constitute part of the situation, the set of means and conditions, within which the actor operates.[3]

Though the definition of the functional prerequisites of a society logically precedes the development of a scheme of structural prerequisites—which tell *how* the functional prerequisites may be met—in actuality the theoretic development of the two approaches is indivisible.

I. A DEFINITION OF A SOCIETY

The unit we have selected for analysis is a *society*, such as a nation, tribe, or band, and not any social

system in general. The statement of the functional prerequisites of *any social system*—a monastery, a church, or a town, for example—would be on too general a level for the present discussion, though it may be an important task. Furthermore, once the functional prerequisites of a society are outlined, it becomes easier to state those of other types of social systems, often by dropping certain prerequisites from the list, since most of these other types of systems are parts of a society (or result from the interrelations of two or more societies) and depend for their perpetuation on the existence of a society.

A society is a group of human beings sharing a self-sufficient system of action which is capable of existing longer than the life-span of an individual, the group being recruited at least in part by the sexual reproduction of the members.

The identity and continuity of a society inhere in the persistence of the system of action in which the actors participate rather than in the particular set of actors themselves. There may be a complete turnover of individuals, but the society may survive. The individuals may survive, but the society may disintegrate. A system may persist in a situation while its component relationships change. Its persistence inheres in the fact that it maintains its separation from the situation, i.e., it inheres in the *integrity* of the organism, not in its fixity or unalterable character.

A system of action always exists in a situation. In the case of a society this situation includes the nonhuman environment and, in almost every case, it includes other societies. The viability of a social system and its recognition as a society within the terms of this definition depend upon the particular set of conditions in which it functions. Study of the system itself cannot alone determine whether the system meets the criteria of the definition. What is crucial is that a social system contain successful arrangements for meeting the chronic and recurrent features of its milieu.[4]

"Longer than the life-span of an individual" re-

---

[2]Thus all societies must allocate goods and services somehow. A particular society may change from one method, say business enterprise, to another, say a centrally planned economy, without the destruction of the society as a society but merely with a change in its concrete structures.

We seek to avoid the limitation inherent in defining the function of a social element solely in terms of its contribution to the survival or maintenance of the particular system of which it is a component. Structural analysis, which has recently undergone notable development, is prone to focus attention on static equilibriums. We consider *what* must be done in *any* society and hope our effort may be of use in considering the alterations that take place in *how* things are done in a society while that society persists.

[3]Neither the nature of the dependence of our formulation on this theory of action nor the theory of action itself can be further elaborated here. The theory of action is outlined briefly in Talcott Parsons, *Essays in Sociological Theory* (Glencoe: Free Press, 1949), pp. 32–33.

[4]This point receives further treatment below. A social system need not be copperplated to meet the definition of a society. Natural catastrophe may terminate a concrete society. Such an event does not represent a failure to meet the functional prerequisites but is rather to be considered the result of a change in the nonhuman environment beyond the limits assumed here as the setting of a society. Many concrete societies have been assimilated by the expansions of groups with which these societies had had little or no previous contact. This, too, represents an alteration in the situation of the society beyond the limits within which it had been meeting its functional prerequisites.

minds us that a society must be able to replace its members with effectively socialized individuals from the maturing generation. The requirement of sexual reproduction excludes from consideration such groups (monasteries, cliques) as depend *solely* on types of recruitment other than sexual. But a society may be recruited in part by non-sexual means, e.g., by immigration and conquest.

The heart of the definition is "self-sufficient system of action."[5] Its full meaning will be developed in the exposition of the functional prerequisites and in the next paragraphs.

A number of questions are bound to arise in the reader's mind as to the application of the definition to particular social systems and as to the basis on which the decision is to be made as to whether such systems fall within the definition of a society. We emphasize that the definition is an ideal type. *A concrete aggregate is a society in so far as it approaches the generalized model.* The following examples, though not definitive, suggest the way in which the definition may be applied.

A society is not a culture. Culture is socially transmitted behavior conceived as an abstraction from concrete social groups. Two or more *societies* may have the same *culture* or similar cultures. Though the Greek city-states shared similar culture patterns, each possessed a self-sufficient structure of action and is hence to be considered a separate society. One society may be composed of groups with some marked differences in culture. The union of agricultural, industrial, and pastoral groups in a single structure of action is an example. We discuss below the limits as to the amount of diversity possible and the conditions under which such diversity may occur without the disintegration of the society.

To some degree two different societies may possess overlapping personnel and even structural elements without losing their identity as distinct societies. The fact that Englishmen live in the United States as diplomats and traders and function, in effect, as actors in both systems, does not destroy the identity or the self-sufficiency of the United States or of Great Britain as action-systems.

To be considered a society, a group need not be self-sufficient with respect to resources. It is the structure of action that must be self-sufficient. Thus,

the United States is a society. While imports and exports are necessary to its maintenance, arrangements for foreign trade are part of its self-sufficient structure of action. It is this, and not the group of individuals, that is self-sufficient. Hence Chinese-American trade does not make China and America parts of a larger society. Trade relationships are limited and relatively unstable. Their existence does not involve the two aggregates in the same self-sufficient structure of action. For parallel reasons the British Empire and the United Nations are not societies but associations.

A series of difficult decisions about the relationships of various social systems can be resolved by the introduction of a point of crucial differentiation. When a social aggregate is not capable of providing a structure, structures, or parts of structures which can meet the functional prerequisites in question, it is not to be considered a society. Thus, occupied Japan does not constitute part of American society, since in the absence of American forces Japan would seem to be able to continue control and the legitimized use of force. A group of American Indians governed by the United States for a sufficient length of time may lack the crucial structures necessary for continued existence as an independent entity and therefore be considered part of American society, in spite of an important cultural variation. An American town does not constitute a society because of its thorough participation in American political, economic, value, and other structures. The early Mormon settlement in Utah, however, did constitute a society.[6]

Under what circumstances do considerations of social change lead us to speak of a "new" society? Whenever social change results in a change of social structure on the most general level under consideration, we shall speak of a "new society" having been brought about. Such transitions may be gradual (evolutionary) or sudden and chaotic (revolutionary). The determination of the exact point of change may be extremely complex but is in theory possible. This criterion for a "new society" will not ordinarily

---

[5]"System" and "structure" will be used interchangeably throughout the remainder of this treatment.

[6]There is no intention of making the political variable the sole criterion for the decision as to what constitutes a society. The nature of economic ties, the degree to which value-systems are shared, and the like are also crucial in making the differentiation between two systems of action.

Thus the decision as to the distinctness of two or more aggregates as societies rests on the analysis of all aspects of the systems of action, and not merely of a single variable, in their consequences for the self-sufficient character of the systems of action. Borderline cases undoubtedly exist, but the treatment made here is sufficiently refined for the purposes at hand.

enter the study of comparative institutions unless the developmental picture of some particular society (or societies) is under consideration.

We assume that social change characterizes all societies. Change may be gradual and peaceful or characterized by severe conflicts. In either case there may be profound structural changes. Societies may split or merge peacefully or violently. In all these instances a society of some sort exists. Whether it is considered the same society or a new one depends on the relation between the level of the structural change and the level of analysis. The changes in question may be analyzed in terms of this frame of reference. We may examine the way in which a society meets its functional prerequisites, the points of tension (those functional prerequisites least effectively met), and the responses to those strains. We do not assume the perfect integration of any society.

We have omitted from our definition any statements regarding territoriality. Action, it has been pointed out, always takes place in a situation, one feature of which is a spatial dimension. The existence of two societies intermingled during a civil war, or any such example, does not negate considerations of spatiality, which are always an essential background feature of any society.

II. FOUR CONDITIONS TERMINATING THE EXISTENCE OF A SOCIETY

The realization of any of the following conditions terminates the existence of a society—the existence of the structure of action, though not necessarily of the members.

A. *The biological extinction or dispersion of the members.*—To arrive at this condition, a society need not lose all its members but need only suffer such losses as to make inoperative its structure of action. Analyses of such conditions may be made at this level in terms of fertility, morbidity, and migration rates, without reference to the highly complex factors underlying them.[7]

B. *Apathy of the members.*—Apathy means the cessation of individual motivation. This condition affects some individuals to some extent in all societies and large numbers in a few societies. That migrant Polynesian laborers have died of nostalgia is well known. It is claimed that whole societies in

Melanesia have withered away from ennui. In these cases, physical extinction is merely an extreme consequence of the cessation of motivation.

C. *The war of all against all.*—This condition appears if the members of an aggregate pursue their ends by means selected only on the basis of instrumental efficiency. Though the choice of means on this basis may result at times in co-operative combinations, these combinations are by definition subject to immediate dissolution if, for example, exploitation or annihilation becomes more advantageous for any one member. Hence a state of indeterminate flux, rather than a system of action, exists. The use of force is efficient only for limited purposes. Force is a sanction, but never the essence, of a society. A society based solely on force is a contradiction in terms that raises the classical question, *Quis custodiet ipsos custodes?*

D. *The absorption of the society into another society.*—This entails the partial loss of identity and self-sufficiency of the total action-system but not necessarily the extinction of the members.[8]

The more fully these four conditions are realized, the more indeterminate is the structure of action, a condition also induced when the rate of social change is very rapid. Hence we may hypothesize that fluctuations in the vital indices, in apathy, and in coercion are to some extent functions of the rate of social change. In fact, revolutions (extreme social change) are characterized by increases in mortality, morbidity, apathy, force, and fraud. The faster the change, the greater the stress, two manifestations of which are force and/or apathy. Viewing coercion as a response to stress should help us to put the discussion of the role of force in social systems on a nonideological basis.

III. THE FUNCTIONAL PREREQUISITES OF A SOCIETY

The performance of a given function is prerequisite to a society if in its absence one or more of the four conditions dissolving a society results. This can be demonstrated clearly in some cases. Less clearly, but still convincingly, the nonfulfilment of certain

---

[7] In this regard certain catastrophic occurrences deriving from marked alterations in the situation are excluded from consideration in accordance with the line of reasoning previously outlined.

[8] It is worth re-emphasizing that a given society may at one time contain arrangements for maintaining its distinctness from other societies that form part of its situation, but that an alteration of that situation (the arrival of a numerically and technically superior group bent on conquest) may render these arrangements ineffective. We would not, therefore, say that the society thus absorbed had never *been* a society, but that in a *new* situation it showed a relative inadequacy of one of its functional prerequisites that resulted in its absorption.

other functions can be shown at least to foster one or more of the conditions negating a society. No specific action-pattern is prerequisite to the existence of our ideal-typical society. We are concerned with *what* must get done in a society, not with *how* it is done.

A. *Provision for adequate relationship to the environment and for sexual recruitment.*—This includes modes of adapting to, manipulating, and altering the environment in such a way as (*a*) to maintain a sufficient number and kind of members of the society at an adequate level of functioning; (*b*) to deal with the existence of other societies in a manner which permits the persistence of the system of action; and (*c*) to pattern heterosexual relationships to insure opportunities and motivation for a sufficient rate of reproduction. In the absence of these provisions, the group will suffer biological extinction through the death of the members or failure to reproduce or it will suffer absorption into another social system.

A society, however, need not provide equally for the physiological needs of all its members. Infanticide, geronticide, limitation of marriage, and birth control may be necessary to maintain certain societies. Which members, and in what proportions, are most important for the functioning of a society depends on its social organization. Every society needs enough adult members to insure reproduction and to man the essential status-positions.

A society must adapt to, manipulate, and alter its situation. Among the features thus dealt with may be chronically threatening aspects of the situation. In a dry region a society may employ techniques of food storage, irrigation, or nomadic migration. If neighboring societies are hostile, an army may be essential and the society thus dependent on the deliberate hazarding of some of its members' lives. The existence of Murngin society depends partly on the destruction of a portion of its adult males by chronic warfare. Resistance is only one possible response to hostile neighbors. Certain "men-o-bush" tribes of New Guinea make but little resistance to raids. These raids, however, do not threaten to extinguish the society. Only if they do can such a passive adaptation be said to be inadequate to meet the functional prerequisitie.

The inclusion of such apparently disparate features as maintenance of the organism, defense, and provision for sexual reproduction under one heading is by no means arbitrary. From the point of view of a social system, the nonhuman environment, the biological nature of man, and the existence of other societies are all part of the situation of action. To none of these aspects of the situation is passive adaptation the only mode of adequate relationship. Thus the biological basis of society itself is molded. Individuals have constitutional differences, but the latter are variously evaluated and dealt with by societies. The biological birth-growth-death cycle is a dynamic process in its own right, yet societies both adapt to it and modify it in a number of ways. In noting the necessity for a society to meet certain biological prerequisities, we remark also upon the great plasticity of individuals. It is scarcely necessary to remark that, concretely, societies alter their modes of relationship to their situations; that technological changes occur, sometimes through loss, more often by invention and diffusion.

B. *Role differentiation and role assignment.* This signifies the systematic and stable division of activities. We will treat under other headings role-learning and the sanctions perpetuating the role structure.

In any society there are activities which must be regularly performed if the society is to persist. If they are to be done dependably, these extensive and varied activities must be broken down and assigned to capable individuals trained and motivated to carry them out. Otherwise everyone would be doing everything or nothing—a state of indeterminacy which is the antithesis of a society and which precludes getting essential activities carried out. The universal problems of scarcity and order are insoluble without legitimized allocation of property rights and authority, and these, in turn, are unattainable without reasonably integrated role-differentiation. While a given individual is often the locus of several roles, he can never combine all the roles of his society in himself. Age and sex differences impose a degree of role-differentiation everywhere; in some societies class and occupation are additional bases of differentiation. Arguments for specialization based on differential ability, while of great force in complex societies, have no clear bearing on societies so simple that any technique can be learned by any individual who is not feeble-minded. Whatever the society, activities necessary to its survival must be worked out in predictable, determinate ways, or else apathy or the war of each against all must prevail. Without reliable provision for child-rearing activities and without their assignment to specific persons or groups, the society invites extinction, since children at birth are helpless. The absence of role-differentiation and of role-assignment thus makes for three of the conditions negating a society. A system of role-differentiation alone is useless without a system of selection for assigning individuals to those roles.

Mention should be made of one particular type of role-differentiation that is a requirement for any society, namely, stratification. Stratification is that particular type of role-differentiation which discriminates between higher and lower standings in terms of one or more criteria. Given the universality of scarcity, some system of differential allocation of the scarce values of a society is essential. These values may consist of such desiderata as wealth, power, magic, women and ceremonial precedence. That conflict over scarce values may destroy a society will be shown in another connection below. Our present point is that the rank order must be legitimized and accepted by most of the members—at least by the important ones—of a society if stability is to be attained. Allocation of ranks may be on the basis of ascribed or achieved qualities or both.

Role-differentiation implies organization. Precedence in specialized activities must be correlated to some extent with rank order. Coercive sanctions and initiative must be vested in specified status-positions. Some individuals will thus receive more than others. These privileges are usually made acceptable to the rank and file by joining to the greater rights of the elite a larger share of responsibilities. The Brahmins stand closer to other-worldly non-existence than do the members of any other Hindu caste, but they also have to observe the most elaborate ritual obligations. The Trobriand chief enjoys a multiple share of wealth and wives; he must also finance community enterprises and exhibit at all times more generosity than anyone else.

Even the simplest societies have hierarchical sex and age grading. Modern societies are much more elaborately stratified. Symbolic activities or ritual must be carefully organized to effect successfully their latent functions of allaying anxiety and re-creating allegorically the basic meanings and affirmations of the society. In group enterprises some roles tend to rank others, though the individuals filling the roles may rotate freely, as in the case of the citizens of the Greek city-state. Regardless of

the type of stratification and authority-system, a normative scale of priorities for allocating scarce values (precedence, property rights, power, etc.) is always a vital portion of the differentiation of roles in any society.

C. *Communication.*—Evidence from deaf-mutes, "wolf children," and bilinguals shows that speech, the basic form of communication, is learned and that only rudimentary communication is possible in the absence of shared, learned linguistic symbols. Without learned symbolic communication only a few highly general emotional states—e.g., anger, sexual passion—in one individual can evoke an appropriate response in another; only a few skills may be conveyed by imitation.

No society, however simple, can exist without shared, learned symbolic modes of communication, because without them it cannot maintain the common-value structure or the protective sanctions which hold back the war of each against all. Communication is indispensable if socialization and role-differentiation are to function effectively. That each functional prerequisite thus depends in part on other functional prerequisites does not vitiate our argument so longs as the functional prerequisites are logically separable. But they need not be empirically distinct activities, since any action-system may contribute to several functional prerequisites.

In a simple society, where relationships are exclusively face-to-face, shared speech forms suffice. In complex societies, other than oral communication is necessary for the system as a whole, though not for subsystems. Thus, in China, writing facilitates the survival of the society despite local dialect differences too great to permit oral communication without bilingual intermediaries. Clearly, no modern society could survive without writing. Thus, communication requires language, a medium of communication, and channels.

D. *Shared cognitive orientations.*—In any society the members must share a body of cognitive orientations which (*a*) make possible adaptation to and manipulation of the situation; (*b*) make stable, meaningful, and predictable the social situations in which they are engaged; and (*c*) account for those significant aspects of the situation over which they do not have adequate prediction and control in such a way as to sustain and not to destroy motivation.

If the first criterion were not met, biological existence would be impossible. If the second were not, interpersonal and intergroup relations could not exist. Private definitions of social situations or the absence of such definitions could lead only to mutually incompatible actions and the war of each against all. In no society are all conditions predictable and controllable; so the frustration of expectations is a chronic feature of social life. Without a reasonably determinate explanation of such areas of existence, the individual would exist in an unstructured world and could not avoid psychological disorganization. In the absence of shared orientations, serious clashes would ensue.

Cognitive orientations must be shared, but only in so far as the actors are involved in the same situation of action. A housewife may not distinguish a colonel from a corporal; a soldier may not appreciate that he is using his hostess' "wedding silver." They must agree, however, that a foot is "so long" and that that gentleman is a "policeman." But though a farmer may pray for rain and an aviator rub a rabbit's foot for good weather with no resultant difficulties between them, both must define the American political system in a roughly similar fashion if they are to vote.

E. *A shared, articulated set of goals.*—To phrase this prerequisite in terms of ultimate ends of action produces a vague and not very useful formulation like Thomas' four wishes. It is equally difficult to operate in terms of motivations, since these are exceedingly diverse and are intricately articulated with the social structure. Our statement in terms of goals seeks a middle ground and is couched in the terms most suitable for considering a system of action.

Because there is role-differentiation in every society, we must consider a set of goals rather than a common goal. The facts of scarcity and of differential individual endowment, features of all societies, also make it necessary to speak of a set of goals. It is the range of goals, however narrow, that provides alternatives for individuals and thus reduces one serious source of conflict in societies. (The possibility of universally sought goals in a society is not ruled out.)

The goals must be sufficiently articulated to insure the performance of socially necessary activities. They must not include too much action which threatens the existence of a society. A cult of sexual abstinence, if universalized, would terminate the society. The goals must be shared to some degree, though this will vary with the differentiation of the society. Finally, the goals of one individual must be meaningful to another in so far as they share a common structure of action.

There will be both empirical and nonempirical goals. Some goals may be mutually incompatible without being destructive to the society. Without an articulated set of goals the society would invite extinction, apathy, or the war of all against all.

F. *The normative regulation of means.*—This functional prerequisite is the prescription of means for attaining the socially formulated goals of a society and its subsystems. It complements but does not overlap the functional prerequisite of "effective control of disruptive behavior." The "normative regulation of means" defines positively the means (mostly noncoercive) to the society's goals.

That these means must be stated clearly for the sake of order and the effective functioning of the society follows from (*a*) the nature of other functional prerequisites and (*b*) the *anomie* that must result from the lack of recognized legitimized means. First, role-differentiation specifies *who* is to act, while the common articulated set of goals defines *what* is to be done. The normative regulation of means tells *how* those goals may be won. Second, the absence of normative regulation of means invites apathy or the war of each against all. Without socially prescribed means, a goal must be either devalued or forcibly seized. As the loss of a bolt may cause a great machine to beat itself to pieces, so the absence of normatively regulated means operates cumulatively to destroy the social structure.

Especially in ritual and initiatory activities must procedures be normatively specified. The content of prescriptions may vary greatly among societies; what is indispensable is simply that socially accepted directives for ceremonial and symbolic action exist. This point emphasizes the necessity for the category of normative regulation of means, in addition to the effective control of disruptive behavior. Moreover, there are often alternative, noncoercive ways of realizing goals, and they must be differentially evaluated for the sake of order, or else some must be ruled out.

G. *The regulation of affective expression.*—In any society the affective states of the members must be mutually communicable and comprehensible. Furthermore, not every affect can be expressed in every situation. Some must be suppressed or repressed. Lastly, there are affects which must be produced in the members if the social structure is to survive.

All these aspects are included in the regulation of affective expression.

In the absence of the first of these conditions, stability of expectations between individuals is destroyed, and apathetic or destructive reactions will occur. This is true alike of states of anger and of affection, of love, lust and the like.[9] Without comprehensibility and communicability, mutually inappropriate responses in affectively charged situations can only result in the destruction of the relationship. In a love affair, if one member's expression of affection has the intended meaning of a flirtation, while to the other it signifies willingness to consummate the affair, the relationship is headed for a crisis. The same state of affairs with respect to the expression of affect in an entire society is clearly incompatible with the continuation of that society. This is not a matter of a lack of a shared cognitive frame of reference; rather, the conflicts are potentially explosive because of the emotional involvement. The cues that make affective expression comprehensible range from obvious and subtle linguistic behavior to posture, facial expression, gesture, and tone of voice. Many of these cues are not consciously recognized by the actors themselves.

In the face of regulated competitive, co-operative, and authority relationships, some of which are entailed in any conceivable system of role-allocation, taken together with disturbances of expectation and scarcity situations, no society can survive if it permits complete latitude of affective expression in all situations. The ungoverned expression of lust and rage leads to the disruption of relationships and ultimately to the war of all against all.

Finally, a society must not only structure the way in which affects are expressed and restrict certain forms of emotional expression; it must actively foster some affects. Unless we adopt the view that all relationships in all societies can be rational and contractual in character, we must take the position that some relationships depend on regulated affects for their perpetuation.[10] In the absence of the production of appropriate affects, the family, for example, would not survive. The question of what affects must regularly be produced in any society is closely related to the way other functional prerequisites are fulfilled. In American society the urban middle-class conjugal family depends heavily on the establishment of strong affective ties between spouses. The American family system in meeting the demands of a highly mobile society is deprived of certain bases of stability which other family systems possess, and the mutual affection of spouses becomes of correspondingly greater importance.

H. *Socialization.*—A problem is posed for any society by the fact that its structure of action must be learned by new members. To each individual must be transmitted so much of the modes of dealing with the total situation—the modes of communication, the shared cognitive frame of reference, goal-system, attitudes involved in the regulation of means, modes of expression, and the like—as will render him capable of adequate performance in his several roles throughout life, both as respects skills and as respects attitudes. Socialization thus is a different concept from the maintenance of the child in a state of biological well-being.

Furthermore, socialization includes both the development of new adult members from infants and the induction of an individual of any age into any role of the society or its subsystems where new learning is required.

A society cannot persist unless it perpetuates a self-sufficient system of action—whether in changed or traditional form—through the socialization of new members, drawn, in part, from the maturing generation. Whatever the defects of any particular mode of socialization, a universal failure of socialization means the extinction of the society, through a combination of all four of the terminating conditions mentioned previously.[11]

One individual cannot become equally familiar with all aspects of his society; indeed, he may remain completely ignorant of some. But he must acquire a working knowledge of the behavior and attitudes relevant to his various roles and identify to some degree with such values as are shared by the whole society or segments thereof wherever his behavior articulates with that of other members of the society. A Brahmin and an Untouchable learn

---

[9]It may be that gross affective states are mutually communicable in the absence of regulation, but such communication is not sufficient to obviate all the problems dealt with here.

[10]This argument is an example of the dependence of our system of functional prerequisites on a theory of action. A theory which includes an affective aspect in the actor's orientation can and must include this functional prerequisite.

[11]The complexities of personality development arising from the interaction of individuals of varying constitutional endowment with the modes of child care and socialization and various other aspects of the social situation, as well as with more random situations, cannot be dealt with in any way here. It is sufficient to say that no socialization system is ideally efficient, i.e., in no society are all individuals equally well socialized nor is any one individual perfectly socialized.

some skills and attitudes unknown to each other. Both, however, must learn that the Hindu world is made up of castes and that this is the way things should be.

I. *The effective control of disruptive forms of behavior.*—Prominent among disruptive modes of behavior are force and fraud. The extent to which such behavior will occur is dependent on the way that various other functional prerequisites are met: role-allocation, goal-system, regulation of means and of expression, and socialization being the more obvious cases in point. All these functional prerequisites, it is clear from the preceding argument, tend to prevent the occurrence of disruptive behavior. In addition to, and separate from, these is the effective control of such behavior when it occurs. To understand why this functional prerequisite is necessary, we must ask: Why would not a perfectly integrated society exist in its absence?

The answer lies in three conditions inherent in any society: scarcity of means, frustrations of expectations, and imperfections of socialization. That many of the desiderata of life are ultimately scarce needs no emphasis. Since sexual objects are differentially evaluated by a society, those few at the top of the scale tend to be sought by a large number of the opposite sex. Wealth, however defined, is basically scarce for the mass of individuals everywhere. Force and fraud are often the most efficient methods of acquiring scarce values. Indeed, only scarce values can be objects of rationally directed coercive effort. To argue that society without coercion and deceit can exist, one must first demonstrate the absence of scarcity. Frustration of expectations is inevitable for many individuals in any society so long as there are such universal realities as unexpected consequences of purposive behavior, scarcity, and uncertainty.

Imperfect socialization results, among other things, in evasions of the normatively prescribed paths of action. Together with frustrations of expectations, it results in explosive outbursts of anger and violence.[12] Thus, both rationally directed exercise of force and fraud and less rational outbursts

of emotion continually press to disrupt stable social relationships. If resort to these disruptive behaviors is restricted only by opportunity, the war of all against all will ultimately result. (Some disruptive action may also tend in the direction of an apathetic breakdown. This does not alter the nature of the argument.)

The system of goals tells *what* must be done; the normative regulation of means prescribes *how*. It also includes pre- and proscriptions regarding the use of force and fraud. In addition, however, the society must have techniques for handling those who, for reasons outlined, use these disruptive means or are subject to these outbreaks. The form of control and the degree of efficiency may vary greatly. What type of action is directly destructive of a society depends on the nature of the society: patricide in a society founded on patriarchal clans, violation of property rights in a property-emphasizing society, and so on. Conversely, some societies can tolerate forms of these behaviors that others cannot. Chuckchee social structure, for example, withstands a high homicide rate.

IV. CONCLUSION

This treatment makes no claim to be final. Our list of functional prerequisites can be elaborated and altered by the reader by making explicit the elements we have left implicit. At present, a statement of the functional prerequisites of a society is primarily useful as a contribution to general social theory rather than as a tool for analyzing individual societies. It should be especially useful for constructing a general system of structural prerequisites that will tell us how the functional prerequisites may be met, and this in turn may lead to a more comprehensive and precise comparative sociology.

Even at the present stage, however, the authors have found this approach useful as a point of reference for analyses of societies and their subsystems, and for suggesting inadequacies in the analysis of given societies and in the empirical data available. It directs attention to features of social systems, relationships among institutional structures, and implications for social change which might otherwise be overlooked.

---

[12]Other disruptive modes of behavior, including apathy, also may occur. But a refined analysis of the problem of deviancy is beyond the scope of this paper.

PART VI

CULTURE IN THE ECOSYSTEM

Though a distinctive *kind* of animal, man still is of the earth. He lives in space and time, and must maintain those life-giving bonds to the environment that characterize all organic forms. In the case of human societies, however, the patterns of exploitation of the environment by which men live are more complicated than they are for other animal species; on the one hand, through the accumulation of knowledge and experience of previous generations that is embodied in a cultural system, adaptive possibilities are greatly widened. At the same time, because of particular other features of man's biological abilities—such as the capacity for symbolization and the actions of the opposable thumb—there has also developed an accelerating technology for use in exploiting the environment, a development that in today's world threatens to be a sorcerer's apprentice. With the readings that follow in this section, we are concerned, then, with further enlarging the perspective in which we see "culture." Our first task was to examine its generic features, such as values and symbols. Then we looked at culture as one dimension of a larger interacting whole called a sociocultural system, or a society. Now it is time to see some of the ways in which culture (as part of a sociocultural system) operates in a context of an *ecosystem*, that is, an even larger framework of dynamic and functional relations between animal populations and their environments. These few readings, of course, can only briefly introduce a topic that is becoming of greater interest to behavioral scientists—and of greater and greater pragmatic importance to human societies as a whole. It is becoming, literally, a matter of life and death that we see the biological and ecological interrelatedness of events in nature, and especially, man's role and man's responsibilities in controlling his own predation and pollution.

MAN AND HABITAT

With this selection we move from considering culture as one system in what has been called a *sociocultural* system to considering it as involved in an even larger and more comprehensive network of relationships, that of an *ecosystem*. We hear a great deal these days about ecology—interrelations of organisms and environment—and with good reason; for all of life rests upon the maintenance of particular kinds of interactions with the physical and biotic environment. This is as true of the life of human societies as it is that of all other species. But while that fact has been commented upon for a long time (both as a "folk notion" and as a scientific assertion), it has been subject to periods of rising and falling popularity so far as its being considered on a *conceptual* basis is concerned. An early form of anthropological theorizing, for example, stressed an almost strict determinism of cultural forms by specific characteristics of the physical environment. An ecological frame of reference has once again entered the social and behavioral sciences, however, one characterized this time by more emphasis on the dynamic *inter*relationships between men and their environment: the environment may create the conditions for certain kinds of developments, but this is only a necessary and not a sufficient condition. The other dimension of this interactive relationship is of a cultural nature: the orientation, values, skills and knowledge that human societies bring to the situation.

This first excerpt, by a well known ecologist, lays out the general point for these several excerpts, namely, that in understanding the forms and structure of human societies we must first start with the land and what it gives or holds back. In that point he gives specific substance to something said in the preceding article by Aberle and his colleagues—that any society must make provision for adequate relationship to its physical environment. But Darling's statement, coming as it does from a biological scientist, also underscores the *inter*disciplinary nature of an ecological frame of reference; he cannot fully understand what happened to the flora and fauna of the Scottish highlands and islands unless he brings into the ecosystem such factors as human cultures and social forms. His insistence on close, detailed observation of the natural setting in which interactive processes are occurring will also be readily accepted by anthropological readers.

THE ECOLOGICAL APPROACH TO THE SOCIAL SCIENCES

F. FRASER DARLING

Some years ago there was a great advance in Britain in the methods of growing grass, the basic food of livestock. We learned how to grow more grass, how to lay down new pastures, to select leafy strains, and to compound seed mixtures which would give early and late grazing. Indeed, such was the thrill of power, some agricultural scientists became grass fanciers and forgot the livestock in what should have been a cow's millenium.

Nobody asked the cow.

Nevertheless, the grass fanciers were sure they were in the position to supply the best of all possible cows' worlds and could point to results in increased

Reprinted with permission of author and publisher from *American Scientist*, vol. 39, no. 2 (April 1951), 244–54.

stocking capacity, more beef, more milk. The problem of cows' lives was solved.

But was it? The cows had a habit of searching diligently in the hedge bottoms and some were so perverse as to break out of heaven and graze the roadside roughage. And lately, investigators have come upon a number of digestive disturbances and conditions which can really only be called poisoning, occurring on these improved, artificial pastures.

Within the last five years, students of animal behaviour have begun to study cows and record their observations. You can present the cow with a questionnaire, but she is inarticulate, like most human beings. Yet she has quite decided opinions and all sorts of little preferences, dislikes, and fussinesses which are important to the good life—of cows. We are learning more of how to keep cows in mental and physical health by watching them. When do they feed, when do they rest, what is it they seek in the hedge bottoms; and if they find it, how much of it do they want; what is the physical and chemical quality of the plant sought? Do cows like trees, and if so, what for—cover, browse, back-scratchers, or what? What is the structure and nature of their community life? A cow's world, you will see, is becoming a complex one, and it is quite difficult to assess scientifically the various environmental factors which influence her well-being. Her life cannot be planned from the material end with such omniscience that she can be popped down in the environment which we are assured provides the greatest good for the greatest number —of cows. She has shown us that the environment should be planned around her as a sentient organism and a personality in a social group. She had forest-roaming ancestors.

So had we.

The much greater complexity of human communities and the more baffling mental and physical sicknesses we suffer as a result of having tried to create for ourselves a grass fancier's world, are the reasons for my choosing this title for my paper. You cannot turn a highly bred dairy cow back into the forest again, and it is quite certain that *we* are not going "back to nature." Yet we must go on learning something of the natural history of man.

I am merely a biologist whose main interest is ecology and animal behaviour in relation to conservation, but during the last seventeen years I have been applying the methods of ecology to studying the life of the West Highland people among whom I have lived; the study was desultory for ten years or more, but has been intensive since then. The underlying principle in conservation today is to study the complexity of the habitat, the wholeness of the environment, and the relations and behaviour of the animals within it in time as well as in space; and if you can keep the habitat going, in sufficient quantity that it is not dying on the fringes, there is no difficulty in conserving any particular animal within it. The social life of the animal is now recognized as being an important part of its environment. Conservation in this sense is closely associated with the pressures between human communities and their environment and between themselves. The study of these is human ecology.

At the end of these six years the conviction has grown that the ecological approach to a study of human communities can be an illuminating one, but I would not be so bold as to say that I could now set down a sound statement of what human ecology is. Rather I have learned what a great deal we do not know, and the good idea of human ecology will need much hard thinking and careful discipline before it is good science. That is what many of us are seeking in our different ways: to make the social investigation of man into good science. Human ecology deals with the structure of animal communities which man dominates and their development through the ecological principle of succession. As Paul Sears says, "The social function of ecology is to provide a scientific basis whereby man may shape the environment and his relations to it as he expresses himself in and through his culture patterns." Perhaps in these early days of human ecology it would be better not to set it up as a science, but rather to say that human problems may be nearer solution if we tackle them ecologically.

I believe that human ecology and social science can be good science, but we should not confuse it with social service. If I may say so, the natural history of man and the emergent social sciences are not missionary endeavor. If, as scientists, we come upon an outbreak of wife-beating, the men's immortal souls and the women's suffering backs are not our primary concern, as investigators. We would seek causes for the phenomenon, and possibly find it in a hectoring foreman and the operation of peck-orders. Doormats among animals and men have a habit of being hard on their females and children.

There are different levels in what might be called the social management of man. These are exploration and fact-finding, research and the development of ideas, application, and maintenance. We should not confuse the first two of these strata with the second two.

I was once asked by a social anthropologist what human ecology was that social anthropology was not. This was a very right and proper question to which the reply should be that there is no difference. But I ventured to say that human ecology deals essentially with *process*. The value of the ecologist will be in his power and accuracy in elucidating causes and forecasting consequences.

THE WEST HIGHLAND PROBLEM

The relatively small West Highland and Hebridean populations live close to their physical elemental environment, and to the natural resources on which they have largely depended for their existence. It seemed to me, when I began the West Highland Survey seven years ago, that the problem of the Highlands should be investigated from the biological point of view, looking on the people—without the least disrespect—as members of the indigenous fauna and social animals, and inquiring what were the factors of change in the environment, or in them, which were rendering man a slowly failing species in that environment. This was an essay in human ecology, the approach of a naturalist in conservation as contrasted with the economic attitude of mind which tends to be that of the grass fancier towards the cow. The West Highland problem cannot be described here in detail, but will serve for illustration of what I consider to be the ecological approach to the study of social behaviour.

Broadly, the Highland problem is that of *a very old and in many ways primitive human culture existing in an administratively awkward and physically refractory terrain set on the fringe of a highly industrialized urban civilization*, which itself is situated in one of the greenest, kindest lands on earth. Highlanders have been part and parcel of our national structure for only two hundred years, having until then lived a very different kind of life, in standards, laws, language, and techniques, than had the rest of Britain. Yet Highlanders are not New Hebrideans or Eskimos over whom, try as we may to the contrary, we feel some kind of mental superiority. Here is a race of people of probably greater average intelligence and intellect than the dominant group,

indistinguishable from it in physical appearance. And as members of this race moved so smoothly and successfully in the dominant civilization, it was overlooked how different were the inner rhythm of life and the style of thought and tradition. The new centralized British government of that day merely extended its administrative, economic, and social regime to include the Highlands, and with some ameliorations and some encrustations this applies today.

In human ecology we can never neglect history, for we are studying process; I would say, therefore, that a cross-sectional social survey is not ecological unless it studies origins and successions, in other words, process. We must always remember the significance of political action as an environmental factor. For example, the manipulation of the Salt Tax in the last part of the eighteenth and early nineteenth centuries had profound results on the lives of Highlanders, and the transposition of the English system of poor relief had some fantastic consequences. Again, imagine the island of Islay being immune from Spirit Duty, as it was in the late eighteenth century: distillers flocked in, the bread corn of the people was deflected to whisky, the distillers were soon making money advances (at their own rates) on the barley crops of small tenants; drunkenness was rife and the people were reduced to an appalling social state. The detailed research into population movement conducted by the West Highland Survey shows that this favoured island has suffered more than any other part of the Highlands from excessive emigration.

Another historical factor at the root of the Highland problem of today, is the exploitation which the natural resources suffered in the past. The Tudor monarchs in England were already conscious that the supply of oak was dwindling, and there were prohibitions on the felling of English oak. This sent the shipbuilders northwards to the Scottish forests; and a hundred years later, when the iron districts of Surrey and Sussex had lost their trees, there was a determined attack on Highland forests to provide fuel and charcoal. The iron ore was shipped up there. The ultimate disappearance of the forests followed the introduction of sheep-farming on the extensive, extractive system in the second half of the eighteenth century.

The countryside was one of steep hills, initially poor rocks, and of high rainfall. The climax vegetation which conserved fertility was broken, and there was rapid deterioration of the habitat. That is the core of the problem today: the people are living in a devastated habitat. And now we come to another important ecological factor, the age of the culture. The Gael is living where he has lived for several thousand years and is tenacious of place and culture. How different from North Wisconsin, where settlers went in to still virgin forests in the 1920's, devastated their environment in a very short time, and left! "Ghost towns" remain. The administration which furthered the movement had forgotten the podsol conditions of the soil in relation to climate. A heterogeneous aggregation of people would not continue to inhabit a devastated terrain in the way an old culture hangs on to its place, even in decay.

Before leaving the historical aspect, we might consider briefly the effect of a change of food habits. Dr. Salaman of Cambridge has recently published his great book, *The History and Social Influence of the Potato;* it is a mine of wealth for the human ecologist. The acceptance of the potato as the staff of life allowed an immense increase in the number of mouths so long as a low standard of existence was accepted. The history of the west of Ireland and the West Highlands and islands of Scotland—both places where wheat was not grown and where the bread corn was relatively difficult to harvest— shows that the potato, coinciding with the practice of vaccination, did bring about a swarming of the population and a very marked depression in the standard of living. Potatoes and maize meal were staples of diet at the most chaotic period. Arthur Young tried to make the potato the food of the rural working class in England; Cobbett fought the potato school tooth and nail, and the English labourer stood firm by his wheaten loaf.

We may take it for granted that when a countryside begins to feed on much the same diet as its pigs, social problems are piling up ahead. And that is the right order; the change in diet precedes the social trouble. The human ecologist will never neglect the belly of the people. Professor Paul Sears has noted an interesting situation that occurred in Mexico. The government had prohibited the fermentation of a beer, pulque, from a plant called maguéy that is grown as a stiff hedge of spiky leaves. The result of the prohibition was a high incidence of diseases associated with deficiency of vitamin B, and only when the plant was ceasing to be grown was it discovered that it was one of the most efficient anti-erosion plants on the plateau.

To return to the Highlands: the destruction of the forests has meant the removal of cover, and this environmental factor is of great importance in human lives. Humanity needs cover for all sorts of things—shelter for crops and stock; cover to enable a man to do a little experimentation which he dare not try if the eyes of every household in the township are upon him; and cover for courting and lovemaking. It is obvious what a social problem lack of cover imposes in certain types of urban communities. In the Highlands it has imposed a set of conventions almost the exact opposite of our own. Darkness is the only cover, but this is supplemented by a build-up of psychological cover. The Tiree crofter visits the Duke of Argyll's factor on the nights of no moon, though he could just as well go in the day. A fellow and a girl in the Hebrides will ignore each other in daytime should they meet on the road, but he will be calling at her home just about the time of night when in our culture we should have taken our leave. Good manners require that he be gone before it is light.

I have mentioned the value of cover in experimentation. We tend to forget how important it is in primitive communities that people should not be different, and the initial attempts to be different are the most dangerous ones. Think how in our own lives we like to experiment in private and avoid being different in the beginning. The Anglo Saxon races have a firm belief in the power of demonstration in changing methods of doing things. This is a fallacy. The Gael or the Mexican is wiser. It does not matter that a changed practice will reap him a bigger material reward. That is not recompense for having to that extent placed himself outside his group. If the material reward is real, he will be envied by his fellows, and that is not a good state to be in. If the reward is illusory, he will be ridiculed, and that is not good either in a society where there is no privacy.

I have seen the sudden loss of cover depress a small community psychologically, because of the sudden cessation of the opportunity to grow flowers and fruit. Nor should we neglect an animate factor such as the rabbit as a creator of deserts, and as an animal weed of poor land. I have seen a community give up all effort at gardening because of rabbits, and looking forth on a deteriorating habitat fostered psychological ills of frustration and ultimate indifference. Village halls do not correct this kind of situation. The first requirement is a coordinated scheme of habitat rehabilitation. It is in this way that the Tennessee Valley Authority has been such a splendid ecological project.

DETERIORATION OF THE HABITAT

The science of ecology deals with causes of observed biological phenomena, and it should be expected to lay bare multiple-factor causation, which is a very difficult field. But it is also concerned with consequences and ramifications. The practical value of ecology, as I have said, is the ability to forecast consequences of certain courses of action and of observable trends. The politician has to be very careful here, and I would suggest that the ecologist is as necessary a servant to the statesman as the economist. Let me take examples from the Highland problem. I have said that the destruction of the region's greatest natural wealth, its forests, was followed by the establishment of large-scale sheep-farming on the ranching, extractive system. The immediate social consequences of this were unfortunate, in that the people were pushed to the coast and suffered a forcible social break. This kind of sheepfarming meant a very heavy preponderance of sheep over cattle, and I have managed to discover in detail how this style of grazing destroys the habitat over a period of a century or so.

The soil is in general sour and peaty, and the roots of trees reaching down to the rock and possible glacial drift were an essential means of bringing mineral matter of a basic nature to the surface. First it went to the leaves, and as a proportion of the calcium-rich young leaves were eaten by caterpillars, there was a rain of their faeces onto the surface of the ground, where they were consumed by earthworms, which are so necessary in the British terrain to the production of a porous, well-mixed soil. Removal of the trees has broken the circulatory system of basic salts and destroyed the continuum. Earthworms disappear if the calcium level of their medium is not maintained; the soil becomes a tough, peaty skin and loses its absorptive as well as its nutritive qualities. Sheep graze much more selectively than cattle and tend to remove the more palatable components of the herbage, especially the ameliorative legumes. Sheep also neglect tall and toughened herbage, so that burning of the terrain is necessary when the sheep-cattle ratio is wide. This practice in itself impoverishes the variety of the herbage, helps the spread of the bracken fern, and tends to produce a biotic climax of a few dominants of poor nutritive quality. Burning on peat slopes also tends to produce an impervious surface which accelerates lateral runoff. This runoff water, being heavily charged with carbonic acid as it runs over the acid peat, itself helps in souring the land in the glens. This is a story of impoverishment of habitat by imposing a foreign land use.

Where the sheep-cattle ratio is grossly disturbed, conditions for a peasantry become desperate. I have now reached the stage in the Highlands when I can say: "Tell me the cattle-sheep ratio in an area, and I shall know the social health of the people." If the ratio is wide, 30–50 or more sheep to one cattle-beast, there is serious trouble; if it is under 10, things are not so bad. One can also correlate the cattle-sheep ratio with the age-structure of the population. Another thing that becomes evident is that it is the children who keep milk cows on the land; when the age-structure gets top-heavy like that of Assynt in 1931, down goes the number of milk cows.

The descending spiral of fertility of the general habitat, as outlined above, is continued on the inbye land of the croft: when a man replaces his cattle with sheep, he finds he has no manure for his arable plot, and the yields go down so far that his capacity for winter cattle is decreased. He also finds that he must bring his ewes onto the inbye land to lamb, and there they stay, nibbling the heart out of the grass until the end of May. Such meadow land cannot be expected to yield a good crop of hay, and being relieved of grazing so late means that the hay crop is not ready to cut until a time when heavy rain is general. This means the hay will not be gotten well and its nutritive value will be poor, so that once more the ability to maintain a cattle stock and the fertility of the arable land is being assailed. It is quite definitely an ecological story, and to attempt to study social and economic problems apart from the biological background would be to blindfold oneself.

Now, where do the politician and economist conflict with the ecologist in the example just given? You may have heard that ten years ago hill sheep-farming was not paying, yet a supply of hill sheep was necessary for the stratification of crosses leading to the low-ground farms, which were paying. The economist finds many good reasons for the discrepancy, though deterioration of the habitat by the hill sheep is not one of them. He says: "We must take some of the high profit from the fat-lamb end of the chain and put it back at the fountain-head." And this has been done by giving a substantial subsidy to hill ewes. The idea may have worked well in the Southern Uplands of Scotland, but in the poor terrain of the Highlands the ewe subsidy might have been specially designed for further deterioration of the habitat and for fostering social unhealth. The politician says we cannot start differentiating between one countryside and another in a measure of this kind. All he could do was to slap a still bigger subsidy on hill cattle and another new one on calves. The economists here will admit that this is a dangerous path to follow, and I as an ecologist will say, from close observation of this particular measure, that the ultimate good it can do is negligible unless it is linked with vigorous rehabilitation of habitat, which is the basis of social health.

OTHER SOURCES OF SOCIAL PROBLEMS

Depopulation and distortion of the age-structure go together and bring a new set of social problems. People in and out of the Highlands have said often enough that industries should be established there, industries of the kind where wheels go round in an important way. But what do we find? Where such industry has been established, there has been even greater depopulation in the adjacent rural areas, yet the big problem is how to maintain dispersion. Fort William and Kinlochleven may have provided Britain with aluminum, but they have created new social problems and solved none.

The remoter areas of the Highlands need roads and better transport, and scarcely anyone can be found to question the benefit that might accrue. But again, this obvious measure of amelioration must be considered ecologically. For example, I happen to know well the townships on either side of a long sea loch, one side of which has a road and the other has not. The living conditions of the people either side are different. Those on the road buy Glasgow bread (untouched by hand) and packeted goods of all sorts, and I have seen tinned porridge sold from the vans. The communities are absolutely dependent on the vans, and their standard of husbandry is low. On the other side of the loch, more cows are kept; cheese and butter are made; homemade oatcakes and porridge are the cereal staple rather than bought bread; the men

fish more, and the standard of husbandry is higher. So what has the road done? It has given those people the benefit of our well-known brands of this and that and a daily paper. But it has not so reorganized the habitat that the so-called higher standard of living can be paid for out of the greater amount of produce exported. Indeed, quite apart from the loss of social health and skills, these people are in a worse economic plight. On the roadless side there is still self-sufficiency, competence, and a realization that the croft must be well farmed. A road can be a benefit only if the environmental factors are closely studied and integrated. Here is seen clearly the effect on this small, old, subsistence culture, of being on the fringe of the most highly developed urban culture of its day. Had most of Britain been like the Highlands, the impact might have been less severe.

The ecologist asks that unquestioned beliefs should be questioned. Good communications is one of these; education is another. Consider, for example, the problem of educating the Reindeer Lapps in Scandinavia. How do you do it? The convenient way is to put the children in schools in the winter season when the Lapps are at the southernmost end of their pastoral migration. But if this is done the families and their reindeer are unduly immobilized, and the secret of pastoralism in poor terrain is to keep on the move. The winter range of the Reindeer Lapps is thus being overbrowsed, and as it is the amount of winter range which determines numbers of livestock, the damage to the birch and willow forests means that the high summer potential of the tundra is being less used. We can still believe in education, of course, but at least let us ponder methods of applying it, in terms of consequences on the habitat.

I have mentioned depopulation and the distortion of the age-group pyramids. The problems of human ecology arising from the phenomenon in small communities are manifold. In the first place, the old remain in power and so prevail that they can initiate an era of reaction in the life of a community, so that in a region of hard-shell Presbyterianism all gaiety for the young is frowned upon. And nowhere do the young show greater consideration for the old than in the Highlands. I know of townships where there are but few married couples now. Brothers and sisters have cared for their old folk, and now that they are gone they continue living in their parents' houses and cannot bring themselves to the considerable upset of getting married. The social urge and necessary gaiety are not there. This depression of the vivid social life of man is likely to lead to such undesirable consequences as burning of the hills in an excitement bordering on hysteria. The crass burnings of the heather are made ostensibly to further the growth of young grass; in actual fact they further the devastation of the habitat. The fires occur at Beltane, which was once the breeding season. Where the social life is in better order, burning is under control. That great American ecologist, Charles Adams, who has now turned his attention to mankind, told me recently of an almost identical phenomenon in one of the southern states, and of how the problem had solved itself with improvement in social conditions.

It is difficult to avoid the impression that religion is a considerable ecological factor, but it must always be related with other environmental characteristics. The areas of most pronounced depopulation in the Highlands have the harshest sects of Presbyterianism; but I do not want to overdo this idea or give a wrong impression, because the area of greatest congestion, Lewis, follows the same faith. What I would say is this: that in the Highlands a small, remote community with poor services would have more chance of survival if it were Catholic than if it were Free Presbyterian. This is because there is more sense of community to be found in the districts of the old, liberal—almost Columban—style of Catholicism. The culture is stronger altogether; music and folk tales have not been dimmed, and the status of women is higher. Birth rates are exactly the same. It is in these small, isolated communities, where the social pattern of humankind can scarcely be completed, that a factor which is associated with the old culture can be critical.

The human ecologist must always be on the lookout for these marginal factors, the comprehension of which may illuminate a much wider field where complexity defeats scientific investigation.

There is one more illustration that I want to give from the Island of Lewis, which, as I have said, is a congested island. The terrain is poor, but the people have been there for 4000 years or so, with various immigrant waves which have accepted the old culture and have not imposed their own. The old Celtic custom of subdivision of land, and the intense conviction that the land is theirs, have re-

sulted in the island's being entirely held by crofters, all doing much the same things. It is one-class society worthy of very close study. Weaving has given prosperity, and though the land is tending to be neglected because it is more profitable to weave, the people cannot effect the social revolution of relinquishing at least lip service to subsistence husbandry, and thereby achieving division of labour and social stratification. There is an intense social life from house to house and among the young in Lewis, who are numerous enough to maintain a fine gaiety in the face of religious proscription, but there is little knowledge of the constructive or artistic use of leisure. Nearly everybody is a peasant except for a handful of professional people in Stornoway. Prosperity has come as money—pound notes—but in rural Lewis there is nothing much to spend money on.* Social evolution would seem to have stuck, and needs a catalyst. Lewis will not allow itself to evolve, and the observer cannot help comparing the tremendous social vitality maintained by the good proportion of young folk, with the stricken life of the dying communities on the mainland shore. The right hand of Lewis reaches out for all that the world can offer, but her left hand holds fast to the croft in the unenclosed township, and she is anchored in time. The fact that the crofting townships are unenclosed, precludes differentiation of husbandry and agricultural improvement.

I want to close these remarks on the natural history of society by pointing the obvious: that tradition and accumulated experience are part of man's environment, and for all the importance of the physical and biological factors I have mentioned, the ethos is still the biggest ecological factor of all on the life of the individual. Here I would digress for a moment on methods of approach in gathering data. The ecologist must distrust the questionnaire so beloved of the sociologists, because it fails to take sufficient notice of the ethos of a people. The questionnaire will not necessarily give you scientific data. In the course of the West Highland Survey we compiled a punch-card Domesday of factual data about crofting townships and it is immensely valuable, but we never asked questions on personal household matters or questions of opinion. Had we

---

*At the moment of going to press, the export market for Harris tweed has suffered a relapse; there is depression in the weaving districts of Lewis.

done so we should either have come up against a brick wall or, with such a sensitive and penetrating people, we should have got the answers they thought we should like. Much the best way is observation and soaking in the culture. Ability to observe closely and interpret accurately, by way of a large grasp of the organism of a society in its habitat, is the essence of human ecology. It is an integrative science as much as an analytical one, with observation as its basis.

If the psychologists could devise courses in development of the power of observation as part of the training for a research career, we should at least be able to pick out at an early stage those graduates who are fitted to study man as a social animal. After that must come the faculty to use several disciplines. Teamwork in human ecology will be essential, but still each specialist will have to have the quality of delighting in another man's work and linking his own to it; and he cannot be the traditionally remote academic type, but must be inquisitive about what humankind is doing to itself.

"CULTURAL" ECOLOGY

Recently there have been many articles and some books by anthropologists dealing with what has become known in the discipline as "cultural ecology." One of the earliest of these is the following article by Hallowell, one of the most influential of American anthropologists. In the spirit of a holistic, unified framework suggested by Darling, he places a question dealing with the land tenure system—the size of Algonkian hunting territories—in an ecological perspective, that is, a framework of the dynamics of adaptation between human populations and their physical and biotic surroundings. Noting that matters such as size of hunting territories are not simply a function of "cultural" factors such as abstract beliefs about property rights, his central point is that, given the fundamental aim of trapping as an exploitative activity, the sheer size of land holdings is meaningless unless it is related to the number of potentially trappable animals found in a given land area. The determining feature is, then, a *functional* one having to do with problems of adaptation: this is the ecological message so far as it relates to human populations trying to survive. And it is a profound and pervasive message, one that is becoming more widely diffused and reckoned with in many behavioral science investigations (even though it may parade under a variety of labels, such as "human ecology," "social ecology," "environmental psychology," and so on).

THE SIZE OF ALGONKIAN HUNTING TERRITORIES: A FUNCTION OF ECOLOGICAL ADJUSTMENT[1]

A. IRVING HALLOWELL

A new note has recently crept into the now familiar discussions of the hunting territory system of the Northern Algonkians. First, there was the initial period of description, begun by Speck more than thirty years ago.[2] At that time, when the crude evolutionary theories of cultural development that prevailed in the 19th century were being outgrown, there was even a certain novelty in the idea that,

Reprinted with permission of publisher. From *American Anthropologist*, 51 (1949), 35–45.
[1]Paper read at the meeting of the AAA, Albuquerque, New Mexico, December, 1947.

[2]Speck's initial paper, based on a lecture delivered at the University of Pennsylvania, was entitled "Basis of American Indian Ownership of the Land." It was printed in the *Old Penn Weekly Review*, Vol. 13, No. 16, 1915.

instead of communal ownership, there were hunting peoples who maintained a system of ownership in severalty.[3] Soon, the geographical distribution of the hunting-territory system among Algonkian peoples was well under way and the land-tenure systems of other hunting peoples in North America and elsewhere were drawn into the discussion.[4] Following this, and in keeping with the intellectual climate of the period, the question of historical depth arose: How far was the observed system of land tenure among the Algonkians completely aboriginal? Despite a few dissident voices, the weight of evidence, when systematically marshalled and analyzed by Cooper (1939),[5] lent support to the aboriginal thesis, at least in so far as certain nuclear features of the institution were concerned. Cooper even went further and advanced the hypothesis that such a system might be a "tarriant" phenomenon from very ancient times, among the marginal peoples of the world.[6] More recently, however, Cooper has expressed doubt about his own hypothesis. He says . . . "It looks as if land tenure among hunting peoples is delicately responsive to ecology, especially to the fauna exploited as the staple food supply. It looks likewise as if such tenure can and does adapt and change readily and swiftly in accordance with changing local ecological conditions."[7]

Thus a new note has been struck in the discussion of land tenure among the Northern Algonkians, similar overtones being clearly perceptible in a previously published article by Speck and Eiseley.[8]

To my mind this ecological hypothesis has some

important methodological implications. It calls for a more dynamic type of analysis than has been previously undertaken. Instead of concentrating upon cultural description, the facts of geographical distribution and problems of historical depth and continuity, the major question becomes in effect: What are the *actual* determinants or controlling factors involved? Once this question has been broached, the level of inquiry is shifted from the plane of description and chronological reconstruction to that of process and the structural dynamics of human adjustment. It involves a more detailed examination of all the conditions under which a given human population makes its fundamental ecological adjustments in a specific locale. Within this frame of reference, however, we are forced to take new data into account, data of a *non-cultural* nature. For we can hardly pursue an ecological hypothesis without giving due weight to relevant demographic facts, as well as those pertaining to the character, incidence and fluctuations of fauna or other pertinent information. Perhaps in this case, as well as in others, our very devotion to cultural description and historical explanation, on the implicit, if not explicit, assumption that culture is a phenomenon, *sui generis* has blinded us to the relevance of some of the way data that are needed if the actual dynamics of the hunting-territory system is to be fully understood or explained. Furthermore, if we begin to ask questions about the controlling factors of the hunting-territory system it is not likely that we shall arrive at a satisfactory explanation if we operate exclusively with generically descriptive traits that purport to characterize the normative aspects of the institution considered as a whole. We need more precise information about the variabilities and constancies that are found in the actual operation of the hunting-territory system under given conditions. If we had more inclusive data at our disposal from different localities, we might then be able to discover some of the factors responsible for the variable and constant features of the system and thus illuminate its basic dynamics. In this paper I have selected only a single variable—the size of Algonkian hunting grounds—as a concrete illustration of the more general problem.

What precise information do we have about this attribute of Algonkian hunting territories that would enable us to state the factors responsible for its great variability? All we can say is that this feature not only varies greatly in magnitude, when we

---

[3]Lewis H. Morgan, e.g., in his characterization of the stage of Savagery, had written "Lands, as yet hardly a subject of property, were owned by the tribes in common." (*Ancient Society*, p. 537).

[4]Speck's "Family Hunting Territories and Social Life of Various Algonkian Bands of the Ottawa Valley," with maps showing the actual boundaries of the hunting grounds of the Timaggami, Timiskaming, Kipawa and Dumoine bands, was published in 1915. A preliminary world-wide survey of similar systems of land ownership appeared in the *Proceedings of the 22nd International Congress of Americanists* (1928). The contributions of Cooper, Davidson and myself to this phase of the problem can be easily located in the literature cited and need not be referred to here. But attention needs to be called to Cooper's discussion of the three major forms of ownership in severalty, since this important contribution is somewhat disguised under the generic title "Land Tenure among the Indians of Eastern and Northern North America" and it appeared in a relatively obscure source.

[5]"Is the Algonkian Family Hunting-Ground System Pre-Columbian?" The world distribution of the family hunting-ground and related systems is brought up to date in this article. For additional bibliographical items see Cooper, 1941, note 87, p. 57.

[6]Cooper, 1939, pp. 84–85.

[7]Cooper, 1946, p. 294. Cf. the same author's discussion of the factors that he deems "responsible in large part for the system of tenure in *severalty*," observable among marginal peoples in his *Temporal Sequence*, 1941, pp. 59–60.

[8]Speck and Eiseley, 1942.

consider intra-band conditions, but even more so when the mean variation reported for different ethno-linguistic groups is taken into account. At one extreme we have the Newfoundland Micmac, the average size of whose hunting territories Speck estimated to be 2,000 square miles,[9] while on the other hand we have an estimate of 8–10 square miles for the White Earth Ojibwa.[10] But even these figures cannot be said to be typical of the ethno-linguistic units referred to, since the Ojibwa elsewhere are known to have much *larger* hunting grounds and other Micmac groups are reported to have much *smaller* territories (Cape Breton Island 400, Nova Scotia 200 square miles). Since this is the case, it is impossible to make any satisfactory statement about the mean size of Algonkian hunting territories in general, particularly in view of the fact that it is doubtful if we actually have on record an adequate sample of the mean size of the hunting grounds of Algonkian peoples throughout their habitat.[11] It is indeed somewhat paradoxical that while many descriptive generalizations have been made about the Algonkian hunting-territory system, mean size is not among them. This is analogous to describing all the morphological characteristics of an animal like the elephant without reference to the size of the creature. The explanation, of course, lies partly in the phenomenon of variability itself. Nevertheless, this variability must have its limits as well as its determinants. And where we have the most precise information, the range of variability *does* seem to have characteristic limits in different localities.

The size and composition of the winter hunting groups that are associated with the hunting territories present another interesting variable. So far as composition is concerned, the small biological family (unmarried children and parents) cannot be taken as typical, and consequently there is a considerable range in size, even within the same locality. If we have data on both the size of hunting territories and the size of hunting groups we can,

of course, discover whether the size of the latter varies concomitantly with the former or in some other way. We also have the necessary information for stating the density of population among one people as compared with another. And, if we likewise know whether the population is increasing or decreasing we may gain some insight into the relation between population dynamics and the functioning of the land tenure system under such conditions.

Another problem of focal interest is the ratio of active hunters to other persons in different locales. How variable or constant is this ratio? If it should turn out to be relatively constant in different regions, despite variations in the size of hunting territories, the size of hunting groups or fluctuations in fauna, it would then appear that we have a ratio that perhaps defines some primary unit in ecological adjustment.

If, in addition to such demographic data as I have mentioned, we also had adequate information about the incidence of the various fur bearers and other animals in given regions, I believe that we could obtain some significant answers to questions of ecological adjustment.[12] It might then be possible to advance a hypothesis, empirically grounded in the structural dynamics of the ecological adjustment of specific groups, that would throw further light upon questions of historical depth and continuity. For we know that, even if such an institution as the hunting-territory system has persisted in time, it has not done so in an ecological vacuum. There must be conditions present that either re-enforce its continuance or lead to change.[13]

---

[9]Speck, 1922, p. 196.

[10]Speck, 1917, p. 89.

[11]In his first paper, Speck wrote: "The districts among the Algonkians seem to average between two and four hundred square miles to each family in the main habitat, while on the tribal frontiers they may average from two to four times as large." This estimate of the range of the mean size of Algonkian hunting territories is repeated word for word in Speck, 1928, except that the phrase "nearer the central range of the tribes" is inserted after "habitat." The need for more precise information is illustrated by the fact that, while one of the groups discussed in this paper falls within the range indicated, the Berens River Ojibwa do not.

[12]Cooper, 1941, p. 59, already has suggested the determinative weight of "migratory or markedly nomadic, and/or gregarious habits of the fauna," upon the prevalence of a *communal* type of land tenure and the contrasting influence of "non-migratory and/or non-gregarious fauna, or fauna of a relatively restricted home range," upon systems of tenure in *severalty*. Both groups of Indians discussed below primarily exploit animals of the latter category and are characterized by ownership in severalty. However, the question of the relative *incidence* of the staple game animals in different localities is another variable of possible weight in the determination of the *size* of hunting grounds.

[13]Cf. the statement of Cooper, 1946, p. 293, that "these various considerations and points of evidence suggest that the family hunting-ground system, as found among the various discontinuously distributed hunting peoples in the coniferous belt of North America and Eurasia, is of multiple rather than of unitary origin, representing local adaptation to differing ecologies and subsistence quests, and that it is not integral to taiga economy as such in the sense that it developed and spread uniformly with this economy." Such a statement is a far cry from the not-too-distant debates in cultural anthropology about diffusion *versus* independent development. It will no doubt become increasingly evident in our studies that any crude choice between such polarities, unless the crucial evidence is available, actually leaves us high and dry so far as the complex realities of the historic process are concerned.

So far as the Northern Algonkians are concerned, one of the conditions of such continuity is the fact that they have lived in the same faunal and climatic zone and no faunal catastrophe has occurred as in the case of the Sioux. And it is true as Kroeber has pointed out,[14] with respect to both Algonkians and Athabascans, that as a result of the demand for furs "the long-run effect of Caucasian contacts was to entrench these peoples more firmly in their occupation as hunters." Nevertheless, the Algonkians have undergone many demographic and cultural readjustments. Today they exhibit various levels of acculturation. It is hard to believe, therefore, that all these processes of readjustment have left their land tenure system *completely* unaffected. If a closer study of the hunting-territory system as it operates today can give us an insight into the actual factors that control its variable features, it should be possible to deduce some of the necessary and sufficient conditions that underlie stability as well as change. It might even be possible to explain such variant and less characteristic patterns of ownership in severalty as the allotment system as an emergent practice that arose under specific local conditions.

By way of illustrating some of the possibilities that an ecological approach suggests I wish now to present some concrete data from two localities within the habitat of the Northern Algonkians. I shall confine my discussion to the one major variable mentioned above—the mean size of their hunting grounds, some correlative demographic data and the controlling factors that may be involved.

The two groups chosen belong to the same ethnolinguistic unit—the Ojibwa-Ottawa Algonkian.[15] One group is the Grand Lake Victoria Indians, located in the Province of Quebec; the other is the Berens River Indians in Manitoba. These Indians not only have the same linguistic and cultural background, they live in the same faunal zone, hunt the same animals with the same technological equipment, dispose of their fur in a market controlled by commercial companies operating throughout the Dominion of Canada, and have approximately the same standard of living. Any local differences, therefore, must be viewed against the broad background of linguistic, cultural, technological and other uniformities.

Davidson collected the data on the Grand Lake Victoria group in 1926;[16] I collected the material on the Berens River Indians between 1932 and 1934.[17] These data comprise, among other things, detailed information on 74 winter hunting groups, 31 representing the Grand Lake Victoria Band and 43 the Berens River Saulteaux (Northern Ojibwa). Only those winter hunting-groups are included for which reliable information in respect to the size of the hunting territory and the number of persons in the hunting groups has been recorded. Consequently a few groups have been omitted, but there are so few that the sample used is thoroughly representative.

I have calculated the areas of the hunting grounds in square miles by the use of a planimeter applied to the original maps on which the boundaries were drawn. These boundaries were outlined in most cases by the Indians themselves or by the investigator under the immediate instruction of the Indians. They represent approximations subject to errors dependent upon the scale of the maps employed and the ability of the Indians to recognize familiar landmarks. In the case of the Berens River people large-scale maps of the National Topographic Series were used. These permitted somewhat greater accuracy than in the case of the smaller-scale maps which Davidson was compelled to use. The resulting figures as a whole offer a sound quantitative basis for a comparison of the mean size of the hunting grounds for the two groups. So far as I know these are the only two groups where we have figures compiled on the basis of direct planimetric measurement.

Quantitative information on the size of hunting grounds, the size of winter hunting-groups, density of population and the ratio of hunters to other persons for the two groups under discussion has been tabulated on page 285.

The mean size of the hunting grounds in the two localities is remarkably different. Those of the Grand Lake Victoria group average more than three times those of the Berens River Indians. *A priori* one might suppose that this difference might be a simple function of the size of the hunting groups. But this is not the case. In fact, the size of the hunting groups in the localities compared bears an inverse relation to the size of the hunting grounds. For the winter hunting-groups of the

---

[14]Kroeber, 1939, p. 96.
[15]Voegelin, 1941, has pointed out the linguistic unity. To my mind there can be no doubt about a parallel ethnic unity.

[16]Davidson, 1926.
[17]Unpublished Ms.

NAME OF GROUP	SIZE OF HUNTING GROUNDS			SIZE OF HUNTING GROUPS		DENSITY OF POPULATION	
	No.	Range (sq. mi.)	Av. (sq. mi.)	Range (no. persons)	Av. (no. persons)	Range (sq. mi. per person)	Av.
GRAND LAKE VICTORIA	31	64–1716	316[18]	2–17	5.6[19]	13–146	55.6
BERENS RIVER	43	13–212	93	4–49	14.9	1–24.5	6.2

NAME OF GROUP	RATIO OF ACTIVE HUNTERS TO OTHER PERSONS					
	Active Hunters		Other Persons		Ratio	
	Range	Av.	Range	Av.	Range	Av.
GRAND LAKE VICTORIA	1–3	1.3	1–14	4.3	1:0.5–1:65	1:3.1
BERENS RIVER	1–10	3.3	2–39	11.6	1:1–1:8	1:3.5

Berens River Indians are *three times as large* as the hunting groups of the Grand Lake Victoria Indians. And when we calculate the mean density of the population the contrast is even more striking. While the picture exhibited by the Berens River Indians is one person to 6.2 square miles, among the Grand Lake Victoria Indians it is one person to 55.6 square miles. The former figure, incidentally, is a little higher than Kroeber's estimate of the aboriginal density of the population north of the Great Lakes (one person per 5.3 square miles) while the latter shows an even greater sparsity than Kroeber's estimate of one person per 34.6 square miles in the eastern sub-arctic.[20]

When we turn to the ratio of active hunters to other persons, however, we get a different picture. The ratio is approximately identical, being 1 hunter to 3.1 non-hunters in the case of the Grand Lake Victoria Indians, and 1 active hunter to 3.5 non-hunters in the Berens River group. This fact is even more interesting when the composition of the hunting groups in the two localities is compared. For the mean number of active hunters per hunting group is 1.3 at Grand Lake Victoria while it is 3.3 among the Berens River Indians. This is explained by the fact that since the Grand Lake Victoria hunting groups are small there is only a single hunter in the large majority of them (70.9%). The reverse is true of the hunting groups in the Berens River region; only 11% of them operate with a single active hunter.[21]

Two important inferences can be made from the analysis of the data just presented. (1) The constancy in the ratio between hunters and non-hunters appears to be independent of either variability in the size of the hunting territories or of the size of the hunting groups. If such a ratio should be supported by information from other groups it would be a basic fact in the ecological adjustment of these northern hunters. When thought of in terms of group composition it is equivalent to a small family consisting of a hunter, his wife and two children. (2) The second inference that can be made on the basis of the data from the two groups compared is that the size of the hunting territories is in no sense a simple function of the size of the hunting group that makes use of them.

What then are the controlling factors in the size of hunting territories? In the first place it may be pointed out that there is nothing in the economic

---

[18]Twice the figure of the area (100–150 sq. mi.) attributed to Australian hordes of 20–50 persons. See Steward.

[19]The Tete de Boule (Davidson, 1928b) also average 5.6 but no group numbered more than 13 persons. My own unpublished data on the St. Francis Abenaki, while not quite so precise, approximates this same figure.

[20]See Steward, p. 338, for these figures. Kroeber's (1934 and 1939) are expressed in number of persons per 100 km². It is also worth noting that the latter's density figure for the Ojibwa north of the Great Lakes, 9.54 persons per 100 km² (1939, p. 141), which is the equivalent of one person per 6.51 square miles, is practically identical with the figure given above for the Berens River Ojibwa.

[21]Of the 31 hunting groups of the Grand Lake Victoria Indians, 22 have 1 active hunter; 6 others have 2, while the remaining 3 have the maximum of 3 active hunters. In contrast, only 5 of the 43 winter hunting-groups of the Berens River Ojibwa have a single hunter, while 15 have 3, 9 have 4, 6 have 5, and the two largest groups of all have 10 active hunters each.

culture of these people to motivate the accumulation of large tracts of land. The products of the land are a primary source of wealth rather than the ownership of land in the sense of "real estate." For land has no value in exchange. Referring to intra-band variations in the size of hunting grounds Davidson remarks:[22] "It will be noted that some individuals own exceptionally large tracts of land . . . such conditions, however, are not the result of willful endeavors on the part of the respective owners to acquire property and wealth. It may be said in this respect that no lust for territory larger than that necessary to insure a reasonable bounty of fur, is at all present in the minds of these people." I can only add that, among all the Algonkian people with whom I have been acquainted, there is also no prestige whatsoever that accrues to the man who hunts over a large tract of land as compared with the man who traps over a smaller area. So we must conclude that so far as intra-band factors are concerned, economic competition is not a controlling factor in the size of hunting grounds nor can variability be connected with any ranking system or the functioning of prestige.

Nor do I think that the size of hunting tracts is in any sense a function of inheritance rules that tend to stabilize rigid boundaries over the generations. While I cannot give the evidence here I can only say that my own data from the Berens River indicate great flexibility in this regard. The hunting territory boundaries of one generation are not *precisely* those that prevail in the next generation.

It seems difficult, therefore, to explain variations in the size of hunting territories in terms of purely cultural factors.

If we now turn to non-cultural influences that might possibly be controlling factors in the size of hunting grounds one factor that conceivably might influence the situation is to be sought in population dynamics. Assuming that migration from the region does not take place, what effect does either increase or decrease of population have upon the size of hunting territories? In the two areas from which I have cited data, we have contrasting pictures in this respect. The Grand Lake Victoria Indians in the period prior to and succeeding Davidson's study show a decline in population (252 in 1912 to 85 in 1929),[23] whereas between 1902

and 1934 the Berens River population increased 69% (527 to 891). While it might appear that the smaller size of the Berens River hunting territories could be explained as a result of population pressure within a limited habitat, I must confess that I see no actual evidence for this. My mapping shows that the boundaries of hunting grounds could be extended but this has not taken place. All I can say is that there seems no economic advantage in doing so, since their needs are met just as well by hunting in more restricted areas. In other words, the decisive factor may be the relative abundance of game and fur-bearing animals available within a given area. Davidson made this general observation twenty years ago.[24] He pointed out that "physically it is possible for a man to cover only so much trapline. His catch for the year, therefore, is not limited by the amount of distance covered but rather by the number of game animals in his district. A normal territory, therefore, would be one which would annually produce the yearly catch of the trapper. *Such a tract would thus depend in size more upon the abundance of game than upon its extent in miles. Given this normal territory, additional lands would be useless to a hunter.*" (Italics ours.) This seems to me a sufficient explanation of the situation observed among the Berens River Indians. But the same principle may be invoked to explain the *larger* hunting territories of the Grand Lake Victoria Indians. That is to say, if it were known that game was less abundant in the region hunted over by the Grand Lake Victoria Indians then it may have been *necessary* for them to range over *larger* areas in order to make a living. Since we know that the ratio of hunters to non-hunters is the same in both areas and that the standard of living is approximately the same, this provides an attractive ecological hypothesis. Unfortunately, I have not been able to secure the necessary data on the relative abundance of fauna in the two regions that would be required to prove that such a differential factor is the crucial determinant of the size of hunting territories.[25]

The situation is complicated by another factor which is present in the Grand Lake Victoria region

[22]Davidson, 1928a, p. 87.
[23]Figures from census (Dominion of Canada). The influenza epidemic of 1918 decimated the band approximately 25%.

[24]Davidson, 1928a, p. 88.
[25]Speck and Eiseley, 1942, p. 221, point out that "we are greatly in need . . . of a more detailed knowledge of the animal and human inter-relationships of the whole Canadian region. An approach to this aspect of the dove-tailing cycles of human and animal fluctuation in number will be a future step in the method of treatment of the economic problems of the area, under ecological conditions."

and absent in the Berens River area. This factor is the direct competition with white trappers for fur-bearing animals among the Grand Lake Victoria Indians. Davidson is quite explicit about this. He says: "Throughout the domain of the Grand Lake Victoria and Lake Barriere Indians, the trapping operations of the white men are yearly becoming more serious. The alarm felt by the Indians may well be realized when we learn from one hunter that as many as twelve white men were trapping on his own territory in the winter of 1925–26. Other Indians report the presence of any number between two and six, and *not one* Indian reported that his territory has not been invaded some time during the season."[26]

From an ecological point of view this means that the actual hunter-game ratio is quite different than is the case if we consider the Indians alone. It also means, of course, that there is less game available to the Indian trappers. Even if we ignore a possible differential in the incidence of the economically valuable fauna in the two regions, the presence of white trappers introduces a new factor whose influence has to be evaluated in the case of the Grand Lake Victoria people. Since this influence has not been studied it is impossible to draw any conclusions. It may even be considered an open question as to whether the factor of white competition bears any relation to the size of the hunting territories in this region. But it cannot be denied that the situation as described is part of the modern ecological picture. At any rate, I must let the solution of this particular problem rest.

It has been the major purpose of this paper to call attention to the need for a type of investigation which goes beyond the bare ethnographic facts of land tenure rather than to give any final solution to particular problems. On the basis of the concrete material presented it has been shown that a number of possible explanations of the mean difference in the size of the hunting territories in these two localities must be rejected. On the other hand, certain factors that appear to be of determinative importance have been pointed out. If investigations based on sound ecological hypotheses were carried through rigorously and systematically on the basis of an inclusive body of relevant facts I believe that we could arrive at an explanation of the actual factors that control the size of Algonkian hunting grounds as well as the basic dynamics of the hunting territory system as a whole.

BIBLIOGRAPHY

COOPER, JOHN M.

1938 Land Tenure Among the Indians of Eastern and Northern North America. *Pennsylvania Archeologist*, 8: 55–59.

1939 Is the Algonquian Family Hunting Ground System Pre-Columbian? *American Anthropologist*, 41: 66–90.

1941 *Temporal Sequence and the Marginal Cultures.* Catholic University of America, Anth. Series, No. 10, Washington.

1946 The Culture of the Northeastern Indian Hunters: A Reconstructive Interpretation. In *Man in Northeastern North America.* Papers of the R. S. Peabody Foundation for Archeology, Vol. 3, pp. 272–305. .

DAVIDSON, D. S.

1928a The Family Hunting Territories of the Grand Lake Victoria Indians. *Atti del XXII Congresso Internaz. degli Americanisti*, Rome, 1926, pp. 69–95.

1928b Notes on Tete de Boule Ethnology. *American Anthropologist*, 30: 18–45.

EISELEY, LOREN C. (See Speck and Eiseley)

HALLOWELL, A. IRVING

(1) The Hunting Customs and the Hunting Territories of the St. Francis Abenaki. (Ms.)

(2) Winter Hunting Groups, Hunting Territories, and Inheritance Rules among the Berens River Saulteaux (Northern Ojibwa). (Ms.)

KROEBER, A. L.

1934 Native American Population. *American Anthropologist*, 36: 1–25.

1939 Cultural and Natural Areas of Native North America. *University of California Pub. in Amer. Archeol. and Ethnology*, Vol. 38.

MORGAN, LEWIS H.

1878 *Ancient Society,* or *Researches in the Line of Human Progress from Savagery through Barbarism to Civilization.* Henry Holt & Co., New York. (Ed. Chas. Kerr & Co., Chicago, 1907.)

SPECK, FRANK G.

1915a Basis of American Indian Ownership of the Land. *Old Penn Weekly Review*, 13: 181–196.

1915b *Family Hunting Territories and Social Life of Various Algonkian Bands of the Ottawa Valley.* Memoir 70, Anth. Series. No. 8, Geological Survey of Canada.

1917 Social Structure of the Northern Algonkian. Pub. of the Amer. Soc. Soc., Vol. 12.

1922 *Beothuk and Micmac.* Indian Notes and Monographs, Museum of the American Indian, Heye Foundation, N. Y.

[26]Davidson, 1928a, pp. 73–74.

1928 Land Ownership among Hunting Peoples in Primitive America and the World's Marginal Areas. *Atti del XXII Congresso Internaz. delgi Americanisti*, Rome, 1926, pp. 323–332.

SPECK, FRANK G., and LOREN C. EISELEY

1939 Significance of Hunting Territory Systems of the Algonkian in Social Theory. *American Anthropologist*, 41: 269–280.

1942 Montagnais-Naskapi Bands and Family Hunting Districts of the Central and Southeastern

Labrador Peninsula. *Proceedings American Philosophical Society*, 85: 215–242.

STEWARD, JULIAN H.

1936 The Economic and Social Basis of Primitive Bands. In *Essays in Anth. in Honor of Alfred Louis Kroeber*. University of Cal. Press., Berkeley, Cal.

VOEGELIN, C. F.

1941 North American Indian Languages Still Spoken and Their Genetic Relationships. In *Language, Culture and Personality*, *Essays in Memory of Edward Sapir*. Menasha, Wis.

SOCIOCULTURAL SYSTEM AND ECOSYSTEM

Ecological ideas and terms have by no means been confined to anthropology in their incursion into the social sciences. There has been a long-standing influence of some of those ideas in certain research areas of sociology, for example. One of the most effective of those uses, to my mind, is illustrated in the excerpt that follows, for Duncan remains faithful to the essential ingredient in an ecological frame of reference—that of the search for *dynamic* interrelations having to do with problems of adaptation, and not simply a static, geographic delimitation of a given area as representing an "ecologic" perspective. Duncan's discussion is also important for refreshing your understanding of the idea of *levels of phenomena* (recall White, Novikoff, and Nadel), which we attempt to study through the conceptual framework of *levels of analysis*. And, with Duncan, we have come to a clear discussion of the point being stressed over the last several excerpts—that, while for some problems it is useful to conceive of sociocultural systems as isolated and operating in a vacuum, for many other problems (especially for those having to do with the dynamics of human behavior) it is far more profitable to think of sociocultural systems as components in an *ecosystem*. Hence Duncan's title, "From Social System to Ecosystem." Though the article was addressed primarily to sociologists, it, like Homans's, can be read in an ecumenical spirit. Certainly the concrete illustrations he offers for his point—air pollution, smog, and automobile exhaust—are not only timely but important enough to concern us all.

FROM SOCIAL SYSTEM TO ECOSYSTEM

OTIS DUDLEY DUNCAN

LEVELS AND SYSTEMS

All science proceeds by a selective ordering of data by means of conceptual schemes. Although the formulation and application of conceptual schemes

Reprinted with permission of author and publisher. From *Sociological Inquiry*, 31 (1961), 140–49.

are recognized to entail, at some stage of inquiry, more or less arbitrary choices on the part of the theorist or investigator, we all acknowledge, or at least feel, that the nature of the "real world" exercises strong constraints on the development of schemes in science. Some schemes, used fruitfully over long periods of time, come to seem so natural

that we find it difficult to imagine their being superseded. One type of scheme is deeply ingrained by
our training as social scientists, to wit, the organization of data by *levels*. Kroeber is only voicing the
consensus of a majority of scientists when he writes:[1]

> The subjects or materials of science . . . fall into four
> main classes or levels: the inorganic, organic, psychic,
> and sociocultural. . . . There is no intention to assert
> that the levels are absolutely separate, or separable
> by unassailable definitions. They are substantially
> distinct in the experience of the totality of science,
> and that is enough.

MacIver gives substantially the same classification,
but instead of using the relatively colorless term
"levels," he chooses to segregate the several "nexus
of causation" into "great dynamic realms."[2]

It is significant that scientists, insofar as they do
accept the doctrine of levels, tend to work *within* a
level, not *with* it. The scheme of levels does not
itself produce hypotheses; it can scarcely even be
said to be heuristic. Its major contribution to the
history of ideas has been to confer legitimacy upon
the newer scientific approaches to the empirical
world that, when they were emerging, had good use
for any kind of ideological support.

Quite another type of conceptual scheme, the notion of *system*, is employed by the scientist in his
day-to-day work. Conceptions of interdependent
variation, of cause and effect, or even of mere patterning of sequence, derive from the idea that nature (using the term broadly for whatever can be
studied naturalistically) manifests itself in collections of elements with more than nominal properties of unity.

No doubt there are many kinds of system, reflecting the kinds of elements comprising them and the
modes of relationship conceived to hold among
these elements. The point about this diversity that
is critical to my argument is this. When we elect,
wittingly or unwittingly, to work *within* a level (as
this term was illustrated above) we tend to discern
or construct—whichever emphasis you prefer—only
those kinds of system whose elements are confined
to that level. From this standpoint, the doctrine of
levels may not only fail to be heuristic, it may actually become anti-heuristic, if it blinds us to fruitful

results obtainable by recognizing *systems that cut
across levels.*

One such system, probably because it is virtually
a datum of immediate experience, is rather readily
accepted by social scientists: personality. Manifestly
and phenomenologically an integration of non-
randomly selected genetic, physiologic, social, and
psycho-cultural elements, personality has a kind of
hard reality that coerces recognition, even when it
can be related to other systems only with difficulty
or embarrassment. If I am not mistaken, however,
the concept of personality system enjoys a sort of
privileged status. We do not so readily accede to the
introduction into scientific discourse of other sorts
of system concept entailing integration of elements
from diverse levels. The resistance to such concepts
is likely to be disguised in charges of "environmental determinism" or "reductionism." An example: The working assumption of some human
ecologists that the human community is, among
other things, an organization of activities in physical
space is criticized (though hardly refuted!) by the
contention that such a conceptual scheme is contrary to "essentially and profoundly social" facts,
i.e., "conscious choice of actors who vary in their
ends and values."[3] We must resist the temptation
to comment here on the curious assumption that
the "essentially and profoundly social" has to do
with such personal and subjective states as "ends
and values," rather than with objective relations
among interdependent living units. (Surely the latter is the prior significance of the "social," in an
evolutionary if not an etymological sense.) The
point to emphasize at present is, rather, that such a
reaction to ecological formulations is tantamount
to a denial of the crucial possibility that one can
at least conceive of systems encompassing both
human and physical elements. The "dynamic realm"
of the psycho-social has indeed become a "realm,"
one ruled by an intellectual tyrant, when this possibility is willfully neglected or denied.

THE ECOSYSTEM

Acknowledged dangers of premature synthesis and
superficial generalization notwithstanding, ecologists have been forced by the complexity of relationships manifested in their data to devise quite
embracing conceptual schemes. The concept of

---

[1]A. L. Kroeber, "So-Called Social Science," ch. vii in *The Nature of Culture* (Chicago: University of Chicago Press, 1952), pp. 66–67.
[2]R. M. MacIver, *Social Causation* (Boston: Ginn & Co., 1942), pp. 271–72.

[3]Arnold S. Feldman and Charles Tilly, "The Interaction of Social and Physical Space," *American Sociological Review*, 25 (December, 1960), p. 878.

ecosystem, a case in point, has become increasingly prominent in ecological study since the introduction of the term a quarter-century ago by the botanist, A. G. Tansley. "The *ecosystem*," according to Allee and collaborators, "may be defined as the interacting environmental and biotic system."[4] Odum characterizes the ecosystem as a "natural unit . . . in which the exchange of materials between the living and nonliving parts follows circular paths."[5] The first quotation comes from an enlightening synthesis of information now available on the evolution of ecosystems; the second prefaces an exposition of principles concerning the operation of "biogeochemical cycles" in ecosystems. Social scientists whose acquaintance with general ecology is limited to gleanings from the essays of Park[6] or the polemic by Alihan[7] might do well to inform themselves concerning current developments in ecological theory by consulting such sources as these. Even more readily accessible is the statement of Dice.[8]

> Ecologists use the term ecosystem to refer to a community together with its habitat. An ecosystem, then, is an aggregation of associated species of plants and animals, together with the physical features of their habitat. Ecosystems . . . can be of any size or ecologic rank. . . . At the extreme, the whole earth and all its plant and animal inhabitants together constitute a world ecosystem.

Later in his text (ch. xv) the same author undertakes a classification of "human ecosystems." This classification presents in elementary fashion much material familiar to social scientists; but it also conveys an unaccustomed emphasis on the "diverse relationships" of human societies "to their associated species of plants and animals, their physical habitats, and other human societies."[9]

Popularization of the ecosystem concept is threatened by the felicitous exposition by the economist, K. E. Boulding,[10] of "society as an ecosystem."

The word "threatened" is well advised, for Boulding uses "ecosystem" only as an analogy, illustrating how human society is "something like" an ecosystem. His ecosystem analogy is, to be sure, quite an improvement over the old organismic analogy. But ecosystem is much too valuable a conceptual scheme to be sacrificed on the altar of metaphor. Human ecology has already inspired a generation of critics too easily irritated by figures of speech.

If the foregoing remarks suggest that general ecologists have come up with cogent principles concerning the role of human society in the ecosystem, then the discussion has been misleading. Actually, the writing of Dice is exception as a responsible attempt to extend general ecology into the human field. Most biological scientists would probably still hold with the caution of Clements and Shelford, that "ecology will come to be applied to the fields that touch man immediately only as the feeling for synthesis grows."[11] There is abundant evidence in their own writing of the inadvisability of leaving to biological scientists the whole task of investigating the ecosystem and its human phases in particular. As a discipline, they clearly have not heeded the plea of the pioneer ecologist, S. A. Forbes, for a "humanized ecology":[12]

> I would humanize ecology . . . first by taking the actions and relations of civilized man as fully into account in its definitions, divisions, and coordinations as those of any other kind of organism. The ecological system of the existing twentieth-century world must include the twentieth-century man as its dominant species—dominant, that is, in the sense of dynamic ecology as the most influential, the controlling member of his associate group.

Symptomatically, even when discussing the "ecology of man," the biologist's tendency is to deplore and to exhort, not to analyze and explain. The shibboleths include such phrasings as "disruption," "tampering," "interference," "damage," and "blunder," applied to the transformations of ecosystems wrought by human activities. Such authorities as Elton, Darling, and Sears state very well some of the dilemmas and problems of human life in the

[4]W. C. Allee, Alfred E. Emerson, Orlando Park, Thomas Park, and Karl P. Schmidt, *Principles of Animal Ecology* (Philadelphia: W. B. Saunders Co., 1949), p. 695.

[5]Eugene P. Odum, *Fundamentals of Ecology* (Philadelphia: W. B. Saunders Co., 1953), p. 9.

[6]Robert E. Park, *Human Communities: The City and Human Ecology* (Glencoe, Ill.: The Free Press, 1952).

[7]Milla Aissa Alihan, *Social Ecology: A Critical Analysis* (New York: Columbia University Press, 1938).

[8]Lee R. Dice, *Man's Nature and Nature's Man: The Ecology of Human Communities* (Ann Arbor: University of Michigan Press, 1955), pp. 2–3.

[9]*Ibid.*, pp. 252–53.

[10]Kenneth E. Boulding, *Principles of Economic Policy* (Englewood Cliffs, N. J.: Prentice-Hall, Inc., 1958), pp. 14–16.

[11]Frederic E. Clements and Victor E. Shelford, *Bio-ecology* (New York: John Wiley & Sons, 1939), p. 1 Cf. F. Fraser Darling, "Pastoralism in Relation to Populations of Men and Animals," in *The Numbers of Man and Animals*, edited by J. B. Cragg and N. W. Pirie (Edinburgh; Oliver & Boyd, 1955).

[12]Stephen A. Forbes, "The Humanizing of Ecology," *Ecology*, 3 (April, 1922), p. 90.

ecosystem.[13] They evidently need the help of social scientists in order to make intelligible those human behaviors that seem from an Olympian vantage point to be merely irrational and shortsighted. Insofar as they recommend reforms—and surely some of their suggestions should be heeded—they need to be instructed, if indeed social science now or ultimately can instruct them, in "The Unanticipated Consequences of Purposive Social Action."[14] If social science falls down on its job, a statement like the following will remain empty rhetoric: "Humanity now has, as never before, the means of knowing the consequences of its actions and the dreadful responsibility for those consequences."[15]

ILLUSTRATION

Now, it is all very well to assert the possibility of conceptual schemes, like ecosystem, ascribing system properties to associations of physical, biological, and social elements. But can such a scheme lead to anything more than a disorderly collection of arbitrarily concatenated data? I think the proof of the ecosystem concept could be exemplified by a number of studies, ranging from particularistic to global scope, in which some such scheme, if implicit, is nevertheless essential to the analysis.[16] Instead of reviewing a sample of these studies, however, I would like to sketch a problematic situation that has yet to be analyzed adequately in ecosystem terms. This example, since it is deliberately "open-ended," will, I hope, convey the challenge of the concept.

The framework for the discussion is the set of

categories suggested elsewhere[17] under the heading, "the ecological complex." These categories, population, organization, environment, and technology (P, O, E, T), provide a somewhat arbitrarily simplified way of identifying clusters of relationships in a preliminary description of ecosystem processes. The description is, by design, so biased as to indicate how the human elements in the ecosystem appear as foci of these processes. Such an anthropocentric description, though perfectly appropriate for a *human* ecology, has no intrinsic scientific priority over any other useful strategy for initiating study of an ecosystem.

The example is the problem of air pollution, more particularly that of "smog," as experienced during the last two decades in the community of Los Angeles. Southern California has no monopoly on this problem, as other communities are learning to their chagrin. But the somewhat special situation there seems to present a configuration in which the role of each of the four aspects of the ecological complex, including its relation to the others, is salient. I have made no technical investigation of the Los Angeles situation and have at hand only a haphazard collection of materials dealing with it, most of them designed for popular rather than scientific consumption. (The personal experience of living through a summer of Los Angeles smog is of value here only in that it permits sincere testimony to the effect that the problem is real.) The merit of the illustration, however, is that ramifying influences like those postulated by the ecosystem concept are superficially evident even when their nature is poorly understood and inadequately described. I am quite prepared to be corrected on the facts of the case, many of which have yet to come to light. I shall be greatly surprised, however, if anyone is able to produce an account of the smog problem in terms of a conceptual scheme materially *less* elaborate than the ecological complex.

During World War II residents of Los Angeles began to experience episodes of a bluish-gray haze in the atmosphere that reduced visibility and produced irritation of the eyes and respiratory tract (E→P); it was also found to damage growing plants (E→E), including some of considerable economic importance, and to crack rubber, accelerating the

[13]Charles S. Elton, *The Ecology of Invasions by Animals and Plants* (London: Methuen & Co., Ltd., 1958); F. Fraser Darling, *West Highland Survey: An Essay in Human Ecology* (Oxford: Oxford University Press, 1955); Paul B. Sears, *The Ecology of Man*, "Condon Lectures" (Eugene: Oregon State System of Higher Education, 1957). See also, F. Fraser Darling, "The Ecology of Man," *The American Scholar*, 25 (Winter, 1955–56), pp. 38–46; Donald F. Chapp, "Ecology—A Science Going to Waste," *Chicago Review*, 9 (Summer, 1955), pp. 15–26.

[14]Title of an early essay by Robert K. Merton, *American Sociological Review*, 1 (December, 1936), pp. 894–904; a recent statement, pertinent to ecology, is Walter Firey's *Man, Mind and Land: A Theory of Resource Use* (Glencoe, Ill.: The Free Press, 1960).

[15]Sears, *op. cit.*, p. 50.

[16]The following are merely illustrative: A. Irving Hallowell, "The Size of Algonkian Hunting Territories: A Function of Ecological Adjustment," *American Anthropologist*, 51 (January–March, 1949), pp. 34–45; Laura Thompson, "The Relations of Men, Animals, and Plants in an Island Community (Fiji)," *American Anthropologist*, 51 (April–June, 1949), pp. 253–76; Edgar Anderson, *Plants, Man and Life* (Boston: Little, Brown & Co., 1952); Fred Cottrell, *Energy and Society* (New York: McGraw-Hill Book Co., 1955); Harrison Brown, *The Challenge of Man's Future* (New York: Viking Press, 1954).

[17]Otis Dudley Duncan, "Human Ecology and Population Studies," ch. xxviii in *The Study of Population*, edited by Philip M. Hauser and Otis Dudley Duncan (Chicago: University of Chicago Press, 1959).

rate of deterioration of automobile tires, for example (E→T). In response to the episodes of smog, various civic movements were launched, abatement officers were designated in the city and county health departments, and a model control ordinance was promulgated (E→O). All these measures were without noticeable effect on the smog. At the time, little was known about the sources of pollution, although various industrial operations were suspected. By 1947, a comprehensive authority, the Los Angeles County Air Pollution Control District, was established by action of the California State Assembly and authorized to conduct research and to exercise broad powers of regulation. Various known and newly developed abatement devices were installed in industrial plants at the instance of the APCD, at a cost of millions of dollars (O→T).

Meanwhile, research by chemists and engineers was developing and confirming the "factory in the sky" theory of smog formation. Combustion and certain other processes release unburned hydrocarbons and oxides of nitrogen into the atmosphere (T→E). As these reach a sufficiently high concentration and are subjected to strong sunlight, chemical reactions occur that liberate large amounts of ozone and form smog. In particular, it was discovered that automobile exhaust contains the essential ingredients in nearly ideal proportions and that this exhaust is the major source of the contaminants implicated in smog formation. It became all the more important as a source when industrial control measures and the prohibition of household open incinerators (O→T) reduced these sources (T→E). Also implicated in the problem was the meteorological situation of the Los Angeles Basin. Ringed by mountains and enjoying only a very low average wind velocity, the basin frequently is blanketed by a layer of warm air moving in from the Pacific. This temperature inversion prevents the polluted air from rising very far above ground level; the still air hovering over the area is then subject to the afore-mentioned smog-inducing action of Southern California's famous sunshine (E→E).

The problem, severe enough at onset, was hardly alleviated by the rapid growth of population in the Los Angeles area, spreading out as it did over a wide territory (P→E), and thereby heightening its dependence on the already ubiquitous automobile as the primary means of local movement

(T↔O). Where could one find a more poignant instance of the principle of circular causation, so central to ecological theory, than that of the Los Angelenos speeding down their freeways in a rush to escape the smog produced by emissions from the very vehicles conveying them?

A number of diverse organizational responses (E→O) to the smog problem have occurred. In 1958 a "nonprofit, privately supported, scientific research organization, dedicated to the solution of the smog problem," the Air Pollution Foundation, was set up under the sponsorship of some 200 business enterprises, many of them in industries subject to actual or prospective regulatory measures. The complex interplay of interests and pressures among such private organizations and the several levels and branches of government that were involved (O→O) has not, to my knowledge, been the subject of an adequate investigation by a student of the political process. Two noteworthy outcomes of this process merit attention in particular. The first is the development of large-scale programs of public health research and action (O→P, E) concerned with air pollution effects (E→P). Comparatively little is known in this field of epidemiology (or as some research workers would say nowadays, medical ecology), but major programs have been set up within the last five years in the U.S. Public Health Service (whose interest, of course, is not confined to Los Angeles) as well as such agencies as the California State Department of Public Health. Here is a striking instance of interrelations between medical ecology and the ecology of medicine illustrating not merely "organizational growth," as studied in conventional sociology, but also an organizational response to environmental-demographic changes. Second, there has been a channeling of both public and private research effort into the search for a "workable device," such as an automatic fuel cutoff, a catalytic muffler, or an afterburner, which will eliminate or reduce the noxious properties of automobile exhaust. California now has on its statute books a law requiring manufacturers to equip automobiles with such a device if and when its workability is demonstrated (O→T).

Some engineers are confident that workable devices will soon be forthcoming. The Air Pollution Foundation has gone so far as to declare that the day is "near when Los Angeles' smog will be only a memory." Should the problem be thus happily resolved, with reduction of pollution to tolerable levels, the resolution will surely have to be interpreted as the net result of an intricate interaction of factors in the ecological complex (P, O, T→E). But if the condition is only partially alleviated, how much more growth of population and increase in automobile use will have to occur before even more drastic technological and organizational changes will be required: redevelopment of mass transit, introduction of private electric automobiles, rationing of travel, limitation of population expansion, or whatever they may be? What will be the outcome of experience with increasing air pollution in other communities, whose problems differ in various ways from that of Los Angeles? And the question of questions—Is the convulsion of the ecosystem occasioned by smog merely a small-scale prototype of what we must expect in a world seemingly destined to become ever more dependent upon nuclear energy and subject to its hazards of ionizing radiation?

CONCLUSION

I must assume that the reader will be kind enough to pass lightly over the defects of the foregoing exposition. In particular, he must credit the author with being aware of the many complications concealed by the use of arrows linking the broad and heterogeneous categories of the ecological complex. The arrows are meant only to suggest the existence of problems for research concerning the mechanisms of cause, influence, or response at work in the situation so sketchily portrayed. Even the barest account of that situation, however, can leave no doubt that social change and environmental modification occurred in the closest interdependence— so close, in fact, that the two "levels" of change were *systematically* interrelated. Change on either level can be comprehended only by application of a conceptual scheme at least as encompassing as that of ecosystem.

The reader's imagination, again, must substitute for documentation of the point that smog, though a spectacular case and full of human interest, is no isolated example of how problems of human collective existence require an ecosystem framework for adequate conceptualization. I do not intend to argue, of course, that sociologists must somehow shoulder the entire burden of research suggested by such a conceptualization. Science, after all, is one of our finest examples of the advantages of a division of labor. But labor can be effectively divided only if there is articulation of the several sub-tasks; in scientific work, such articulation is achieved by employment of a common conceptual framework.

Sociologists may or may not—I am not especially optimistic on this score—take up the challenge to investigate the social life of man as a phase of the ecosystem, with all the revisions in their thought patterns that this kind of formulation will demand. If they shirk this responsibility, however, other disciplines are not unprepared to take the leadership. Anthropology of late has demonstrated its hospitality to ecological concepts.[18] Geography, for its part, cannot forget that it laid claim to human ecology as early as did sociology.[19]

Of even greater ultimate significance may be the impending reorientation of much of what we now call social science to such concepts as welfare, level of living, and public health. Programs to achieve such "national goals" (to use the former President's language), like the studies on which such programs are based, are finding and will find two things: first, each of these concepts is capable of almost indefinite expansion to comprehend virtually any problem of human collective life; and, second, measures or indicators of status or progress in respect to them must be multi-faceted and relational. Public health, to take that example, is surely some sort of function of all elements in the ecological complex; it is observable in any sufficiently comprehensive sense only in terms of interrelations of variables located at all levels of the ecosystem. Extrapolation of current trends over even a short projection period is sufficient to suggest the future preoccupation of the sciences touching on man with much more macroscopic problems than they now dare to set for themselves. It is perhaps symptomatic that spokesmen for the nation's health programs now declare that the "science of health is a branch of the wider science of human ecology,"[20] and that expositions

---

[18]Marston Bates, "Human Ecology," in *Anthropology Today*, edited by A. L. Kroeber (Chicago: University of Chicago Press, 1953); J. G. D. Clark, *Prehistoric Europe: The Economic Basis* (New York: Philosophical Library, 1952); Julian H. Steward, *Theory of Culture Change* (Urbana: University of Illinois Press, 1955).

[19]H. H. Barrows, "Geography as Human Ecology," *Annals of the Association of American Geographers*, 13 (March, 1923), pp. 1–14; William L. Thomas, Jr., editor, *Man's Role in Changing the Face of the Earth* (Chicago: University of Chicago Press, 1956).

[20]President's Commission on the Health Needs of the Nation, *America's Health Status, Needs and Resources. Building America's Health*, vol. 2 (Washington: Government Printing Office, 1953), p. 13.

of the problem of economic development have come to emphasize the necessary shift "From Political Economy to Political Ecology."[21] Even the literati proclaim that the "fundamental human problem is ecological."[22] (Cf. the similar remark of Kenneth Burke: "Among the sciences, there is one little fellow named Ecology, and in time we shall pay

him more attention."[23]) If one holds with Durkheim that the basic categories of science, as well as the interpretive schemes of everyday life, arise from the nature and exigencies of human collective existence, it cannot be long before we are forced to conjure with some version of the ecosystem concept. The question is whether sociology will lead or lag behind in this intellectual movement.

[21]Title of an essay by Bertrand de Jouvenel, *Bulletin of the Atomic Scientists*, 8 (October, 1957), pp. 287–91.
[22]Aldous Huxley, *The Devils of London*, "Torchbook edition" (New York: Harper & Bros., 1959), p. 302.

[23]Kenneth Burke, *Attitudes toward History*, Vol. I (New York: The New Republic, 1937), p. 192.

THE UNITY OF THE ENVIRONMENT

Although it was published some years ago, I include this article by Bernard for several reasons: first, for its clear, forceful statement of the issues involved; and, second, to illustrate the point that good ideas will live, transcending the tides of faddism and popularity. Much of Bernard's discussion is, of course, directed at the writings of his day—some of the names you will already have heard about in earlier anthropological theorizing about relations between human societies and their environment. But the principal point Bernard is making is the one recently placed under the rubric "ecosystem"— namely, that "culture" and "environment" should be seen as parts of an interacting whole. "Culture" is as "natural" as any other element in the field of determinants of human behavior, having effects upon and being affected by other elements in that network of relationships. Human culture does, however, add something to what other features of man's biological endowment create, for the environment that the humanized man (one living in a human social group) deals with is as much—or *more*—that "psychosocial" environment created by the very fact of group living and the press of value systems as it is the sheer geographic and biotic features of a habitat. But that psychosocial dimension of the environment remains nonetheless as "natural" as any other feature. It simply expands the field of inquiry when the matter is one of dynamics and structure of human behavior, and underscores what has been said earlier—that culture is a primary element in man's adaptation, *as well as in what he is adapting to.*

CULTURE AND ENVIRONMENT

L. L. BERNARD

There is a strong recent tendency on the part of those who deal much with the concept of culture to place the concepts of environment and of culture in opposition and to think of them as mutually ex-

Reprinted with permission of publisher. From *Social Forces*, vol. 8, no. 3 (March 1930), 327–34.

clusive. This implied distinction between culture and environment is, in my opinion, essentially erroneous and is likely to be the source of much unscientific analysis and partisan or sectarian writing. Already the orthodox or strict culture interpretationists have erected the concept of culture into an underived *ultra qua non* similar to the soul, the old time free will, the first cause, logos, etc., which are prone to be used as axiomatic starting points in casuistical discourse and thus become the mothers of much error and of more intolerance. What the culture interpretationists have to defend apart from the concept of culture and the methodological independence of anthropology (which always has been annoyingly confused in subject matter and mixed in administrative control with sociology) I am unable to say. However, the concept of an underived cultural entity may possibly be regarded as a sort of substitute defense for routed biological determinists who can no longer appeal to instinct as the final explanation of the genesis of human behavior and who must perforce transfer their system of causal explanation from a hereditary to an environmental basis. It is also perhaps an equally good substitute defense for those who were formerly worshippers at the shrines of custom and tradition, taking their oracular pronouncements as valid and final.

Perhaps it is useless, and somewhat psychoanalytical, to seek the motivation back of the culture entity or culture-in-a-vacuum dogma. If science ends in the discovery of the fact and eschews speculation as to the why of the fact, we may begin with this indubitable datum that the orthodox cultural interpretationists are loath to seek the origins of culture in environment and that they practically uniformly conceive of environment as natural environment. The evidence for the former assertion will appear in the course of this article. The recent work of R. B. Dixon, *The Building of Cultures* (1928), may be taken as an illustration of the truth of the latter statement. Dixon expressly limits the term environment to the physical,[1] specifying such phases of the natural environment as climate, topography and raw materials[2] and geographic position.[3] Practically the same limitation to the term environment is made by most of the other social anthropologists. Wallis speaks of the geographic environment, ignoring other forms.[4] Goldenweiser criticises the environmentalist interpretations of culture of such men as Montesquieu, Taine, Buckle, Ratzel, Semple, and Huntington and specifies the factors of the environment—which he appears to regard as exclusively physical—as "climate, flora,

fauna, geographical position."[5] Boas,[6] Kroeber,[7] and Lowie[8] likewise confine their use of the term environment to the physical natural environment, although Kroeber at least recognizes a superorganic factor[9] which might as well be termed environment as culture. Wissler[10] also writes with the same limitation upon the concept of environment, dealing specifically with such natural environmental factors as "land and sea, climate, plant and animal life, etc,"[11] but he also recognizes specifically the social environment under the more anthropological (as contrasted with sociological) term of "ethnic environment."[12] This ethnic environment is the culture-carrying environment. Tribal groups react against each other and thus spread their culture. "Hence, the environment that really counts for most is the ethnic environment, the culture setting."[13] But even with this strong recognition of a social environment, there is no analysis of it by Wissler as environment, but only as culture.

In 1925 I published a paper[14] designed to show that the concept of environment must be expanded to include not only the natural environment, but also a series of evolving and cumulative social or cultural environments, whose content is essentially the same as the "culture" of the anthropologists. In this paper I offered what is in effect a theory of the origin of culture from the impact of one term in the natural environment (man) upon another term in this natural environment, the inorganic and organic worlds to which man must make his adjustment and which he must learn to control in order to survive and develop his culture. In 1926 I published another paper[15] with the definite purpose of demonstrating the relationship between environment and culture,

---

[5]*Early Civilization* (1922), p. 292.
[6]*The Mind of Primitive Man* (1911) pp. 161 ff.
[7]*Anthropology* (1923), pp. 181 ff.
[8]*Culture and Ethnology* (1917), Ch. III.
[9]"The Superorganic," *Amer. Anthropologist*, XIX: 163–213 (1917).
[10]*Man and Culture* (1923), Ch. XV.
[11]*Ibid.*, p. 321.
[12]*Ibid.*, pp. 321–325.
[13]*Ibid.*, p. 321. Lowie likewise speaks of the cultural environment, which he is inclined to regard as more important in shaping human behavior than the natural environment (*Culture and Ethnology*, p. 58). However he does not make active use of this concept of cultural environment as such in developing his theories.
[14]"A Classification of Environments," *Amer. Jour. of Sociol.*, XXXI: 318–332 (1925). See also *An Introduction to Social Psychology*, 1926, Ch. VI. This classification is in bare outline as follows: I. The Natural Environments; 1. Inanimate; 2. Organic. II. The Social or Cultural Environments; 1. The Physico-Social Environment; 2. The Bio-social Environment; 3. The Psycho-Social Environment; 4. The Derivative Control of Composite Social Environment.
[15]"The Interdependence of Factors Basic to the Evolution of Culture," *Amer Jour of Sociol.*, XXXII: 177–205 (1926). See also F. A. Cleveland (Ed.), *Modern Scientific Knowledge of Nature Man and Society*, pp. 454–455.

---

[1]*Op. cit.*, p. 8.
[2]*Ibid.*, p. 13.
[3]*Ibid.*, p. 18.
[4]*An Introduction to Anthropology* (1926), Ch. VII.

both as to their origin and as to their content. I wish in this paper to attempt to make more pointed and specific the argument for this relationship, supported by an analysis and a criticism of the cultural and environmental concepts of the culture anthropologists.

There were at least three fundamental weaknesses of the old anthropogeography. One of these was its necessary disregard of the social environmental factors. Another was the inadequacy of its detailed analyses of the relation of the natural environment to behavior. A third weakness was that it lacked any adequate classification of the environments—even of the natural environmental factors—which would enable the student and the investigator readily to place or classify their data when procured. As a result of the first deficiency analyses were incomplete. Because of the second, the subject lacked concreteness and precision. This difficulty is in part now being removed by the more detailed field and laboratory analyses of the new school of human geographers. The third deficiency was the cause of a perennial confusion of the antecedents and conditioners of behavior. The writer recalls a long and fruitless controversy in his student days between his instructor and himself as to whether human behavior was to be interpreted "environmentally" or "psychologically." It is now clear that neither disputant understood adequately the contention of the other, simply because there was available no scheme of classification which would place, delimit, and define the two supposedly opposing concepts. As a matter of fact, the two concepts of behavior determination were not wholly distinct and unrelated, when viewed from the standpoint of a more inclusive classification of environments, but were (as used by the two contestants) very decidedly assimilable. The difficulty was that there was no schema available for bringing about this accommodation and partial assimilation of the two concepts. The classification of environments published in 1925 was designed to provide such a schema.

In this classification I separated the natural from the social or cultural environments, not because environment as a whole suddenly ceases to be "natural" and becomes all at once "artificial" or "cultural," but because I wished to illustrate the fact that man, in his struggle to make an effective adjustment to his world, creates new environment as a means to this end. It is in this way that he learns to control his environment. The environment to

which he must adjust thus becomes decreasingly "natural" and increasingly "artificial" and "cultural" or "social." Thus he creates environment to be used as a tool in the control of his world and he creates incidentally and cumulatively a new environment to which it is easier for him to make adjustment and which it is easier for him to control because, for the most part, this environment has been created to meet his needs and it has been created as a tool. Of course there are incidental phases of this environment, by-products and unanticipated developments, as it were, which may produce complications in his cultural environmental evolution and which possibly may interfere with the adequacy or the facility of his adjustment to and control of (really one and the same process viewed from opposite angles) his world. The danger that the utilization of modern technical inventions may be used in warfare for the destruction of civilization is a good example of the unexpected and incidental results of the human creation of environment. The creation of new cultural or social environments is itself at first a process purely incidental to the more fundamental process of adjustment to the environments previously existing. The behaviorist sees all human activity as a phase of adjustment, or of the reciprocal interrelationships of organisms and environments.[16] The creation of social or cultural environments is at first merely incidental to this reciprocal interrelationship, but with the development of thinking and language as phases of this incidental development, the purposive or projective creation of cultural or social environment to be used consciously as tools or means to the control of the adjustment process may and does come into play in the adjustment situation.

It is scarcely necessary of course to say that it is not intended to imply that primitive man worked out the theory of all this process of the creation of cultural environments as tools and as means to the modification of the relatively hard and austere natural environments before he started to work to accomplish the results he has achieved. In a behavioristic interpretation of social phenomena there is no definite dividing line between the purposive and the non-purposive whereby to separate them into two distinct kingdoms of human action. Such a separation is the work of metaphysical logic, not

---

[16]Cf. M. Basov, "Structural Analysis in Psychology from the Standpoint of Behavior," *Jour. of Genetic Psy.*, XXXVI: 267–290 (1929).

of human experience. Moreover, consciousness does not come suddenly into the adjustment process and radically transform it. It also is a gradual growth and, where it functions constructively and intelligently instead of destructively and emotionally, it appears to be correlated with a refinement and further particularization of the adjustment process. When the adjustment process could be slower and could work by generations rather than by individuals, in the prehuman days of the world, it seems to have occurred largely through the mechanism of natural selection. But individual habit modifications appear even then to have been important in mediating differential adjustments to the environments. When habits became conscious and conceptual or verbal with the development of some sort of symbolizing and objectivating technique, that is, some sort of language, the adaptation of the organism to the environment began to pass decisively from the subjective (the modification of inheritance and of neuro-muscular habit merely) to the objective (the permanent and conserved modification of the environment transmitted through language symbolization) phase. The development of verbal communication or language symbolization aided greatly in the maintenance of these external and environmental modifications or in the creation and perpetuation of culture.[17] It is not necessary to suppose that all the persons concerned knew what was happening in the production of artificial or cultural environment, or even that any one realized the wider and more ultimate significance of the process at these earlier stages of the control of adjustment through tradition. Relatively few persons in our present civilization have achieved with any degree of adequacy this second realization or power of objectifying the process through the philosophic or scientific utilization of language. But, at whatever stage it occurred, this external modification of the environment, whether unconscious or conscious, whether its social significance was understood or not, was an invention; and invention, or the adaptive modification of the environment of man, has now become a recognized and honored profession.

It was by means of invention that the original natural environments were modified and new cultural or artificial environments were created. These artificial environments varied in character according to the materials out of which they were constructed. Out of the inorganic materials of the natural (and later of the artificial) environments, and out of the organic materials rendered inorganic through the process of utilization, was created a physico-social or material cultural environment. This environment began at first as tools, shelter, ornaments, and later evolved into machines, the equipment for transportation and communication, cities, etc. Out of living things, not transformed into inorganic materials by the process of utilization, was created a biosocial environment, or a culture of behavior and performance rather than a culture of things. This field of culture lies between the material and the nonmaterial culture of the culture classificationists and its presence would seem to make necessary a four-fold classification of culture, to take the place of the old dual classification into material and nonmaterial culture, somewhat as follows:[18]

1. Cultural objects
   (1) Material objects or things (involving changes of form or of content)
   (2) Symbolical objects (involving objectivated symbolic behavior such as art and written language.
2. Cultural behavior
   (1) Overt behavior (neuro-muscular adjustment forms)
   (2) Inner behavior (neuro-psychic adjustment or symbolical behavior forms in action)

This second phase of cultural environment, the bio-social, is produced by means of the breeding and training of plants and animals and includes, under the category of training, both domestication and education. To these processes we do not ordinarily apply the term invention, since by precedent and practice we have been accustomed to limit the application of the concept invention to direct modification of inanimate things or cultural objects rather than of living beings and their cultural behavior. Thus we speak of invention when we make new modifications of significance in the inanimate physical environment or in the organizations of symbols. We approximate the application of the term invention to modifications of behavior when we plan or put into administrative functioning a

---

[17]Cf. "Neuro-Psychic Technique," *Psy. Review*, XXX: 407–437 (1923).

[18]Cf. "Neuro-Psychic Technique," loc. cit.; also *Instinct: A Study in Social Psychology* (1924) Chs. V. and VI, and *An Introduction to Social Psychology* (1926), Ch. X, for underlying statements of this point of view by the author.

new organization of human relationships, but in this last case the emphasis seems to be primarily upon the plan or system of behavior; rather than upon the behavior itself. These three types of inventions have been denominated physical, method (methodological), and social inventions.[19]

The two types of cultural modification of the environment indicated above—physico-social and bio-social—were originally visible modifications of the inorganic and organic natural environments and have remained visible modifications of the form and content of the material objects, or of the behavior of living things corresponding to categories 1, (1) and 2, (1) of the classification of culture suggested above. In both cases the transformation is essentially objective and visible. A third type of environmental transformation or cultural creation is essentially symbolical. It began in the subjective modification of the adaptive behavior of the individual who was under the necessity of making a more refined adjustment to his environment, which would at the same time be coadaptive or social. Language undoubtedly had its beginnings in the process of natural selection or the modification of inheritance, but it has had preëminently its greatest development as a phase of acquired modification of behavior. As long as language remained in the gesture and vocal phases it was essentially a form of behavior and was to be grouped under the second or bio-social phase of environment corresponding to category 2, (2) of our culture classification scheme. Of course, in large measure it is to be classified there still, for most communication remains in the gesture and vocal stage. But the most advanced and socially significant environmental aspects of language are in its objectivated or symbolical forms (symbolical cultural objects, corresponding to category 1, (2) of our culture classification scheme), and in this aspect it really constitutes a third most important phase of social or cultural environment. I have called it psycho-social environment, because its roots are psychic and subjective rather than material and objective.

In its phases distinct from the bio-social environment, out of which it grew, this psycho-social environment has developed into several successive forms. Inclusive of the symbolical element in both the behavior and post-behavior or symbolically objectivated aspects, the chief forms of the psycho-social environment or culture may be represented in a condensed manner as follows:

Gesture language ⎫
Vocal language   ⎬ when meanings are standardized
Written language ⎭

Traditions, beliefs, etc.—composite residual vocalizations (having quasi independence of carriers)

Art in all its forms   ⎫
Philosophic discourse   ⎪ Objectivated symbolic
Scientific discourse   ⎬ language content,
Creeds, codes, systems,   ⎪ (having actual independence of carriers)
    etc.   ⎭

Museums, art galleries   ⎫ Collections of objectivated symbolic language content (condensers and carriers of all the above)
Libraries   ⎬
Periodical press   ⎭

This as a whole is what the culture classificationists call non-material culture and what I have indicated under the second subdivision of each of the two general types of culture suggested in my proposed revision of the classification of the types of culture (1, (2), 2, (2)). It partakes of both of these major divisions of culture because in the long process of its evolution it develops from the subjective or internal behavior phase to an objectivated or superorganic and super-object phase. In this second stage of objectivated development it does not itself consist of material objects, but is carried by material objects, usually of an inanimate character, just as in the first stage of development it is carried by living objects who manifest its symbolic meaning through their behavior.

In my classification of social or cultural environments I have included a fourth phase of artificial environment, which I have called the derivative control environment. It is in the main institutional in character and is a composite of the other three artificial environments, and even of as much of the natural environments as may survive untransformed to the stage of institutionalization and as can at the same time be integrated into a social control system. This environment is primarily conceptual in character and its function is to serve as a system of norms, expressed primarily through its psycho-social or symbolical content for the standardization and regulation or control of the coadaptive or social adjustment behavior of individuals in the presence of their environment. The physico-social and bio-social phases of his environment, in so far

───────────

[19]"Invention and Social Progress," Amer. Jour. of Sociol., XXIX: 1–33 (1923).

as they are included in the institution which directs his adjustment, serve as means to the adjustment. Important examples of these lower forms of the social environment are the material equipment and administrative organization of the directive institution. The psycho-social environment may consist of such important elements as constitutions, laws, creeds, codes, traditions, beliefs, scientific knowledge and principles, etc. This phase of the cultural environment is distinct from the other phases only in a functional sense, but this functional integration constitutes it a new and distinct phase of culture.

It is not possible to determine exactly when each of these four phases of culture began its existence. It is certain that in their more primitive forms all are very ancient. Nor is there any intention to maintain that each type of culture thus evolved is wholly distinct from and unlike the other forms. In their beginnings they are very closely related, but in their more developed aspects the lines of distinction become more marked, but never absolute. The point selected for emphasis here is that all of these phases of culture developed originally out of the old natural environments as a result of man's attempt to make more successful adjustments to these natural environments. If today each additional increment to culture is the result of an adaptive transformation of previously constructed cultural environments, it is because man has so far progressed in his adaptive and transforming adjustment to his environment that he lives primarily and most immediately in a world of culture, that is, in an artificial or socially created environment, and only secondarily or derivatively in a natural environment. The derivation of the physico-social and the bio-social environments from the natural environments in the manner here described is easily enough understood. But when it is recalled that the psycho-social environment begins in language and that language begins in behavior, even in instinctive behavior, the analogous naturalistic derivation of this environment likewise is made clear. The derivative control environment, primarily of institutions, being made up of functional integrations of the other three cultural environments must therefore be ultimately derivable from the natural environments.

If the foregoing are facts rather than fancies—and surely they are easily observable and demonstrable facts—how can it be said that culture is an underived social entity? Nor is there any other method of deriving culture from environment than that of invention, although culture when thus derived obviously may be transmitted by borrowing. I do not mean to contend that any culture interpretationist makes verbal denial of these facts. The denial is only by implication based largely on their limitation of the concept of environment to the natural environment, as demonstrated above. Of course, it might be asserted, in contravention of the viewpoint here presented, that culture proceeds from revelation, or that it is the result of the human reason uncovering the natural laws that are inherent in the universe, of some sort of innate ideas,[20] or, finally that it is the result of the maturing of our inherent or instinctive powers and potentialities.[21] In the past such contentions have been made with the intention of "confounding" such a "materialistic" doctrine of culture as that set forth above. It is scarcely to be believed, however, that the modern culture interpretationists are so tied up in their sympathies or by their training with these old theological and metaphysical systems of explanation of a pre-scientific age of thought as consciously to offer any one of them in defense of their tacit viewpoints.

[20]Bastian did actually hold to a theory of innate or elementary ideas. See Boas, *Mind of Primitive Man*, p. 159 and Barnes, *History and Prospects of the Social Sciences* (1925), p. 211.

[21]Possibly Wissler's "drive to produce cultures," which he finds in man's protoplasm and which "carries him forward even against his will" may belong to this instinctive category (*Man and Culture*, p. 265).

PART VII

THE CASE STUDIES

At the beginning of the introduction to this series of readings, I included several statements of problems extracted from case reports on technological and medical innovations in the developing world. We return now to the second installment of those selected case studies—in which are presented the authors' own analyses of the relevant course of events and the interacting factors that they see as being involved in the problem. The case reports are included here primarily to put back together what has been somewhat taken asunder in the readings up to this point; we were trying to abstract out discrete dimensions or concepts, to get at least the beginnings of an understanding of such ideas as culture as a system of values and symbols, or of social relationships and their patterned character. Now it is time to return to the wholeness of reality once again and see how some of these concepts basic to more behavioral scientists than just the cultural anthropologist appear to work in the context of real problems, problems in real time and with real people. For it is this kind of "holistic" summing up, this synthesis following the analysis, that the anthropologist is called upon to do after he has dissected the flow of events and considered them with relation to his working concepts. In these reports, then, we will see the importance of understanding such cultural factors as values systems or symbolic meanings of things and events, elements of social structure such as status and power relations, a "functional" analysis of events in a social system, and the importance of bringing to bear upon events in human society a more embracing conception, that is, an ecologic frame of reference.

HEALTH

We return now to the first of the four case studies in human problems that were suggested in the introduction as illustrating the importance of understanding cultural and social factors in the dynamics of human adaptation and change. Recall that among the Zulus health conditions were extremely poor, and that a variety of approaches were attempted in an effort to improve both nutritional status and general health standing, and to create new social patterns that would contribute to preventive health measures. In the account that follows, several points emerge. One of these is that knowledge of the cultural system and social structure is of critical importance in understanding how a people respond to new stimuli in their environment; in a fairly fundamental way, the culture shapes the reality they see (illustrated, for example, in the incident of the diagnosis of tuberculosis, when who, or what, caused the disease was viewed very differently by the doctor compared to the elder in the family). Another example is the introduction of powdered milk—not seen as "really" milk and therefore acceptable as food for pregnant women. The influence of deeply held values that structure environmental resources as well as social relations is seen in beliefs regarding the symbolic importance of cattle in Zulu culture (as also in many other east African societies), or generally in the indigenous theories about causation of disease and misfortune—that such misfortunes are the result of displeasing one's ancestors. But also underscored by Cassel's account is another theme throughout this reader, namely, that social and cultural systems operate in a physical setting and are best seen as part of an ecosystem. In this instance, illustrations are the fact of extreme soil erosion, or of the migration of men to industrial centers (which, in turn, had its effect upon family structure). In all, Cassel's discussion presents us with an example of the fruitfulness of bringing to bear a comprehensive framework for understanding, one in which cultural factors are a vital dimension in understanding the dynamics of human adaptation.

A SOUTH AFRICAN HEALTH PROGRAM (Continued)

JOHN CASSEL

THE SITUATION

The Zulu People

In the mountainous, wooded, and grassy country surrounding the Polela Health Centre live some 16,000 Zulu tribesmen. Their mud-walled, thatched-roofed huts are occupied mainly by women, children, and old men; the adult male population spends the major part of the year working in the neighboring towns. An occasional small store, some scattered mission schools made of mud or wood and iron, the one main dirt road through the area, the German print dresses of the women and ragged

shirts of the men—these form the only outward signs of contact with western civilization. Many less apparent evidences of culture contact exist, however. Of these, the disruption of family life caused by the migrant labor system and the inadequacy of the old codes and mores in a changing world have perhaps the most important health implications.

The ancestors of these people originally belonged to a small clan of Central African Zulu tribesmen. They traveled south in the great migrations from Central Africa and in the early part of the seventeenth century settled in what is now Zululand, in northern Natal. At the beginning of the nineteenth century, the clan's chieftain, Chaka—a man of extraordinary military genius and insatiable political ambition—embarked on a campaign of imperial

Reprinted with permission. From John Cassel, "A Comprehensive Health Program Among South African Zulus," in *Health, Culture, and Community*, ed. Benjamin D. Paul, © 1955 by Russell Sage Foundation, Publishers, N.Y., pp. 17–41.

conquest. He conquered most of southeastern Africa and united all the various clans into one great empire, the Zulu nation. Even today the Zulus pride themselves on their warrior tradition and tend to look down upon the other Bantu peoples of South Africa.

The disintegration of the Zulu empire, started by internal dissension, ended in conflict with the whites. The last major clash occurred as recently as 1906. During the reign of Chaka, war and starvation had set in motion great waves of refugees, and clashes with the whites caused further dislocation. The people of Polela today are remnants of many clans scattered by Chaka and the European wars.

Today Zulus comprise some one and one-half to two million of the eight million Bantu inhabitants of the Union of South Africa, whose total population is about 12 million. In common with the majority of Bantu tribes of Africa, the basic unit of Zulu society has not been the individual or the married couple and their children, but the "extended" family centered around the male family head. Until recently polygamy was prevalent, and the family was an extended polygamous unit. Grown sons continued to live with their parents, along with their own wives and children. Obtaining a wife necessitated the exchange of cattle between the families of the groom and bride. This was no mere matter of buying and selling, but a kind of social contract between the two families designed to guarantee good faith and good behavior on both sides.

Today, owing partly to poverty and the relative scarcity of cattle and partly to the influence of Christianity, polygamous families are becoming increasingly rare. Furthermore, one of the effects of contact with Europeans has been the increasing disruption of Zulu family life, and today small husband and wife families, as well as "broken" families, are far more common than the extended type of family of a few generations ago.

In spite of three centuries of change wrought by contact with western culture, traditional concepts and beliefs still govern many attitudes and activities of the vast majority of people. This is certainly true in regard to health. Of particular importance is the belief that all natural phenomena, including crop failures, lightning and storms, as well as sickness, are caused by the spirits of one's ancestors.

The advent of Christianity and the increasing number of Christian converts have changed many of the outward manifestations and rituals concerning these beliefs. Today some 60 per cent of the people in this area are Christians. Christianity has done little, however, to change underlying beliefs; the vast majority of those served by the Polela Health Centre would feel defenseless in a hostile world unless they could undertake appropriate ceremonies of propitiation, however disguised for the benefit of the missionaries.

For example, it is considered essential to have a feast one year after the death of the head of a family to propitiate his spirit. This feast involves the ritual slaying of an ox and several goats. To protect the home, incantations are made over the contents of the gut of the ox, since it is believed that these contents can be used to bewitch the home if they fall into the hands of an ill-wisher. The entire kin group and neighbors assemble to dine on meat and beer. Each person eats a prescribed part of the ox, depending on his age, sex, and relationship to the family. Certain choice pieces of meat and blood are placed in a designated section of the hut for the use of the spirits.

Since this ceremony has been banned by missionaries, today converts to Christianity hold a "feast of remembrance" one year after the death of the family head. At this feast the ox and goats are slaughtered with the same rituals, the contents of the gut are protected in the same manner, the meat and blood are placed in the appropriate place for the use of the spirits, but the people eat from tables instead of sitting on the ground and sing Christian hymns while they eat those parts of the ox appropriate to their sex, age, and relationship to the family!

One effect of culture contact, however, has been of fundamental importance. Following the mid-nineteenth-century discovery of diamonds in Kimberley and gold in the Transvaal, the industrial revolution came to South Africa. This led to the growth of towns and cities and an ever-increasing demand for labor. The masses of Bantu peoples provided a ready source of labor for mines, industries, and domestic work. But the dominant white population refused to accept those Bantu who came to the cities as a permanent part of the urban population. This gave rise to a system of migrant labor, whereby adult males were encouraged to come to cities while their wives and children had to remain in specially designated rural "Native Reserves." Over the years, the increasing poverty of these reserves has accelerated the townward migration of the adult males, and today the majority of able-bodied adult males spend less than two months a year with their wives and families. The disproportionate sex ratio in the urban and rural areas during the major part of the year has led to ever-increasing promiscuity, illegitimacy, and a weakening of family ties, in the face of which traditional codes of morality are virtually powerless. This situation has had the further deleterious effect of increasing the incidence of venereal disease and juvenile delinquency and subjecting women to ever greater emotional strain.

These, then, are some of the main features of the community which the Polela Health Centre began to serve in 1940.

The Polela Health Centre

The staff of the Polela Health Centre was organized into a number of multi-disciplined teams, each team consisting of a family physician, a family nurse, and a community health educator (health assistant). A team functioned in a defined geographical area consisting initially of approximately 100 families. Periodically this area was extended, until today each team serves between 300 and 500 families. In this area over the years, the major health problems were defined through analysis of the clinical records maintained by the Centre teams, augmented by especially designed surveys.

These problems were broadly classified into those needs that were "felt" and those that were "unfelt." In general, "felt" health needs were those expressed by the people themselves in the course of group discussions; for example, a desire to do something about the high incidence of infantile mortality and morbidity and a desire for healthy children. "Unfelt" needs included, among others, the totally inadequate diet, the poor state of environmental hygiene, the lack of immunization, and the desirability of changing some of the child-rearing practices.

Health programs were then initiated on two planes, in which the promotive-preventive and the curative aspects of health and medical care services were integrated. The one approach, community health education, was the responsibility of the health educators. Through periodic routine home visits and small group discussions, they attempted to make the "unfelt" needs of the community "felt," and to motivate people to make those

changes in their way of life that were necessary to meet these needs. Simultaneously, the other approach, curative and preventive services to individuals within their family unit, was the responsibility of the doctor and nurse on the team. Each individual was offered complete periodic health examinations, followed by family conferences to discuss the health problems peculiar to that family. An illness in any of the families would be treated by the same doctor and nurse who had been endeavoring to keep them healthy.

Details of these periodic health examinations and the illnesses that had been treated were recorded in the clinical records. These records supplied one of the sets of health indices used in analyzing and assessing health problems and evaluating progress. Team meetings were held daily, and all aspects of the total program were reviewed and assessed. Future programs were evolved at these meetings in accordance with progress made or obstacles encountered. The meetings also assured the fullest possible integration between the promotive-preventive and curative aspects of the program. Thus, for example, if syphilis were found to be a major problem, the staff would arrange group discussions in the community designed to discover local concepts about the nature of the disease. The discussions would highlight differences between these concepts and those held by the Centre staff, particularly as to the relationship between syphilis and abortions and stillbirths. At the same time, facilities for treatment would be improved. While under treatment, the patient would receive further instruction from his doctor and nurse concerning the nature of his disease and the aims of treatment. A fundamental working principle was that new concepts and practices should never be imposed upon the community; rather, they should be integrated into the culture through active popular participation. The majority of the guiding principles and concepts were developed by Dr. Sidney L. Kark, founder and original medical officer in charge of the Polela Health Centre. At the time of writing he is medical officer in charge of the Institute of Family and Community Health, Durban, with which the Centre is associated.

The details of four specific areas of health action in the Zulu community served by the Centre will illustrate the general concepts that have been outlined. These will be described in the order of difficulty presented, each successive effort encountering increased popular resistance to change. Two of the illustrations involve attempts to improve the diet, one by the introduction of home-grown vegetables, the other by greater use of eggs and milk. It will be seen that the second was harder to accomplish than the first. The third effort, an attempt to control tuberculosis, proved still more difficult. Most difficult of all was an effort to control soil erosion, a condition basic to many of the health problems.

Reeducation for Better Nutrition

As already indicated, severe malnutrition was a major community health problem. Many factors served as predisposing, precipitating, and contributory causes. Food surveys indicated that the prevailing monotonous, often grossly deficient, diet was one of the major causes. The high incidence of chronic disease, particularly tuberculosis, syphilis, and recurrent bouts of dysentery and diarrhea, was another cause. Still another was the great physical effort required, particularly from women, in their day-to-day life. The program to change the food habits of the community involved a detailed knowledge of the existing diet, an analysis of the factors responsible for it, and an investigation of current attitudes and beliefs about food.

The diet consisted principally of maize (corn) prepared in numerous ways, supplemented by dried beans, negligible amounts of milk, and occasionally meat and wild greens. Potatoes and pumpkins were eaten seasonally, and millet (sorghum) was fermented to brew beer, which was consumed in large quantities. Whenever funds allowed, sugar and white bread were also bought. Even though this was a rural agricultural community, poor farming methods and poverty of the soil made it impossible for the vast majority of the people to raise adequate food supplies. About half of the families produced less than one-quarter of the maize necessary to feed themselves, and consequently a large percentage of their food consisted of refined maize meal purchased with money sent home by the migrant laborers. Furthermore, during the best month of the year, even if all the milk had been equally distributed, only one-twentieth pint per head per day would be available. In addition to extreme poverty and extensive soil erosion, factors responsible for the poor diet included certain traditions as to which foods were customary, ignorance of the nutritional values of food, inefficient use of available resources, and

cooking methods that frequently destroyed a large fraction of the nutrients.

As anticipated, early attempts to demonstrate the causal relationship between poor diet and low standard of health encountered considerable skepticism. People maintained that their diet was the diet of their ancestors and had always been the diet of their people. On this same diet, had not their ancestors been strong and healthy, mighty men of valor and military deeds? It was difficult to refute this point without having any reliable information about the health of their ancestors.

A search of the available literature, however, revealed that the present diet had not always been the traditional diet of the Zulus and other Bantu-speaking tribes. Prior to the arrival of the whites, the indigenous cereal had been millet, maize having been brought into the country by the early settlers. Because of its greater yield, maize had gradually supplanted millet as the staple cereal, millet being reserved solely for brewing. Furthermore, historically the Zulus were a roving pastoral people owning large herds of cattle; milk and meat had played a prominent part in their diet. So important was milk as an article of food that no meal was considered complete unless milk was included. Milk is consumed in the form of thick soured curds, and consequently the process is described as "eating" rather than "drinking" milk. The relatively fertile nature of the land at that time and the extensive wild game resulted in further additions of meat to the diet and a plentiful supply of wild greens. Roots and berries gathered from the forests were also extensively used.

The health educators attempted to make people aware of these facts through group discussions at informal gatherings held at various places in the area. As the "key" homes came to be recognized—homes visited frequently by many people—the group discussions were increasingly held there. Most of the people did not speak English, but this was no handicap; all the health educators were Africans, and all discussions were held in Zulu. These discussions were supplemented by routine periodic home visits, during which the occupants of each house were engaged in a conversation about the diet of their ancestors as compared with their present diet.

Surprisingly enough, once the facts about the diet of "the olden times" were presented, they were readily accepted by many of the older people.

Fairly frequently they would make comments such as these: "Now that you come to mention it, I remember my grandmother telling me those same things." "Yes, those were the good old days when we all had good things to eat." Almost in the same breath, however, they maintained that their present diet was traditional. Once they saw the anomaly, however, a certain measure of interest was aroused and cooperation achieved, particularly among the older people, who were more likely to remember former conditions. This was of great importance in gaining acceptance for the program. The assistance of the older group was particularly gratifying in view of the fact that this group usually forms the most conservative element in any community. At Polela the older people were those most consistently opposed to the introduction of new ways.

Interest in the subject of food was further aroused by discussion on the commonly held concepts of digestion and the functions of the different articles of diet. It was widely, though not universally, held that in some manner food entered the blood stream. What happened to it thereafter was unspecified. Greatest interest was aroused by considering how a fetus was nourished *in utero;* discussion on this point would sometimes continue for hours. Many women were of the opinion that there must be a breast in the uterus from which the fetus suckled, for as they said, "We all know the baby in the mother's womb grows, and all growing things need food, and the only way a baby can get food is through suckling." Others indicated that calves *in utero* also grow and, therefore, must be receiving food, and who had ever seen a breast in a cow's uterus? Some women maintained that the fetus was nourished by the placenta; the Zulu term for placenta literally means "the nurse." But when challenged, they were unable to explain how the placenta could feed the baby.

The result of these and similar discussions was to arouse a desire for further knowledge. When the functions of the placenta and umbilical cord were explained by use of posters and models, the interpretation was readily accepted. Some of the posters were remarkably effective in stimulating curiosity and discussion at this stage. One picture showed a longitudinal section of a uterus with a fetus *in situ.* At one discussion group, an old woman remarked indignantly, "I never believed I would live to see the day when such pictures would be shown us in public—and by a man at that!" Never-

theless, she was one of the most eager to get a good view of the poster and took a lively part in the conversation.

As concepts about the digestion and absorption of food began to change, it was possible to direct discussion to the function of different types of food. The view generally held was that all food had only one function, to fill the stomach and relieve hunger. This view was immediately challenged by a number of people, however, who maintained that certain foods gave strength and others were fattening—a bodily attribute much valued in this community. Over a period of time it became more generally accepted that different foods had different functions; the value of milk, eggs, and green vegetables especially for growing children came to be understood.

Increased interest and changing attitudes toward food created a favorable climate for the next step, a program to induce changes in diet. The reults of this action program may be indicated by focusing attention on efforts to increase use of vegetables and of eggs and milk.

Increasing Production of Green Vegetables

From its inception, one of the cardinal principles of the health education program was to demonstrate how better use could be made of available resources and, by so doing, how these new needs could be met in part. Since all the homes had adequate space around them, a home vegetable garden program was initiated. A demonstration vegetable garden was grown at the Health Centre, where members of the staff could gain gardening experience and where local families could have the methods demonstrated. The more cooperative families were assisted in starting their own vegetable gardens; as the number of gardens increased, a seed-buying cooperative was initiated. The establishment of a small market where families could sell their surplus produce and annual garden competitions were some of the more successful techniques used.

In addition, cooking demonstrations were held to show how these home-grown vegetables could be cooked to suit the tastes of the community and still preserve their nutrient value. Garden surveys conducted four times a year gave an indication of the progress made at different seasons. In 1941, the year of the first survey, 100 homes were surveyed; three vegetable gardens, growing a total of five different varieties of vegetables, were found to exist.

In 1951, during the same season, 1,000 homes were surveyed and nearly 800 vegetable gardens, growing a total of more than 25 different varieties of vegetables, were in existence.

Not only had this program resulted in a marked increase in vegetable consumption, but it was possible to associate it with another program aimed at improving environmental hygiene. In order to improve the fertility of the soil for vegetable growing, families were shown how to make compost in pits instead of scattering it indiscriminately. All household refuse could immediately be placed in these pits and would eventually aid in producing better vegetables.

Eggs, Milk, and Taboo

While the home vegetable garden program was thus relatively satisfactory, greater difficulty was initially encountered in attempts to increase the consumption of eggs and milk. Of those families surveyed, more than 95 per cent had fowl, and eggs were fairly plentiful at certain seasons of the year. However, eggs were infrequently eaten. There were a number of reasons for this. It was considered uneconomical to eat an egg that would later hatch and become a chicken; egg eating was regarded as a sign of greed; and, finally, eggs were thought to make girls licentious. None of these notions, however, was associated with powerful emotions, and with patience it was possible, over a period of years, to overcome to a great extent the aversion to eggs.

To accomplish this, the function of eggs in promoting growth and "strengthening" the blood was discussed during group meetings and home visits. Cooking demonstrations showing how eggs could be incorporated in the diet, particularly of infants, were held periodically in the homes and at the Centre. Well-child sessions were called "mother and baby" sessions, since both mother and child were cared for. At these sessions mothers were advised how and when to introduce eggs into their children's diet, and the reasons were again discussed. People were encouraged to buy better breeds of cocks to improve the strain of their fowl and shown how to build nests to protect eggs from dogs and small wild animals.

As a result of these efforts, eggs today form a relatively common article in the diet of infants. While the aim of the Health Centre—an egg daily for children over six months—has not yet been achieved, many of the children do get from three to four eggs a week in the productive seasons of the year. Because of the shortage in supply, adults cannot have eggs so often as their children, but eggs are bought by many families for the use of adults whenever they are available—something almost unheard of twelve years ago.

The question of milk proved a more difficult and complex problem. In addition to the extremely limited supplies available, the "eating" of milk was associated with very deep-seated and powerful customs and beliefs. Only members of the kin group of the head of a household can use milk produced by that man's cattle. In fact, one of the methods of establishing relationship to a family is to request milk on entering the hut. While this restriction applies equally to men, women, and children, so that no family could supplement its milk supply from another family outside the kin group, the situation is more complex in the case of women.

During her menses or when pregnant, a woman is thought to exert an evil influence on cattle and may not pass near the cattle enclosure or partake of any milk. This applies even in her own home. Since it is usually impossible for men to know when a woman is menstruating, it is customary to exclude milk from the diet of the majority of girls once they have passed puberty. When a woman marries and goes to live with her husband's family group, she falls under a double restriction. Not only is she a woman, but she is now in the home of a different kin group. Consequently, of all people in the community, married women are most rigidly excluded from partaking of milk. The only conditions under which a married woman might have it are these: if her father presented her with a cow at the time of her marriage, she could use the milk; or if her husband performed a special ceremony involving the slaying of a goat, she would be free to use milk in his home. Because of the poverty that prevails, neither of these two procedures is common in this area today.

The reasons for these customs are lost in the mists of antiquity, not even the oldest people in this community being able to explain them. "This is our custom, and this is how it has always been" is the only explanation offered. In all probability it is likely that the customs are closely related to native religious beliefs centered around ancestors. Even today when some 60 per cent of this community are Christians, ancestors play a very important part. A person feels himself to be dependent upon the good will of his ancestors to protect him from all manner of ill luck, ill health, and misfortune. The link between a man and his ancestors is his cattle, and ceremonies of propitiation involve the slaying of cattle. Accordingly, anything that might have an evil influence on the cattle would anger the ancestors; in addition, a married woman continues to have her own set of ancestors and must not interfere with her husband's.

Whatever the underlying reasons, it soon became evident that the taking of milk by girls and especially by married women had powerful emotional connotations. In the face of those deep-seated beliefs, no mere conviction of the nutritional value of milk could be expected to change the practice. This became an important problem, since the nutritional state of expectant and lactating mothers was a subject of major concern to the Health Centre, and these were the individuals most rigidly excluded from using milk. Fortunately, it was possible to overcome this difficulty to a considerable extent by introducing powdered milk into the area. Even though people knew that this powder was in fact milk, it was not called milk in Zulu but was referred to as "powder" or "meal" and accepted by all families without protest. Even the most orthodox of husbands and mothers-in-law had no objection to their wives or daughters-in-law using this powder, and each year a greater number of people have bought milk powder to supplement the limited amounts which could be prescribed by the Health Centre. Cooking demonstrations designed to show various methods of incorporating this powdered milk into the diet increased its popularity. For some years now the Health Centre has been prescribing 800 pounds of milk powder every month, and this supply falls far short of the mounting demand.

While the introduction of milk powder has provided a partial solution to the problem of increasing milk consumption, it is by no means a complete answer. Many people, particularly the women, still do not make the best use of available milk supplies.

The Problem of Pulmonary Tuberculosis

While the problem of inadequate egg and milk consumption was more difficult to overcome than that of vegetables—and is still not entirely solved—the resistance encountered in the attempt to combat pulmonary tuberculosis was even greater. The difficulty in controlling tuberculosis stemmed mainly

from reactions of the people toward the disease, although technical difficulties associated with case-finding procedures and therapeutic techniques were also involved. The recent advent of drugs that produce more dramatic results has been of immeasurable value, not only in treating cases but in changing local concepts of disease.

As already stated, pulmonary tuberculosis was a potent factor contributing to the poor nutritional state of many people in the community. At the same time, tuberculosis was itself a reflection of this poor nutrition. While it is difficult to give an accurate figure of the prevalence of this disease due to inadequate case-finding facilities, it is estimated that there are 15 cases of active tuberculosis per 1,000 population in this rural area. In a recent survey of roughly 100 families, one home in every four was found to harbor an active case, including primary tuberculosis in children. In addition, tuberculosis is now one of the leading causes of death in this community. Of even graver importance, there is every indication that during the past twelve years the incidence of the disease has increased rapidly, and it would appear that this area is suffering from an epidemic of tuberculosis.

Many factors have been responsible for this rapid spread and the failure of the Health Centre to control the disease. These include continuous introduction of new cases into the area by returning migrant laborers, the lack of isolation facilities, the difficulty of adequate case-finding in a mountainous rural area, and the poor nutritional state of the people. None of these aspects, however, has proved so great a handicap as the intense resistance and noncooperation of the people in regard to tuberculosis control. Reluctance is manifested mainly in the case of adult patients, there being far more cooperation where a child is the sufferer. It has been the general experience at the Centre that even though an individual may have been attending the clinical sessions at the Health Centre for several years, an announced diagnosis of tuberculosis would terminate attendance. Some of the reasons for this lack of cooperation are to be found in local concepts and attitudes concerning tuberculosis.

According to the Zulus, any disease associated with labored breathing, pains in the chest, loss of weight, and coughing up bloodstained sputum is attributed to the machinations of an ill-wisher. This person causes poison to be put in the victim's beer or food; he may do this personally or through the services of a "familiar" over which he has control. This poison is not excreted through the bowel but remains indefinitely in the stomach causing a person to vomit blood and lose weight. Eventually the influence of the poison affects the lungs and causes pains in the chest. The treatment consists in taking an emetic specially prepared by a "witch doctor" skilled in treating this disease. Once the emetic causes the poison to be vomited, the patient will be cured. If he is not cured, not enough of the poison has been brought up.

It is maintained by the Zulus that this syndrome is one of the oldest known to them and that cases occurred frequently, long before contact was made with the whites. Objective evidence, however, indicates that tuberculosis was extremely rare, if not absent, among the Zulu and other Bantu tribes until comparatively recent times. In discussing the history of tuberculosis in South Africa, one authority has this to say: "Up to the time of Livingstone who in his 'Travels and Researches in South Africa' states categorically that tuberculosis did not exist among the tribes, there is no evidence that clinically recognizable tuberculosis among the Bantu was other than a rarity."[1] It is likely that this syndrome originally was produced mainly by cases of pneumonia and congestive cardiac failure.

People in this community were thus firmly convinced that patients presenting symptoms of pulmonary tuberculosis were suffering from a disease that had always been treated by their own medical men, and about which a white doctor could be expected to know little. In addition, it was known that if a diagnosis of tuberculosis was made, hospitalization would be advised. The nearest tuberculosis hospital is 100 miles away, and since the majority of patients who had agreed to be hospitalized had been practically moribund before giving their consent, it was generally accepted that hospitalization was synonymous with death. The worst feature of such a death was that it would occur in a strange place, many miles from home, relatives, and the protection of the ancestors. Even if a patient refused hospitalization, it was known that strenuous efforts would be made by the health workers to isolate him, and what could be more unreasonable than to separate an individual from his friends and relatives at the very time he most needed their

presence to comfort and cheer him and assist in his recovery?

A firm belief in the efficacy of the indigenous medical methods in treating such diseases was thus coupled with an intense fear of accepting a diagnosis of tuberculosis. It must be admitted that the prevailing concepts constituted a logical chain of thought. Granting the original premise, that an ill-wisher had poisoned the patient, it could logically follow that such poison would cause vomiting, eventually bloodstained, and a loss of weight. Further, the obvious treatment would be to give an emetic; since this was no ordinary poison, a special emetic prepared by a skilled person would be required.

Only a limited number of approaches appeared feasible in any attempt to alter these concepts. It would be extremely difficult, if not impossible, to convince people that the original premise was false. No one ever saw the ill-wisher put poison in the food; it was just automatically assumed that this was the case. Assuming this premise, the rest of the argument was difficult to refute. One vulnerable point was the belief that the influence of the poison spread from the stomach to the lungs and caused pains in the chest and coughing (recognized as an essential feature of the syndrome). The health education program decided to exploit this weak point, demonstrating that the lungs were separate from the stomach, and presenting an alternative and equally logical set of deductions for consideration. That no connection existed between the lungs and stomach was demonstrated by means of models, posters, and reference to the anatomy of cattle and goats. It was then suggested that the "poison" responsible for the disease could be inhaled rather than swallowed, and that its dissemination might be a matter of accident rather than design. Once inhaled, this "poison" would attack the patient's lungs and could be spread unknowingly by that sufferer in turn.

As can be imagined, this type of education was tedious and demanded great patience and prolonged discussion. Fortunately, the community programs were directed mainly toward healthy people. The majority of people involved were not tubercular and thus the element of intense fear was not present. It was the responsibility of the doctors and nurses to demonstrate their ability to treat the disease should any person contract it. Prior to the advent of the new antibiotics, this was a very dif-

[1]Gale, G. W., "The History and Incidence of Tuberculosis in South Africa," *The Leech*, vol. 16, August, 1945, p. 7.

ficult task, since no short-term dramatic results could be anticipated. The use of these newer drugs has materially assisted the entire program by giving people more confidence in the ability of their doctor and nurse.

In the course of time, a slight decrease in the resistance of the community could be detected. Progress was painfully slow, however, and only by accident was it realized that there was yet another powerful reason preventing the acceptance of a diagnosis of tuberculosis. During a family consultation this additional factor was brought to light in a dramatic fashion.

Four years ago, a daughter of this family had married and contracted tuberculosis in her married home. Her disease had been diagnosed by the Health Centre, but all recommended treatment had been refused. Subsequently, the daughter returned to her maiden home; it was presumably thought that the influence of her ill-wisher was too powerful at her married home. Over the years, eight individuals became infected in her maiden home, four of them dying. With four more of his household seriously ill, the head of the family eventually agreed to discuss his plight with the Centre doctor.

It was known that this man was a part-time "witch doctor," one who was skilled in the arts of Bantu medicine but practiced his profession only occasionally. The consultation opened with a long discussion of Bantu concepts of disease, the father wishing to be convinced that the doctor knew both aspects of the problem—not only the medicine of the whites. Fortunately, the doctor came out of this "quiz" relatively well. After another hour and a half of conversation, the father pronounced himself satisfied. He said he would accept the doctor's recommendations and hospitalize the patients. The doctor then decided to give a résumé of the course of the disease through the family, beginning with the return home of the married daughter suffering from tuberculosis.

This review brought surprising results. Instead of reinforcing the father's decision, as was intended, it suddenly made the old man completely uncooperative; he withdrew his consent for hospitalization. Eventually, after long and patient discussion, the reason for this anger was discovered.

By suggesting that the daughter had started the disease process in this family, the doctor in effect had accused the daughter of possessing the power to spread disease. In this community only sorcerers and witches are recognized as having that power. When the full implications of the doctor's concepts became clear to him, the father realized that by accepting them he would be party to agreeing that his daughter was a witch. Eventually it was possible to obtain consent for hospitalization once more, but only after withdrawing the suggestion that the daughter was in any way responsible for the spread of this disease.

Effects of the Combined Approach

One of the more successful features of both the nutritional and tuberculosis programs was the combined use of clinical sessions and neighborhood health education, the one reinforcing the other. A major goal of the health education program was to convince parents of the importance of regular prenatal and well-child care. The techniques employed here were based on the same principles that governed the programs already described. As a result, the percentage of expectant mothers attending the prenatal sessions increased from fewer than 20 per cent in 1943 to more than 80 per cent in 1952. Similarly, the percentage of mothers who made use of the regular mother and baby sessions increased from a negligible percentage to more than 85 per cent in 1952. At the mother and baby sessions, detailed dietary advice was given to mothers by the family nurse and doctor. Women who had already been exposed to neighborhood health education programs now found this general knowledge applied specifically to themselves and their children.

In the sphere of nutrition, the combined programs yielded dramatic results. An infant mortality rate of 276 per 1,000 live births has been reduced in ten years to just under 100. The major factor influencing this reduction appears to be the improved nutritional state of the babies. Vital statistics available from other parts of Bantu South Africa show that this trend is not general.

Further results are equally evident. The incidence of gross cases of nutritional failure such as pellagra and kwashiorkor has dropped markedly; the incidence of kwashiorkor fell from 12 or more cases a week to fewer than 12 cases a year. The average year-old baby at Polela today weighs two pounds more than the average baby did some six years ago. In addition, the diet of infants has changed quite radically. In 1941 a one-year-old Zulu baby was fed breast milk and maize products. This diet was supplemented seasonally with wild greens, pumpkins, potatoes, and negligible amounts of milk. Today, besides breast milk and maize products, a baby receives powdered milk, eggs, tomatoes, spinach, cabbage, pumpkins, potatoes, peas, fruit in season, and millet.

One index of the greater difficulty experienced in controlling tuberculosis is that no significant decrease in the prevalence of the disease or in mortality rates has yet appeared in spite of the fact that efforts to curb tuberculosis were equal to or greater than those in the nutritional field. What has occurred, however, is a marked change in the attitudes of the people and greater cooperation. This has been evidenced by the increasing willingness of tubercular patients to seek treatment at the Centre. Further, while people at first refused to submit to x-ray examination, the present demand for x-ray services is greater than the Centre can meet. These changing attitudes, along with recent therapeutic advances, in all likelihood will produce improvements in the tuberculosis situation within the next few years.

Health, Soil Erosion, and Ecological Balance

The varying degrees of success achieved by the Polela Centre's programs show that change has been possible in spite of difficulties. A greater effort was required to produce less change in controlling tuberculosis than in improving diet; similarly it was more difficult to effect change in relation to milk and eggs than in regard to vegetables.

However, the relative success of these programs cannot disguise the fact that the critical circumstance associated with the low standard of health in the Polela area is soil erosion, which continues unchecked. Indeed, the very successes attained by the Health Centre will eventually aggravate the problem by increasing the pressure of population on the limited land. Soil erosion is not only the most critical factor in the overall program of improving standards of health; it is also a problem which cannot possibly be solved by a health agency acting alone. Many different approaches have been made to the question of soil conservation in native reserves in South Africa. In this community the two main features of the conservation program have been attempts to improve agricultural practices and to prevent overstocking and overgrazing by cattle.

In an effort to improve farming practices, Africans have been trained in agricultural colleges as "agricultural demonstrators" and stationed in native reserves among their own people. To prevent overstocking and overgrazing, the right of entry of cattle into an area has been strictly controlled and strenuous efforts have been made to persuade cattle owners to reduce the size of their herds. In spite of these and all the other procedures that have been tried, soil erosion is increasing at an alarming rate. Some of the efforts, particularly in regard to reducing the number of cattle, have had the unfortunate effect of increasing hostility and resistance. Explanations for this unhappy state of affairs must be sought in the natural and cultural history of soil erosion in South Africa.

Originally the Bantus were a roving pastoral people owning large flocks and herds. They would farm a plot of land until it was exhausted and then migrate to a more fertile area. From the latter part of the nineteenth century, their right of movement has been restricted and rural Africans have been confined in reserves. In these reserves, families had relatively small plots of land which they cultivated season after season without changing their original agricultural practices. Returning little of the waste products to the soil and oblivious to crop rotation, they have steadily deteriorated the fertility of the land.

Furthermore, the use of migrant labor in all industries and domestic work has drained the men from the fields, and in consequence the care of the land has become the job of women and children. Increasing poverty of the reserves in turn has accelerated the migration of men to the towns, further aggravating the situation. Since women in Zulu society have the legal status of minors and lack authority to change existing practices, it is not surprising that the efforts of the agricultural demonstrators have been of so little avail, women and children being their only audience for the greater part of the year. Thus, poor farming methods continue unabated, perpetuating the vicious cycle of deepened poverty, longer absences of the men to work for wages, and decreased possibilities of altering prevailing agricultural practices.

Additional forces abet this downward spiral. One is the mountainous nature of the land which makes large tracts unsuitable for agriculture even if modern technology were available. Another is the overcrowding of the reserves by man and beast. Still others are the destruction of the soil cover by deforestation to obtain fuel and burning pastures in spring to hasten the appearance of green grass in order to relieve starvation of the animals.

The efforts of administrators to ease this pressure on the land have centered mainly on attempts to control the cattle and reduce their number. Much hostility has been aroused by these methods, largely because insufficient account was taken of the function of cattle in Zulu culture. People with European background have found it easy to assume that the major uses of cattle are to produce milk, to serve as draught animals, as an index of wealth, and—among native Africans—as payment for the "bride price" necessary to obtain a wife. Accordingly, it has also been assumed that fewer cattle of better stock would be acceptable, since they would produce more milk. Compensation for reducing the herd could be made in cash, which should also become an index of wealth, and a wife could then be obtained by a cash transaction or payment in kind.

All these assumptions overlook the deep symbolic value of cattle. The transference of cattle involved in a marriage is more than a matter of buying or selling a wife. To the Zulus, it guarantees the good behavior of both marriage partners, for which the families of the bride and groom hold themselves responsible. Moreover, since cattle form an essential link between a man and his ancestors, loss of cattle means a weakening of this bond, leaving one defenseless in a hostile world. Finally, the deep attachment of men for their cattle must not be underestimated. Any man in this area could, without hesitation, describe each of his cattle in minute detail, depicting not only appearance and color but character and habits as well. Many Zulu men probably know far more about their cattle than they do about their children.

Thus, it is evident why attempts at cattle reduction should encounter resistance. But even if this reduction were accomplished, the problem would scarcely be solved in view of the many additional and interrelated factors responsible for the accelerating soil erosion. Furthermore, while the reduction of the number of cattle might ease the pressure on the land to some extent, stock limitation alone would have unfavorable effects on the health of the people unless this move was part of a much more comprehensive program. Initially, stock reduction would mean a still further limitation of the already inadequate milk supply, since pedigreed cows could not survive without good pastures. The numbers of oxen available for draught purposes is already limited inasmuch as most of the cattle are owned by only a few families. Many families, therefore, have to borrow oxen from their neighbors for plowing. The delay in plowing some of the fields results in frequent crop failures caused by early frosts; a further reduction in cattle would only aggravate this situation.

It thus becomes apparent that soil conservation, on the scale necessary in this area, is beyond the scope of a health agency. It would require a broadly based community program integrating the activities of various agencies and a thorough knowledge of relevant social and cultural forces.

IMPLICATIONS

While no attempt has been made to present an exhaustive discussion of all the factors involved in maintaining health, enough has been said to show that the improvement of health conditions cannot be conceived as an isolated effort; rather, it must be seen in its total context. In the Polela area this context includes economic, political, and ecological considerations, as well as many features of the local culture.

Recognizing that most health problems among these people are fundamentally related to soil erosion, poverty, and the system of migrant labor, one can envision a solution that makes maximum use of local resources. Specifically, such a plan would begin by building a dam across the river that flows through the valley, using the impounded water to irrigate the lower flat slopes. In this way, crops could be grown the year round, and not merely during the wet summer months as at present. The rest of the area, which is too mountainous for extensive cultivation, could be put into timber. The climate is eminently suitable for pine trees, and within ten to twelve years these would begin yielding returns. Once the timber was mature, after eighteen years, hydroelectric power could be developed from the dam to start timber industries.

Such a scheme would check soil erosion and gradually restore fertility. It would also provide sufficient occupational opportunities to slow down the migration of men to the towns. The increased productivity of the area would offset the population increase that would come with improved health. Under these circumstances, a comprehensive health program could be expected to yield enduring results. While this kind of program would appear to solve many community problems, the power to implement it obviously far exceeds the scope of a health agency. This being so, it becomes the obligation of the health agency to attempt motivating other agencies to cooperate in carrying out some such scheme, and at the same time to recognize realistically the magnitude of changes that are possible through its own efforts.

Once a health agency has delineated those areas in which change is feasible, it is important to distinguish tasks in terms of the amount of effort that will be required to overcome local resistance. It has been shown that the control of tuberculosis among the Zulus was more difficult than the improvement of diet. Within the dietary program, it was more difficult to increase the consumption of milk and eggs than vegetables. In all the programs it was necessary to bear in mind the limiting factors of low productivity and the system of migrant labor, which would permit changes only up to a certain point.

It will be readily appreciated, however, that improving the productivity of an area by itself would not automatically solve all health problems. A comprehensive health program closely integrating neighborhood health education with medical care has proved effective in the Polela area even though certain conditions beyond the control of the health agency have set limits to the changes that could be effected. The techniques developed by the Centre have been found useful, not only in this particular community but in other communities of South Africa as well.

In addition to combining the promotive-preventive approach with the curative approach, new ideas have been communicated to the people with lasting results. This happened because the new ideas were brought into correspondence with existing ideas, rather than being imposed from above. As a result, there have been increased cooperation and confidence in the Health Centre on the part of the community. To achieve these ends, the small-group discussion method was found to be much superior to a mass approach. It in turn has necessitated operating in a limited sphere and gradually increasing the area of influence centrifugally. Attempts were made to build into the programs themselves techniques for appraisal and evaluation. This has been a constant feature of the work of the Centre, rather than a spasmodic occurrence.

SUMMARY

Examples from the work of the Polela Health Centre serving a Zulu community in the Union of South Africa illustrate the different degrees of resistance encountered in trying to make a variety of changes in the health status of the people. Changes were progressively more difficult to effect in these four aims: improvement of diet by the cultivation of vegetable gardens, increasing the consumption of milk and eggs, the control of tuberculosis, and, finally, soil conservation, which is basic to problems of health.

Thorough understanding of local ways and values and the importance of fitting new ideas into the existing cultural framework of the people were shown to be essential if lasting results were to be achieved. The experiences of the Centre demonstrated the advantages of an integrated service wherein the promotive-preventive and curative aspects of health practice are combined and made the responsibility of the same team.

SELECTED REFERENCES

Cohn, Helen D., "The Educational Nurse in Health Centre Practice," *Health Education Journal* (Central Council for Health Education, Tavistock Square, London), vol. 8, October, 1950, pp. 178–184. A nurse cites in detail the case of a Bantu family served by one of the health centers to illustrate the necessity of integrating promotive, preventive, and curative work.

Gluckman, Max, "The Kingdom of the Zulu of South Africa" in *African Political Systems*, edited by A. Meyer Fortes and E. E. Evans-Pritchard. Oxford University Press, London, 1940, pp. 25–55. A scholarly analysis of Zulu power structure and the effect upon it of European impact written by a primary anthropological authority on the Zulu.

Kark, Sidney L., "Health Centre Service: A South African Experiment in Family Health and Medical Care" in *Social Medicine*, edited by E. H. Cluver. Central News Agency, Johannesburg, 1951, pp. 661–700. A comprehensive background article on the Polela program, its scope, its development, and the respective functions of team members—doctor, nurse, and health educator.

Kark, Sidney L., and John Cassel, "The Pholela Health Centre: A Progress Report," *South African Medical Journal* (Johannesburg), vol. 26, no. 9, 1952, pp. 101–104 and 132–136. A report of specific programs, techniques, and results.

Krige, Eileen J., *The Social System of the Zulus*. Long-mans Green and Co., New York, 1936. Zulu past and present, based mainly on a survey of published sources.

Richards, Audrey I., *Hunger and Work in a Savage Community*. The Free Press, Glencoe, Ill., 1948. A British anthropologist with extended field work in Africa provides a compact and readable outline of

Zulu life in the course of following out the implications of the Zulus' "nutritional system."

Simons, H. J., "Race Relations and Policies in Southern and Eastern Africa" in *Most of the World*, edited by Ralph Linton. Columbia University Press, New York, 1949, pp. 271–330. A competent regional survey emphasizing contemporary economic and racial conditions.

WELLS

Holmberg's discussion of the wells that failed brings out a different set of events and relationships. In this case the need for more water was clear; what was not clear to the outsiders bringing in the needed wells was that there was a preexisting sociocultural system into which the new technology would be placed. The needed improvement was entering an ongoing system—and the homework regarding the outlines and functioning of that system had not been sufficiently well done by the improvers so as to increase the chances for acceptance. There were deeply held beliefs relating to social differences and the social hierarchy in the village of Viru, beliefs that interlocked with status systems, and social relationships that differentially distributed political and economic power. Again, the anthropological analysis of this case underscores the need for more holistic and comprehensive view of the total sociocultural system. In the context of such a view, Holmberg's discussion also points to some of the other strategies that, if used, might have led to acceptance of the innovation.

THE WELLS THAT FAILED (Continued)

ALLAN R. HOLMBERG

1. Before deciding to drill the wells, the Peruvian government sent a geological commission to survey the possibilities of ensuring the success of the venture. In company with the water commissioner of Viru, the geologists made a reconnaissance of the upper part of the valley near the village. Their report was favorable, and a number of sites most likely to yield water were selected and marked.

2. The one chosen for first drilling lay on private land near the main irrigation ditch about two miles

up the valley from the village. Shortly thereafter, two technicians arrived and the well-drilling equipment was hauled into the village. Before operations could start, however, it was necessary to repair and widen a road which passed near the site and to open a trail from the main road to the spot where the first well was to be drilled. This was a community responsibility.

The *Junta* had trouble finding people who were willing to help, even though at this time of year (September) no agricultural work was going on. The harvest in Viru is generally in July and the farmer cannot again begin to prepare his fields for sowing until December, when there is some hope

Reprinted with permission. From Allan R. Holmberg, "The Wells That Failed," in *Human Problems in Technological Change*, ed. Edward H. Spicer, © 1952 by Russell Sage Foundation, Publishers, N.Y., pp. 114–23.

that water for irrigation will soon descend from the mountains. Moreover, there were no funds in the municipal treasury to hire the necessary workers. The *Junta* went into debt, therefore, to pay for the labor needed to widen and repair the road. Even then few people responded to the call. Finally, with great difficulty, the machinery was hauled to the site.

3. Meanwhile, the technicians themselves encountered trouble in finding a place to live or even a place to eat. Moreover, working at a distance of two miles from town with no way of getting out and back except on foot, it was both exhausting and uneconomical for them to return for lunch each midday; yet, at first, no one could be induced to send lunch to them or to pack it so they could eat at the site.

Nevertheless, they had a job to do and they began work at once. The drilling itself went smoothly enough because the technicians could carry out this operation with machinery alone.

4. While the well was being drilled, however, few people showed enough interest even to visit the site. Exceptions included the water commissioner (part of whose job it was), the man on whose property the operations were taking place, and some members of the *Junta*. In the village, reactions to the well were varied: a few were enthusiastic about it; some were skeptical of its possible success; and others knew nothing about it. Still others spoke openly against it, saying that it was all politics, that the geologists and technicians did not know their business, that the site selected was a poor one, and that if water were struck the village would not benefit by it anyway. The technicians were somewhat surprised by such hostile attitudes and lack of interest, since the well was not costing the village a centavo, but they went about their work without seriously complaining until their first job was done—and a hard one it was, for it took them more than thirty days to drill through a hundred feet of solid rock. At this depth the well gave a constant flow that was considered adequate to justify the drilling of another. However, in view of the lack of sufficient help and favorable response from the villagers, both the engineer and the technicians recommended termination of the project.

5. On the part of the villagers the reaction to this conclusion was one of "I told you so." The technicians left, the equipment was withdrawn, and by April, 1948—the last time the writer visited the village—a pump had not even been installed on the well that had been drilled. Thus Viru, as far as its water supply was concerned, was in the same condition that it had been before the project was started. Meanwhile, hostility toward the national government had increased and thousands of dollars had been uselessly spent on a project that might have resulted in success.

RELEVANT FACTORS

In order to understand why events took the turn they did, it will be necessary to call attention to a few facts about the culture of Viru and to a few of the circumstances that existed at the time the well was being drilled.

In the first place, the village itself is made up largely of small landowners and sharecroppers. The majority of these are natives of the valley who depend for their subsistence on small plots of irrigated land from two to ten acres in size but some of whom, for commercial purposes, also sharecrop on large haciendas outside the village, paying as rent 25 per cent of the crop.

At the same time, the village contains a few large landowners not all of whom are native-born, but some of whom through unscrupulous practices and unfair dealings have managed to accumulate land holdings of considerable size. In some cases, for example, these large holdings include parcels which formerly belonged to the community and the church and which were secured through shady deals. As a result, the community is normally split along two main lines: on the one hand, there is a dichotomy between large and small landowners; on the other, between natives born in Viru and *forasteros* (people from the outside). Needless to say, members of these groups do not always see eye to eye, especially on serious matters. Moreover, outsiders in general have less status than the natives and the large landowners are more prestigeful than the small.

In the second place, national political conditions existing at the time bear considerable relevance to an understanding of the course of events. The political party then in power was the so-called liberal or APRA (Alianza Popular Revolucionaria Americana), one of the main planks of whose platform was to break up the large estates and wealthy power groups and to return the lands and the rule to the people. Being underdogs, the majority of small farmers and sharecroppers in Viru—that is to say, the bulk of the population—were either members of the liberal party or gave considerable lip service to it. On the other hand, certain power groups as represented by the larger landowners and the priest—some of whom were highly respected in the community—were violently opposed to the liberal party and thoroughly disapproved of its aims. The community was therefore further split along political lines, and rather widely so.

In the third place, municipal affairs were in the hands of a Transitory Board. Until this time local government had been the charge of a Municipal Council, the principal members of which had always been appointed by the prefect of the Political Department, who was himself an appointee of the national government in Lima. This system made for strong central government which had always been the policy of dictatorships in Peru. The liberal party planned to change all this; in fact, their congress was discussing a bill to legalize municipal elections for the first time in Peruvian history. But as a temporary measure and to give time to prepare rural areas for this change, Transitory Boards were set up (in the same way that Municipal Councils had been previously appointed) to govern at the local level. Because of a scarcity of enlightened liberal party leadership in the rural areas, however, the government was sometimes hard put to find educated local personnel to appoint to these boards. As a result, it was necessary either to make appointments from the outside or to be satisfied with inferior local personnel. In appointing the Board of Viru, a combination of these two alternatives was resorted to.

For a further understanding of this case, attention should be called to another cultural factor, namely, the status system. Positions of prestige in Viru are not assigned only to those of good family and wealth; they may be gained also by those of more humble birth and means. The principal channels for acquiring prestige in the community are wealth, education, the institutions of *compadrazgo*, and the religious fiesta. Having reached the pinnacles of success in this system—as reflected by being a man of means, of some learning, the godfather to many children, and having been the first steward of the religious fiesta of the patron saint— one is in a position to assume the highest responsibilities of leadership and power as expressed by being appointed mayor of the Municipal Council.

Under normal circumstances one cannot arrive at such a position, which takes a long period of time, without at least having been born in the village.

A final cultural factor to which some attention should be directed is that of the value system. Not long before the well was drilled, Viru was a relatively isolated village; actually, it was put in ready contact with the outside world only after 1939, when an asphalt highway connecting it with other coastal valleys in Peru was completed. Until that time ideas of change and progress, as typified by modern science and technology, had hardly entered the minds of most villagers; rather, their outlook on life, as typified by religion and magic, was essentially static and pessimistic. Lacking scientific knowledge and techniques to control their water supply, they had for years relied on religious beliefs to explain their lack of water and on magical means to ensure whatever supply they did enjoy. In other words, such natural phenomena as the water were thought to be controlled by supernatural forces—as represented by images of the Catholic saints—which could be influenced only by the observance of magico-religious rites, specifically by the celebration of the feast days of certain saints. In Viru, for example, the first water of the new agricultural year generally appears in the irrigation ditch soon after the celebration of the fiesta of the Virgin of Sorrow, which occurs on the twelfth of December. If the year is dry, it is believed that this fiesta has not been properly celebrated and that the Virgin is castigating the people. If the year continues to be dry, the image of St. Isidore, patron of farmers, may be taken out on a religious procession and worshipped at the river until water comes. If crops fail completely, people are being punished for their sins. On the other hand, if the year has been good and the harvest bountiful, it is attributed to the fact that the Catholic saints, who control the weather, the insect pests, and the water supply, have been abundantly honored by religious fiestas and are thus favorably disposed toward man. In this connection it is significant to remember that at the time the well was being drilled many of the people of Viru subscribed to these magico-religious ideas and practices with respect to the water supply.

ANALYSIS

We are now in a position to disclose a number of significant reasons for the failure of this project.

In the first place, local people, many of whom knew a great deal about the water supply of the valley, were little consulted by the technical commission or the technical staff; in fact, they were almost completely ignored. One of these people, for instance, had had considerable experience in drilling wells on his own land and was thoroughly acquainted with water conditions in the valley; yet, he was by-passed by the technical commission. Moreover, he was a native of the village, with wealth, prestige, and power, and had formerly been a member of the Municipal Council. Actually at the time, he was the most powerful informal leader in the village. While strongly against the political party then in power, he opposed the project not so much on political grounds as on the grounds that he was not consulted in the planning stage and that he was slighted by the technical commission and even members of the Transitory Board, who regarded him as their political enemy. Consequently, he used none of his influence and prestige to support the project but spoke openly against it, saying that it was sure to fail.

In the second place, the site for drilling the first well fell on the property of a large landowner against whom—although he was a native of the village—there was considerable hostility on the part of some of the large landowners and many of the small ones. For this reason, many people suspected that the owner of the property alone would benefit from the drilling of the well. Moreover, some of the sites selected by the commission were located on public lands, so that the people thought that the first operation at least should have taken place on them. It should be mentioned, however, that the first site picked by the technical commission was in no way related to the question of whose land it was situated on; it was selected solely because of its likelihood of yielding an abundant supply of water and because of its proximity to the village. Nevertheless, many of the villagers believed otherwise and thought that they would never benefit from a well drilled on this particular site.

In the third place, the local governing body was transitory and its principal members were neither native-born Viruñeros nor representative of the real leadership of the community. The principal member of the Transitory Board, the mayor, did not even reside in the village but on a neighboring *hacienda*. He only rarely visited the village and

delegated most of his duties to the lieutenant mayor. Although a resident of the village, he had been born in another part of Peru. He was besides a *curandero* (native medical practitioner), whose reputation for healing among many of the people was not high. In addition, he had the reputation of being a meddler and an opportunist who was generally insincere. A third member of the board, the secretary, although not an official of much importance, was a local boy and a member of an old family in Viru. But he was unmarried and was so young that he had not gained much prestige through the channels previously mentioned. Moreover, he typified the younger progressive members of the community, who were at this time far in the minority.

In the fourth place, members of the Transitory Board themselves showed a lack of interest in the project. Neither was there support from the prestige elements in the community, such as the priest, the director of the school, the public and lay-religious officials. For that matter, even the people of the village were little informed about what was going on and therefore became suspicious of the motives of the *Junta* and the activities of the technicians. As a result, malicious rumors about the project circulated freely and many people became hostile to it simply for a lack of accurate information.

Finally, quite a large group of prestigeful men in the village conceived of this operation, consciously or unconsciously, as a threat to an old way of life which they valued highly and which for some time they had been fighting to conserve. To be sure, it had been a losing battle ever since it began, for the termination of the asphalt highway had made possible a considerable flow of modern technology and new ideas, one of the results of which was that the old value system—as typified by the patriarchal family, the *compadrazgo* system, the religious fiesta, and the cult of the saints—had already begun to break down. Actually, a lack of water during the intervening years between the completion of the highway and the drilling of the well was explained by these people as the consequence of the waning of the customary religious practices. In fact, many members of this conservative element were heard to remark that before the coming of modern influences there seldom had been any lack of water in Viru because the cult of the saints had been strictly practiced.

This idea, of course, received reinforcement from the priest, who bitterly railed against the increasing secularization that had accompanied the modernization process. Consequently, this group, while it did not openly oppose the project, gave it no support.

In view of the foregoing circumstances, what might have been done to have enhanced the chances for the success of this project? In an *ex post facto* analysis of this kind, of course, no one solution can be final. But a number of possibilities come to mind.

1. More advice should have been sought from local people, even though most of them knew little about the technical aspects of the potential water supply of the valley. Such a suggestion does not mean that the technical commission would have had to accept as final the decision of the villagers as to where to drill the well. But had the question been discussed with the local people (with a committee of leaders, at least)—not an unknown practice in Viru—it would have been possible to explain the objectives of the project and why it was necessary to select the sites exclusively with reference to their potential water supply. If such a meeting had been held during one of the important religious fiestas, for example, when almost everyone comes to town, it might have been possible to have broken down resistance to, and gained considerable support for, the project even before it began.

2. The first well should have been drilled on land other than that of a large landowner who was little respected in the community; particularly since good potential sites had already been located on public lands by the technical commission. Such a step would have helped to eliminate the suspicion of many people that the village as a whole would not benefit from the drilling of the well, and it would have provided a sound basis for wide community participation.

3. The Transitory Board, since it did not repre-sent the real leadership of the village, should not have been the only local group consulted. Every community contains informal leaders who are often more influential than the people actually holding office. In this instance, therefore, some attempt should have been made to find out who these leaders were and to gain their support for the project. As it happens, it would have been relatively easy to have enlisted the aid of the priest, the director of the school, members of the local sports club, and many farmers and merchants who were highly respected in the community. And if in gaining this support it was found impossible to work with the *Junta*, attempts should have been made to change its membership or by-pass it rather than to let the project fail.

4. The central institution of the religious fiesta itself, or the cult of the saints, might have been employed to publicize and dramatize the scientific techniques of drilling wells. Had the support of the priest and the lay-religious officials been gained, for example, the site could have received the proper religious blessing, or a religious procession could have been held to it, all of which would have helped to enlist the support of the conservative elements who later opposed the project.

These are but a few of the possibilities that could have been tried in order to enhance the likelihood of success in this venture. It happens that the gathering of data presented here was incidental to a larger study under preparation at the same time. But if a capable social scientist had been sent in beforehand specifically to investigate the factors likely to lead to success or failure in a project of this kind, the significant ones could have been discovered in a relatively short period of time—say, a month. And had such a course been adopted and had the social scientist's recommendations been taken into account in planning the project, there is every likelihood that Viru, after 400 years of suffering from lack of water, would have at least obtained a secure supply.

AXES

The following selection is already widely known to many beginning students in the social and behavioral sciences. The reason is clear: it dramatically illustrates the "functional" analysis of a sociocultural system, the articulation of the parts or elements of such a system, so that introduction of change in any one part may have far-reaching effects on many other features of group life. Take a simple change such as introduction of steel axes in place of stone axes. See how widely this new element in the sociocultural field alters status structures, self-image, relationships between men and women, trade relationships beyond the group, and even such diffuse matters as world view or "ethos" of the culture, those deeply held values systems that for the Yir Yoront organized man, time, and space into one coherent whole.

STEEL AXES FOR STONE AGE AUSTRALIANS (Continued)

LAURISTON SHARP

1. In 1623 a Dutch expedition landed on the coasts now occupied by the Yir Yoront. All cultural items (although few in number) recorded in the Dutch log for the aboriginals they encountered were still in use among the Yir Yoront in 1935. To this inventory the Dutch added pieces of iron and beads in an effort to attract the frightened "Indians." They remained at this spot for two days, during which they were able to kidnap one and shoot another of a group of some hundred males. Today metal and beads have disappeared, as has any memory of this first encounter with whites.

2. The next recorded contact in this area occurred in 1864, and here there is more positive assurance that the natives concerned were the immediate ancestors of the Yir Yoront community. These aborginals had the temerity to attack a party of cattlemen who were driving a small herd from southern Queensland through the whole length of the then unknown Cape York Peninsula to a newly established government station at the Peninsula's northern tip. As a result there occurred what became known as the "Battle of the Mitchell River," one of the rare instances in which Australian aboriginals stood up to European gunfire for any length of time. A diary kept by the cattlemen records the incident: ". . . ten carbines poured volley after volley into them from all directions, killing and wounding with every shot with very little return, nearly all their spears having already been expended. . . . About thirty being killed, the

leader thought it prudent to hold his hand, and let the rest escape. Many more must have been wounded and probably drowned, for fifty-nine rounds were counted as discharged." The European party was in the Yir Yoront area for three days, then disappeared over the horizon to the north, not to return.

During the anthropological investigation some seventy years later, lasting almost three years, there was not one reference to this shocking contact with Europeans, nor anything that could be interpreted as a reference to it, in all the material of hundreds of free association interviews, in hundreds of dreams and myths, in genealogies, and eventually in hundreds of answers to direct and indirect questioning on just this particular matter.

3. The aboriginal accounts of their first remembered contact with whites begin with references to persons known to have had sporadic but lethal encounters with them beginning about 1900, and it may be noted that from that time on whites continued to remain on the southern periphery of Yir Yoront territory. With the establishment of cattle stations or ranches to the south, occasional excursions among the "wild blackfellows" were made by cattlemen wishing to inspect the country and abduct natives to be trained as cattle boys and "house girls." At least one such expedition reached the Coleman River, where a number of Yir Yoront men and women were shot, apparently on general principles. A stick of trade tobacco, the natives now claim, was left with each body; but this kindness was evidently unappreciated, for the leader of the excursion was eventually speared to death by a native fighting party.

4. It was about this time that the government

Reprinted with permission. From Lauriston Sharp, "Steel Axes for Stone Age Australians," in *Human Problems in Technological Change*, ed. Edward H. Spicer, © 1952 by Russell Sage Foundation, Publishers, N.Y., pp. 70–90.

was persuaded to sponsor the establishment of three mission stations along the seven hundred mile western coast of the Peninsula as an aid in regulating the treatment of natives. To further this purpose a strip of coastal territory was set aside as an aboriginal reserve and closed to further white settlement.

In 1915 an Anglican mission station was established near the mouth of the Mitchell River in the territory of a tribe neighboring the Yir Yoront on the south and about three days' march from the heart of the Yir Yoront country. Some of the Yir Yoront refused to have anything to do with the mission or to go near it, others visited it on occasion, while a few eventually settled more or less permanently in one of the three "villages" at the mission.

5. Thus, the majority of the Yir Yoront continued to live their old self-supporting life in the bush, protected until 1942 by the government reserve and the intervening mission from the cruder realities of the encroaching new order which had come up from the south. To the east was poor country, uninhabited. To the north were other bush tribes extending on along the coast to the distant Archer River Presbyterian mission with which the Yir Yoront had no contact. Westward was the expanse of the shallow Gulf of Carpentaria, on which the natives saw only a mission lugger making its infrequent dry-season trips to the Mitchell River. In this protected environment for over a generation the Yir Yoront were able to recuperate from former shocks received at the hands of civilized society. During the 1930's their raiding and fighting, their trading and stealing of women, their evisceration and two- or three-year care of their dead, their totemic ceremonies continued apparently uninhibited by western influence. In 1931 they killed a European who wandered into their territory from the east, but the investigating police never approached the group whose members were responsible for the act. In 1934 the anthropologist observed a case of extra-tribal revenge cannibalism. The visitor among the bush Yir Yoront at this time found himself in the presence of times past, in an essentially paleolithic society which had been changed, to the casual eye, chiefly by the addition of oddments of European implements and goods put to a variety of uses.

6. As a direct result of the work of the Mitchell River mission, all Yir Yoront received a great many more western artifacts of all kinds than they ever had obtained before. As part of their plan for raising native living standards, the missionaries made it possible for aboriginals at the mission to earn some western goods, many of which were then given or traded out to natives still living under bush conditions; or they handed out gratis both to mission and to bush aboriginals certain useful articles which were in demand. They prevented guns, liquor, and damaging narcotics, as well as decimating diseases, from reaching the tribes of this area, while encouraging the introduction of goods they considered "improving." As has been noted, no item of western technology that was available, with the possible exception of trade tobacco, was in greater demand among all groups of aboriginals than the short-handled steel axe. A good supply of this type of axe was therefore always kept in stock at the mission for sale; and at Christmas parties or other mission festivals steel axes were given away to mission or visiting aboriginals indiscriminately and in considerable numbers. In addition, some steel axes, as well as other European goods, were still traded in to the Yir Yoront by natives in contact with cattle stations established south of the missions. Indeed, such axes had probably come to the Yir Yoront along established lines of aboriginal trade long before any regular contact with whites had occurred.

RELEVANT FACTORS

If we concentrate our attention on Yir Yoront behavior centering about the original stone axe, rather than on the axe—the thing—we should get some conception of the role this implement played in aboriginal culture. This conception, in turn, should permit us to foresee with considerable accuracy some of the results of the displacement of stone axes by steel axes acquired directly or indirectly from Europeans by the Yir Yoront.

The production of a stone axe required a number of simple skills. With the idea of the axe in its various details well in mind, the adult men—and only the adult men—could set about producing it, a task not considered appropriate for women or children. First of all, a man had to know the location and properties of several natural resources found in his immediate environment: pliable wood, which could be doubled or bent over the axe head and bound tightly to form a handle; bark, which could be rolled into cord for the binding; and gum, with which the stone head could be firmly fixed in the haft. These materials had to be correctly gathered, stored, prepared, cut to size, and applied or manipulated. They were plentifully supplied by nature, and could be taken by a man from anyone's property without special permission. Postponing consideration of the stone head of the axe, we see that a simple knowledge of nature and of the technological skills involved, together with the possession of fire (for heating the gum) and a few simple cutting tools, which might be nothing more than the sharp shells of plentiful bivalves, all of which were available to everyone, were sufficient to enable any normal man to make a stone axe.

The use of the stone axe as a piece of capital equipment for the production of other goods indicates its very great importance in the subsistence economy of the aboriginal. Anyone—man, woman, or child—could use the axe; indeed, it was used more by women, for theirs was the onerous, daily task of obtaining sufficient wood to keep the camp-fire of each family burning all day for cooking or other purposes and all night against mosquitoes and cold (in July, winter temperature might drop below forty degrees). In a normal lifetime any woman would use the axe to cut or knock down literally tons of firewood. Men and women, and sometimes children, needed the axe to make other tools, or weapons, or a variety of material equipment required by the aboriginal in his daily life. The stone axe was essential in making the wet-season domed huts, which keep out some rain and some insects; or platforms, which provide dry storage; or shelters, which give shade when days are bright and hot. In hunting and fishing and in gathering vegetable or animal food the axe was also a necessary tool; and in this tropical culture without preservatives or other means of storage, the native spends more time obtaining food than in any other occupation except sleeping.

In only two instances was the use of the stone axe strictly limited to adult men: Wild honey, the most prized food known to the Yir Yoront, was gathered only by men who usually used the axe to get it; and only men could make the secret paraphernalia for ceremonies, an activity often requiring use of the axe. From this brief listing of some of the activities in which the axe was used, it is easy to understand why there was at least one stone axe in every camp, in every hunting or fighting party, in every group out on a "walk-about" in the bush.

While the stone axe helped relate men and women and often children to nature in technological behavior, in the transformation of natural into cultural equipment, it also was prominent in that aspect of behavior which may be called conduct, primarily directed toward persons. Yir Yoront men were dependent upon interpersonal relations for their stone axe heads, since the flat, geologically recent alluvial country over which they range, provides no stone from which axe heads can be made. The stone they used comes from known quarries four hundred miles to the south. It reached the Yir Yoront through long lines of male trading partners, some of these chains terminating with the Yir Yoront men, while others extended on farther north to other groups, having utilized Yir Yoront men as links. Almost every older adult man had one or more regular trading partners, some to the north and some to the south. His partner or partners in the south he provided with surplus spears, and particularly fighting spears tipped with the barbed spines of sting ray which snap into vicious fragments when they penetrate human flesh. For a dozen spears, some of which he may have obtained from a partner to the north, he would receive from a southern partner one stone axe head. Studies have shown that the sting ray spears become more and more valuable as they move south farther from the sea, being passed on in recent times from a native on one cattle station to a native on another where they are used during the wet season, when almost all aboriginal employees are thrust into the bush to shift for themselves until the next cattle-working dry season is at hand. A hundred and fifty miles south of the Yir Yoront one such spear may be exchanged for one stone axe head. Although actual investigations could not be made, presumably still farther south and nearer the quarries, one sting ray spear would bring several stone axe heads. It is apparent that links in the middle of the chain who make neither spears nor axe heads receive both as a middleman's profit simply for passing them back and forth. While many other objects may move along these chains of trading partners, they are still characterized by both bush and station aboriginals as lines along which spears move south and axes move north. Thus trading relations, which may extend the individual's personal relationships out beyond the boundaries of his own group, are associated with two of the most important items in a man's equipment, spears and axes, whether the latter are of stone or steel. Finally, most of the exchanges between partners take place during the dry season at times when the great aboriginal fiestas occur, which center about initiation rites or other totemic ceremonials that attract hundreds and are the occasion for much exciting activity besides trading.

Returning to the Yir Yoront, we find that not only was it adult men alone who obtained axe heads and produced finished axes, but it was adult males who retained the axes, keeping them with other parts of their equipment in camp, or carrying them at the back slipped through a human hair belt when traveling. Thus, every woman or child who wanted to use an axe—and this might be frequently during the day—must get one from some man, use it promptly, and return it to the man in good condition. While a man might speak of "my axe," a woman or child could not; for them it was always "your axe," addressing a male, or "his axe."

This necessary and constant borrowing of axes from older men by women and children was done according to regular patterns of kinship behavior. A woman on good terms with her husband would expect to use his axe unless he were using it; a husband on good terms with his wives would let any one of them use his axe without question. If a woman was unmarried or her husband was absent, she would go first to her older brother or to her father for an axe. Only in extraordinary circumstances would she seek a stone axe from a mother's brother or certain other male kin with whom she had to be most circumspect. A girl, a boy, or a young man would look to a father or an older brother to provide an axe for her or his use, but would never approach a mother's brother, who would be at the same time a potential father-in-law, with such a request. Older men, too, would follow similar rules if they had to borrow an axe.

It will be noted that these social relationships in which the stone axe had a place are all pair relationships and that the use of the axe helped define and maintain the character of the relationships and the roles of the two individual partici-

pants. Every active relationship among the Yir Yoront involved a definite and accepted status of superordination or subordination. A person could have no dealings with any other on exactly equal terms. Women and children were dependent on, or subordinate to, older males in every action in which the axe entered. Among the men, the younger was dependent on the older or on certain kinds of kin. The nearest approach to equality was between brothers, although the older was always superordinate to the younger. Since the exchange of goods in a trading relationship involved a mutual reciprocity, trading partners were usually a kind of brother to each other or stood in a brotherly type of relationship, although one was always classified as older than the other and would have some advantage in case of dispute. It can be seen that repeated and widespread conduct centering on the axe helped to generalize and standardize throughout the society these sex, age, and kinship roles, both in their normal benevolent and in exceptional malevolent aspects, and helped to build up expectancies regarding the conduct of others defined as having a particular status.

The status of any individual Yir Yoront was determined not only by sex, age, and extended kin relationships, but also by membership in one of two dozen patrilineal totemic clans into which the entire community was divided. A person's names, rights in particular areas of land, and, in the case of a man, his roles in the totemic ceremonies (from which women are excluded) were all a function of belonging to one clan rather than another. Each clan had literally hundreds of totems, one or two of which gave the clan its name, and from any of which the personal names of clan members were derived. These totems included not only natural species or phenomena like the sun, stars, and daybreak, but also cultural "species": imagined ghosts, rainbow serpents, heroic ancestors; such eternal cultural verities as fires, spears, huts; and such human activities, conditions, or attributes as eating, vomiting, swimming, fighting, babies and corpses, milk and blood, lips and loins. While individual members of such totemic classes or species might disappear or be destroyed, the class itself was obviously ever present and indestructible. The totems therefore lent permanence and stability to the clans, to the groupings of human individuals who generation after generation were each associated with one set of totems that distinguished one clan from another.

Among the many totems of the Sunlit Cloud Iguana clan, and important among them, was the stone axe. The names of many members of this clan referred to the axe itself, or to activities like trading or wild honey gathering in which the axe played a vital part, or to the clan's mythical ancestors with whom the axe was prominently associated. When it was necessary to represent the stone axe in totemic ceremonies, it was only men of this clan who exhibited it or pantomimed its use. In secular life the axe could be made by any man and used by all; but in the sacred realm of the totems it belonged exclusively to the Sunlit Cloud Iguana people.

Supporting those aspects of cultural behavior which we have called technology and conduct is a third area of culture, including ideas, sentiments, and values. These are most difficult to deal with, for they are latent and covert or even unconscious and must be deduced from overt actions and language or other communicating behavior. In this aspect of the culture lies the "meaning" of the stone axe, its significance to the Yir Yoront and to their cultural way of life. The ideal conception of the axe, the knowledge of how to produce it (apart from the purely muscular habits used in its production) are part of the Yir Yoront adult masculine role, just as ideas regarding its technical use are included in the feminine role. These technical ideas constitute a kind of "science" regarding the axe which may be more important in relation to behavioral change than are the neurophysiological patterns drilled into the body by years of practice. Similarly there are normative ideas regarding the part played by the axe in conduct which constitute a kind of "morality" of the axe, and which again may be more important than the overt habits of social interaction in determining the role of the axe in social relationships. More than ideas regarding technology, ideas regarding conduct are likely to be closely associated, or "charged," with sentiment or value. Ideas and sentiments help guide and inform overt behavior; in turn, overt behavior helps support and validate ideas and sentiments.

The stone axe was an important symbol of masculinity among the Yir Yoront (just as pants or pipes are among ourselves). By a complicated

set of ideas which we would label "ownership" the axe was defined as "belonging" to males. Everyone in the society (except untrained infants) accepted these ideas. Similarly spears, spear throwers, and fire-making sticks were associated with males, were owned only by them, and were symbols of masculinity. But the masculine values represented by the stone axe were constantly being impressed on all members of society by the fact that non-males had to use the axe and had to go to males for it, whereas they never borrowed other masculine artifacts. Thus, the axe stood for an important theme that ran all through Yir Yoront culture: the superiority and rightful dominance of the male, and the greater value of his concerns and of all things associated with him. We should call this androcentrism rather than patriarchy, or paternal rule. It is the recognition by all that the values of the man (*andros*) take precedence over feminine values, an idea backed by very strong sentiments among the Yir Yoront. Since the axe had to be borrowed also by the younger from the older, it also represented the prestige of age, another important theme running all through Yir Yoront behavior.

Important for an understanding of the Yir Yoront culture is a system of ideas, which may be called their totemic ideology. A fundamental belief of the aboriginal divided time into two great epochs, a distant and sacred period at the beginning of the world, when the earth was peopled by mildly marvelous ancestral beings or culture heroes who in a special sense are the forebears of the clans; and a second period, when the old was succeeded by a new order that includes the present. Originally there was no anticipation of another era supplanting the present; the future would simply be an eternal continuation and reproduction of the present, which itself had remained unchanged since the epochal revolution of ancestral times.

The mythical sacred world of the ancestors with which time began turns out on investigation to be a detailed reproduction of the present aboriginal world of nature, man, and culture altered by phantasy. In short, the idea system expressed in the mythology regarding the ancestral epoch was directly derived from Yir Yoront behavior patterns—normal and abnormal, actual and ideal, conscious and unconscious. The important thing to note, however, is that the native believed it was just the other way around, that the present world, as a natural and cultural environment, was and should be simply a detailed reproduction of the world of the ancestors. He believed that the entire universe "is now as it was in the beginning" when it was established and left by the ancestors. The ordinary cultural life of the ancestors became the daily life of the Yir Yoront camps, and the extraordinary life of the ancestors remained extant in the recurring symbolic pantomimes and paraphernalia found only in the most sacred atmosphere of the totemic rites.

Such beliefs, accordingly, opened up the way for ideas of what *should be* (because it supposedly *was*) to influence or help determine what actually *is*. Dog-chases-iguana-up-a-tree-and-barks-at-him-all-night had that and other names because, so he believed, his ancestral alter ego had these same names; he was a member of the Sunlit Cloud Iguana clan because his ancestor was; he was associated with particular countries and totems of this same ancestor; during an initiation he played the role of a dog and symbolically attacked and killed certain members of other clans because his ancestor (conveniently either anthropomorphic or kynomorphic) really did the same to the ancestral alter egos of these men; and he would avoid his mother-in-law, joke with a distant mother's brother, and make spears in a certain way because his and other people's ancestors did these things. His behavior in these rather than in other ways was outlined for him, and to that extent determined, by a set of ideas concerning the past and the relation of the present to the past.

But when we are informed that Dog-chases . . . had two wives from the Spear Black Duck clan and one from the Native Companion clan with such and such names, one of them being blind; that he had four children with such and such names; that he had a broken wrist and was left-handed, all because his ancestor had exactly these same attributes, then we know (though he apparently did not) that the present has influenced the past, that the mythical world has been somewhat adjusted to meet the exigencies and accidents of the inescapably real present.

There was thus in Yir Yoront ideology a nice balance in which the mythical world was adjusted in part to the real world, the real world in part to the ideal preexisting mythical world, the adjustments occurring to maintain a fundamental tenet of native faith that the present must be a mirror of the past. Thus, the stone axe in all its aspects, uses, and associations was integrated into the context of Yir Yoront technology and conduct because a myth, a set of ideas, had put it there.

ANALYSIS

The introduction of the steel axe indiscriminately and in large numbers into the Yir Yoront technology was only one of many changes occurring at the same time. It is therefore impossible to factor out all the results of this single innovation alone. Nevertheless, a number of specific effects of the change from stone axes to steel axes may be noted; and the steel axe may be used as an epitome of the European goods and implements received by the aboriginals in increasing quantity and of their general influence on the native culture. The use of the steel axe to illustrate such influences would seem to be justified, for it was one of the first European artifacts to be adopted for regular use by the Yir Yoront; and the axe, whether of stone or steel, was clearly one of the most important items of cultural equipment they possessed.

The shift from stone to steel axes provided no major technological difficulties. While the aboriginals themselves could not manufacture steel axe heads, a steady supply from outside continued; and broken wooden axe handles could easily be replaced from bush timbers with aboriginal tools. Among the Yir Yoront the new axe never acquired all the uses it had on mission or cattle stations (carpentry work, pounding tent pegs, use as a hammer, and so on); and, indeed, it was used for little more than the stone axe had been, so that it had no practical effect in improving the native standard of living. It did some jobs better, and could be used longer without breakage; and these factors were sufficient to make it of value to the native. But the assumption of the white man (based in part on a realization that a shift from steel to stone axe in his case would be a definite regression) that his axe was much more efficient, that its use would save time, and that it therefore represented technical "progress" toward goals which he had set for the native was hardly borne out in aboriginal practice. Any leisure time the Yir Yoront might gain by using steel axes or other western tools was invested, not in "improving the conditions of life," and certainly not in developing aesthetic activities, but in sleep, an art they had thoroughly mastered.

Having acquired an axe head through regular trading partners of whom he knew what to expect, a man wanting a stone axe was then dependent solely upon a known and an adequate nature and upon his own skills or easily acquired techniques. A man wanting a steel axe, however, was in no such self-reliant position. While he might acquire one through trade, he now had the new alternative of dispensing with technological behavior in relation with a predictable nature and conduct in relation with a predictable trading partner and of turning instead to conduct alone in relation with a highly erratic missionary. If he attended one of the mission festivals when steel axes were handed out as gifts, he might receive one simply by chance or if he had happened somehow to impress upon the mission staff that he was one of the "better" bush aboriginals (their definition of "better" being quite different from that of his bush fellows). Or he might—but again almost by pure chance—be given some brief job in connection with the mission which would enable him to earn a steel axe. In either case, for older men a preference for the steel axe helped create a situation of dependence in place of a situation of self-reliance and a behavior shift from situations in technology or conduct which were well structured or defined to situations in conduct alone which were ill defined. It was particularly the older ones among the men, whose earlier experience or knowledge of the white man's harshness in any event made them suspicious, who would avoid having any relations with the mission at all, and who thus excluded themselves from acquiring steel axes directly from that source.

The steel axe was the root of psychological stress among the Yir Yoront even more significantly in other aspects of social relations. This was the result of new factors which the missionary considered all to the good: the simple numerical increase in axes per capita as a result of mission distribution; and distribution from the mission directly to younger men, women, and even children. By winning the favor of the mission staff, a woman might be given a steel axe. This was clearly intended to be hers. The situation was quite different from that involved in borrowing an axe from a male relative, with the result that a woman called such an axe "my" steel axe, a possessive form she never used for a stone axe. (Lexically, the steel axe was differentiated from the stone by an adjectival suffix signifying "metal," the element "axe" remaining identical.) Further-

more, young men or even boys might also obtain steel axes directly from the mission. A result was that older men no longer had a complete monopoly of all the axes in the bush community. Indeed, an old man might have only a stone axe, while his wives and sons had steel axes which they considered their own and which he might even desire to borrow. All this led to a revolutionary confusion of sex, age, and kinship roles, with a major gain in independence and loss of subordination on the part of those able now to acquire steel axes when they had been unable to possess stone axes before.

The trading partner relationship was also affected by the new situation. A Yir Yoront might have a trading partner in a tribe to the south whom he defined as a younger brother, and on whom as an older brother he would therefore have an edge. But if the partner were in contact with the mission or had other easier access to steel axes, his subordination to his bush colleague was obviously decreased. Indeed, under the new dispensation he might prefer to give his axe to a bush "sweetheart" in return for favors or otherwise dispose of it outside regular trade channels, since many steel axes were so distributed between natives in new ways. Among other things, this took some of the excitement away from the fiesta-like tribal gatherings centering around initiations during the dry season. These had traditionally been the climactic annual occasions for exchanges between trading partners, when a man might seek to acquire a whole year's supply of stone axe heads. Now he might find himself prostituting his wife to almost total strangers in return for steel axes or other white men's goods. With trading partnerships weakened, there was less reason to attend the fiestas, and less fun for those who did. A decline in one of the important social activities which had symbolized these great gatherings created a lessening of interest in the other social aspects of these events.

Not only did an increase in steel axes and their distribution to women change the character of the relations between individual and individual, the paired relationships that have been noted, but a new type of relationship, hitherto practically unknown among the Yir Yoront, was created in their axe-acquiring conduct with whites. In the aboriginal society there were almost no occasions outside the immediate family when one individual would initiate action to several people at once. For in any average group, while a person in accordance with the kinship system might be superordinate to several people to whom he could suggest or command action, at the same time he was also subordinate to several others, in relation with whom such behavior would be tabu. There was thus no over-all chieftainship or authoritarian leadership of any kind. Such complicated operations as grass-burning, animal drives, or totemic ceremonies could be carried out smoothly because each person knew his roles both in technology and conduct.

On both mission and cattle stations, however, the whites imposed upon the aboriginals their conception of leadership roles, with one person in a controlling relationship with a subordinate group. Aboriginals called together to receive gifts, including axes, at a mission Christmas party found themselves facing one or two whites who sought to control their behavior for the occasion, who disregarded the age, sex, and kinship variables among them of which they were so conscious, and who considered them all at one subordinate level. Or the white might impose similar patterns on a working party. (But if he placed an aboriginal in charge of a mixed group of post hole diggers, for example, half of the group, those subordinate to the "boss," would work while the other half, who were superordinate to him, would sleep.) The steel axe, together, of course, with other European goods, came to symbolize for the aboriginal this new and uncomfortable form of social organization, the leader-group relationship.

The most disturbing effects of the steel axe, operating in conjunction with other elements also being introduced from the white man's several subcultures, developed in the realm of traditional ideas, sentiments, and values. These were undermined at a rapidly mounting rate, without new conceptions being defined to replace them. The result was a mental and moral void which foreshadowed the collapse and destruction of all Yir Yoront culture, if not, indeed, the extinction of the biological group itself.

From what has been said it should be clear how changes in overt behavior, in technology and conduct, weakened the values inherent in a reliance on nature, in androcentrism or the prestige of masculinity, in age prestige, and in the various kinship relations. A scene was set in which a wife or young son, his initiation perhaps not even yet completed, need no longer bow to the husband or father, who was left confused and insecure as he asked to borrow a steel axe from them. For the woman and boy

the steel axe helped establish a new degree of freedom which was accepted readily as an escape from the unconscious stress of the old patterns, but which left them also confused and insecure. Ownership became less well defined, so that stealing and trespass were introduced into technology and conduct. Some of the excitement surrounding the great ceremonies evaporated, so that the only fiestas the people had became less festive, less interesting. Indeed, life itself became less interesting, although this did not lead the Yir Yoront to invent suicide, a concept foreign to them.

The whole process may be most specifically illustrated in terms of the totemic system, and this will also illustrate the significant role which a system of ideas, in this case a totemic ideology, may play in the breakdown of a culture.

In the first place, under pre-European aboriginal conditions in which the native culture has become adjusted to a relatively stable environment in which there can occur few, if any, unheard of or catastrophic crises, it is clear that the totemic system must serve very effectively to inhibit radical cultural changes. The closed system of totemic ideas, explaining and categorizing a well-known universe as it was fixed at the beginning of time, presents a considerable obstacle to the adoption of new or the dropping of old culture traits. The obstacle is not insurmountable and the system allows for the minor variations which occur about the norms of daily life, but the inception of major changes cannot easily take place.

Among the bush Yir Yoront the only means of water transport is a light wood log, to which they cling in their constant swimming of rivers, salt creeks, and tidal inlets. These natives know that forty-five miles north of them are tribes who have a bark canoe. They know these northern tribes can thus fish from midstream or out at sea, instead of clinging to the river banks and beaches, and can cross coastal waters infested with crocodiles, sharks, sting rays, and Portuguese-men-of-war without the recurring mortality, pain, or anxiety to which they themselves are constantly subjected. They know they lack any magic to do for them what the canoe could do. They know the materials of which the canoe is made are present in their own environment. But they also know, as they say, that their own mythical ancestors lacked the canoe, and therefore they lack it, while they assume that the canoe was part of the ancestral universe of the northern tribes. For them, then, the adoption of the canoe would not be simply a matter of learning a number of new behavioral skills for its manufacture and use. The adoption would require at the same time a much more difficult procedure, the acceptance by the entire society of a myth, either locally developed or borrowed, which would explain the presence of the canoe, associate it with some one or more of the several hundred mythical ancestors (and how decide which?), and thus establish it as an accepted totem of one of the clans ready to be used by the whole community. The Yir Yoront have not made this adjustment, and in this case we can only say that ideas have for the time being at least won out over very real pressures for technological change. In the elaborateness and explicitness of the totemic ideologies we seem to have one explanation for the notorious stability of Australian cultures under aboriginal conditions, an explanation which gives due weight to the importance of ideas in determining human behavior.

At a later stage of the contact situation, as has been indicated, phenomena unaccounted for by the totemic ideological system began to appear with regularity and frequency and remain within the range of native experience. Accordingly, they cannot be ignored (as the "Battle of the Mitchell River" was apparently ignored), and an attempt is made to assimilate them and account for them along the lines of principles inherent in the ideology. The bush Yir Yoront of the mid-1930's represent this stage of the acculturation process. Still trying to maintain their aboriginal definition of the situation, they accept European artifacts and behavior patterns, but fit them into their totemic system, assigning them as totems to various clans on a par with original totems. There is an attempt to have the myth-making process keep up with these cultural changes so that the idea system can continue to support the rest of the culture. But analysis of overt behavior, of dreams, and of some of the new myths indicates that this arrangement is not entirely satisfactory; that the native clings to his totemic system with intellectual loyalty, lacking any substitute ideology; but that associated sentiments and values are weakened. His attitudes toward his own and toward European culture are found to be highly ambivalent.

All ghosts are totems of the Head-to-the-East Corpse clan. They are thought of as white, and are, of course, closely associated with death. The white man, too, is white and was closely associated with death, so that he and all things pertaining to him are naturally assigned to the Corpse clan as totems.

The steel axe, as a totem, was thus associated with the Corpse clan. But it is an "axe," and is clearly linked with the stone axe, which is a totem of the Sunlit Cloud Iguana clan. Moreover, the steel axe, like most European goods, has no distinctive origin myth, nor are mythical ancestors associated with it. Can anyone, sitting of an afternoon in the shade of a ti tree, create a myth to resolve this confusion? No one has, and the horrid suspicion arises that perhaps the origin myths are wrong, which took into account so little of this vast new universe of the white man. The steel axe, shifting hopelessly between one clan and the other, is not only replacing the stone axe physically, but is hacking at the supports of the entire cultural system.

The aboriginals to the south of the Yir Yoront have clearly passed beyond this stage. They are engulfed by European culture, in this area by either the mission or cattle station subcultures, or for some natives a baffling, paradoxical combination of both incongruent varieties. The totemic ideology can no longer support the inrushing mass of foreign culture traits and the myth-making process in its native form breaks down completely. Both intellectually and emotionally a saturation point is reached, so that the myriad new traits which can neither be ignored nor any longer assimilated simply force the aboriginal to abandon his totemic system. With the collapse of this system of ideas, which is so closely related with so many other aspects of the native culture, there follows an appallingly sudden and complete cultural disintegration and a demoralization of the individual such as has seldom been recorded for areas other than Australia. Without the support of a system of ideas well devised to provide cultural stability in a stable environment but admittedly too rigid for the new realities pressing in from outside, native behavior and native sentiments and values are simply dead. Apathy reigns. The aboriginal has passed beyond the reach of any outsider who might wish to do him well or ill.

Returning from the broken natives huddled on cattle stations or on the fringes of frontier towns to the ambivalent but still lively aboriginals settled on the Mitchell River mission, we note one further devious result of the introduction of European artifacts. During a wet season stay at the mission, the anthropologist discovered that his supply of tooth paste was being depleted at an alarming rate. Investigation showed that it was being taken by old men for use in a new tooth paste cult. Old materials of magic having failed, new materials were being tried out in a malevolent magic directed toward the mission staff and some of the younger aboriginal men. Old males, largely ignored by the missionaries, were seeking to regain some of their lost power and prestige. This mild aggression proved hardly effective, but perhaps only because confidence in any kind of magic on the mission was by this time at a low ebb.

For the Yir Yoront still in the bush a time could be predicted when personal deprivation and frustration in a confused culture would produce an overload of anxiety. The mythical past of the to-temic ancestors would disappear as a guarantee of a present of which the future was supposed to be a stable continuation. Without the past, the present would be meaningless and the future unstructured and uncertain. Insecurities would be inevitable. Reaction to this stress might be some form of symbolic aggression, or withdrawal and apathy, or some more realistic approach. In such a situation the missionary with understanding of the processes going on about him would find his opportunity to introduce religion and to help create the constitution of a new cultural universe.

MEDICINE

Dealing with his experience in trying to introduce "modern" medicine into an Indian village, Carstairs recounts many instances where persons acting in terms of two different cultural systems (that of modern medicine and that of an indigenous system) interpret a given objective event in very different ways. As we have seen in many of the readings presented thus far, there is no "single" reality to which persons coming from divergent cultural systems are responding, especially in such life-threatening matters as illness and impending death. Rather, the cultural environment of a person influences his perceptions and responses; the capacity for, and act of, symbolization creates worlds that only partly overlap, with many gaps being left between these realms of meaning. Such cultural orientations toward events in nature define not only the nature of life and death, but also many areas of social expectation in human relationships, as illustrated in this case by incidents in which Carstairs interprets his inability to cure as a failure, while the Indian villagers, on the contrary, define his actions in a different value framework. Or take the nature of beliefs about the body and its functioning (recall the readings in Part I); how different these are between the Western doctor and the Indian villager—and each is shaped by a cultural system of ideas and values. In all, Carstair's experiences speak to the profound role that belief systems (what are being called here "cultural systems") have in governing daily behavior.

MEDICINE AND FAITH IN RURAL RAJASTHAN (Continued)

G. MORRIS CARSTAIRS

THE SITUATION

Village Life in Rajasthan

In 1950 and 1951 I had the opportunity to spend

Reprinted with permission. From G. Morris Carstairs, "Medicine and Faith in Rural Rajasthan," in *Health, Culture, and Community*, ed. Benjamin D. Paul, © 1955 by Russell Sage Foundation, Publishers, N.Y., pp. 109–34.

a number of months in two different villages in Rajasthan, where until recently the maharajahs ruled with medieval splendor and unrestrained autocracy. It is a lovely country, although harsh to the eye like the Bad Lands of Wyoming, and the people are handsome in their bearing and in their bright peasant costumes; but still, I was rather disappointed at first that my sociological research should be carried out here. I had hoped to go and live among really primitive peoples—Sea Dayaks, perhaps, or Melanesians—whereas to my mind the people of Rajasthan were not at all primitive.

To begin with, I had been brought up among them. My earliest memories were of playing field hockey, marbles, and other local games with a pack of little Hindu boys; of riding through dusty villages on my shaggy country-bred pony; and of special occasions when we toured the countryside by bullock-cart, living under canvas. My father was a missionary, and there was nothing he liked better than these excursions away from the beaten track. At dusk or before sunrise he and I would scour the surrounding jungle for quail or duck or partridge for our next day's dinner. I well remember one such occasion when we saw from our bullock-cart a cavalcade of Rajput horsemen, lance in hand, galloping in chase of a wild boar. That night we camped beside the mud-walled fortress of the chief who had led the hunt and listened to his minstrels extemporizing songs in honor of the day's sport.

The Rajputs are far from being the only inhabitants of this region, but they do constitute its aristocracy and set standards of valor, self-respect, and pride of bearing to which many of the lowlier castes also aspire. The great historian of Rajasthan, Colonel James Tod (who was himself a Scot) was the first of many who have pointed out similarities between the clans of Scotland and the 36 principal lineages of the Rajputs, and in my first experience of life in a Rajput village I had many occasions to remember this. The village is called Sujarupa, and it is situated on the fringe of the jungle-covered slopes of the Aravli Mountains, in the extreme north of Udaipur State.

Sujarupa is a compact little hamlet of stone-walled cottages, each surrounded by a thorn fence that serves as a corral for the family herd of goats and one or two heads of cattle. The people are all farmers, cultivating fields that they or their immediate forebears have cleared from the jungle. Men and women work hard in these fields, the women covering their faces with a head cloth if a stranger approaches. The children work too; from the age of eight or nine they learn to drive the village flocks through the dry foothills. Like David, each carries a sling and practices throwing jagged stones that roar as they fly through the air, to scare off jackals, hyenas, and an occasional wolf. It is a hard-working community, accustomed to a minimum of comfort;

and yet the people are usually sure of a meal twice a day. Except for years in which the rains fail—and this happens on an average every fourth year in Rajasthan—they are able to raise enough wheat to sell some for cash.

Nearly everything in the village is homemade. The plows and sickles that the villagers use are manufactured by artisans in the nearest large village, as are their cooking pots, their shoes, and their clothes. Their houses and their wells are made with their own hands. They are all Hindus, and on feast days some of them may visit a distant temple of Mahadev or Sri Krishna, but throughout the year they are more concerned with the local gods whom they regard as intermediaries between them and the remote Great Gods whom the Brahmans worship. It took me many weeks to distinguish the numerous stones and trees that were severally consecrated to these gods.

Almost all the farmers in Sujarupa, as well as those of the surrounding district, are Rawat Rajputs; and when we sat and talked together, or walked through their fields, or set off in a party to visit the nearest small township, I often thought how similar they were in many ways to the only other farming community that I knew at all well— my own kinsfolk, living in the Western Highlands of Scotland. Sometimes I used to think of those small clusters of houses, the hamlets of Clachan or Glenbreckrie, and wonder how those Highland farmers would react if a stranger with a different colored skin were to settle among them for a few months and presume to analyze their way of life. It was a profoundly discouraging reflection.

What Prognosis Meant to the Villagers

Fortunately, the farmers of Sujarupa were comparatively forthcoming. The very day after I had pitched my tent on some level ground near the village, a young man called Govind Singh came to summon me to his house. He had heard that I was a "Daktar Sahib" and he begged me to do something for his young wife, who was possessed by a devil and in great pain.

I found myself bitterly regretting the shortcomings of my training at Edinburgh University, which was all too light on exorcism; but bearing my stethoscope like a talisman, I followed him to his hut. Inside, a girl of seventeen was rolling about on the floor, wailing loudly. I examined her nervously at first but with more confidence as it dawned on me what was going on; and then I told Govind Singh that hers was a very healthy little devil, as he would soon see for himself. In fact, her first baby was born that evening, a lively boy. Govind Singh himself came to my tent with a present of milk and rich pudding to tell me the news. Afterward, he pretended that he had known all along what was the matter: "But these young women, you know, Sahib, they get frightened over nothing."

From that moment the people of Sujarupa were very cordial toward me. They said it must be drafty and uncomfortable out there in the tent, which was true, and invited me to live in the large *paul* or guestroom of their hamlet; and I received numerous requests to treat their children for sore eyes and their old people for chronic bronchitis. I was agreeably surprised at this welcome, but a little puzzled. It was only much later that I realized that although I had done nothing for the young mother, I had spoken the magic words: "She will be all right. She will have a healthy baby." And events had proved me right. In their opinion, pronouncing a prognosis is one of the most important functions of a healer, but with this difference: when their healers say, "He will recover," they are not expressing a personal opinion but are speaking with the authority of the supernatural power, which is the real agent of their cure.

Curers and Treatment in Sujarupa

Throughout my five months' stay in Sujarupa, I carried on a small and intermittent dispensary practice; but I soon realized that my remedies were only one of several sorts of healing, and by no means the most popular. My village friends were not narrow-minded; they were willing to give my sort of medicine a trial, but they did expect immediate results. This did not mean that they always demanded immediate results from their own forms of cure—but that was a different matter, because they already had faith in these, and so once the condition was diagnosed and the prescription given, they felt assured that the correct steps had been taken and recovery was bound to follow. My sort of medicine carried no such aura of conviction, and therefore it was required to justify itself dramatically, and without delay.

I was naturally curious to hear about my rival practitioners, and to see their work; and I did not have long to wait. Within a week of my settling in Sujarupa village, my neighbors called me out one

night to attend an open-air celebration of worship. A throng of men and boys sat around a great log fire beside a hilltop shrine and sang the praises of the god of that place, one Kagal-Devji, a black snake-god. Sometime after midnight, when the singing had worked up to a high pitch of excitement, an elderly man sitting at the side of the fire gave a loud cry and began to dance and shake convulsively. It was whispered in my ear: "Look, he's begun to 'play.' The breath of Devji has come into him." Then the possessed individual, who was the priest of the shrine, ran indoors and saluted the idols; he then appeared in front of us still twitching and gasping for breath and called out a number of rather cryptic prophecies about the coming year. After this he sat trembling before the image, and people came before him one by one. They poured out small offerings of grain and begged the god to tell them the cause of their own, or their children's, or their cattle's illness; and what they must do to be well.

At this stage I knew too little of the local dialect to understand what was going on; one or other of my new friends had to keep prompting me in Hindustani. Several weeks later, however, I went with two families of Sujarupa to attend the weekly "possession" at a shrine which lay some seven miles off in the jungle. This was the shrine of Danaji, a local demon-god, who had acquired a special fame as a healer of all sorts of ills. It was generally conceded that it was better to go instead to Devji if one were bitten by a snake (cobras and kraits being the common local venomous varieties) because after all he was a snake-god himself. In such an emergency, the priest would invariably become possessed and then throw himself upon the patient, noisily sucking at the wound and supposedly drawing out the poison. For all other troubles, however, Danaji was regarded as the more reliable authority.

The importance of Danaji was brought home to me by an event in the hut next to the one which I came to occupy, in Sujarupa. This was the home of Nol Singh, his wife, and two sons, one of whom was a sturdy boy of twelve years, the other a sickly baby named Lum Singh. The father had served in the Indian Army, and hence was one of the three men in the village who had traveled far afield and who were literate. In keeping with his knowledge of the world, he professed to have great faith in "Sahibs' medicines" and called me in twice to attend to Lum Singh, first for acute conjunctivitis and next for dysentery. But Lum Singh fell sick again, and this time his father did not consult me but went to Danaji. Some days later, when there was a small waning moon, I saw Nol Singh enter the village carrying an all-black goat, which he had bought.

Two nights later, at the blackest of the moonless period, he came to ask for the loan of my sharp *kukri* knife. I was now sure that some curative rite was in progress, but he was very reluctant to talk about it, promising to tell me everything in due course. Next day he returned the knife and explained that the Danaji had diagnosed that a witch was eating Lum Singh's liver. In order to appease her, a black goat had to be killed at midnight, five men each putting a hand to the knife, and then the head and entrails were to be set in a broken pot at a place where three paths crossed. This was a striking demonstration of the parallels between folk beliefs about witchcraft in medieval Europe— the goat, the midnight sacrifice, the offering in the broken pot, and the place where three paths cross all are to be found in accounts of European witchcraft—but it had a tragic sequel.

Late one night a few days after the sacrifice, Nol Singh called me to his house. He was very anxious about his child's health, and with good reason, for I found him in a state of profound toxemia, suffering from diphtheria. There was nothing in my box of medicines that could meet the case, but I knew there was a government dispensary and a doctor in the large village a few miles off. So I set off by bicycle in the starlight and woke up the doctor. Unfortunately, he had no anti-diphtheritic serum in his stock, not even any penicillin. I cycled back and gave the child an injection of atropine, simply in order to let the distracted parents feel that something was being done. The boy died in a few hours, and I went with all the men of the village to his hurried burial, piling thorn branches and stones over the grave so that the hyenas could not dig up the body. Then we all went to bathe and wash our clothes at the well, to cleanse ourselves of the pollution of contact with death.

I thought that perhaps this time I would be blamed, because I had given Lum Singh an injection and he had shortly died; but I was wrong. Throughout the rest of my stay I had to listen again and again to Nol Singh's graphic account of my heroic ride on his son's behalf, braving countless ghosts, and twice crossing a stretch of the road

which was known to be frequented by leopards. At the time, I was not aware that there were leopards about; and I am sure that I would not have enjoyed my ride so well had I known. In fact, neither I nor the Danaji was blamed. After the first outburst of grief, the family repeated the traditional formula: it was his fate; his day had come; he was a loan from God, to whom he had returned.

After this, I was curious to see the celebrated priest of Danaji at work. Accordingly, one Sunday night when two families of the village announced that they were going to his shrine to consult the oracle, I set out with them. The moon was big once more, and we enjoyed our seven-mile walk under the brilliant Indian night sky. The shrine was in an out-of-the-way little valley, and from some distance off we could see the flickering glow of a fire, and then as we drew nearer we could hear occasional loud cries from the priest, who was already in a state of possession. We removed our shoes and laid aside our swords and staves a little way from the sacred place, where many other visitors had already done the same, and then sat near the priest, who crouched, trembling violently, and now and again gave a sudden wild shout. The Spirit had come to him strongly this night.

There was something particularly dramatic in the way that he summoned certain of his supplicants. He would interrupt the series of patients who came before him with a cry: "A man and a woman of Kachabli," or "Three brothers from Taragarh!" and these would press forward from the waiting crowd. One of his summonses was for "Two men from Mandawar road!" and my companion of the walk nudged me, saying, "That means us, Sahib; we came by that road." He sat before the priest first and consulted him about his little boy, whom the Danaji had saved from witchcraft. He was told to perform certain offerings, and then to carry the child three times around the shrine. Then it was my turn. The priest gave me a pinch of grain. "How many?" he said. "Four grains." He gave me one more, to bring it up to the auspicious number, looked to the shrine for inspiration, and then shouted out his prophecies: "The British will return to rule again. You will get a promotion—a new post, with great power and much pay. When this happens, come back and honor the Danaji." With this he gave me a small dried lemon, telling me to guard it carefully. Then he continued to attend a series of sick people and anxious parents, presenting their whimpering children for his advice. I watched about 30 of these consultations and noted his remedies, which all involved soliciting the help of the Danaji and other gods.

Late in the night the session came to an end. The priest raised his arms with a loud cry, and then became an ordinary villager once more as the Spirit left him. He came to talk with us, professing to recognize me for the first time. "I saw you once before, Sahib," he said. "Don't you remember I was lying sick in the government hospital, and you came and examined my chest with those tubes and said, 'It is all right; you will get well.' "

I did remember having seen him a month or so before, when he was acutely ill with pneumonia. Again I was reminded of the magic power ascribed to a confident prognosis. I replied, "You and I do the same work, helping the sick get well." But the priest replied at once, "It is not I, Sahib; God alone can do that,"—and I was reminded, as every practitioner must often be reminded, that our individual skill is only one part of the complex business of healing.

Village Concepts of Illness

It might be argued, by those who are accustomed to our pragmatic tests of the efficacy of treatment, that surely these magic prophecies must become discredited over and over again, and in time lose their efficacy. The answer to this is that these villagers do not, as we tend to do, believe that one can influence the course of events simply by the exercise of a technical skill. To them, the Supernatural is everywhere immanent, and events can be influenced only by enlisting supernatural aid. They naturally assume that there is a magic quality in the prescriptions of western medicine as well; and this is one reason why the administration of intramuscular injections, with its ritual of aseptic precautions and the dramatic quality of the act of acupuncture, is especially highly valued among those who have had some contact with allopathic doctors.

There was one young man in Sujarupa who, when he came home on leave from his work as a laborer in the distant city of Ahmedabad, used to beg me to give him just one very powerful "objection" in order to make him strong. He knew only two or three words of English, and this was one of them. I remember him particularly because he was

a singularly robust man, and I used to tease him when he insisted that he felt weak, as though he were wasting away. During my few months' practice in this region, I frequently encountered patients who simply complained of weakness; and my head was so filled with anticipation of vitamin deficiency, of malnutrition, chronic malaria, dysentery, anemia, tuberculosis, and so on, that I sought and fancied that I had found one or another of these conditions in every case. It was not until the following year, in Delwara village, that I came to realize the true significance of this complaint.

In the meantime I gradually widened my circle of acquaintances in the nearby hamlets and encouraged some of the divinely inspired healers to share some of their secrets with me. One old man, who had recovered from an acute attack of dysentery after taking a course of sulfa drugs which I had sent him, was kind enough to explain to me how he could tell that a sick person was possessed by a witch or a demon, by felling his pulse. What the old man actually did was to lay his forefinger gently across the patient's wrist and wait to see whether he could feel a tremor in one of the flexor tendons of the fingers. There was, however, no consistency in his interpretation of the sign; it served, rather, as the cue for an immediate intuition, as a clairvoyant will hold an object belonging to an absent person and then claim to have a direct awareness of details of his appearance and personality. The most important aspect of this procedure is that the patient and all the onlookers know what the healer expects to find. If there is deception, to our way of thinking, it is one in which they all participate; and one in which the western doctor can find himself unwittingly caught up. We take the act of feeling the pulse so much for granted that we can easily overlook the fact that this may have a quite different significance to the patient and to us.

Every practitioner is familiar with the misunderstandings that so readily occur in everyday practice. Patients and relatives, when keyed up with anxious fears, often place a wrong interpretation on their physician's smallest gesture, or his misheard remark. This is naturally still more likely to happen when patient and physician approach the illness with totally dissimilar systems of ideas. It is, of course, not only oriental peoples who have a non-scientific conception of their own bodily processes; one can find abundant instances much nearer home.

Elementary instruction in the physiology of reproduction is now recognized to be an essential part of prenatal care; and the experienced practitioner learns to elicit from his patients something of their own (often fantastic) beliefs about what is happening inside them to make them feel ill. Where the general level of formal education is low, an understanding of physiology can only grow slowly, in relation to what most intimately concerns the health of each particular community. For example, there are already many parts of India where the relationship between malaria, mosquitoes, and quinine has become part of everyday knowledge, whereas in less heavily endemic areas the onset of a malarial rigor is still believed to be the possession of the patient's body by a god. There is no propaganda agent so effective as a demonstrable cure; but it may take many years before conservative villagers are convinced that it is the western drug which has in fact effected the cure.

I remember one night when I was working with a neighbor (one of the priests of Devji) by the light of my pressure-lantern. We were interrupted by a young farmer who lived about a mile and a half away on the fringe of the jungle. He said that his wife was struck by a fierce witch, or so it seemed to him, and he came to ask the priest for help. They both invited me to accompany them, and so we set off in single file along a series of field paths. When we approached the house, we could hear loud moans and shrieks. The young woman crouched in the yard, giving full expression to the pain and terror she was suffering. A string bed was drawn forward to serve as a seat for the priest and myself, and then there followed a polite altercation: he urged me to attend to the patient, while I insisted that it was his help the family desired. Accordingly, he felt her pulse and confirmed the husband's diagnosis, then spoke a charm over a small brass pot of water and gave the woman a few drops of this sanctified water to drink. The pot was then placed on the roof-top, so that no one's shadow might fall across it and thus impair its virtue.

As soon as this was done, I was told that now it was my turn. With some difficulty, I managed to persuade the patient to calm down long enough to allow her to explain that she suffered from a severe pain in the chest, which had begun the day before;

now it was much more severe, and she felt sure that her destruction was imminent. At the thought, she began to cry out once more. In the presence of her husband and strangers, it was impossible for her to unveil her face, but she was persuaded to reveal the side of her chest, where I found vesicles of herpes zoster. The husband led me back to Sujarupa, and I entrusted him with codeine tablets and with spirit for local application. He returned the next day for more, saying that his wife was very much better already.

In that instance everything was done so politely and with the exchange of so many flattering speeches that both the priest and I felt assured that we had made the significant contribution to the patient's recovery. The same was not the case, however, with another patient to whom I was summoned a few nights later. He was a merchant from a large village 20 miles away and lay on the bullock-cart on which he had made the journey. I examined him on the roadside by the light of my lantern and found him very ill indeed. He had had typhoid fever six weeks previously and now his heart was grossly enlarged and his pulse very rapid. On auscultation I could hear a gallop rhythm. He was extremely agitated and begged me to save his life. I felt doubtful of my ability to do this but encouraged him as best I could, and gave a heroic dose of digitalis. The cart took him to the nearest large village, where he stayed at a kinsman's house, and there I visited him daily. For the first two days he still looked and felt acutely ill, and his pulse did not fall below 120/minute; but on the third day there was a remarkable change. The pulse was 96, the patient sat up and talked cheerfully, and for the first time showed some desire to eat. I wondered if this was attributable to my therapy, and soon found that it was not. What he had omitted to tell me until then was the reason for his state of panic: he had become convinced that some enemy had caused fatal sorcery to be placed on him. Against this belief, neither my medicine nor my reassurances had been effective. He knew that Sahibs tend to make light of sorcery, and so he had not liked to discuss it with me. Instead, he had obtained the services of a local man who possessed a powerful charm, and on the previous night this man had brought it into play with a dramatic performance, at the end of which he branded the back of the patient's neck with a red-hot iron. This drove out the evil spell; and it was the relief that the patient experienced at his feeling of escape from mortal danger which had brought his pulse-rate down.

What Is Expected of a Healer

This case, and many others of my village cases, served to impress upon me that the expectation of my patients here was different from that to which I had been accustomed. There was not the same attribution of personal responsibility to the physician for the success or failure of his treatment, because a sovereign fatalism determined the patients' attitude to events; whatever happened was coming to one anyway. What was expected from the healer was reassurance. So long as the illness was nameless, patients felt desperately afraid, but once its magic origin had been defined and the appropriate measures taken, they could face the outcome calmly. The parallel with our own clinical experience is obvious.

The few months I had spent in Sujarupa gave me a little insight into local preconceptions about sickness and cure, and this proved invaluable next year when my wife and I made a ten months' stay in the larger, more sophisticated village of Delwara, which lay only 18 miles from Udaipur, the capital and indeed the only large town of this state. Delwara was almost a small town in itself, having 2,500 inhabitants and a row of merchants' shops in its central street. Unlike Sujarupa, but like most other large villages in India, it included households belonging to a wide variety of castes, both the upper crust of the "twice-born" (the landlord, priest, and merchant castes) and no fewer than 36 different groups of hereditary artisans, all interrelated in a complex pattern of traditional obligations and rewards. Besides their varied occupations, almost every family had a stake, however small, in the land. Until the recent change of government in India, Delwara had been the seat of authority of one of the powerful feudal landlords, the Raj Rana of Delwara. The former ruler's vast fortress-palace still towered above the village; and at a high window the Raj Rana himself sat every day, brooding over the slightest occurrences in the bazaar below. He generously put a section of his palace at our disposal for our kitchen and sleeping quarters, but in order to carry out my work I had to hire a room in the center of the village.

During my stay in Delwara I learned much more about village ideas concerning medicine; and some things I learned only slowly and painfully. In this category I should put my long and unsuccessful struggle to plan my day on western lines, by the clock. I tried to adhere to the rule that I would see patients only the first thing in the morning (this was at 6:30 a.m. in the hot weather) and again in the late afternoon, but it simply did not work. The villagers themselves preferred to wait until they saw me coming down their lane, and then would call me in with every sign of desperate urgency to see a patient who had been sick for days; and peasants from the surrounding countryside would just walk into my "office" and sit patiently on the floor until I attended to them. Often they would beg me to go with them to their hamlets to see a close relative who lay very sick, but after one or two such excursions I learned to harden my heart and stick to my rule of refusing these requests, the majority of which proved to be cases of advanced phthisis.

One day, however, during the first month of my stay, a powerfully built young farmer appealed to me with great earnestness to help his brother, who lay ill in a hamlet two miles off. He had a high fever and had coughed up a blood-stained sputum, which sounded ominous; but his brother insisted that the whole illness was of only a few days' duration. No doubt what finally persuaded me to go was that the young farmer had borrowed a horse from the palace and held it saddled for me to make the journey. I was very glad in the end that I did go, for the patient was suffering from double pneumonia and was acutely ill. I gave him a massive injection of penicillin and followed it up with sulfamerazine, and as I cantered home I wondered what his chances of survival were. He gave me the answer two weeks later by walking into my office with a *dali* (a ceremonial tray of gifts) of sweet corn and other produce of his fields.

At the time I thought that this might lead to my dispensary practice growing to uncomfortable proportions, but such was not the case. Throughout my stay both villagers and country folk remained very skeptical of the quality of my medicine. They had three grounds for distrusting it. First, I did not describe their illnesses in the terms they had come to expect from their own healers. Second, I failed to prescribe elaborate dietary restrictions as did practitioners of classical Hindu medicine. Again and again my patients would pause after receiving their pills and say, "*Kattay parhez?*" which is the customary opening formula: "No bitter condiments, avoid this and this. . . ." In the end, I adopted a simple and familiar list which would do them no harm and seemed to make my treatment at once more comprehensible. Finally, they were dismayed to find that I did not invariably, and in dogmatic terms, assure them that my medicine would immediately cure them. In their eyes, my failure to do so amounted to malpractice. As many of them pointed out to me, it is not so much the ingredients of the prescription which effect the cure as the patient's unhesitating belief in its efficacy. For this reason, every homely recipe (of which everyone knew two or three) ended with the peroration: "Take that and you will *certainly* be cured of your fever within a day."

Near the end of my stay in Delwara I was called to a house to treat a merchant who seemed to be suffering from a cancer that obstructed the portal vein and gave rise to ascites. After we had tapped several pints of fluid from his abdomen, his son asked me how ill his father really was, and I told him the prognosis. That same evening a friend who had been present reminded me of this, with a smile; he found it simply incomprehensible that one could say a thing like that. "You know," he said, "our custom here is that even if a man is sure to die, we never say so. We always say something like 'If it is God's will, he will get better.'"

I realized that just as in the past I had been given credit for a decisive intervention simply because I had uttered a hopeful prognosis, now the reverse was the case. I had committed a serious impropriety in stating that the patient would not recover. . . .

A Cultural Body-Image

In Delwara, as previously in Sujarupa, I was frequently asked by apparently robust men to give them medicine—or better, an injection—to make them strong. At first, I continued to regard them as cases of anemia or malnutrition until my eyes were opened one day to the real condition by the interpolations of a bystander, who was watching me examine one of these patients: "Of course he's weak!" he said. "He was such a libertine when he was a young man that his semen got spoiled, and it's been leaving him ever since."

The patient seemed relieved to have it stated for him in this blunt manner. What he really wanted, he explained, was some medicine that would remedy this condition and cause his semen to stay inside his body instead of leaking away and making

him feel weak. From that day on, whenever a man asked me for strength-giving medicine, I urged him to tell me more about his trouble, and once he realized that he and I "talked the same language" in terms of symptomatology, a similar story always came out. Perhaps it is important to mention that this preoccupation was quite independent of the recognition of venereal disease and the fear of having contracted it. Gonorrhea was specifically mentioned as being only one of many ways in which "spoiled semen" might leave the body.

I found that a consistent belief about the nature and functions of the semen was held by all these patients, in different degrees of complexity according to their education. They were all able to describe how blood is made by the digestion of good food in a sort of low fire contained in the stomach, from which comes the warmth of the body; and that from every 40 drops of blood one drop of semen is laboriously formed. This semen, in which lies the source of a man's strength and of his subjective sense of well-being, is stored in a reservoir in his skull, which has a capacity of about 20 fluid ounces. The amount of well-formed semen which a man carries in this hidden store is not merely an indication of his state of health; it is also a measure of his moral and religious status. This is made clear when one learns what factors are conducive to the increase of semen, and what detrimental. In the former category come "cool" foods, such as dairy products, wheat flour, sugar, some fruits, and a number of the milder spices; in the latter, the cheaper and heavier cereals, unrefined sugar, vegetable oil, strong spices, and some of the commonest fruits. An especial anathema is placed upon eating meat and eggs, and drinking all forms of alcohol.

The striking thing about these food preferences is that all the foods in the approved class are the more expensive ones, which only the wealthier members of the high castes can afford to eat regularly. The mass of low-caste peasants and artisans eat meat and cheap cereals and drink wine; it is only on feastdays that they treat themselves to wheat cakes and pure sugar and dishes made with milk.

Even more important than these dietary restrictions, however, is the belief that the quality and amount of one's stored semen can be diminished by a failure to observe "right behavior." Obviously, it will be dissipated by an excessive indulgence in sex; but it will be lost more quickly and irretrievably if this indulgence is extramarital, and the bad effect will be intensified if the sex partner is of a low-caste community. Indeed, any act that incurs the condemnation of the elders of one's caste is believed to militate against the formation of the "Royal Principle." For example, many people told me that the reason the present generation of young men is so puny is this: it is a consequence of the growing habit of sitting in tea-shops, drinking "English tea" (known in England as Indian tea). This habit is condemned, first, because it implies a disregard for the serious, ritualistic practice of eating the two meals of the day; second, because it is a frivolous extravagance; and most important of all, because it exposes one to the ritual pollution of sitting to drink in company with others of lower caste. In general, it can be said that any violation of the many strict rules of behavior which concern the orthodox Hindu is regarded as detrimental to his store of semen, and thus to his mental and physical well-being.

Now at last these reiterated complaints of weakness began to make sense. They were the expression of chronic anxiety engendered by feelings of guilt. Small wonder, therefore, that my iron tonics and vitamin concentrates had little effect; what these people really wanted was a release from their burden of guilt, and this release they could find only in their own traditional way, by making a pilgrimage and bathing in one of the many sacred lakes or rivers which have the property of washing away one's sins, or by one of the elaborate and costly ceremonies of purification at which the Brahman priest is always ready to preside. Actually, these drastic measures are seldom taken; for the most part, they seem content to go on worrying and resolving to do something about it one day. There are even some who appear to derive a certain pleasure in describing their impending physical decay, like Calvinists who dwell lugubriously upon the prospect of hell-fire.

I have emphasized the element of guilt in this "general weakness" syndrome because there it was etiologically important. In time, however, I came to realize that it entered to some extent into every form of illness. The patient and his extended family always had the feeling that they were temporarily in a state of ill favor with some divine agency. One is reminded of the description of depression which is put forward by psychoanalysts of the Melanie Klein school as a phantasy of ingesting "bad ob-

jects" so that the whole self feels bad. Be that as it may, the village patient did not feel relieved of his illness unless he had the subjective assurance that the divine agent had been placated at the same time as his physical symptoms were relieved.

Sacred and Secular Diseases

This was dramatically shown in their treatment of snake-bites. All snakes, but especially the black cobras, were believed to be the embodiment of powerful godlings. For example, every plot of cultivated fields had a protector-god here known as Radaji, and in the form of a black snake the Radaji often patroled the fields entrusted to his care. Should anyone trespass or otherwise offend the god, he would get bitten. Here, as in Sujarupa, there were priests of the snake-god whom the sufferer might consult. They would become "possessed," suck out the poison, and be placated with an offering.

There was, however, another and more popular remedy. This was to consult one of the four elderly men in the village who were known to possess powerful charms against just such an occurrence. One of these, a handsome bearded Brahman called Nathu Lal, told me about an instance that occurred two years previously. A blacksmith called Partab had cut across a neighbor's cornfield and was bitten on the foot. One of the other healers was summoned, and a great crowd gathered in the yard of the blacksmith's house, Nathu Lal among them. It soon became clear to him that the other healer's charms were not strong enough to meet the case because this was evidently the work of a more than usually powerful god—probably the very Radaji whose shrine was set up to protect the main entrance of the village. At last, Nathu Lal himself decided to intervene. He took a pinch of dust between his fingers, whispered his strongest charm over it, and blew it toward the patient. "The dust did not touch him, Sahib, but the air of it was enough."

At once, compelled by the charm, the god entered the body of his victim, who shrieked with rage and flew at Nathu Lal, but he had anticipated this and dodged into a room, closing the door behind him, and calling out to the bystanders to tie Partab securely to a pillar. There then followed a heated discussion between him and the god speaking in the body of the patient. In the end, the Radaji promised to spare him if he made certain sacrifices before his shrine, and the "possession" came to an end. The case was not yet closed, however, because when Partab came to his senses, he maintained that the offering was more than he could afford and refused to make it. The onlookers were scandalized, but after he had had his face well slapped he did as he was told.

It was, of course, common knowledge that such possession might occur. Every adult villager has seen it happen many times; indeed, his familiarity with the expected behavior is presumably what causes the patient's trancelike state of dissociation to take this particular form. One patient of mine recalled how when he was a boy of five or six, both he and his mother were bitten by a snake. They went to an old man famous for his charms, and he took the precaution of tying them to a tree before magically summoning the snake's spirit. "My mother became possessed," said this young man, "I remember seeing her shake all over and cry out and struggle as she tried to attack the healer, but the Spirit did not come to me."

In later years, after he had seen two or three dramatic instances of possession and cure, suggestion would have told, and he too would be possessed— or so one might think. But actually the situation was quite different. This youth, whose name was Prithwi Singh, became a devoted worshiper of the Goddess Vijayshan-Mata, whose shrine stands just outside of Delwara. Like his soldier uncle before him, Prithwi Singh attended at all occassions of worship of his goddess, and it was he who performed the sacrifice of goats and sometimes young buffaloes in her name, decapitating them each with a single cut of his sword.

In the summer of 1950, Prithwi Singh was bitten on the finger by a cobra one afternoon as he was returning from his fields. This happened about a mile and a half from the village, and by the time he reached home, the poison was working in him. He felt thick-headed and confused, and could hardly drag his legs along.

"Sahib," he said, "at that time I really thought that I was about to die. But I managed to make my way to the shrine of Mataji, and I prayed to Her that if it was Her will, She should make me well. Then I went back to my house to an inner room where I have a little brass image of the Goddess, and I lay down below it on the floor, and at once I became unconscious. I lay there for some hours in a fever, and they said that I groaned in my sleep;

and then I had a dream. In my dream I saw the Goddess come into the room and stand beside me. She lifted up my hand and sucked the poison from my finger, and then She turned and went away. I woke up, wet with perspiration and quite weak; but from that moment I began to get well."

Among my stock of medicines was a set of dried polyvalent antivenin serums for intravenous injection in cases of snake-bite. I let it be known that this was available, but although I heard in due course of several such cases, two of which were fatal, no one asked for this treatment. I believe now that this was on account of the close association of the illness and the god. A physician who was perversely insensible to the all-important divine agent could not inspire confidence in treating this condition.

In the same way there was bitter opposition to the efforts of governmental authorities to promote universal vaccination against smallpox. Here, as all over India, this disease is believed to be due to the wrath of the demon-goddess, locally known as Sitala-Mata. Epidemics always occur in the hot weather, when flies are most abundant. High fever is taken as a sign that the goddess is hot. She is angry. She devours children in her rage. For this reason at the beginning of the very hot season, there is a placatory ceremony at the goddess' shrine, and this is repeated should there be a spell of especially hot weather or should smallpox break out in the vicinity. On such occasions, the image of Sitala-Mata is bathed with cool water, and garlands and fruits are laid before her. "We are cooling her down," say the women.

In contrast, there were some afflictions that were less decidedly associated with divine intervention. For example, there was no talk of "possession" when one was stung by a scorpion, although every practitioner who had charms against snake-bite seemed also to know one of the lesser charms against such a sting. My local-analgesic oily preparation was in great demand during the hot weather nights, when stings were most frequent. On one occasion I came upon a group squatting in the dusty village lane. A young man had received a severe sting. His leg was swollen and very painful. My old friend Nathu Lal was engaged in exorcising the poison, stroking the leg over and over again with a twig of nimleaves and whispering the appropriate charm. When he saw me squat beside him, he paused and suggested that I should apply my medicine, but I knew that at this stage it could do nothing to relieve his pain, so I persuaded Nathu Lal to continue his good work.

The Role of Faith in Curing

There were so many lesser healers and magicians at work in Delwara that one tended to overlook the fact that there was also a government dispensary, with a doctor trained in Ayurvedic medicine, and a dispenser. Their services and their medicaments were available free; and yet strangely enough they found very few clients. In all the many conversations I had with them in their sparsely equipped premises, I can remember only thrice being interrupted by the arrival of a patient. This state of idleness, it must be confessed, was not uncongenial to the doctor's temperament; indeed, he tended to encourage it by maintaining that these free medicines provided by the government were not very good anyway—let people come to his house privately, and he would let them have others, which would cost a good deal and which were correspondingly effective. In this way, he carried on a desultory sort of practice among the better-off families but earned the resentment of the poorer majority.

In Delwara, as in Sujarupa, the chief resort of families afflicted with sickness (or indeed any other trouble) was to the priests of a number of shrines in the vicinity; and here, too, there was one shrine that enjoyed an outstanding reputation in this respect. It was the shrine of Vijayshan-Mata, of which Prithwi Singh was one of the attendants. Every Sunday night without fail the priest became possessed and sat quivering on the floor in front of the image of the goddess, while a long succession of patients and supplicants came before him to be diagnosed and treated. In time I got to know the priest quite well, and I could see that sometimes he seemed genuinely in trance, while at others he was wide awake and made only a pretense at still being "possessed." In fact, this was evident the first time I attended his ceremony, a few months after my wife and I had settled in the village. When the priest had worshiped Vijayshan-Mata to an accompaniment of gongs and conch-shell music, her spirit came to him and he flailed himself ecstatically with an iron chain, and then began to utter his divinations. At this point I found myself thrust forward to the door of the temple and voices said,

"Go on, ask Mataji anything you want to know, and she will tell you the true answer."

After racking my brains for a moment, I asked a question which in fact had been exercising my wife and me for several weeks: "Mataji, this baby that we are going to have shortly, will it be a boy or a girl?" The quivering priest forgot himself for one moment and nearly burst out laughing. To conceal this, he turned toward the image as if seeking guidance, and then cried out, "*Choro vaygo*," (village dialect for "It'll be a boy"). And for days everyone in the village made us repeat this prophecy and then congratulated us upon our coming good fortune; but the baby proved to be a girl after all.

I sat beside this priest for many hours watching villagers and peasants present their sickly children or themselves for the blessing of the goddess' treatment, and I became familiar with the small range of common complaints: fever, dysentery, tuberculosis, childlessness, and, above all, witchcraft, which covered a multitude of women's and children's illnesses. One thing impressed me especially: these patients did not give a history of their complaint in the way to which we are accustomed. They took it for granted that the divine healer would know at once what was wrong. (Here, as many times in these villages, one was reminded of analogies to the Gospel stories.) This observation reminded me of the many occasions when country people had come up to me and silently extended a hand for me to take their pulse. And when, after doing so, I asked, "What is troubling you?" they would answer, "Sahib, that is for you to say. We are only poor ignorant people; how should we know?"

This attitude bespoke their ready trust. It meant that, having once decided to believe in a certain healer, they would accept uncritically whatever he told them. It was an indication also of their faith in the physician's cure. And that faith was always absolute; they knew no half measure. My village informants were quite explicit on this point. "Medicines are all very well," they would say to me. "But really, Sahib, it is *tassili* (faith) that makes a sick man well. No matter how rare a medicine you give a patient, unless both you and he have faith in it, he never will be cured."

In the case of the priest's therapy, this was certainly true, because he seldom applied any physical treatment at all. Watching the scores of peasants who passed before him, I came to realize that what they asked from him (or rather, from the goddess) were two things: that the affliction should be given a name and so become less terrible, and that the priest should utter his prediction, "He will get well." It mattered not that this formula was repeated to every other patient, every night. To each one it was like a personal communication from the goddess herself and put new heart into him.

At first, I must confess, I was filled with scorn and hostility toward this charlatan; but in time I came to realize that he was no less convinced than all his patients of the worthwhileness of his work. After all, he was simply performing what is one of the most important functions of the general medical practitioner, by letting these sick people feel that they were not alone and helpless but part of a succoring community, both real and supernatural. In my boyhood in Scotland I knew an eccentric old country physician who was remarkable for two things: for his detestation of internal combustion engines ("Damn these motors! Damn these motors!" he would cry when an early Model-T Ford made him skip to the side of the road) and for his habit of falling to his knees and "putting up a prayer" whenever one of his patients chanced to die. Unkind critics pointed out that he had more scope for this exercise than had his younger competitors, but his practice remained a large one to the end of his days. Our Presbyterian neighbors felt that in him they had a guide through life and the hereafter.

IMPLICATIONS

Nowadays simple piety is at a discount in the western world. In its place we offer the assurance of a securely based scientific training, which enables us to treat our patients and utter our prognosis with a sincere, if measured, confidence. It will be a long time before the scientific approach to the understanding and treatment of disease reaches remoter villages such as Sujarupa and Delwara. Until the material resources and the educational level of the public permit us to give them something demonstrably better, it would be a disservice to these people to try to undermine the chief solace they have in time of trouble.

By this I do not mean that we are justified in adopting a defeatist attitude toward the problem, but simply that we have to work from below upward. There were evidences of such new ideas in Delwara in 1951. Young men who had left the village to work in the city or to serve in the army came home with a smattering of new ideas about hygiene and sanitation. They spoke up at the village council in favor of cleaning up the lanes and building proper city-style latrines. A young Congress-party worker read in the newspaper about infections spread by water and persuaded the council to disinfect the main well of drinking water during the fly-infested season. It was here, I felt, at the village level itself, that the new ideas must take root if they were ever to command the confidence, the all-important "tassili" of the village people, which alone could make them work.

Perhaps the most significant lesson of my stay in these two villages was the realization that it was not enough to bring good medicines and efficient hygienic techniques to these country people. Before they can take effect, they must be *accepted*, and this will never come about so long as a wide gulf separates the thinking and the experience of western doctors from that of their village patients. There are three ways in which this gulf can be bridged: by the slow diffusion of information about sepsis and infection; by a better understanding of the expectations with which the people approach the doctor; and by presenting new techniques in a way which will link them up with what they are expected to supersede. Just as the earliest "horseless carriages" evolved only slowly and as if reluctantly toward the streamlined efficiency of a modern roadster, so we must expect new ideas in medicine to take root, at first by emphasizing their continuity with old traditions. To confront the villager with radically new departures from all that is familiar in the domain of health and sickness will only alarm and bewilder him and forfeit his cooperation, as has so frequently happened.

SUMMARY

This paper has been devoted to the recording of a number of lessons that I learned in the course of my attempts to practice medicine in two country villages of northern India. I was forced to recognize the seriousness of certain obstacles to the acceptance of western medicine, obstacles whose true nature could be understood only when I had learned a good deal about the villagers' own beliefs concerning sickness and cure. Misunderstandings were found to arise from false expectations on both sides, based on different theories of etiology, different techniques of cure, and different conceptions of the role of the physician.

After a period of practical experience, I realized that one can scarcely expect village people to change their whole cosmology simply to accord with the outlook of a western-trained doctor. Scientific knowledge seems likely to be disseminated throughout India as education becomes widespread and the products of western technology become a part of everyone's environment—but one cannot afford to wait for this to happen. In the immediate future, it devolves upon those who are introducing western techniques in public health and medicine to study how best they can adapt the roles of the doctor, the pharmacist, and the public hygienist to fit into the existing cultural expectations. In the process, they may have to consent to assume the mantle of the priest or the magician. This does not mean, of course, that they will themselves subscribe to non-rational beliefs, but simply that they will accept the inevitable fact that their own techniques of healing will be accepted "irrationally," as indeed they are for the most part in the West. Western health personnel can, however, turn this fact to advantage by dramatizing the concepts of infection, sterilization, and chemotherapy for all they are worth and by accepting as an asset the quite unscientific awe which the ritual of even minor surgery can inspire.

Public health workers will have to formulate their measures so that they can be linked with the old teachings, and above all must aim to enlist the support of the leaders of village opinion. These considerations may sound devious and Machiavellian, but so long as western-trained workers remain clear in their own minds about the worth of the contribution they have to make to the community's well-being, they will be able to play their roles with that conviction and assurance of ultimate success which the villagers themselves recognize as the hallmark of truly potent therapy.

EPILOGUE

Man is, to be sure, the "time-binding animal," as some writers have characterized him, the animal who can worship the past and fear the future and live in a world far from the here and now. And without this binding from one generation to the next, without this bridge heavy with the traffic of one generation's gifts to another, we would see about us none of the familiar sights now surcharged with symbolic reference, nor hear sounds that prick a wealth of memories and of imaginings. For, in one view, culture is that body of ideas, sentiments, and skills learned by man as a member of society —a generalized image of conduct and orientation of man toward man and toward nature, a complex image which carries with it, in addition to its pragmatic functions, the persuasions of moral legitimacy.*

*Charles C. Hughes, "Cultural Conflict: Dialect of Man in Nature," *The Centennial Review*, vol. 9, no. 3 (Summer 1965).

PRINTED IN U.S.A.